MARIA THERESA: EMPRESS

MARIA THERESA: EMPRESS

The Making of the Austrian Enlightenment

RICHARD BASSETT

YALE UNIVERSITY PRESS
NEW HAVEN AND LONDON

For information about this and other Yale University Press publications, please contact:
U.S. Office: sales.press@yale.edu   yalebooks.com
Europe Office: sales@yaleup.co.uk   yalebooks.co.uk

Set in Van Dijck MT by IDSUK (DataConnection) Ltd
Printed in Great Britain by TJ Books, Padstow, Cornwall

Library of Congress Control Number:2024945269

ISBN 978-0-300-24398-7

A catalogue record for this book is available from the British Library.

10 9 8 7 6 5 4 3 2 1

In memory of Dr Raimund Kerbl
(Herr auf Grödig)
1943–2023

You have the honour of serving the greatest monarch in the whole world. So you must incline yourself to carrying out all reasonable orders with a willing heart and bear with patience all the hardships which you may endure through heat, cold and rain, comforting yourself with the thought of better times ahead.

Prince Joseph Eszterhazy's address
to his regiment, Eisenstadt, 1747

How much happiness had she not provided for her subjects? Open ports, improved roads, the flag at sea respected and secure, manufacture increased and protected with benefit for her subjects and to the admiration of all peoples.

Elia Morpurgo, Jewish communal leader, Gradisca, 1781

Contents

Part III (i) The Legacy: Politics and Trade

Part III (ii) The Legacy: Culture and Piety

CONTENTS

A Note on Structure and Titles

THE STORY OF THE Great Empress is first and foremost one of personally struggling against seemingly impossible odds, then politically delivering a radical reform programme which transformed central Europe, while finally bequeathing a cultural and geopolitical landscape whose characteristics continue to reverberate to this day. I have therefore felt it best to divide the narrative into three clear sections which reflect these three components.

The first section describes the struggle for Maria Theresa's inheritance with all its peaks and troughs. The second section focuses on her achievements in domestic policy and the astonishing programme of reform which remade Austria into a modern state. In the final section, divided into two, the lasting legacy of those achievements in the political and cultural spheres is examined, in particular the extraordinary variety of activity which so enriched the Habsburg empire in the late eighteenth century and provided the foundations of central Europe's glorious and unique contribution to so many strands of modern civilization in the early twentieth century.

In this way I hope that the astonishing breadth of Maria Theresa's legacy can be examined without the constraints that a solely chronological approach might impose.

The reader will perhaps wonder at the circumstances which made the 'Great Empress' in name and deed but only gradually and informally in title. Maria Theresa was born an Archduchess of Austria. On her marriage in 1736 to Francis Stephen of Lorraine she acquired the title of

Archduchess of Lorraine and Bar. A year later, on her husband receiving the Grand Duchy of Tuscany (in return for surrendering Lorraine), Maria Theresa became Grand Duchess of Tuscany. In 1740, on the death of her father Charles VI, she became Queen of Hungary and Queen of Bohemia as well as ruler of 'all the lands, kingdoms and domains of the monarchy of the *Casa Austria*'. Francis, until his coronation as Holy Roman Emperor in 1745, possessed neither land nor estates. Indeed, with Tuscany assigned to secundogeniture and Modena given to tertiogeniture, he was landless, owing everything to the House of which his wife (and not him) was the head. His influence, if he chose to wield it – which he did exceptionally rarely – stemmed entirely from the power invested in his wife by her inheritance.

Contemporaries at this time, notably Frederick of Prussia, referred to her as the Queen of Hungary. In 1745, although not crowned herself as Empress at the side of her husband (she did not wish to detract from a jot of Francis Stephen's glory at his coronation as Holy Roman Emperor – it was all the glory he could ever formally enjoy given the reality of his situation), she acquired the right to the title of Empress and was so addressed by her family, her court and her subjects. Following the First Partition of Poland in 1772 she also assumed the title of Queen of Galicia-Lodomeria. The title Empress-Queen was rarely used during her reign and is a later German invention.

Frederick, meanwhile, was always only King *in* Prussia until the First Partition of Poland enabled him to acquire West Prussia and so allow him finally to call himself King *of* Prussia. This was on account of the Holy Roman Empire only recognizing the Kingdom of Bohemia and the Kingdom of Hungary as 'proper' kingdoms, compared to the tapestry of principalities, electorates, prince-archbishoprics and dukedoms which made up the extraordinary, varied fabric of the empire, and of which the sandy wastelands of Prussia, first elevated in 1417 to membership, were to play an increasingly important if fractious role.

Acknowledgements

It is my pleasure to thank many friends, relatives and colleagues, sadly often long dead, who have helped over the many years this book has been in preparation. Maria Theresa was during my childhood the one Austrian personality who received positive treatment at the hands of my infant reading of English illustrated history books. The Collins *History of the World*, published in the early 1960s, even provided a modern-coloured illustration of the Great Empress in her apartments at Schönbrunn. Later, when I visited Vienna for the first time post my undergraduate studies in 1977, the preparations for celebrating the imminent 200th anniversary of her death were in full swing and I was privileged to encounter *Hofrat* Dr Walter Koschatzky, the then ebullient director of the Albertina, and be given a personal tour of some of the eighteenth-century drawings in the Theresian collection. Dr Koschatzky was working on the imminent 200th-anniversary celebrations of Maria Theresa's death and showed me a rare portrait of Maria Theresa as Judith holding the head of Holofernes (Frederick of Prussia).

Dr Koschatzky personified, with his charm, courtesy and impeccable good manners, an Austrian sophistication which I was probably encountering in a conscious way for the first time. For better or for worse, my subconscious has ever since made a connection between this Austrian sensibility, noticeably different from Bavarian or German approaches, and the Great Empress. Over the years, this Austrian mindset, so very useful for dealing with the unexpected and demanding, has been reinforced by countless other encounters which have left me more and more convinced that the differences in mentality and culture between modern-day Austrians and Germans are indelibly written

ACKNOWLEDGEMENTS

in an ink first manufactured during the reign of Maria Theresa, even though she herself extolled the virtues of '*Deutschtum*'.

In more recent times, I am especially grateful in Salzburg to the late Dr Raimund Kerbl and the late Frau Rosemarie Büttner-Chaimowitz, who both exemplified these differences. In Vienna I am grateful to Dr Christopher Brennan, Professor Lothar Höbelt, Professor Erwin Schmidl, as well as the late Dr Christoph Allmayer-Beck, the doyen of Austrian military historians. I also would like to record my thanks to the late Professor Renate Wagner-Rieger who received me with great warmth in 1977 and gave me letters of introduction affording me access to many Theresian government buildings in Vienna, usually at that time 'off-limits' to scholars. In Cambridge I owe much to discussions on Theresian subjects with Dr Will O'Reilly and Professor Jo Whaley and the establishment there of the Cambridge New Habsburg Studies Network. The network afforded an early opportunity to encounter Derek Beales, the undisputed authority on Joseph II and Josephinism.

In London the late Dr Ihsan Toptani, an Albanian aristocrat educated at the Theresianum shortly after the First World War, and the late George Ramsden helped me deepen my knowledge of the eighteenth-century Enlightenment over many years of happy discussion. I am also immensely grateful for the help of the late Professor Christopher Duffy and the late Gottfried Pils, both experts on the Theresian military era. My knowledge of the Maria Theresa Order was encouraged by the late Baron Geoffrey or, as he was known in Italy, Goffredo (Gottfried) Banfield, the last surviving holder of that illustrious decoration, who welcomed me so generously in Trieste when I came to work there in 1979.

I owe thanks to Martin Randall who encouraged me, as we emerged from the rigours of the Covid lockdown, to present some of the ideas contained in this text to an educated audience during a series of lectures on central European topics which he organized through the medium of Zoom. The appetite for more information about the Great Empress was always satisfying to behold and there can be no doubt that a serious revival of interest in her life and achievements is under way not just in Germany but also in the Anglo-Saxon world.

I should also like to thank many friends who have chipped in on the more arcane points of manners and Theresian court protocol: Dr Philip

Mansel, Sir Jonathan Marsden, Daniel Spička, Dr Claudia Lehner-Jobst and Countess Monika Czernin. I owe an enormous debt of thanks to the Comunità Israelitica di Trieste, in particular Annalisa di Fant who helped me research the community's eighteenth-century archives.

The librarians of the Austrian State Archives, in particular the late Dr Rudolf Jezabek, proved invaluable and I wish to record here my thanks to the unsung heroes of those archives and the British Library, who discharged their anonymous duties with such courteous efficiency in the happy, far-off days before the BL was permanently paralysed by cyberattack.

A consistently invaluable source of material has been Florian Bernd's bookshop in Vienna which supplied many of the more obscure post-1800 texts unavailable in libraries. The material available on Maria Theresa is so enormous and nearly constantly updated that the aid of that increasingly rarest of species, the highly educated antiquarian bookseller, is of vast assistance. The late Mario Cerne of the Umberto Saba bookshop in Trieste also provided me with several immensely helpful texts.

No less important were my spiritual directors over many years, beginning with the late Monsignor Alfred Gilbey and the late Father Anthony Meredith S.J., continuing through to many fruitful discussions with their successors. Finally, I must thank Heather McCallum and her highly capable team at Yale, especially Rachael Lonsdale and Katie Urquhart, but also Robert Sargant whose copy-editing saved me from many 'unforced errors'.

Living with the Great Empress for the last few years has been very congenial, opening many insights into the Theresian world and providing a refreshingly different perspective on eighteenth-century Austria to that with which most English-language readers are familiar. Her legacy, as I hope these pages show, powerfully resounds to this day.

London, 1 May 2024

BRANDENBURG-
PRUSSIA

Berlin

NETHERLANDS

Brussels

POLAND

Warsaw

Rhine

LUXEMBOURG

SAXONY

SILESIA
(lost 1742)

Habsburg possessions

0   200 miles

0   200 km

Prague

BOHEMIA

Kraków

Lemberg

GALICIA
(1772)

BAVARIA

MORAVIA

BREISGAU

INN QUARTER

Salzburg

Vienna

Pressburg

ZIPS
(1770)

FRANCE

Innsbruck

AUSTRIA

TYROL

STYRIA

Danube

Budapest

BUKOVINA
(1775)

CARINTHIA

H U N G A R Y

MILAN

Milan

Trieste

CARNIOLA

BÁNÁT OF
TEMESVÁR

Genoa

PARMA

Belgrade

Florence

TUSCANY

O T T O M A N
E M P I R E

Austria in 1740.

Introduction

THE NAME MARIA THERESA rolls off Anglo-Saxon tongues more easily than the German Maria Theresia, and thus has the 'Great Empress' come down to us as a figure of matriarchal fortitude, feminine grace and simple courage in adversity. In the days when European history was considered a mainstream subject in our schools and universities she came to occupy a unique position among Whig historians not generally known for their sympathy for anything to do with the Habsburgs. If the English school textbooks relished documenting the failures of the Habsburgs throughout the age of nationalism in the nineteenth century, there was a distant glow, hazy but nonetheless distinctive, around the achievements of their eighteenth-century predecessors, although much of this tended to be directed towards Maria Theresa's son, Joseph II, the darling of Enlightenment historians to this day.

The cult of Frederick II (whom the Germans, and the English, call 'The Great')[1] also brought Maria Theresa to a wider English audience, although as an altogether less striking, inferior figure, constantly harassed and chivvied along the path of her Prussian rival's road to military glory. As the reputation of Frederick was artificially inflated by the birth-pangs of German nationalism in the late nineteenth century, Maria Theresa experienced a similar injection of fervour in the Austrian crown lands as a counterweight to exclusively Prussian consciousness. If, between her death in 1780 and the accession of Franz Josef in 1848, not a single monument was erected to her memory, the blossoming of a multi-national empire, in particular the need to pacify the Hungarians, and the elevation of its capital to the leading rank of European cities, soon changed all that. The Ringstrasse created magnificent open spaces and one of its most opulent was reserved for a monument to the *Grosse Herrscherin*.

Some of Austria's greatest artists were harnessed to this cause and, if Maria Theresa's reign was depicted through the most ecstatic of scores in the German Richard Strauss's great opera *Der Rosenkavalier*, it was left to his librettist, the Austrian Hugo von Hofmannsthal, to immortalize for the non-Prussianized German world the sense of Maria Theresa's peculiarly Austrian brand of *Milde und Munifizenz*.

In an essay which still resonates through our perception of the Empress to this day, Hofmannsthal enumerated her achievements, always contrasting them with the developments of Prussian Germany: 'If the Prussian kings saw with the sharpest of vision the concept of caste as something to be determined by rank, lifestyle and function, then Maria Theresa had a wider if more naive view of "the people" for which Austrians must be eternally grateful because it is inexhaustible and intuitive.'[2]

For Hofmannsthal, it was this combination of 'high spiritual qualities and security of instinct' ('humanity and femininity perfectly combined') which enabled her to cut through to the essentials of any problem. Fortunate in her choice of confidants, she assembled around her the most gifted and capable men of her time, a tribute to her ability to measure the worth of people and trust them: 'In which powers she trusted and in which she did not, does not stand in any catechism and yet from generation to generation it is carried silently in the heart.' The deep suspicion Maria Theresa had of the abstract was the inevitable consequence of a 'strong soul' fashioned by a piety which, in the words of the Prussian ambassador Podewils, 'offered her a sanctuary where all the dangers of the world cannot reach her'.[3]

Yet piety, if a refuge, did not signify any retreat from the demands of imperial rule and it remains to this day an indisputable fact that virtually no public institution in central Europe can fail to trace its origins to Maria Theresa's reign. Between 1740 and 1780 she remade the relationship between Church and State, the provision of primary and secondary education, the establishment of elite academies of further education, and the introduction of a public health system. To these years came a myriad of other reforms: the introduction of indirect taxation, the abolition of serfdom and the freeing of the peasantry, the creation of rights and privileges of servants, the establishment of medical excellence and the development of building and health regulations, all to be administered by an incorruptible and increasingly meritocratic civil service.

Social mobility undreamt of in the socialist 'liberal' regimes of the late twentieth century was surprisingly common in Maria Theresa's Austria: how else can one explain the extraordinary rise of Johann Amadeus de Paula Thugut, a teenage orphan who may have caught the Empress's eye rowing her across the Danube and, after an unashamedly elitist education, paid for by her, rose to the rank of imperial chancellor before Metternich?[4]

At the same time, this combination of fecund intuition and iron will moved the Casa d'Austria's 'Weltidee' away from what was unrealistic and fantastical. If her father had constructed the magnificent Klosterneuburg palace with its centrepiece as the *Reichskrone*, Maria Theresa's Schönbrunn was decorated on its façade with the less universal *Hauskrone*.

This little architectural detail, which today goes mostly unnoticed, reflected a subtle shift. Maria Theresa's husband Francis Stephen (Francis I) was Holy Roman Emperor after 1745 but he held neither lands nor possessions. In fact, he owned nothing which did not stem from his wife. It was she and not he who was the head of the Habsburg house where power resided. When the *Grand Renversement* of alliances sealed Austria's rapprochement with France, many of the traditional 'functions' of the old Holy Roman Empire ceased to exist, in particular its centuries-old mission to defend the western frontiers of *Deutschtum* along the Rhine. If France, thanks to Maria Theresa's chancellor Kaunitz's brilliance, no longer threatened that frontier, Francis Stephen's role as emperor was really limited to just *Sitz und Stimme* (a seat and a vote).

This focus on the Casa d'Austria made it imperative to introduce the administrative machinery of state. But the *Oberstaat* which ruled over Germans and Italians also ruled over Hungarians, Serbs and Croats as well as Czechs, Slovaks, Ruthenes and Romanians. This meant that, while administrative reform was largely in the hands of German-speaking bureaucrats and French-speaking aristocrats, the Empress could never represent an exclusively German state, and thus was born the German

Dualismus which was arguably only 'resolved' with the *Anschluss* of 1938 and then only for seven unhappy years. Even German nationalists eventually came to rue the day of 'Austria's return into the Reich'. The state Maria Theresa bequeathed, despite later historians dwelling on her 'teutsches blut' and teutonic mercantile immigration policies, proved ultimately impervious to enduring *Germanisierung*.[5]

Yet though keen to harness some of the centralizing lessons of the Prussian state for Austria, Maria Theresa never wished to reproduce it. Recent historians have echoed the pan-German nationalist sentiments of Heinrich Ritter von Srbik and argued that Maria Theresa and Frederick of Prussia were similar and 'had much in common'. According to this interpretation, both were 'ruthless' and 'determined' and Maria Theresa as aggressive as Frederick. This theory fits neatly into the *Gesamtdeutschtum* of German historiography but confuses human qualities with spiritual values. Unsurprisingly, modern historians find it difficult to come to grips with the imperatives of Catholic dogma and the overwhelming influence it had on the Empress. Yet, in the eighteenth century, the house of faith and reason in Austria was less divided than in France or Prussia. In the belief and values system of Maria Theresa, every personality defect of Frederick — vindictiveness, aggressive atheism, moral cowardice and insincerity — was mostly absent. When, as on occasion every mortal does, Maria Theresa succumbed to feelings of revenge and realpolitik, it was the exception rather than the norm.

Radical change in the Habsburg lands was never implemented with Prussian efficiency, and Hofmannsthal was quick to stress the difference between two worlds: 'The Theresian world was earthly (*irdisch*), naïve and full of piety: it embraced nature and God and its pride was genuine without stiffness and hardness: Haydn, Gluck and Mozart are the legacies of this spirit.' Just in case the point might have been lost on the less 'earthly' north Germans, Hofmannsthal concluded by pointing to the qualities associated with Maria Theresa: 'Mildness and mercy (*Milde und Gnade*), piety and humanity in these less easily grasped traits, less sharp in design than those of her son, Joseph, Maria Theresa personified the drawing together of all those threads which make up the Austrian soul and this proved decisive for all that followed.' 'Unsurprising,' the Austrian writer insisted, 'that Germans might find this transition from their world into ours rather uncomfortable.' Such discomfort was 'entirely due to her'.

This approach to Maria Theresa unsurprisingly was met with incomprehension by German nationalist historians, including those of Austrian descent, not least during the years following the *Anschluss* between Austria and Germany in 1938. Heinrich Ritter von Srbik, certainly one of Austria's most brilliant historians, but also a committed supporter of the Nazis, delivered the perfectly scripted German National Socialist response to any lingering *Rosenkavalier* nostalgia. Writing in 1942, he noted that 'like Frederick the Great she spoke only German', like him she was a great centralizer and a military reformer and (of course), like him, she was 'an instinctive anti-Semite'.[6] She had promoted German colonization of south-eastern Europe and had maintained that Hungary could only be conquered 'allein mit teutschem Blut' (with German blood alone). But even Srbik admitted that this 'Deutsche Frau' had 'old Habsburg thoughts' and was always convinced of the 'universal character' of her inheritance.[7] Srbik's imitators of late have not usually granted such a dispensation to the Austrian Empress.

Yet historians, despite their best efforts to strip away the prejudices of generations, have always found it difficult to dispel entirely the enduring significance of Maria Theresa's 'myth' for Austrians. It is easy to place her in the context of religious intolerance and focus on the concrete pinnacles of her constitutional and political achievements, as if these were somehow separate and somehow the Empress compartmentalized her statecraft from her piety.

This transposition of modern religious practice, limited in a post-Christian world to the private sphere, to the eighteenth century where it enjoyed a far wider public identity, leads to much misunderstanding. The confusion is not helped by the later generations of intellectuals who have regarded Catholicism and the Enlightenment as incompatible. The reign of Maria Theresa, even more than that of her son Joseph II, disproves this assertion. The groundwork of the golden age of the Enlightenment in Austria was laid by men who were often both practising Catholics and Freemasons. Not all Freemasons were enlightened and not all enlightened men were members of Masonic lodges but, as the initial oath of Freemasonry sworn 'in the presence of Almighty God' indicated, mutual exclusion was, notwithstanding repeated papal bulls denouncing Freemasonry, not the divisive issue it later became.[8]

In fact, Maria Theresa's reign saw a harnessing of the newest achievements of philosophy and science often to defend the essential dogmas of Catholicism. Many of those minds with which the Empress surrounded herself believed that Catholicism had to modernize if it wished to remain a viable intellectual alternative to the persuasive arguments of anti-clericals. Thus, in Salzburg, in the 1740s, it was the Benedictines who established at the university the first European discipline of experimental physics. Maria Theresa's reign was thus a powerful catalyst for what we now refer to as the 'Catholic Enlightenment'.

Her well-documented anti-Semitism is also too easy to characterize out of context. It was never racially motivated but mostly theological and political. When the Jewish community collaborated with her enemies, she flew into a rage, incensed by their betrayal. When she ordered the expulsion of the proud ancient Jewish community of Prague, following reports of their fraternizing and helping the Prussian and French occupiers, she refused for several months to listen to pleas for mercy, not only from her most powerful advisers but even the King of England. Eventually, she relented, and it is significant that while at other times she vented her spleen on them, even calling them a 'plague' on one memorable occasion, she never permitted any general persecution of the empire's Jews.

Moreover, long before her son introduced his famous Patent of Toleration in 1782, extending confessional freedoms to Protestants and Jews, Maria Theresa had permitted the erection of a public synagogue and school (Scuola) in Trieste in 1745. The Jewish community in that city flourished under her benevolent eye and, as early as 1754, the Venetian agent Alvise Foscarini, in a secret dispatch to the Doge, noted critically the presence and freedoms of Jewish merchants, especially the Ashkenazi Morpurgo family, in the city (in contrast to their ongoing persecution in Venice). The Empress issued patents encouraging the Jewish community in Trieste which were approved in 1747 and 1762.[9]

It is this pragmatism which is perhaps the most enduring legacy of the Empress. It meets with scant acknowledgement from some of her recent biographers, but perceptions, especially in central Europe, are real and it would be a foolish historian who failed to acknowledge the power of this pragmatism in fashioning the identity with which Maria Theresa invested modern Austria.

As recently as 1979, Walter Koschatzky could write, 'new interpretations try to aid our understanding and dispel legends and emotions but when all is said and done the Theresian mosaic with which we are left combines courage, the powerful idea of a state and Austria. . . . to be an Austrian never meant to belong to any nationality but to enjoy a certain approach to life (*Lebenshaltung*). This was followed by a conviction of modesty, indifference to the blows of fate and discretion in reaching conclusions. Above all the acceptance of life's failures and successes, never losing the ability to laugh and never relinquishing a selfless sense of service' (*selbstlose Gesinnung des Dieners*).[10]

All these traits are found in the subject of this study, a woman who personified not only the special relationship that exists within the Austrian psyche towards the female and the motherly but the umbilical cord which links Austria to the rest of Europe and will always prevent her from any enduring or exclusive absorption into the German nation. Even at the height of the 1848 revolution, so often cited as a grand moment of 'German Nationalism', one revolutionary, Karl Beitel, could address the Frankfurt parliament in these words: 'Austrian Germans will be German as long as you do not unreasonably insist that they cease to be Austrian.'[11]

PART I

THE CRISIS

CHAPTER I

The May Child

MARIA THERESA'S ARRIVAL IN May 1717 on the grand stage of European politics was nothing if not low-key. No-one can say that Maria Theresa's birth brought rejoicing either to the Habsburg lands or even her parents. The presence of a daughter rather than a son heralded disappointment on many fronts and even astrologers rued the fact that the child had not been born under the star sign of Leo, as favoured traditionally for its leadership qualities by the Habsburgs, but under the far less auspicious constellation of Taurus. There was little comfort in the fact that, according to most students of the zodiac, the sign, though famously weak in the male line, offered resilience, conscientiousness and strength in the female.

Her names were chosen conventionally but were not without significance. If Maria, the Mother of Christ, was a given as the common honouring of the Virgin, Theresa was less obvious. The Theresa referenced by this gesture was the great Theresa of Avila, the sixteenth-century Carmelite known for her discipline and austerity, as well as a powerful mysticism. If the future Empress's third, fourth and fifth names – Walburga, Amalia and Christina, signifying Benedictine and family connections – were of importance, it was Theresa of Avila who was to become a lifelong source of inspiration and courage.

Even today, Catholics who are perhaps unfamiliar with the story of the great Spanish saint can often vaguely recall Theresa of Avila's 'bookmark'. It is worth quoting here as it could have been composed to serve as a daily spiritual rampart in Maria Theresa's challenging life. In the Viennese German Maria Theresa learnt as her mother tongue, it reads:

Nichts soll Dich ängstigen	(Nothing should make you afraid
Alles geht vorüber	Everything passes
Nur Gottes Wege bleibt	Save the way of the Lord)[1]

However well-chosen the names, they were to emphasize, as well as piety, the enduring nature of the Habsburg dynasty. If the birth of a girl at that time was for any ruling house a disappointment, there would be no indication of such impatience during the elaborate ceremonies which followed Maria Theresa's birth. Everything from the guest list to the choice of godparents underlined that, whatever her gender, the new child was accepted to one day be worthy of the discharge of the duties of a sovereign. Two Empresses, Eleonore Magdalene and Wilhelmina Amalia (the widows of Joseph I and Leopold I), together with Pope Clement XI (represented by the Papal Nuncio, Spinola), headed the list of godparents.

But one looks in vain for representatives of potential allies which doubtlessly would have accompanied the baptism of a son. Maria Theresa was for her father a kind of reinsurance policy if a son remained elusive, but the hope remained for a male heir. This allowed the future Empress considerable freedom and not least the luxury of a degree of self-definition free from the aspiration and obsessive hopes of oppressive dynastic parenting. Her greatest ally in all her adolescent trials was her faithful *aya*,[2] Countess Fuchs, a virtual surrogate mother whose advice was always full of practical good sense. Countess Fuchs helped her charge to absorb the inevitable weight of parental expectation and disappointment.

Maria Theresa's father, Charles VI, was well-used to disappointments. His personality expressed the last embers of the Habsburgs' Spanish inheritance. The great victories in the War of the Spanish Succession, of Marlborough and Prince Eugene, had been partly won to ensure Charles's claims to the Spanish Habsburg inheritance were honoured, but the series of treaties concluded at Utrecht in 1713 confirmed the wishes of the maritime powers who, having fought successfully to prevent the crowns of Spain and France being united, had little appetite for the crowns of Austria and Spain to be reunited by a single Habsburg.

London, in particular, was always suspicious of the ghosts of the great Catholic universal monarchy which had been personified by

Charles V and which had, through Philip of Spain's marriage to Mary Tudor, briefly incorporated England into the Habsburg system.

Charles bore his losses arising from 'The Great Betrayal' of Utrecht with dignity, wearing the sombre black doublet and flash of scarlet stocking favoured by the Spanish court in which he had spent some of his formative years. The Spanish rules and etiquette (*Spanische Hofzeremoniell*) he favoured at the Vienna court continued to be enforced rigidly right up until the end of the monarchy in 1918. At Klosterneuburg on the banks of the Danube not far from Vienna he remodelled a twelfth-century Augustinian monastery, constructing his own personal *Escorial* complete with an arresting skyline of massive crowns and crucifixes wrought in copper.

In 1703, at the height of the Grand Alliance, he had landed in England where he had an audience with Queen Anne at Windsor. From this encounter we have the charming portrait of an eyewitness, Rapin:

> The court was very splendid and much thronged; the queen's behaviour towards him was very noble and obliging. The young king charmed all present: he had a gravity beyond his age, tempered with much modesty. His behaviour was in all points so exact that there was not a circumstance in his whole deportment that was liable to censure.[3]

Rapin's account went on to notice a certain Hispanic severity:

> He paid an extraordinary respect to the queen and yet maintained a due greatness in it. He had the art of seeming well-pleased with everything without so much as smiling once all the while he was at court, which was three days. He spoke but little and all he said was judicious and obliging.[4]

The Venetian ambassador Francesco Donaldo confirmed this image when he wrote, after being presented to the Emperor: 'His face is serious, unsmiling and pious. His qualities are clearly his faith and loyalty to his word combined with an iron resilience in the face of all destiny's blows.'

Such was the character of Maria Theresa's father. Her mother was hewn of altogether different stock; north German and a cradle Protestant, Elisabeth-Christine was the eldest daughter of the Duke of Brunswick-Wolfenbüttel and his wife, a Princess Oettingen-Oettingen. This north German sobriety was, on reflection, not as incompatible with Charles's Hispanic Catholicism as it might have seemed at first glance. After a visit to the great Marian pilgrimage village of Mariazell, the *Magna Mater Austriae*, in 1706, Elisabeth-Christine embraced the faith of her husband, converting in Bamberg the following year. Perhaps the simplicity of the medieval carving of the Madonna and child – at that time not yet adorned by the baroque genius of Joseph Emmanuel Fischer von Erlach's opulent silver canopy – impressed the young princess along with the remoteness of the Styrian Alpine landscape. In any event, her conversion was hastened by one of her companions on that pilgrimage, a young Jesuit by the name of Michael Pachter, whom later she would engage to teach her daughter.[5] In time, Maria Theresa would receive her first Holy Communion in this *Gnadenkapelle* high in the Styrian Alps.

Such Catholic piety notwithstanding, both parents could lay claim to significant Enlightenment credentials. Elisabeth-Christine's forefathers had assembled a century earlier the greatest library north of the Alps. In the years of Maria Theresa's reign this library would enjoy the presence of one of the leading Enlightenment writers, Gotthold Ephraim Lessing.

Meanwhile, Charles VI, defined by the loss of his Spanish inheritance, sought solace in the company of merchants and sailors who promised that, largely landlocked though Austria appeared to be, she had in the form of the port of Trieste a potentially prosperous window on the world. It was Charles VI who granted Trieste in 1719, two years after his daughter's birth, its Free Port status and, as the statue of him near the Piazza Unità (Grande) in Trieste – and that of his father Leopold I, a few steps distant – illustrates to this day, Charles saw the potential of linking the Mediterranean with the Alpine worlds. It was a vision his daughter would fully embrace.

Neither of Maria Theresa's parents could thus be described as out of tune with some of the more stimulating ideas of their times. Yet it was Elisabeth-Christine's principal duty to furnish the Habsburg emperor with a male heir and when, in 1716, her infant son Leopold died after seven months, the pressure became more acute; hence the degree of understatement which greeted the arrival of Maria Theresa a year later.

Yet, however intensely felt, such disappointment could not be allowed to detract from the ceremonies surrounding the new arrival's birth. As noted earlier, the guest list for Maria Theresa's christening and the choice of her godparents all strongly underlined the infant's future destiny as a sovereign.

As Maria Theresa grew up, her parents still hoped for a male heir but there are signs that, in the choice of her tutors, both parents were aiming for something more than just a frivolous superficial upbringing for their daughter. The Jesuit Michael Pachter was joined by a colleague, Franz Xavier Vogel. The two men were put in charge of Maria Theresa's formal education and the teachers they assembled for the young Maria Theresa were an early lesson in the merit of discernment. Without exception, each of the young archduchess's tutors was not only an expert in their field but also, more importantly, a first-rate teacher.

Her mathematics and astronomy teacher was one of the leading scientists of the day, a member of both the Russian and Prussian academies of sciences. Giovanni von Marinoni was Friulan by birth and famously compiled the cadastre of Milan. By the time he was teaching Maria Theresa about the constellations, he had already made a reputation for himself as one of the leading cartographers of Europe. Later as Empress, Maria Theresa would surprise her military advisers with her firm and easy grasp of cartographic detail, especially with regard to frontiers.

For history, the choice was perhaps even more inspired: Gottfried Spannagl introduced the archduchess to the reign of Emperor Henry III who deposed three Popes in 1048 before installing his preferred candidate Clement II. At the same time, Spannagl criticized the emperor's successor, the later Emperor Henry IV, for undertaking the humiliation of begging forgiveness from the Pope at Canossa in 1077. Henry had surrendered the secular power to the ecclesiastical and Spannagl never allowed his pupil to forget that this had been a grave error. It was a lesson Maria Theresa always remembered.

Given that, after the Reformation, Henry IV was seen by German Lutherans as a prototype defender of Protestantism (the 'First Protestant'), these ideas were rather remote from what later historians imagined was a 'conventional Catholic upbringing'.

In addition to these courses, there were many lighter lessons in music and dance, in both of which the archduchess excelled. This instruction was without doubt as important as any of her other studies. Her ability to dance gave her poise and dignity while the much-underestimated qualities inherent in musical study offered above all the ability to listen, arguably the most invaluable tool of statecraft and diplomacy.

As well as these imparted skills there was also time in the curriculum for regular instruction in the most important European languages: Spanish, Italian and French. Although Maria Theresa never spoke any German other than Viennese dialect with its melodic cadences and affectionate diminutives – she was always known as *Reserl* – she quickly mastered perfect court French. To this day the predominance of languidly pronounced French adjectives in Austrian German is a legacy of the fashion for speaking either French or Viennese dialect, or a combination of the two, in court circles.[6]

Her drawing instructor was Daniele Bertoli, a highly gifted artist, while her singing teacher was Pietro Metastasio, the librettist of Mozart's *Clemenza di Tito*. It should be noted that neither of these teachers was of noble birth and the fact that both, despite their plebeian origins, were given access to the highest court circles suggests that Maria Theresa's schooling was at times remote from the stiffness of court etiquette espoused by her father. So successful was Maria Theresa's musical education that her voice soon became widely celebrated.

Unsurprisingly, she grew quickly to be something of a high-spirited young girl with tomboyish traits. She was a crack shot and passionate aficionado of the card table (where later as Empress she lost significant sums). Once, after hearing the depressing reports of her senior officers smarting from some battlefield setback, she would invite them to forget their woes by playing *schnaps*, that ever-absorbing Austrian variant of *Bezique*, still favoured throughout central Europe by those fortunate in a digital age to have time on their hands.

Above all, however, a Jesuit education, then as today, stressed the importance of conscience. It was not enough, the priests insisted, to do something well; it had to be done to the best of one's ability. The invigilator of every action and even word spoken was not necessarily some external force but first and foremost one's conscience. Ignatian spiritual exercises were designed to give the recipient, through the device of colloquy, a glimpse of the verities of the faith, in particular an awareness of evil and the snares of the devil. A thrice-daily five-part examination of conscience was the prelude to a deeper thought process which demanded a constant awareness of answerability to higher authority. Without doubt, this part of her studies Maria Theresa absorbed completely.

It gave her both boldness and resolution: how could she fail if God was at her side? At the same time, it offered her comfort and sanctuary, that place, as Podewils, the Prussian ambassador, observed, where 'all the dangers of the world cannot reach her'.

By the time her teenage years had arrived, Maria Theresa had emerged as an accomplished fun-loving woman with a growing reputation for what would today be called a considerable 'force of personality'. It was, needless to say, all the drama of unrequited love which brought out this early demonstration of iron will.

Among her earliest letters are to be found a correspondence with someone she addresses in typically Austrian affectionate terminology as 'Mäuserl' (lit. little mouse), adding in perfect French (and Italian), 'je vous embrasse de tout mon Coeur; menagez vous bien, adieu caro viso; je suis la votre sponsia dilectissima'.[7]

'Mäuserl' was a childhood sweetheart, Francis Stephen, Duke of Lorraine and Bar, a distant cousin whose family had long felt completely at home in the Austrian court. He was short, stout, lacking in much of what would be called finesse but he was warm-hearted, fun, adventurous and unambitious for either political or social prestige. The two had known each other for years and it appears, according to British diplomatic documents, that Maria Theresa was already thinking ahead to the time when, with no male heir in sight, she would inherit the mantle of rule and require a suitable spouse.

The British ambassador, Thomas Robinson, later Lord Grantham, observed in a dispatch, dated 1735, how the young archduchess was developing into a 'princess of the highest spirit . . . she reasons already. Her father's losses are her own. She admires his virtues but then she condemns his mismanagement and is of a temper so formed for rule and ambition as to look upon him as little more than her administrator.'[8]

Robinson's evaluation was shared by other members of the diplomatic circle in Vienna. Some years earlier, the Venetian ambassador, Alvise Pisani, had written that 'no woman might be so well-fitted to succeed' her father. She had behaved with the greatest of tact and discretion while 'never losing sight of her future position'.

The future doge of Venice concluded: 'No woman in the world could have humoured her father in his obsession with male heirs without for a moment relinquishing her own claims.' The Venetian also observed something else, that beneath the charm and vivacity was steel: 'When she comes into her inheritance, those who are summoned to her councils will find that the decisions rest with her not with them.'[9]

Her perceptive eye was certainly not blind to the *difetti piccoli* of her future husband but she was in love with him despite any limitations. Francis Stephen's misfortune (if that is the right word) was to be a harmless, benign mediocrity in the shadow of one of the greatest women and sovereigns of the age. His advice in statecraft was useless and his military leadership qualities were, as would soon be painfully proved, virtually non-existent.

Yet he was a wonderful companion on the hunt, highly sexed and of a homeliness which offered, if not practical solutions to the challenges ahead, at least some respite and intimacy from a hostile world. His acumen in business affairs and his curiosity for scientific developments led him into avenues of Freemasonry current throughout Europe, attending lodges in The Hague and at Houghton in Norfolk where he was inducted by Robert Walpole, then British Prime Minister.[10]

Preparations for Maria Theresa's wedding to Francis Stephen had begun in 1735. Maria Theresa's father was mostly focused on the costs involved and instructed his ministers to ensure that in 'these penurious times' the wedding could be arranged as economically as possible.

Nonetheless, everything was relative and the Emperor insisted on, at the very least, an opera being performed to mark the occasion. On 31 January, Francis Stephen formally asked Charles VI for his blessing on the marriage of his daughter. This was an elaborate semi-public ceremonial symbolizing the mutually binding agreement. It involved an open procession to pay respects to the Emperor in his private apartments before approaching the audience chamber where the young archduchess accompanied by her mother and her *aya*, Countess Fuchs, awaited her suitor.

Spanish etiquette demanded that the young man genuflect thrice before the Empress but, after his second kneel, she approached him 'in a particular mark of favour', to show how pleased she was to see him. After a glance at her mother, Maria Theresa was allowed to receive a portrait of her suitor and a brief kiss. Every detail of this ceremony had been thought out by courtiers who, like courtiers everywhere, saw in each movement a vital moment of pregnant symbolism. But as in all courts, the formal panoply of pageantry on display was a carefully constructed façade behind which informal intimacy flourished.

The wedding took place a year later, in February 1736. Like the courtship, it was solemnized in front of a congregation of courtiers. The bridegroom was brought from Pressburg by coach and, once installed in the robing room, was attired entirely in white to meet his bride, also dressed in pure white. In the Augustinerkirche, the ritual of a Catholic wedding, which insisted that God as well as the married couple was present in the fate of any wedding, was painstakingly enacted. The ritual was familiar to anyone who had been married and followed usual conventions. Only in one respect did the imperial status of the bride make itself felt when, before acceding verbally to her vow, she looked at her parents for their approval.

After the ceremony, the entire wedding party led the imperial couple to their rooms in the Hofburg where, once all the guests had withdrawn, the Emperor and Empress undressed the married couple and left them to each other's now barely concealed passions. Several days of celebration followed, concluding with the obligatory masked ball, until Ash Wednesday and Lent brought all such festivities to a halt and the newly-weds set out for the great pilgrimage church of Mariazell in the Styrian Alps to pray for the blessing of the *Magna Mater Austriae* on their union.

The court settled down to its usual pursuit of rivalry and intrigue which was the main pastime of the two thousand courtiers who, whatever their differences in social status, were united by the common thread of ambition. Maria Theresa well understood this world and knew how to move effortlessly from the formal ceremonies to the informal intimacies. Francis Stephen's position was more precarious. He was, after all, the duke of a non-existent duchy living in an 'alien' court. Yet he had always been a favourite of the Emperor Charles VI and he fitted into the Viennese court with great ease.

Although Frederick of Prussia enjoyed poking fun at Francis Stephen as the 'Gasthaus landlord who leaves the running of everything to his wife', the young prince undoubtedly offered a strong emotional prop to Maria Theresa. She soon discovered that he was a serial adulterer but she harboured little malice towards him or even his mistresses, preferring to 'notch it up as another cross' to bear, although she proceeded against prostitution and vice with merciless vigour. But the affairs of state left little time for personal rancour and, whatever his 'distractions', their physical relationship flourished even when, after sixteen pregnancies, Maria Theresa's nocturnal energies began to flag. As Robinson observed, 'she sighs and pines all night for the Duke of Lorraine. If she sleeps it is only to dream of him; if she wakes it is but to talk of him.'[11]

Undoubtedly, it was the loneliness of her earliest childhood which inflamed this love. Youthful Company was rare and the death of her infant brother and another sibling, a sister who died aged five, meant that Maria Theresa enjoyed in the early days of the nursery only the company of her younger sister Marianne. At the same time, her mother Elisabeth-Christine was remote and diffident and the young archduchess came to rely for emotional support more and more on her *aya*, Countess Fuchs. When the young Francis Stephen had arrived at court aged nine, in order to be educated, Maria Theresa had just been born, but as she grew up it was hardly surprising that she was drawn to the elder boy and that in this vacuum *Reserl* would soon find an *Anschluss* with her 'Mäuserl'.

But any discussion of marriage involved high European diplomacy and ultimately Maria Theresa's desires and wishes had to be subordinated to the interests of *haute diplomatie*. Ironically, however, it was precisely as a result of this that Maria Theresa eventually *was* allowed to marry her beau. British diplomacy was keen that the future husband of the Habsburg heiress be a nonentity on the chessboard of European power politics. This at a stroke removed many eligible suitors.

Originally, it had been planned for her to wed Francis's elder brother, Clement. By all accounts, he was a splendid and talented young man but on the eve of his first visit to Vienna he died of smallpox. Thus did the gaze, already advanced, begin to intensify on Francis. It of course helped that he was the best of shots and the most companionable of men. Maria Theresa's father was enchanted but he knew better than most that ultimately the decision would have to reflect diplomatic sensibilities.

If the War of the Spanish Succession had proved the wisdom of not placing one's faith entirely in the resort to arms, the conflict had also left Charles VI with an abiding respect for England as an arbiter of Europe's destiny. It was a lesson his daughter would learn very quickly when, against her better judgement, she was 'persuaded' by London no less than three times to make peace with her arch-enemy Prussia.

In the 1730s all that lay ahead, but it was clear to the Habsburg emperor that it was Walpole and Cardinal Fleury who kept the peace of Europe and that whoever married his heir could not be a matter of indifference to England or France. Fortunately, Francis Stephen was only Duke of Lorraine and the sensitivity of Paris towards an extension of Austrian influence to her borders could be nullified by an adroit sleight of the cartographical hand. Much to Francis Stephen's chagrin, it was made clear that he would have to surrender the lands of his birthright. As the Emperor's principal adviser Baron Bartenstein made brutally clear in a message to Francis Stephen: 'No surrender of Lorraine, no archduchess.'[12]

This little matter of European power politics could be dealt with at once.

Defeat in the Polish War of Succession and the Austro-Russian Turkish war had unwound many of the victories of Prince Eugene, surrendering Belgrade to the Ottomans and, by the Treaty of Vienna of 1738, Francis Stephen was prevailed upon to formally cede Lorraine to the outgoing King of Poland, Stanislaus I. In return, Francis received the Grand Duchy of Tuscany and, as he had already married his childhood love on 12 February 1736, Maria Theresa became, in addition to an archduchess of Austria, the Grand Duchess of Tuscany. When the two visited Florence in January 1739, a triumphal arch designed by Jadot was erected to greet the happy couple, both of whom were unaware that they would never set foot in their Tuscan Duchy ever again, though not before the young duchess had moved a Florentine audience to tears by singing a duet with the celebrated Italian tenor Senismo. So enchanted was he and the other listeners at the unmistakeable musical talent displayed that the performance was interrupted by rapturous applause.

If the marriage in 1736 of Francis Stephen to Maria Theresa had seemed to offer a cloudless future, the storm clouds soon began to gather in central Europe. Not only had military defeats reversed earlier Austrian success in the Balkans, they had exposed bitterly the shortcomings of an army woefully neglected following the death of the great *Feldzeugmeister*, Prince Eugene, in 1736.

At the same time Charles VI, increasingly distrustful of military security, had already, some years earlier, moved his obsession from achieving a male heir to safeguarding the inheritance of his eldest daughter. The struggle *um das Erbe* was waged first and foremost by the diplomats and it was they who came up in 1717 with a means of ensuring Charles's offspring, as yet unborn, could inherit in preference to the daughters of his predecessor, his elder brother, Joseph I. Joseph's sudden death without a male heir in 1711 had already highlighted the Habsburg weakness in producing male heirs. Austrian diplomats knew all too well that if in France and England a royal house died out it could be replaced by another dynasty. Such a luxury did not pertain to Austria. The extinction of the Habsburg line would signify the collapse of imperial power in central Europe.

The absence of a male heir would also create a significant barrier to the Habsburgs retaining the title of Holy Roman Emperor which since 1438 had been an instrument of Habsburg influence in the heart of Europe. The Holy Roman Emperor enjoyed precedence over all continental European sovereigns. Powerful German states such as Bavaria and Saxony had to acknowledge this influence while the countless smaller states which made up the fabric of the *Reich* were all too familiar with the interference of Vienna through the *Reichshofrat* and *Reichsfiskal*. Thus was the way cleared for a *pactum mutuae successionis* or, as it came to be known, a *Pragmatic Sanction*.

This established the right of sole inheritance by the eldest son or, if no sons were born, eldest daughter. By its terms, the Austrian Habsburg line was finally, in theory, freed from the risk of a divided inheritance. The 'Sanction' certainly ensured harmony internally within the Habsburg dynasty but, when it came to securing the agreement of the European powers, the issue not only became more complex but forced Vienna to make many harmful concessions in return for pledges of support, few of which, as it transpired, proved worth the paper they were written on.

CHAPTER 2

The Struggle for the Inheritance

THAT A EUROPEAN MONARCH should have staked so much on paper promises betokened a certain naivety but the lesson of the sanguinary Spanish
War of Succession was not lost on Charles VI. The Habsburg dominions
could only exist with the support of other powers and the need to stabi-
lize the dynasty's future required new diplomatic techniques. Each
government which formally recognized the Pragmatic Sanction exacted
a considerable price. Most rapacious of them all was England which
demanded Austria surrender the ambitions to become a global trading
power through the ports of Trieste and Ostend which had been so close
to Charles's heart.

The imperial Ostend East India Trading Company had the potential
to rival the British East India Company. With ships captained by English,
German and Dutch seamen, the company had already mounted several
expeditions to the Far East, carrying the Habsburg ensign as far as
China, when Charles reluctantly agreed to close it down in return for
English support.[1] It had been a last link with the universality of the
Habsburgs but it had been consistently denounced in London as a threat.
Indeed, the British Prime Minister, Robert Walpole, was accused of
taking bribes from the company so that he would acquiesce to its
continued existence, but its activities filled the House of Commons with
anxiety and distrust and it remained, until its eventual suppression, the
most serious thorn in the side of positive Anglo-Austrian relations. The
port of Ostend would only lose its significance with the Treaty of Paris
between Austria and France in 1757, long after the imperial East India
Company had been shuttered but, until then, British merchants and

statesmen were always wary of the trading potential of the Austrian Lowlands.

One of the imperial Ostend East India Company's most intrepid ships, the *San Carlo*, sank just off the coast of Trieste in 1740 at a spot marked by the present Molo Audace (formerly called Molo San Carlo). Its foundering seemed to mark symbolically the formal end of all Austria's and Charles's wider ambitions.

There would be a brief revival in the 1770s under the British-Austrian sailor William Bolts, but it was a pale shadow of the Ostend Company's ambitions and reach. An unintended consequence of all this would be Austria's eventual consolidation in central Europe, but at the time it seemed a humiliating concession. Yet so large did it loom in British domestic politics that it was impossible for any government in London to tolerate its continued existence.[2]

At the same time, France demanded, as we have seen, Lorraine and made it a term of recognizing the Pragmatic Sanction.

Everywhere, Austria's diplomats worked tirelessly to secure recognition of their Emperor's wishes but only Prince Eugene warned, before he died in 1736, that a strong army was worth a dozen Pragmatic Sanctions. Two years later, Maria Theresa saw the sense of such advice when her husband returned from the Turkish wars, not as a hero but as just one Austrian military incompetent among a sea of others. The Turkish war, which forced Vienna to give up all the territory including Belgrade which had been won by Prince Eugene, was an early lesson in the failure of the Habsburgs' advisers to confront their sovereigns with the truth. The two most prominent Austrian generals in the Turkish campaign, Wallis and Neipperg, were court-martialled and placed under house arrest, scapegoats for the debacle which could only partially be attributed to them.

In addition to England's calculation and France's greed, Spain, Bavaria and Saxony all bided their time and awaited the death of Charles and the accession of a young and, as they calculated, inexperienced daughter. Cardinal Fleury insisted that he did not wish for the Austrian domains to be partitioned among her neighbours. Rather, he wanted only to 'tear out a few feathers' from the fattened goose.[3]

However, in the event, it was the new King of Prussia, Frederick II, who would be the first to make a move. His father, Frederick William I, had died on 31 May and, in the four months which ensued before Charles's death, the young Prussian king pondered how he could 'make a splash'. He had inherited an army of 80,000 men and a treasury which, thanks to the parsimony of his father, could well withstand the shock of limited conflict and fund all the necessary sinews of a *blitzkrieg*.

Such is the ingratitude of monarchs that Frederick felt no compunction in turning on the very house which had established him as king. It had been Charles VI who had argued, following Prussian support during the War of the Spanish Succession, that the Electors of Brandenburg be granted the title Kings in Prussia. The self-styled *roi-philosophe* who had praised the supremacy of moral law less than one year earlier in his essay on 'Anti-Machiavel' had had a conversion to realpolitik which egocentrics might recognize the world over as the first slippery step towards total moral degradation.

It now mattered even less to Frederick that he, too, had personally pledged to defend the Pragmatic Sanction and recognize the indivisibility of the Habsburg inheritance. As Macaulay acidly observed:

> The selfish rapacity of the King of Prussia gave the signal to his neighbours. The whole world sprang to arms. On the head of Frederick is all the blood which was shed in every quarter of the globe. The evils produced by his wickedness were felt in lands where the name of Prussia was unknown; and in order that he might rob a neighbour, whom he had promised to defend, black men fought on the coast of Coromandel and red men scalped each other by the Great Lakes of North America.[4]

The beginning for Frederick, as for many a later megalomaniac, was promising: he achieved total surprise – neither his relatives nor his ambassadors were informed before he mobilized twenty thousand troops to march into Silesia. Just before they entered Silesia, Frederick sent a personal envoy, Count Gotter, to Maria Theresa to offer a draft convention whereby he would support Austria on condition of her surrendering Silesia. This was merely a gesture, and he could not have expected a serious response, but Maria Theresa's firm refusal to meet the envoy while Prussian troops menaced her possessions was an unexpected snub, causing dismay in court circles in Berlin where hopes of an eventual settlement after the initial incursion ran high.

Silesia was undefended and the 3,000 troops stationed there were no match for the well-drilled overwhelming numbers of Prussians who entered Breslau on New Year's Day 1741 with Frederick at their head.

Shocked and affronted, Maria Theresa saw the very inheritance of her father threatened by the Hohenzollern upstart. Cynics – and certainly Frederick belonged to their number – might say that, as the Pragmatic Sanction was bereft of positive stipulations and relied entirely on goodwill, it could be violated with moral impunity. Frederick, as an admirer of Voltaire, would have seen little to sanction him for such behaviour but Macaulay was surely right when he later wrote:

> Even if no positive stipulations had existed, the arrangement was one which no good man would have been willing to disturb. It was an arrangement acceptable to the great population whose happiness was chiefly concerned. It was an arrangement which made no change in the distribution of power among the states of Christendom. It was an arrangement which could be set aside only by means of a general war. The sovereigns of Europe were therefore bound by every obligation which those who are entrusted with power over their fellow creatures ought to hold most sacred to respect and defend the rights of the Archduchess. Her situation and her personal qualities were such as might be expected to move the mind of any generous man to pity, admiration and chivalrous tenderness.

But Frederick was not alone in ignoring such considerations. England, whose King, George II, feared for the integrity of his 'country seat', Hanover, urged his ambassador in Vienna, Robinson, to bring heavy moral pressure on Maria Theresa to seek an 'accommodation' with Prussia. Robinson was instructed by London to 'expiate on the dangerous designs of France . . . of the powerful combination against Austria'. Maria Theresa's response was somehow typically Viennese: she dismissed this form of 'British support' as 'yet another burden on the nerves'.[5]

France, Bavaria, Spain and Saxony watched on with interest as Frederick's troops won a resounding victory at Mollwitz, although

Frederick, terrified by his first experience of war, hastened off the battlefield and was not there to see it. The Austrian cavalry had, as it was so often to do, easily defeated the stationary Prussian horse but the superb fire-discipline of the Prussian infantry, advancing as on a drill square, won the day for Frederick.

When Maria Theresa was confronted with the news of the defeat she asked hard questions of her advisers and officers, who finally told her the truth: that her army, with the exception of some cavalry regiments, was largely decrepit, her infantry and artillery no longer capable of waging modern warfare and, above all, her treasury completely empty, incapable of financing even the most basic requirements of war.

The old men who advised her offered only caution and retreat. Taking their cue from the British minister, they counselled accommodation and compromise. Maria Theresa would later observe that 'If God himself had not arranged for the death of them all, I should never have survived.'[6]

It did not help that in Silesia, while the partly mixed German-speaking and Polish peasantry remained loyal to Maria Theresa and the Austrian troops, the Silesian nobility swiftly embraced the Prussian occupiers. In the words of the Austrian commander in the province, Maximilian Ulysses Browne: 'From all outward appearances we can promise ourselves nothing but good from the country people, I only wish we could be sure of the same from the whole of the nobility.'[7]

While Maria Theresa's outnumbered and outgunned troops struggled in Silesia, several German intellectuals rallied to her defence in an early example of what might be termed a military PR campaign. Jean Ignace de Roderique wrote a widely disseminated article in the *Gazette de Cologne* which criticized Frederick and praised the moral cause of the Austrians. The Prussian king was furious when he read the article and characteristically ordered dockers to beat Roderique up when he appeared a few days later in Cologne harbour. Freedom of expression was not something this 'enlightened' sovereign tolerated.

At the same time, Dutch newspapers carried cartoons lampooning Cardinal Fleury and Frederick as twisted greedy men eager to violate the fresh beauty of the fair Austrian Maria Theresa.

Frederick, whose eye for published news was acute, stamped and raged when these articles were shown to him by his ambassadors but, like many an invader in Europe after him, he found he could not easily win the 'hearts and minds' of those he sought to conquer. In an act of cerebral vindictiveness rather typical of this Prussian *soi-disant* intellectual, he ordered, after the victory of Mollwitz, a Te Deum to be sung in every Prussian church. Frederick carefully chose the readings and these included Timothy 2: 11–12: 'A woman should learn in quietness and full submission. I do not permit a woman to teach or assume authority over a man; she must be quiet.'

At this early stage in her fortunes, Maria Theresa indeed was quiet. It is said that when she heard the true details of her inheritance's finances she asked to leave the room for a moment and on entering the nearby anteroom burst into tears for five minutes before regaining her composure and returning to her advisers.

Gradually, she began to trust her instincts. She knew that in Browne and Khevenhueller she had competent commanders but she still felt at this stage compelled to bow to the 'wisdom' of other advisers. Count Kinsky, her Bohemian chancellor, was fearful that his estates in Silesia would be ravaged by war and so counselled his sovereign against choosing too 'vigorous' a commander for her forces. He had recommended Neipperg, recently released from prison, following his failure in the Turkish wars. But Mollwitz had shown Neipperg to be lacking in all the energy and force needed for a successful general; above all he was unlucky.

No doubt, Kinsky and the other members of the high aristocracy felt, with that frivolity which was even apparent a hundred and fifty years later in 1914, that Neipperg would recover and perhaps knock Frederick quickly out and, if not, their estates would be largely preserved under Prussia. But Mollwitz galvanized the young sovereign in a way that was to have far more profound aftershocks than the effect on Austrian arms. Mollwitz had shown that the promises and sweet words of support from Russia and Saxony and especially France were worthless. Their greed far outweighed their fear of the growth of Prussia. France was busily arming, nobody could rely on Russia and, if the Dutch were divided in their response, the Elector of Bavaria egged on by Paris was ready to mobilize.

Later historians have nearly always chosen to focus on the loss of Silesia as the principal cause of the wars of the Austrian Succession. In fact, France not Prussia was the main antagonist. Paris had developed a highly elaborate plan aimed at dismembering Austria and eliminating her from the first rank of European powers. Bohemia and Upper Austria were to go to the Elector of Bavaria who would also, for good measure, usurp the traditional convention whereby the Holy Roman Emperors were nearly invariably Habsburg sovereigns. Lower Silesia and Glatz would of course go to Prussia while Moravia (Vienna's 'back garden', to quote a later Austrian chancellor[8]) would, along with Upper Silesia, go to Saxony. Austrian Lombardy would, meanwhile, be absorbed by Spain, deluded into recovering the old territories of the 'Spanish Roads'.[9] The Habsburg 'empire' would at a stroke be reduced to the territories of 'Inner Austria' (Styria, Carinthia and Carniola), Vienna, Lower Austria and the permanently rebellious Kingdom of Hungary, still recovering from centuries of Ottoman rule. This was not 'tearing out a few feathers' from the Austrian goose, this was devouring most of the carcass with alacrity.

But every game bird usually contains some undissolved, teeth-breaking shot and it was Maria Theresa's destiny to ensure her predators choked on the object of their greed. The 'betrayal' of France – Marshal Belle-Isle was quickly dispatched to coordinate a campaign with Frederick – was a wake-up call. Yet while London, and indeed most of Maria Theresa's advisers, including even her husband, counselled an accommodation with Frederick, something occurred which awoke a stubborn refusal by the young Empress to give in. To this day it is impossible to ascertain with certainty, save for her developing iron determination, why, despite all the intense pressure brought to bear, she refused to comply.

She remained obdurate even when, on 5 June, France signed a treaty with Prussia. That which a few weeks earlier had seemed unthinkable had happened. At the English King George II's urging, the British ambassador to Vienna, Robinson, once again urged the 'Queen of Hungary' to compromise with Prussia. Maria Theresa listened politely but it was another example of the Englishman 'getting on our nerves'. After hearing the diplomat's carefully prepared advice, the young sovereign erupted in emotion 'with exclamations and sudden starts of passion'. This was a performance entirely alien to the mindset of the bloodless Robinson who was taken aback by the sheer force of female outrage which now met him. As the Austrian calmed herself, she consented (it would be the first of many times under English pressure) to open negotiations with

Frederick, but she made it abundantly clear to the hapless Englishman counselling appeasement that she was not going to waver in her determination to safeguard her inheritance:

> Not only for political reasons but from conscience and honour, I shall not consent to part with much in Silesia. You will see that no sooner is one enemy satisfied than another one starts up; another and then another must be appeased, and all at my expense. I am convinced of your *bonne volonté* but your mission will be as fruitless as that of Graf Gotter: remember my words![10]

This interview resonated throughout Vienna. Maria Theresa's outburst marked something new and powerful. Her words might not shift British policy but Robinson was clearly impressed and, if he might be forced by London to remain unmoveable, the same could not be said of the Queen of Hungary's closer advisers. They took their lead from their sovereign's husband. Francis felt no longer able to influence his wife's opinions. In affairs of state, Francis was beginning to learn that, however devoted she might be to him, his *Reserl* was utterly indifferent to his political opinions: just because he had had to surrender Lorraine, that did not mean she was going to renounce Silesia. He fell quickly into line.

Maria Theresa's internal public relations effort was as successful as her external one. Her advisers, seeing the complicity and loyalty of Francis, quickly realized that any failure to obey their Queen would lead to the charge of desertion and, devastating at any time in a court, ostracism. The Sovereign felt the change immediately, her instincts quickly gauging the new mood of compliance.

She began to understand that in a crisis most men need leadership. She was determined to give it, even if it was in the teeth of contrary advice. Her older advisers, Harrach, Kinsky, Sinzendorf, she began to ignore and circumvent. Only one of the 'old men' managed to cling on to her confidence and he repaid it amply in becoming her staunchest defender at court. Johann Christoph Bartenstein had been brought up a devout Lutheran but had converted to Catholicism in 1715 at the age of 25 in order to advance his career. His Catholicism apparently was sincere, although it seems to have had a rather Jansenist flavour. This supported strong local churches and bishops over unhesitating obedience to Rome, views which found favour with Maria Theresa even if Jansenist theological arguments over the foundations and exigency of grace left her unmoved.

Perhaps the strict Lutheran upbringing of Bartenstein reminded Maria Theresa of her mother's childhood. In any event, although Bartenstein had been involved in the ill-fated Pragmatic Sanction, he quickly demonstrated his fealty to his new sovereign. When, on her accession, he had prostrated himself, knowing all too well that she had a dim view of his abilities, he had offered her his resignation. But with that intuition which served her so well and seemed to be free of all personal vindictiveness, she had simply told him to get up, observing: 'You had much better stay and try to do what good you can; I shall see to it that you do no harm.'[11]

Thus did Bartenstein become the most faithful of stewards and most loyal of courtiers. He would also, most importantly for Maria Theresa, become the most implacable enemy of Prussia, a masterly publicist who ensured all the legality of Austria's claims were published in accessible and legally defensible documents. Gradually, under Bartenstein's guidance, even the ministers she had bypassed began to sense the strength of their sovereign. She acquired at this time an ability, widely noticed, to make the most arrogant and powerful members of her court obedient slaves.

Her charm became legendary and later historians have accused her of weaving a spell of 'male fantasies' for centuries afterwards, but the attraction men felt in her presence is too well and extensively documented to be so easily dismissed. Outstanding among the documents is her famous letter, with its portraits of Maria Theresa and her son Joseph, to Khevenhueller following his conquest of Munich in 1742:

Dear and faithful Khevenhueller,

Here you behold the Queen who knows what it signifies to be forsaken by the whole world. And here also is the heir to the throne. What do you think will become of this child? To you as a true and tried servant of the State, your most gracious lady offers this picture of herself and therewith her whole power and resources – everything indeed that her kingdom contains and can do. You, the hero and trusted vassal, shall dispose of all things as you think fit and according as you would render account before God and the world in general. May your achievements be as renowned as those of your master, the great Eugene, who rests in God. Be fully assured that now and always you and your family will never lack the grace and favour and thanks of myself and my descendants. A world-wide fame will also be yours. Fare well and fight well.[12]

When Maria Theresa wrote this letter, she might be forgiven for giving vent to powerful emotional forces. She had a few weeks earlier given birth to a son and heir, Joseph, but Prague had been occupied by the Bavarians and their elector had already crowned himself King of Bohemia, thus paving the way for his election as Holy Roman Emperor. On the day Maria Theresa penned this letter, the upstart Wittelsbach was actually crowned Holy Roman Emperor in Frankfurt. Yet these hammer blows were partly reversed by Khevenhueller's destruction of a French army at Linz, a Tyrolean uprising which slaughtered various Bavarian relief columns and, sweetest of all, the Austrian occupation of Munich. On the day Charles Albert, Elector of Bavaria, was crowned emperor in Frankfurt, Khevenhueller occupied Munich and sent the usurper an unequivocal message: he torched the Elector's palace.

The election of a non-Habsburg emperor posed immediately a practical challenge for Maria Theresa's soldiers. Accustomed to fighting under the standard of the famous double-headed eagle of the Holy Roman Empire, Maria Theresa ordered the 'temporary' removal of the insignia from her battle standards. In its place came a bold image of the Madonna, an inspired choice uniting, as it did, the *Magna Mater Austriae* (Great Mother of Austria) with the Mother of Christ in a fierce *Mater Castrorum* (Mother of War) which combined all the divine prestige and purity of motive of the Virgin Mary with the steely determination of her soldiers' sovereign.

This showed yet again Maria Theresa's public relations skills but nothing demonstrated better their outstanding potential than her dealings with her eastern flank, Turkey and Hungary. The Ottomans were busy digesting the Serbian territory they had won by the Treaty of Belgrade concluded by Maria Theresa's father. His daughter quickly assured the Ottoman representatives that they need fear no renewal of hostilities from the side of Vienna. There would be no compensation for territories lost elsewhere at the expense of the Porte. She was true to her word and for thirty-two years not a single Austrian soldier fired a shot in anger at the Ottoman forces.

Hungary was altogether a more complicated affair. Here, however, Maria Theresa was able to benefit from the wise guidance of Count Janos Palffy, a keen diviner of the Magyar temperament who had negotiated the Peace of Szatmar of 1711 between Maria Theresa's father and the unruly Hungarian nobility who had raised the standard of rebellion under 'prince' Rakoczi. That the Magyar aristocrats had deserted their 'prince' for the Habsburgs was due in no small way to the skill of Palffy. Fearless, having fought in the Turkish wars under Prince Eugene, he was in his eighth decade when he encountered the desperation of his young sovereign. Slightly deaf and increasingly blind, his political instincts remained undimmed.

Those who have enjoyed the unique riches of a relationship between a 20-year-old and someone nearly 60 years older will well know that such a friendship enjoys a dynamic rarely present in friendships developed between contemporaries of similar vintage. When Palffy, aged 78, first encountered his 23-year-old Queen there was an immediate magnetism on both sides. Palffy, the Judex Curiae (Judge Royal), personified moral authority in Hungary. Universally respected and in some cases feared, he was the embodiment of those higher values which are at the heart of every great historical nation's consciousness and which are invariably brought into play in moments of crisis.

Palffy had also served as viceroy (Ban) of Croatia and knew when to compromise and when to be intransigent in his dealings with that notoriously difficult warrior nation. He quickly saw that his young sovereign was made of character and courage, two qualities essential to Magyar concepts of chivalry.[13] With the wisdom of his years, he quickly realized that by helping Maria Theresa cement a relationship with his country he would also bring Hungarian interests into a more favourable constellation in Vienna.

Indeed, such would be the depth and stability of the new Queen of Hungary's relationship with her Magyar subjects that her reign would be remembered fondly as offering a greater period of tranquillity in Hungarian affairs than at any other time past or future. That this was to be possible was the result of Palffy impressing upon Maria Theresa the unique qualities of her Magyar subjects and their capacity for fearless devotion to their sovereign. In return, Maria Theresa would, despite initiating one of the greatest periods of centralization and reform in European history, allow her Hungarian lands the absolute guarantee of autonomy in the governance of her subjects there.

In accordance with Hungarian tradition, Maria Theresa would have to be crowned 'King' of Hungary (the Hungarian Constitution did not formally recognize a queen). The same tradition required then, as it would for nearly two more centuries, that the monarch canter on horse-back and ascend the 'Royal Mount' of Pressburg,[14] fifty miles to the east of Vienna. Wearing the historic robes of St Stephen and the famous Hungarian crown with its crooked cross, the sovereign was expected to take the slope at a brisk canter and, with the ancient sabre of the Hungarian kings, point to the four axes of the compass in turn, swearing to defend with her life the integrity of the 'Hungarian' lands.

It was the first full-dress occasion of her reign and it has rightly come down to us as the most dazzling achievement of 'impression management' of her entire career.

CHAPTER 3

The Hungarian Concordat

Maria theresa's treasury was empty but Palffy had advised her well that the Magyar spirit responded above all to generosity and extravagance and that parsimony along with cowardice and discourtesy were capital offences in the Hungarian almanack. Ignoring the imminent bankruptcy of her court and the mounting debts arising from a rapidly increasing military budget, Maria Theresa spared no expense in the expedition to Pressburg. A cortège of barges was arranged, bedecked in the Hungarian colours of red, white and green and crewed by men attired in the most lavish *attilas* of traditional Hungarian costume. The late afternoon sun glittered on the gold braid of these men, each chosen for their physique and handsome appearance. At the head of this resplendent procession sailed the flagship in which a vast tent had been erected for Maria Theresa and her husband. If the new 'King' of Hungary was to conquer this notoriously rebellious and proud people, there would have to be a sense that they were part of something spectacular, not just in sentiment but also appearance. Impression management, Palffy had advised his sovereign, was something that could have been invented by the Magyars.

As the sun moved lower in the sky, the Austrian flotilla tied up on the western side of the Danube. Leaving all her ministers on board, Maria Theresa, accompanied only by her husband and a white-coated bodyguard of imperial cuirassiers, equipped with blackened breastplates, was met at the border by six hussars in a uniform of gorgeous blue and gold, the colours of the princely Eszterhazy family. The hussars conducted the royal couple to a meadow trimmed and decorated with two pavilions in the Turkish style with vast canopies and colourful swirls. One of the pavilions was reserved for Maria Theresa, who now changed into a dress with Hungarian devices; in the other were assembled the deputations from the chambers of the Hungarian Diet.

The coronation was attended by, among others, the cautious British diplomat Robinson but he, too, seems, as his *diamanté* prose indicates, to have surrendered entirely to the spell of the young woman:

> The coronation was magnificent. The Queen was all charm; she rode gallantly up the royal mount and defied the four corners of the world with the drawn sabre in a manner to show she had no occasion for that weapon to conquer all who saw her. The antiquated crown received new graces from her head and the old tattered robe of St Stephen became her as well as her own rich habit.[1]

Robinson was not the only eyewitness to be captivated; a diplomatic colleague observed that, even without the crown, Maria Theresa's appearance was invested with 'an air of delicacy occasioned by her recent confinement' becoming 'most attractive, the fatigue of the ceremony diffused an animated glow over her countenance while her beautiful hair flowed in ringlets over her shoulders'.[2]

After a night's rest, the political and constitutional duties began. Maria Theresa had two guides to help her through the tortuous negotiations which now unfolded. Palffy was one but the other was perhaps even more useful in this situation where stalemate and fractiousness seemed to dominate.

Count Antun Grassalkovich had not been born a Magyar; his family origins were Slav and could be traced first to Slovakia and then to Croatia. His grandfather had been called Horvath, a name which in Magyar means Croat. His wealth, which derived mostly from a fortuitous marriage, had established him in Pressburg where his palace today serves as the residence of the Slovak state's president. In 1741 he was still in his early forties and could reinforce Palffy's elder statesman wisdom with energy and determination.

When the Hungarian magnates baulked at the idea of a governor imposed upon them from Vienna, it was Grassalkovich who came up with the compromise whereby the Diet chose their own Palatine (viceroy) of Hungary with Vienna's approval. A range of smaller constitutional points were argued but eventually conceded by Maria Theresa in the teeth of her Austrian advisers' resistance.

It was a sign of how much friction was in the air that day that, as the Austrian high aristocracy in their robes of the Order of the Golden Fleece sought to line the steps of the cathedral, they were rudely pushed away by the Hungarian nobles claiming precedence. The commotion of feathers and dolmans on the one hand and medieval ermine on the other was an unedifying sight. As this struggle continued, Maria Theresa emerged from her carriage, tired and pale. The atmosphere was anything but festive. Most displeasing of all, she had been separated, by protocol, from her husband. The Hungarians were adamant that he be excluded from the ritual and that any role as co-regent be denied to him.

Maria Theresa was alone as she faced a sea of unknown and unsmiling faces. Yet the majesty of the crown, to this day still the most powerful symbol of Hungarian sovereignty, played a pivotal role. As Palffy placed the crown with its crooked cross on her head, it was as if a sea-change came over all the participants. Petty arguments over protocol and precedence were suddenly forgotten and the crowds beyond catching a glimpse of Maria Theresa's head burst into wild cheering and cries of *Eljen Hurra!* Not even the most heartless of the magnates could fail to be moved by this display, and the proceedings took on an intensity bordering on hysteria.

Later, as she settled down to the state banquet, shorn of her crown, her natural colouring impressed all who came near to her. Above all, reunited with her husband, she could savour the admiration (and relief) Francis Stephen clearly felt at the way the festivities had developed. It mattered little to him that he could not share his wife's titles, and not for the first or indeed last time was he content to bask in her reflected glory. Her consort looked on happy for his wife's undoubted success and sufficiently self-deprecating to be not in the slightest offended that his was a role of only secondary importance.

Whatever the demands of her newly faithful subjects, one thing and one thing only appeared to matter to the young Queen: would the Hungarians, with their Slovak and Croatian subjects, provide her with an army with which she could recover Silesia?

Brutal reality began to intrude once the passions of the day had subsided. News arrived of the treaty between France and Bavaria at Nymphenburg which at a stroke began to implement French machinations for the dismemberment of Maria Theresa's domains. On 24 July the hapless Robinson renewed his pleas to the young sovereign to come to an agreement with Frederick.

Eventually, Maria Theresa would make peace with Frederick under English pressure no less than three times, but in the afterglow of her Hungarian coronation she was in no mood for compromise and a violent argument ensued which Robinson found 'highly disagreeable'. But with the help of her husband and her Austrian ministers, Robinson was able to persuade Maria Theresa to at least explore an agreement with Frederick.

In this early negotiation Maria Theresa found she was capable of the bluntest of deceptions. An agreement with Frederick, which offered most of Silesia in return for hard cash and Frederick's support for her husband's candidature for the imperial crown, was hedged around with so many conditions by the young sovereign that when Robinson warned it might prove unacceptable, Maria Theresa flared up at him shouting, 'I wish he may reject it!' She eventually calmed down and resigned herself to discussions with Berlin along these lines but her heart was far from in it.

A curious letter to her Bohemian chancellor Kinsky hints at a capacity for subterfuge not usually associated with Maria Theresa's character, and the fact that the letter was sent *en clair* indicates that such deception did not come naturally to her:

I have found it necessary to deceive my ministers but since you are the only one I trust, I do not include you and I shall confide in you my true intentions. Today we shall inform Robinson of our conditions; since he has gone so far as to threaten us it is necessary to keep the door open behind us and indulge him. Perhaps by doing this we may obtain better terms from the other side.

It is my firm resolve never to give up any part of Silesia, still less the entirety of Lower Silesia; I have meanwhile indicated to Robinson through the Chancellor that hypothetically I might surrender Breslau in return for a payment of two million to compensate us and Saxony.

If Prussia will then bring all her force against our enemies and support our claim to the Imperial crown, I shall allow myself to be bargained with a little; in this way we should be able to tide Robinson over his difficulties. God preserve me from really wishing this! No I wish only to give the impression to the ministers so that they will circulate this rumour and thus keep Robinson in play until a reply comes from Bavaria. Nobody knows of this idea and we can discuss it with Bartenstein this evening when I shall be alone.[3]

In its naivety and contradictions this letter offers very little that might be termed mature diplomacy. In later years, with more sophisticated advisers, especially with men of such stature as Kaunitz and Lacy, she would be capable of the most daring and accomplished strokes of statesmanship, but at this stage she was a young girl foundering, ill at ease in the sharks' pool of European diplomatic practice while nonetheless determined to swim with them.

Frederick's response to Robinson's suggestion was predictably contemptuous. His grenadiers had already seized Breslau by the time the British envoy arrived in Berlin and, when Robinson dared to remind the Prussian king of the guarantees he had once made under the Pragmatic Sanction, Frederick erupted:

Who observes guarantees in these times? Has not France 'guaranteed' the Pragmatic Sanction? Has not England? . . . Why have you all not rushed to the aid of the Queen? I am at the head of an invincible army, I am already master of a country which I must and which I will have. My ancestors would rise out of their tombs to reproach me were I to abandon the rights they have transmitted to me.[4]

When Robinson asked simply what answer he should bring back to Vienna, Frederick coldly observed: 'Return with this answer: They who wish for peace should give me what I desire. I am weary of ultimatums and I shall have no more of them. My position is immoveable. This is my final answer and I shall give no other.' At which point, with a sweeping gesture removing his hat, Frederick indicated the interview was at an end and that Robinson could withdraw.

By mid-summer the vultures were gathering. A French army under the command of the Duke of Broglie crossed the Rhine. Saxony, having initially allied herself with Austria, changed sides and the Bavarians, recovering from their earlier setbacks, swept across Upper Austria towards Linz.

Truly, the situation was desperate: Prussia was ensconced in Breslau and Lower Silesia; the Bavarians were making swift progress along the Danube valley; Belle-Isle, the French envoy, was progressing with an overpoweringly brilliant retinue from court to court in Germany, 'insinuating, cajoling and intimidating'; Saxony, Cologne and the Palatinate were joining forces with Charles Albert while French troops disguised as Bavarian auxiliaries (there had been no formal French declaration of war) were heading in the direction of Vienna. A junction between the French, Bavarians and Prussians outside the gates of the Austrian capital seemed not inconceivable.

If that were not enough, George II of England, while pledging support for Austria, was declaring to Prussia his 'neutrality' so as to safeguard his beloved Hanover. At the same time, Spain was about to attack in Italy, and Sardinia was about to join forces with France.

There appeared to be no alternative but surrender. The young sovereign had learnt the most bitter of lessons and she had finally resigned herself to realities. But not for the first or indeed last time did those around Maria Theresa fail to get the measure of her.

Bartenstein drafted a note of surrender and Maria Theresa scribbled simply one word, *Placet*, adding underneath 'as there is no other way but with profound grief'. But Maria Theresa, even if she was prepared to lose her composure, did not lose her nerve. The Hungarian coronation had been a salutary reminder of the difficulties that surrounded dealings with her most fractious subjects, but she had seen enough of the Magyar hussars who had escorted her at Pressburg to realize that, whatever their demands, the Hungarians could deliver soldiers – and so she returned to Hungary to appeal to their chivalry and their honour. She would throw herself on their mercy and summon them to arms.

On 7 September she arrived at Pressburg and four days later, on the 11th, she summoned the magnates to the castle where she addressed the Hungarians with a skilfully worded speech. The original has survived with its handwritten alterations, all in Latin and all carefully calibrated to arouse the deepest of emotions among its audience. Like the accomplished musician she was, the Queen judged crescendo and climax perfectly:

> The disastrous situation of our affairs has moved us to lay before our most dear and faithful states of Hungary the recent violation of Austria. I lay before you the mortal danger now impending over this kingdom and I beg to propose to you the consideration of a remedy. The very existence of the kingdom of Hungary – of our own person – of our children and of our crown are now at stake! We have been forsaken by all!
>
> We therefore place our sole resource in the fidelity, the arms and the long-tried immemorial valour of the Hungarians, exhorting you, the states and orders, to deliberate without delay in this extreme danger, on the most effectual measures for the security of our person, of our children and of our crown, and to carry them into immediate execution. In regard to ourselves, the faithful states and orders of Hungary shall experience our heartfelt cooperation in all things which may promote the immaculate contentment of this ancient kingdom and the honour of its people.[5]

This appeal had been described as exuding a certain sobriety but the Latin text is of a Roman majesty which, in its rhythms and vitality, is very far from being 'matter-of-factness'. Perhaps it was forgotten that the Austrian pronunciation of Latin with its explosive consonants was a more emotive sound than the clipped English pronunciation so beloved of Oxbridge-educated parsons.[6] Her speech was not so much a plea for help as a summons to arms.

Her Austrian advisers had feared the consequences of bringing the Magyars to an insurrection. 'Immaculate contentment' was not a state of affairs usually associated with Hungary. Was this not a gesture fraught with risk? Was this not potentially just another nail in the Habsburg coffin? But this speech certainly had the desired effect. The difficult, arrogant men could not but be moved by the tenderness of the figure before them voicing all the power of cadence, dynamic and crescendo in her speech. Dressed as she was in solemn black, against which her blonde ringlets shone like amber in the morning sun, the visual and aural effect was simply devastating.

It was Maria Theresa's calculation that if she appealed to these men as equals, rather than as her subjects, they would put aside their *amour propre* and respond chivalrously. She may well have understood what the response might be but even Palffy, her aged adviser, could not have imagined the power of the response.

The Hungarian magnates assembled drew their swords and cried *Eljen!* Eyewitnesses relate that they also cried 'vitam et sanguinem pro nostro rege!' Few chose to hear the phrase several of the magnates present, according to Hungarian sources, also muttered under their breath afterwards: 'Sed non avernam!' (But we shall not pay!)[7]

Irrespective of their reluctance to offer any financial backing, they were prepared to supply men and horses. They pledged 40,000 troops and 25,000 horses. More, they urged her to relocate her court to Győr and place her security and that of her son in their hands. This generous offer the sovereign resisted but Hungarian experience taught her perhaps the most useful lesson of her reign to date: namely that if she eliminated the 'forbidden zone' which normally surrounded the monarch, she could appeal directly to them and bend them to her will. As she advised Khevenhueller, busy preparing the defences of Vienna with regard to that city's inhabitants: 'Never forget the Viennese will do anything if talked to kindly and shown affection.'[8]

The Magyars were nothing if not hard-headed beneath their gestures and this promise of support came at the price of concessions to help them achieve 'immaculate contentment'. Hungary's taxation would be left largely to the magnates, who would retain their traditional exemption from state levy. This compact would run for more than a hundred years and, in return, Maria Theresa would gain recognition of her husband as co-regent and retain direct control of the beautiful lands of Transylvania. By preparing to display her son to the Magyar nobility, Maria Theresa was sealing this compact for generations, promising that one day the Magyars would indeed have a male sovereign as their king.

Three days later, the French and Bavarians occupied Linz and the Elector of Bavaria, with extravagant *folie de grandeur*, promptly declared himself Archduke of Austria and offered himself to the Hungarians as a 'worthy candidate' for their crown. The Magyars listened to the Bavarian envoy before showing him politely the door. They had just sworn their fealty to Maria Theresa. They were Hungarians not treacherous Germans. Nobility and honour were not just titles but qualities earned by action. The message to be taken back to Charles Albert was short but sincere: anyone setting foot in Hungary hoping to come between that nation and their Queen 'would return home in a coffin'.

CHAPTER 4

The Turning of the Tide

THE HUNGARIAN PROMISE OF arms and men was not long in coming. Three new regiments of hussars were raised within days. In addition, six regiments of infantry swore an oath of allegiance to their sovereign the following month. The numbers fell far short of the 40,000 men initially imagined but, as well as these regular regiments, there were also from the Kingdom of Hungary's borderlands significant irregular reinforcements. The Theresian palaces of Trieste's old town boast many a martial-looking head gazing down on the passer-by from the keystone above the main arch of the entrance. These faces, fiercely bewhiskered, invariably wear an exotic headdress. The *Pandours* had arrived.

These warriors were brigands of various ethnicities from the 'wrong side' of the Military Frontier but, martialled under a gifted Austrian officer by the name of Trenck, they were soon to prove their worth.[1] Irregulars with a fearsome reputation for cruelty – babies, women and children were regularly 'ins Feuer geworfen' – the *Pandours* were welcomed into imperial service, even though they possessed no conventional officer corps. An informal system of command sufficed whereby units of fifty men obeyed their *Harumbascha*. They were paid a pittance (6 kreutzer a day) out of Trenck's own estates and, as this left little over for expenditure on uniforms, their appearance was highly exotic.

When they first appeared in Vienna in the late spring of 1741, the *Wienerisches Diarium* could write:

Two battalions of regular infantry lined up to parade as the Pandours entered the city. The irregulars greeted the regulars with long drum rolls on tall Turkish drums. They bore no colours but were attired in picturesque oriental garments from which protrude pistols, knives and other weapons.

It was characteristic of Maria Theresa that, despite their appearance with their knees and elbows stitched with scarlet material in the shape of hearts, she ordered that a dozen of the tallest and most handsome be invited to her quarters where they could be paraded in front of her mother-in-law, the dowager Empress Christina.

These *Pandours*, when deployed, soon struck terror into the French and Bavarian troops menacing Vienna. They were prone to unruliness and Neipperg had to constantly remind them that they were 'here to kill the enemy not plunder the civilian population'. When Neipperg attempted to have Trenck replaced, a mutiny resulted which only Khevenhueller managed to resolve by confirming Trenck in his command. On the other hand, the irregulars were dazzlingly successful in guerrilla tactics and ambushes which demoralized an enemy that, until their arrival, had largely enjoyed success on the battlefield. Within a year, just the rumour of their presence was enough to clear terrain of their opponents' scouts.

When Maria Theresa returned to Vienna, she found Khevenhueller well advanced in his preparations to defend the city, still fortified with the redoubtable bastions and walls which had defeated the great Turkish siege of 1683. The Bavarians with their French supports had little appetite for a rerun of that disastrous investment of the Austrian capital and were easily tempted to turn north from Linz and attack Prague. A month later, in November 1741, reinforced by Saxons and French troops, they surprised the small Austrian garrison under Ogilvy and stormed into the city largely unopposed.

A glimmer of hope appeared as Khevenhueller cleared Upper Austria of the Bavarians and French. He had blockaded Linz which was held by 10,000 French troops under Ségur. He had then gone on to seize Schärding on the Inn, cutting the French off from any relief from their Bavarian allies.

A secret armistice with Prussia was signed at the Dietrichstein castle of Klein Schnellendorf in October 1741. Frederick needed a breather but he had no intention of honouring any truce. As he characteristically wrote to Podewils: 'If anything is to be gained by honesty, then we shall be honest but if deceit on the other hand is called for, then let us rejoice in being knaves.' Five months later, Prussian troops invaded Moravia, hoping to link arms with the French in southern Bohemia. By 19 February his leading formations had reached Znaim, barely a couple of days march from Vienna.

Once again, Maria Theresa revealed her feelings in a letter to her minister Kinsky:

Prague is lost and perhaps even worse will follow if we cannot secure three months supplies. Austria cannot find them and it is far from clear that Hungary will be able to do so. We have reached the moment of truth when only courage can save Bohemia and the Queen, who, without Bohemia, will indeed be but a poor princess. My own resolve is firm; we will do everything – win or lose – to save Bohemia. It may involve destruction and desolation which twenty years will be insufficient to restore but I must hold *Grund und Boden*.

Then, continuing in words which might have dismayed her newly won Hungarian adherents, she insisted to Kinsky: 'All the Hungarians shall die before I surrender an inch of this territory. This is the crisis: do not spare the country, only hold it.' Here was the *Mater Castrorum* indifferent to human loss and as callous as Napoleon in her determination to wage war, whatever the cost. Yet even in this seemingly resolute command, Maria Theresa allowed a glimmer of her humanity, *Milde und Munifizenz*, to shine through as she continued:

Do all you can to help your people (the inhabitants of Bohemia) and to keep the troops contented and lacking nothing; you know better than I the consequences of failure in this. Help my poor husband who feels so deeply for the suffering of the troops and the countryside that their condition fills him with pity.[2]

Yet this letter dispels any idea that Maria Theresa was in some way an unnatural *Mater Bellum* or inadequate war leader. She was ruthlessly resolved to the harshness of war and the terrible effects of it on her peoples: 'You will say that I am cruel: that is true. But I know that all the cruelties I commit today to hold the country I shall one day be in a position to make good a hundred-fold. And this I shall do.'

The omens seemed more positive as Prince Charles of Lorraine, Francis Stephen's brother, and a descendant of the illustrious Prince of Lorraine who had helped relieve the great Turkish siege of Vienna, assumed command. However, Maria Theresa was going to learn that the Prince, whatever his pedigree, was loud, uncouth and, most unfortunate of all, like his brother, her husband, a military incompetent. But at first his incompetence seemed minor compared to that of his brother's and the Austrian troops prepared to meet their enemies beneath the walls of Prague.

Lorraine, however, needed much prodding from Vienna to engage the Prussians. They, in turn, were becoming overstretched and vulnerable but, compared to Khevenhueller's minor *blitzkrieg* down the Danube valley, Lorraine was all caution and reserve.

Eventually, he collided with Frederick's army near the village of Chotusitz east of Prague. The battle, like Mollwitz, began rather promisingly and the Austrian cavalry once again drove their opponents from the field but, as the solid Prussian infantry held its ground, a certain over-zealous Austrian colonel, Livingstein, had the idea of setting fire to the village, oblivious to the fact that the flames and smoke would effectively bring the Austrian attack to a halt and allow the Prussian defence to re-form. As if that was not enough of an error, the Austrian hussars began to plunder the Prussian camp, allowing Frederick to regroup his reserve and rapidly clear the battlefield of the Austrians.

After four hours of heavy fighting, Charles felt compelled to order a withdrawal. This the Austrians did in good order, having captured fourteen standards and inflicted 7,000 casualties on the Prussians. The Prussian cavalry had been so severely handled that it was no longer an effective fighting force but once again the rock-like Prussian infantry had saved the day. This was not the crushing victory Frederick, who had finally distinguished himself in battle without panicking, had wanted in order to support his demands in Bohemia and he was keenly aware that another hard-fought 'victory' along the lines of Chotusitz could cost him dearly. As Podewils remarked, referencing Cardinal Fleury's earlier famous expression: 'Some lovely feathers may have been torn from Austria's wings but the bird is still capable of flying quite high.'[3]

The severity of Frederick's losses highlighted the asymmetry in manpower and strategic depth upon which both armies relied. The Austrians could draw on far greater numbers for recruitment and Chotusitz illustrated vividly Frederick's manpower dilemma were he to continue hostilities.

The situation in Bohemia was moving slowly in Austria's favour. The moment for rapprochement had arrived. Podewils signed the preliminaries at Breslau and Prussia gained Upper and Lower Silesia together with Glatz. Even though Austria retained only a sliver of Silesia around Troppau and Jaegersdorf, Bohemia, as close to Maria Theresa's heart as Silesia, appeared to be secured. The Habsburg armies could now turn their full weight against other enemies, notably the French. Frederick was prevented from achieving one of his main objectives, the release of French troops locked up in Bohemia, and Paris was quick to express its dismay. But the Prussian king was well versed in the art of what we should call today the 'blame-game'.

'I have done everything possible to support the designs of your King,' he wrote to Fleury, 'with inviolable fidelity', but it was time to 'cease carrying the burdens of others unaided'.

These modest Austrian successes had a significant effect on public opinion in northern Europe. An address by an eminent German lawyer to the merchants and tradesmen of Antwerp was widely published in 1742 and distributed in London, translated by a barrister of the Inner Temple. Entitled 'In Praise of Her Most Serene Majesty Maria Theresa, Queen of Hungary etc. upon the Happy Success of Her Arms', the anonymous speech had an impact out of all proportion to its length or audience.[4]

It began by emphasizing the strong bonds which tied Maria Theresa to Germans and all Europeans desirous of peace and stability:

Since there is so strong a connection between your love of your country and the interests of Her Most Sacred Majesty . . . anyone who shall be base enough to separate them or even give a hint that his inclinations tend that way must be deemed a parricide to the vision of his ancestors.

This was rousing stuff and there are sadly no eyewitness accounts of its impact on the stolid diamond merchants and other tradesmen of Antwerp but in London the pamphlet circulated everywhere. It contained several passages which depicted Maria Theresa in the helpless yet noble light of which official circles had been informed following her coronation in Budapest.

As the pamphlet insisted: 'If ever a falling tear disdained her glorious cheek it was because she wept for her country more than for herself.' Amid all the 'horrors and alarms of war and rapine', she alone preserved 'concord and serenity'. Her opponents, meanwhile, especially Prussia, offered 'peace and mediation on the point of a sword besmeared with the blood of butchered infants and their martyred parents whose dying groans are the only harmony that usher in the march of Maria Theresa's foes'.

Focusing on Maria Theresa's fortitude, the pamphlet noted that Maria Theresa would sooner let Germany be destroyed than stoop to such 'inglorious terms — let Frenchmen flatter, fawn and infamously betray their trust' but she would rather receive their 'swords in her bowels' than admit 'falsehood to her heart'. Rather, 'soft persuasive ardour flowed from every word she spoke and from her invincible mind'. She had overcome difficulties which would 'have seemed insurmountable to any but a princess of her superior penetration and resolution'. Here was another masterly propaganda offensive which showed Austria's diplomats' mastery of the art of public relations, but it was the widening of Austria's cause to that of Europe which perhaps was the most extraordinary theme of this pamphlet. Maria Theresa 'saw the wounds of her bleeding country and the liberty of Europe and applied her hand to heal them'. The authors clearly felt Austria's mission to be consonant with that of saving Europe. This was a theme Maria Theresa and her advisers would develop with relish.

In denouncing the fickleness of British policy and that of the other non-Catholic European states, the pamphlet spared no country's blushes: 'Where were then the various potentates of Europe, particularly those of the reformed religion whose chief interest it was to support her? Did they supply her with arms or the sinews of war? No! Did they order their respective ambassadors at the courts of her enemies to make pressing demands in her favour? No! A dead sleep seemed to have fallen over all of them.'

Without naming Walpole, it was clear that the pamphleteer had the British Prime Minister and his lukewarm policy towards Austria well in his sights. Instead of focusing on the Balance of Europe, a statesman, unnamed, had preferred to support France and conceal a 'black scene of corruption and iniquity'. The pamphlet now urged: 'Blush, blush, blush you supple cringers to deceitful France.'

The pamphlet may well have contributed to the fall of the British government a few months later, while its impact on Germans was gauged by the shifting sands of alliances within the German-speaking world. As an example of English eighteenth-century oratorical skill harnessed to a European cause it can arguably boast no equal.

The Treaty of Breslau a few weeks later allowed the Austrians to gain the initiative. Broglie sought to bring his beleaguered French troops out of Prague. The position of his garrison was pitiable. Meanwhile, the coalition against Vienna was disintegrating. The Saxons no longer wished to be involved and in London, with the removal of Walpole, the Austrian party was once again in the ascendant and large supplies of money and material were approved in parliament to support Maria Theresa. Her defiance had not just showed that she could 'hold on' but had highlighted even to the most parochial of English politicians that the destruction of the House of Austria could only result in the aggrandizement of the House of Bourbon, a development which, as England moved towards vast hostilities with Paris across far-flung parts of the globe, could only be viewed with dismay. Meanwhile, in Russia, a new government, suspicious and contemptuous of the arriviste, watched with increasing scepticism how an aggressive Prussia was emerging from provincial obscurity.

All these changes were noted with pleasure in Vienna and Maria Theresa had the confidence to rebuff Fleury's overtures, convinced after Chotusitz that her armies could make short work of the French in Bohemia. With fighting words she rejected French peace-feelers: 'I will grant no capitulation to the French army; I will receive no proposition or project. Let them address my allies!' It was a reasonable assumption, but the young Queen had not reckoned with the ineptitude of her commander in the theatre of operations, Charles of Lorraine.

The French commander Belle-Isle slipped out of Prague unnoticed by the pickets posted by Lorraine and, in an epic retreat, brought most of his men with all their colours and guns back to France two months later. A detachment of hussars under Lobkowitz left by Lorraine to 'keep an eye on things' failed to notice 11,000 infantry and 3,000 cavalry steal away. The Bohemian women appear to have distracted them quite effectively from their duties. As a result, the French army passed some thirty miles through open country without receiving the slightest check.

To be fair to Lorraine, Austrian military incompetence at this stage offered a very tight field. Austrian plans to seize Naples had failed miserably and the entire Italian campaign would have ended in ignominious defeat had not Sardinian troops rescued their Austrian allies in Parma and Modena.

But even these events did not deter Maria Theresa from vowing retribution on those who had crossed her. Another document reveals all too clearly her determination at this headstrong young stage of her life to neither forgive nor forget. Another peace overture from Belle-Isle met with uncompromising severity:

> I am astonished that he should make any advances; he who by money and promises excited almost all the princes of Germany to crush me . . . I can prove by documents in my possession that the French endeavoured to excite sedition even in the very heart of my dominions; that they attempted to overturn fundamental laws of the empire and to set fire to the four corners of Germany; and I will transmit these proofs to posterity as a warning to the empire.[5]

Meanwhile, in London, the mood music had not only changed, so that Maria Theresa was no longer being constantly badgered into coming to terms, but she was now even being offered troops as well as subsidies.

A 'Pragmatic Army', so named because it was to protect the Pragmatic Sanction, took to the field as a kind of anti-Bourbon league, made up of Austrian, Hanoverian and British contingents. The Austrian minister in London, Wasner, from his handsome abode at Chandos House, entertained and cajoled the leading Whig luminaries, reporting to Vienna that London wished to 'chase the House of Bourbon from Italy, return

Lorraine to the House of Lorraine to round off a bit the states of Her Majesty to compensate in that way for the sacrifices just made to the King in Prussia'.[6]

The 'Pragmatic Army' soon demonstrated its worth at the Battle of Dettingen where George II, famously, if briefly, led a cavalry charge.[7] Of the 20,000 Austrian troops that participated in the battle, the majority were from the Austrian Netherlands and at least at one point in the battle they stabilized the broken British lines. Dettingen placed the French on the defensive and, as the Pragmatic Army crossed the Rhine, the mood in Vienna was buoyant. In the winter of 1743, a couple of months after Dettingen, Saxony concluded a defensive alliance with Austria.

Frederick looked on uneasily. Recalling his failure to take Bohemia and anxious lest a *Pax Austriaca* heralded the prelude to a renewal of hostilities in Silesia, he conceived of a new plan to repeat an attack on Prague. Skilful diplomacy would revive the alliance with Louis XV and the Bavarian monarch who still held the imperial crown. This would ensure that the Austrian forces, thinly stretched across the Netherlands and along the Rhine, would be unable to march to reinforce Austrian troops to the east. Little over a hundred years later, a Prussian army would eject Austria from her leadership of Germany at the Battle of Königgrätz. Frederick was attempting something similar, although with the added Frederician dimension of naked avarice and lust for territorial expansion, in this case for the rich crown lands of Bohemia.

For her part, Maria Theresa still refused to recognize the Bavarian usurper as emperor and she contemptuously rejected the advances of the diet at Frankfurt. She did not conceal her ambition to humble France with England's help, appropriate Bavaria and eventually reduce, with Saxon help, Prussia to sackcloth and ashes.

As an Austrian army entered Lorraine, Frederick waited no longer and, on 15 August 1744, he led his troops into Bohemia. It was, Frederick insisted, 'just a pre-emptive attack' as Austria was 'preparing to attack'. The Prussian eruption into Bohemia was, in a phrase favoured by tyrants throughout the centuries up until our own age, 'protective'.[8] It would even offer, Frederick insisted, 'repose for Europe'.[9]

With Maria Theresa's army now more than 400 miles away from Bohemia, Frederick undoubtedly chose his moment well but he had once again underestimated his opponent and, perhaps more dangerously, overestimated his Bavarian and French allies.

Three Prussian columns descended on Prague and, after a brief siege which hit the Marian column in the city's old town, the Bohemian capital capitulated. Nevertheless, help for the Austrians was at hand. Another appeal to Hungarian chivalry produced 40,000 troops and, at the same time, the illness of Louis XV distracted French strategy to the extent that an Austrian army under Lorraine escaped across the Rhine with just a few trifling attacks on its rearguard. By 22 October more than 75,000 troops were marching towards Frederick, carefully coordinated by Count Traun who, deploying Fabian tactics, relentlessly harassed and confused his opponents. Although less dynamic than Khevenhueller, who had died suddenly at the age of 60 earlier that year, Traun was a serious military strategist who compensated for Lorraine's lack of experience. He, too, was slow and excessively cautious but he carefully uncoiled his forces, slowly bringing each of the Prussian columns relentlessly into a deadly net.

Once again, the *Pandours* spread panic and fear among the Prussian *piquets*. Their reputation had become 'enhanced' by their behaviour in Bavaria a few months earlier where they had torched whole villages, throwing babies into the fire. The disciplined Prussian infantry were useless against the sudden night attacks of the terrible *Pandours*. If these were not enough to cause his garrisons distress, the tough Bohemian peasantry, mostly Czechs, fell upon Frederick's outposts with a ferocity born of an enduring hatred for the *Saupriessen* ('pig-Prussians'). Disease and poor logistics completed their work and the Prussian military machine collapsed, almost disintegrating in front of the King's eyes.

In desperation, Frederick sued for an armistice but Maria Theresa was implacable, demonstrating a hardness, some would say ruthlessness, which astonished her advisers. Frederick rapidly realized that only the swift evacuation of Bohemia could stave off disaster. Abandoning his army yet again, he decamped to Silesia, all too aware of where hostilities would now lead. His army was left to march out, to the jeers and stone-throwing of the mob, to stagger back to Silesia. But even here there was no respite; by Christmas, all of Upper Silesia had been recovered by the Austrians. Frederick's 'protective' operation had cost him 30,000 men.

To reinforce the sense of Austrian triumph, there was excellent news from Bavaria where the usurper Elector, following his coronation as Holy Roman Emperor, Charles VII, had now succumbed to a violent attack of gout on hearing from one of his domestic servants the tidings of Austrian victory. He expired some days later, on 20 January 1745, a broken man.

The hapless upstart who had dared to seize the Holy Roman imperial title and crown left, in the words of a contemporary, 'a memorable example to his posterity not to aspire to a dangerous pre-eminence without power or resources, or those transcendant abilities which so arduous a situation required'.[10]

On his deathbed he testified to his regret that he had brought ruin to himself and his country in order to have become 'an imperial pageant in the hands of France'. With the wisdom that comes often all too late, he urged his son to renounce any aspiration to the imperial title and come to an agreement with Maria Theresa as soon as possible.

Meanwhile, in Italy, Piedmontese (Sardinian) troops, together with several Croatian Austrian regiments, routed the retreating French, and when Frederick surveyed the constellation of events, he realized that the wheel of fortune had moved decisively against him. 'Never had a crisis been greater than mine', he wrote that winter. 'Pray help from my lucky star.'[11] (As an Aquarian, well might he seek astrological succour.)

Certainly, his horoscope could have offered pause for reflection, but more tangible circumstances were now asserting themselves and the news from London that the Whig government had granted a new £200,000 subsidy to Austria could not have brightened the outlook, whatever the astrologers might have said.

So radiant were the reports from London that some of Maria Theresa's advisers even suggested the imminent partition of Prussia but their sovereign had learnt, despite the power of her emotions, to be rational and even cautious. With her practical common sense she coolly observed that 'before dividing up the bear's skin it is necessary first to kill it'.[12]

CHAPTER 5

The Prussian Recovery

BAVARIA HESITATED BEFORE COMING to an accommodation with Vienna and on 21 March 1745, two gifted generals, Batthyany and Browne, launched a veritable *blitzkrieg* against the armies of the Electorate. In a matter of a few weeks virtually every Bavarian garrison in their way fled or surrendered. At Pfaffenhofen, a small French force under Ségur attempted to make a stand but found themselves surrounded by the dreadful *Pandours* who proceeded to slaughter every Frenchman they could find, including the dying and wounded. As Ségur escaped with a few men, the Habsburg hussar squadrons harassed their flanks, and only nightfall brought Ségur any respite. Of his force of 6,500 troops, barely 2,000 survived.

Once again, the Austrians entered Munich as victors and the Bavarian peace party, all too cognizant of the destruction visited on the city the previous time it was occupied, soon sued for an armistice. Within a week Bavaria had recognized the terms of the Pragmatic Sanction and signed a treaty at Füssen.

Although the treaty was a great celebration of the success of Austrian arms, cementing Bavarian recognition of Maria Theresa's claims, it was also lenient. With a masterly insight into the tempers of the peoples she ruled, she offered the following olive branch to her vanquished rival: 'Everything which is harmful has its origins in the division of our two houses' was her opening message to the Bavarians.

In return, the Electorate, like Saxony, would move into the anti-Prussian camp and recognize Maria Theresa's husband as the new Holy Roman Emperor. Maria Theresa had not only safeguarded her lands but vanquished Wittelsbach pretensions to the Habsburg inheritance. Moreover, with Bavaria knocked out, there was no longer any geographical cohesion to the Franco-Prussian strategy. From now on, Austria would engage in two entirely separate wars in different theatres against enemies who, though united by their common distaste for the House of Austria, were no longer able to form a cohesive alliance. Nevertheless, just as all seemed to be running in Austria's favour, everything began to go wrong.

First at Fontenoy, though the Austrian contingent of the Pragmatic Army consisted of only eight squadrons of dragoons and hussars, the gifted Maurice de Saxe outwitted a large force commanded by the inexperienced Duke of Cumberland, crushing the British infantry in one of the most decisive campaigns of the entire war. The victory was enduringly traumatic for the British: Irish regiments had fought magnificently – on the French side. But for the Austrians the defeat was relatively insignificant. Frederick summed up its importance for his struggle with Vienna, observing that it had 'no more advantage than the capture of Pekin'.[1]

Then, less than a month later, at Hohenfriedberg, an entire Austrian army supported by the Saxons, both under the command of Charles of Lorraine, fell into a brilliantly conceived and executed trap of the Prussians. London, confronted with this run of defeats, began to wobble in its support. It did not help that the Young Pretender, Charles Stuart, chose this moment to raise his standard in Scotland.

Maria Theresa remained defiant, although she was beginning to learn that her brother-in-law was incapable of bringing lasting military honours either to the House of Lorraine or the House of Austria. Lorraine's ascendancy had been hitherto unstoppable but his hubris had led swiftly to those twin demons of sluggishness and complacency: vices which would so often cast a long shadow over the Habsburg military effort.

Hohenfriedberg marked a new era in the Frederician military effort. Impressed by the Hungarian hussars of his opponents, the Prussian king had recruited some disaffected Magyars of his own and these skilfully acted as a screen to disguise his movements. Moreover, a network of spies consistently misinformed the Austrians that Frederick was ill and in no mood to give battle. This was precisely what Lorraine wanted to hear and so, as he entered Silesia, he undertook no detailed reconnaissance, preferring to rest; he even allowed his cavalry to set up camp some distance from their horses so that they were dismounted when the battle began.

When Frederick attacked at five in the morning, the Saxons bore the brunt of the onslaught and were soon cowed by the Prussian war-cry of 'Kein Pardon an den Sachsen' (No pardon for the Saxons), an order Frederick had insisted be read that morning to his troops in revenge for the fickle friendship the Saxons had offered him in deserting their alliance.

The battle, nonetheless, was fiercely contested. Austrian losses, by the standards of the time, were appalling. Lorraine left 10,000 of his troops dead or dying on the battlefield. Sixty-six standards, scores of guns and eight pairs of silver kettledrums fell into Prussian hands. Lorraine's initial bulletin to Vienna was terse: 'At Hohenfriedberg we have suffered a total defeat in one of the finest positions imaginable.'[2]

Lorraine retreated with his shattered remnants into Bohemia and soon received reinforcements, including fresh Hungarian cavalry. Nadasti, perhaps the finest light cavalry commander in Europe, conceived of a bold plan to roll up the Prussian lines of communication, fearfully overstretched as they approached Bohemia. Unfortunately, the time that elapsed between this plan's conception and its execution was too long and it was once again the Prussians who seized the initiative. At Soor on 30 September, the Prussians 'surprised' the Austrians with their boldness. Despite a devastating artillery barrage, the superb Prussian infantry wheeled with perfect discipline to effect a 90-degree change of front. The Austrian cavalry fared little better than at Hohenfriedberg and the Hungarian hussars preferred to plunder Frederick's tents, capturing his greyhounds (but not his orders or letters) rather than engage with the Prussian horse. The Austrians were forced to retreat and this they did in good order under a young officer, soon to become a Theresian hero, named Daun.

Soor, more than any other battle, destroyed the reputation of the Austrian cavalry and, as reports came back to Vienna, it became abundantly clear that root-and-branch reform was necessary if Austrian arms were going to ever stand up to the Prussians. Soor showed all too clearly that a Prussian army, even though inferior in numbers, could still defeat the Austrians. As Frederick himself wrote: 'If the Austrians could not beat me at Soor I shall never be beaten by them.'[3]

As 1745 drew to a close, the peace party in Vienna, encouraged relentlessly by London, gained the upper hand, and once again, British diplomacy, desperate to have Austria's undivided attention devoted to the mortal enemy of France, brought enormous pressure to bear on Maria Theresa to sue for peace with Prussia. And thus, for the second time, British diplomats brought about a ceasefire with Frederick and an end to hostilities between Austria and Prussia.

Partly influenced by the fate of her ally Saxony, whose territory was now invaded by Frederick, Vienna sued for peace. Under the terms of the Christmas Day Treaty of Dresden, Silesia together with Glatz was signed over to Prussia along with its 1,220,000 hard-working inhabitants and some of the richest mineral deposits in the Habsburg domains. In return, Frederick agreed to recognize and support Francis Stephen's candidature for the Holy Roman title. Maria Theresa may not have thought much of the machinery of the Holy Roman Empire but, as a vehicle for her husband's rank, as the cost of Prussia's recognition shows, it was clearly worth a great deal to her.

Maria Theresa also even pledged not to resort to arms ever again to recapture her lost territory and, indeed, when hostilities resumed nearly a decade later, it was she who kept her word and Frederick who once again committed the initial aggression.

The year 1745, which had started so promisingly for the Habsburg cause, ended with Austrian armies in Bohemia demoralized and exhausted. In the Netherlands the cause fared little better. British support was distracted by the emergency at home over the Stuarts. In the Dutch provinces, the Francophile party gained more momentum and was sceptical of the arrangements with Austria.

Yet the crowning of Maria Theresa's husband Francis Stephen in the autumn of 1745 offered some recompense after the trials of the last five years. The imperial election was a stabilizing hard-won triumph. Since the Golden Bull of 1356, the seven members of the Electoral College had consisted of three archbishops – Mainz, Cologne, Treves – and four secular sovereigns – the Elector Palatine, the Duke of Saxony, the Margrave of Brandenburg and the King of Bohemia.

There were, needless to say, frictions. There was first the argument as to whether Francis, as a Prince of Lorraine, was a Prince of the Empire at all. Then the Prussian and Palatinate sovereigns objected to the validity of Maria Theresa's vote as King of Bohemia. In a gesture of defiance, these two initially withdrew but their abstention was smoothed over and, as clearly there was no rival candidate any more, the path for Francis Stephen was free.

To witness her husband parading in the medieval splendour of the imperial title was, together with the recovery of Silesia, arguably the consuming passion of Maria Theresa's youthful life. She accompanied Francis to Frankfurt in great style. With that sense of sacrifice for which Austrian matriarchy for centuries afterwards became renowned, she adopted an attitude of secondary privilege, resolutely refusing to detract in any way from her husband's glory by even participating in the formal ceremonies.

For some time now she had already behaved as an Empress, and through the agency of her unquestioned power she could afford to avoid the solemn theatricals of the coronation. Even if she was now *Kaiserin* in name, this mattered far less to her than the support and shoring up of her husband's confidence after his brief but disastrous military career.

Frederick, with his usual acidic acuity, observed that Maria Theresa's absence from the ceremony only underlined the fact that the imperial crown had become a 'worthless bauble'. In any event, Francis was making history alone; he would be the last non-Habsburg to hold the imperial crown. The Holy Roman Empire would be dissolved under the innovative shocks of another rapacious warrior-monarch sixty years later.

Meanwhile, without Prussia, fighting continued for three years. The Pragmatic Army proved no match for the French once Maurice de Saxe cemented his command. In Italy, Austrian forces fared better but the allies – Dutch, Sardinian and the ever-challenging Hungarians – bickered among themselves while the 'butcher's bill' from the campaigns grew with each month that passed. Every belligerent began to explore a way to escape the relentless bloodshed and logic of combat. Only Maria Theresa, determined not to yield an inch further of territory in her

Italian possessions, stubbornly insisted on the fighting continuing in Italy.

Austrian arms had undoubtedly improved and the return of the double-headed eagle, following Francis's coronation, to the Austrian regimental colours fused the terms 'Imperial' and 'Austrian' unequivocally for the next century and a half.

Yet the series of conflicts collectively known as the War of the Austrian Succession had been sanguinary in the extreme. The civilian casualties and dislocation had been enormous. The so-called age of 'civilized warfare' had seen appalling atrocities carried out by all the belligerents. The British army in the Rhineland pillaged churches and regularly burnt villages. The Prussians occupied Saxony and Bohemia with exceptional severity, administering what one historian has called 'exemplary brutalities'. The French, too, were more than capable of barbaric behaviour towards civilians. And the Austrians, for all the talk of the *Austria Clementia* of Maria Theresa, proved they could be as merciless as any of their opponents. The *Pandours* famously spared no civilians, male or female, infirm or child.

Moreover, Maria Theresa showed, at this stage of her reign, a hostility towards Jews which resulted in her ordering the expulsion of all Prague's 20,000 Jews in 1744.[4] This decree was later widened to include all of the Jews of Moravia and Bohemia.

Maria Theresa's anti-Semitism was never racially or ethnically inspired, and the immediate cause of this singular instance of political anti-Semitism on a large scale during her reign was reports alleging the Prague Jews had collaborated with the French and Prussian occupiers. She neither questioned nor analysed the reports but vowed immediate retribution.

To the consternation of her advisers, she flew into one of her most fearful rages and vowed vengeance on the Prague 'collaborators'. In time, her feelings towards Jews would soften. Two years later, through patents, she would offer significant privileges to the Jews of Trieste. But in the mid-1740s, it was only the direct intervention, again, of British diplomacy – London's Sephardic Jewish community had lobbied George II to implore the Empress to rescind the order – which prevented the dispersion of the Jewish diaspora of Bohemia.[5]

Eventually, following this British démarche and the advice of her most trusted intimates, Maria Theresa relented and the proud Jewish community of Prague was allowed to return in 1748 and enjoy the imperial *Gnade*.

This protection formed part of the informal discussions around the Treaty of Aix-la-Chapelle which finally brought hostilities to a close. Once again, British diplomacy had forced Maria Theresa to the negotiating table and while none of the signatories could express much satisfaction, anything seemed preferable to the protracted state of exhaustion which had consumed all the belligerents.

Above all, on reflection, when the Empress surveyed the internal arrangements of her hard-won inheritance, she realized that there was a critical need for reform. Such reforms could not be implemented while the distraction of war consumed her statesmen's best energies. Her advisers were not just military reformers but men of immense intellectual depth. The men who had come into her inner circle were a mixture of practicality, charm and intellect. They were very different from each other, but they all bore the signs of a certain authenticity and it was this quality, above all others, which the young Empress prized most enthusiastically. Gradually, these men would develop almost an alchemy over their Empress, fashioning from a headstrong inexperienced sovereign of emotional volatility the greatest reforming ruler of eighteenth-century Europe.

PART II

THE ACHIEVEMENT

CHAPTER 6

The Age of Reform I: The New Men

WHO WERE THESE MEN who would exert such influence that they would never undermine their sovereign but only use that power to strengthen her domains, to such an extent that a new modern state was created in barely a decade?

One of the most exotic was the Portuguese aristocrat, Don Manoel Telles de Menezes e Castro, Count of Tarouca (and later from 1755 Prince of Silva). Due to circumstances arising from the Spanish War of Succession, Tarouca's father had served the Habsburgs in the Austrian Netherlands. His son had been appointed a page at the court of Charles VI. He had later accompanied the great Prince Eugene against the Turks, fighting bravely at Peterwardein and Temesvar. He had even accompanied the Prince back to his bedroom for the last time before the *edler Ritter* died.

On retirement from the army, he had transferred to the Austrian Netherlands where he had occupied an important but minor post in the Viceroyalty. In this role he had distinguished himself, first by handling with great delicacy certain issues of state concerning Maria Theresa's mother, and second by offering to take a substantial cut in remuneration from 26,000 Gulden to 16,000. When Maria Theresa eventually came to the throne, he astonished everyone by tearing up an IOU for 100,000 Gulden which he had been offered by her mother, and accepting that he would, in the straitened circumstance now facing Austria's depleted treasury, be unlikely to receive more than the 15,000 Gulden advanced to him the previous year.

Tarouca's family were well-to-do but their wealth was relatively modest compared to the scions of the high aristocracy who gathered around the court and so his sacrifice was no easy gesture. But his austerity followed that of his father who, as Portuguese ambassador in Vienna, had impressed the emperor Charles VI by his resolute avoidance of all unnecessary expenditure and debt, a rarity among diplomats of those times.

Tarouca, unlike many courtiers, had another supreme gift: he was very good with children. As a page at court, he had delighted Maria Theresa and, as soon as she came to the throne, she lifted him out of the obscurity of the Viceroyalty and made him president of the Ministerial Council for the Netherlands. This promotion only served to disguise a more intimate relationship, born of that familiarity of childhood which to this day is one of the most powerful foundations of nepotism at court.

In the late nineteenth century, Professor Theodor Georg von Karajan, an authority on Haydn in London, was granted access to the Tarouca archives then lodged on their estates in Moravia. These contained forty-four letters in French from Maria Theresa to her 'oldest and best friend'.

In Tarouca's case it was truly an example of 'nihil sine nepote'. His advice soon spread to all affairs of state but his detachment from any outward signs of worldly ambition gave Maria Theresa the confidence to share her innermost doubts and fears with him. During her great ordeals at Pressburg, she asked Tarouca to devote himself exclusively to her service, to act as her conscience, to visit her daily, and to advise her in all matters and, above all, tell her the truth about all things, including herself.

In her own words, Tarouca's task was to 'show me my faults and make me recognize them . . . this being necessary for a ruler since there are few or none at all to be found who will do this, preferring out of awe or self-interest to remain silent'. In her own original commission she under-lined what she meant: 'From now on, without intermission, you are to tell Her where she errs, and to explain with perfect openness Her faults of character.'[1]

Tarouca discharged this obligation with all the love born of true friendship, unsullied by the ostinato of familial reproach which, for reasons known to all, rarely can rise to the heights of disinterested advice. He made no secret of the fact that he 'hated' this work and that it brought many challenges personally to him. Tarouca spoke little German, in common with many courtiers of Maria Theresa of Latin descent, but his French was vivid and articulate. Advising her was a 'hateful' business: 'How was it possible to point out your mistakes,' he wrote to Maria Theresa, 'without incurring the envy and jealousy of your ministers and courtiers?'[2]

How could he remain objective and not 'awake my own ambitions'? The Portuguese continued: 'I ask you to inform me whether I have been on the right track or whether I should follow some different route . . . only my ambition and love and obedience have kept me on the right path because I have long believed that all honours are nothing compared to your confidence.'[3]

In another letter, Tarouca insisted: 'My character is only made of love and interior ambition. I have never sought my fortune in money or external riches.'

It may have helped that the diminutive Tarouca, almost North African in appearance, and blessed with what one female admirer called the 'finest legs ever to be wrapped in silk stockings',[4] was both an outsider as well as the ultimate insider in the Austrian court. Tarouca was intelligent and loyal with a good brain and that Portuguese sobriety which even today is the hallmark of their finest servants of state. He quickly attempted, with a degree of success, to impose a strict timetable on the court's weekly calendar, turning what had been almost a lottery for ministerial audiences and diplomatic conferences, sporadically sandwiched between dancing lessons and children's parties, into a regular pattern of events.

In Tarouca's 'system', Wednesdays and Saturdays were reserved for meetings with foreign envoys while Sundays from 9 to 11 am were given over to ministerial meetings which were brought strictly to a close by 11 so that the court could proceed punctually to High Mass. Tarouca, with a practical piety which matched that of his sovereign, insisted that the general audiences, often devoted to dealing with petitions from orphans and widows, be reserved for Sunday afternoons and feast days. Such audiences were a 'true Sunday penance' to be 'enjoyed' with a good word or deed to the more desperate of her subjects. Thus was the *Landesmutter* able to lift the spirits of the *kleiner Mann*.

'Sprechen Sie nur fort' (Just tell me as it is), Maria Theresa once said to him, urging the older man that she was in reality just his pupil (*Schülerin*).[5]

As news filtered out of Tarouca's favour, the other courtiers – like most courtiers, a breed not widely known for their sense of compassion or magnanimity – sharpened their intellectual weapons and predilection towards intrigue in the face of Tarouca's effortless rise. Khevenhueller, never one to hold back in relaying court gossip, noted somewhat acidly after Tarouca had arranged a festival at Schönbrunn to celebrate the feast of St Francis, that this 'cadet of a foreigner minister [had] somehow risen [to become] *directeur des Plaisirs de la Reine*'.[6]

The Portuguese, as his letters show, sensed this precariousness and his sovereign's appeals were at first spurned. The responsibility was too great and not to be undertaken lightly but, after several months of prevarication, Tarouca did accept and for the best part of the next fifteen years provided, as best he could, that sounding board for his Empress's conscience. Even after the 1750s, when the Empress found many other advisers, she remained faithful to her 'Ami'.

The affection between the two appears to have been genuine. It was also, despite a secret passage linking Tarouca's palace (the site of today's Albertina gallery) with the Hofburg, an entirely platonic friendship. In 1766, after the death of her husband, Maria Theresa lamented her poor state of mind, noting that Daun and Tarouca were her best friends. Daun had died a few weeks earlier and the Empress added: 'Poor Daun I have lost, but my oldest and most reliable friend still lives well, unlike his pupil.'[7]

When Tarouca suggested his retirement, she would hear nothing of it, accusing him of abandoning her like some child deprived suddenly of her nurse. Their friendship she insisted was as 'deep' as it had ever been during the previous fifteen years. In another letter written after her husband's death in 1765, she urged: 'My dearest Tarouca: I am in a terrible state; I have no interest in anything that I might share with my friends and so share my troubles. I do not know what I am doing or what I am saying.' When Tarouca tried to console her with logical argument, reminding her of her wider responsibilities, she answered: 'Your head has always served you well and although one cannot avoid occasionally someone doing something bad to one, on the whole you have been fortunate – unlike me! I am to blame, and I am so demoralized that I am losing what little understanding remains to me.'[8]

It is clear from these words that Tarouca was an important emotional prop, especially after Francis Stephen's death. The Empress's words reveal a depression and mental demoralization in advancing years which serve as a marked counterpoint to the passionate exuberance of her youth.

The relationship with Tarouca was platonic, mentally mutually intimate and rich in the devotion two people, despite the separation of over twenty years in age, can sometimes have if they enjoy each other's trust. If, during her childhood, her *aya*, Countess Fuchs, had been her great emotional prop, and during the years of her marriage, her husband, Tarouca supplied a support which combined elements of both relationships.

Tarouca's ongoing advice and company stimulated and comforted the Empress. The historian looks during the successive decade in vain for that wallowing self-pity which so marked her demeanour in the immediate aftermath of her husband's death in 1765. Instead, stoicism mingled with resignation and detachment form part of her character.

In 1769, in more playful mode, she wrote to Tarouca congratulating him on his birthday: 'I have not forgotten that your small treasure (*kleines Schatzerl*) Therese has come to celebrate your birthday; the fat Therese will join her so that you can be congratulated from the entirety of her soul.'[9]

We know from the correspondence that Tarouca urged his 'Schülerin' to appear more regularly at court and we also know that, in addition to personal observation, he readily engaged in discussion of court policies. As the Grand Reversal of Alliances planned by Kaunitz assumed more tangible form with the betrothal of Marie Antoinette to the Dauphin of France, Tarouca did not shirk from airing his misgivings about the new diplomatic constellation. 'We Portuguese and Austrians know all too well that France is just a nest of Frankian knavery (*Fränkische Knechtenschaft*) . . . time will tell who is right and who is mistaken about this'.[10]

But if the Empress felt embarrassed or put out in any way by the advice of 'her oldest friend', she never gave Tarouca any cause to think their friendship was in any way diminished by his oblique criticism of her and her ministers' policies. In the last letter Maria Theresa ever penned to Tarouca, she stressed the great service he had performed for her: 'If I keep going at all it is only on account of all the lessons you have taught me on different occasions. They are lessons whose validity I have learnt to see and value . . . believe me I did not accept them just to please you . . . your devoted and loyal friend Therese.'

This devotion was mutual and unhesitating. Tarouca's two children were named Maria-Theresa and Francis Stephen. At Schönbrunn, where Tarouca was made director of planning and building works (*Hofbaudirektor*), the courtier quickly established himself as an instrument for his sovereign's wishes, constructing a palace that would later be her brother-in-law Charles of Lorraine's summer residence.

Of course, Tarouca's presence at court aroused gossip but, despite the prevailing convention whereby in court circles it was permitted for every husband effectively to have two wives, one for material advantage and one for affairs of the heart, there was no real risk of infidelity as far as the Empress was concerned. Maria Theresa enjoyed the company of practical and devoted men but she was as serially monogamous as her husband Francis Stephen was serially polygamous. As Podewils the Prussian ambassador observed, the imperial couple were 'made for conventional marriage'. Certainly, any affair would have been very difficult to conceal among the ever-observant servants of court. But as her last letter to the Portuguese reveals, Tarouca was the most 'special' of 'special friends'. News of his death in 1771 provoked Maria Theresa to exclaim that she too was now ready to bow out: 'Death fills me with impatience rather than fear.'

We have given Tarouca this prominence not only because he was in so many ways *primus inter pares* among her male advisers but also because their relationship throws into sharp relief the insecurities and anxieties of an absolute ruler. The limitations on absolute power are both internal and external. The relationship Maria Theresa enjoyed with Tarouca vividly illustrates her determination to improve and be worthy of her role.

Tarouca was, of course, far from being the only one of the Empress's close advisers, even if the others did not share the same intimacy with their sovereign. As the 1740s progressed and the Austrian realm avoided disintegration and dismemberment, the glaring need to modernize her possessions became more acute, and here Maria Theresa found several additions to the beleaguered Bartenstein and ageing Palffy to guide her through the labyrinths of statecraft, just as Tarouca had helped her navigate her more personal challenges.

It was always one of Maria Theresa's convictions that the loss of Silesia condemned more than a million of her erstwhile subjects to the strictures of an over-centralized Prussian rule: 'My poor lands can experience no worse and unfortunate fate than to fall into the hands of the Prussians.' Yet the Austrian machinery of state was in *dira necessitas* of overhaul. If Tarouca had brought a degree of *Ordnung* into the timetable of the court, it was a reform in miniature of what her empire needed. The other men with whom Maria Theresa came into contact at court vigorously defended her rights but, like Tarouca, they were frank about the shortcomings of her inheritance.

Two men in particular, both in their forties, at this time sought to impress upon her the need for change. One was a physician by the name of Gerard van Swieten, the other was Wilhelm Haugwitz. Both were very different in appearance and mindset but both would exert a profound influence on the Austrian state that was beginning to emerge following the loss of Silesia. Like Tarouca, they were personally austere, largely unmotivated by material gain and scrupulously honest.

Van Swieten was a handsome, independently minded Dutch physician, possessed of great charm and a brilliant mind and imagination. Haugwitz, on the other hand, was, according to Frederick II's chancellor, Fürst, a man who 'really looked more like a lunatic than a great statesman'.[11]

It did not perhaps help appearances that Haugwitz had a nervous twitch which kept one eye in near-perpetual motion but when one of Maria Theresa's courtiers dared to question her faith in Haugwitz, the Empress responded firmly. 'He is honest, straightforward and utterly without ambition,' she insisted, singling out three qualities she esteemed highly and adding: 'He knows what is good, he is disinterested and has a great capacity and joy for work. Above all he is not afraid of the light or the ungrateful jealousy of others.'[12]

Haugwitz was the son of a Protestant general who had been in the service of the King of Saxony. In 1725 he had converted to Rome and entered the Silesian civil service. The Prussian seizure of Silesia put him quickly out of work. Aged 41, 'poor with no prospects', he popped up in Vienna to find, to his great surprise, that Maria Theresa's husband, with his interest in finance, seemed to know all about him. Haugwitz was Francis Stephen's 'discovery' and this patronage gave the new arrival massive influence.

Thus it was that, in the words of one jealous courtier, 'this seeming half-wit'[13] was now entrusted by Maria Theresa to bring her empire into the 'bureaucratic absolutist model' of the rococo age.

The Habsburg possessions had always been in the first rank of Europe and under Maximilian I they had developed new methods in politics, trade and warfare against the French. Later, Ferdinand I in Spain had laid the foundations for an imperial entity of different, widely dispersed possessions. The Battle of the White Mountain of 1620 had umbilically tied Austria to Bohemia, yet the dynasty had, on the other hand, never been able to eliminate the resentments of the Hungarian nobility or break the power of the *Reichsstände* and the maintenance of their aristocratic privileges.

Haugwitz saw more clearly than most that these Austrian aristocrats with their personal fiefdoms (*ständischer Adel*) were a 'brake' on progress. His experience in Silesia had taught him that the Prussian model was not without its merits. If he could weaken the local nobility and the influence of the Church, he might just be able to give the Empress's possessions a coherence and centralized revenue stream which could defend them from further attacks. The *ständische* structures had to be transformed into the *staatliche*.

The French and the Prussian examples of centralized absolutism would need to be modified to fit the Austrian dimension but they offered a new way of administering Maria Theresa's territories, introducing a tax system which could weather the storms of the 1740s and finance a modern army. The ideas were not new; long before Maria Theresa's birth, Charles VI had already noted the efficiency of the more centralized system of administration in Holland and England. Yet the high aristocracy, the *Landesfürsten*, were unlikely to surrender willingly their privileges, which included exemption from taxation.

On 2 May 1746 Haugwitz introduced the new system to all the territories of the empire, except Hungary, Italy and the Lowlands. Adapting the Prussian *Generaldirektorium*, he created a *Directorium in publicis et camer-alibus*. This new body would administer the far-flung territories with a new consistency and efficiency, hitherto unheard of in the Habsburg domains. The new administrative apex of the pyramid was to be large but not unwieldy, and at a stroke it marked the most important step in central Europe's history in its transformation from a medieval state into a modern one. Its remit would only extend to the western part of the monarchy, leaving Hungary with its quasi-feudal social structures untouched. Nevertheless, the *Directorium* would act as a 'Super-Ministerium' exercising responsibility for all policies in the empire except war, foreign policy and justice. It tied the Bohemian-Austrian *Landesgruppe* together into an *Einheitsstaat* until 1918 (and some would argue even beyond). Most importantly, it signified the withdrawal of the aristocracy from power in the local political and financial sphere. In their place came the new centralized bureaucracy, a new centralized army and a new centralized treasury. It was a *Hauptsystem* which could double revenues to more than 15 million Gulden and thus finance a standing peacetime army of at least 100,000 men, in theory a significantly improved deterrent to the greed of Austria's neighbours.

Haugwitz forged a centralized state out of a hotchpotch of feudal lands but not, unsurprisingly, without stiff opposition from the aristocracy he strove to disenfranchise. Carinthia and the Duchy of Krain had offered a useful guinea pig for Haugwitz. In Carinthia especially, under the self-interested Khevenhuellers, who had ruled Carinthia as a personal fiefdom, huge financial losses and speculative failures threatened to nullify any attempts at transparency and reform.

Together with the Kinskys in Bohemia, the Starhembergs and Herbersteins in Styria, the Khevenhuellers engaged in bitter criticism of Haugwitz but, with the Empress at his elbow, he was unstoppable. She was a most unlikely revolutionary but Haugwitz instigated perhaps the only genuine revolution the House of Austria ever undertook. It was deeply unpopular and at one stage the Empress had to order a permanent bodyguard for Haugwitz of four cuirassiers.

Even when another of her most powerful courtiers, Count Harrach, threatened to resign in protest, Maria Theresa loyally supported Haugwitz, giving the haughty Harrach ten days in which to either rethink his resignation or 'vanish from my sight'. By the time Haugwitz's reforms had cemented the union of the Austrian and Bohemian chancelleries, imposed statutory taxation on the *Stände* and separated judicial and executive powers, Maria Theresa had silenced most of his critics by appointing him (concurrently) Chancellor of Austria and Bohemia, Finance Minister and Interior Minister.

At a stroke she had made him the most powerful man in the state. She invested him with such confidence that he would be eclipsed in power and influence only by his later rival, Kaunitz, a man Haugwitz subsequently described with Viennese double entendre as that most 'illumined' (*erläuchteste*) of statesmen.[14]

Haugwitz's contribution to the modernization of Austria was never forgotten by Maria Theresa. Writing to his widow on his death, she observed: 'He alone in 1747 was capable of bringing the state out of its confusion and installing order' (*aus der Confusion in eine Ordnung gebracht*).

Haugwitz's overhaul of the system of taxation had been specifically required to create a standing army of over 100,000 men with a budget of 14 million Gulden out of a total revenue of 40 million. 'Church mice do not make wars' and Haugwitz's familiarity with the Prussian war machine in Silesia meant that he had seen at first hand how the Frederician army had been supported by the ample funds left by Frederick's parsimonious father.

Conscious that such austerity was difficult to replicate in the Austrian crown lands, Haugwitz nonetheless agreed with the Estates that they would have to subscribe every ten years large sums in cash to the central government which would recruit and equip the army.

In addition to this intrusion of the *Staat* into the Estates and Lands, Austrian military reform benefited also from private financing. On 8 February 1748 a distinguished group of senior officers met to coordinate the military reforms necessary to modernize the Austrian army. Prince Wenzel Liechtenstein offered to fund the overhaul of the artillery arm. He had been wounded at Chotusitz and had been impressed by the eighty-two well-served Prussian guns which had compared so well with the antiquated Austrian cannon. With his military career cut short by wounds, he was determined to devote the rest of his life to giving the Habsburgs the finest artillery in Europe.

Assisted by his immense private wealth – his estates ran to over 200,000 hectacres in Bohemia and Moravia – he invited at his own expense the foremost artillerists of Europe to advise him: Alvson from Denmark, the brothers Feuerstein from Kolin, the precision-obsessive Schroeder from Prussia, 'Fire Devil' Rouvroy from Saxony and the formidable Gribeauval from France.

In a move which was to have far-reaching consequences for the development of central Europe's armament industry, the Prince realized that artillery could not be left to ordinary soldiers and that the quick-witted Bohemians, Czech and German, were the most suitable for training in the artillery arm. They were tough, imaginative, humorous and energetic. Cool under fire, these Bohemians were to provide the backbone of Habsburg artillery right up until 1918.

By anchoring the artillery depot in Budweis (České Budějovice), the Prince also supported his local communities and offered his estate workers an alternative profession. When Wenzel Liechtenstein began his work, there were only 800 trained artillerists in the Habsburg army. By 1755 there were 2,000 master gunners providing the majority of three artillery brigades, made up of some thirty-three companies, a ten-fold increase.

So much for the army which Haugwitz's structural reforms were to finance. His new systems of taxation, understandably, enjoyed no such supportive private initiative from the aristocracy. Rather, an incorruptible army of civil servants was to be established to implement the levies which were to be based on the value of everyone's immoveable property, land and fixtures and rents.

Income was calculated at 5 per cent of the relevant capital sum, and on this income the landowning nobility had to pay a one-hundredth part. The peasantry were required to pay one fiftieth. This was innovative. For centuries the nobility and the clergy had been exempted from such levies. The nobility's commitment to defence in time of war had largely been the reason for this exemption but the wars of the Austrian Succession had highlighted all the weaknesses of the system. Military matters were too important to remain solely the concern of the aristocratic generals.

Resistance was sporadic but, as we have seen in the case of Count Harrach, at times vociferous. Harrach's resistance to reform had been far from unique. Haugwitz had also had to contend at first with the passive resistance of the existing *Hochbürokratie*, a caste of imperial servants whose tactics and ethos would arguably long outlast the Habsburg monarchy.

Haugwitz adopted persuasive measures and argued the case with each of the individual estates. Those closest to Prussia understandably became the most compliant. Those most remote proved the most intransigent. It did not help that Haugwitz had selected Carniola and Carinthia to be the guinea pigs for the *Neuordnung*. The Khevenhueller stronghold of Carinthia, secure behind the great Karawanken range of mountains, held out longest, and the Hungarians, ever indulged since Pressburg, avoided paying barely half of their levy and it would be another hundred years before the magnates paid even a single heller of tax.

Yet gradually, Haugwitz succeeded in cajoling the provinces into recognizing that their own partial interest was linked to the interest of the whole and that, if decline was to be arrested, a degree of centralization would have to be enacted. Writing many years later, Maria Theresa raged at the lack of coherence which reigned over her possessions, noting that without doubt 'the greatest crime was the separation of the Bohemian and Austrian administrations'.[15]

A loose collection of states with no common interest was how she described them before her reforms, and it was undoubtedly the case that for her the concept of a 'personal union' was meant to be not just theoretical or symbolic but practically unifying. Yet Austria, even with Haugwitz's diligence and zeal, could never be Prussia. The independence of the *Länder*, the rivalries and petty jealousies of the local 'bigwigs' – these would persist in Austria long after the House of Habsburg had withdrawn from all political life in central Europe.

Nevertheless, it was a sign of Haugwitz's skill that by 1747 he had secured his 14 million Gulden for a standing army of 108,000 men. In the teeth of intrigues and widespread corruption, the *Systema Nova* was first implemented in Moravia and Bohemia, Lower and Upper Austria and finally Styria, Carniola and the ever-fractious Carinthia, which was granted the privilege of a three-year recess, as opposed to the other provinces' ten-year recess. The local *Stände* renounced their *Grundrechte*. It was arguably the beginning of a new era.

THE AGE OF REFORM I: THE NEW MEN
THE AGE OF REFORM I: THE NEW MEN

Two years later, in 1749, a *Grundsteuerreform* confirmed the abolition of the tax exemptions of the aristocracy and established the two principles of Haugwitz's reforms: uniformity and consistency. The rivalry of the various chancelleries was abolished and once again the *Directorium in publicis et cameralibus* was given authority over the various *Hofkammern* which had hitherto held disparate reins of power. At a further devolved level, the local *Gemeinden* were henceforth limited to authority over trade, corporations and local business policies.

Although Maria Theresa removed the dualism between the *Landesherren* and *Landstände*, she noted that the latter were at least supportive of monarchical absolutism and thus Haugwitz's creation of a unified state was rightly perceived, even at the time, to be *cum grano salis*. The Empress may have cut the wings of the *Stände* but she did not abolish them. It would be left to her son, Joseph, to attempt to destroy their remaining power and that effort would lead, like so many of his other policies, to confusion, disarray and friction. Eventually, Leopold II would restore calm, principally by reverting to this Maria Theresa compromise.

Haugwitz's reforms thus can be seen as embodying, for all their innovation, a certain spirit of *Ausgleich* (compromise), and it was this spirit which invested all further structural reforms. Hungary remained constitutionally inviolate and the new organizational structures were deemed 'incompatible' with the 'Rights and Interests' of the Magyars. Once again, it would be left to Maria Theresa's son, Joseph, to attempt to cross these 'red lines', with disastrous results a few decades later.

Haugwitz, nonetheless, could survey his achievement with a degree of satisfaction. Fiscally and constitutionally, his reforms ushered in a modern state. Vienna was finally unequivocally the centre of the monarchy. The Austrian-Bohemian *Einheitsstaat* Haugwitz's reforms created would endure well into the twentieth century and only be irreparably ripped asunder by the Nazis and later the Beneš decrees of 1948 and the forced expulsion of 3.5 million ethnic Germans from Bohemia and Moravia in the months that followed.

Haugwitz's state was not the well-oiled machine that Descartes envisaged in comparing the state with the workings of a clock, but the idea of the state as a well-made machine was familiar to Haugwitz. Johann

Heinrich Gottlob Justi had been appointed to teach at the recently established Theresianum in 1746 and his book on public finances was not only read by Haugwitz, it seemed to owe much to some of his ideas. Justi was a Protestant from Thuringia who had studied law and pioneered the newly emerging discipline of cameralistics (the administration of public finance).

In his inaugural lecture at the Theresianum, Justi was teaching that the state was potentially a machine which depended on the systematic coordination of all its constituent parts. 'All the parts,' said Justi, 'all the cogs and springs must fit together.' The apex of power over this machine was, of course, the sovereign but the sovereign needed advisers to help realize the objectives of the state. Above all, the machinery of the state needed to be constructed on a rational basis. Like a clock, it would need regular supervision but, like a clock, it could also be expected to run by itself 'and show all the forces and actions of which it is capable'.[16]

Haugwitz had no problems in digesting this approach and Justi was quickly brought into Haugwitz's inner circle to help advise on the overhaul of the Austrian state. Both men seem to have cross-fertilized each other with their ideas and Haugwitz's reforms appeared to be the basis for many of Justi's later writings. Like Haugwitz, Justi saw reform as a methodical strategy directed at transforming the differing strands of public administration into a fully unified, structured system in which each element had to justify its contribution to the ultimate aims of the state.

This conceptual framework would have to await Joseph's accession to the crown in 1780 before renewed energy could transform Haugwitz's efforts into Justi's vision, but as ever the foundations of these reforms of the Josephine era were laid during his mother's reign. Yet Maria Theresa was instinctively against anything which subordinated the individual to the systemic, or the tangible to the abstract. Haugwitz's genius was to proceed with caution along a radical route, never allowing himself to be suborned by the intellectual attraction of the exclusively abstract. This, he realized, was the only way he could bring his Empress with him and it proved to be highly effective in so far as it went, but the crown lands were not a well-made timepiece and each part of the 'clock' needed to be approached with care. No 'one system fits all' approach stood the remotest chance of success. Reform had to be piecemeal in order to be effective and the logic deployed had to be of a kind which did not conflict with the day-to-day functioning of the monarchy. The fragile balance between the sovereign and the vested interests of her possessions always demanded an acknowledgement of the monarchy's complexities and peculiarities.

Having focused his considerable mental gifts on revenues and structures, Haugwitz turned his attention to other parts of the 'clock', in particular the fulfilment of one of his sovereign's *Lieblingsideen*, the separation of the machinery of justice from the machinery of administration. For someone who was generally considered to be 'unintellectual', Maria Theresa appears to have digested from a very early time in her reign the elementary principles of the 'separation of powers' and the need for an 'independent judiciary'. 'Nothing less,' she wrote, than a 'gänzliche separate des Justizwesens von deren publicis und politicis der Länder' was necessary.[17]

Undoubtedly, Maria Theresa's mind was benefiting from the exposure to the great brains with which she was surrounding herself. If Haugwitz with his constant tick was the rather unlikely statesman behind one set of radical change, he was the perfect foil to Gerard van Swieten, the second engine of domestic reform in her lands.

Van Swieten had studied with the great Dutch medic Herman Boerhaave. Despite offers of well-paid positions in Vienna and London, he had resisted the temptation to leave Holland, but when, on account of his Catholicism, he was rejected for any public position or promotion at the University of Leiden, he realized that even that cradle of the Enlightenment laboured under limitations.

A devout Catholic, he attended Mass every day, and although he was also an enthusiastic Freemason the 'intolerance of the tolerant' denied him any career prospects in his native land. No Catholics were eligible for public office in Holland and their churches were hidden and their bells silenced for many years to come.

Maria Theresa had known of Van Swieten's reputation for some time but it was only when her sister, Maria Anna, gave birth to a stillborn baby in 1744 and fell seriously ill that Van Swieten responded to her overtures and attended her sister in Brussels. Although she died a few weeks later, in December 1744, Van Swieten had impressed everyone with his calm, methodical manner and seriousness. A year later he finally succumbed to Maria Theresa's entreaties and was appointed Prefect of the Court Library and court physician. It was not an easy decision: 'I am a small republican who abhors all the pomposity of titles and dress at court', he wrote to a relation.[18]

His arrival in Vienna caused something of a sensation as he refused to wear court dress, rejected both lace cuffs and a sword and never wore a wig. His dress was the austere simple black coat and white shirt of the Dutch Enlightenment.

Yet if Maria Theresa might have entertained any fears of secular heresy and the preachings of Voltaire creeping into her court with this exotic Dutch import, Van Swieten's simple honesty and devotion – it was noted he took Communion every month – served to offer her evidence that the Enlightenment and her faith need not be at daggers drawn. Van Swieten personified the interface between Catholicism and Freemasonry, freely drawing on both sensibilities and cultures to establish what he believed was best for the efficient discharge of his responsibilities. For him, as indeed for his sovereign, the house of reason and faith was not a divided one.

Together with Paul von Riegger, a pupil of the Jesuits, and his own pupil Karl Anton Martini, another eminent brain, Van Swieten contributed to the atmosphere of intellectual debate which marked the last three decades of Maria Theresa's reign. He was also a great supporter of another lawyer, Joseph von Sonnenfels, a converted Jew, whose father had been a rabbi in Moravia. These eminent minds owed their security and stability to a city whose daily structures permitted their unimpeded dialogue and exchange of ideas. Van Swieten contributed to that atmosphere more than perhaps any other single personality of that time.

Sonnenfels was another perfect exemplar of the 'new' atmosphere encouraging the 'new' men. His rise paid tribute to a society which was increasingly meritocratic. After military service in the ranks of the 'House' regiment of Vienna, the illustrious *Deutschmeister*, he found a job as an accountant in the *Arcieren* Life Guard. For a man who had taught himself nine languages and was possessed of a formidable intellect, this was small beer. By 1765, his writings on jurisprudence were becoming widely known and the 'Nikolsburger Jew' became the subject of heated debate in court circles. It was Maria Caroline (Maria Carolina), Maria Theresa's most intellectual daughter, who brought Sonnenfels's ideas to the 'all-highest'. In 1765 appeared the first volume, 'Polizey', of what would in time become the Austrian Juridical code. The Empress found this and the two subsequent volumes, 'Treatment' and 'Finance', sufficiently groundbreaking to allow Sonnenfels the unique privilege of interrupting her games of piquet when he needed urgently to consult the Empress. This 'Austrian Montesquieu' became increasingly important especially in the field of education where he counselled his sovereign: 'More knowledge for the people, more insight for the monarch.'

But Sonnenfels, with the supreme self-confidence of the self-made man, found that he could not limit his activities simply to legal and educational reform. He was a passionate defender of the German language, attempting to lure the greatest of German-speaking playwrights, Gotthold Ephraim Lessing, from Hamburg to Vienna, but Lessing found Sonnenfels 'too hot to handle'. He wrote:

> You cannot believe how many enemies in Vienna this man has . . .
> the entire city loathes him . . . the more I get to know about him
> the more it does not surprise me that his star rises and falls so
> dramatically . . . his pride and self-esteem cross all frontiers . . .
> everything that I hear from him suggests he is the most intolerable
> lunatic ever to have set foot on God's earth.[19]

Certainly, Sonnenfels, for all his 'Vaterlandsliebe', was egotistical. Entrusted by his sovereign with drawing up a new system of lighting public spaces in Vienna, he proudly, if slightly ironically, remarked to a colleague who was impressed when the moon came out behind clouds to illuminate Schönbrunn: 'Yes it's true I am even responsible for all that.'[20]

Nothing, however, illustrated Sonnenfels's gifts more acutely than his persuasion of his sovereign that Austria should finally make an end of torture in her lands. In 1768 Maria Theresa replaced the existing death penalty regulations with a new code, the *Constitutio Criminalis Theresiana*. This was not an attempt at humanity and moderation. On the contrary, it listed in detail the different instruments and practices of torture to be applied to malfeasants, even distinguishing between a 'severe' death penalty and a 'merciful' death penalty. The former involved quartering and disembowelling, the latter beheading or hanging.

Sonnenfels was not a person to accept unquestioningly such a code. From his teaching position at the University of Vienna, he openly criticized the new code until a directive from the court came to silence him under the threat of 'Entfernung' (exile). In reply to this threat, he asked 'Her Majesty to allow him to deliver personally a presentation on his thoughts on the matter'.

An audience was granted and, on the appointed day, Sonnenfels entered the audience chamber and, immediately seeing the Empress seated, fell on one knee to genuflect as protocol demanded. However, Sonnenfels did not rise but proceeded to deliver in faultless paragraphs of ideas a detailed analysis and logical deconstruction of the new code and in particular its articles referencing torture.

The Empress began to be moved by her supplicant's words. She reached for a handkerchief as tears filled her eyes. As Sonnenfels saw her distress, he immediately stopped speaking and rose to his feet. In the silence that followed, Sonnenfels chose his words wisely: 'When Europe sees these tears in the eyes of the greatest monarch of our times, they will not doubt for a second that torture in Austria has been abolished.'

The Empress stood up, dried her tears, placed her hand on Sonnenfels's shoulder and said to him: 'Let it be so; Torture will be abolished.' On 2 January 1776 the abolition of torture in the Austrian domains was formally proclaimed, an example soon to be followed throughout Europe.

How did Van Swieten, whose friends were Freemasons (or, in the case of Sonnenfels, even members of the 'Illuminati'), manage to gain the confidence of the devout Empress, whose natural instincts recoiled from the musings of the *philosophes*? The simple answer is that she trusted them, and the complex answer leading from that is that she trusted them largely because Van Swieten was a devout Catholic and, like her, had been trained as a child by Jesuits.

The Jesuits are depicted by many historians of the eighteenth century as reactionary. The unhappy story of the centuries-long persecution of the Jesuits in England continues to influence the Anglo-Saxon historiography. One recent biography of Van Swieten devoted many pages to what was described as his bitter struggle against the Jesuits in the Vienna University.[21] Yet this is a gross simplification. Certainly, Van Swieten's arrival in Vienna and his ability to draw students from all over Europe to his lectures in the Hofbibliothek put many academic noses out of joint, but imperial patronage silenced them as Maria Theresa made it known that any criticism of her *Leibarzt* was criticism of her person.

In many ways, Van Swieten personifies the Catholic Enlightenment, many of whose ideas were expressed by Jesuit teaching in Vienna. If Kaunitz, the 'most illumined' of committed Freemasons, could see no contradiction between the exercise of absolute power and the full panoply of Enlightenment ideals, a more secular age, reared on the divided house of faith and reason, may well question how a Catholic Enlightenment could have enriched Maria Theresa's reforms in the mid-eighteenth century.[22]

Van Swieten defies modern categorization: opulence, excessive piety, Counter-Reformation baroque immoderation and ultramontanism, attitudes could be rejected while never questioning the basic premises of Catholicism and its dogma. That acceptance of Catholic dogma created common ground, a framework within which more radical ideas could flourish. For Van Swieten this was ingrained, having been denied a university position in a country renowned for its tolerance, on account of his Catholicism.

Unlike the French high aristocracy and the *philosophes*, Maria Theresa and the men around her were not religious hypocrites. Voltaire had written: 'I want my servants, tailor, valets and even my wife to believe in God. I think that if they do, I shall be robbed less and cheated less.'[23] In aristocratic French circles, as the late Professor Owen Chadwick has observed, the unspoken rule in discussing secularist ideas was 'not in front of the servants'.[24]

Nothing could have been further from Maria Theresa's own concepts, her faith being so solidly anchored that she could happily discuss from an early age with her *aya* and other servants all the complexities of the gospel parables.

These discussions moved onto a higher level with her advisers, especially Van Swieten, whom she put in charge of censorship and with whom she had many spirited arguments about the role of the Jesuits in her empire. Van Swieten had no qualms in criticizing the Society of Jesus where he felt it abused its near monopoly on education in his sovereign's realms but he also judged Jesuits individually rather than collectively and, like his Empress, had cordial relations with many of them.

These discussions could never have taken place had not Maria Theresa tacitly understood that on the religious fundamentals of social and moral life, she and Van Swieten were entirely in agreement. It was this shared belief system, rather than just Van Swieten's devotion to his sovereign, that gave him the authority and confidence to advance his ideas. He did not, therefore, 'reluctantly' ban Voltaire but was rather enthusiastic in preventing his 'harmful' writings from gaining wider currency in the monarchy. But under Van Swieten, the baleful practice of burning books and raiding bookshops was ended.

Irony, however, continued to be the Empress's blindspot and when Van Swieten attempted to defend a Bavarian article lampooning 'in a constructive and improving way' some of her contemporaries she would have none of it. 'As far as I am concerned I dislike irony in any form; it improves nothing, it only embitters and I consider it uncharitable. Why waste time writing or reading such things? There are so many better things to be done, to which we should apply ourselves.'[25]

Yet if Van Swieten could accommodate his sovereign's wishes on matters of style in articles, he was skilful in defending his protégés when they came under imperial attack. Thus in 1766, he proffered his resignation rather than ban some writings of Sonnenfels which had incurred clerical censure. The Empress immediately climbed down. By then, Van Swieten had become a towering figure in the empire. Although not an outstanding physician in any practical way, he raised the level of medical practice to new heights. Inoculation against smallpox, a practice he had at first opposed, soon became, after the Empress nearly died of the disease in 1767, standard procedure, with free inoculation offered to the poor in order to give the Viennese doctors further practice in the technique. Maria Theresa attributed her recovery from the illness – 'the prolongation of the days of a useless old woman', as she described it – first and foremost to God, and then to Van Swieten. Twelve impoverished girls from an orphanage who had prayed daily for her recovery were rewarded with an annual pension of 30 guilders, a demonstration which more than anything underlined Maria Theresa's belief in the power of prayer.

The physician was rewarded with the honour of the Order of St Stephen and inoculation, already well established in England, became quickly widespread in German-speaking parts of Europe. Even Frederick, apprised by Voltaire of its efficacy, rapidly adopted it, giving Maria Theresa paradoxically the final spur to approve its use throughout the monarchy. According to a letter she wrote to her cousin, Antonia of Saxony, she had even congratulated Frederick: 'You have given me the courage to take this step and I have you to thank for saving my children.' The words offer an insight into Maria Theresa's moral sensibility and sincerity. Despite all her detestation of Frederick, she was prepared to acknowledge in this instance the personal debt she owed him.[26] It had by no means been an obvious method of prevention. Although the fashion for inoculation had by then become prevalent in the Ottoman lands, there were still many pockets of resistance in the German-speaking parts of Europe. The Elector of Saxony, Max Joseph, had refused to allow himself to be innoculated and died of smallpox in 1777.

Moreover, there were risks of infection in the procedure and Robert Sutton and his son Daniel, who were the English pioneers of the technique, could not, despite a personal invitation from Maria Theresa, be persuaded to visit Vienna. Daniel Sutton, despite having no medical training, had quickly identified the cause of the disease's contagion as skin contact. His father, meanwhile, had modified the inoculation technique so that it involved just a simple jab into the flesh. The result of these two men's research meant that the 'Suttonian method' gained a reputation well beyond the shores of England, enabling them to set up franchises across Europe and in Vienna. Even though Daniel Sutton, who made a considerable fortune by personally inoculating more than 22,000 people in the space of a couple of years, could not be persuaded to come to Vienna, his agents brought the details of the technique to the monarchy and by 1768 Van Swieten felt he must take the technique seriously and establish an experimental practice to test the method.

The first guinea pigs were orphans whose condition was documented with great detail. Some sixty-seven children between the ages of five and fourteen were inoculated with no ill effects and Van Swieten swiftly embraced the new capability. By 1768 Maria Theresa had even overseen the construction of an inoculation centre on Vienna's Rennweg, visiting the building frequently to observe the procedures taking place. By September of the same year, she authorized her own children to receive the treatment. Joseph permitted his daughter, Therese, to join the arch-dukes, Ferdinand and Maximilian, to be inoculated by the 'Suttonian method', administered in their cases by an English-trained Dutchman, Jan Ingenhousz. As the technique proved successful, Maria Theresa char-acteristically responded by awarding a pension to the three-year-old boy who had supplied the 'variolous poison' for the puncture. The boy and his parents were granted an annual income of a hundred guilders a year.

By 1777 Maria Theresa could write: 'The more I observe this method the more I am taken with it.' By then, thanks partly to her own open-mindedness and Van Swieten's scientific rigour, Vienna had become a centre of considerable medical expertise.

The city began to attract skilled physicians from all parts of the monarchy. One, Leopold Auenbrugger, arrived from Graz where his father had asked him to measure the wine in his barrels at the family *Gasthaus Zum schwarzen Mohren*. The young doctor developed a technique of tapping the barrels and then realized that tapping the chests of his patients revealed the outline of the heart and enabled him to plot impor-tant symptoms of diseases. Thus did Austria under Maria Theresa pioneer the introduction of percussion diagnostics.

Nevertheless, in his capacity as physician to the family of the Empress, Van Swieten had to witness several failures. Despite his most conscientious efforts, Maria Theresa's son Karl and her two daughters Johanna and Josepha as well as both of Joseph's wives all died despite his interventions. Yet he remained much loved by the imperial family. One of the Empress's daughters hated eating fish until Van Swieten took her to a clear river and showed her how to fillet anatomically the cooked trout so that no bones survived. Another child simply refused to eat until Van Swieten began feeding her vegetables preceded by a cup of hot chocolate.

But to look after the imperial family, however time-consuming, was the least of the Dutchman's duties. The *Leibarzt* was to become *Reicharzt* and the care he lavished on the imperial family was replicated by reforms in the way public health was organized and administered in central Europe. New schools of Botany, Chemistry and Medicine were established and the renowned plant expert Nicholaus Joseph Jacquin returned from his trip to the West Indies with a mahogany tree newly named after the great physician, *Swietenia*.

Van Swieten was not at the forefront of all these developments by any means. He summoned enlightened scientists from all over Europe to join him; Franz Zeiller, Joseph Valentin Eybel and Karl Martini all followed his lead in a later age which was perhaps riper for such discoveries. Van Swieten's delay in recognizing the efficacy of inoculation cost the Empress one of her daughters and a daughter-in-law. Auenbrugger's invention of percussion diagnostics needed to be discovered by French physicians before they became standard practice, but Van Swieten's presence enabled large numbers of capable scientists to see in Vienna a place where they could flourish. Nowhere was that to be more visible than in the other great area of reform desperately needed by the crown lands: education.

CHAPTER 7

The Age of Reform II: Religion and Education

THE COUNTER-REFORMATION, FOR ALL its dramatic visual and emotional projection of ritualized forms of baroque piety, had failed to eliminate 'heresy'. Jansenism, with its ideas of the specificity rather than universality of grace, various strands of scholasticism and, above all, where it survived, often underground, crypto-Protestantism all embodied the reaction against the baroque display of innumerable feast days, extravagant wealth and a combative, often nepotistic, clergy.

Maria Theresa, as a pupil of the Jesuits, did not need to be told that, for all its seeming glories, the Counter-Reformation merited indictment both at an intellectual and political level. The Jesuits had spearheaded the Counter-Reformation but they were intelligent enough to realize that a new age needed new techniques to serve the 'greater glory'. The indictment would be best expressed in practical terms by Sonnenfels a few years later when he asked simply: 'Why is the prosperity of the Protestant lands so much greater than that of the Catholic territories?'

In this context, religious renewal in Austria could not be left to theologians and clerics; it was far too important for that. It was an affair of state and the Empress was the personification of a reform Catholicism, bringing the strands of economic, civil and political religious activity into a new relationship between Church and State, under the aegis of a sovereign who was *Defensor et Advocatus Ecclesiae*.

This had several consequences, the first and most easily recognizable being a dismissal of ultramontane curialism. The papacy under Benedict XIV had not endeared itself to Maria Theresa by supporting Bavaria in the War of the Austrian Succession. Her early lessons as a child on the 'humiliation of Canossa' came back to her with renewed vigour and the establishment of the *Hofkommission in Religionssachen* reflected a robust indifference to Vatican priorities. Already the new mood was reflected when the Prince-Archbishop of Salzburg, Firmian, who had inflicted enormous economic damage on the city by expelling in 1731 its 20,000-strong Protestant population, was retired and a more reform-minded episcopate encouraged. In the Austrian crown lands an awareness quickly grew that cameralist statist ideas could work hand in glove with reform Catholicism to the benefit of both Church and State.

Commentators have often dwelt on the idea that Maria Theresa's educational reforms began only in 1773 with the Papal Suppression of the Jesuits, but in fact she quickly realized after the First Silesian War that the prosperity of her lands would rest on commercial and educational opportunity. Writing to her chancellor, Ulfeld, in 1743, she noted with almost forensic logic: 'The longer I look at it, the clearer I see that no proper care is being taken of commerce and manufacture in any of the Lands; and yet these are the sole means of bringing prosperity to my domains and attracting foreign gold.'[1]

In order to allow commerce to flourish, the state needed an administrative machine greased with the oil of an encouraging and effective bureaucracy. The Theresianum, housed in a former royal palace of *La Favorita*, was to be the academy of the central European elite for the next two hundred years, creating a new class of largely, but by no means exclusively, aristocratic administrators. In 1746 Maria Theresa sold the palace to the Jesuits who, within a decade, had shown with their customary energy that Austria provided fertile ground for creating a new intelligentsia, loyal to Church and State.

By 1760 a *Schulhofkommission* was established to explore whether the reforms to secondary education could be complemented by the introduction of primary education. To the amusement of Frederick of Prussia, Maria Theresa actually wrote to him to ask permission for her to 'borrow' the Augustinian priest Johann Ignaz von Felbiger, whose educational reforms had worked marvels in Silesia among Frederick's newly won Catholic subjects.[2]

As with religion, so, too, with education, the priority of the Austrian state vanquished all other considerations. As the Empress was fond of reminding those who criticized her didactic zeal: 'Education is and remains at all times a political matter.' Beneath this expression of power was without doubt a belief that the fate of her possessions could not be guaranteed without advances in education. 'The education of the young of both sexes,' she wrote later, 'is the most important foundation for the genuine well-being of nations.'[3]

Five years after the establishment of the Theresianum, another famous bastion of state education was created with the introduction of an Oriental academy for the study of Eastern languages so that trade with the countries of the Levant and beyond could be developed. If the Theresianum was to provide the new cadre of the Austrian state's internal administrators, the Oriental academy would equip a caste of consuls and diplomats with the language and diplomatic skills critical to any awakening of trade with the Orient.

The victories of Prince Eugene had established a new relationship with the Orient and trade with Constantinople, not war, was Maria Theresa's vision of Austria's commercial future. In this she was truly the daughter of Charles VI, the benefactor of the great port of Trieste.

Historians, keen to burnish the Enlightenment credentials of Joseph II, continue to dwell on Maria Theresa's supposedly reactionary views – but nothing perhaps gives the lie to this more than her resolute promotion (in the teeth of protectionist opposition from Joseph, who feared for local Austrian industries) of the benefits of free trade.

The loss of Silesia had destroyed the centuries-old trading patterns. The privileges and exemptions from customs duties which the emerging port of Trieste had enjoyed were all withdrawn by Prussia. All Austrian cloth was forbidden access to Prussian markets and by 1766 the entire export trade to Silesia had collapsed.

Maria Theresa proposed the abolition of tariffs and customs duties for her crown lands and even introduced favourable terms for trade with England. 'I and His Majesty,' she ordered, 'are determined to remove the bureaucracy which currently infests our trade and the lazy execution of business. We shall immediately tear up the roots of this *Vielschreiberei* (excessive scribbling) with the following orders which are to be carried out immediately.'[4]

These sentiments would not be shared in the following years by her 'enlightened' son who held steadfast to the protectionist ideals of an earlier (and later) age, always afraid that 'globalization' would herald the end of local industries which he believed survived only because of tariffs and customs duties. It was only one powerful example of how the 'darling' of the eighteenth-century Enlightenment favoured autarkic policies whose inflexibility appeared at odds not only with his 'conservative' mother but with the prevailing zeitgeist.

Meanwhile, the reforms initiated in these early years of Maria Theresa's reign laid the foundations for much that followed, especially when, fifteen years later, a full-blown *Bildungskrise* erupted with the suppression of the Jesuits in 1773.[5] The 1750s saw under Van Swieten radical reforms to the universities in an attempt to mobilize not just material but intellectual forces in the service of the state. The decade after Maria Theresa's hard-won enthronement brought peace and, with that, the freer flow of ideas into the universities from France, England and Germany. Numbers of students rose significantly and Maria Theresa quickly saw that, if entry tests to the universities were not introduced, there would be nothing to prevent the creation of an utterly useless graduate class: what she termed an 'Academic Proletariat'.[6]

As always practical, the Empress insisted that the entry tests were to be especially rigorous in the 'new' scientific subjects. Her commentary on the *Akademieplan* was rich in practical advice, especially with regard to entry which, she insisted, should not be limited to the offspring of the 'best families'.

Here, the so-called 'arch-Conservative' possessed a sense of the benefits of social mobility which arguably later Marxists or socialists could only dream of. 'The domestic condition of the monarchy is the first and most important consideration which must be assessed in all policy deliberations,' she wrote. To this end, she fully agreed with her advisers who urged that educational reform must not result in a 'restrictive hierarchy' but a multi-track educational stream which allowed provision for 'the poor but exceptionally talented'.

The *Verwaltungsstaat* created in 1749 by Haugwitz needed these talented minds to administer the structure in which the dynasty and the bureaucracy alone could try to organize a modern state. 'Your Majesty,' wrote one of Maria Theresa's greatest advisers, 'needs the services of intelligent people who owe their position not to the accident of birth but first and foremost to the circumstance of their ability. Ability not birth should always count in the service of the state.'[7]

These last words were written by Count Wenzel Kaunitz. His ascent in the court of Vienna as the troubled decade of the 1740s drew to a close was a portent of imminent, even more radical change – first and foremost for Count Haugwitz, whose ageing career was entering its sunset phase as the new decade began, but most of all for the Austrian state and, by extension, the peace and stability of Europe.

CHAPTER 8

Enter Kaunitz

WENZEL KAUNITZ-RIETBERG MIGHT HAVE enjoyed, despite his overarching ambition, a relatively obscure life had he not, like so many ambitious courtiers, made a highly favourable marriage, in his case to a daughter of the great Starhemberg family whose ancestors had saved Vienna from the Ottoman siege and whose scions would play a leading role in Austrian affairs of state right up until the Nazi *Anschluss* in 1938. It was only old-fashioned nepotism that gave this obscure Moravian count from an insignificant village, Kaunitz (Koudnice in Czech), after which he was named, the opportunity to demonstrate his talents.

Although his father had held a position as a *Geheimrat* at court, the stiffness and conventions of Maria Theresa's father's Spanish-oriented protocol was not encouraging of new blood.

The Austrian court was dominated then by the great house of Liechtenstein, *primus inter pares* among the high Austrian nobility, combining as they did the 'triple lock' of vast *latifundium*, Catholic orthodoxy and unwavering dynastic loyalty. Kaunitz enjoyed none of these advantages. Other members of the court would have no doubt moved swiftly to marginalize Kaunitz in 1736 when he joined the Imperial Court Council at the age of 24, had he not married Maria Ernestine Starhemberg a few months later and entered the ranks of the *Hochadel* through marriage.

Kaunitz was, however, well able to make his mark. His education had been most carefully arranged by his father who appointed Johann von Schwanau, a Jesuit-trained intellectual, as his son's tutor. Wenzel was one of nineteen children but he was quickly perceived to be by far the brightest of the clan. Early plans to enter holy orders foundered on a combination of young Wenzel's academic brilliance and his most sober frugality. The hard work, self-discipline and emotional restraint were apparent from his early studies and his enlightened tutor, who appears to have held Jansenist views on grace through diligence and effort, encouraged Wenzel to pursue studies in Leipzig where he excelled in law, rhetoric and music.

From there he travelled to Holland and England, enjoying the atmosphere of those Protestant lands, and learning much from their different social structures.[1]

In 1740 he was in Copenhagen and, to all intents and purposes, had entered the imperial diplomatic service. Two years later, his sovereign sent him to Turin where great efforts were being made to encourage Charles Emmanuel of Sardinia to join the Austrian cause. The young Kaunitz and the 62-year-old Carlo Vincenzo Ferrero Rosaio, Marchese d'Ormea, Charles Emmanuel's foreign minister, hit it off. Both were highly intelligent and the Austrian was more than content to flatter the Italian by sitting at his feet learning about the ruthless pursuit of diplomatic statecraft. Sardinian support would come at quite a price – Ticino and Piacenza – but it would be paid by others.

D'Ormea was sympathetic to Kaunitz's mindset and he proved perhaps the young Austrian's greatest tutor in the intrigues of eighteenth-century diplomacy. It was the Italian who disabused Kaunitz of the notion that interstate relations were a 'gentleman's game'; rather, the Italian insisted, it involved some of the dirtiest of dealings imaginable. It was a lesson Kaunitz never forgot.

From his success in Turin, the young Austrian was given the position of head of household to Maria Anna, Maria Theresa's ill-fated sister, in the Netherlands. It was a brilliant opportunity to be close to the imperial family while learning to negotiate through the strange intellectual and political labyrinth which was at that time the Austrian Netherlands, a kind of joint stock company administered by the Habsburgs with British military support, for the mutual benefit largely of British and Austrian trade.

The position and his diplomatic success appear to have had quite an effect on his character. The man who was famously frugal and of 'few words' became rather sybaritic. He avoided 'enthusiasms' but adored the company of actresses. A talented cellist, he was also a total hypochondriac. His disdain for confessional intolerance was born of his happy days in the Netherlands and he never forgot that Flanders was a rich tapestry of different races, not unlike his native Moravia.

The Netherlands experience helped bring Kaunitz closer to his Empress. It was a mark of her patience with him that, although he returned from the negotiations of Aix-la-Chapelle – the 'Great Betrayal' – with largely empty hands, he had proved to be an accomplished diplomat, well versed in the art's baser methods and disappointments. At Aix-la-Chapelle, it had been Paris and London which had called the shots and Kaunitz had represented a country totally relegated to the sidelines of the main negotiations.

This brutal reality reflected not only the weakness of the Austrian state and its sovereign throughout the 1740s but also the new state of affairs in Germany, where the emergence of Prussia was a constant thorn in the side of Austrian prestige and ambition.

Kaunitz saw himself as perhaps better able to understand this new reality than most of his fellow courtiers. The question for him was simple: could this diplomatic weakness be reversed? Could the reforms which were beginning to transform the Habsburg lands into something approaching a modern effective state be matched by a diplomatic revolution which would once and for all eliminate Prussia from the ranks of the major European powers, returning it to its well-merited, sandy heathland obscurity?

As Kaunitz mulled these ideas over in his mind, he continued to consolidate his position at the Vienna court. He lavished patronage on sculptors and musicians, promoting the work of the sculptor Zauner and offering 'high protection' to the composer Christoph Willibald Gluck and later the young Mozart whose *La finta semplice* was even rehearsed in Kaunitz's palace in Mariahilf.[2]

The young Austrian diplomat was also the foremost proponent of French theatre in the monarchy, much preferring it to the *Sturm und Drang* of contemporary German works whose sentimentality found little resonance for those possessed of an Austrian sensibility. The odes and dramas of Friedrich Gottlieb Klopstock, arousing much enthusiasm in

Germany, could never be taken seriously by the bittersweet frivolity prevalent in Vienna audiences.

Stubbornly autonomous in his thinking, Kaunitz was nonetheless capable of deploying a charm which persuaded many of the great talents of the time. Mozart, Zinzendorf, Liotard and even Voltaire only wrote of Kaunitz's charm. The fairer sex was no less impressed and both Countess Altenburg and Lady Bentinck were smitten by his manners. Unsurprisingly, perhaps, only the Prussian ambassador was more critical, preferring to dwell on his view that the young Austrian was 'an affected parvenu' who was not only easily offended but 'easily offensive'.[3]

It probably helped that Kaunitz had impeccable connections to the Viennese world of the lodges – unsurprising given some of the names listed above. Although a report by the Vienna police would emphatically insist Kaunitz himself was not a Freemason, this report dates from 1790 when, in the wake of the French Revolution, official attitudes towards the 'Craft' had changed dramatically.[4] By 1790 the eclipse of the secret societies in Vienna was imminent. Many men were distancing themselves from earlier affiliations and, in the new era of violent revolutionary activity in France, it would not have helped even the most well-connected to be identified as belonging to a lodge.

Yet it is inconceivable that Kaunitz was not a Freemason and that the support he received at court for his policies would have been impossible without the backing of other well-disposed Masons who occupied, like Van Swieten or the influential officer Franz Moritz Lacy – a man with 'fascinating manners' – important positions of trust at court.

Moreover, it is an indisputable fact that Kaunitz's father was inducted into a Vienna lodge in 1743.[5] The hereditary principle was highly prized in eighteenth-century Austria and it is hardly likely that the young Kaunitz would have been exempted from it. Finally, the world of diplomacy in the eighteenth century – as the Marchese d'Ormea, that 'shining light of equivocation', would have been the first to impart to the young Austrian – was largely run by members of their respective countries' lodges.

This network of support was immensely helpful to Kaunitz. Later commentators, distracted by the standard later nineeenth- and twentieth-century narrative of Masonic–Catholic antagonism, have failed to realize that in eighteenth-century Vienna, Freemasons like the Emperor Francis

Stephen, Kaunitz and Van Swieten were members of lodges while at the same time exercising, without questioning its fundamental dogma, the rituals of their faith.[6]

Kaunitz exuded the intellectual curiosity of his peers. The British ambassador was astonished to find, when he presented a copy of Adam Smith's seminal work, *The Theory of Moral Sentiments*, to the Austrian court in 1759, that Kaunitz had already read it and was 'eager to discuss the value of labour as a measure of net product'.[7] Yet neither the full power of intellect nor the most supportive of 'networks' could have prevailed had Kaunitz not been able to win over his Empress.

By the early spring of 1749, Maria Theresa asked each member of the Ministerial Council to put into writing their recommendations for the future course of Austrian policy. In an elaborate memorandum, Kaunitz put his thoughts on paper and extolled the virtues of a completely new and daring Austrian foreign policy.

His starting point or premise was quite simple: Prussia was par excellence the dissonant factor (*Störfaktor*) in European politics; it therefore had to be eliminated from the front rank of nations. The stability not only of the Habsburg domains but indeed of all Europe could only be assured by a reversion to the four great powers of Europe (Austria, France, Russia and England) which existed at the conclusion of the Spanish War of Succession.

Preserved in the Austrian war archives is a memorandum penned by Kaunitz of significant insight into the future problems of Europe. In it he argues that without victory Austria and then 'all the nations of Europe' would have 'no option' but to introduce a 'militarist form of government in the Prussian manner' until 'finally the whole of Europe would be subjected to this intolerable burden'. For Kaunitz it was clear that 'this and other evil consequences can only be prevented by weakening the King in Prussia'.[8]

The question was how to effect this development, and here Kaunitz came up with a plan which was to bring him the laurels of the 'greatest diplomat of the age', even though it would plunge not just Europe but vast tracts of the wider world into the bloodiest of conflicts.

England had to be kept 'on side'. Her purse strings were too long to risk conflict with the great maritime power but, Kaunitz argued, England had no interest in the recovery of Silesia, an utter irrelevance to British interests. Moreover, as the mixed record of the 'Pragmatic Army' had shown, the English military contribution was rarely decisive. What Austria needed was a first-rate military ally with an army sufficiently powerful to help Vienna annihilate the Prussian war machine.

It was Kaunitz's inspiration to believe – at a time when no tangible evidence existed to support his thesis – that Austria could persuade its *Erbfeind* (hereditary enemy), France, to come over to its side. This was a novel idea but Kaunitz was nothing if not mentally prepared and he played skilfully on the Empress's passionate feelings for Silesia by arguing that unless Silesia was recovered, Bohemia and Moravia would in time be lost. Just as Silesia could never be recovered while a Franco-Prussian force opposed Austria, it was logical that only French assistance could help Austria drive Prussia out of Silesia.

Kaunitz was no warmonger. He always saw war as 'a disturbance of the natural order' and compared it to an illness of the body. Moreover, he knew better than most that if a 'defensive and peaceful' foreign policy were to fail, the shocks of war would require a robust state to withstand them. To this end, he noted that 'the domestic conditions of the monarchy are the first and most important considerations and these must be assessed in all diplomatic deliberations'. Furthermore, he continued, 'causing a war is a pernicious undertaking and can be justified only when the issue of survival necessitates it'.

Thus was born the idea of the great *Renversement*, but it was to be supported by renewed internal reform. Maria Theresa admired the diplomat's acuity and sharpness of mind but she understood that diplomacy never functions in a vacuum. Therefore, the architect of the *Renversement*, in order to persuade his sovereign, needed linkage with internal policy. This fitted in with Kaunitz's own ideas. He believed that 'foreign policy should truly aim to improve internal conditions'. He added in a later aside: 'It is only through wise statutes of state, that Austria can demonstrate a strength which even the most glittering of victories cannot match.'[9]

It would be seven years before Kaunitz's foreign policy revolution bore fruit and during those years he built on his predecessor Haugwitz's era of reform to ensure that, as he prepared the international constellation against Prussia, Austria continued to modernize as a state. That these policies were able to be so easily transformed into action was partly the result of the absolutism that 'enlightened' thinkers such as Kaunitz were supposed to abhor. But Kaunitz, like the other great brains around Maria Theresa, supported absolutism, recognizing that absolute power was a long way from arbitrary power and that even the Empress was no *deus ex machina* but simply the apex of a pyramid whose upper reaches were a larger decision-making process.

No fan of Prussian-style centralization, Kaunitz saw the need to expand the chain of command emanating from the Hofburg. Eventually, he would create an advisory council, the *Staatsrat*, which would attempt to offer all the advantages of a prime-ministerial government with none of the mood swings and inconsistency that such a system, as practised in England for example, risked.

The *Staatsrat* was a quintessentially eighteenth-century Enlightenment structure. It provided, on the one hand, an instrument whereby monarchs and their advisers could present and develop reform ideas. On the other hand, it could keep a watchful eye on the inevitable expansion of bureaucracy and ensure that it did not develop into the huge monster of devoted bureaucrats which Frederician Prussia had created.[10]

In the meantime, the consummation of an alliance with France was to take up Kaunitz's next few years. As the idea was his, it was logical that he should go in 1750 to Paris as ambassador to explore the possibilities. This was a mission after his own heart. Surrounding himself with the utmost splendour, he sounded out the leading French aristocrats but quickly discovered that barriers of habit and realpolitik stood in the way of any rapprochement with Austria. How could Austria – which had never declared war against England (and until 1914 never would) – help Paris in her life-and-death global struggle against London?

Moreover, a triumphant Austria could easily, with the leadership of Germany and a weakened Prussia, become a mortal threat to France. And was not Francis Stephen burning with a desire to recover Lorraine? The scepticism which greeted Kaunitz was perfectly disguised in the courtesy extended to him; his invitations were accepted and his presence tolerated but his task appeared, as Count Colloredo in Vienna had warned, 'thankless and futile'.[11]

But Kaunitz began to display the qualities which made him such an outstanding diplomat. As well as intelligence, tact and charm, he brought the indispensable diplomatic and spiritual virtue of patience.[12] As has been noted, a lesser man would have been cast down by the sheer scale of the task he had set himself. As usual, there were countless courtiers back in Vienna predicting his failure and relishing the banishment from the 'inner circle' such a fate would bring. Haugwitz, to his dying day, remained highly sceptical of the entire initiative and, when the plan was first mooted to Francis Stephen, he denounced it as utterly impossible.

Three years passed during which Kaunitz achieved nothing other than a reputation for giving good parties. At one point, he appeared so much to despair of success that he even wrote to his sovereign asking to be relieved of his duties so that he could be better deployed patching up her quarrel with Prussia. But Maria Theresa was also blessed with patience and she insisted Kaunitz persist. After all, his career did not at this stage suggest he had any other options available to him. He was the 'right man in the right place', but he needed some luck. 'Tell Count Kaunitz that he knows my intentions better than anyone,' wrote the Empress to him in 1751:

> . . . that I certainly have no preference for France but that nothing would be more repellent to me than to bind myself to the King of Prussia in the way he suggests at the end of his dispatch and thus for ever renounce all chance of one day recovering possession of Silesia . . . that I certainly do not flatter myself that Silesia may be won back in my lifetime, that I desire the continuance of peace more urgently than anyone. But having said all that, I refuse to bar the way to the reconquest of Silesia on the part of my successors, as I should do by adopting the Prussian proposal.[13]

Kaunitz resumed his task with all the skill and energy at his disposal, but his tales of Prussian treachery and his character assassination of Frederick fell on deaf Parisian ears. It did not help that Frederick used the 1750s to consolidate quietly his absorption of Silesia and refrained from obvious acts of perfidy.

Yet Kaunitz had won the attention of Louis XV and, perhaps most importantly of all, had secured the sympathy of Madame de Pompadour, the most influential woman in Paris, the principal mistress of the King, and perhaps, in many ways, one of his most trusted confidantes. Kaunitz had sowed the seeds carefully, and when Prussia, as he believed it sooner or later would, acted with its ingrained ambition and ruthlessness, Austrian views would receive a fair hearing.

Like many a great diplomat before and since, it was of course not enough for Kaunitz simply to wait for such an occasion to arrive. Perhaps events could be given a helping hand. But if that were to be the case, he would have to draw the reins of foreign policy together from Vienna rather than just from Paris.

On his return to the Austrian capital in 1753, his personal qualities quickly came to the fore. He had not a scintilla of personal greed and his strong hostility to academic traditionalism endeared him to his sovereign. Above all, Kaunitz personified the Catholic Enlightenment; he was perceived by the Vatican to be a 'ministro eretico' but there is absolutely no evidence to suggest Kaunitz, despite his membership of a Masonic lodge, was an atheist. Rather, like his monarch, he was fiercely protective of the dynasty's privileges in the face of papal encroachments. Together with his sovereign, he was critical of clerical opulence and English Catholic pieties but also, like her, he never questioned the dogma of Catholicism or the Jesuitical mantra that to do well was not enough if performing to the very best of one's ability was possible.

The abilities of Kaunitz aroused at first much jealousy but, against the support and patronage of Maria Theresa, there was little the old guard could achieve. Ulfeld and Bartenstein were already in their sunset phase. Kaunitz did not disappoint. As Chancellor, he moved swiftly to draw all the strands of Austrian internal and foreign policy into his orbit.

A new professionalism invested the conduct of foreign policy. Prussian diplomats who had enjoyed the easy-going gossip of the Bartenstein–Haugwitz era now found Austrian decision-making impenetrable: 'Now not only is Count Kaunitz himself incorruptible and much too circumspect to betray himself but his staff are also inaccessible', lamented the Prussian ambassador Podewils.[14]

Kaunitz moved swiftly to strengthen internally the provinces of the monarchy. His experience of the Netherlands gave him insights into the temper of what is today modern Belgium and Luxembourg while his time at the Sardinian court had left him with a profound respect for the potential of northern Italy. In the appointment of Count Beltrame Cristiani he found a perfect candidate to organize Lombardy into the modern era. To underline Cristiani's Italophile credentials, and thus make him more acceptable to the sophisticated Milanese, the Count was to act not as Viceroy, as had hitherto been the custom, but as Minister Plenipotentiary. Cristiani was as unprepossessing in appearance as Haugwitz, in fact more so as none of his clothes ever fitted. Addicted to snuff, he was constantly covered in powder, a great test of his sovereign's patience.

Yet Cristiani had a brilliant mind and during his office the immense Census of Lombardy was undertaken, the *Catasto Teresiano*. Cristiani's achievement was all the more notable given that Rome, despite the pliant Clement XIII, was demonstrating a new inflexibility with regard to Austrian influence. In 1758, with the appointment of Cardinal Luigi Torrigiani as Cardinal Secretary of State, there was a clear attempt to 'stop the drift' in Austrian policy under Kaunitz away from the interests of the Vatican. Whatever Kaunitz's personal religious feelings, he became more and more confrontational with the Vatican, denouncing Torrigiani's 'exorbitant presumptions'. For Kaunitz, like his monarch, it was a *sine qua non* of Habsburg outlook that 'no Pontiff dictate laws to a temporal prince'. Dealing with Rome for Kaunitz was a matter, as he confided to his sovereign, of 'denari o bastioni' (money or truncheons).[15]

Kaunitz's personal views on the Catholic hierarchy would be considered innovative even today. While not flinching from his conviction that he was answerable to his maker, he nevertheless was highly critical of the law of celibacy which, in his view, caused 'irreparable harm to future generations'. He was especially scathing of the proliferation of contemplative orders which deprived the state of 'many thousands of potentially useful citizens'.

When in 1754 a slew of papal prohibitions was issued with regard to feast days, Kaunitz ordered that they be ignored. Corpus Christi could be celebrated on Sunday rather than Thursdays which interfered with commercial activities. The 'obsession with pilgrimages' was deemed 'very harmful' and their scope and practice stringently curtailed. All these measures were portents of the Josephinian era but under Maria Theresa such radical measures were always accompanied by pragmatism and a sensitivity to existing practices. When the response to the proposals to limit pilgrimages proved overwhelmingly hostile, Kaunitz did not push it. Moreover, while Kaunitz could fulminate on the 'threatened propagation of the human race' posed by monastic celibacy, he was loath to push for reform of the contemplative orders by frontal assault. Instead, he introduced regulations which limited entry to monastic orders before the age of 21 and ruled that no girl could enter a convent until she had 'lived in the world' for at least one year.

Again, it would be left to Joseph II to build on these reforms and then take them to extremes and instigate a virtual dissolution of the monasteries with disastrous effects for Austrian prestige in northern Italy. Here, a generation later, the local populace, incensed at the destruction of the monastic fabric of their society, would, ironically, welcome the 'godless' Napoleon with open arms.

Even the Jesuits who would face suppression a decade later[16] would find in Kaunitz a staunch defender. They were very far, in his view, from the 'reactionary' forces of Enlightenment mythology. Rather, they were 'useful, innocent subjects'.[17] He would later write of the Suppression: 'I could never regret enough the senseless chasing out of the best brains from their teaching posts in order to replace them with the worst.'[18]

These examples show the pragmatism which was at the heart of Kaunitz's decision-making. The Enlightenment depended on absolutism and the fundamental beliefs and dogma of the Catholic Church but these were not incompatible with intellectual freedom, clerical reform and even a degree of secularization. It is this paradox which is at the heart of Maria Theresa's reign and which allowed her to achieve so much.

It is a paradox which extended to judicial and social reform under Kaunitz, who was in many ways far more radical than Haugwitz. Unlike Haugwitz, who tolerated with good humour the views of his aristocratic peers and superiors, Kaunitz was impatient of his fellow aristocracy. His intellectual vanity made him a vicious verbal opponent of any loose thinking and a staunch meritocrat. In a note written to the Empress about this time, Kaunitz observed: 'The higher interests of the state require the brightest and most reliable minds you command. My regard for your service requires me to stress that only ability in your service should influence your decisions . . . Austrians should become accustomed to obeying non-aristocrats.'[19]

This was a view espoused with equal enthusiasm by Sonnenfels who, in his publication *Der Vertraute* (The Confidant), had lambasted the privileges of the aristocracy until the censors had after eight issues banned the magazine. A later publication, *Der Mann ohne Vorurteil* (The Man without Prejudice), was more successful and proclaimed: 'An enlightened populace is obedient because it desires to be obedient. A prejudiced populace is obedient because it must be obedient.'[20]

Through constitutional reforms, Kaunitz brought the middle classes and even eventually the peasantry into the *Stände*. Judicial reforms gave these new classes a protection which they had hitherto not necessarily enjoyed. An independent judiciary abolished at a stroke the worst excesses of the subservient position of the lower classes to the nobility. As Kaunitz wrote later, after the French Revolution, 'No-one, neither state nor crown, is above the law.'

Determined that the state be seen as the support rather than tyranny of the people, Kaunitz even observed: 'The carrying out of the law should never lead to a corrupt espionage system and random incarceration.'[21]

If an independent judiciary removed one level of oppression in the monarchy, the regulation of Church and State limited the ability of clerical structures to retard progress. Kaunitz was always a bitter opponent of superstition and what he termed *fanatischer Pfaffenunsinn* (literally, fanatical priestly nonsense).

Within another decade, a *Concessus in publico ecclesiasticis* would regulate Church–State relations in the monarchy. Again, it would reflect a triumph of pragmatism as well as absolutism. If, internally, the checks and balances achieved by the establishment of an independent judiciary, capable of administrative service, and a council of state, offered some mitigation to the exercise of absolute power, it was never a brake on reform. Rather, this combination of enlightenment and absolutism created first and foremost a state in which all classes from the dynasty downwards could have faith. This was perhaps Kaunitz's enduring achievement more than his celebrated *Renversement*.

The great chancellor, who had originally accepted his elevation only on the condition that it was 'temporary', remained at the helm of state affairs for forty-one years, outliving Maria Theresa and even surviving beyond the reigns of Joseph II and Leopold II into the era of the *Bieder Franz* (Francis I of Austria). While later events completely nullified his greatest diplomatic achievement and a later generation of biographers chose to dwell on his personal vanities and hypochondria, the *Grand Renversement* remains arguably the most dazzling diplomatic event of the eighteenth century and therefore repays closer examination.

CHAPTER 9

The *Grand Renversement*

JUST AS ENGLAND HAD brought Maria Theresa to end her conflict with Prussia in 1748, it was paradoxically England which set in train the momentous events which would lead to the reopening of hostilities. It was Pitt who had observed that, in European affairs, it was always England which had 'the longest purse strings'. As a colleague of Pitt concurred: 'As we pay the piper, it is not unreasonable for us to have the tune we like.'[1]

As the decade of the 1750s progressed, the conflict between France and England for trade and empire overseas became an obsession for British and French statesmen. In this context, London was acutely aware that the 'joint stock company' of the Austrian Netherlands was guaranteed by the 'Barrier Treaties' as a buffer zone between France and the Dutch Republic. Conscious as they were of the great victories of the Grand Alliance of Eugene and Marlborough a generation earlier, it rarely crossed the minds of the English diplomats and politicians that Austria had any choice but to remain a steadfast ally of London.

Kaunitz, like Thugut and Metternich after him, saw the 'joint stock company' in different terms. The Austrian Netherlands were indefensible, a huge drain on resources which benefited nobody except England. Maria Theresa could protest that they supplied her and her court with 'the most reliable of domestic servants' but that appeared a minor consolation to the imperial treasury. English cash subsidies came with so many conditions that Maria Theresa felt constantly deprived of financial independence.

Kaunitz saw that any petty disputes were brought to his sovereign's attention and exaggerated. The language used by the British envoys in Vienna was deemed harsh and unfair. At the same time, the Austrian ambassador in London was snubbed and criticized and communication between the two courts degenerated into a 'paper war'. While this was happening, a correspondence facilitated by Kaunitz between Maria Theresa and Madame de Pompadour skilfully established a counterpoint sense of incipient harmony.

In order to secure France, Kaunitz was under no illusions that he would have to break with London, but he dared not encourage openly that break until he was assured of French compliance. He now moved remorselessly and ruthlessly to advance his plans. In 1755 matters came to a head and the Empress listed her grievances against England and the maritime powers, noting that she had 'never had the satisfaction of seeing her allies do justice to her principles'.

When the British envoy retorted that England had 'spent so much blood and treasure to support the House of Austria', the Empress rounded on him saying 'to those efforts England owes its present great-ness, riches and liberty'.[2]

London sensed that something was moving and peremptorily demanded a guarantee of military aid to Hanover in the event of French aggression. The démarche was less of a concrete demand than an attempt to discover the 'real intentions of the Court of Vienna'. Kaunitz simply referred them to the Empress's words, knowing full well that this would provoke the ever-sensitive King of England to focus on the security of Hanover to the exclusion of everything else. King George II acted predictably and began to extend feelers to Frederick of Prussia. This, as Kaunitz predicted, could only have a detrimental effect on Franco-Prussian relations.

When London panicked and signed a treaty with Prussia in January 1756, the so-called Convention of Westminster, Maria Theresa took the moral high ground and accused England of 'abandoning the old system first'. The British move certainly helped the Empress prevail with Kaunitz over the dissenters at her court. First of these was her own husband who, when told of the projected new diplomatic alignment, flew into a rage shouting: 'Such an unnatural alliance is impracticable and shall never take place.'[3]

However, the 'unnatural and impracticable' took place. The news of Prussia's agreement with London was met with fury at the French court, and an anti-Prussian war party, led by none other than Kaunitz's carefully flattered and nurtured la Pompadour, began to gather momentum. Louis XV had never liked Frederick and now, with the news of the Convention of Westminster, he felt betrayed. In this febrile atmosphere it was not too difficult to persuade, as Kaunitz later wrote, 'that a great power's true interests had been directly opposed by the whole political system it had hitherto pursued'. Kaunitz had skilfully created a *casus foederis* and now needed simply to sit back and await events.

Back in Vienna, a reserved Maria Theresa on 13 May 1756 expressed her 'disappointment' with England and told the British envoy that she was finding London increasingly 'unhelpful'. Not by one breath did she admit that, two weeks earlier at Versailles, Austria and France had signed their own treaty whereby Austria pledged to defend French interests in Europe, while maintaining her traditional neutrality towards England. In return, there was a French guarantee of Austria's frontiers and possessions. A secret codicil to the agreement, the *sine qua non* of most Austrian treaty agreements, pledged that each country would put an army of at least 24,000 men into the field if attacked by any *continental* power. Thus, at no cost to Austria – she did not need to break with England or surrender her Netherlands – France's military support was assured for her struggle against Prussia. The treaty was undoubtedly one-sided, a triumph for Austrian diplomacy,[4] and Kaunitz personally. Two hereditary arch-enemies had seemingly buried the hatchet. Europe looked on, as well it might, astonished.

The maturing of the alliance with France was only the keystone of Kaunitz's new diplomatic architecture. In order to destroy the 'King in Prussia', he intended to secure more allies. To this end, he opened negotiations with Russia, promising huge tracts of Pomerania and East Prussia to the Empress Elizabeth in return for a Russian army descending on Berlin. A second Treaty of Versailles was signed in January 1757. For good measure, Kaunitz also cooperated with France to bring Sweden into the anti-Frederician coalition. A part of Pomerania was vouchsafed to Sweden in return for Swedish forces crossing the Prussian frontier. Finally, this deadly constellation received understandably the support of Saxony, Prussia's neighbour and detested rival.

Maria Theresa saw in such a coalition the guaranteed return of her beloved Silesia. Kaunitz also hoped for this outcome but wisely set his eye on the greater prize: the elimination of Prussia as a factor in European politics. His diplomatic revolution did not achieve the former, but it certainly went a long way in establishing the latter; when the Seven Years War ended in 1763, Prussia, while territorially intact and still holding onto Silesia, was a financial, military and social wasteland. For just over a hundred years she remained largely an irrelevance in European affairs until Bismarck and the Schleswig-Holstein question propelled her, to the future detriment of all Europe, again to front stage in 1864. But to have kept the Prussian spirit in check for the best part of a century was perhaps the most enduring of Kaunitz's legacies.

By the spring of 1756 the dispatches reaching Berlin from her European envoys were disquieting. Kaunitz's diplomatic pivoting was causing unease. Frederick refused to believe that the French would seriously fight on behalf of their hereditary enemy, Austria, but his envoys had also noted Austrian military reforms and a general improvement in Austrian arms was not to be discounted. If Vienna was set on retaking Silesia, it would be better to confront Maria Theresa with a simple question sooner rather than later: Did Austria intend to attack?

Podewils was instructed to pose the question until he received a 'satisfactory and unambivalent reply'. This he signally failed to get. Twice Kaunitz was asked and twice, to the consternation of members of the Austrian court and at least one of Maria Theresa's ministers, Kaunitz refused expressly to rule out military action. The House of Austria could not, he insisted, give undertakings which might limit Austria's 'freedom' to pursue her 'vital interests' in the coming months. Frederick did not need to read the reports of his extensive network of spies to interpret these words correctly.

Kaunitz, for his part, was perfectly aware that he was giving Prussia very little choice but to take 'preventative measures', and the sooner Prussian troops crossed the Austrian frontier into Bohemia, the sooner the clauses of the Versailles treaty triggering French military assistance could be activated.

It is more than likely that Frederick knew of these clauses and thus, to avoid their enaction, he chose to disrupt Kaunitz's diplomacy not by invading Bohemia but by occupying, without any declaration of war, Saxony in what today would perhaps be called a 'special military operation'.

On 29 August 1756 the Prussian army marched into Saxony. In a dispatch sent to Maria Theresa dated a few days earlier, Frederick assured her that his troops were only there 'temporarily' until she gave him his word that Austria did not mean to attack. Kaunitz, from his sleepy little castle in Moravia with its fruit trees lining the roads to Vienna, counselled silence and mobilization. Maria Theresa's final reply to Frederick was not encouraging: 'In the present crisis I deem it necessary to take measures for the security of myself and my allies which tend to the prejudice of no-one.'

Frederick began to realize that the Convention of Westminster had been a diplomatic blunder which had bought him neither time nor a credible ally on the mainland of Europe. English troops could not help Frederick in his struggle with the deadly alliance threatening to encircle him. There was no naval dimension to renewed campaigning in central Europe; the struggles which would erupt in Canada and India between the British and the French were, from Berlin's point of view, utterly meaningless in terms of the equation of power in Europe.

As Frederick occupied Saxony, he rapidly brought up to full strength an army of 150,000 but speed and meticulous planning were not the only elements in his strategy. In an attempt to discourage his enemies taking the field against him, he now instigated a campaign of what today might be called 'terror bombing' to cow the local population into surrender and warn others to desist from attack. Saxony was ruthlessly pillaged to support the Prussian war effort. Not since the Thirty Years War had destruction on this scale been visited on cities in Germany. Within a month of the first Prussian troops entering Saxony, the Saxon army was neutralized and bottled up in the fortress of Pirna while Dresden was systematically stripped of her wealth and looted. Of Saxony's 6 million Thaler annual revenue, no less than 5 million would be sequestered for the Prussian sinews of war. Any of the Saxon nobility who resisted the claims of the Prussian invaders soon discovered that Frederick's Enlightenment credentials did not extend to his military terms.

Indeed, Frederick's vindictiveness at this point was unlimited towards those who dared to defy him. He appears to have taken particular delight in ordering the Prussian Freikorps's detonation of the Saxon statesman Count Brühl's *Schloss*.[5] Frederick delighted in the demolition and ransacking of the aristocracy's properties, causing the British representative at Frederick's court to comment, after the wanton sacking of Hubertusburg castle, that these actions demonstrated on Frederick's part 'a meanness that I am really ashamed to narrate'.[6]

Frederick's vindictiveness came in small as well as large doses. In the fortress of Glatz, Frederick had ordered the internment of various Austrian soldiers. In September 1757 two of these, Josef Rentwig and Johann Veit, escaped. The penalties for escaping prisoners under Prussian military law were predictably harsh. While enjoying the status of prisoners of war while interned, enemy soldiers who escaped were liable for summary execution as 'deserters'. When Rentwig was caught, he tried to save himself by blaming his confessor, a 46-year-old priest by the name of Andreas Faulhaber. According to Rentwig, he had confessed his plans to escape to the priest but had not been warned about the consequences. He had supposedly asked the priest, 'Is it a great sin if I desert and do not keep my oath to a Lutheran king as a Catholic?' The priest was alleged to have answered, 'Of course this is a great sin but not too big to be forgiven.' The priest was immediately arrested and interrogated but he remained loyal to that seal of confession which had been personified by his fellow Bohemian, St John Nepomucene.[7]

News of Faulhaber's silence reached the Prussian king who became enraged at the perceived challenge to his kingly authority. It was of no consequence to Frederick that the Prussian military investigators concluded that Faulhaber was innocent and that Rentwig had been lying. It helped even less when Rentwig retracted his statement and confessed to having lied. Even when the judge declared the priest innocent, Frederick insisted he remain imprisoned. Faulhaber had placed the salvation of the soul above the importance of an oath and this injured Frederick's self-esteem. It suited him to demonstrate to his newly acquired Catholic subjects in Silesia that the Church should be subordinate in all things to the Prussian crown. Frederick personally ordered Faulhaber's execution and, in an act of characteristic petty-mindedness, explicitly forbade the priest to receive the last rites. He was also, after his execution, denied a funeral; his body would remain on the gallows decomposing until the Austrians recaptured the city many months later and gave this latest martyr to the seal of confession a Christian burial.

The reaction to the Prussian eruption into Saxony proved that Frederick's worst fears were justified but like many an aggressor, he simply 'doubled down' and moved on Bohemia before his enemies could gather their strength to resist him.

The Saxon army in Pirna would eventually surrender once it was made clear to them that they could receive no relief from any Austrian force in Bohemia. But this time, despite Frederick taking Teschen and Aussig, the Austrians were prepared for hostilities in Bohemia. To counter Frederick's Prussian advance guard were some 52,000 Austrian troops under the newly promoted Field Marshal Ulysses Browne. He was about to demonstrate that Austrian military reform, like administrative and educational reform, had yielded considerable benefits; the Prussian advance was about to be stopped in its tracks.

CHAPTER 10

Mater Castrorum

BROWNE'S TASK WAS INITIALLY to relieve Pirna but Frederick's rapid advance on Bohemia made the defence of that kingdom the priority. Browne devised a plan to fix and hold the Prussian advance while organizing a relief column to the Saxons through the difficult but picturesque terrain of the 'Saxon Switzerland' via a 'flying column'.

Browne skilfully deployed a force of Croatian irregulars on the tangled slopes of the volcanic Lobosch hill. Behind this was the right flank of his army but most of his troops were cunningly concealed behind the marshy banks of the Morellen stream. It was a plan of some subtlety and Frederick might be forgiven at this stage for falling into the trap; he had a low view of Austrian military capabilities and, despite the many reports of army improvement emanating from Vienna, he could not imagine anything Austrian could seriously impede his own war machine.

Seeing the Croats, he quickly jumped to the logical conclusion that they were simply the rearguard of a retreating Austrian force and ordered the Duke of Bevern to clear the hill so that he could stage a traditional flank attack on the withdrawing Austrians.

The Battle of Lobositz that ensued was to remain a bitter memory for Frederick for the rest of his life. As Bevern advanced to drive the Croats from their positions, he was met by murderous fire from skirmishers in concealed positions. Within twenty minutes the Prussians stalled. If this was not enough of an irritant, Frederick was suddenly given a vivid example of the progress the profession of artillery armaments had made under Liechtenstein. As Frederick ordered his cavalry to chase what he thought was a retreating Austrian cavalry division, the

Austrian horsemen led their Prussian pursuers directly on to the guns of several batteries drawn up behind the Morellen stream. They opened fire with case at 300 paces. The Prussian horse was cut down in a matter of a few minutes and was soon fleeing in utter disorder.

The cavalry were so disordered that Frederick ordered his own infantry to fire on them to prevent the horsemen throwing his entire centre into disarray. They briefly rallied but their second charge unhorsed more than half of them and, as the fog cleared, Frederick became demoralized and, realizing that his cavalry had ceased to be an effective fighting force, he did what he did best, and fled the scene of battle, leaving Field Marshal Keith to save what could be saved. Keith saved the day for Frederick but, as another Prussian officer present noted with a degree of concern:

On this occasion Frederick did not come up against the same kind of Austrians he had beaten in four battles in a row. He was not dealing with people like Neipperg or the blustering Prince Charles of Lorraine. He faced Browne and Lacy, the former who had grown grey in the service but whose talent and experience had raised him to one of the heroes of his time. He faced also an artillery which Prince Liechtenstein had brought to perfection at his own expense. Above all he faced an army which during ten years of peace had attained a greater mastery of the arts of war.[1]

Browne stole away with 9,000 men through the wooded hills on the left bank of the Elbe and, in an impressive series of forced marches, unheard of in an Austrian army of the previous decade, he arrived to try to rally the Saxon troops. But their morale had been pulverized by Prussia and they consistently failed to communicate with Browne, forcing him to withdraw to Bohemia. Shortly afterwards, the hapless Saxons surrendered to Frederick, giving Austro-Saxon military cooperation a very poor name.

Nevertheless, Frederick's position in Bohemia was untenable. Browne's irregulars began plundering the Prussian lines of communication and harrying his supply chains so effectively that Frederick faced no choice but to pull his forces back to Saxony and consolidate. The Austrian army had passed its first great test.

The Saxon army, on the other hand, met a fate which was considered highly innovative for the time: it was simply incorporated into the Prussian army. Its officers were mostly cashiered or incarcerated and the infantry and famously impressive heavy cavalry, the pride of Saxon arms, were asked to burn their white and gold uniforms and don Prussian blue.

This extraordinary move even evinced protests in Prussia but, with his usual cynical approach to moral questions, the Prussian king simply observed: 'I take pride in being original.'

In the event, the move quickly backfired as the Saxons proved, as they would two generations later under Napoleon, the most unreliable of allies. More than two-thirds deserted, while the incorporation of a nation's entire fighting forces into new uniforms, oaths and drills was widely perceived as sinister proof of Kaunitz's warnings that Prussia was only set on expansion.

Maria Theresa did not hesitate to encourage the monarchical outrage which spread at the news of Frederick's behaviour in Saxony. France, in particular, reacted badly to the Prussian absorption of Saxony; the Dauphin, after all, was married to the daughter of the Elector.

If Kaunitz moved swiftly to play up Frederick's moral weaknesses with Paris, he also ensured that the Prussian reputation was no less blackened in St Petersburg. Frederick was lulled by the wildly over-optimistic reports of the incompetent and boorish British envoy Charles Hanbury-Williams. Hanbury seriously believed that if Frederick bribed the Russian minister Bestuzhev, Russia would remain neutral. On Hanbury's advice, Frederick ordered the transfer of a vast payment and even denuded his units in East Prussia. So convinced was Frederick of the Welshman's dispatches that he refused to believe the reports that Russia was mobilizing until finally, on Christmas Day, Hanbury's Christmas 'present' arrived in the form of a report of a Russian army 100,000-strong marching on Königsberg.

In order to head off the lumbering Russian threat, Frederick pursued the classic Prussian strategy of holding the 'key to central Europe', in Bismarck's later phrase – Prague. A four-pronged invasion of Bohemia would regain the initiative and deliver what Frederick called a 'Grand Coup'. On 18 April 1757 a formidable Prussian invasion force crossed the frontier, causing panic and consternation throughout the Bohemian crown lands.

To Kaunitz's concerns came a heated debate over who should command the Austrian forces in Bohemia. Kaunitz favoured Browne and a relatively untested but reputable general by the name of Leopold Joseph Daun but he soon realized that court precedence would return the command to the cautious Charles of Lorraine. So vexed was Kaunitz by the fears expressed by senior officers should Lorraine be reinstated that, even after the decision was taken, he sent one of his personal physicians to Prague to instil some coherence into the Austrian strategy and, above all, iron out the differences in style and thinking between the two commanders, Browne and Lorraine.

The Austrian strategy was simple: Lorraine and Browne would await the Prussian advance on Prague while Daun would bring his forces to bear. But Austrian logistics were slow and Daun was a day's march away when Lorraine's clumsy incompetence neutralized all Browne's plans and resulted in a hard-fought Prussian victory.

True, the battle for Prague did not go entirely Frederick's way. The Austrian infantry revealed the benefits of its previous years of drill and training and, as they advanced on the Prussians firing a withering volley every fifty seconds, several Prussian regiments were overwhelmed. As Field Marshal Schwerin attempted to rally his infantry, he fell in a hail of musket balls from the Austrian line.

But once again, the fate of Austrian generals would decide the ebb and flow of battle. Browne was wounded and his leg blown away by a cannon ball. As he was carried off the battlefield, the Austrian attack faltered. The crisis of the battle had arrived and Lorraine chose this moment to have a minor heart attack, fainting with chest pains. Without the apex of leadership, the subordinate commanders felt compelled to organize a fighting rearguard action to cover the army's withdrawal into the city. It was near-suicidal but somehow the Austrians avoided annihilation. Once again, the Prussians had won but their casualties, nearly 15,000, were significantly higher than those of their opponents.[2]

In Vienna, the news of the threat to Prague filled the court with gloom. For Maria Theresa, while she may have thought of the Bohemian crown as 'just a fool's cap', she was all too aware that the loss of Prague would damage her prestige irreparably and leave the way open for Frederick's armies to advance on Moravia and even Vienna. Any ensuing armistice would be entirely on the Prussian king's terms. Kaunitz was promptly dispatched to Daun to ensure the Austrian general did not tarry in his plans.

The news that the Austrian chancellor was on his way to Bohemia was immediately interpreted by the hubristic Frederick as a sign that the Austrians were about to initiate peace talks, and that Kaunitz would shortly appear in Prague begging for an audience to advance the terms of Maria Theresa's surrender.

Instead, on 7 May, Daun's trumpeters announced in a fanfare the arrival of the Austrian statesman in his camp some fifty miles east of the Bohemian capital. Daun did not need Kaunitz's presence to understand the situation was critical and he complained bitterly about Lorraine's anaemic leadership. He also asked the Chancellor for the reinforcements which alone could give Daun the superiority in numbers that could help him engage the Prussian army on his own terms. Kaunitz immediately returned to Vienna, arriving three days later on 11 May with his boots still covered in the mud of Bohemia.

Notwithstanding his fatigue and appearance, he brushed past the apoplectic court chamberlain and went straight to his Empress. A *Konferenz in mixtis* made up of privy councillors and generals cooled their heels for two hours while Kaunitz patiently answered his sovereign's discerning questions about the strategic and military situation. The reverse at Prague was put into context and the Empress took much solace from Kaunitz's confidence in Daun to deliver a victory, if he could only receive the reinforcements he needed. An eighteen-point plan was drawn up to mobilize forces to march to Daun without any further delay.

By the first week of June, barely a month later, Daun's forces numbered 156 guns and just over 50,000 men, enough to undertake an offensive and bring relief to Prague.

Frederick, meanwhile, had not been idle; his artillery had shelled the city, damaging countless buildings around the Old Town square. His cavalry screen observed the build-up of Austrian forces to the east and Frederick soon decided to crush the enemy before their strength grew further. At this stage of his career, the name Daun meant very little to Frederick. A hazy memory of some of the officers involved in Austria's military reforms might have been a *Begriff* but Frederick, despite his bruising encounter with Browne a few weeks earlier, was largely disparaging of Austrian generalship, and felt he could rely on the ponderous Lorraine to inhibit any attempts to raise the energy levels of the Habsburg chain of command.

A fierce skirmish at Kutna Hora (Kuttenberg) between Daun's advance guard and the Prussian screen alerted Frederick to the fact that he could not simply ignore the build-up on his eastern flank but should move swiftly to annihilate the Austrian force.

Daun, meanwhile, had with meticulous care brought the bulk of his army to a strong defensive position near Kolin above the main Vienna-to-Prague *Kaiserstrasse*. It was an open invitation for one of Frederick's favoured outflanking movements but this time the Austrians anticipated him and Daun's infantry executed a faultless 90-degree redeployment. When the Prussian lines advanced they were met with withering volleys front and flank which cut them down by the score before they came anywhere close to the Austrian position.

Frederick now changed tack. Imagining that the other parts of the Austrian position must have been denuded by the sudden change of front, he ordered six of his finest regiments to advance on Daun's centre. As an eyewitness noted:

> The Austrians saw nothing of the Prussians save their brass caps through the thick corn and as soon as these brave but doomed men had climbed one third of the steep slope with unspeakable difficulty they were met and thrown back by the rolling volleys of the infantry and the frightful rain of canister from the Austrian batteries which maintained a cross-fire from every side.[3]

The Prussian army was nothing if not stoic and they simply re-formed and marched up the hill again. At a nearby oak wood the fighting was particularly fierce as Prussian infantry met Croatian irregulars and the elite Hoch und Deutschmeister regiment, the 'House' regiment of Vienna, distinguished by sky-blue facings and an almost familial sense of loyalty. At a time when there were no decorations or medals for the ordinary rank and file, Maria Theresa would reward these men with a personal distribution of the *Gratifikations* money when they returned to Vienna.

As the golden sun drew lower in the sky, Frederick refused to give up and, shortly after 6.30 pm, he committed his reserve, the Prussian Guard, in a final effort against Daun's centre. It was the seventh attack the Prussian infantry had put in that hot day and few on either side were under any illusion that the crisis of the battle was now at hand. Daun reorganized his lines with coolness but the sheer intensity of the battle had shaken many of his staff and a discussion on the merits of a withdrawal took place. The troops were so low on ammunition that the order was given to the drummer boys to cut open the tops of their drums and fill them with ammunition from the pouches of the dead and wounded and redistribute it as quickly as possible.

Sources to this day are unclear as to what happened next and whether, as the final Prussian attack appeared to overwhelm the Austrian front line, the order to withdraw was in fact given, only to founder on the reluctance of the front-line troops to disengage and risk destruction as they retreated. In the heat of the battle, any thought of withdrawal to a new rallying point struck the forward Austrian commanders as suicidal and best ignored. It may also have been the case that the legendary poor logistics of Austrian military communications were actually helpful in this instance.

In any event, the de Ligne dragoons received the order to cover the withdrawal and were stupefied by the request. Recruited from the Netherlands and wearing dark blue coats, they were distinguished from most Austrian cavalry by their absence of moustaches. On receiving the order to cover the retreat, their colonel rode up to Daun and, in a heated exchange, demanded he be allowed to charge. Daun looked at the dragoons and somewhat impatiently asked if 'these *blancs becs*' were really ready to attack. The tone of dismissive scepticism was well calculated and the insult spurred the dragoons to charge the advancing Prussian infantry in the flank, crying 'we do not need moustaches but only steel blades to prove our valour'.[4]

The Prussian infantry reeled and unsurprisingly broke. Unsupported by their own cavalry and by now utterly exhausted they turned and fled, leaving their colours and drums on the field. The myth of Prussian invincibility had been shattered. As so often happens in battle, the line between overwhelming victory and rout was far thinner than most non-combatants can ever imagine. At Kolin, barely fifteen minutes divided the moment of seemingly inevitable Prussian victory and overwhelming defeat.

Daun might have turned the defeat into a rout had he ordered a pursuit; he had several regiments of light cavalry under Nadasti ready precisely for that purpose but he hesitated, perhaps exhausted mentally by the long day or perhaps, as one of his staff officers observed, 'he did not want to let the sun go down on his anger'.

In any event, Austria could claim a great victory. Just how great a victory, Daun was only just beginning to appreciate.

CHAPTER 11

Austria Resurgent

KOLIN MARKED A TURNING point, not only personally for Daun's military career, but also for the Empress's prestige. It changed the view in the German lands of Maria Theresa. In addition to *Milde und Munifizenz*, there was now steel. Her armies could march to victory and her generals could measure swords with arguably the most disciplined army in Europe. It was the beginning of a new phase in a war which would bring many further victories against Prussia. As Frederick was bitterly to recall, waging war against Maria Theresa was 'like dying a thousand times every day'.[1]

Frederick had undoubtedly experienced a dramatic reversal of fortune. From being about to complete the destruction of one army trapped in Prague and the marginalization of another under Daun, he had been totally defeated, with great loss of men and materiel. Austria, recently so vulnerable, had been saved.

For Daun, the spoils of victory made this once rather obscure officer into a household name throughout Europe. Favours and honours were showered upon him. He had been Kaunitz's protégé and Kaunitz made sure no detail of Daun's achievement went unnoticed. Above all, Maria Theresa bestowed all the riches of imperial favour to the man who had 'saved the monarchy'.

Two days after his great victory, the Empress established a new honour of chivalry. The Order of Maria Theresa was from that day onwards the supreme military decoration of the Habsburgs, with its 'birthday' firmly anchored to 'Kolin Day', 18 June. Until the empire fell in 1918, this order was to retain quasi-mystical status as the highest award for gallantry in the old Austria and one of Europe's most coveted awards for bravery.[2] Daun was nominated Commander of the Order though, contrary to popular belief, he was not to be its first candidate for recognition. That honour was to befall the luckless Charles of Lorraine, whose career, now completely overshadowed by that of Daun, needed some sweetener to accompany his imminent, well-deserved, demotion from the status of overall commander.

The Empress presented to Daun's son a map of Bohemia, on which the name of Kolin was entered in gold lettering. The map's golden case bore the inscription in the Empress's hand: 'Toutes les fois que vous regarderez cette carte geographique, souvenez vous de la journée ou votre pere a sauvé la Monarchie.'[3]

Kolin also marked a diplomatic turning point for Kaunitz. Nothing succeeds like success, and the alliances he had been carefully constructing now bore fruit. Two French armies crossed the Rhine, while a Swedish army advanced into Pomerania, and a Russian force closed in on East Prussia. Courtiers in Vienna began to boast of the imminence of *Prussia delenda est*.

Kaunitz himself was taken up by the enthusiasm which enabled him to bask in Daun's glory. Prussia was to be dismembered: Silesia and Glatz would revert to the Habsburgs, Magdeburg and Halberstadt were to be given to the King of Poland, Ravensberg to the Elector Palatine, most of Prussian Pomerania to the Swedes, and parts of East Prussia to Russia. Thus would Frederick pay for his 'rape' of Silesia. In fifteen years, thanks to Kaunitz, the tables had indeed been turned on Prussia and it was now the Hohenzollern dynasty that appeared to be facing eclipse.

Another Prussian defeat, at Moys, cost Frederick one of his favourite generals, Winterfeldt, while in Berlin a large Austrian reconnaissance force found the Prussian capital undefended. Andreas Hadik, the Austrian commander, enjoyed five days of unopposed looting and the pleasure of humiliating the austere Berliners as his hussars stormed and robbed their way through Charlottenburg.

As Frederick rushed back to his undefended capital, his troops in Saxony and Silesia were defeated piecemeal. The fortress of Schweidenitz fell to the Austrians, yielding 6,000 Prussian troops as prisoners of war, while shortly afterwards Breslau was retaken. In East Prussia the news was equally grim: a Russian army defeated a Prussian force at Gross-Jaegersdorf.

Arguably, Frederick never proved himself a more brilliant adversary than in the few months that followed these setbacks. Just as everything seemed lost, his energy pushed him into regaining the initiative in Saxony and Silesia. He well knew that, if he was to have any cards in his hand at the imminent negotiations for a ceasefire, he would have to win some battles.

Choosing the weakest of his opponents, he routed a small French force under Soubise around the village of Rossbach and crushed a *Reichsarmee* under Hildburghausen whose troops, with the exception of two Austrian cuirassier regiments, 'all ran like sheep'. The 'battle' was over in half an hour and Prussian losses amounted to 168 dead, but the effect on Prussian morale was uplifting and Rossbach put Frederick firmly back in control of Saxony.

To make any significant impression on his enemies, Frederick understood he would have to defeat the Austrians and here he was helped enormously by the reappointment – in the teeth of Kaunitz's opposition – of Lorraine as Commander-in-Chief of the Habsburg forces. Lorraine's supporters at court had not been entirely eclipsed by Daun at Kolin, and he himself knew this was his last chance to win back the laurels of command. Against all the advice of his senior commanders, Lorraine insisted on giving battle. It was 5 December 1757 and Daun's victory of the summer was about to be squandered at Leuthen. Frederick chose his ground well and a fold in the hills concealed the movements of his troops from Lorraine.

Once again, Frederick decided to 'roll up' the Austrian flank, but this time the Austrian centre did not notice as the Prussian infantry changed front and moved invisibly towards the weak Austrian left flank which was defended only by second-division imperial troops and Bavarians. When the Prussians suddenly erupted in front of these, two volleys were enough to disperse them. Within barely half an hour, Lorraine's flank had vanished. The Austrian centre collapsed an hour later and a further hour saw a third of Lorraine's army surrender. Leuthen was undoubtedly Frederick's most dazzling victory and, if Kaunitz needed any further ammunition to ensure Lorraine's long-overdue retirement from command, Leuthen provided all that was necessary.

Not even Maria Theresa's husband, Charles's brother, could save him now. On 16 January 1758 Lorraine was finally removed by way of a letter from Maria Theresa which even his thick skin could not fail to interpret correctly. Daun would assume overall command.

Leuthen, for all its staggering success, was, unlike Kolin which saved Bohemia, strategically insignificant. It did not, in Frederick's phrase, 'rid him of the Austrians completely'. Austria was richer than Prussia in materiel and manpower and a setback like Leuthen was not going to force either Kaunitz or his Empress to deviate from their course of eliminating Prussia from the equation of European power. Frederick hoped to induce panic and *pourparlers* by advancing on Moravia but, even if some of the Empress's courtiers packed their bags to flee Vienna, the Empress and her chief minister were not going to show their backs to Prussia. Daun called a meeting of corps commanders at Skalnitz and began with the help of two talented officers, Lacy and Loudon, to restore the Austrians' morale. By the spring of 1758, Daun had overhauled his infantry and even reinforced the Moravian fortress of Olmütz, provoking Frederick to remark acidly: 'I cannot believe (these reinforcements) are Austrians! They must have learnt to march!'[4]

Prussian attempts to resupply their siege force were frustrated by ambushes carefully planned by Loudon's irregular cavalry units. In one successful ambuscade, more than a hundred wagons were captured and the accompanying escort of 3,000 hussars put to flight. Austrian losses were barely six hundred. Loudon skilfully introduced the art of guerrilla warfare to the unfortunate Prussians. Outmanoeuvred by Daun, Frederick felt compelled to raise the siege of Olmütz and withdraw.

Yet Frederick believed he still needed to bring the Austrians to another battle if he was to survive. As he observed: 'If we beat the Austrians we will have nothing to fear from the others.' But Frederick found that Daun was a master of positioning and that he would only give battle on terrain of his own choosing. The months passed and as winter turned to spring and spring to summer, Vienna began to share Frederick's frustration at Daun's caution.

Daun could not be rushed; there was too much at stake to repeat the rash errors of Lorraine. Moreover, the forces closing in on Prussia on other fronts were having a demoralizing effect on his opponents: a

Russian army had occupied Königsberg, the city of Leibniz and the Prussian Enlightenment. An action at Zorndorf had been a bloody stalemate, with the stubborn Russian infantry still in control of the battlefield.

Yet by the time autumn arrived, expectations in Vienna were exerting considerable pressure on the Austrian commander-in-chief to give another demonstration of his skills. On 24 September, Maria Theresa urged him to undertake a 'decisive operation at all costs if an unfavourable peace was to be avoided'. Frederick shared the Empress's impatience: 'If His fat Excellency of Kolin (Der dicke Excellenz) would only do me the honour of sticking his neck out, I should be delighted to smash it off.'[5]

On 13 October, the urgings from Vienna became more terse: 'Look seriously for an opportunity to give battle', came a missive from Maria Theresa's husband. British diplomatic pressure for a settlement was again being applied in Vienna and London.

Daun, urged on by his commanders, especially Lacy, now felt the moment arriving when he would satisfy both foe and friend. As the doyen of military historians, Christopher Duffy, has written, 'it was just when Daun's slow uncoiling lulled Frederick into the deepest torpor that Daun was apt to listen to the bold counsel of someone like Lacy'.[6] Just such a moment was now imminent.

Frederick, arranging his army east of Dresden, was aware that Daun had placed himself between the Prussian forces and Silesia and, as he moved his forces gingerly towards it, he anchored his right flank around the village of Hochkirch which sat on high ground.

The woods around it were seething with Loudon's *Pandours* and it was left to the heroic Keith, one of Frederick's most experienced generals, to express what many Prussian officers felt: 'If the Austrians allow us to remain peacefully here then they really deserve to be hanged.' To which Frederick replied: 'True, but I hope they fear us more than the hangman.'[7]

When Frederick's quartermaster also protested, refusing to pitch his tents in such an exposed position, he was promptly put under arrest. Perhaps Frederick was assured by his intelligence reports which all seemed to concur that Daun would never undertake so uncharacteristic an action as a surprise attack.

The reports were not entirely misleading. It was Lacy, the officer with 'the most fascinating manners', who persuaded Daun. Lacy devised a plan whereby a large part of the Austrian army would steal away in the night only to reappear a few hours later in columns which, in a star-shaped formation, would advance on the Prussian position. The epicentre of this formation was Frederick's exposed salient on the spur at Hochkirch.

Everything was done to lull the Prussians into a false sense of security. Even the Austrian tents and fires were maintained in their original positions with woodsmen encouraged to make as much noise as possible, felling trees and singing songs.

Promptly, as the village church bells struck five, the Austrians struck. Croat irregulars rushed the Prussian outposts and began their murderous work with the bayonet. Cutting the tent ropes of the encampments, they began systematically bayoneting the writhing mass of trapped humanity inside. The streets literally ran red with blood along what would be called thereafter the *Blutgasse*.

The Croats achieved total surprise and an hour later the Austrian artillery opened up against the disorientated Prussians with devastating effect. The Duke of Brunswick drew his sword but it and his head were carried away by a cannon ball. Brave Keith, who had dared to question his sovereign's dispositions, formed his infantry into two lines and attempted to rally his grenadiers, only to fall with two musket balls through his chest. Prince Maurice of Dessau and a score of other Prussian officers fell in the first hour of Daun's assault.

Three hours later and Frederick ordered a full retreat. By 10 am, the battle was won for the Austrians. Thanks to the fierce firepower the disciplined Prussian infantry, even in retreat, could bring to bear on their pursuers, the Prussians escaped annihilation. The Croats and *Pandours* preferred in any event to pillage the Prussian camp rather than risk their lives chasing an already defeated foe.

The spoils of war were indeed rich that day. By midday, a third of Frederick's army lay dead or dying; the entire Prussian artillery park of 101 guns had been captured, along with 30 standards and immense amounts of baggage. Many of the Prussian generals were wounded or dead.

Keith's body was carried off by the Austrians who left it covered by a *Pandour*'s cloak in the church. When, later that afternoon, Lacy and Daun entered the church, they saw the corpse and, sensing that it must be that of a senior Prussian officer, Lacy gently tugged away the cloak, recoiling in shock and horror as he recognized his distinguished opponent. Turning to Daun, he quietly said: 'That is my father's best friend', before, to the consternation of their Croat sentries, both men burst into tears.

Lacy was all for renewing the attack but the scale of Austrian casualties, although lower than the Prussian losses, was significant. The Prussians in retreat had sold their lives dearly; more than 7,000 Austrians were dead or wounded.

Yet there was no denying Daun had won another great victory and the news, when it reached Vienna two days later, occasioned universal rejoicing, not least for the Empress, who could finally boast an army in the first rank of the European powers. Her meticulous attention to detail had moved her ever closer to the military machine her talented advisers had created over the previous ten years, and she had insisted at every stage that she be informed of the progress of reform. Hochkirch was as much her victory as it was Daun's.

Maria Theresa's personal equestrian skills gave her particular insights into the use of light cavalry and she had bombarded her officers with advice often heavily leavened with what might be termed feminine common sense. Her 'suggestions' often met with resistance from her more conservative commanders but her sincere commitment to the army's improvement made many of her recommendations inescapable.

She asked why all her regiments could not present arms in an identical fashion; she complained that there were too many words of command: 'The shorter the better', she insisted. So acute was her sense of equestrian drill that she quickly condemned any aspects which seemed effete or unnecessary, penning the command that it should be abolished forthwith as 'it strikes me as decidedly unmilitary'.

Nor were Maria Theresa's strictures confined to the parade ground; she immersed herself in the study and practical application of cavalry tactics. During a long debate among her senior officers on the efficacy of cavalry firing in formation, she observed tersely, 'ich halt nicht viel' (I do not think much of it).[8]

Her cavalry commanders soon realized that any change, however minor, even if it only concerned the importance of equestrian kettle-drummers rather than trumpeters, needed to be 'signed off' by their Empress. When the Croat irregulars, who had inherited the mounted kettle-drum tradition from their Ottoman opponents, baulked at the removal of their traditional percussion instruments and threatened even mutiny, Maria Theresa reluctantly gave in, but she insisted that she personally thought them 'completely unnecessary'.

It was largely at Maria Theresa's own instigation that the officer corps, which proved itself so ably at Hochkirch, had emerged from under the baneful shadow of the proprietary colonels who were inconsistent in quality.

As they soon quickly realized, there was no detail of military affairs which seemed insignificant enough to escape the Empress's attention. Whether it was the make of riding gloves, which shade of green to be used as facing colours, the use of pomades and powder in the hair or the cut of riding boots, Maria Theresa was, to use the modern phrase, 'across it'.

Some regiments found that, in order to escape the cloak of Theresian uniformity which descended on them, they had to lobby personally their sovereign. The Latour dragoons, after their splendid showing at Kolin, petitioned their Empress to continue to have the right to be exempt from the prevailing fashion for moustaches. The Savoy dragoons had also fought well, and their Colonel Lyndon was granted an audience with the Empress so that he could argue, successfully as it happened, that his regiment continue to enjoy the unique privilege of wearing red coats with black facings. When a senior commander questioned this blatant exceptionalism (the entire Austrian regular heavy cavalry was attired in white, save for the *Schvo-ley*'s[9] green coats), Maria Theresa ended the discussion with the simple phrase: 'Lyndon's regiment is good.'

Once Maria Theresa had demonstrated her tastes with regard to her wilful cavalry regiments, the infantry quickly submitted to her requirements for the removal of excessive ornament. A new, shorter and lighter infantry uniform was introduced following Maria Theresa's injunction that the old uniform was unsatisfactory. As the Empress noted:

One of my principal ambitions is and always shall be to make such arrangements as will promote the upkeep of the private soldier and alleviate his duties. Bearing this in mind I have decided to try out a new kind of uniform among my infantry regiments which will give the ordinary soldier's body better protection against cold and wet and yet be no heavier to wear.[10]

Maria Theresa's personal intervention in the details of her military did not always meet with universal approval and Podewils noted that her attempts to change uniforms often foundered at first on the stiff resistance of her officers.

But it was on the drill square that Maria Theresa perhaps exerted her greatest influence over her infantry. In 1749 she issued a proclamation which heralded radical change: 'It has come to Our notice that Our imperial infantry possesses neither a uniform drill nor consistent observation of military practice. These two shortcomings not only give rise to various disorders but promote a dangerous, harmful and damaging situation.'[11] Thus emerged the Imperial-Royal *Regulament und Ordnung des gesammten Fuss-Volcks*.

Nor were these reforms of the three arms of war carried out in a vacuum. Just as in 1746, Maria Theresa had founded first the Theresianum as a *collegium nobilium* to educate a cadre of future civilian administrators and servants of the state, and then the Imperial-Royal Oriental Academy, to train her diplomats in the languages of the east, so too she turned her attention to military education.

A castle in imperial ownership twenty-five miles west of Vienna at Wiener Neustadt was converted into an 'aristocratic cadet school' (*Adelige Kadettenschule*). The decree issued by Maria Theresa on 14 December 1751 bears all the hallmarks of her specific interests in creating a meritocratic officer class rather than a finishing school for the high aristocracy. She envisaged an officer training academy with a corps of cadets divided into two companies of 100 men. One company was reserved for young aristocrats while the second was the reserve of the sons of senior officers, some of whom might have been ennobled. As the prestige of the officer corps was raised, all officers with thirty years' service were routinely ennobled. The cadets were admitted in their thirteenth year, having been prepared for the entrance exam by a 'Vorschule' established for boys between the ages of 8 and 13.[12]

A further keystone of Theresian military reform was the Empress's belief that the decision-making process during times of conflict needed streamlining. As early as 1745, she had issued a proclamation reforming the *Hofkriegsrat*.

Quartermaster functions and judicial oversight were designated separate departments while the members of the court war council were limited to eleven. Under Van Swieten, a programme of military medical capability was also rolled out. The full benefits of these reforms would only arrive after the Seven Years War was over, but they fully underlined Maria Theresa's commitment as *Mater Castrorum* to making Austria's military effort a match in every way to that of Prussia.

CHAPTER 12

The Humbling of Frederick

FREDERICK ADMITTED THAT HOCHKIRCH had been a 'disaster' and that he was 'a beaten man'. Though barely 46 years of age, Frederick was showing signs of physical and mental deterioration. The British envoy was shocked to see him after Hochkirch, describing him as 'an old man lacking half his teeth, with greying hair, without gaiety or spark, or imagination'.[1]

To these obvious, if premature, signs of age came the further debilitations of gout and influenza. Foreign envoys noted the careworn face and the more slovenly mien, not helped by his reluctance to change his uniform, which gradually became moth-eaten and covered in food stains. He had lost his best generals, his best friends, and the casualty rate among his subalterns, the future promise of any army, had been as high as 70 per cent in most of his battalions. Several regiments had in fact ceased to exist as the supply of native Prussian manpower simply dried up.

Writing to Frederick of Brunswick on Christmas Eve 1760, the Prussian king noted: 'Do not expect big things. We are thoroughly dilapidated and our defeats as well as our victories have robbed us of the flower of our infantry.'[2]

Of all his enemies, the Austrians had transformed themselves into the most feared. The French were, in Frederick's phrase, 'experienced but careless', and the Russians 'wild and incompetent'. Maria Theresa's Austrians, on the other hand, had become his 'most professional adversary'.

Still Frederick hung on. He debased the Prussian coinage to keep the sinews of war going, with some financial help from London, but Prussia had neither the resources nor the materiel of Austria, let alone his other opponents. The scions of the Junker families who had made up the backbone of his infantry officers had been so enormously winnowed that he had to face recruiting officers from the middle classes, men whom Frederick, despite his Enlightenment credentials, believed were 'very poor officer material' as they were too 'devoted to materialism' and thus 'unfit for the honourable profession of arms'. The social mobility enjoyed by Austrians under the supposedly socially 'conservative and bigoted' Maria Theresa was unheard of in Frederick's Prussian Enlightenment. While the Theresian army welcomed all confessions, Prussia's officer corps remained an exclusively Lutheran caste.

Yet Frederick, kidnapping young men from Magdeburg and bribing his enemies to return their prisoners, gradually rebuilt his army. The reports reaching Vienna from Berlin were ominous. Was the Prussian eagle about to become its most dangerous in its hour of greatest weakness?

Kaunitz arguably saw more clearly than anyone what Frederick and Prussia meant for the future security and stability of Europe. As we have seen, he was keen to remove the evil 'of remaining armed beyond our means and burdening loyal subjects with still more taxes rather than granting relief from their burdens'.[3] In this one sentence, Kaunitz almost predicts the entire history of Europe in the twentieth century up to 1991.[4]

Austria redoubled its efforts to crush Prussia and, in another defeat for Frederick, an Austrian force under Loudon, supporting a large Russian army under Soltikow, annihilated Frederick's forces at Kunersdorf. The new raw Prussian recruits had none of the discipline of the old Prussian army defeated at Hochkirch. When confronted by a massive combined Austrian and Russian cavalry charge, they disintegrated on contact. Even Frederick, exhibiting for a change a complete indifference to his personal safety, failed to rally his troops. At one point surrounded by Cossacks, the Prussian king was only saved by a quick-thinking officer, Prittwitz, who gathered hastily a few squadrons of hussars to rescue Frederick.[5]

Even by the standards of Kolin and Hochkirch, Kunersdorf was victory on the grandest of scales. Unlike Hochkirch, there was no orderly retreat with disciplined Prussian firepower to help the shattered remnants escape. Again, an entire artillery park, this time 178 guns, was captured and barely three thousand Prussian soldiers escaped, less than a tenth of Frederick's original force. The taciturn, moody Loudon, whose cavalry charge had won the day, could perhaps never have dreamt of a more complete revenge on the Prussian king who had had the temerity to reject Loudon for service in his army some years earlier.

'I believe all is lost,' Frederick wrote that evening, adding with a flourish of the melodramatic, 'Adieu forever.' It was, above all, a personal defeat as Frederick had chosen the position and tactics for his army. This initial mood of resignation soon passed and, in characteristic form, Frederick soon found a scapegoat in the guise of his infantry, whose fault the 'entire collapse' was.

To ram home the point, Frederick ordered that every soldier who had fled the battlefield, and returned later to the colours, be flogged with twenty strokes of the cane. Thus did this idol of Enlightenment, whom the Germans (and British) dubbed 'the Great', evade once again any personal responsibility for the disaster he had brought upon his army.

Frederick ordered the evacuation of the royal family from Berlin but he need not have feared; he was about to be saved by the petty jealousies of his opponents. Loudon was rightly seen as the man of the hour but the Russian commanders could not help feeling that Vienna was rather too happy to fight on to the death of the last Russian soldier. Soltikow's campaign had already cost him 27,000 men. Were he to secure another victory on these terms, he would have no choice but to return to Moscow 'alone with a truncheon' to confront his Empress.

Russian caution was complemented by Daun's characteristic aversion to rushing things. While Daun delayed, Frederick rebuilt his army and artillery park.

The moment for Austria to combine again with her Russian allies and wipe Prussia off the map came and went. The Austrians captured the Prussian garrison in Dresden but Frederick began to withdraw as many troops as he could find to a formidable position in Torgau.

General 'Winter' helped the Prussian king and Daun felt he should withdraw his forces to Bohemia for the winter months. His army now consisted of a largely imperial force comprising the troops of various princedoms whose reliability was inconsistent. They were not of the calibre of his Austrian forces and he was wary of deploying them against a strong defensive army well dug in for the winter. Frederick was determined to avenge his recent defeats and told his senior commanders that the 'Fat Consecrated Excellency' (Daun had been recently invested with a papal decoration) who had 'accumulated all the symbols of human vanity about him' needed to be 'sent packing with a colossal kick up his fat ass'.[6]

To administer this 'colossal kick', Frederick sent a force under General Finck to take up a strategically threatening deployment near Maxen, from where it could harass Daun's communication lines and generally 'encourage' Daun's withdrawal to Bohemia. Once again, it was Lacy who saw the potential and, despite the driving rain and sleet, he brought three columns and artillery into a position which surrounded the Prussians. The hapless Finck saw what was happening and sent repeated requests to Frederick for reinforcements but the Prussian king never received them. Lacy's Croat scouts intercepted all Finck's messengers and so, faced with no possibility of relief and imminent annihilation, Finck, after a brief but disastrous skirmish, surrendered.

For barely 900 casualties, the Austrians had inflicted 3,000 losses and captured 14,800 men, 549 officers, including 16 generals, and another large (71-gun) artillery park.

Maxen secured Austria's position in Saxony. Frederick was dumbfounded and quickly moved to blame others for what had in effect been his own strategic miscalculation. Finck (in Austrian captivity) was informed that his career was at an end and that the surrender of an entire Prussian corps was an 'unheard-of precedent'. For good measure, the unfortunate Finck was also told that a court martial awaited him once hostilities paused to allow his return to Berlin. With one exception, all his fellow generals were also cashiered, while the regiments which had been present at Maxen were formally disgraced and declared the object of the king's *Ungnade* for the rest of Frederick's life. The contrast with Maria Theresa's long-suffering patience with her unsuccessful generals could not have been more marked.

The *Finckenfang* (literally, Finck-snare) brought 1759 to an end but sadly, despite the disasters of Frederick, no respite for the combatants. English subsidies ensured Frederick fought on and that Silesia remained unconquered. Another Prussian army was defeated by Loudon a few months later at Landshut and the fortress of Glatz also fell to the Austrians. Lacy even managed to enter Berlin again with a large raiding force made up of Austrians and Russians in October 1760, recovering many Austrian trophies and standards captured in earlier campaigns and even procuring as a souvenir for a brother officer (O'Donnell) one of Frederick's flutes.

Yet, despite Russian infantry 'marching knee-deep in shattered Meissen' in Charlottenburg, Frederick fought on and the news that he was heading back west at the head of another army encouraged Lacy to abandon Berlin. A month later at Torgau, a large battle finally brought an end to the long weeks of manoeuvring. Daun was wounded in the midst of battle and the Austrians, after first sensing victory, became overconfident and were surprised by a spirited Prussian cavalry attack under Ziethen who forced the Austrians to withdraw.

Torgau was a costly but limited victory for Frederick; the Prussian army was received by an Austrian artillery cannonade which, in the eyes of one witness, was of an intensity such as 'had never been experienced since the invention of gunpowder'. The extent of Prussian casualties was so high that Frederick insisted it be kept secret. 'It will cost you your head if this gets out', he warned his staff.[7]

After Torgau, Daun wanted no further offensive operations, preferring to remain in a strong position around Dresden and await the increasing demoralization of Frederick's forces to take effect as the Prussian finances continued to deteriorate. But Maria Theresa and Kaunitz smelt blood and were convinced that one more great victory was necessary to keep Frederick subdued before the precarious diplomatic constellation which Kaunitz had so carefully constructed began to fall apart.

Kaunitz was acutely aware that the illness of the Russian Empress and the growing influence of the Tsarevich, the future Peter III, were investing Russian policy with serious doubts over the continuation of the war; Russia was gradually becoming more interested in peace rather than war. The anti-Austrian party in St Petersburg was gaining momentum. Time was running out for the decisive blow against Prussia.

Loudon did his best and, with the help of 800 wild and inebriated Russians, his force of Austrians captured the great fortress of Schweidnitz, the anchor of Prussia's position in Silesia. Silesia was thus largely in Austrian hands and, for the first time since 1740, an Austrian army could winter in the disputed province.

Yet this was to be the high-water mark of the Empress's military efforts. Had Austria been able to launch one colossal final effort, there is no doubt that the Empress's and Kaunitz's war aims of Prussia being eliminated once and for all from the map of Europe would have been achieved. As Frederick himself admitted: 'Unless some miracle happens, I do not see how we can be saved.' Less than a month later, on 10 December, he could note 'the time for miracles is over, all that remains is deadly reality'.[8]

In fact, as 1762 arrived, miracles began to occur with almost biblical profusion. First, a financial crisis which had been slowly developing in Vienna suddenly flared up and threatened to compromise the Austrian war effort. The Empress had no desire to go down the Prussian route of debasing the currency and, reluctantly, Maria Theresa ordered stringent cuts to the numbers of her standing army; each regiment was immediately to be reduced by two companies. The Empress's husband and even her son, Joseph, who wrote the first of many memoranda on military affairs, protested vigorously, but the Empress was adamant: she would not follow Prussia into financial dependency on outside powers. Of this she had already had enough experience a decade earlier. Maria Theresa's fiscal prudence thus saved Berlin.

Meanwhile, in Russia, on 5 January the celebrated 'miracle of Brandenburg' had taken place with the death of Frederick's bitter opponent, the Empress Elizabeth. The new Tsar, her nephew, was not only an admirer of Frederick's but detested his late aunt and he moved swiftly to reverse her policies. Mischievously referring to the Prussian king as 'The King my master', he immediately sent a message to Frederick asking him to participate in a 'new enterprise'.

Frederick took the hint and promptly released all his Russian prisoners of war and sent a trusted envoy, von der Goltz, to bestow a diamond-encrusted Order of the Black Eagle on the new young Tsar. Peter's 'new enterprise' was nothing less than a joint Prussian–Russian offensive against Austria. He offered an 'auxiliary corps', a guarantee of Silesia and Glatz and a proposal to surrender all claims on Russian-occupied Prussian territory.

The third 'miracle' was that deeds accompanied the new Russian ruler's words. Almost overnight, the Russians evacuated East Prussia, freeing up all the available manpower and resources of that province to be harnessed to Frederick's crippled sinews of war.

The arrival of Prussian prisoners of war brought further 'manna from heaven'. They included some of Frederick's best and most experienced officers. From being on the edge of the abyss barely a month earlier, Frederick's position looked altogether more promising. He even planned to send troops to join a raid on Vienna, spearheaded by 6,000 Tatars. So taken was he with this idea of revenge for the Austrian occupation of Berlin that Frederick, typically, even ordered that the occupying troops 'should commit more excesses than usual . . . so that they can see the flames in Vienna as . . . the inhabitants are reduced to wild screams and disorder'.[9]

Fortunately for Maria Theresa, there was never any real danger of the Prussians marching on Vienna. A blocking force under Beck barred their way and the Prussian advance guard soon beat a hasty retreat back to Silesia.

Finally, in this year of stupendous fortune for the beleaguered Prussian king, Kaunitz suddenly fell ill. By the time this frail hypochondriac had recovered several weeks later, the Empress noted that he appeared to have lost some of his earlier belligerence. The new diplomatic constellation had perhaps brought all too clearly home to him that the only way forward now was peace before events brought an even more negative conjunction of hostile circumstances.

Saxony was keen for peace, Russia was hostile to Austria, and Sweden had also dropped out of the anti-Prussian coalition. France, meanwhile, was nursing its wounds as it emerged from its vast conflict with England. The struggle for Silesia had played no role in stemming the loss of Canada and India.

Six years of war had cost Austria nearly half a million men but the reputation of Maria Theresa's arms ran high: 'her armies in which the first Princes of Germany reckoned it was an honour to serve, returned to her lands in a stronger and finer state'.[10]

The same could not be said for Frederick, whose armies were, like his country, in far worse shape than when he had inherited them. Prussia at the end of the Seven Years War was, as he himself put it, 'like a man with many wounds who has lost so much blood that he is on the point of death'.[11]

With that pragmatism which was Maria Theresa's greatest gift, she perhaps realized that the annihilation of Prussia was undesirable if, instead, its neutralization could be achieved. This was probably her and Kaunitz's most laudable diplomatic aim. It was an objective the Peace of Hubertusburg more than handsomely confirmed. Although Maria Theresa never regained Silesia – her armies had wintered there for the last time – her and Austria's prestige and leadership in central Europe were unchallenged for a century. So weakened by the struggle with Maria Theresa was Prussia that, while Austria could, a generation later, fight five coalition wars and even defeat Napoleon, Prussian militarism had been so impaired that by 1806, it could be vanquished on the fields of Jena and Auerstedt in an afternoon and only painstakingly and slowly rebuilt.

CHAPTER 13

The Queen of Peace

THE TRANSFORMATION FROM WARRIOR-QUEEN into the monarch of *Milde und Munifizenz* was not the swift seamless transition of legend. Maria Theresa's hunger for reform was, from the first years of her rule, almost an obsession; in fact, later psychiatrists might point to addictive tendencies in all her activities. If she was to rule, she was to brook no opposition to her wishes, and the never-ending quest for improvement in domestic affairs would even rival her unquenching thirst for military reform illustrated in the previous chapters.

If she was to be a conscientious monarch, she was to be answerable to God and give herself up to her prayers, daily examining her conscience in the five-part confessional regime of the Jesuits. If she was to be a pleasing wife, she must detach herself from weaknesses and bear her husband as many children as possible. If she was to be a great tribal mother in the Austrian tradition, then she must create the context of a family life which, for all its domesticity, never deviated from a strong sense of dynastic duty. Her House had almost been extinguished by the absence of a male heir. That deficiency she could at least generously correct.

To help carry all these significant self-imposed restraints, she shamelessly harnessed, as we have seen, the most gifted men of her empire but on a parallel plane she devoted as much time as affairs of state permitted to her family. The memory of her own lonely childhood with just her *aya*, Countess Fuchs, to look after her made her keenly aware that there should not be the 'forbidden zone' that had limited her access to her own parents when she was growing up.

To that end, as the celebrated gouache by her talented second daughter Marie Christine poignantly depicts, Maria Theresa also took the responsibilities of familial duty very seriously. The gouache dates from 1753 and shows a harmonious if rather staged scene where Maria Theresa is pouring coffee, her husband is reading by the fire, and four children including the young Joseph are absorbed by their toys and dolls. Francis Stephen is wearing a towel around his head after his early morning *levée* and the entire scene exudes a bourgeois homeliness later Habsburgs strove hard to replicate in the more 'socially progressive' Biedermeier times of the following century.

Duty was the leitmotiv of Maria Theresa's life, and long before the German poet Heinrich Hölty wrote the words 'üb immer Treu' und Redlichkeit bis an dein kühles Grab und weich kein kleinen Finger breit von Gotteswegen ab', and long before Mozart immortalized them by writing the music (for an altogether different text) in *Die Zauberflöte* (*The Magic Flute*), the sentiments of this popular folksong expressed fully the dutifulness which Maria Theresa expected at every turn from all those who came into contact with her.

Yet this stoic expectation – the Viennese folksong became such a hit in Prussia that it was chimed every hour at the garrison church in Potsdam – was always tempered by pragmatism and compassion in Vienna. In her philandering husband, Maria Theresa saw all too clearly that even those who could not practise 'loyalty and sincerity' (Treu' und Redlichkeit) must also be loved. For all his faults, Maria Theresa never deviated from her devotion to her husband. In a notebook found after her death, she had calculated the precise duration of her marriage as 29 years, 6 months and 6 days as '258,744 hours of happiness'.

The end of hostilities in 1763 in theory meant Maria Theresa could devote more time to her family. She had experienced by then sixteen confinements and there were now, following the death of Maria Johanna from smallpox at the age of 12, only eleven children.

As far as the young archduchesses were concerned, they were reared very much in the tradition of their house to become consorts of other ruling houses. *Bella gerant alii, tu felix Austria nube* (Let others wage war; you, happy Austria, marry) had been the courts of Europe's early verdict on the Habsburgs' policies of accumulating new domains through marriage rather than war. Maximilian I's grandson had thus gained Bohemia and Spain. Centuries later, the daughters of the Empress were reared for similar dynastic priorities.

Yet Maria Theresa resisted all attempts to give her daughters an education that might prepare them for such a role in the eighteenth century. Her own training at the hands of the Jesuits had been good enough for her and she was happy to entrust them with the upbringing of her children. The idea, however repugnant to modern tastes, especially in an era when women's liberation has changed attitudes markedly towards what was once called 'the fairer sex', that daughters must be obedient was not without realism in the eighteenth-century world where, unless you were fortunate to be Empress, the role of women was formally one of subservience. Maria Theresa herself put it with her customary terseness: 'My daughters are born to obey and must learn to do so in good time.'[1]

Pragmatism and the looser conventions which invested Viennese court life undermined such formal subservience in countless ways. The robust femininity which to this day is a recognizable trait in much of Austria suggests that the mental and physical repression bequeathed in more northern climes by the stiff austerities of, for example, Victorian England was happily not one of the consequences of Maria Theresa's imperative of formal female compliance.[2]

Moreover, the command to obey was accompanied by instructions to avoid any complacency or imperiousness entering the young archduchesses' characters. As Maria Theresa observed: 'They must not be allowed to talk to door-keepers and stokers or to give them orders.' There was always to be a certain *Unnahbarkeit* (remoteness) but this was never to extend to displays of public arrogance. This upbringing achieved a combination of grandeur and modesty which is arguably still a defining characteristic of any well-bred aristocracy.

Despite Maria Theresa's best efforts not to indulge her children, there is ample evidence that they were nonetheless horribly spoilt. Their mother may have forced them to eat fish, which most of them detested, three days a week, and treats were in theory strictly limited: 'I don't like to see them eating much sugar, see that they have as little as possible', Maria Theresa instructed the children's *aya*, Countess Lerchenfeld. Yet the sweet tooth of all the children was evidenced in the proliferation of family puddings which spread through the court and have subsequently become stalwarts of Austrian cuisine.[3]

The daughters of later generations of high-born families might well find these traits familiar. Certainly, Maria Theresa's comments on personal hygiene would have been well received even in the twenty-first century: 'Cleanliness is to be observed most strictly,' she ordered of her children, 'they must be properly washed and combed every day without exception.'

These instructions underline again that Maria Theresa was determined to be abreast of all her responsibilities, whether they be house, home or state. She applied herself with the same energy towards her household as she did towards her Councils of War, and her frequent confinements slowed her down only briefly. She refused to allow them to exhaust her and they became punctuation marks in her routine rather than serious interruptions.

Not that in this world of duties and responsibilities there were not moments of fun. The Empress was nothing if not a devotee of the distractions of concerts and plays. Her courtiers found the continual succession of entertainments far from congenial but even they remembered how in the darkest, earliest days of her reign she had celebrated her survival with an equestrian *Damenkarussell* in which she and her female friends had turned the great hall of the Hofburg's Winter Riding School into a firing range. The targets, much to the consternation of the Prussian ambassador, had been portraits in papier mâché of Frederick and his principal advisers. Two teams, each of sixteen 'Amazon' ladies, had on that occasion charged their targets and, led by the Queen herself, had decapitated their 'enemies'. As an aficionado of such displays, the Empress could never have wished to deny such frivolities to her own daughters, even if older members of the court may have found the endless round of festivities exhausting.[4]

Yet not all such court parties were just superficial divertissements. Many involved the leading performers of their time. Inevitably, therefore, in 1762, just as the wearying conflict of the Seven Years War was ending, the sovereign commanded a seven-year-old boy from Salzburg with his sister to perform at court. Wolfgang Amadeus Mozart and his sister Marianne had, thanks partly to their father's connections with the Vienna Masonic lodges, found Vienna a city of warm welcome and appreciation for his talent. But nothing could compare with the reception the Empress prepared for him. As his father Leopold wrote in a letter to his wife: 'Now there is barely time to say that we were so graciously received that as I relate it seems a fairy-tale. Suffice it to say our little Wolfgang sprang onto the lap of the Empress and put his arms round her neck and vigorously kissed her. We were with her from three to six.'[5]

Here was more evidence that the 'forbidden zone' which had surrounded her forefathers had been eliminated by the Empress. Maria Theresa may have sensed the talent and genius in the child; certainly, the boy was dazzlingly precocious, but what this story really illustrates is the ease with which even the most powerful sovereign of the eighteenth century could be amused and genuinely enchanted by a gifted child of obscure background.

In time, the daughters would rise to the obligations of their 'vocation' with impressive courage. Even Maria Antonia (Marie Antoinette) would mesmerize her persecutors with her calm dignity at the moment of her execution. Although her other daughters were spared the dreadful fate that awaited this most buoyant and fun-loving of her daughters, both Maria Carolina, who became Queen of Naples, and Maria Amalia, who married Ferdinand of Parma, faced almost as great a challenge as sovereigns in febrile times.[6] Both would skilfully navigate their husbands' domains through an era of vast uncertainty. Both would display that intoxicating combination of seriousness of purpose and gaiety which so invested their mother.

Of the sons, the shadow cast by the young heir, Joseph, generally eclipsed his other brothers, Maximilian, Leopold and Ferdinand. From the beginning, as the prized male heir, the young Joseph stood apart from his siblings, all too aware that the future hopes of the dynasty rested on his shoulders. As Maria Theresa recalled, writing on Joseph's birthday in 1777:

> What a great day for me which thirty-six years ago reinforced all my actions and reinvigorated me, affirming that the good God, this divine Providence still desired to maintain the sceptre in our House, granting me at the most critical juncture a son when I no longer

possessed a single undisputed land and did not even know where I might give birth to my next child, as I could not stay in Vienna with Bohemia and Upper Austria lost, Lower Austria threatened by the Bavarians, Italy and the Netherlands invaded, and Hungary so infected by Plague that when my baggage arrived at Pest, the gates were shut because of the contagion, and it had to be returned.[7]

Contemporaries, and not least the Empress herself, were all too acutely aware of what happened when the male line in succession failed. The risks to dynasty and state were immense. One unavoidable drawback of a female succession was that no woman could become Holy Roman Emperor, and the struggle for the influence that title conferred during her own lifetime made the arrival of Joseph reason enough for the child to command devotion.

Joseph's birth, occurring in the time of emergency, was virtually the only good news with which the sovereign could console herself in the difficult years between 1740 and 1745. In the words of the Venetian ambassador: 'As soon as the news spread, people crowded to the royal palace with shouts of joy and ran through the streets in ecstasy . . . the hopes of the entire nation had been directed to this and the House of Austria appears confirmed'.[8]

The baptism of the child reinforced the celebrations. In Prague, the Archbishop distributed, from the first-floor windows of his baroque palace next to the Hradčany castle, hundreds of gold coins to the eager celebrating crowd below. In Vienna, details of the baptism were widely disseminated: the water used had come from the Holy Land and the River Jordan where Christ himself had been baptized. The relics of the crown of thorns and the cross were displayed during the ceremony so that the divine could accompany the earthly in helping the child survive the fearsome rates of infant mortality then prevailing.

By the time Joseph had reached childhood, the attention lavished on him had in no way diminished, but any affection demonstrated could only be effected within the tight constraints of court etiquette administered at that time by Count Khevenhueller on the basis of 'tradition'.

As the last time there had been a male heir to the throne had been at the end of the previous century, the protocols were, unsurprisingly, especially claustrophobic. Already at the age of five, Joseph showed signs of developing a lifelong aversion to court ceremony.

Yet by the standards of the time, Joseph's upbringing was largely happy and his childhood compares favourably with that of the male heirs to the British and French thrones, Louis (XVI) and George (III), who had miserable, parentless upbringings. Even the heir to the throne of Denmark, Christian (VII), had had to put up with losing his mother when he was three. In addition, the hapless young prince was inflicted with both an alcoholic father and a sadistic tutor. Of course, the laurels of the most brutal royal childhood had long been won by Frederick (II) of Prussia; he had been beaten, imprisoned and publicly humiliated by his tyrannical father, who had even ordered the execution of his best friend.

In comparison with all these vagaries of upbringing, Joseph's childhood was exemplary. Supported by both his parents, he soon had his 'own' regiment and by the age of nine was even given his own court, complete with secretaries, military and civil.

But Maria Theresa, while undoubtedly more devoted to her children than most eighteenth-century sovereigns, was an unpredictable parent, given to moments of harshness towards her children, on the heels of sincere displays of public affection.

Nothing illustrates the volatility of her moods better than the memorable occasion when, having dressed up her infant son in the specially tailored uniform of the Althan dragoons, she found the compliments showered on the handsome child so grating that she immediately sent him to his room to eat alone. At other times, she did not shy away from corporal punishment, and when told that it was 'without precedent' for an archduke to be beaten, she answered: 'it is high time (*höchste Zeit*) for the experiment to be made'.

The ever-present Podewils reported to Berlin the following characterization of the six-year-old Joseph which, perhaps unsurprisingly, set the 'ton' for many subsequent descriptions: 'In a room adorned with portraits of his ancestors he greeted one visitor with the words, "that is the emperor, my grandfather, that is Empress so-and-so" before turning to the Lorraine portraits and dismissing all the Lorraine personalities depicted.' This haughtiness was perhaps exaggerated for the Prussian ambassador's benefit but the precociousness of which Podewils complained was certainly present.

What distressed Joseph's mother more was his habit, as an adolescent, of mocking people's physical and mental weaknesses, knowing that he could be rude with impunity on account of his rank. But these were the flaws of any privileged child's upbringing and Joseph soon learnt to develop a courtesy which certainly did no dishonour to his House and, above all, an intellectual curiosity which made him a vivacious interlocutor far removed from the myth of 'horrid youth' propagated by some writers.

In contrast to his sisters, his education was discussed by his parents with almost forensic obsession. A medal was struck in 1750 to commemorate the completion of his first studies. His tutors were again Jesuits and they directed his education with their usual discipline and devotion. Although in 1748 they were joined by an Augustinian monk, the direction of study, with its weekly confessions, rosary and daily morning and evening prayer, produced a timetable in which formal religious observance was clearly the priority. Every day, reports of his progress were made to the Empress.

Joseph appears to have enjoyed Latin, reading Virgil's *Aeneid* more than once. He was particularly fascinated by the drama of the Trojan Horse and the terrifying destruction of Laocoon's sons by the marine serpent. Above all, he enjoyed all his lessons which touched on the military arts. As for many young men, especially one able to don the fine uniform of a cavalry officer at the head of 'his' regiment, the military world was the most enticing and, throughout his life, Joseph would imitate his mother's great Prussian adversary, Frederick, and have his portrait show him invariably in the green uniform of one of his elite *Schvo-ley* cavalry regiments. Significantly, the green was associated with Protestant Holland rather than Catholic Austria whose troops were traditionally attired in white. Above all, Joseph relished the simplicity of the military life, freed from traditional court formality, and, in time, as we shall see, would focus his energies most aggressively on further reform of his forces.[9]

While Joseph continued at his books, his mother's reforms continued to invigorate the Austrian state but there is no evidence that innovative thinking was brought to bear on the young prince's education, which remained as conventional as that of his sisters, despite the greater attention paid to it by his mother. Her radicalism was the result of practical realities rather than any theoretical principles. Her reforms sprang out of the emergency of the situation of the moment. There was no long-term *Gesamtkonzept* or series of systemic uninterrupted reforms. Rather, Maria Theresa appeared to favour the removal of abuses as and when they arose to threaten the monarchy.

Joseph's role in this monarchy was envisaged as a staunch defender of the Roman Catholic faith and a wise administrator of the possessions of the House of Austria, choosing his advisers carefully, and avoiding extremes which could only disrupt the harmony of the whole. But from an early age, Joseph always favoured a more energetic and dynamic course, irrespective of its consequences. In short, as the Prince de Ligne, one of Joseph's closest confidants, wisely wrote of the training of the archdukes: they were taught 'everything except what they ought to have known'.[10]

In 1760, at the age of 19, his formal studies ended, and he was betrothed to the Infanta, Isabella of Parma. At the same time, he was admitted into the inner councils of his mother's government, thus experiencing the novelty of political engagement simultaneously with the adventure of marriage. Although brought up in Spain, it was Isabella's French connections which attracted Maria Theresa. Her mother was the daughter of Louis XV and the Duchy of Parma was heavily dependent on Paris.

No expense was spared for the marriage, despite the rising expenditure of war, and the cost was estimated to be in excess of 3 million florins.[11]

Although the Infanta would tragically die within three years, Isabella enchanted all who came into contact with her. She played the violin perfectly and had a gift for choosing attractive turns of phrase which fascinated and amused. It was agreed that she was no great beauty but Joseph was fully aware, now that his education had ended, that the business of statecraft was to become his greatest priority and that the transitory superficiality of conventional beauty was a matter of little import.

In the intelligence and sombre reflective thoughts of his bride he found, all too briefly, much solace. Isabella was no ordinary princess and her surviving letters illustrate beautifully the subtlety of her mind. Discussing with her sister-in-law, Marie Christine, with whom she enjoyed an intimate physical relationship, she listed the advantages and disadvantages of marriage:

What should the daughter of a great prince expect? Her fate is unquestionably most unhappy. Born the slave of people's prejudices, she finds herself subjected to the weight of honours, innumerable etiquettes, while the rank she holds, far from procuring her the least advantage, deprives her of the greatest pleasures of life, which are given to everyone else, i.e. company, for she is obliged to live in the middle of the 'great world' where she has neither acquaintances nor friends.

This is not all. In the end the effort is made to establish her. There she is condemned to abandon everything, her family, her country and for what? For an unknown person whose character and manner of thinking she does not know, a sacrifice to a supposed public good, but in fact rather to the wretched policy of a minister who can find no other way for the two dynasties to form an alliance which he pronounces indissoluble but which, immediately it seems advantageous, is broken off.[12]

These feelings of frustration would undoubtedly be shared by Joseph as he came to realize that he, too, would have to play his role in the 'wretched policy' of his mother's ministers whose world he was now to enter. It was a world rich in paradoxes and contradictions, a world where – as Mozart's great *Singspiel*, *Die Zauberflöte*, makes clear – reality and display were often at great variance and where the first lesson of survival was never to be taken in by appearances.

CHAPTER 14

The Austrian Enlightenment

IT WAS ANOTHER OF the paradoxes of the Theresian era that a Vienna imbued with all the piety, the celebrated *Pietas Austriaca* of the Habsburg monarchy, personified by the devotion of their monarch, should at the same time become one of the great centres of European Freemasonry, an organization dating from the year of the Empress's birth.[1] Historians have made much of the contrast, a black-and-white distinction, between reaction and progress, conservatism and Enlightenment, the Catholic Church and 'philosophy'. Yet these distinctions, while eagerly embraced in the nineteenth century by a new generation of anti-clerical thinkers and even more widely affirmed in the secular twentieth and twenty-first centuries, are simplistic and, as we have seen in earlier chapters, flawed.

The 1740s brought Maria Theresa to her inheritance but, at the very time when threats, internal and external, rained down upon her from every side, there was not the slightest resistance to the arrival in Vienna of Freemasonry. Established in London in 1717, its development was an almost convex mirror of Maria Theresa's own pious upbringing. Yet both Archduchess and 'craft' appear to have been perfectly compatible. In the 1740s the ideals of brotherhood, cosmopolitanism and tolerance were not yet tainted by the later violence of social upheaval and revolution. It was somehow typical of the already existing tradition of pragmatism and tolerance in Vienna that, despite the Papal Bull *In eminenti apostolatus* of Clement XII denouncing Freemasonry as 'heresy' in 1738, two years before Maria Theresa came to the throne and threatening excommunication to any who practised it, the predominantly Catholic Viennese court was more than comfortable with the activities of the lodges.

Maria Theresa was fully aware of the fashion for Masonic lodges which was taking hold in Vienna. Tarouca, Van Swieten, Kaunitz and Haugwitz, Sonnenfels and Lacy were all well-known Freemasons, while her husband's induction into an English lodge at Houghton in Norfolk was certainly not kept secret from her.

Francis Stephen had first become acquainted with Freemasonry during his time in The Hague as a young man. Maria Theresa certainly was suspicious of the ritual of Freemasonry, as far as she was informed of it, but her attitude appears to have been overall one of passive acceptance. That she however held certain reservations concerning it is clear from a letter to her son-in-law, Albert of Saxony-Teschen, in which she urges him: 'Albert, how lovely it would be if you could drop your Freemasonry.'[2]

With the establishment of the lodge *Aux Trois Canons* in Vienna in 1741, the practice of Freemasonry in the Empress's capital quickly gathered momentum. It became such an inescapable feature of Viennese court circles that Maria Theresa not only accepted its presence but actively contributed to its financial good works, even publicly endowing a Masonic orphanage in Prague. This act alone merits closer examination, for the question here is not what direct effect Freemasonry had on the policies of the emerging Austrian state, but whether the existence of a collective disposition and vehicle to promote talent, irrespective of birth or money, and to tolerate men of different religious persuasions, offered the chance of promotion to those who would not normally have enjoyed such opportunities.

Orphans were an especial interest of the Empress and in one case this concern of Maria Theresa for her less fortunate subjects brought quite spectacular results. One summer in the year of 1748, the Empress found herself visiting her Hungarian possessions and was about to cross the Danube by boat when her attention was drawn by a handsome young boy, with an almost Gypsy colouring, who, confidently striding up to her, asked if he might have the honour of rowing her across the river. This impertinence was overlooked by the Empress who noticed that the boy's confidence was tempered by poverty, a winning smile and an expressive intelligent countenance.

Who was this boy who seemed so eager to please and so attractive, the Empress asked. The boy was an orphan purchased from a convent by a lowly military clerk and, although christened 'Thuegutt' ('do good'), he was universally known as and called 'Nichtthugut' ('do no good'). With her instinctive eye for young male intelligence, Maria Theresa found the 'orphan' was not only handsome but also quick-witted and charming. By the time the young man had finished rowing her across the river, the Empress had been captivated by his manner and conversation. Such a young man's talents were unlikely to flourish while he was called 'Nichtthugut' and the Empress, on hearing further details of the boy's impoverished background, decided on the spot to look more closely into his education. The teenage Thugut, as he soon became known, quickly found himself the recipient of the Empress's *Gnade* in unimaginable ways. Maria Theresa informally adopted him and, out of her own *Gratifikationsfond*, paid for the boy to receive an education at the hands of the Jesuits in the recently opened Imperial Academy of Oriental Studies. This education bore such fruit that within five years the young Thugut was posted to the imperial embassy in Constantinople, from where he would rise so brilliantly in the service of the empire that he would eventually become imperial chancellor.

Thugut's extraordinary career, and his seemingly effortless rise from impoverished boat-boy to First Minister of the most illustrious court in Europe, underlines vividly the capacity for social mobility of which the Austrian Enlightenment, exploiting the educational capabilities of the Jesuits, was capable.[3] Thugut's meteoric rise has no parallel in Europe and was only possible because of a combination of a sovereign's quasi-absolutist power, first-rate educational opportunity, and a universal moral framework which permitted even the highest in the land to feel a bond with the lowest.

Unlike Voltaire, the protagonists of the Austrian Enlightenment, Maria Theresa included, did not allow their exasperation with the Church to lead to total disbelief in a creed. Catholicism had not failed as a social force and Maria Theresa, whatever her frustrations with the profusion of miracles, feast days and other elaborate trappings of the Church, or her contempt for the Vatican's attempts to interfere in her state's affairs, never for a moment thought of overthrowing Catholic theology. The House of Faith and Reason was not the divided one it would become in later centuries.

The Austrian Enlightenment was therefore very different from contemporary movements in other parts of Europe. Jansenism, with its hostility to baroque display and the structures of the Church, was present but there is ample evidence that Jansenism's core theological beliefs – the overthrow of the Council of Trent, the denial of man's free will to accept or reject God's call, the primacy of predestination – were of irrelevance to most of the Austrian courtiers around Maria Theresa. The wave of Jansenism, which Voltaire rode so effectively in France, had no parallel in Austria. Indeed, had it existed in such a form, Thugut's destiny would have been decided at birth and Maria Theresa's intervention would have merited censure.

Another example of the porous nature of Austrian social strata under Maria Theresa was the cult of her perceived accessibility to everyone. Maria Theresa's court, like every court, was governed by conventions, protocol and ceremony. These were then, as now, designed to shield the monarch from the outside world while protecting the interests and ambitions of a cast of courtiers, court servants, pages, ladies-in-waiting, heralds and other minor figures, whose capacity for scheming, intrigue and exclusivity was carefully nurtured by an accepted recognition that influence and power were dependent on proximity to the sovereign.

Left to its own devices, such a court created an aspic which prevented external disturbance while paralysing innovation, the injection of fresh ideas and fresh blood. The ceremonial aspects of the court served as an outer rampart which sealed the monarch from their subjects. If Joseph detested the claustrophobia this wrought, there is much evidence to suggest that his mother, while seeing the value of public ceremonies, also found them boring and tiresome.[4]

In such an environment, the proliferation of newly established Masonic lodges provided a route for talented Austrians facilitating access to elements of the court. Far from preserving the rights of mediocrity in the face of the challenge of meritocracy (a common accusation against modern Freemasonry), the lodges at this stage sought to achieve the exact opposite. In addition, Maria Theresa introduced various procedures which bypassed some of the protective armour of ceremony that shielded her from circles beyond her court. She appears to have agreed with those of her advisers, such as Kaunitz, who strongly criticized the monopoly over important positions which the high aristocracy exerted.

Another young man who caught Maria Theresa's attention was Peter Prosch. In this case the young boy, also thirteen, was serving as an acolyte at the Capuchin church when in 1757 he caught the Empress's eye. Maria Theresa summoned the boy to her and for what followed, we have only the words of Prosch who wrote a bestseller about Austria's 'True Mother' in 1789. Prosch was from Tyrol and spoke the dialect of that region, which was immediately familiar to the Empress. With her characteristic curiosity, the Empress asked him about her Tyrolean subjects' views of her. 'Do they love me?' she reportedly asked the boy, who flatteringly answered: 'Everyone in the province from the first to the last says you are the very best of women and one whom the world will never see the like of again.'[5]

This encounter prepared the young boy for a successful career as a court entertainer, in which he was the butt of many harsh pranks but always universally esteemed for his good humour, which was proof against sexual abuse (he was, it appears, regularly assaulted), violent pranks (fireworks were planted on his clothes) and other physical hardships (he was tethered to a galloping horse) which mischievous pages and courtiers designed for him. It is hard to accept much of Prosch's narrative but other sources appear to confirm that this court jester indulged in overfamiliar banter on the few occasions Maria Theresa consented to see him, and was an object of amusement rather than an indication of social mobility.

The Empress was not averse, as we have seen, to promoting the unfortunate but her capacity to do this was circumscribed by her senior courtiers, directed as always by the Chamberlain who enforced the strict rules of etiquette.

Nevertheless, Maria Theresa encouraged (and her son was equally if not more enthusiastic) the concept of the public audience as a forum for requests and petitions. Tarouca was strongly in favour of a regular audience to be held each Sunday after divine service. There were no formal entry requirements, though a strict filtering system imposed its own limiting dynamic, but the tradition Maria Theresa evolved here was to endure. The institution of the *Freie Audienz* persisted in Habsburg

Austria until the end of the monarchy in 1918. Joseph, as he grew older, supplemented these events with endless travels incognito.[6]

There were other points of contact which Maria Theresa did nothing to limit. The Empress, on her frequent walks in the park of Schönbrunn and the garden of the Hofburg, was open to anyone wishing to throw themselves at her feet or approach her through the ranks of her entourage. Moreover, the tradition of a paper petition 'at ten in the morning' to submit to Her Majesty via one of her chamberlains was also in theory open to anyone who possessed the necessary writing skills. These were small gaps in the carapace of the court ramparts but they could be exploited with a degree of success. Thus a 'dishonoured' publisher, Johann Trattner, waylaid the Empress, hiding at first behind her ladies-in-waiting before throwing himself on her mercy. Thanks to his eloquence and sincere mien, he was granted an imperial pardon.[7]

It was only following a violent scene in 1753, when a supplicant had drawn a sword and injured the chamberlain on duty, that access to these audiences began to be constrained by new regulations requiring a form of 'pre-registration'.

This gradually impeded wider access but it must be stressed that, in comparison with the courts of France, England and Prussia, Maria Theresa allowed herself to be far more accessible than any other monarch in Europe. Informal channels abounded and, while these could give rise to abuse and personal intrigue, they created another avenue of access. In most cases they involved a plea for funds. Unpaid fees for opera singers, the costs of medical provisions for the destitute, pay increases for kitchen staff – these all usually met with the Empress's approval. In time, her reputation for *Munifizenz* only increased. The sclerosis of local administrations reinforced Maria Theresa's aura of benevolence. She insisted that, in the first instance, supplicants take up their grievances with the local authorities, but these were understandably loath to highlight their incompetence by righting a wrong which should not have been committed in the first place. This bureaucratic inertia ironically helped create a situation whereby the subjects of the monarchy gradually came to believe, whether they were in Transylvania or Tyrol, that the only redress for their complaints was through their sovereign.

Where possible, Maria Theresa trusted her advisers to sort out the problems of the supplicants once she had written *Placet* on the relevant documentation. She remained largely remote from the *Volk* when at court but her relaxed demeanour on the few occasions when the bastions of court protocol were breached by 'commoners' appears always to have revealed an openness to chance encounter.

The stiffness within the court was maintained by the Lord Chamberlain or High Steward who, for much of Maria Theresa's reign, was the formidable Count Khevenhueller-Metsch. A Carinthian nobleman, whose spectacular castle of Hochosterwitz still dominates the approaches to southern Carinthia, Khevenhueller was an assiduous recorder of events at court and his many-volumed diaries form, along with Arneth's documentary collection, the foundations of most biographies of the Empress.

Khevenhueller was a stickler for imperial protocol and exhibited all the stubbornness and suspicion of meritocracy which is often, even today, one of the *difetti piccoli* of a great landowner burdened by the immensity of his pedigree. Any deviation from the norms of protocol were threats to the social order as far as he was concerned. In 1743 he noted in his journal: 'so far as our etiquette is concerned, despite the imperial honours acquired since, not much has changed for the better . . . I should gladly see the court restored to its old decorum.' Yet how could one speak of decorum when there were so many informalities permitted at court, in particular the obsession by all, from the Empress downwards, with card games, played usually for the highest of stakes?

We have Lady Mary Coke's journals to thank for the account of how much time the entire aristocracy, especially female nobility, appeared to devote to card games after dinner each evening. The most fashionable game was what Lady Mary called 'Lu'; known in German as *Lombar* but in Austria as *Lumbar*, it was a variation of the card-play known as *Ombre*. By the 1770s it had swept most other games off the card tables and had come to occupy a position which today is arguably only the preserve of contract bridge.

'Lu', the 'greatest card game of the western world', was the indoor recreation par excellence of Maria Theresa's court and involved three-sided tables as the game was usually played in threes. Small holes carved into the three corners of each table held tokens of varying denominations known universally as 'fish' on account of their shape. Thanks to Lady Mary's accounts of her evenings spent playing 'Lu' with the ladies of the high aristocracy in Vienna, we have detailed indications of the stakes and the frustrations of the game. On many evenings, the ladies lost in excess of 'a hundred fish' which, as these were valued at ten guineas each, represented a considerable sum in today's money.[8]

Maria Theresa was certainly no exception at court to the passion for 'Lu' and she was known to play well into the early hours and often lose heavily, '*in grossem Stil*'. For the Empress, the games were almost an extension of her many battles with the world: with Prussia, with fate, the threats to her domains and the general blows of destiny. Cards mirrored these but they also offered an avenue of distraction and escape from the anxieties of daily policy-making. Lady Mary, as a wealthy English aristocrat, appears to have lost spectacularly too, suggesting that the game was played only by ladies with substantial financial resources behind them. The packs of cards (deck of 40) were often of great beauty, with manufacturers in the Austrian Netherlands producing arguably the finest, but this Habsburg passion for card games would stretch well into successive centuries and give rise to many playing-card manufacturers in the empire whose products' design and beauty are still today familiar to card sharps throughout the world.[9]

In addition to the ubiquitous 'Lu', there was also an interest in chess and here the fascination of Maria Theresa's husband in scientific matters came into play when a court official produced a spectacular automaton which could apparently make moves across a chessboard. Wolfgang Kempelen (1734–1804) had been born in Pressburg and entered Austrian service in the late 1750s when Francis Stephen had encountered him and helped have him appointed as director of salt-mining. Kempelen, it would seem, had been recommended to the Emperor through one of the Viennese lodges.

After the Emperor's death, Maria Theresa was intrigued to hear of a 'playful distraction' which Kempelen had constructed, namely a chess-playing automaton Turk. This apparatus consisted of a life-size model of a Turk, complete in Oriental dress and turban, sitting behind a wooden table on which was a chess set. In fact, the cabinet concealed a human operator who if sufficiently skilled at the game could defeat most opponents. In time, the chess-playing Turk would travel throughout Europe and even America, defeating both Napoleon and Benjamin Franklin, if local accounts are to be believed.[10]

Trick or not, the device with its cross-legged Turk delighted the Empress and, partly out of memory for her scientific late husband, she supported Kempelen in his work. He later produced a manually operated speaking machine and a typewriter for Mozart's blind friend, Maria Theresia von Paradis. In 1771 the Empress honoured him with a substantial pension of a thousand ducats a year but this was rescinded by her son Joseph as soon as he came to the throne as sole ruler, one of many decisions expressive of his own impatience with 'charlatans' but in flagrant breach of the terms of his mother's will.

Acts of munificence on the part of the Empress provoked resentments even while she was alive. Khevenhueller lamented the spontaneous generosity of his sovereign and refused to countenance anything which could undermine the prestige of the court. It was not just his mistress's spontaneous and unpredictable gestures of kindness and generosity, it was the general informal approach to certain details of etiquette which aroused his distemper. To this end he became obsessive about ceremonial detail and even criticized the Empress on occasion for the informality of her arrangements. Was it really necessary, he asked pedantically, to receive the French ambassador sitting on the same sofa? Such were the challenges in Khevenhueller's mind.

As a counterpoint to the spontaneous mixing of the sovereign, the great public ceremonies of imperial marriages, baptisms and funerals brought sovereign and *Volk* together in collective rituals. The Empress's subjects were encouraged to participate in these – nothing was more 'adored than adoring subjects' – and many techniques were deployed to ensure crowds turned out. Coins were distributed along with free wine and food, a kind of medieval 'feast' to be shared by the highest and the lowest in the land. The Empress became accustomed on these high days to showering coins from her carriage as she passed by, cementing a perception that she was not only sovereign but also infinitely generous.

Other occasions when the doors of the Hofburg and the all-highest were opened to the public were the famous ladies' *Karussells*. In addition, there was the tradition of the 'open table' on gala days when the court sat down in public with just a simple rope to separate them from the general public. Anyone was permitted to enter the banqueting hall and watch the feast as long as they were 'in clean and neat clothing'. The untidy and unhealthy were excluded lest the high table lost their appetite.[11]

Maria Theresa also continued and fortified a tradition her father had instituted of bestowing particular grace and munificence on specially selected 'unfortunates'. At every one of her birthdays there had been invited a corresponding number of destitute girls who were granted not only access but gifts. This was a model of philanthropy she embraced. On the occasion of Joseph's second marriage, to Maria Josepha of Bavaria, she endowed twenty-five newly-wed couples with a dowry of 200 guilders each. In addition, she was happy to act as godmother to carefully chosen orphans. In this way, the Empress represented the 'true mother of us all'.

One of the celebrated rituals for any Catholic sovereign was the washing of the feet on Maundy Thursday, the first great solemnity of the Easter Triduum. An English aristocrat watching, Lady Mary Coke, observed:

> I never saw the Empress look so graceful . . . she placed all the dishes on the table and removed them but with a grace that is not to be described; her manner of holding the napkin was so genteel that I could have looked at her forever and if you had heard her talk to those three old women you would have been delighted.[12]

The submission before God of the imperial couple implied by this ceremony was more important than the actual practicalities as to whether the feet were properly washed or not. The Empress continued to kneel as she wiped the feet until arthritis made it impossible, and she delegated the task to one of her daughters. She nevertheless spoke kindly to all the beneficiaries of her grace and Maundy Thursday, with the great feast of Corpus Christi and, in time, that of the Immaculate Conception, became the foundation of Habsburg piety well into the twentieth century. Lady Mary also observed the Empress's son Joseph participating in these ceremonies and was impressed by his devotion to the men he served, although she noticed that, unlike his mother, he did not speak to the men whose feet he was washing. When, however, Lady Mary subsequently congratulated Joseph on the dignity and humility with which he had invested the service, the Emperor asked, apparently sincerely: 'But does not the King of England perform the same duties every Easter?'[13]

Later commentators have disputed the significance of the ceremony, accusing the Empress of never questioning the 'great social divide' her reign embodied, but this is to view such ceremonies through the prism of a later post-Christian age. The humility and servitude the ceremony inflicted on the sovereign were sincere and tangible. The ritual offered arguably a glimpse of a human equality which transfigured notions of an unbreachable social divide through the, today much devalued, concept of 'service'.

Finally, a technique of informality which Maria Theresa, and in particular her son Joseph, much enjoyed, namely the use of incognito, also frayed the edges of the 'forbidden zone'. The privileges of imperial etiquette could be forgotten when a member of the ruling dynasty was in disguise. It was accepted that such a decision automatically cancelled the expectations of deference usually offered in the presence of the sovereign. The relief of not having to uphold continuously one's formal status was especially appreciated by Joseph, who loved travelling under an alias. He was arguably never more satisfied than when he appeared as 'Count Falkenstein', with just a simple footman and valet.

This manner of disguise he had learnt from his mother, who had enjoyed being in disguise during her famous *Damenkarussell* in 1743 and at times relished being mistaken for one of her ladies-in-waiting. This desire to escape the straitjacket of convention and etiquette was one of the reasons Maria Theresa also delighted in the frequent masked balls which flourished in her court.

Maria Theresa's domains extended over what could be called the most religiously diverse fabric in Europe: Luxembourg, Belgium, Bohemia, Hungary and northern Italy made the loose union of sovereign states that comprised the Holy Roman Empire a virtual laboratory for different approaches to religion. The empire had not only been a hotbed of the

Reformation but, after the Peace of Westphalia, an experimental chamber for new ways of coexistence and religious toleration. Westphalia is often seen as marking the birth of the nation state; certainly, thereafter in Europe men were asked to die not for their fellow co-religious but for the state, but by institutionalizing the three mainstream Christian denominations, Lutherans, Calvinists and Catholics, it initiated a most elaborate discussion of religious toleration in central Europe.

A Bavarian Jesuit, Vitus Pichler, could denounce toleration as a 'weakness' but he articulated the default position of his order when he noted that it was 'a lesser evil' than a 'Holy War'. Other Jesuits developed the notion that there was perhaps more than one way to approach God, even if in their view by far the most satisfactory and effective was that of the Catholic faith.

Throughout Maria Theresa's reign, the Catholic Church was divided between 'enlightened Catholics' and what today would be called 'hardline' zealots. What is clear is that those around the Empress belonged, partly as a result – rather than, as is often thought, in spite – of their Jesuitical training, to the former.

The Jesuits proved time and again that their value to the intellectual formation of enlightened thought was very powerful.[14] There could not have been an Austrian Enlightenment without them. All the protagonists of toleration and progress in the monarchy (including Joseph II) were educated and taught to read, write and reason by the Jesuits.[15]

Hard-line Catholicism was in any event on the decline, even if towards the end of her life Maria Theresa was to become highly exercised by the reports of the presence of thousands of 'crypto-Protestants' in her realm. Administrative reform of the Austrian possessions had stripped the provincial clergy of their power and the most strident conservative voices of resistance to religious toleration were emasculated by the new organization of the Austrian state.

Further inroads into reactionary dogma were made by the exigencies of Austrian foreign policy. More Protestant Saxons were settled in Hungary under Maria Theresa's recalibration of her eastern frontier and it was Count Philip Nerius Kolowrat, a Bohemian nobleman, who encouraged the Empress to settle as many Orthodox Serbs as possible within the Hungarian parts of her empire so as to create a useful counterpoise to the ever-tricksome Hungarians. When, after the First Partition of Poland in 1772, the empire gained a significant Uniate population of Orthodox rite worshippers in communion with Rome, Maria Theresa felt the term Uniate implied second-class status and insisted they be called 'Greek Catholics'. A degree of religious toleration was therefore written into the DNA of Maria Theresa's empire.

Much credit would be rightly given to Joseph II's Patent of Toleration but the foundations of the Patent were already set by Maria Theresa and were inspired by her. The later Josephinian Church reforms were already begun by the Empress with her measures in *publico ecclesiaticis*. By the time of her death, the new reform school catechism had also already been agreed.

Yet all these reforms were not incompatible with a solid commitment to the Catholic faith and, to the day of her death, Maria Theresa remained utterly convinced of the benefits of a Catholic upbringing. In her last letter before she died, she wrote to her son Leopold in Tuscany: 'You are Christian-minded (*Christlich gesinnt*) and virtuous and that comforts me . . . may God preserve you.'

Similarly, judicial and land reform implemented by Joseph were grounded in the policies of his mother. As early as 1753 she had opposed the wishes of the local grandees who had resisted a unified justice system. The *Codex Theresianus* would be the foundation for all later judicial reform throughout central Europe. By 1765 the monarchy enjoyed, for the first time, a unified formal legal system of equal weight throughout Habsburg lands with the inevitable exception of Hungary.

The Queen of Hungary was fond of pointing out that she was 'eine gute Ungarin' and while she followed her advisers' policies of trying where possible to dilute Magyar influence by settling Saxons and Serbs in their kingdom, she never lost sight of the fact that social structures there lagged far behind the conditions prevailing in Vienna and further west.

She proceeded cautiously but there was no doubting her appetite for reform. The formal abolition of serfdom may have had to wait until the statutes enacted by Joseph in 1781 but the way had been cleared already by his mother as early as 1750, when she had sent a royal commission to Bohemia to discover why tax receipts had declined so markedly in the last years. This commission quickly established that the peasants could only afford to pay taxes if they were released from the more restrictive obligations they owed the landowners. The Empress moved swiftly to change this state of affairs. Influenced by Karl Martini, a south Tyrolean who came to Vienna to fill the newly created chair of Natural Law, Maria Theresa fully subscribed to his idea that the basis of any successful state was the social contract.

Rules preventing peasants from selling their produce in the free market were abolished, the rights of independent judicial review of all disputes were confirmed while the peasantry were also given the right to submit complaints about their landlords to imperial officials. All fees paid by the peasantry to their landlords were henceforth to be regulated by central authority in Vienna.

Revolutionary though this may have seemed, it was not applicable to land owned by the high aristocracy and, although Maria Theresa extended the reforms to her own crown lands, she failed to bring the high aristocracy and indeed her son with her in extending the *Robotpatent* (the abolition of compulsory labour – *robot* – of serfs) to estates in Bohemia and Moravia.

'This is the crisis in which we find ourselves', Joseph wrote. 'She wants to change the entire system of landownership so that the peasants (*Untertanen*) are relieved of all debts and efforts without the slightest regard for the landowners whose concerns depend on the status quo. This will drive them into bankruptcy.'[16] Once again, it was Joseph rather than his mother who was applying the brakes. For all his Enlightenment credentials, Joseph never wanted to break the foundations of the feudal system and Maria Theresa's efforts to continue to build on her land reforms failed not, as many historians have claimed, on account of subsequent indecision but rather because of her son's decision to oppose it.

In fact, Maria Theresa's belief system enabled her in many ways to take decisions that were far more radical than those of her son. She was always concerned with the effects of reform on Catholic belief and this gave her the confidence to challenge not only the high aristocracy but the Vatican. Far from narrowing horizons, her faith made her anxious to explore how it might improve the condition of her subjects. Nowhere did the debate become more intense than in the field of education, always a keen subject of interest for the Empress but, as the 1770s advanced, education moved suddenly to the very forefront of her political considerations. In 1773 the Pope, bowing to monarchical pressure from Portugal and then Spain, did the unthinkable and suppressed the Jesuit Order. At a stroke, the entire fabric of the monarchy's educational system was torn asunder.

CHAPTER 15

The Great Suppression: Educational Upheaval

WITH HIS PAPAL BRIEF *Dominus ac redemptor*, Clement XIV banned the Society of Jesus with immediate effect: 'Having considered that the Company of Jesus can no long produce those abundant fruits . . . we move to suppress and abolish the Company forthwith.'[1]

That the Jesuits had long been in the crosshairs of their enemies, both secular and clerical, did not come as a surprise in Vienna. Yet the Austrian attitude towards the Order was altogether far more tolerant than that of any of the other Catholic monarchies. Austria, significantly, did not have any colonies and it was striking that those monarchies that sought most aggressively to expel the Jesuits were those whose colonial interests seemed most threatened by them.[2]

When a transfer of Latin American territory from Portugal to Spain deprived Jesuit missions of their autonomy, a native uprising, possibly encouraged by the Jesuits, erupted, causing vast inconvenience to both Spanish and Portuguese colonial authority. Portugal, in any event, under the guidance of its first minister, the Marquis de Pombal, was virulently hostile to the Society and deeply resented its influence.[3]

It is often forgotten that the Jesuits were not just concerned with the erudition and souls of those with whom they came into contact but were also at this time a formidable trading force with powerful commercial interests. Voltaire might have railed against them as the personification of the old society and the strongest rampart of Catholic thinking, but for the commercial instincts of Pombal the morality and intellectual paradigms of the Jesuits were an irrelevancy. By the middle of the eighteenth century, the Jesuits had become a significant trading corporation and it was as merchants rather than spiritual directors that they came into collision with secular authority, first in Portugal, then in Spain, and finally in France.

Pope Clement XIV was a notably weak pontiff who quickly submitted to the growing pressure from these three monarchies to limit the power of the Jesuits. In France, the attack had been led by Jansenist sympathizers but this did not really concern the Pope, who felt far more vulnerable to the threats of loss of prestige if he continued to support an order which was being systematically removed from the principal Catholic powers of Europe.

Austria alone refused to play this power game, but even the Habsburgs could not escape a degree of compliance with developments that seemed to embrace not only the apex of Catholic authority but also every continental Catholic kingdom.

Jesuit authority in Austria had also been on the wane, although not out of commercial rivalry but rather from a keen sense that their monopoly on education and censorship was incompatible with the prevailing intellectual commitment to what was called 'the light of truth'. In 1760 Van Swieten had successfully lobbied his Empress to take over from the Jesuits the responsibility for censorship in the monarchy. This had already been diluted by a 'silent tolerance' (*Stille Duldung*) which had left many books on the Vatican's *Codex librorum prohibitorum* available for use in private libraries.

Nevertheless, any bookshops found selling forbidden tomes were threatened by Maria Theresa with closure and fines if such books were not immediately confiscated, and the Empress seems to have had a particular sensitivity to subversive literature right up to her death. One of her last decrees, in October 1779, was a reorganization of the book trade in her domains. Two years earlier, she had dispatched Count Clary to Prague to 'strangle the roots' of subversion by carrying out a widespread inspection of Prague booksellers.

But if Jesuit involvement in censorship had diminished in recent years, their grip on education was notably firm. With the exception of the Theresian military academy in Wiener Neustadt, under the control of Field Marshal Daun, all Maria Theresa's principal educational establishments were organized and directed by Jesuits. Many of these were among the most knowledgeable teachers of the empire.

Kaunitz, as we have seen, summed up the feelings of most enlightened Austrians when he wrote after the Suppression: 'I could never
regret enough the senseless chasing out of the best brains from their
teaching posts in order to replace them with the worst.' Kaunitz was
happy to acquire on behalf of the Austrian state Jesuit property and
material wealth but, as a pupil himself of the Jesuits, he knew all too
well what was in danger of being lost.

Another pupil of the Jesuits moved to take practical steps to limit the
damage. Joseph, too, was ambivalent. He remained, despite having
purportedly accused them of 'spreading darkness over the earth', keenly
respectful of them. When asked for his views on the Order in 1769 during
a tour of Italy, he adopted a tone of neutrality, avoiding any criticism of
them. In fact, there are several reports of his praising them. Both Count
Papini and later Catherine the Great reported that Joseph was a staunch
defender of the Jesuits. The Jesuits' formidable teaching tradition gave
them a practical role which Joseph, like Kaunitz, no friend of the contemplative orders, would have appreciated.

The threat to the existence of the Jesuits never came from within the
monarchy and Maria Theresa took several steps to mitigate the papal
instruction, allowing Jesuits to pursue where possible their calling
within the constraints of the Suppression which was implemented in a
typically Austrian half-hearted fashion. But if the Empress's neutrality
saved them individually, it did not preserve them collectively and her
studied refusal to engage more robustly on their behalf can be best
understood in the wider context of her diplomatic engagement with
France. The fragile alliance with France, the sole guarantee against a
resurgent Prussia, did not need a defiantly pro-Jesuitical Vienna just at
that moment.

Yet the Austrian court interpreted her neutrality as support for individual Jesuits even as the corporate body was dissolved. Joseph insisted
that 'it was desirable but necessary for the good of religion especially in
the higher schools'. But he realized that it would be quite impossible to
replace these men with people of calibre from the other orders or secular
clergy. In this way many Jesuits remained *en poste*.

A similar Austrian compromise was enacted with regard to the
Jesuits' huge real estate portfolio. Kaunitz was more than delighted to

have these estates absorbed by the Austrian crown but he was hindered by the Vatican's express request that the property remain at the disposal of religious activity. In practice, it was accepted in Vienna that the former Jesuits themselves must have the first charge on it. Surplus property should be used for educational purposes.

Maria Theresa established a commission to consider all these points. The members included some of the finest minds in Vienna. Karl Anton Martini, Van Swieten's protégé and a prominent University teacher, was one member. Ignaz Müller, Maria Theresa's confessor extraordinary, was another. He had more or less replaced the ageing and increasingly decrepit Jesuit confessor Fr Kampmiller. Müller was the provost of the convent of St Dorothea and had been called in to be the Empress's confessor when she fell seriously ill in 1767. His scepticism and jealousy of the Jesuits was well known but it was perhaps the commission's chairman who was the most remarkable choice. Baron Franz Kressel was a prominent Freemason who later was appointed Bohemian and Austrian chancellor. He was a member of both the Prague lodge, *Zu den drei gekrönten Sternen*, and the celebrated Vienna lodge, *Zur gekrönten Hoffnung*.

This, on the face of it, was about as anti-Jesuitical a line-up as could be imagined. Conventional wisdom suggests that Jesuits and Freemasons were always at daggers drawn. The distinguished historian Frances Yates once described European history in terms of a centuries-old struggle between these two forces, 'the most basic and most secret of European patterns'.[4] But once again the reality is more complex than a simple black-and-white analysis would suggest.

Maria Theresa was reluctant to acquiesce in Vatican demands and, from the beginning, regarded the Papal Bull suppressing the Society as flawed. Clement XIII, Clement XIV's predecessor, had planned a consistory to suppress the Jesuits but died on the eve of its first meeting. Before his death he had, throughout the 1760s, provoked Maria Theresa's indignation by trying to reassert the prerogatives of Rome after the largely complaisant pontificate of Benedict XIV.

Maria Theresa's points of conflict with the Vatican gathered increasing friction. First her plans for clerical taxation were opposed, then the pontiff appointed Lombard bishops without consulting Vienna, and then he finally refused to receive the Empress's representatives in protest at the way his own representatives had been treated at the election of Joseph as King of the Romans. The Pope criticized Maria Theresa and compared her most unfavourably with her father and predecessors, a slur which sent the Empress into a well-documented emotional outburst. At one point the relationship became so fractious that Maria Theresa even refused to receive the Pope's letters.

This deterioration between Vienna and Rome has usually been interpreted as encouraging Maria Theresa's anti-Jesuit stance but in fact, if anything, it had quite the opposite effect. The Vatican wanted the Jesuits suppressed but in Vienna a modus vivendi, supported by those around the Empress, soon undermined any hopes Clement XIV might have had of seeing the Jesuits eliminated as a factor in the Habsburg lands. Delay and indecision, two weapons which Austrian statecraft was over the coming centuries to fashion into almost reflex responses to external pressure, caused Vatican commands to run into the sands. A stand-off with the Vatican over the Jesuits' property – Maria Theresa, like Kaunitz, insisted it revert to the crown – applied brakes to the process while a particularly dry and dusty summer had an enervating effect on all decision-making. By the end of September, little progress had been made in the implementation of the Papal Bull and, by the time eventually the Jesuits' property had been seized, most of the former Jesuits were still employed.

When the aggressive Papal Nuncio, Cardinal Migazzi, tried to accelerate measures to seize the Jesuit property, he was met with courteous prevarication. Maria Theresa supported the retention of the Jesuits in universities and schools and the preservation of much of their wealth if only to secure the pensions of their many dependants.

To demonstrate a degree of compliance, the Order's principal buildings in Vienna, including its imposing headquarters, were given over to the state and Lacy enjoyed a palatial office in the former main Jesuit *palais* as it was converted a month later into the seat of the *Kriegsrat*.

Despite the implementation of the Papal Bull in the Austrian lands, the intellectual standing of the Society of Jesus frustrated any extreme measures. Eventually, the Society was formally suppressed but there was to be none of the radical dissolution which marked Joseph's later removal of the north Italian monasteries. Maria Theresa proceeded slowly and carefully. Her son failed to learn this important lesson, and the resentments which were the result of his moves twenty years later against the contemplative orders in Lombardy would leave such a legacy of bitterness that devout Italians would welcome even the godless Napoleon to deliver them from the tyranny of *Josephinismus*.

The Empress took great care to ensure that the intellectual property of the Order remained untouched. Jesuits' libraries were incorporated into the University of Vienna's library (administered by former Jesuits). This had the paradoxical result of ensuring that the Vienna University library not only was enriched with rare manuscripts on theological subjects but was furnished with copies of some of the greatest products of the culture and Enlightenment of the seventeenth and eighteenth centuries.

The works of Winckelmann, Voltaire, Newton, Boyle, Samuel Johnson and Adam Smith were all meticulously catalogued by the former Jesuits and thus, thanks to the supposed 'enemies of progress', did the University of Vienna acquire one of the greatest libraries in the world.

The suppression of the Society, however, gave great impetus to educational reform, although the imperative for far-reaching educational change had been building up for some years before. As early as 1765, nearly ten years before the Suppression, Maria Theresa's government had been steadily increasing its claims to control education. The subsequent reforms are still visible throughout central Europe today and are rightly seen as having been as important in the monarchy's history as anything done under the Empress.

The Empress, as always, was motivated by the imperative to improve the dismally low standards of popular education which were evident throughout the masses of her people. The Prince-Archbishop of Passau, Count Firmian, appealed personally to Maria Theresa to take action. She then instructed Count Pergen, to whom she had entrusted the direction of the Oriental Academy, to investigate what could be achieved and at what cost.

Education, as we have seen, was *ein Politicum* for Maria Theresa, and Pergen's recommendations chimed with the Empress's views. He was mainly concerned that pupils should learn only 'what is useful to them and to the state'. In 1770 he submitted a paper to Maria Theresa outlining a scheme of radical educational reform. The language of instruction throughout the monarchy should be German and he suggested bringing in educationalists from north Germany to advise and assist.

Here, Maria Theresa's instinctive suspicion of Protestants blocked Pergen's way forward. She was happy to countenance the Jesuits losing their monopoly on education but her own Jesuitical formation was sceptical of an invasion of Protestant *Aufklärer* suddenly taking over the reins of her subjects' education.

Even Joseph felt compelled to protest: 'Count Pergen's plan, though I have never read it, by common consent contained much good. But as for using foreign advisers this seems to me very inopportune. We must first of all try to ensure that every subject learns to read, write and calculate. We need schools together with the funds to pay able teachers.'

But Joseph was no less committed to social mobility than his mother and he continued: 'there must be scholarships for exceptionally gifted subjects irrespective of their social class. They should receive the means to devote themselves fully to study the branches of knowledge most illuminating to them according to their varying talents . . . and be maintained out of public funds or by foundations.'[5]

Like his mother, Joseph was only articulating ideas that the ruling caste in Vienna, Jesuit-trained but mostly Freemasons, had long embraced. Like Kaunitz, Joseph believed that, when it came to finding university graduates posts in imperial service, class distinctions should fall away and only merit be given precedence.

When the suppression of the Jesuits made major changes in education inescapable, Maria Theresa had, as we have seen, already taken the highly unconventional step of writing to her arch-enemy, Frederick, suggesting an innovative exchange of 'intellectual property'. Might Frederick wish to receive some of the eminent Austrian former Jesuit scholars to minister higher places of learning for his recently acquired, largely Catholic population in Silesia, in return for having lent her the Augustinian Johann Ignaz von Felbiger who had pioneered, at Sagan, not only a new primary-school system and teaching method but also a new catechism?

Felbiger had quickly introduced a blueprint providing for universal and compulsory elementary education. There would be three sorts of school: the *Normalschule*, which was the model set up in each Land; the *Hauptschule*, of which there was at least one in every district; and the *Trivialschule*, which would offer education in every parish. Contrary to popular belief, attendance between the ages of 6 and 12 was not 'obligatory'. To this day, school attendance in Austria is not obligatory: what the Theresian educational reform insisted on was 'education' between the ages of 6 and 12 but then, as now, such an education could be received at home by private tutors unless 'neither resources nor desire' were available.[6]

By the end of 1774, the first general school ordinance (*Allgemeine Schulordnung*) for the crown lands (aways excluding Hungary) was enacted, with Felbiger in charge of the whole operation. By the time Maria Theresa died, there were more than 500 new schools employing the new methods but the former Jesuit *Gymnasien*, the backbone of secondary education, were often taken over, at least formally, by Piarists who introduced fee-paying structures which inevitably led to a falling-off in pupils, especially from classes that would have most benefited from the schooling on offer. Ironically, this brought many Jesuits back into the equation as they were now employed to give private tuition to many pupils.

This introduction of compulsory elementary education would follow the reforms to the other segments of schooling which would be equally long-lasting. Thus, throughout central Europe, the 'Matura' remains to this day the gold standard of completing secondary-school education (its conclusion celebrated throughout the Czech Republic, Austria and Italy, Hungary and Slovakia, by the *Matura Ball*).

Thus did the Jesuits manage, in one way or another, to continue to contribute to the monarchy's educational progress after their formal elimination. The clergy, though subordinated to the state, were still to play by far the largest part in education. In consequence, not only did many Jesuits, Piarists and other former clergy go on teaching after 1773, but Church and State were inextricably bound together in education and it was Maria Theresa's firm conviction (shared, though not often admitted, by her 'anti-clerical' son) that this state of affairs be the foundation of all Habsburg educational policy. As Felbiger wrote shortly before the Empress's death: 'In no state in the world is so much care devoted to the lowest schools as in Austria.'[7]

CHAPTER 16

Physical Well-Being: The Arrival of a Public Health System

IF THE MENTAL AND educational well-being of her subjects preoccupied Maria Theresa in the late 1760s and 1770s, her interest in the medical progress of her subjects was, as we have seen, no less acute in earlier years. It had been the military requirements for better medical provision which had inspired her as early as the 1740s and we have seen how her personal physician, Gerard van Swieten, had, whatever the shortcomings of his own practice, nevertheless quickly gained Maria Theresa's confidence. The story is told of how, when she was concerned about losing weight, he deployed an unusual method to encourage her to eat less. This involved a footman bringing to her each evening a soup tureen filled with the equivalent amount of food to that which she had eaten during the day. This 'cure' was instructive and within weeks the Empress began to lose weight.

The interest in physical health was not born out of imperial philanthropy. Rather, it was the need for her armies to have access to healthier human material which was the practical reason for the monarchy to raise standards of public health. Unsurprisingly, the first tangible reforms of medical services were initiated in the military sphere.

On 29 January 1744 the chief physician of the army, the *Protomedicus*, an Irishman named Brady, delivered to the Empress a blistering letter in which he listed the shortcomings of medical provision, including the dire state of medical organization and, above all, the state of anarchy which seemed to prevail with regard to military hospitals and medical staff postings.

Van Swieten's reforms touched every aspect of medical health. Departments of Obstetrics were established in Prague and Vienna where trained midwives were employed. In Vienna the medical faculty of the university was entirely reorganized, with practical examinations at the core of a new curriculum. Only doctors who had qualified by passing the faculty's exams were allowed to enter the military medical staff. Nurses and field orderlies were subject to professional examinations in anatomy and physiology and in a very short time a corps hitherto made up of quacks and amateurs conforming to no regulation was transformed into a professional body whose training and discipline would quickly become the envy of other European countries.

These reforms combined also with the development of inoculation against smallpox, a practice born, as we have seen, partly out of the suffering the disease had inflicted on the Empress's own family. Apart from the death of her daughter and daughter-in-law from the disease, the illness left scars on Maria Theresa's own face for the rest of her life.

Despite significant opposition from the medical profession in Vienna, she welcomed the use of inoculation even though at that time it involved the variolization method whereby the patient was injected with material taken from human smallpox pustules, a procedure not without attendant risks.

Such reforms culminated in 1770 with the proclamation by the Empress of a *Generale normativum sanitatis* regulating healthcare throughout the monarchy. Especial provision was made for the lands along the eastern frontier of the monarchy, the so-called Military Frontier which bordered the Ottoman empire and was ethnically and confessionally very diverse.

Quarantine arrangements for travellers entering the monarchy across the Military Frontier were institutionalized, while regulations for sanitary burials and the requirement for all patients dying in hospitals to be examined post-mortem[1] rapidly brought the medical arrangements of the monarchy onto a new level of transparency and efficiency.

As public health improved, the state's role in it was expanded, dovetailing neatly twenty years later when Joseph's dissolution of the monasteries throughout the crown lands removed from the medical sphere the last vestiges of social services which the contemplative orders had preserved. The traditions of the monasteries, however, still persisted and herbal remedies and what would be called today homeopathic medicine continued to hold significant sway over the Habsburg lands for many centuries to come. Yet just as the Swiss physician Paracelsus had revolutionized medical thinking centuries earlier by his emphasis on observation in diagnosis, so too did Theresian medical reforms change the way in which the health of Maria Theresa's subjects was perceived. No longer were they just the victims of indifference and incompetence. By 1770 they could theoretically rely on common standards of proficiency and support. Once again, it was left to Joseph to build on his mother's foundations of reform and introduce even greater centralization into the medical profession throughout the monarchy but, once again, the path had been opened by his mother.

Such reforms ushered in a new, however discreetly discussed, frankness with regard to the relationship between medicine and sex. Not only did the Empress take a dim view of adultery, she elevated the public health issues surrounding prostitution into state policy. At the same time, she regularly asked Van Swieten for (and received) detailed advice on how she could 'perform' for her husband as she advanced in years after her multiple pregnancies.

Perhaps she was informed that her son Joseph was a regular visitor to prostitutes after the death of his first wife. Joseph's physical and emotional needs were certainly more complex than those of his parents and he wrote to his friend de Ligne:

> I'm always a little uncertain of myself in relation to prostitutes, of whom there are a great many shoddy merchandise. So I go to bed peacefully; happy to lie on my own mattress where at least, without the slightest inconvenience and without disturbing my peace, I am my own master, stretching and rolling about as I please.[2]

But this austerity and self-denial was rare, as Joseph often confided at other times to de Ligne that he preferred to go to a prostitute before going to the house of a society woman whom he might hope to seduce so as 'not to be tempted to take advantage'. Later, Joseph defended his 'distractions' with the words:

> What is to be done? Either you remain on your own or you go slumming, or you put up with the company that the locality supplies. You

would take the first option and perhaps if I had a wife and children, too, so would I. But to spend the evening alone with just a *valet de chambre* after working the whole day. Well, that is a life I really could not bear in the long run without falling into despair. The second option, to go out looking for women. Well, I have tried that and there are so many physical drawbacks. It is also brutalizing and leaves such a great void that there really is no other option but to take what advantage one can, make light of the rest and try to spend the evening distracted from business.[3]

This candour was mirrored in the dialogue which Maria Theresa shared with her own physician concerning her declining – and, as she felt it, irreversible – ability to attract her husband and serial philanderer, Francis Stephen. The language exchanged was discreet but it was clear that Van Swieten had no inhibitions in recommending 'certain techniques' and 'mind games' to help Maria Theresa remain physically active.

But sex within the confines of marriage was very different from condoning lax morals outside the marital bedchamber and, perhaps frustrated by her failing ability to monopolize Francis Stephen's sexual appetites, the Empress conducted a veritable crusade against prostitution.

The *Constitutio criminalis Theresiana* demanded severe penalties, including incarceration and even exile, for prostitutes found guilty of soliciting their trade. The infamous *Temesvarer Wasserschube* exiled hundreds of prostitutes to the outer fringes of the empire in the Banat while the clients of prostitutes were also spied upon and fined or even in some cases discharged from their offices in the service of the crown. There is no evidence to suggest that the surveillance techniques applied in such cases were directly, as some have speculated, on the initiative of Maria Theresa, who was happy to see them deployed even when only extramarital affairs were in progress. That was an attempt to paint her as more austere than in reality she ever was. She was anything but a prude.[4]

CHAPTER 17

The King of the Romans

IF JOSEPH SPORADICALLY MANAGED to console himself with the ladies of the night after the death of his first and adored wife, he was soon offered another bride, Princess Josepha of Bavaria. After the exquisite delicacy of the teenage Isabella, with her pretty mouth and hair, the Bavarian was a bit of a shock. When he first saw her, Joseph wrote: 'She is twenty-six. She has never had smallpox, her figure is short, thick-set and without a hint of any charm. Her face is covered with spots and pimples and her teeth are horrible.'[1] Not a promising beginning but, as ever with the Habsburgs, greater issues were at stake and it was Kaunitz who believed the axe needed to be buried with Bavaria – and how better than to secure a union between the houses of Habsburg and Wittelsbach through the marriage of the crown prince to the Bavarian princess?

In March 1764 the title Rex Romanorum (King of the Romans) had been granted to Joseph, confirming him as set to become elected as Holy Roman Emperor on his father's death. While an emperor was alive, it was possible for the nine electors to elect a King of the Romans who would then automatically become emperor on the death of the incumbent, thus avoiding any interregnum. In the early '50s much negotiation had proceeded to procure the election of Joseph as King but these efforts had failed, partly because of their being involved in a much resented British diplomatic initiative to inject new ginger into the Anglo-Austrian alliance which, unbeknown to London, was falling apart under Kaunitz's great *Renversement*. With the end of the Seven Years War, the restoration of the status quo ante appeared to leave Austria with little to show for Kaunitz's great démarche but Maria Theresa obtained one advantage from the Peace of Hubertusburg in February 1763: Prussia's support for Joseph as King of the Romans (and therefore later Emperor).

In 1764 it seemed as if that eventuality was remote. Francis Stephen was only 57 and enjoying his life to the full but then, suddenly, he died on his way to his rooms, returning from a performance of Goldoni's *Il Tutore* in Innsbruck. The seizure was swift and dramatic. At first, the courtiers tried to keep Maria Theresa away but when she saw the lifeless body laid out she knelt and prayed without weeping. An hour later she had to be dragged away by force.

The King of the Romans, without formality, automatically became the Emperor Joseph II. Externally, the title was devalued currency and, as Frederick observed already in 1752: 'It seems to me likely that the power of the emperors will continue to diminish because the electors, now that they are powerful princes, can match imperial authority and power by uniting together and calling on the help of France.'[2]

Internally, the title had deep implications for Austria and the monarchy: a new co-regency was born. Joseph, according to the terms of his father's will, was the sole heir to the financial fortune his father had constructed. It was vast; Joseph became master of something like 20 million florins in bonds and money alone and estates worth over 13 million. Francis Stephen had belied his 'uncomplicated' personality with an acumen for accumulating wealth worthy of a later Rothschild.

Unlike that between Maria Theresa and her late husband Francis Stephen, during which the Emperor had always been resigned to the background, the new co-regency was from the very outset fraught with tension. Maria Theresa declared Joseph as co-regent on 17 September, while noting that she made this arrangement 'without however surrendering the whole or any part of our personal sovereignty over our states'. She was shattered by her consort's death and many biographers have seen Joseph's appointment as a prop for her in its wake. She also needed to bind Joseph to her and to a certain extent limit his freedom of action as Emperor. To a considerable degree, Joseph owed his co-regency to the fact that as Emperor he was the senior crowned head of Europe, but the realpolitik of his mourning mother was, despite her grief, not to be underestimated. The co-regency bound the prestige, rights and powers of the imperial title to the service of the monarchy.

Perhaps there is no better visual evidence of the difference between mother and son than their tombs in the Capuchin crypt in Vienna. Maria Theresa's is the most opulent and ornate construction, bursting out of its domed canopy with magnificent carvings depicting the greatest of her military victories. Joseph's, on the other hand, is a simple wooden and copper coffin with a faded inscription, designed in every way to contrast with the celebration of his mother. The simple inscription runs: 'Here lies the body of Joseph II who failed in everything he tried to achieve.' As in death, so in life Joseph, once the mantle of power had been invested in him, demonstrated that, however significant his mother's reforms of the previous twenty-five years had been, they were in his eyes only the beginning of a much more radical overhaul of the Austrian state.

Nothing perhaps illustrated this better than the first responsibility Maria Theresa ceded to him in 1765: the governance and organization of the army. This suited Joseph as he admired – much to his mother's horror – the ruthless clinical approach to life of Austria's great adversary Frederick. Frederick was callous, cynical and undoubtedly a warrior-king remote from the easy-going *Gemütlichkeit* of Joseph's father and the high-minded piety of his mother. If Maria Theresa had once said, 'You would have to kill me to prevent my trying to do good', Joseph's mantra would have been, 'You would have to kill me to prevent my trying to make this monarchy more efficient, centralized and controlled.' Like Frederick, Joseph always wanted to be portrayed in uniform and his determination to exercise sole control in his responsibilities was manifest at an early age. When only nine, he had written to Haugwitz demanding he 'lay off my own regiment' (1st Chevaux-légers) 'with your meddling reforms'.

Convinced that it was his destiny to modernize his empire and to prepare its armies for the great victories to which he would surely lead them, Joseph scorned tradition. If Maria Theresa was the Queen of the Night in Mozart's *Die Zauberflöte*, Joseph resembled Sarastro, the all-controlling promoter of a new order where all is regulated by his own arbitration.

Military structures were treated with nonchalant irreverence and the clash between 'reform' and 'tradition' was piquant. First on the block was the traditional white Austrian tunic. There must be cheaper colours, Joseph insisted. We have seen how he himself never wished to be portrayed in 'Catholic white' and always preferred the green uniform of his *Schvo-ley* regiment. A commission was set up to investigate the rival merits of wolf-grey and pike-grey.

Keen at all times to emulate Frederician military practices, Joseph also wanted to reorganize the Austrian infantry along cantonal lines. This, too, would save money. As an early memorandum, the first of many delivered in May 1761, warned: 'We should not reduce our forces; rather we must dismantle all the luxury and excesses of an unaffordable system.'[3]

Court dress for officers was to be replaced by uniforms as befitted the servants of the state's 'first servant' and, like Frederick, Joseph affected a military lifestyle of austerity and discipline. 'To be a soldier has always been my profession and favourite occupation.'[4]

Following a long tour in Bohemia in 1766, the new Emperor appointed new inspectorates for cavalry, artillery and infantry. Daun's death the same year gave Joseph's idea added momentum. The 'expensive' Swiss Guard was abolished, the army staff reorganized and the infantry elevated into the 'Queen of Arms'. A tide of *Nüchternheit* (austerity) enveloped the officer corps: their canes were to be unadorned, their boots and tunics of simpler cut. All excessive ornamentation was to be removed, epaulettes banned. All facing colours were for the first time subject to manuals which laid down the precise shades of colour for each regiment. Thus was born the *Farbkastel* (box of colours) which included such exotic names as 'sulphur yellow' (*Schwefel-gelb*), carmine red, parrot green and *Krapprot* (madder red).

The cavalry, whose traditions and dress had always been jealously guarded privileges, felt this wind of austerity especially keenly. Regimental standards and guidons were reduced by half; all drum horses were abolished, and the number of cavalry regiments significantly reduced. By 1775 Joseph had conducted his reforms so effectively that he could proudly write to his mother: 'Nothing of the old army remains.'

Maria Theresa hoped that the army would suffice to keep Joseph occupied, but his interests were too wide-ranging and his obsession with change so intense that she soon found her co-regent adopting an altogether far more intrusive role than her late husband.

Joseph devoted particular attention to the affairs of Hungary and Transylvania. In the case of Hungary, his words anticipated all too well the problems that would follow in those lands upon his mother's death in 1780. Unlike his mother, who scrupulously avoided direct conflict with the magnates, Joseph was altogether more robust: 'I would judge that before we can reasonably expect anything more from this country we must reform their internal system, increase their population and educate their youth . . . We must be especially careful to create no suspicion that we want to infringe their privileges, although in private we feel no respect for them at all.'[5]

Joseph felt none of his mother's sentimental affection for the Hungarians who, in her most desperate moment of crisis, had ridden to her rescue. Rather, it was just another territory to be exploited: 'If Hungary contributed taxes of which I don't despair in the long run, it would be another Peru', he insisted.[6]

When his mother pointed out that the Hungarian magnates were not known for their compliance or subordination, Joseph replied: 'The great nobility ought to be kept quiet either by honours or by fear; the lesser nobles should be supported against the great and won over by appointing them to all types of offices which the sovereign ought to keep within her control.'

This generally cavalier approach to the aristocracy was something Joseph appears to have learnt from Kaunitz. It was very different from the Prussian model in which Frederick always supported the nobility, especially the landed class which supplied the backbone of his officer corps.

But Joseph's views, which became even more radical when he came to the throne on Maria Theresa's death in 1780, revealed not just Puritan rigour, they showed a certain prescience of future events. Joseph was always a young man in a hurry, determined that the social explosions, which he clearly saw were imminent, happened in other European states rather than his own. As he wrote in a memorandum of 1765: 'I was just astonished that people had lived so long in this crass ignorance, and I regarded everything that had been previously done as though it was a creation of the Iroquois Indians.'[7]

The far-reaching aims of Joseph's *Rêveries* were never acceptable to Maria Theresa but from the start Joseph bombarded his mother with ideas. 'I have a hundred thousand projects in my head, as many good as bad,' he told his brother Leopold, adding, 'I shall tell you about them as soon as they are sorted out a little.'

The contrast with his mother's mourning and melancholy could not have been greater. While she proclaimed herself in private to be 'half-dead; I live without spirit and reason', Joseph ran about 'overwhelmed by business and audiences'. Maria Theresa lamented that she got up at five, went to bed late and did nothing all day.

Maria Theresa wrote on hearing the news of Daun's and Haugwitz's deaths:

> The good God takes away from me the two men who possessed, and justly, my entire confidence. They were both Christians, zealous and devoted, true friends who told me the truth roundly and to whom I could always open my heart without restraint. This sadness affects all my senses, memory, hearing, sight and judgement. I feel as if I am beginning to lose them all.

But Maria Theresa continued: 'I have not found comfort in anything but absorbing myself in my work more deeply than ever.'[8]

She remained active and strong enough to maintain her control over the affairs of the monarchy but, with Daun and Haugwitz gone and Kaunitz slowing up, only Tarouca and Lacy remained with Starhemberg, recalled from Paris, to guide her confidence. When Kaunitz, feeling the pressure of his thirty-six years of advancing the Austro-French alliance, tendered his resignation, she stubbornly refused to contemplate it. In an astonishingly intimate rebuttal, she wrote back to him:

> How unhappy we are if we can have no true friend! I thought I had one, I was calm and happy. Imagine my disillusionment. With another I venture to suggest you would run many risks but with me who has had only too long to get to know men, I am indulgent and kind. I am incapable of rancour and I can entirely forget things so let us go and die with our swords in our hands or we can both go and hide in the gloomy mountains of Tyrol to finish our days in obscurity, aban-doned by everyone else and the universe.[9]

Kaunitz remained but in this power triangle between Maria Theresa, her son and the ageing, increasingly vain minister, the tensions of state-craft were almost daily apparent. Yet Empress and Emperor continued to work together without personal bitterness. Maria Theresa found her son alien in his manner and sarcasm but he was her son and no doubt she meant it when she said, as she frequently did, that she only 'continued to rule out of love' for him.

In effect, together with Kaunitz, Emperor and Empress comple-mented each other. On the one hand, outside the prerogative of the army, which his mother had ceded to him in 1765, Joseph was unable to achieve anything significant in the way of political action. He was only a nominal lord over ungovernable vassals yet he was crowned with medi-eval religious pomp and expected to take pride in his largely symbolic status. His mother, on the other hand, was an absolute ruler, also working long hours for the state and good of her subjects. Prone to personal caprice and piety, she was, in her respect for tradition and pomp, far removed from her son's obsessive disdain for ceremony and mystique.

This triumvirate ruled the monarchy until Maria Theresa's death. Although Maria Theresa often talked of abdication she never, apart from a brief moment in 1773, offered it. Kaunitz resigned two more times, in 1776 and 1779, but on each occasion his wishes were rejected. The Empress exerted the ultimate authority, relying heavily on Kaunitz while Joseph struggled to make what impact he could on this powerful combination.

After her near-fatal illness in 1767, Maria Theresa staged something of a public comeback. She always wore mourning but her social activities increased significantly, masked balls were revived, elaborate family cele-brations devised and even a trip to the rocky landscape of distant Carniola planned. In 1770 the prohibition on the wearing of rouge was withdrawn. Nevertheless, a marked physical deterioration, largely caused by excessive corpulence, began to prevent her travels and the trip to Gorizia was cancelled. Eventually, by the time of her final five years, her shortness of breath was preventing her climbing stairs or even walking in the Hofburg gardens. A lift had to be installed at Schönbrunn to enable her to reach the summer palace's upper floors.

Meanwhile, Kaunitz grew ever more eccentric and slow. But he could still verbally rout his rivals in any intellectual confrontation and

Starhemberg gave up trying to replace him. By 1771 Joseph had reached the age of 30, his mother was 54 and Kaunitz 60. Joseph had energy and dynamism on his side but most of his more radical schemes in civil affairs were frustrated by his mother and her chancellor.

Despite these frustrations, Joseph continued to exert considerable influence over military affairs, and a later painting of him in 1788, surrounded by his staff at Minkendorf, a new military training ground, illustrates a small group of cavalry hitherto not visibly part of the regular Austrian army. Instantly recognizable by their *tschapkas* and *plastrons*, they are a troop of Polish lancers and their presence marked an act in 1772 of unprecedented callousness which threatened not only to splinter the triumvirate which ruled the monarchy but to break it into disparate pieces. Few things caused Maria Theresa more grief than the First Partition of Poland but, as Frederick cynically observed: 'She cried, but she took.'

CHAPTER 18

The Terrible 'Betrayal': The First Partition
of Poland

AT FIRST GLANCE, THE removal of an entire country from the map of
Europe in peacetime appears an act of unparalleled political violence.
Certainly, the First Partition of Poland was so described in the late nineteenth and twentieth centuries, in an age when nationalism took root in
popular consciousness. Some commentators have even described it as
excusing in advance the activities of Stalin and Hitler, while even in the
twenty-first century, the attempt by Russia to liquidate the recently
independent state of Ukraine might be interpreted as another variation
on a theme first composed by Maria Theresa.

In fact, the First Partition of Poland was largely unviolent and as far as
the Kingdom of Galicia-Lodomeria, the area incorporated into Austria in
1772, is concerned, largely benign. Maria Theresa brought the benefits of
her emerging state apparatus – an independent judiciary, a largely honest
administration and a predictable system of taxation – to lands which were
peopled by an oppressed peasantry, skittish aristocracy, utterly incapable
governing class and dysfunctional monarchy. Compared to the structures
imposed on parts of Poland by the centralizing Prussians and the unpredictable Russians, Maria Theresa brought a stability and harmony which,
even as late as the 1980s, was remembered fondly in Cracow and Lemberg.[1]

Although large in both area and population, Poland by the 1770s had
declined to a condition of internal anarchy and external impotence. A
completely unmanageable aristocracy obstructed their elected kings in
any attempts to strengthen the power or increase the revenue of the
government. An insignificant army of barely 20,000 men could play no
meaningful role in the defence of the kingdom and Poland's three

powerful neighbours, Russia, Prussia and Austria, were kept at bay only by their own failure to reach any kind of agreement among themselves.

The imminent end of the Seven Years War brought that artificial state of affairs rapidly to an end when in 1762 Russia and Prussia began to edge closer to each other. The following year, Augustus III, the Elector of Saxony and King of Poland, died and Frederick supported the Russian candidate at the subsequent royal election. This candidate, Stanislaus Augustus Poniatowski, was a former lover of Catherine the Great, and became king largely thanks to the presence in Warsaw and the surrounding districts of Russian bayonets.

Russian troops remained in the country after the coronation and Prussia acquiesced in St Petersburg's determination to dominate Polish affairs. When in 1764 a formal alliance was made between Russia and Prussia, alarm bells rang in Vienna as Kaunitz saw not just an unfavourable change in the balance of power but a tangible threat to the monarchy. Russian interference in Poland's sovereignty was bound to result in Prussian claims to Polish territory.

When Frederick suggested a meeting with Joseph to discuss Poland, Maria Theresa shuddered at the thought of her impressionable son encountering her arch-enemy and was greatly relieved when the idea was dropped. But following the Russo-Turkish war which broke out in 1768, Kaunitz felt compelled to strengthen Austria's eastern frontier and in particular absorb the 'Zipser' region of the Carpathians which was formally Hungarian territory but had been mortgaged to Poland in 1412. The local Hungarian landowners put pressure on Vienna, as did Lacy who, influenced by his local commanders, believed the entire district should be occupied immediately. This occurred in 1769 and, while the rights of Poland were publicly acknowledged, the sovereignty of Hungary and the monarchy were reasserted.

A further widening of this 'cordon' took place following Joseph's visit to the region when the co-regent declared 'the inhabitants themselves assured me they would be pleased to see it . . . the yield would be 16,000 ducats'.[2]

Finally, there took place in Neisse in Silesia on 27 August 1769 a formal meeting between Joseph and Frederick, organized by Kaunitz. Policies on either side were not advanced but the contact was successful in so far as the Emperor and the King clearly enjoyed each other's company.

This was followed just over a year later by a secret encounter at Neustadt in September 1770. The Prussian king knew well how to flatter Joseph and, in an elaborately arranged ruse, he appeared on the fringes of an inspection of Austrian troops, dressed in disguise in a white Austrian uniform (*Divisa Austriaca*). Joseph was even more impressed when the Prussian king confided that he thought the Austrian troops had improved their drill and appearance to such an extent that they were really 'Prussians in white uniforms'.[3] This was a flattery to which Joseph was all too susceptible.

Nothing of concrete diplomatic import seems to have been concluded at this meeting but undoubtedly personal acquaintance between Joseph and Frederick brought the day of Poland's demise closer. Kaunitz accompanied Joseph, and Maria Theresa described the encounter as 'this pompous interview' and felt it boded only trouble ahead. Writing as the storm clouds gathered, she strongly implied that her hopes for peace over war were frustrated by her son:

> I was induced to approve a camp in Hungary of 30,000 men; that was three months ago. Little by little it has been pushed up to 60,000 – always on specious grounds . . . I am no longer of any use save to serve as a cloak for the plans of others . . . Kaunitz goes along with all this to avoid bother . . . the Emperor knows this well and takes advantage of these weaknesses to attain his ends.[4]

Then, in an astonishing admission by an old woman growing ever more lonely, she observed: 'I have no-one: Khevenhueller, Batthyany, Colloredo are of no comfort to me; they no longer know what is going on.'

Few letters of Maria Theresa's offer up such a frank picture of the frustrations and weaknesses of increasing age. The note of paranoia is striking but at the root of the discontent, expressed to her old friend the Marchioness de Herzelles, is a sense that all she had striven for since becoming sovereign was being frittered away by her son:

> Opposed in this way, continually distressed I am the first to admit I succumb and just let things happen. I am fated to survive all my family and recover from mortal illness at the age of fifty in order to

see the work of thirty-one years of rule perish; in order to see the Monarchy collapse as well and make all my subjects unhappy by war, plague and famine.[5]

A famine in Bohemia in 1771 reduced dramatically the Austrians' sinews of war. A robust foreign policy towards Russia was never on the cards without Prussian support which Maria Theresa despised. Kaunitz played his hand skilfully and bluffed both the Russians and the Turks with the kind of creative ambiguity which diplomats of a certain stamp adore but which only a master like Kaunitz could play without it leading to unpleasant complications.[6]

Kaunitz's skill even duped his Emperor and he advanced time and again arguments for war precisely so that they could be demolished by military logic and the obsession with a defensive military stratagem for the monarchy advanced by Lacy.

Russia, meanwhile, was secretly working with Prussia to partition Poland and extended feelers to Kaunitz as to the Austrian attitude to such a move. Kaunitz saw such a move in purely balance-of-power terms but Maria Theresa was resolutely opposed to partition of any territory, whether Turkish or Polish, however substantial Russian advances had been in the Russo-Turkish war.

She even sought to surrender the Zipser territory of her Hungarians, much to the indignation of Joseph who, in a letter to his brother Leopold, complained:

> in a conversation she had with the Prussian minister Rohde she overturned our entire plan – we wanted to put pressure on Russia and Turkey, threaten them with war etc. She strongly assured him that she would never want or permit war, that the possession of the Crimea seemed to her only a small point that she did not mind at all if Russia retained it.[7]

What changed Maria Theresa's mind was brutal realpolitik. Poland would be partitioned by Prussia and Russia with or without Austria. It was diplomatic suicide to stand by and allow such an aggrandizement of those two powers' territory without some quid pro quo. The quid pro quo was, however, to be quite considerable, larger in population than the acquisition made by Russia and significantly larger in territory than that made by Prussia.

Joseph with his keen eye during his travels in the region had immediately espied the jewels of the potential partition for Austria. These were first and foremost Lemberg (Lvov/Lviv), the salt mines of Wieliczka and a route of access from Upper Silesia to the new territories. Prussia and Russia were shocked. Suddenly from seemingly resisting all attempts at what Maria Theresa called 'a cruel necessity' she was now demanding the lion's share. The statesmen in Berlin and St Petersburg scratched their heads: who was really in charge in Vienna?

As head of the army, Joseph had certain levers of influence denied to his mother and he promptly ordered troops to occupy the districts he wanted. Maria Theresa still resisted the partition, calling it both immoral and unfortunate. Kaunitz, who had long reconciled himself to the inevitability of the partition, congratulated himself but admitted to Stormont, the British envoy, that the whole affair was *très louche*.[8]

Glimmers of moral scruple abounded. Maria Theresa herself raged against the partition at every turn:

> What right have we to rob an innocent nation that it has hitherto been our boast to protect and support? I do not understand the policy whereby for the sake of present convenience and future advantage it is made incumbent on a third ruler to imitate the wickedness of two others who are destroying an unoffending Power. This appears to me to be an untenable proposition . . . the greatness and strength of a state will not be taken into account when we are called to render our final reckoning. Only prove to me the contrary and I shall gladly submit.[9]

In the end, the Empress did submit but not before she had approved the relevant papers with the memorable, regretful words: '*Placet* since so many great and learned men will have it so, but long after I am dead it will be known what this violating of all that was hitherto held sacred and just will give life to.'

To others, even distant friends such as her ambassador in France, Mercy, she admitted: 'j'en suis inconsolable'. Maria Theresa was right to fear the impact of the partition on the regard other nations had for Austria, a country which elevated its loyalty to treaties and its commitment to honesty in its international relations to an almost sacred commitment. The duplicity and secrecy surrounding the partition shattered Maria Theresa's carefully cultivated image as the sovereign of an innocent power armed only for reasons of defence.

In London, Lord Suffolk wrote to the new British envoy in Vienna, Murray Keith, noting, 'The Court where you now reside for long habituated to a more civilized system and so well-informed of her own interests has in direct opposition to the one and the other . . . blindly laboured . . . to establish in Europe *de Droit de plus fort*.'[10]

The moral argument, however, was the only issue to fill the dispatches of the diplomatists recording the event. There was not the slightest awareness of any insult to Polish national pride. The notion that the partition of Poland was some great crime against national feeling was a late nineteenth-century indulgence, inflated by the encouragement of Slavic nationalism in the run-up to the Great War and then cemented at the Peace Conference in 1919 in the creation of a buffer state between the two shattered empires of Germany and Russia.

The First Partition was not the end of the story. Austrian aggrandizement continued and, in 1773, Joseph visited a sliver of Turkish territory which, although only 'a real desert', could be 'a most useful object'. Maria Theresa was incensed at this new ambition, saying, 'We are completely in the wrong', but Kaunitz saw the Bukovina as the land between Transylvania and Galicia and a vital strategic acquisition. He worked tirelessly to secure it. Seeing, like many a later statesman, that possession was 'nine-tenths' of the law, he connived with Joseph to occupy it with troops ahead of its formal surrender in 1775 to the monarchy by the Ottomans, already humbled by the Treaty of Kaynarca and the Russian occupation of Beirut.

If matters on the 'Eastern front' consumed Maria Theresa's dwindling energies as she entered the last half-decade of her life, there were soon pressing concerns bearing down on her from the western fastnesses of her empire. A year after the absorption of the Bukovina into the empire, Joseph's and Kaunitz's gaze fell on the always tiresome neighbour of Bavaria where, in 1777, Joseph's brother-in-law, Maximilian Joseph, died without an heir. The ensuing diplomatic conflict was to cause Maria Theresa yet more headaches as the temperament of her son demonstrated again an unhealthy appetite for expansionist policies.

CHAPTER 19

Bayonets and Potatoes: The Bavarian Succession Crisis

MAXIMILIAN JOSEPH'S DEATH DID not come as a great surprise. As the last of his line, the succession question had long been debated at leisure. Maria Theresa knew well the crisis that engulfed the death of sovereigns without a male heir and the parallels with her own experience were considerable.

Just as Charles VI had laboured to establish in the Pragmatic Sanction a seamless succession for his daughter, so too had the Bavarian elector overseen the publication of no fewer than 288 treatises on the subject of his succession. These had generally agreed that the heir to at least the largest part of Maximilian's inheritance was the head of his family, his distant cousin, Karl Theodor, already the Elector Palatine. But the Bavarian lands were not unified in title and could be divided into at least six classes depending on their title, often attaining to fiefdoms held by 'vassals' of the Holy Roman Emperor.

It did not help that Karl Theodor had no direct male heir himself save for his nephew, the Duke of Zweibrücken. To paraphrase Palmerston speaking of the Schleswig-Holstein question a hundred years later, the question of the Bavarian Succession was only perhaps understood by three people: 'one of whom had died, one was mad, and the third [he, Palmerston] had long forgotten what it was all about'.

Joseph was certainly eligible for the title of one of these Bavarian claims as his own imperial rank gave him several points of intersection with the succession. He was of course Holy Roman Emperor and therefore undisputed sovereign over certain of the territory's fiefdoms. His union with the Bavarian Elector's daughter, Josepha, gave him further rights as he acquired through marriage several 'allodials' (freeholds which could be inherited through the female line).

As early as 1764, in connection with Joseph's marriage to Josepha, Kaunitz had composed a memorandum on the subject, noting that 'the most striking and desirable outcome [of the Succession], if it were feasible, would be the union with Austria of the entire complex of Bavarian lands . . . there is no harm in contemplating it'. In churches in Munich and elsewhere, elaborate altars were constructed graced with the arms of Habsburg and Wittelsbach richly entwined.

For the diplomats, unlike the baroque church artists, the matter was less straightforward. Kaunitz was, of course, far from seeing such a development as a linear process. He noted that the Palatinate would have to be 'placated', France would have to be assured, as would the maritime powers and the empire. 'Above all,' he wrote, it would be 'essential to keep the King in Prussia out of the game.'[1] Fourteen years later, this position had evolved into a practical course of action to be undertaken in the event of the Elector's death. Joseph was to occupy his fiefdoms, pending consultation with the diet of the Holy Roman Empire. All revenues thus accrued would temporarily go to the Emperor. The mobilization orders were drawn up and a discreet line of communication was opened with Frederick and Karl Theodor.

Frederick watched with interest, keen to extract whatever prestige he could out of the predictable debacle. Karl Theodor in his Palatinate territory found the thought of his Bavarian inheritance an unwelcome distraction and hoped to be able to exchange Bavaria for the altogether more congenial and geographically relevant Austrian Netherlands. Maria Theresa, whose public fondness for that province was, as we have seen, limited mostly to her much repeated observation that it produced the 'best domestic servants in the empire', accepted that the proposition should be at least explored, and negotiations proceeded throughout 1777.

These talks were virtually complete when Maximilian Joseph died. The news of his death prompted Joseph to advise a more forward policy. 'There is no time to discuss the matter, we should take possession of Lower Bavaria and promise to discuss in a friendly manner the extent of our frontiers,' he wrote to Kaunitz.[2]

Maria Theresa listened to her son and agreed that she would not say a word about the succession at the formal New Year's Day celebration at court but, with regard to her son's desire to occupy Bavaria militarily, she absolutely refused.

A few days later, the convention between the monarchy and the Palatinate was signed. Austria received most of Lower Bavaria, the exact frontiers of which were to be determined by further 'historical' research in the Austrian archives, while Karl Theodor's ambitions towards the Austrian Netherlands were to be subject to 'further discussions'. Maria Theresa felt that, with the agreement signed and sealed, Austrian troops could enter Bavaria unopposed. She congratulated Kaunitz as 'the greatest statesman in Europe' for securing such an outcome without resort to arms. As Joseph wrote a month later: 'Our Bavarian affairs have turned out in the best possible way. The Elector has been dead for barely a month and we have signed and ratified a convention, we are in possession of the entire district with the fiefs that had lapsed to us and so far no-one has uttered a word . . . everything is quiet.'[3]

Maria Theresa was, against her better instinctive judgement, assured by Kaunitz's words that rarely had the international constellation proved so favourable to Austria's action. France and Britain were about to be locked into conflict over colonies in America. Russia was still embroiled in the Crimea and digesting the fruits of her victory over the Turks. In Germany, Saxony was Austria's long-time ally and Frederick was believed to be sufficiently wary of the reformed Austrian army to not wish to risk yet another conflict with the arch-enemy. Prussia was still recovering from the destruction a decade earlier wrought on her finances and material during the Seven Years War.

But Frederick was not prepared to allow the Habsburg monarchy to make gains as a result of the failure of the Bavarian line if Prussia was to go empty-handed. His claims to the principalities of Ansbach and Bayreuth were legally weak but strategically strong. They both occupied the important buffer zone between Bavaria and Prussia. Frederick demanded that his right to these principalities, long ventilated, was recognized.

Kaunitz, still basking in the compliment of 'the greatest statesman in Europe', deliberately ignored Frederician sensibilities, refusing to make even the slightest acknowledgement of Prussian interests in the two duchies. But nothing showed the deterioration in his abilities more than his lack of any grip on the reality of the diplomatic situation developing around him. Did he seriously believe that an agreement signed with an irrelevant German princeling, Karl Theodor, could be made without any consultation with more significant powers? Did he believe in Karl Theodor's fantasies about the Austrian Netherlands? Or Joseph's faith in his army to deter any intervention? Or in the hastily assembled archival research to silence all arguments against the Austrian claims?

No doubt, the pragmatism and intelligence of the statesman was more than capable of seeing that there might be 'complications' but that these would eventually yield some diplomatic and even territorial gain. He had failed to learn the lesson of his great *Renversement*: that even the most elaborate schemes, perfectly executed, can fail to achieve their objectives. The unhappy diplomacy which surrounded the imminent *Kartoffelkrieg* would confirm this lesson resoundingly.

Frederick sprang into action and, in a series of skilful démarches, demonstrated that, however weakened Prussia might be, she could still cause mischief. First, Prussian envoys suborned the hapless Karl Theodor's heir, the Duke of Zweibrücken, into withdrawing his consent to Karl Theodor's plans. Saxony, recently offended by Austrian troops occupying Schönburg, a hamlet claimed by Dresden, indicated it might enter an alliance with Prussia. England, ever conscious that King George III was also Elector of Hanover, supported Prussia. France, aware of its old alliances with Bavaria, said it would observe strict neutrality. The *grande alliance* on whose altar Maria Theresa had just sacrificed her daughter, Marie Antoinette, only committed France to come to Austria's aid to defend the status quo. Meanwhile, Catherine II of Russia, herself a German princess, made it known she would also support Prussia. Thus did the 'greatest statesman in Europe' bring about as hostile a constellation against Maria Theresa as any she had experienced since her tumultuous accession to the throne nearly forty years earlier.

Frederick mobilized but he had no intention of fighting unless he had to. He was now 66, taut, decrepit and embittered, but also much the wiser. Measuring swords with Maria Theresa had been, as he wrote, 'like dying a thousand times a day'. War with Austria had brought

Prussia to the brink of total ruin already once during his reign. Thus, he worked hard at the diplomatic effort before returning to head an army in the field.

Joseph, on the other hand, was desperate to prove his military credentials. He was untried and yet convinced he was a greater soldier than his father (not very difficult) or his uncle. He was too inexperienced to realize that war was unpredictable, and too headstrong to heed his mother's advice that campaigns might bring victories but only moderation brought lasting peace.

In the shadow of the Prussian ultimatum, Maria Theresa composed a heartfelt letter to her son:

> No sacrifice is too great to ward off the disaster of the overthrow of our house, the Monarchy and complete revolution in Europe . . . Even if our army should be lucky, an initial success would lead to nothing. Winning two or three battles did not win for us any part of Silesia. 1757 was enough to prove to us that our enemy is not to be destroyed so easily . . . We must reckon that even if we were lucky we should have to go on fighting for three years or four and this would be time enough for all Europe to join in the struggle to ensure that we do not grow too strong. We are distrusted enough as things are. I cannot think of a single friend or ally on whom we could count.[4]

This remarkable letter – prescient in its anticipation of imminent revolution in Europe, sensible to the important European states' commitment to the balance of power and, above all, conscious of the ephemeral quality of military victory – shows Maria Theresa's wisdom perhaps better than any other words she penned. It is a remarkable document and, having dictated it to her secretary, she summoned both Joseph and Kaunitz to her rooms where she read it out to them. The two men advanced all the arguments they could muster and the resulting stalemate persuaded Maria Theresa to add a postscript to her original draft: 'If it comes to war then count on me no more. I shall retire to the Tyrol to end my days in total isolation, lamenting the unhappy destiny of my House and my Peoples and seeking a Christian end to my miserable life.'[5]

The moral imperative was uppermost in Maria Theresa's mind and she did not hesitate to use it to advance her arguments against the Bavarian scheme of her son and chief minister. 'It is we who are at fault,' she insisted, 'we covet that to which we have no right.'

This candour strikes an alien note in a later age when the motives of realpolitik are rarely examined from the point of view of moral conscience, but it is precisely this quality of Maria Theresa's which made her the great sovereign she was. In matters great and small, the daily examination of conscience which the Jesuits had instilled in her from the earliest of ages forced her, as she became older, to see almost every act of statecraft in terms of personal responsibility before God.

This quality was also fast running out in eighteenth-century Austria. Joseph's emulation of Frederick's ruthlessness had none of the Prussian's cunning and skill. When Frederick threatened hostilities, Joseph convinced himself that he was only bluffing. When Frederick finally mobilized, Joseph doubled down and began to beat the drums of war with enthusiasm. His enthusiasm would have been perhaps contained if hubris had not been conjured up in the grand style to accompany it. Writing to Frederick, Joseph insisted: 'If it gives Your Majesty pleasure to lead 200,000 men onto the field of battle I shall be there with the same number; if you wish to discover whether you are still a successful general I am ready to satisfy your lust for fighting.'[6]

Maria Theresa was appalled. How could her son regard the serious and vicious business of war in such a trivial light? Did he not realize that his decisions affected 'the well-being of thousands upon thousands of men'? In one sense, Joseph was right to 'tease' his adversary; Frederick had no intention of giving battle. Both armies, enormous by the standards of eighteenth-century warfare, lumbered across each other's supply lines without making contact.

Maria Theresa continued to utter dire warnings but she also offered the commander-in-chief her confidence and devotion. She was happy that he celebrated the feast of St John Nepomucene in Prague on her birthday and that he remained safe even after Frederick penetrated Bohemia shortly afterwards, on 5 July.

Although, once again, Prussia was the aggressor, Frederick had improved the art of public relations in war and it was not difficult for

Prussian envoys to portray the monarchy as Goliath and the Prussian kingdom as David. This inhibited Austrian military strategy which Lacy insisted had to be 'purely defensive'.

Into this stalemate Maria Theresa now decided to intervene through a secret intermediary with her arch-enemy. She dispatched none other than the young orphan who had rowed her across the Danube a decade earlier, Thugut, to make contact with Frederick.

Maria Theresa's trust and confidence in the young man had reaped many rewards for both patron and protégé. After schooling at the Oriental Academy where he had frequently come top of all the language exams, Thugut had been dispatched to Constantinople and proved himself to be a canny diplomat in the service of the Austrian state. Maria Theresa knew she could trust him completely and that his abilities, in an emergency such as the one the monarchy now faced, could be indispensable.

Thugut, disguised in the green uniform of a high-ranking Russian diplomat – he spoke the language well – made his way into Bohemia. In his dispatch box he carried a peace plan which not only compromised on Austrian claims to Bavaria but vouchsafed Ansbach and Bayreuth to Prussia. Although advised by Kaunitz, the proposal was advanced as a 'personal offer' of the Empress. The presence of Thugut, whose loyalty to the Empress could not be questioned, invested the proposal with unique authority.

Thugut also bore with him a 'covering' letter, written in the Empress's own hand, in which she spoke of her maternal anxiety for Joseph and his brother and brother-in-law, Max Franz and Albert, who were both serving with the army. Most persuasively of all, she confided to Frederick that she was writing without the Emperor's knowledge.[7]

In the meantime, Joseph, with that volatility of personality which made him so difficult to deal with, had, after a brief spell of campaigning, executed a 180-degree turn in his views on war: 'It is certain that war is a horrible thing. The evils that it leads to are frightful and it is much worse than I had visualized.'

Joseph's contrition was accompanied by a solemn declaration of filial loyalty: 'Dear Mother, rest assured that I shall redouble my efforts to serve you . . . how happy I am to have such a sovereign and mother . . . I see again the great, the incomparable Maria Theresa.'

Unfortunately, these words of unhesitating obedience did not survive contact with news three days later of Thugut's mission. Joseph erupted in anger bordering on hysteria: 'The King of Prussia is certain to make unacceptable propositions . . . I declare I find Thugut's mission as injurious as possible . . .'

Joseph's ego was wounded, above all, by the thought that negotiations were taking place behind his back: 'The honour of the Monarchy and both our reputations are compromised by this move,' he concluded, adding that he would have no choice but to withdraw into Italy, avoiding the embarrassment of passing through Vienna where he would be 'compelled to make a public demonstration pointing out Your Majesty's personal weakness'.[8]

Thugut, with his intuitive brilliance, would have recognized that his career was unlikely to flourish under his future sovereign as a result of this action, but he was nothing if not steadfast in his loyalty towards the sovereign who had rescued him from poverty, oblivion and insignificance. When, at her urging, he attempted to visit Joseph, the Emperor refused to even receive him. In a blind rage, he wrote to his mother threatening to retreat beyond Prague and leave Bohemia again to the tender mercies of marauding Prussian troops.

Maria Theresa's response to this thinly veiled threat was magisterial and, drawing on her experience as *Mater Castrorum* in earlier years, she could not resist pointing out that she had never had so many troops at her disposition as Joseph now commanded in Bohemia. 'That at least restores the reputation of Charles of Lorraine and Daun who were accused of lacking an adventurous spirit. At least they held things together.'[9]

Maria Theresa redoubled her efforts with Frederick and the Thugut mission was repeated, this time with carefully marked maps indicating the areas Austria would relinquish any claims to. But Frederick rejected the overture, telling his brother that it looked as if they would have to 'beat the Austrian swine' on the field of battle to bring them to a more reasonable frame of mind.

But the Prussian army, for all the fear it instilled in Joseph, was in a bad way as the summer progressed. Illness and a lack of supplies sapped their morale as the soldiers were reduced to digging out potatoes from the fields with their bayonets in order to find food to live off.

By the end of September, this *Kartoffelkrieg* had still brought not a single meaningful clash and the Prussian forces evacuated Bohemia. Lacy's defensive strategy had intimidated the Prussians into refusing any frontal or flank assault. But there was, in keeping with Austrian military tradition, no vigorous pursuit of the retreating Prussians. Lacy, like Daun, was nothing if not a master of the Austrian art of preserving one's forces as intact as possible in order to fight and defend the monarchy at some future point.

Peace negotiations dragged on. The chemistry between Thugut and Joseph was so poor, Maria Theresa felt compelled to find a new intermediary, Count Rosenberg. A 'scarcely honourable' peace was devised in which Austria abandoned all claims to Bavaria. A war without battles had failed to advance the Emperor's claims and in the end the failure to test the Austrian army against the Prussians inevitably spelt doom for Joseph's designs.

War, as Maria Theresa was fond of pointing out, always was unpredictable. Her reluctance to wage a war undoubtedly infected her generals. Even the courageous victor of Kunersdorf, Loudon, failed to display his legendary aggression. He, like Lacy, was all too aware that Maria Theresa disapproved of the war. In Joseph they found a commander-in-chief who was unpredictable, egotistical and often completely unrealistic in his expectations of what war could achieve. Everything about the campaign suggests that Maria Theresa's priority, after her initial enthusiasm, was to preserve the empire and her inheritance and not risk it in some irrelevant adventure. Her generals owed their allegiance to their Emperor but their careers had been made under her suzerainty and their default response to her wishes had always been to seek her favour.

Joseph may have suspected this interference, but he seems genuinely to have been so caught up in the novelty of war that his focus on his mother's interference could only limit itself to the vagaries of the ill-starred Thugut mission.

Once hostilities began, Maria Theresa reasserted her latent absolute power and her generals knew all too well that the safety of her son was valued far above his honour or skill as a soldier. It was a humiliation for the commander-in-chief and ultimately it destroyed the last vestiges of trust in the relationship between Maria Theresa and her son.

Externally, however, Maria Theresa's approach to Frederick through Thugut began the process of restoring the monarchy's international position. As soon as the details of the negotiation and the fact that Austria was prepared to relinquish all claims to Bavaria became known, the monarchy's standing dramatically improved. Prussia's refusal to abandon her claims on Ansbach and Bayreuth as a quid pro quo now appeared rapacious. Austria's apparent disinterestedness removed any threat of Russian support for Frederick.

From the acceptance of mediation in late November 1778, it took almost six months to secure a lasting settlement in March at Teschen. Austria secured a small strip of land, east of the Inn, to be incorporated into Upper Austria as the *Innviertel*, a term devised by Joseph which has remained to this day its Austrian name. Prussia was acknowledged heir to Ansbach and Bayreuth.

Both Austria and Prussia appeared to have lost but in fact gained. The Austrian Treasury had expended a million florins on the campaign but the monarchy was preserved and the gain of the Innviertel distracted from any thought of humiliation. This was the only example during Maria Theresa's reign of any accretion of territory within the *Reich*. Joseph visited the province in the autumn of 1779. He found the frontiers unsatisfactory and his stay at the gloomy Burg at Wildshut was uncomfortable. But, as he told his mother afterwards: 'When one considers what might perhaps have come to pass, it is a petty thing, but in itself, this morsel is satisfactory, and very convenient for Upper Austria.'[10]

Maria Theresa by then had less than two years to live. She was overjoyed at the treaty and experienced huge relief that the threat of war had been lifted. It even brought about a kind of reconciliation with 'the Monster', as she had always referred to Frederick.

'I am overjoyed. Everybody knows that I have no partiality for Frederick but I have to do him justice now and recognize that he has acted nobly. He has promised to make peace on reasonable conditions and he has kept his word.'[11]

In this way Maria Theresa, in the sunset period of her life, mended fences with old deadly enemies while increasingly alienating her son, Joseph. Perhaps their characters were too similar: both were emotional and prone to outbursts. Yet their outlooks were too different. They occupied not only different generations but also different worlds. The Bavarian War of Succession had highlighted Joseph's mercurial nature but it had also underlined his mother's grip on power even as increasingly she sought refuge in contemplation and memory.

The *Kaiserin, Wittib* (Empress dowager) remained, despite all her mourning and prayer, fully informed of all the affairs of state. Yet the more she prayed, the more the tensions with Joseph increased.

CHAPTER 20

Kaiserin, Wittib: The Mourning Empress and the Struggle for Constancy

NO-ONE COULD DENY that Maria Theresa's mourning for her late husband Francis Stephen was anything but sincere. She allowed her beautiful hair to be cut and for three days after his death saw no-one but her children. Thenceforth, she wore mourning and black for the rest of her life. All her ballgowns and coloured dresses she gave to her ladies-in-waiting.

That in her moments of prayer and meditation she often recalled her days with Francis Stephen is attested to in a note written into the margin of her prayer book. It simply recorded: '29 years, 6 months and 6 days = 258,744 hours of happiness.'[1] This was the length of time she had been married to her 'Mäuserl'. Whatever his infidelities and other weaknesses, however jealous and explosively resentful she became towards some of his lovers, with every day that passed after his death, the years of their union assumed an almost mystical quality.

A life in which prayer and statecraft are the daily twin foundations is perhaps hard in the twenty-first century to imagine. Yet an earlier generation would have had no problem entertaining the combination in the most unlikely of political environments. Even as late as the 1980s, the immensely influential Italian statesman and seven-times Prime Minister of Italy, Giulio Andreotti, not only began each day with an early-morning Mass but also regularly received the sacrament of confession.

We have seen how the misguided War of Bavarian Succession brought out, on the one hand, the most lovingly matriarchal, but on the other, the most devious behaviour with regard to Joseph. Age, piety and experience of war and government gave Maria Theresa arguably more wisdom than she had ever possessed. In military affairs she could out-argue both Loudon and Lacy. In diplomatic affairs she could see through all the weaving and spinning of Kaunitz's ill-fated webs. In her advice to her children she turned a bank of human experience into a virtual manual for royal adult responsibility.[2]

Her judgement of men and matters had become a byword for understanding and wisdom. Had not the education lavished on her protégé Thugut shown that all posts in her monarchy were open to talent? But all this accumulated wisdom in old age failed to light the spark of religious tolerance. The *Kaiserin, Wittib* certainly prayed more but the prayers did not broaden Maria Theresa's theological thinking. Toleration of Jews and Protestants had been permitted by the Empress as an exception born of commercial necessity with regard to the Free Port of Trieste. But Trieste was miles away from Vienna, far beyond – until the railway was constructed a century later – the then remote Styrian and Karawanken Alps. A similar dispensation affected Hungary and Transylvania and the Military Frontier where many faiths coexisted happily for the benefit of the monarchy, but when it came to dealing with religious toleration nearer to home, notably in Bohemia, the Empress's pragmatism became rather frayed.

In Vienna, she was aways prepared to treat Protestant envoys with the greatest of politesse. The same courtesy was extended to the Ottoman representatives of the Porte. Protestant worship was permitted in the embassies of the maritime powers and, true to her theological training, any Protestant who converted to Catholicism was treated with precisely the same confessional intimacy as any Catholic born to the faith. Haugwitz, Zinzendorf and others all benefited from this. Some Protestants who served her well – Baron Bruckenthal, for example, in Transylvania – were ennobled and encouraged. Yet, as she daily lost herself more and more in prayer and as the struggle for power with her son took up more and more of her energy, she appears to have become more rigid in her interpretation of Catholic dogma and more and more determined to make her lands as secure in the faith as possible.

This did not mean any increased subservience to Rome and the Vatican, but it did lead to a belief that it was her sacred duty as a Catholic monarch to help reform the Church in order to make her possessions more rather than less Catholic. This inevitably made her encourage Catholicism to the detriment of other religions. Although often accused of being virulently anti-Semitic, it is likely that her anti-Semitism was social as well as ideological. True, she described Jews as 'a public plague' but, as we have seen, her experience of their disloyalty towards the dynasty when the French occupied Prague left bitter memories for her.[3] Yet, like most Habsburg sovereigns from the time of the Great Siege of Vienna, she was dependent financially on Jewish money-lenders with whom she regularly met, although usually separated by a silk screen. She did not, however, have the blanket detestation of them as a race that has sometimes been ascribed to her and she gave written permission frequently for Jews to settle in Vienna. To Jews such as Joseph Sonnenfels, who had converted to Catholicism as a child, she extended the warmest of feelings. Moreover, her treatment of the Jews of Trieste was exceptionally benign (see Chapter 25).

Where, however, a rival religion threatened the integrity of her lands, she moved swiftly and ruthlessly to suppress it. Of the central Catholic lands of the monarchy, Bohemia and Moravia still contained significant numbers of Protestants, despite the aftermath of the Battle of the White Mountain and the Counter-Reformation.

It was a tribute perhaps to Maria Theresa's great ancestor Rudolf II's policies of inclusion in Bohemia that the remnants of Protestantism survived clandestinely at first and then increasingly openly. By the 1770s there was a widespread 'revival' of Protestantism, especially in Moravia. In 1777 Catholic 'missionaries' arriving in a remote part of the province found there were more than 10,000 of these 'heretics'. When news of their existence reached Vienna, the Empress was appalled.

At the same time, coercion, as practised in the 1730s before her accession to the throne, was out of the question. The forced emigration by Archbishop Firmian in 1721 of the entire Protestant population of Salzburg could not be repeated on the grounds of justice and humanity as well as practicality. Expelling thousands of hard-working subjects or even uprooting them to the far-flung corners of the empire exacted an economic cost which was totally unacceptable. Religious toleration was umbilically bound to the financial requirements of the empire and, following the costly Bavarian War of Succession, these were urgent demands.

Yet the emergence of the truth concerning the religious persuasion of so many Moravians, barely half an hour's ride from Vienna, could not but have consequences in an area which controlled one of the major invasion routes from Prussia to Austria and whose strategic importance was therefore far from negligible. Moravia was 'Vienna's back garden'.

Joseph was in France visiting his sister Marie Antoinette and attempting – only to be frustrated by the British envoy in Paris – to meet up with Benjamin Franklin.[4] Kaunitz was apprised of the Empress's distress but could only counsel improvements in the local Catholic clergy who had clearly failed to carry their nominal parishioners with them.

In times past, a few more Jesuits would have been dispatched and within a decade Protestantism would have been most probably overshadowed by *deus ex machina* methods, but the Jesuits were collectively no more and their military order had been disbanded. The entire baroque Counter-Reformation had in any case been overtaken by the Enlightenment practised by Maria Theresa's chief advisers and above all her son. Joseph wrote from France to his mother: 'As long as the state is served, the laws of nature and society observed and your Supreme Being is in no way dishonoured but actually respected and adored what grounds can there be for interference . . . there must be either complete freedom of worship or you must logically expatriate everyone who does not believe as you do . . .'[5]

The movement for Church reform extended well beyond court circles. Baroque piety, expressed by the final flourishes of rococo design as Maria Theresa's reign drew to a close, was about to be replaced by the penitential austerities implied by the severe neo-classicism of Canova. As the art historian the late Anthony Blunt was fond of observing, if the aim of every baroque architect was first and foremost to induce a 'feeling of astonishment at the divine', the straight lines of the classical tradition imposed an unemotional, cool, 'calm reflection'.[6]

The failure of the local clergy needed to be remedied. The reason for the mass 'Apostasy' lay in the decayed state of the Moravian Catholic Church which had been practically untouched by the reforms of Trent. The Empress, with her customary vigour, set about rectifying this state of affairs immediately. Reforms were promulgated. A new diocese was created around Brünn (Brno) and forty new churches were constructed.

A theological commission consisting of a most enlightened priest, Leopold Hay, the brother-in-law of Joseph Sonnenfels, and two other reform-minded Catholics, was dispatched to report back to her on conditions within 'her' church. On 14 November 1777, she agreed to tolerate tacitly the Moravian Protestants although legislation discriminating against their holding public office and participating in certain trades was maintained while the commission pursued its work.

The commission quickly discovered that disillusionment with Catholicism was so widespread in Moravia that only radical steps would be able to halt the rot. If the Catholic Church was to be made more attractive to the Moravians then they would need a better education about their faith, delivered by priests of calibre and intellectual rigour. Once again, the suppression of the Jesuits deprived the monarchy of a well-tried weapon capable of re-educating both clergy and parishioners. Nevertheless, Hay's reforms attempted to instil in the clergy a need to relinquish all extreme fanaticism and argument and concentrate instead on charity and clemency. Hay went so far as to recommend to Maria Theresa that Protestants be allowed to build their own churches – they had hitherto worshipped only in private houses. He saw that a degree of legitimization would remove at a stroke the attraction of semi-secret worship and force the Protestants to compete openly with the established Church.

Much has been made of Maria Theresa's virtual deathbed denunciation of this suggestion as 'evil' but it was the Cardinal-Archbishop of Vienna who convinced the Empress to take such a hard line. Her exchanges with the dogmatic Papal Nuncio, Cardinal Migazzi, who pushed the Austrian primate in this direction, demonstrate that she was very far from surrendering her pragmatism in this debate, and loath to fall into line with the Vatican's paranoia with regard to the subject.

For Cardinal Migazzi, any non-Catholics were insufferable criminals who threatened the very existence of the Church. Maria Theresa held altogether more enlightened views than these, although in her declining weeks she held a dogmatic line more rigidly as she felt everything slipping inexorably away from her.

'What is the point of possessing the true religion if you value and love it so little that you consider it unimportant to maintain it and strengthen it,' she wrote, adding, 'I do not notice such indifference among any of the Protestants.'[7]

Even as she faced death with all the piety and courage her upbringing had imparted to her, Maria Theresa refused to countenance harsh measures against the Moravian Protestants. 'Certainly, no spirit of persecution but still more no indifference or systemic toleration.' That 'systemic toleration' led only to 'imaginary freedom which can never exist and which results in licence and total confusion'.[8]

As Joseph was fond of pointing out to Maria Theresa, her understanding of the word 'toleration' was too wide, and she confused the spiritual with the temporal. 'Toleration for me means only that in purely temporal matters', he wrote. Maria Theresa certainly agreed that she did not wish to emulate the intolerance of Protestant states and the conservatism of republics compared with monarchies.

When the Moravian Protestants began to block access to the newly constructed Catholic churches, Maria Theresa felt compelled to accept the *Staatsrat*'s advice to send in the army, take more punitive measures and round up the ringleaders. Few decisions of the Empress revealed more painfully her ebbing judgement as she approached the end.

Joseph was furious and another heated exchange occurred with his mother: 'Can anything imagined be more absurd than the content of these orders? Do you really think you can convert people by enforced conscription, sending them to the mines or public works?'[9]

The reactionary Migazzi could only rejoice in a policy which, in Joseph's words, was 'unjust, impious, harmful, impossible and ridiculous' but it also sat uneasily with the theological commission of Leopold Hay which Maria Theresa herself had ordered. Kaunitz, too, saw the dangers of such an extreme policy and now persuaded the Empress to row back from such harsh measures.

Arguing with his usual logic, he advanced the view that a lay ruler had no business interfering in matters of conscience. Forcible conversion was entirely incompatible with the teachings of the New Testament. From a practical point of view, resettlement was costly and inhumane, the separation of children from exiled parents a slur on the *Milde und Munifizenz* of the Empress's reign, and the loss of valuable skills precipitated by such a dislocation so costly to the empire.

Maria Theresa was not sufficiently disorientated not to see the sense of her trusted adviser's words. Eventually she agreed and the Protestants were left in peace to be encouraged by the example of their Catholic neighbours and the reforms of the Church. In time, many would be reclaimed by the Catholic Church. This minor example of toleration was significant and would form the basis of all that Joseph a few years later introduced with his Patent of Toleration. Predictably, Kaunitz's wise words were met with angry opposition from both the *Staatsrat* and the Papal Nuncio but Kaunitz was too wily an operator to allow such criticism to deflect him. He had formally no *locus standi* in the Austro-Bohemian *Staatskanzlei* but, on 14 November 1777, he embodied all his recommendations in a secret instruction to the Moravian government.

A year later, a further act approved by Maria Theresa also foresaw future reform. The port of Trieste had been given Free Port status by her father Charles VI who, as we have seen, relished the Spanish maritime trading opportunities which his Habsburg forefathers had so brilliantly exploited. Trieste under Maria Theresa had seen the construction and the development of a new commercial district, to this day known as the *Borgo Teresiano*. A special dispensation had allowed Jews and Greeks as well as Serbs and Dalmatians to live and work in the city free from petty religious discrimination. In 1778 Maria Theresa approved a proposal that a Protestant church be constructed for the Lutheran merchants operating in the city. This set a happy precedent and one the Moravian Protestants were eager to exploit.

On 13 May 1780 some five thousand Moravian Protestants gathered to celebrate the Empress's birthday and then held a service of thanksgiving. Unfortunately, the preacher and some other leaders were arrested by over-zealous local officials. In one of her final acts as Empress, Maria Theresa insisted their hardship was mitigated by a gift of a hundred Gulden for each family from her own purse.

Here was the typical pragmatism of an experienced ruler, wary of trends, fashion and sudden changes of direction. Everything about the tragicomedy of the Moravian Protestants reveals a completely Theresian approach to the burning issues of the time. Taking advice from all sides, a resolute course of action was adopted which, when superior advice pointed to its failings, was reversed.

While Maria Theresa never reached the point of advocating the 'full-blown toleration of the modern state' it is a mistake to brand her as 'reactionary', as she did not block measures which led in that direction.

She developed a statecraft which, right up until the end of her life, bore the hallmarks of her intuitive pragmatism. The great crisis which had attended her accession in 1740 had taught her many things. Above all, it had taught her the precariousness of imperial structures. If, in her view, change was to be effective, it had to be carefully prepared and, where possible, promoted by consensus, and where not possible advanced by persuasion. Surrounded by men completely at ease in abstract thought and articulate exposition, she had that sharpness, almost simplicity of perception which in a later age has become associated with dyslexia.[10]

Maria Theresa's detractors fall regularly into the trap of judging her by the intellectual standards of her most brilliant advisers. Yet, as Maria Theresa learnt as a child, knowledge is not wisdom and wisdom is not understanding. From a practical point of view, this outlook represented a firm conviction that change was not to be feared but always needed to be managed.

The Moravian Protestant controversy turned out to be the last major confessional distraction in Maria Theresa's reign. As she grew weaker during the summer of 1780, she busied herself with the affairs of her children, urging Marie Antoinette to share her husband's bed so that she 'could live in the German way and enjoy that certain intimacy which comes of being together'. Increasingly, she spent more and more time in prayer, sensing her time on this earth was drawing to a close.

In a letter to her son Leopold, she noted that she had withdrawn almost entirely from public affairs and was virtually in seclusion, disinterested and unapproachable, 'constantly engaged in her devotions and prayers'. No doubt her prayers would have included, as they would for all those reared in the faith, the plea for a *bona mors*, a good or easy death.

This wish was granted when, after watching a shoot at Schönbrunn, she caught a fatal chill after some minutes in the pouring rain of a sudden thunderstorm. Until then her physical energy had appeared undimmed despite her increasing immobility and isolation. Joseph, like many offspring of a strong formidable matriarch, believed his mother to be indestructible and confidently predicted she would live for some years yet, but her body had become increasingly an affliction, with breathing ever more difficult.

She continued to work, as much as she could, at her desk, but she developed a light fever which was followed by fits of coughing. She insisted that she was perfectly well but those around her saw the deterioration and alerted her favourite daughter Marie Christine and Albert to come from Pressburg. When they arrived on 24 November, they found many things had changed and that the Empress's physical condition was much weakened. Only the force of her willpower seemed to enable her to get out of bed. Joseph, ever suspicious, wondered if his mother's physician had simply exaggerated her condition to satisfy his own personal ambitions.

A day later, on 25 November, Maria Theresa summoned her confessor without telling her children. She was talking in her sleep and coughing fits arose more frequently. Yet she could still talk to her children and attend state banquets. She appears to have agreed with Joseph that the last rites were still unnecessary while she could receive Communion but, on the night of the 26th, Joseph, having spent the evening in her antechamber, heard her terrible coughing. When on 26 November the Empress coolly informed Joseph that she had asked for the last rites to be administered to her, even he was shocked into reality.

He began to 'lose all hope' and the following day news that the Empress was dying was made public. The Lord Chamberlain announced that, as a result of Her Imperial Majesty's serious illness, 'grave consequences were to be expected'. Throughout the monarchy as the news spread, prayers were offered up in churches, monasteries and convents. The Blessed Sacrament was exposed and novenas for the soul of the Empress offered. All public theatres were closed. Finally on 28 November, she received the sacrament of Extreme Unction and Viaticum in the company of most of her children.

Thanks to her devoted and devout daughter, Marianne, we have the following account of what followed:

> when the ceremony was over we all stood up and left her with her confessor. After a quarter of an hour, she bade us all to enter; the emperor, Maximilian, Marie, Albert, Elisabeth and I sat in a circle around her chair and she addressed us without any change in the

timbre of her voice for about fifteen minutes. She commended us to the emperor, thanked us for our love of her and said the most touching things . . . even as we all dissolved in tears she retained her composure . . . the emperor wanted to answer her but he broke down sobbing and knelt before her. She gave him her blessing, he kissed her hand, she kissed him . . . finally she looked at us and said, 'Away with you, it costs me too much to see you like this.'[11]

But the end was still to come. Marianne and the Emperor saw her again. The Empress showed no signs of fear or of a troubled conscience. At five o'clock in the morning of 29 November she held one final conference with all the children. In the words of the official protocol: 'She turned to Joseph, the heir to the throne and appointed him father over them. Finally, she sent her daughters away as she did not want us to see her die.'

Joseph, Maximilian, Albert and her physician, Anton von Störck, remained with her and she continued to refuse to fall asleep: 'How can I wish to sleep when I may be called before my judge at any moment. I fear sleep as I do not wish to be taken by surprise. I want to see death coming.' No doubt, the Empress would have been made aware from an early age by her Jesuit teachers of the words of her namesake, Theresa of Avila: 'I want to see God and in order to do so I must first die.'[12]

A few minutes before nine o'clock, she got up suddenly from her chair and tottered towards a sofa before collapsing. As she was helped up, Joseph, seeing her sitting uncomfortably, rushed to bring her some more cushions, saying, 'Your Majesty is uncomfortable' (*Majestät liegt schlecht*). Maria Theresa's reply was terse: 'Comfortable enough to die' (*Gut genug zum sterben*). A few moments later she was dead. It was a death Maria Theresa had always prayed for and certainly 'nothing became her more in this world than her style of leaving it'.[13]

This, at least, was Marianne's account and none of the other records contradict it in its essentials. The Great Empress had died a 'true Christian heroine'. The last days had brought a final harmony into the relations between mother and son. Joseph spent days at her side, watched over her at night, and performed all the temporal and spiritual obligations with a perfection that was commendable and that could serve as a model for any son. A calm, composed, resigned death was a sign of God's grace, the *bona mors*.

For the members of her family who could not be with her the news was received with various outpourings of public grief. Leopold in Tuscany, Marie Antoinette in Paris – both publicly wept. In Vienna, hardened Hungarian grenadiers openly shed tears for the death of their 'King'. A veritable cascade of odes and funeral eulogies flooded the German-speaking world. A period of official court mourning was prescribed throughout Europe. In accordance with Habsburg tradition, the imperial body was embalmed and the heart removed. The body was laid out in the Augustinerkirche rather than the Hofburg and Joseph, in the first of many actions which reversed his mother's wishes, allowed members of the imperial family to pay homage to her corpse.

He lost no time in striking the new notes of his reign and within twenty-four hours he had ordered the doors to Schönbrunn palace to be nailed shut, banned courtiers from genuflecting and kissing his hand and generally began that era of 'Enlightenment terror' which was greeted by some contemporaries as the 'year of salvation' and others as the tragic end of the era of *Milde und Munifizenz*.

PART III (i)

THE LEGACY:
POLITICS AND TRADE

CHAPTER 21

The Mother (I): The Daughters

MARIA THERESA'S UNION WITH Francis Stephen of Lorraine brought, as well as a welter of internal reform and external armed conflict, no fewer than sixteen pregnancies. Of the eleven daughters and five sons, ten survived into adulthood. It was undoubtedly a substantial achievement but one which reflected the risks and dangers inherent in dynastic marriages at that time. It also symbolized the strength and fecundity of the dynasty. A profusion of children was seen as a sign of power across all strata of society. If it allowed for skill across the dynastic chessboard for the highest in the land, it also permitted a supply of human material for the poorest who could on Sundays parade in their best clothing, however threadbare, as they entered church and show, like the pipes of a baroque organ, their encompassing of a natural order in which youth deferred to age, supporting it as the burdens of physical decrepitude advanced. A large family offered the *Volk* a common bond of physical empathy between ruler and ruled which, at arguably the most demanding moments of any woman's life, childbirth, was a shared experience. It brought not just a mystical union between divine and earthly but practical insight into the stresses and pains of pregnancy which was shared by all, irrespective of their place in the social hierarchy of the monarchy.

Unlike earlier, and indeed later, unions between Habsburg sovereigns, there was no obvious risk from inbreeding in Maria Theresa's marriage to Francis Stephen; they were at best distant cousins and their degrees of relationship would have satisfied any pioneers of eugenics, but this did not eliminate other risks.

The first and eldest child was Maria Elisabeth, a sickly child who died aged three in 1740. The second child was Maria Anna (Marianne), who appears to have had an extreme form of scoliosis which made her considered unsuitable for marriage, not least on account of the restriction imposed by the condition on childbirth.

Marianne would live well into old age and accompany her mother right up to the latter's death in 1780. Thereafter, she retired to a convent in Carinthia where she lived as abbess until her death in 1789, leaving her considerable estate to the convent.

A third daughter, Maria Caroline, died in infancy and it was thus with much rejoicing that she was followed by a son, Joseph, in 1741. The next birth was particularly happy, too, and Marie Christine (1742–1798) would become Maria Theresa's favourite child. Pretty, gifted and of an artistic temperament, she was destined to marry Albert of Saxony-Teschen and was said to be the only one of Maria Theresa's children to be allowed to marry for love rather than interests of high politics. Her favoured position with her mother made her inevitably somewhat resented by her siblings who felt often that she 'could never do anything wrong'. Even after her death, caused by drinking unclean water, she bequeathed to Vienna's Augustinian church unique riches in the form of Canova's arguably finest neo-classical funerary monument.[1]

Marie Christine (Maria Christina) was the fifth child and was from the moment of her birth auspicious. She was born on 13 May, the same day as her mother's birthday, and was encouraged from infancy to share the Taurean qualities of the Empress. These included constancy, an overriding sense of duty, and faultless conscientiousness. All these qualities, either on account of her astrological good fortune or on account of other myriad circumstances, Marie Christine inherited from her mother and quickly manifested. As has been pointed out, Marie Christine was the only child of the Great Empress whom she appears never to have criticized in her writings. She quickly established her ascendancy over her siblings and charmed by her general vivacity everyone who came into contact with her at court. She also inherited her mother's good ear for music and languages. Unlike her mother, however, she was prepared to give discreet vent to her sexual impulses long before she was married. A brief affair with the rather unsuitable and 'fast' Prince Louis of Württemberg might have got out of hand had Maria Theresa not moved swiftly to ban the libertine from court. More passionate still appears to have been Joseph's first wife Isabella of Parma's infatuation with Marie Christine. More than two hundred letters have survived from Isabella to the young archduchess and they underline a powerful affection for her sister-in-law. Both were highly musical and played duets together on most days up until Isabella's tragically early death at the age of 22. Interestingly, Marie Christine's letters to her sister-in-law have not survived other than a rather indifferent character sketch of the melancholic sensitive princess.

It was Maria Theresa's husband's wish that the beautiful and talented Marie Christine marry the son of his sister, the Queen of Sardinia, Benedetto of Chablais. But in 1760, Prince Albert of Saxony arrived at the Viennese court to fight in the Seven Years War. Albert was the sixth son of the Elector of Saxony and King of Poland. He was smitten immediately when he saw Marie Christine performing at a chamber concert but the Saxon prince was impoverished and his prospects were dim, to say the least. He had not the slightest chance of inheriting either Saxony or Poland. As a suitor for the lovely Marie Christine, he was entirely inappropriate, at least in the eyes of Francis Stephen.

But for reasons still debated to this day, Maria Theresa was determined this favourite child of hers marry, like she had, for love, not dynastic aggrandizement. For five years she secretly supported Albert and when, in 1765, Francis Stephen suddenly died, Kaunitz was instructed to end the negotiations with Chablais and refocus on Marie Christine's upcoming betrothal to Albert. This was all testament to Maria Theresa's affection for her favourite child. She was impressed by Albert even if he was impoverished. He was handsome, in a Germanic kind of way, *anständig* (reliable), kind and brave. She perhaps feared that her daughter's strength of character might cause immense turbulence were this match not to be blessed, but Maria Theresa openly conceded that it was not a union in accordance with the finest points of statecraft but almost a 'beggars' wedding'.

To ensure that it would nonetheless not be any such thing, the Empress ordered an exception to be made to the prevailing marital law which ordered a wife to take on her husband's marital status. By the terms of the marriage contract of 5 April 1765, drafted by Kaunitz, the bride's privileges of birth and titles were all preserved in the union. A generous endowment, more than 666,000 guilders, so vast it was deemed necessary to conceal its extent from her siblings, was settled on Marie Christine. In addition, she received a dowry of 100,000 guilders, the rich estates of Altenburg and Mannersdorf as well as the usual silver, porcelain and silks provided for any newly wedded imperial couple. The endowment was an exceptional gift and, as has been pointed out, amounted to half the size of the funds allotted to all the rest of Maria Theresa's children combined.

A fine palace, once in the ownership of Tarouca's family, at the edge of the Hofburg complex in Vienna, was put at the disposal of the couple and, in time, became the home of the finest drawings collection in Europe, named, to this day, the Albertina, after the fortunate prince.

The newly-weds seemed to remind Maria Theresa of the happiest days of her early married life and she showered titles and privileges on Albert so that he would not for a moment feel inferior in status to his imperial bride. The dukedom of Teschen, the governorship of Hungary, the future governorship of the Netherlands: the gifts were generous. The close bonds between the Saxon royal family and the Habsburgs, which would prove so powerful a hundred years later in the Austro-Prussian war, were cemented in gold and diamonds in this union.

Inevitably, the favouritism displayed was jealously resented and became the subject of much diplomatic gossip. Certainly, the Empress appeared to be impervious to any criticism of her daughter and the fact that she was, in the eyes of all her other children, ruthlessly being exploited by Marie Christine does not seem to have diminished her joy at the match between Albert and Marie Christine: 'It so gladdens my heart to see the married couple together . . . if anything at all can still give me joy, they remind me of my former pleasures.'

After Marie Christine came Maria Elisabeth, who enjoyed a dazzling beginning in which her infant manners made her the 'most *angenehm* of companions'.[2] Later, she became rather melancholy and cantankerous, remaining unmarried up to her death in 1808 and retiring to a convent in Innsbruck. A fierce bout of smallpox had disfigured her once pristine looks and made her unattractive. The Tyroleans dubbed her 'die kropferte Liesl' (neckful Liz).

The next child, Karl Joseph, was by all accounts highly charming and less introspective than his elder brother but smallpox carried him away by the time he was 16. Maria Amalia was born in 1746 and was compelled as part of the Habsburg–Bourbon rapprochement to marry the Duke of Parma. A natural rebel, she never forgave her mother for denying her a love match with her preferred lover, the Duke of Zweibrücken. Her adolescence was marked by the rapidity with which she reduced her governesses to tears. But her singing voice and charm captivated foreign dignitaries even if such talents left her mother less impressed. Amalia was, as we shall see, a handful; she hated the French and was four years older than her chosen husband.

The next child was a boy, Peter Leopold, later Emperor Leopold II. He was granted the Duchy of Tuscany which, the reader might recall, had been given to Francis Stephen in exchange for his surrendering Lorraine.

The next two daughters, Maria Caroline and Johanna, both died young. The next daughter, Josepha, had been contracted to marry the Neapolitan crown prince. With her death at the age of 16, her place was taken by the next daughter, also named Maria Caroline (Maria Carolina).

Maria Carolina was perhaps the most impressive of all Maria Theresa's daughters. As Queen of Naples, she even outdid her mother's formidable series of births by having eighteen confinements. Like her mother she was forceful but pragmatic. She remained a devout Catholic throughout her life but encouraged and even subsidized out of her own pocket several Masonic lodges in Naples.

Then came Ferdinand Karl Anton who founded the Habsburg d'Este collateral branch of the family when he married the heiress to the Duchy of Modena. By all accounts a grey personality with none of the easy quick-wittedness of his brothers, he died in 1806.

Finally came the two youngest. The first, Maria Antonia, better known after her marriage to the Dauphin of France as Marie Antoinette, was destined for martyrdom and eternal fame. The youngest, Maximilian Franz, became Elector of Cologne. As his health was never very robust, he entered holy orders in order to rise to the archbishopric, one of the most important as it carried the right of a vote in the election of the Holy Roman Emperor.

Maria Antonia has come down to our generation, despite the best efforts of Antonia Fraser and Sofia Coppola, as a byword for frivolity, superficiality and extravagance. Stefan Zweig painted a slightly different picture and the Rosminian priest Father Jean-Marie Charles-Roux, son of an eminent French diplomat, in his weekly sermons at the parish of Ely Place in London in the 1990s, portrayed her in terms of hushed reverence compatible with martyrdom and sanctity.

Indisputable is the fact that Maria Antonia was supposed to provide the sealing glory to Kaunitz's great *Renversement des Alliances* and, by marrying the future King of France, was destined to preside over the culmination of Kaunitz's crowning achievement. This pressure to succeed in this duty towards her House was inescapable and imposed protocols, sacrifices and innumerous demands on a young teenage girl.

That Maria Antonia was charming was attested to in the eyewitness accounts of countless contemporaries. That she was quick-witted, intelligent and beautiful is less well known. After a slow start (her early education dwelt predictably on theological verities), she was given a crash course in French and encouraged to perfect her considerable equestrian skills. Her marriage was contracted on her eleventh birthday and she was married by the time she was nineteen.

By then, her reputation for fecklessness was beginning to emerge in anti-Austrian circles in Paris who disapproved of the marriage and the implications of an alliance with the Habsburgs. These circles detested the House of Austria and all for which it stood. France's model of empire, of government and of intellectual and religious life was diametrically opposed in their eyes to everything for which Vienna stood. Marie Antoinette, as she now was known, was an easy tool to exploit in their chiselling away at the daily 'humiliation' which alliance with Austria implied.

Maria Theresa certainly felt great responsibility for her youngest daughter and a sense of guilt that her preparation for the throne of France had been very inadequate.

In the remaining weeks before Maria Antonia set out for Paris, Maria Theresa insisted that she stay with her overnight in her own private apartments so that she could at every moment take the opportunity to correct her daughter on issues of extravagance, mental flightiness and empty-headedness. The rebukes were frequent but Maria Theresa quickly learnt that whatever qualities Maria Antonia might have enjoyed, an ability to concentrate was not one of them. Nonetheless, the letter she gave her on her departure was far longer and far more explicit than any she ever wrote to her other daughters. The length reflected Maria Theresa's anxieties but also the realization that it was already too late to expect her daughter's character to change. She made her daughter swear solemnly to read it diligently every month.

Maria Theresa's worries are clearly articulated in another letter to the Austrian ambassador at Versailles, Count Florimonde Mercy d'Argenteau: 'I am apprehensive about my daughter's youth,' she wrote before continuing with a candour few proud parents would dare utter to a relative stranger: 'I am also apprehensive about her susceptibility to flattery, her idleness and general disinclination towards any serious activity.' Mercy, a rich and unambitious man, was utterly discreet, and there arose a parallel correspondence between him and the Empress, while she wrote and exchanged letters with her daughter.

How was a Habsburg princess to be changed into the Dauphine of France? How was the protocol to symbolize this transformation without offending either the pride of France or the majesty of Austria? The solution to this conundrum is well documented and has now, thanks to the medium of film, become available to an even wider audience. On a small island no more than a sandbank in the Rhine, opposite Strasbourg, an elaborate marquee was erected. This was a theoretical 'no-man's-land' where an elaborate ceremony had been prepared. The space was divided into four rooms, two facing west and two facing east. Between them was a domed central hall hung with tapestries and containing a throne and baldachin.

The rooms facing east were Austrian and would represent the last of Marie Antoinette's tangible geographical links with the land of her birth. After entering these, she was stripped naked by her ladies-in-waiting, surrendering every item of jewellery, memento and dress. A completely new set of clothes of French manufacture awaited her. With jewels, powder and fabrics sent from Paris, the young Austrian archduchess was to be reborn a French princess.

Far worse than the discarding of her familiar Viennese petticoats, stockings and chemise was the abandonment of her servants which now ensued. As they withdrew, new unfamiliar faces with severe frowns entered to take control of her every next move. Marie Antoinette behaved as any girl of her tender years would and burst into tears, throwing herself into the arms of the startled Comtesse de Noailles, her first new lady-in-waiting, who, unaccustomed to such a display of intimacy, stood frigidly stiff as the young girl sobbed on her shoulder. The relationship between these two would be rich in paradox but their first frosty encounter would set the tone for much that followed. 'Madame Etiquette', as Marie Antoinette called her, was a martinet for observing the detail of the French court's conventions and the young Austrian bridled almost from the first day at the avalanche of instruction which descended upon her at the hands of the Comtesse. So constrained by the strict etiquette that was imposed upon her, Marie Antoinette's spontaneity only became more exaggerated, a form of protest at the prevalence of suffocating protocol. The Comtesse ensured that the young Austrian knew that she could not just play with the children of her servants or greet her Lorraine cousins with familiarity. Marie Antoinette was the future Queen of France and, by definition, was unapproachable.

So fractious did the relationship between these two become that at one point, after a riding accident, Marie Antoinette felt compelled to ask only half in jest what the protocol was for the Dauphine remounting a mule. When she became Queen, it was among the Austrian's most delightful duties to receive the Comtesse's resignation. A few years later these two would be reunited as equals under the blade of the guillotine.

Maria Theresa, meanwhile, offered in a letter some important 'props' for her daughter's emotional and spiritual life. The advice underlines the degree to which the Empress believed that the sacramental life was indispensable to everyday existence. It was important to begin each day with prayer. After greeting the day on her knees, Marie Antoinette was to study some religious text for five or six minutes, taking great care not to talk to anyone during this time. 'All depends on beginning the day well and the intentions with which you begin it . . . pray during the day as often as you can.'[3]

In this first of many letters of advice over the years, Maria Theresa interestingly appears to have had religion and the spiritual formation of her daughter uppermost in her mind but she also offered practical

warnings. Her daughter, having begun the day with prayer and meditation on a religious text, was to make sure that she 'never uttered a
comment on the Jesuits'. They were detested in France. Moreover, all
letters were to be torn up after reading.[4]

Another theme of this first letter dwelt on the 'ideal' of female marital
submission. It is important here to stress that Maria Theresa was formu-
lating an ideal rather than a dogma. She knew better than anyone that the
following advice would have to be modified over time as the relationship
and equation of power of two personalities developed. This had been her
own experience with Francis Stephen who, after failure in military leadership, gradually stepped back into the obscure foothills of government.
Maria Theresa might have desired her husband to be a brilliant political
mind or gifted military leader but, once he had demonstrated he was
neither of these, marital subservience could not run unchecked.

Thus, the following lines should be read as an aspiration rather than
a rigid set of parameters: 'The wife must completely submit to her
husband and must have no business other than to please him and obey
him . . . all depends on the wife, on her being sweet, willing and amusing.'
Maria Theresa was perhaps on firmer ground when she simply observed:
'The only true happiness in this world is a happy marriage.' With these
words all attempts to cast the Empress in the guise of a 'proto-feminist'
encounter resistance.[5]

The Empress did not hesitate to proffer other useful tips as to how to
deal with the personages in the French court: 'Do not be familiar, you
will flatter no-one because it is too ordinary – kindness is what reassures
and brings everyone closer.'

From the beginning of her daughter's arrival in France, the Empress
had instructed her ambassador Mercy to keep her informed daily of her
daughter's progress. Mercy's letters are models of diplomatic tact and
over the years he became the invisible third party in the correspondence
between Marie Antoinette and her mother. Mercy noted early on that
the 'princess knows how to deploy wit and sarcasm so as to make her
observations biting'. He also picked up early on her 'extreme distaste for
reading and other serious occupations'. The Empress took the hint and
many of her letters at this time include strong pleas for her daughter to
inform her mother of her current reading material.

Mercy also saw very quickly the asymmetry in strength of personality between the young Austrian princess and her husband. Already in 1770, writing on 14 July, the ambassador could relate, 'there can be no doubt that with a little caution she will be able completely to dominate him'. The young Austrian had already ordered that the Dauphin be deprived of all pastries following an attack of indigestion. 'Marie Antoinette,' wrote Mercy, 'rules him in all little things and he never contradicts her.'

There followed a long correspondence on the relative merits of Parisian and Viennese corsets. It seems that Marie Antoinette had some form of minor scoliosis as Mercy noted in the same letter that her right shoulder was out of kilter with her left. Maria Theresa eagerly pounced on this as evidence of her daughter's 'general carelessness'.

Meanwhile, Marie Antoinette stressed in her letters to her mother that her husband was really, despite his small defects, a good-natured man whose weaknesses were just the result of his 'poor education'. She had clearly got the measure of him very early on. Her mother had no illusions about the lack of solidity at the French court. Over the years she had had ample evidence of French perfidy and lack of seriousness. For all their intellectual brilliance the French were completely lacking in that *Menschenkenntnis* which was second nature to Maria Theresa, and many other Austrians.

'The French royal family are in no way capable of appearing to advantage in public,' the Empress observed, adding, 'they are incapable of setting the *ton* and there are always many malcontents . . . it is therefore for you to set the tone at Versailles.' This belief in the superiority of the Viennese court and the Habsburg dynasty remained a theme of the correspondence for many years. 'The solidity and frankness of the German' was always contrasted with the superficiality and insincerity of the French. Marie Antoinette put her finger on the difference early on when she confessed to her mother that the French ladies at court despised her gaiety and spontaneity, preferring her to adopt 'their ways of unsmiling stiffness' with people. This was so different to the world that the young Austrian had been brought up in, a place in which, as her mother recalled, 'making people like us smile is the only amusement and happiness of our royal condition'. The future Queen of France was to 'further the glory of God and the welfare of man', the Empress advised in a formulation of two concepts which could be said to have defined her rule.

When Marie Antoinette was reported to have given 1,000 livres to the Hôtel-Dieu charitable institution, her mother immediately scolded her for such public munificence. 'These acts should be known only by God.'[6]

By 29 August 1773 the lack of any pregnancy in her daughter was beginning to be a factor in their correspondence. The Empress was especially concerned at reports of her daughter's passion for riding, in particular galloping across rough terrain: 'A married woman can never be sure she is not pregnant, therefore this sport is highly unsuitable.'[7]

In the meantime, problems of related significance stretched before the royal couple. The Dauphin suffered from a phimosis which inhibited all physical activity. Letters from Marie Antoinette to her mother, referenced by Stefan Zweig more than a century later, dwelt on the difficulties of the Dauphin's unfortunate condition. At first, Maria Theresa was at pains to present a relaxed response (*Gelassenheit*) to these difficulties. There was, after all, plenty of time: 'On no account display any irritation,' she wrote to her daughter in 1771, 'only tenderness and caresses. Too much eagerness could ruin everything; gentleness and patience are the only things that help . . . you will both grow stronger. But, of course, it is only natural that we old parents pine for [news of] of the consummation.'

Maria Theresa's advice disguised the fears (always a sensitive nerve point for her) that news of the lack of an heir always evinced in her. The whole point of this union, Kaunitz's jewel in the crown of the great *Renversement*, was the production of an heir to the throne of France through whose veins would course Austrian blood. Only then could the Empress rest easy that the future risk of a great war between these two erstwhile rivals could be discounted.

Eventually, it would be Joseph who, dispatched to confront his brother-in-law in 1777, encouraged the Dauphin to screw up his courage for the painful but brief circumcision which would solve the problem.

Such problems were straightforward and, while they absorbed much of Maria Theresa's thoughts – she demanded to know the precise details of her daughter's monthly menstruation cycles – they were manageable. Less easy to deal with were the countless intrigues at court which flourished in Paris and soon ensnared the young Dauphine in their machinations.

For some time, the King of France's mistress, Madame Dubarry, had enjoyed a prestige at court which had increasingly offended members of the sovereign's family. These now saw in Marie Antoinette a simple way of exacting revenge. This could be orchestrated by encouraging the young princess to assert her precedence at all formal occasions. As court etiquette insisted that the Dubarry could not initiate a conversation with the Dauphine, Marie Antoinette snubbed the commoner at every occasion, enjoying with childlike glee the ensuing commotion it caused, blissfully unaware that she was storing up for herself all the venom a royal mistress spurned could muster.

The news of this intrigue soon reached Maria Theresa. Mercy, her ambassador, did his work well and the Empress was informed almost hourly of the progress of the dispute. Whatever the moral arguments for or against the Dubarry, Maria Theresa did not hesitate to take a firm line on her daughter's behaviour. It was not a question of reprimanding a monarch's mistress for any failure of morals, it was far more a question of *Staatspolitik*. Kaunitz was dragooned into writing a warning letter. This resorted to simple logical arguments to set Marie Antoinette on a more conciliatory path: 'To refrain from showing civility towards persons whom the King has adopted as members of his own circle is derogatory to that circle; and all persons must be regarded as members thereof whom the ruling monarch himself looks upon as his confidants, no-one being entitled to ask whether he be right or wrong in doing so. The choices of a reigning monarch must be unreservedly respected.'[8]

Sadly, Marie Antoinette was far too headstrong to take this advice, even if it was from the man who perhaps more than anyone else in Austria was responsible for her being where she was. Louis XV's daughters encouraged her to continue her vendetta against the Dubarry and it was only when the King decided to get involved personally by summoning Mercy and letting the Dubarry explode in tears and rage against him that signs of compromise began to emerge. Mercy confronted the princess directly and, with all the authority of her mother behind him, he reminded her in no uncertain terms that it was not her personal feelings which counted in 'cette affaire' but her duty and responsibility towards her House. Marie Antoinette conceded and agreed to greet the Dubarry but when the encounter took place, the young Austrian's plans were derailed by one of the fractious aunts.

Mercy was horrified; the King was incensed but failed to see that it was one of his own relations rather than his daughter-in-law who was at fault. Maria Theresa, on hearing this news, felt compelled to pen a withering letter to her daughter: 'What a to-do about saying *Bonjour* to someone, a kindly word concerning dress or some trumpery . . . you seem to have allowed yourself to have become so enslaved that neither reason nor duty can persuade you.'[9]

Stressing that she could 'no longer keep silent on this matter any longer', Maria Theresa's advice now exuded authority and command. Of maternal affection there was no hint:

After all Mercy told you about the King's wishes and your duty, you actually dared to fail him! What possible reason can you offer for such conduct? Nothing at all! It is not acceptable for you to regard the Dubarry in any other light other than that of a lady whose right of entry to the court is confirmed along with her entry to the King's society. You are His Majesty's first subject and as such owe him obedience and submission . . . all that is expected of you is that you should say an indifferent word. If some baseness or intimacy was asked of you I should of course not advise consent but that you should look at her courteously, not for her sake but for the sake of your master and benefactor![10]

On New Year's Day 1772 Marie Antoinette deigned to grant the Dubarry a glance and the observation: 'Il y'a bien du monde aujourd'hui a Versailles' (There are a lot of people in Versailles today). She then turned back to another lady but it was enough. In the words of a later biographer, the court was 'all smiles and the alliance was saved'.

Marie Antoinette continued to cause her mother anxieties – were the reports true that she rode astride a horse rather than side-saddle? – but the long-awaited child was duly born in the summer of 1778. Eleven years before revolution and war were to upturn everything Kaunitz had striven to achieve, there seemed to be some guarantee of future harmony.

Reports of Marie Antoinette's personal behaviour, however, continued to cause Maria Theresa unhappiness, especially after her daughter became Queen in 1774. It distressed her particularly that her daughter had developed a French cynicism dismissive of people's weaknesses and frailties. The birth of an heir did not lead to any lasting intimacy with her husband, whom the Queen dismissed as 'un pauvre homme' and 'une quantité negligéable'.

When Joseph visited Paris, even he was struck by the complete absence of any tenderness between the couple. Somehow his youngest sister had absorbed all the superficiality of the French court and discarded any of the compassion to be found in the court of her mother. There was a hardness now in her character, born perhaps of the traumatic uprooting of her adolescence when she had been woefully ill-prepared for the alien strictures of a foreign life. Psychologists, had they existed in those days, would have pointed out the hidden depressive tendencies her constant yearning for distraction hinted at.

Above all, it was the young Austrian's superficial dismissiveness which injured the personification of Austria's reputation for *Gnade* and *Pietas*. How was it, despite all the extenuating circumstances, that her mother's daughter could have developed into what a later age might have referred to as 'such a load of rubbish'?

Maria Theresa saw very clearly the need for her daughter to be loved in France. 'Our two monarchies,' she wrote on 30 May 1774, 'only need quiet to arrange our business. If we remain tightly linked no-one will trouble us and Europe will enjoy all the happiness of its tranquillity.' This advice came as a response to a plea for help from the new French King. On the Dauphin succeeding to the French throne, as King Louis XVI, he had written the following impassioned plea for counsel from his mother-in-law: 'protect us all as we are too young to reign . . . I would much like to have your advice.' This, in Mercy's opinion, was the 'decisive moment'. All Europe watched carefully to see what unfolded. A future British minister, visiting Paris, was enchanted to see the Queen dancing. As he commented to a courtier next to him on the grace and elegance of Marie Antoinette's steps, the courtier acidly observed that she was out of synchronization with the music. 'Then it must be the rhythm that is wrong', countered the minister.[11]

Certainly, for Maria Theresa the fact that her daughter was now Queen of France gave her the kind of satisfaction that was afforded a century later to Queen Victoria at the thought of her relations and descendants succeeding to the thrones of Germany and Russia. In both cases, the carefully laid plans of a gifted matriarch in order to secure peace and stability in Europe through dynastic proximity were doomed to failure.

Yet the Empress seems to have underestimated the risks of an anti-Austrian reaction in Paris if the French elite came to believe their new king was being manipulated by the stronger personality of her daughter. It did not help that the new Queen embarked on extravagant gestures which could only alienate her subjects. The Queen refused to engage in what her mother called the 'right sort of economizing'. In June 1775, barely a year after coming to the throne, a bread riot erupted in protest at rampant inflation in the price of wheat. Maria Theresa, apprised of it as it happened by her ambassador, wrote to her daughter, warning her of the new mood of discontent stalking Europe.

Once again it revealed a 'finger on the pulse' of European political and social development not usually ascribed to the Empress. 'I think there is something behind it', she wrote to her daughter on hearing the news of the riots. 'Our people in Bohemia used just the same language . . . the spirit of rebellion is becoming familiar everywhere. This is the consequence of our enlightened century.'[12]

For more than one and a half centuries, until discovery by Stefan Zweig and others, Maria Theresa's most intimate criticisms of her daughter lay hidden in the Vienna archives, never to see the light of day until the monarchy had fallen. The following is perhaps one of the most poignant:

Where is the good and generous heart of the Archduchess Antoinette? I see only intrigue, vulgar spite, delight in mockery and persecution. Intrigues which might do very well for a Pompadour or a Dubarry but never for a Queen, still less for a great princess, kindly and good of the house of Lorraine and Austria.

All winter long I have trembled at the thought of your too easy success and the flatterers surrounding you while you throw yourself into a life of pleasure and preposterous display. This pursuit of one pleasure to another without the King, knowing that he takes no happiness and only permits you to do as you please out of sheer good nature . . . has made me write to express my fears.

Maria Theresa's fears for the future are all too apparent in this letter. Historians have often attributed Joseph's frenetic haste to secure as much radical reform as quickly as possible to an acute sensitivity to the imminent risk of a seismic revolutionary explosion. That may be true but what is certain is that this prescience and lack of complacency was inherited from his mother, whose next words of warning to her daughter strike an eerily prophetic note:

Your luck can all too easily change and by your own fault you may well find yourself one day plunged into the deepest misery . . . One day you will recognize the truth of this but by then it will be too late. I hope I shall not live until misfortune overtakes you and I pray to God to end my days quickly, since I am no longer of any use to you, and I could not bear to lose my dear child . . . whom I shall always love tenderly until I die.[13]

Maria Theresa was evidently so well-informed by Mercy, not only of her daughter's activities in Paris but also of wider political and social developments, that she could even foretell Marie Antoinette's nemesis.

As well as political developments, the Empress showed her equally firm grasp of practicalities by her comments at the same time to her daughter concerning the latest news of her marital arrangements. In particular, the reports from Mercy and other sources that her daughter no longer shared her husband's bed occasioned much alarm in Maria Theresa. Here, her advice appears to have been as sure-footed as her political instincts and certainly might be considered as acutely relevant to married couples today as it was in the eighteenth century: 'If the King no longer sleeps with you, you will have to give up your friendship; your habit of always being together will also end and I foresee only misfortune and sorrow . . . Your only endeavour must be to be his best friend', adding some advice that any modern marriage counsellor would no doubt enthusiastically endorse: 'a best friend in whom he can confide; so do try to be up on things so as to discuss them with him and help him; he should find pleasure and serenity nowhere but in your company'.

The ever-thorny issue of extramarital friendships, hinted at by this last sentence, considerably exercised Maria Theresa. She found her daughter's friendship with the Prince de Ligne especially difficult to accept, despite his long-standing friendship with her son Joseph. In a particularly perceptive comment on the dashing prince, she observed: 'The Prince de Ligne is full of wit and pleasant qualities, but his character does not rise to them because he is a frivolous boaster.'[14]

The combination of marital separation – there was never the slightest question of infidelity – importunate friends and bouts of material extravagance all combined with the young ruling pair's political inexperience to threaten to light the fuse which would explode years later.

Reports of some sudden whimsical piece of expenditure on Marie Antoinette's part, the purchase of some vastly overpriced bracelets, also incurred all of Maria Theresa's wrath: 'these kinds of anecdotes pierce my heart'. It was despicable behaviour and symptomatic of her daughter's life of 'constant dissipation': 'A sovereign cannot abase herself in so adorning her person . . . why are you not listening to music and reading? . . . all I find is horse races, gambling and late nights.'

Notwithstanding her own lifelong personal addiction to card games, the Austrian sovereign felt compelled to warn her daughter that 'gambling was the very worst . . . bringing bad talk, bad attitudes and bad company'.[15] This chimed with Joseph's reports that his sister was 'not doing her job'. As Joseph laconically warned, 'that may well have consequences in the future'.[16]

In 1777 Joseph had paid his first incognito visit to Paris and confirmed to his mother all her fears about her daughter's 'state of continual apathy'. He had noted that, as Mercy had earlier reported, the King loved Marie Antoinette but 'feared her more'. In bed, as well as in government, they were 'two complete blunderers'. Joseph's graphic accounts of Louis's 'issues' in bed illuminated his complete absence of squeamishness in discussing intimate physical affairs.

Luckily, as we have seen, Joseph's advice to seek medical help solved the problem and soon Maria Theresa was beaming with the joy of the future prospect of a royal French grandchild. When it arrived in 1778, her disappointment that it was not a son was cogently expressed.

In the weeks before her death, Maria Theresa felt compelled to warn her daughter of the machinations of England and the deadly threat she perceived it posed for France. The British armies were not invincible and the French were 'always so brave' but her daughter's kingdom remained fragile. The same letter ends with the desperate entreaty: 'We absolutely need a Dauphin.'[17]

Increasingly, even though she felt the succession in France was heading for resolution, she dwelt on political affairs and her letters, written barely two years before her death, reveal her ongoing perspicacity on issues of geopolitics. On 17 May 1778 she took the opportunity to reiterate her contempt for the Prussian King Frederick. 'For thirty-seven years, he has made Europe wretched through his despotism and violence as he renounced all the verified principles of truth and honesty. Not a single European prince has been spared his perfidy.'[18]

But try as she might not to worry about the reports of frivolity and trivialities, Maria Theresa felt she could not refrain from warning her daughter of the danger of a sudden irruption of anti-Austrian feeling. The American Revolution was a straw in the wind of the volatility of the times.

The Empress wrote: 'I am not at all pleased with the situation in America.' Yet aware that her daughter now personified the union of the houses of France and Austria, the Empress increasingly took a more critical line on the English. She had always been sceptical of English promises and never forgave the English for forcing her three times to the negotiation table with Prussia when all her instincts cried out for a war à l'outrance against Frederick. Yet, as her daughter's adopted country and England became deadly rivals across the globe, there is no doubt the Empress's attitude towards England hardened while retaining always considerable admiration. 'The resources at England's disposal are immense,' she wrote to Marie Antoinette in January 1780, adding warningly, 'their fanaticism is unbelievable.' But, as Maria Theresa had to admit, Austrian public opinion and the Austrian aristocracy were all pro-English: 'an old prejudice', she lamented.[19]

Six months later, in June 1780, as the Gordon Riots erupted in a renewed frenzy of anti-Catholic feeling, the Empress was given another occasion to ventilate her thoughts on England: 'a terrible riot without example in a civilized country: there it is: that liberty, so often praised; that unique way of legislating! Yet without religion and without morality nothing endures.'[20]

Maria Theresa's scepticism towards England was not just on account of that country's well-known persecution of Catholics, by far the longest of any European country; she was also aware that England's power was growing exponentially, largely at the cost of her daughter's kingdom, France.

Apart from warning her daughter of England's immense resources, long purse strings and 'unbelievable fanaticism', the Empress felt compelled to share with her daughter her sense of England's unstoppable rise: 'That nation for the last few years has been gaining terribly everywhere; one cannot be too careful in taking precautions and preventing their seduction and influence in everything.'

Maria Theresa would not live to see the birth of the new Dauphin, a year later, in 1781, or his tragic death from tuberculosis nine years later and the even more distressing fate of his brother, who died in captivity aged 10.

In her last letter to her daughter, Maria Theresa stressed the importance of 'public ceremonies'. The 'little inconveniences they inflicted were well worth their value', especially with regard to 'such a lively people as the French'. Maria Theresa shared her daughter's desire to escape the rigidities of the court; 'much court life is dull and empty', she commiserated, but from a practical point of view she urged her daughter to 'not let herself go' and give up on these tedious duties which always served a purpose, if only that of keeping the sovereign in touch with opinion.

Ultimately, notwithstanding all this sound advice, the temper of history was against Marie Antoinette and the Austro-French alliance would not survive either her execution or the five coalition wars Austria would wage to arrest Napoleonic France from dominating Europe.

In contrast to the vagaries and challenges of Maria Antonia, Maria Carolina was to provide ample evidence that at a different court, Naples, the sybaritic life need not lead to dissolution and endless frivolity. The marriage between Maria Carolina and Ferdinand of Naples was contracted, as we have seen, following the death of Maria Josepha who had originally been chosen by Maria Theresa for this dynastic union and had been struck down by smallpox.

Maria Carolina and Ferdinand were married by proxy in April 1768 when Maria Carolina was only 15. The same year, she travelled to Naples to begin a new life no less daunting than that of Marie Antoinette but without the tyrannies of protocol and intrigue which greeted her youngest sister. Naples was an altogether more relaxed court, one where the codes of behaviour were very different from what Maria Carolina was accustomed to in Vienna.

Maria Theresa, here, too, gave her departing daughter some useful advice: 'Do not talk always about Austria or draw comparisons between our habits and theirs. Never forget there is good and bad to be found in every country. In your heart and in the uprightness of your mind remember you are a German; in all that is not important, though in nothing that is wrong, you must appear to be Neapolitan.'[21]

Maria Carolina was certainly of a temperament stronger than that of Marie Antoinette and she skilfully avoided the obvious traps, embracing – who could not? – the magnificence of the city, its celebrated location, dubbed by Humboldt, along with Salzburg and Constantinople, the 'finest of any city in the world', and above all the spontaneity and indefatigable exuberance of its inhabitants.

Her husband, Ferdinand, provided perhaps a greater challenge than any cultural malaise. In contrast to the beauty of his surroundings, the King of Naples was ugly and crass. In Joseph's description, he was disfigured and crude: 'His head is relatively small, surmounted by a forest of coffee-coloured hair which he never powders. His nose begins in his forehead and gradually swells in a straight line as far as his mouth which is very large with a jutting lower lip, filled with good but irregular teeth. The rest of his features, his low brow, piggy eyes, flat cheeks, and long neck are unremarkable.'[22]

To be fair to Ferdinand, he was not, at first, entirely enamoured by his young bride, observing that 'she sleeps the sleep of the dead and sweats like a pig'.[23]

Maria Carolina's position was much easier than that of her sister in Paris. The two had always been exceptionally close; it was said that as soon as one fell ill the other immediately followed suit. Yet nothing could have been more different to Marie Antoinette's via dolorosa in Paris than Maria Carolina's political success in Naples.

It helped that her husband was more interested in hunting than government and that his vulgar physicality did not repel Maria Carolina as much as it did startled visitors, who had to become accustomed to Ferdinand suddenly taking their hand and making it feel the hardness of his manhood by unbuttoning his waistcoat. When the English diplomat William Wraxall was treated to this gesture, he almost fainted. Like her mother, Maria Carolina was not focused on superficialities, nor averse to sophisticated techniques of dealing with them.

Maria Theresa advised her daughter to feign an interest in the 'boredom of shooting' so that Maria Carolina gained her husband's confidence. Increasingly, Ferdinand followed his wife's suggestions. When in 1775 their first male child was born, Maria Carolina, thanks to a clause astutely inserted into the marriage agreement by Maria Theresa, was admitted into the Neapolitan Privy Council where her tact and perception soon gained her many admirers. Meanwhile, her seventeen subsequent confinements suggested that if she slept the 'sleep of the dead' it was largely as a consequence of her husband's exhausting nocturnal performances.

From the outset, Maria Carolina was struck by the progressive and intelligent thinking of certain members of the council in Naples. Although she had left Vienna as a young teenager, she was well aware through her brother Joseph that Freemasonry played a very important role in Viennese cultural and intellectual life. Shortly after her first confinement she was introduced to several Neapolitan Freemasons who not only impressed her but convinced her that her irrepressible subjects could only be governed with the help of secret societies. Maria Carolina was not, unlike her mother, theologically dogmatic to the degree that she could harbour the scepticism Maria Theresa occasionally felt towards the 'craft'. Rather, Maria Carolina realized that as so many of her mother's principal advisers were Freemasons there was little to fear from them as individuals and much to benefit from their participation in the reform of the Neapolitan state.

Certainly, what became termed as the Neapolitan Enlightenment found no greater champion than Maria Theresa's second-youngest daughter. Ferdinand increasingly was happy to leave the difficult decisions of government in her hands. He had neither the attention span nor the literacy skills to focus himself on affairs of state and the Queen's abilities to make political decisions grew decidedly.

So supportive did she become of the secret societies that when the Neapolitan minister Bernardo Tanucci sought to ban the lodges after the discovery of one in a royal regiment, Maria Carolina exploited the dispute to harness the lodges to her support, persuading her husband to dismiss Tanucci, and gradually open the city to Austrian rather than Spanish influence.

Court life was immeasurably enriched by the Austrian queen who attracted some of the greatest minds and painters to establish themselves there. She generously supported painters such as Angelica Kauffmann and Philipp Hackert. In particular, she strengthened ties with representatives of England.

William Wraxall, an astute observer of court life, felt particularly drawn to the Queen's sincerity and frailty: 'Though neither possessing beauty of face nor liveliness of person yet was she not absolutely deficient in either and, if her figure might be esteemed too large, still it wanted neither grace, dignity nor even attraction . . . she was the only Queen I ever saw weep in public.'[24]

In Wraxall's case, he had chosen to be presented to her on the anniversary of the Queen's son's death and, as Maria Carolina had mentioned it, tears had filled her eyes. The Englishman was won over immediately, later noting: 'It was difficult not to be favourably impressed towards a princess capable of giving such involuntary testimony of maternal tenderness in a place and situation where it was impossible to suspect her of any artifice or affectation.'

Another English visitor commented more favourably on Maria Carolina's beauty:

Her Majesty is a beautiful woman, she has the finest and most transparent complexion I ever saw. Her hair is of that glossy chestnut I so much admire and her eyes are large brilliant and of a dark blue, her eyebrows exact and darker than her hair, her nose edges towards the aquiline, her mouth small, her lips very red, while her teeth are beautifully white and even. When she smiles two dimples appear which invest her with a sweetness, while her figure is perfect.[25]

The British envoy, Sir William Hamilton, was also smitten by Maria Carolina and spent many happy hours introducing her to his well-furnished mind and his wide acquaintance of scholars, philosophers and poets. Emma Hamilton also fell under the Queen's spell and the two enjoyed a certain intimacy which may not have been entirely platonic. As the European scene darkened in the 1780s, Hamilton played a key role in encouraging Maria Carolina to enlist the support of Sir John Acton who was serving her brother, the Grand Duke Leopold, in Tuscany by building up the naval forces of the Grand Duchy. Both Hamilton and Acton's tireless energy helped reduce Spanish and French influence at the Court of the Two Sicilies.

'In the evenings I go to her,' Emma wrote, 'we are *tête-à-tête* for two or three hours . . . no person can be so charming as the Queen. She is everything one might wish for – the best mother, wife and friend in the world. I live constantly with her and have done intimately so for two years and I have never in all that time seen anything but goodness and sincerity in her . . . she could not be kinder to me even if I were her daughter. I love her with all my soul.'[26]

Emma Hamilton's relationship with Maria Carolina became even closer after she smuggled Marie Antoinette's last letter to her sister out of France following the Revolution of 1789.[27]

The Revolution which finally exploded in Paris nine years after Maria Theresa's death might not have come as a great surprise but the subsequent execution of the royal couple in 1793 shocked the world. Austria had declared war on revolutionary France after a French army menaced her possessions in the Netherlands. In October 1793 a bloody two-day battle at Wattignies forced the Austrians to raise the siege of Maubeuge which had threatened Paris. With the threat averted, Marie Antoinette, who had been kept prisoner as a possible bargaining chip for negotiations, was now deemed expendable.

Marie Antoinette's calm demeanour on the day of her execution and dignified bearing on the scaffold impressed even her persecutors. She graciously apologized to the executioner for inadvertently stepping on his foot. Huge black clouds drifted across the Paris skyline as she mounted the block; the crowd fell silent as the sun was suddenly hidden by a cloud. Eyewitnesses recounted that as the blade fell there were neither shouts nor cheers; by her bearing Marie Antoinette had shown she was a true child of the Great Empress, facing death with all the resignation and equanimity with which her mother had faced it thirteen years earlier.

For Maria Carolina, the execution of her sister was all she needed to complete the reorientation of Neapolitan foreign policy towards a philo-British stance. A defensive treaty with London was quickly signed in 1793. Britain was already allied to Austria against France and the move was logical, but powerful forces in Naples were against the monarchy and Jacobins had already infiltrated malcontents into the capital. As the year progressed, Maria Carolina and her husband narrowly escaped assassination. 'I go nowhere,' the Queen wrote, 'without wondering if I shall return alive.'

The great British naval victory at the Battle of the Nile eventually proved to Maria Carolina that the young, short, unprepossessing naval officer Hamilton had introduced her to a few years earlier had indeed been, in Hamilton's phrase, 'far from handsome but will live to be a great man'. But Horatio Nelson's great victory came too late to save Naples from an advancing French army on land. Maria Carolina's cousin, Francis, Holy Roman Emperor after her brother Leopold's death in 1792, sent General Mack to help reorganize the Neapolitan forces which on paper numbered in excess of seventy thousand men. But the 'malheureux Mack en personne', as he would identify himself to his French captors a few years later at Ulm, was not a vigorous commander and he soon earned the soubriquet of 'retiring Mack'.

Maria Carolina, so as not to risk the fate of her sister in Paris, made a dash with her family for Sicily, arriving on Boxing Day 1798 at Palermo. 'God help us', she wrote to her daughter, who after her marriage to her cousin, Francis, was now Empress. 'We are saved but ruined and dishonoured.'[28]

Maria Carolina was destined to experience almost as vividly as her younger sister the turbulences of the prevailing zeitgeist. After a brief but unsuccessful restoration, she finally was forced to leave Naples in 1813 and return to Vienna via Odessa and Lemberg several weeks later. She did not live to see her enemy Napoleon defeated and exiled but she always treasured the back-handed compliment he paid her when, after her return to Naples in 1802, he conceded, 'The Queen is the only man in the Kingdom of Naples.' It echoed beautifully, if unconsciously, Frederick of Prussia's verdict on her mother, half a century earlier, when he had written: 'Finally the Habsburgs have a real man at their helm, but that man is a woman.'

The third of Maria Theresa's daughters who was born to marry into a ruling house was Maria Amalia. This girl, unlike her sisters, Marie Antoinette and Maria Carolina, was undoubtedly taking a step downwards with her marriage to the Duke of Parma. In truth, Maria Amalia had been unlucky in childhood. As the eighth child she had been far removed from her eldest siblings, and her youngest sibling had died early so that she was raised almost as an only child. Her relationship with her mother was challenging, to put it mildly, and Maria Theresa maintained that, however charming she had been as an infant, she was undoubtedly the child with whom she got on least well.

Maria Amalia was certainly blessed with good looks and was said by many contemporary observers to be the most beautiful of all the Empress's daughters. But beauty was not to guarantee happiness and she was contracted at an early age to marry Ferdinand, Duke of Parma, the brother of Joseph II's first wife Isabella. Unfortunately, Maria Amalia had fallen in love with Prince Charles of Zweibrücken, a minor royal figure whom Maria Theresa did not consider *standesgemäss* (of equal social rank) for her daughter, or capable of positively influencing the Franco-Austrian alliance. Ferdinand of Parma was a Bourbon and therefore Maria Amalia's marriage to him would reinforce the union between the two houses embodied in her younger sister's marriage to the Dauphin.

In this way, the star of European geopolitics poisoned relations between mother and daughter. Maria Amalia never forgave her mother for refusing her love match with Charles of Zweibrücken. The Parma contract did not lead in any way to a conventionally fruitful union. It did not help that Ferdinand of Parma was by royal standards virtually a pauper and that the duchy was controlled as a client state of France. Maria Amalia hated the French and was older than her husband.

Yet unhappy and unamused by the visible reduction in her circumstances which the Duchy of Parma offered her, Maria Amalia displayed her mother's talents for reforming local government. She first engineered the dismissal of Francophile ministers, then thwarted attempts by Spain to impose its influence on the duchy. She then saw off attempts to facilitate the duchy's incorporation into the new Napoleonic Kingdom of Etruria. Once again, her husband was content to leave her fully in command of the reins of government and these she proceeded to deploy skilfully, eventually appointing a cabinet of local Parmesan politicians who were personally loyal to her.

While her husband sought solace in the arms of countless peasant women, whose simplicity and warmth contrasted so sharply with the forceful character of his wife, Maria Amalia set about a series of affairs with the uncommonly handsome men of her ducal guard, hand-picked by her for their physical beauty. Maria Theresa was scandalized when she received reports of Maria Amalia's behaviour but her daughter merely doubled down on her habits and began cross-dressing, going about the duchy incognito in uniform, playing cards twice a week at the Parma officers' club.

Yet she understood, like her mother, the importance of public duties. She gave lavish quarterly gala banquets where she invited the poor to join the Parmesan nobility, ensuring that, while seated at different tables, the two sets of guests nonetheless received the same food. Moreover, she demonstrated considerable diplomatic skills. Having freed the duchy from French and Spanish influence, Maria Amalia was unamused when her mother sent Count Franz Xaver Orsini-Rosenberg to her court as Austrian ambassador with instructions from the Empress that her daughter obey everything Orsini recommended.

Maria Amalia summoned the hapless Rosenberg and told him politely but firmly that, as 'he might have noticed, she was the one in charge here' and that henceforth she did not wish to be in communication with Vienna 'at any time'.

The Austrian envoy was staggered; he had never been treated so peremptorily in his career.[29] When Maria Amalia's sister, Marie Christine, arrived on a visit she wrote immediately to her husband that she found her sister 'far less beautiful' than when she had left Vienna and that her glamour and beauty had been replaced by an altogether more masculine form of dress and carriage.

There can be no doubt that this most wayward of all Maria Theresa's daughters found, like her sister in Paris, that she could 'bend her husband to her will' and that realization, along with her determination to satisfy her libido by serial adultery with the members of her personal guard, made her into the 'less gay, less discriminating' figure her sister described.

But whatever hardness crept into Maria Amalia's character, she was still capable of intense affection for members of her family. When the news of Marie Antoinette's execution reached Parma, Maria Amalia first giggled before suddenly going white and collapsing in front of one of her daughters. One of the last letters Marie Antoinette had smuggled out of her prison before her execution had been to Maria Amalia.

Eventually, she was forced by Napoleon to abandon her duchy in 1802, when her husband was poisoned by the French. The horrors of this transition had a sobering effect and Amalia was able to flee to Prague, where she lived an altogether less racy life, dying peacefully in 1804.[30]

Thus did the third of Maria Theresa's daughters destined for political power also surrender all the prestige to which she had been born and lose all the status she might have been promised. Given that both Leopold and Joseph died equally youthfully, one can almost sense a combination of genetics and zeitgeist working to the detriment of the calculated dynastic network of Habsburg alliances Maria Theresa had hoped to create.

Although the dynastic arrangements involved for three of Maria Theresa's daughters have rightly assumed a prominence in discussing her daughters' legacy, we cannot forget the daughters for whom circumstances dictated a very different fate. It was a tradition in most families, irrespective of their social status, that at least one daughter remained at home to care for her parents in old age. This imposed upon them the low status of lifelong spinsters and was considered especially humiliating in the grander families. Maria Theresa's sister-in-law, Princess Charlotte of Lorraine, believed she cut 'an absurd figure' when, despite her 40 years of age, she was expected to follow, head bowed, the younger and more beautiful archduchesses 'like an old hag with the air of a duenna'.

Of the Empress's remaining daughters, both Marianne, born in 1738, and Elisabeth, born in 1743, were consigned to this fate. However, it was not, as is sometimes stated, a fate imposed upon them entirely by their mother. Marianna was considered dynastic marital material until her teens. She had even been regarded as a possible bride to the Duke of Savoy but the evidence of a serious scoliosis, an inherited illness which then as today caused in a woman several issues relating to childbirth, put pay to all such thoughts. By the time Marianna was 18, the deformity was so great that the physicians declared she would find it virtually impossible to give birth. This was disguised at court at the time as a 'catarrh' and indeed at one point she contracted such a virulent illness that she was even administered extreme unction. She recovered but it was considered too humiliating to expose Marianna's reputation as a daughter of the fecund Maria Theresa to the label of 'barrenness'. Unable to give birth, and increasingly bent double by her degenerating deformity, Marianna had no other option but to remain with her mother. Her marital prospects were nil.[31]

Her physical deformity kept her in relative obscurity but those who came into contact with her were impressed. She was vivacious, witty and humble. Her piety was of that positive nature which saw all events as part of God's providence and which therefore allowed her to accept her situation with complete resignation to the wishes of higher authority.

She was clearly highly intelligent and a keen reader of texts on natural history but the scientific interest was combined with her own deep Catholicism. In the animal and mineral world she explored, she saw always confirmation of God's existence.

In 1765 she was appointed prioress of the newly founded Theresian *Adeliges Damenstift* in Prague. This was yet another of Maria Theresa's projects to bind more closely the aristocracy to her while raising revenues through the establishment of an institution which could provide a home for aristocratic spinsters. The *Damenstift* did not have an exclusively religious character, even though it was devoted nominally to the

1. *La Belle Chocolatière*: from humble servant to Countess Dietrichstein. An enduring Viennese tradition: hot chocolate served with the obligatory glass of water.

2. Johann Amadeus Thugut: from simple boat-boy to Chancellor of Austria. Educated at the Empress's expense, few at court questioned his humble origins.

3. Angelo Soliman (Mmadi Maki): from Nigerian slave to prominent Austrian courtier and Freemason. Promoted by the princely Liechtensteins, Soliman was treated as an equal in the many games of chess he played (and won) with the Liechtenstein princes.

4. Joseph Sonnenfels: from Jewish corporal to Europe's greatest legal reformer. It was Sonnenfels's public denouncement of torture which moved Maria Theresa to abolish the practice throughout her domains.

5. Maria Theresa as Judith with the head of Frederick II as Holofernes. A rare depiction of the Empress as the victorious biblical heroine.

6. Destruction of the Prussian army in the *Blutgasse* at Hochkirch. Taken totally by surprise in a dawn raid by the Austrians, Frederick lost his best generals and over a third of his army in this action.

7. Wenzel Kaunitz: diplomatic revolutionary, Chancellor of Austria and architect of the *Grand Renversement* which laid Prussia to waste during the Seven Years War.

GERARDVS L. B VAN SWIETEN

8. Gerard van Swieten: Catholic refugee and medical reformer. He transformed Austria's health provision and was Maria Theresa's personal physician.

9. Franz Xaver Messerschmidt: a conventional sculptor enjoying imperial patronage in this depiction of Maria Theresa in 1764.

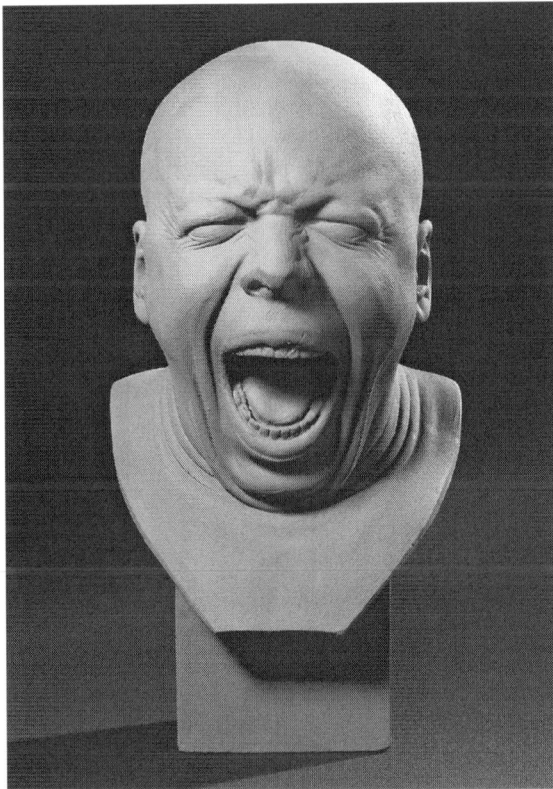

10. Franz Xaver Messerschmidt: an unconventional sculptor breaking the bounds of expressionist modernism while financed by imperial funds until his death in 1783.

11. The Empress's husband, Francis Stephen. A highly capable businessman, he had a shrewd eye for administrative talent and helped ensure the state's finances were put onto a more solid and stable footing.

12. One of the Empress's favourite generals, Franz Moritz Lacy. Of Jacobite stock, Austria's youngest and most charming field marshal was described by the Empress as having 'the most fascinating manners'.

13. Playing cards with her generals and advisers. The Empress was a compulsive gambler and regularly lost thousands of ducats on the baize. Her partners here are Batthyany, Nadasti, Daun and Loudon.

14. The one object the Empress always carried with her until the day of her death: her rosary, later bequeathed to her daughter Marianne in Klagenfurt.

15. Maria Theresa 'alla turca'. The painter Liotard brought the Turkish costume from Constantinople and the Empress eagerly embraced it as an opportunity to demonstrate her philo-Levant policies.

16. Maria Theresa at Pressburg rallying the Magyars to her cause. The presentation of her infant son Joseph as she addressed the Hungarian nobility added a note of feminine vulnerability, well calculated to appeal to the Magyar chivalry.

17. The Enlightenment symbol par excellence enjoyed pride of place in the Empress's favourite summer residence of Schönbrunn in the suburbs of Vienna.

18. On closer inspection the obelisk contains this allegory of Maria Theresa's achievements, rich in Masonic images and the icons of her Catholic monarchy, symbolic of a house of faith and reason undivided during her reign.

19. Familial duty and almost bourgeois homeliness: Maria Theresa pouring morning coffee for her husband while the children play with their toys.

20. Archduke Joseph (later Emperor Joseph II). Brilliant but fanatic and in a hurry to reform and head off revolution, Joseph's character revolted against his mother's pragmatism. Embittered by the death of his first wife Isabella of Parma, his reforms, however well-intentioned, drove Austria to the brink of collapse.

21. Archduke Leopold (later Emperor Leopold II). As Duke of Tuscany, Leopold undertook wide-ranging reforms which have benefited Tuscany to this day. Later, as Emperor, he inherited the chaos his brother's reforms had created and spent his all-too-brief reign carefully steadying the shaken Austrian ship of state.

22. Marie Christine: Maria Theresa's favourite daughter and the only one she permitted to marry 'for love' rather than dynastic politics. Pretty, gifted and musical, despite her marriage to Albert of Saxony-Teschen she was also involved in a passionate relationship with her beautiful sister-in-law Isabella of Parma.

23. Marianne. An intellectual and attractive personality, Marianne was considered ineligible for marriage on account of her severe scoliosis. She retired to a convent in Klagenfurt where she appears to have fallen in love with a local Freemason who founded a lodge in her name.

24. Maria Antonia (Marie Antoinette). It was Marie Antoinette's composure on the scaffold which impressed onlookers far more than the reports of her frivolities and venialities. At the moment of her martyrdom she revealed herself to be a true daughter of the Great Empress.

25. Lady Mary Coke: probably the most acute of the many female devotees of Maria Theresa. However, her indiscretions in a letter to Walpole concerning the Empress's expenditure brought her abrupt ostracism from the Vienna court and the full force of the Theresian surveillance state to bear on her travels through the Habsburg domains.

26. The Gloriette at Schönbrunn, arguably Vienna's most celebrated monument. Few who walk up the hill realise that the architect Johann Ferdinand von Hohenberg's great creation commemorates the defeat of Frederick of Prussia's armies at the Battle of Kolin in a 'just war'.

27. Europe's most celebrated order of chivalry, the Order of Maria Theresa was also inspired by the Austrian victory over Prussia at Kolin. Its last surviving member, Geoffrey (Gottfried) Banfield, died as recently as 1986.

28. Monument to Maria Theresa in Trieste. Erected in 2022, it commemorates not only the Empress but the most successful coin ever minted, the Theresian Thaler, which inspired the US dollar.

29. Monument to Maria Theresa in Prague. Erected in 2022 behind Prague castle, it is a symbol of the Czech state's long overdue reconciliation with its Habsburg history and reverses the post-war communist narrative of the Empress as an enemy of the Czech people.

30. Mozart's *Magic Flute*: the Queen of the Night. Mozart's *Singspiel* underlines the largely happy co-existence between Austrian Catholicism and eighteenth-century Austrian Freemasonry. The Queen of the Night dressed in mourning for her late husband would have been instantly recognisable to contemporary audiences as the Empress Maria Theresa.

31. Hertha Töpper as Octavian in Richard Strauss's *Der Rosenkavalier*. Hugo von Hofmannsthal's masterly evocation of the Theresian world has left generations of opera-lovers with an enduring image of the Great Empress and Austria's 'golden era' of *Milde und Munifizenz*.

'Holy Angels', and its first inmates were rich enough to afford donations which amounted to more than eighty thousand Gulden a year.

Marianne, as she quickly became known, visited it several times but appears to have found Prague and the atmosphere of public grandeur around the Hradčany castle not to her taste. Perhaps on account of her deformity, she always hated having to appear in the beau monde and she also thought that her piety was misinterpreted.

Thanks to her intellectual interests, Marianne's life in Vienna was rich in distractions. She organized a catalogue of commemorative medallions for her mother, even illustrating them with copperplates engraved by her own hand. Both the imperial engraving academy in Vienna and her brother Leopold's Academy of Arts in Florence granted her honorary membership. On her mother's death, Maria Theresa's will expressly arranged for Marianne to retire to a convent in Klagenfurt, Carinthia, a provincial backwater where she could devote herself to good works, reading and prayer. Marianne had fallen in love with the simplicity of the convent in Klagenfurt – the humility of the nuns and their indifference to any outward displays of rank or wealth. She had first seen the convent on her way to Innsbruck for her brother Leopold's wedding and it had immediately made a favourable impression on her. The nuns had asked her to remember them and Marianne was impressed by the good works they carried out for the poor, sick and infirm. She wrote a letter to her mother, preserved to this day in the convent, in which she asked for the privilege of becoming a resident of the convent on her mother's demise.

She did not wish to become a 'Klosterfrau aber doch in der Einsamkeit und im Dienste zu schliessen' (a nun but rather end my days in the loneliness and service of the convent). Under the terms of her mother's will, a 'modest' palace, designed by Maria Theresa's favourite architect, Nikolaus Pacassi, was constructed for her.

Like her mother before her, Marianne's days began always with a disciplined five-part examination of her conscience. Surviving documents in her hand detail one of these and, for a modern post-Christian society, they appear almost 'masochistic'. Yet they sound perfectly normal expressions of humility for anyone familiar with the sacramental life and are models of sincerity. One part of the five-fold examination of conscience involves a supplication for the grace to know what one's true weaknesses and sins are. One of the writings of Marianne shows that she had digested this lesson almost to perfection. She enumerated her faults, especially her frivolous activities. These included dancing, reading novels and gambling. She had pursued a life of trivialities and had only realized the folly of her ways with the blows of fate, notably her physical condition and the death of her father. But with God's help she could 'tame' her 'volatile and extreme temperament'. For any confessor then and even now, such self-awareness was not a sign of merciless cruelty at the hands of an unforgiving Lord but rather, in its negation of all feelings of pride, an indication of the bestowal of the highest grace.

She also believed that she enjoyed, thanks to God granting her a 'tender and constant heart', a platonic relationship of the most sublime nature with a man of whom we know nothing. Again, the modern world of instant gratification is quick to see unrequited love as proof of a lonely and joyless life. Yet, as an earlier generation once recognized, if only in literature, such unrequited love is the very essence of great romance. In its limitations, so often self-imposed, and in its suppression of physical passion, it acquires a richness and intensity which was well known to the ancients.

In the eighteenth century an archduchess could not easily just 'let herself go' and allow her feelings to lead to an intimacy which, for all manner of reasons, offended against the morality of her upbringing.

We do not know who the object of Marianne's affections was, only that she saw him regularly over a period of many years before breaking off all contact with him. Klagenfurt was in the 1780s a backwater offering barely a handful of grand aristocrats for company – the Thurns and Khevenhuellers between them carved up the county – and even these were often in Vienna. The few men of enlightened thought that worked in the town might not normally have been considered *standesgemäss*. It seems likely that this 'special friend' was married and completely 'unsuitable'.

Such an *amitié amoureuse* could only end in moral sanction and tears and therefore had to be broken off. No easy matter. As Marianne confided in a heart-rending note: 'once I loved I thought of no-one else and I loved constantly through twenty-one years, the last just the same as the first'.

We do not know if these feelings were reciprocated. The relationship was, like all such attractions, undoubtedly asymmetrical – how else could it have remained platonic for so long? Ultimately, only Marianne alone could decide whether the friendship should be continued or terminated. 'I cannot deny,' she wrote, that 'this battle was the greatest . . . Of my own free will I had to tear myself away from a passion I have never disputed.'[32] Only God could give her the supernatural strength required to oppose her own heart.

There has been some speculation that Ignaz von Born, who had served as her mentor in Vienna, might have been the object of her affection but it is equally likely that Marianne's 'special friend' may well have been one of the offspring of the high aristocracy, or even a humbler tradesman of Klagenfurt who helped her with the myriad of good works with which she supported the local community. The peculiar provincial intimacy of the town – it was not Graz or Innsbruck, two cities with imperial heritage – may have encouraged social interaction across the classes.

Her generosity was legendary, and such was the esteem with which the Carinthians held her Enlightenment credentials that two years after her arrival in Klagenfurt she appears to have inspired the foundation of Klagenfurt's first Masonic lodge. In 1783 a lodge was established with the name *Zur wohltätigen Marianna* (To the beneficent Marianne). Whether Marianne attended any lodge meetings is impossible to discern but that she encouraged their activities is indisputable. She had, after all, been the pupil of Ignaz Born, a well-known Viennese Freemason, and in her many discussions with him concerning minerals and medals it is certainly hard to imagine that they might not have touched on the existence of the lodges. There were secret societies for ladies as well as men in the Theresian world. The eighteenth-century predilection for depicting in porcelain female members of lodges with a tell-tale pug dog at their feet was just one sign of this.[33]

Whatever Marianne's relationship with Freemasonry, she could not influence her brother Joseph's famous Patent on Freemasonry which officially tolerated but in practice strictly limited Masonic activity, with the result that the lodge dedicated to her was formally closed in 1786.

Nor could she deter her brother from his campaign of dissolution of monasteries and convents which he did not deem useful. Just as her own convent was threatened with closure, Marianne invited him to spend a day with her there. At first, he was sceptical: 'treatment and medicine is surely a better way to deal with the sick than meditations and prayers', he said on his arrival. But ten hours later, he had revised his views: 'I must say I am impressed by the cheerfulness and energy of the sisters', he admitted to his host.[34]

Klagenfurt offered Marianne refuge from all the trappings of court which, on account of her scoliosis, she found so irksome. By devoting herself to scientific studies, good works and prayer, she found an equilibrium and satisfaction which a more material world might find hard to understand but which in many ways represented the apogee of personal, emotional and spiritual fulfilment. Her unrequited love interest assumes naturally in a more material age the aspect of hardship, if not extreme emotional damage, but an earlier age, with a mindset informed by austere dogma, would see the frustrations and denial in terms of something more positive.

Marianne's sister Elisabeth was five years younger than her and at first appeared destined for anything but a life of spinsterhood. She was beautiful and there were many candidates for dynastic union. The King of Poland, Stanislaw Poniatowski, the lover of Catherine the Great, had been considered along with the Duke of Chablais but the smallpox epidemic of 1767 so ravaged her beautiful face that she, too, was also considered ineligible for marriage. A half-hearted attempt by the French court to push Louis XV in her direction foundered on the understandable reluctance of the monarch to commit himself to an archduchess he had never seen. Any attempt at 'inspection' was out of the question and in any event the old king was thirty-three years his prospective bride's senior and, as a well-known philanderer, entirely unsuitable.

The effect the ravages of smallpox wrought on Elisabeth did not promote any humility or resignation along the lines of her more pious sister Marianne. Instead, Elisabeth reacted to her destiny with increasing bitterness. In one encounter with the British ambassador she sarcastically said that even a 'hole in the cheek' from a rotten tooth was a welcome distraction from the tediousness of her life. In her relations with her long-suffering governesses, she was almost schizophrenic, one moment angelic, another demonic. Her mother was so exhausted by the reports of the Marchioness de Herzelles that she ordered Elisabeth to be locked up (*eingesperrt*), adding, 'I shall treat her like a madwoman' (*wie eine*

Verrückte).[35] So driven to helplessness was the Empress that she confided to one visiting diplomat that she would be reluctant to marry any of her daughters off to the King of Spain but Elisabeth she would happily (*mit Freude*) send him as a present.[36]

Elisabeth never ceased complaining about her fate and when she heard of the lavish sums earmarked to secure her brother Maximilian's elevation to the archbishopric of Cologne she had a near-hysterical fit, insisting that she would not under any circumstances allow herself to remain at court. As Maria Theresa later wrote to Marie Christine: 'We all had difficulty getting her to calm down.'

Maria Theresa was more than just aware of Elisabeth's difficulties. She sympathized that she 'faced nothing but boredom all year round' and moreover had to put up with her bad moods. It did not help that the only 'amusements' the Empress felt she could arrange for Elisabeth involved her siblings whom Elisabeth increasingly could not stand. Her sarcastic wit was feared and loathed by her brothers, especially Leopold, who referred to her 'terrible tongue'. Yet Elisabeth, like her mother, was given to sudden impulses of great kindness. An abandoned orphan was adopted by her and brought up under her strict but kind supervision. Visitors who were not relations were treated to the full spectrum of Theresian charm. She could be vivacious, generous and compassionate. On her mother's death, in accordance with Maria Theresa's will, she was made abbess of the *Adeliges Damenstift* in Innsbruck.

CHAPTER 22

The Mother (II): The Sons

OF THE EMPRESS'S SONS, we have already encountered Joseph as co-regent, and a further chapter will explore that part of his mother's legacy which historians have chosen to call *Josephinismus* (Josephinism). His younger brothers now merit closer examination. Maximilian (Max) Franz, born in 1756, we encountered as generally of feeble health and therefore destined for the Church rather than the more physically demanding pillars of state service.

The Peace of Teschen, which had ended the War of Bavarian Succession, gave little indication at first to the chancelleries of Europe as to who had gained most from the expensive 'war without battles', but historians are generally agreed that the international standing of Austria was vastly improved while that of Prussia and its internal condition rapidly deteriorated. An early sign of this asymmetrical development was the election of Max Franz as coadjutor in Cologne and Münster.

Maximilian was the youngest son and predictably something of a *Lieblingskind*, favourite child. He had been considered for many important positions while still a child but his physical and mental lethargy excluded most of them. At the age of 10, he had been awarded the Grand Cross of the Order of St Stephen, suggesting that he might play some as yet undefined role on behalf of the dynasty in Hungary. Another possible bauble was the Grand Mastership of the Order of Teutonic Knights. Max had been inducted into the order, with special papal consent, at the tender age of 14.[1] But Maximilian's lack of mental robustness seemed to suggest that even that position, dealing with the fractious debates of aristocrats squabbling over petty privileges, could prove too demanding.

Moreover, whatever affection Maria Theresa may have had for this boy was tempered by great disappointment over his development spiritually and mentally. A child's education was, as Maria Theresa herself wisely admitted, 'the consequence of the thousands of circumstances which ensure that we really can never achieve perfection in anything in this world'.[2]

Maximilian had been sent abroad to widen his intellectual capacity, but the Empress left, as always when it came to her children, extensive instructions for those 'monitoring' their behaviour. According to Khevenhueller, the decision to send Maximilian to visit the foreign courts of Italy and France was taken partly as a result of certain 'faults', to coin a term much used in weeding out disappointing novices. In Maximilian's case, these faults were external as well as internal. He was cold, *unnahbar* (unapproachable) and brusque in his manner, lacking any of the basic charms of his siblings. Maria Theresa insisted on daily reports on her son's behaviour during his travels and even ordered her long-suffering courtier, Orsini-Rosenberg, to not let the archduke out of his sight: 'My son will decide nothing on his own and he will not take a step without your knowledge.' Whether Maria Theresa was more worried about the reputation of her House rather than the danger of infectious ideas in circulation in foreign courts is hard to gauge. She certainly was worried, as always, about anything which might challenge the strict moral upbringing all her children had enjoyed but she was also concerned that her son make a 'good impression' on all those with whom he came into contact, despite his extreme *Schwermut* (melancholy).[3]

She need not have worried on either score. Her youngest son comported himself with dignity and modesty. On the whole, Maximilian appeared completely indifferent to intellectual debate. He seemed to possess a languor which bordered on the listless. Leopold, writing to his mother from Tuscany, insisted that his passivity suggested a lack of any ambition or drive towards physical or mental exertion. He preferred the company of servants to courtiers and, while this might have been seen as a sign of considerable discernment, it was accompanied by what Leopold described as 'an almost fanatical distrust of everyone and everything'.

When the *Kartoffelkrieg* broke out over the Bavarian Succession, Maximilian briefly accompanied Joseph on the campaign in Bohemia, only to be felled by an infection of his leg which severely hindered his mobility. The incompetence of various field surgeons exacerbated the lesions on one of his legs and he was sent back to Vienna to recover.

Like Ignatius of Loyola, the 'wound' was the making of the archduke. Suddenly, his utter lack of empathy and general indifference to the world became useful props to recovery. Everyone was impressed by his stoicism, lack of regret and complete absence of self-pity. Maria Theresa's judgement of him underwent a complete transformation. If fortitude, as all the family had learnt from an early age, was a valued gift of the Holy Spirit, then young 'Maxi' appeared to possess it in vast quantities.

Where might such qualities be best deployed? The lesions on his leg eventually cleared up but he walked with a slight limp thereafter, so any thoughts of a military career were abandoned. Fortunately for the young recovering archduke, Kaunitz had already identified a possible role for the seemingly unemployable, over-serious prince.

In the ecclesiastical principalities of the *Reich*, the dynamic between emperor and prince of the church was governed by many imponderables which limited the direct power of the emperor. His relationship to these fiefdoms was that of a constitutional monarch rather than an absolute ruler. This made the personality of the prince-archbishop important, but neither the Pope nor the emperor could control the choice of each successive ruler who was elected by the cathedral or monastic chapter.

Since some of these states played an important role in the balance of power and controlled substantial revenues, their rulers were not negligible factors in European diplomacy. The case of Salzburg, which defended its interests in the teeth of many failed attempts by Vienna to influence its affairs, offered one example of the autonomy and wealth the principalities enjoyed. In practice, the only way in which such autonomy could be brought under closer imperial control was to ensure the candidate elected was supported by a strong caucus of ecclesiastical figures suborned by imperial interests.

When in 1761, Clemens August, the Bavarian princeling who was archbishop-elector of Cologne, died, the vacancy was first contemplated by a candidate from the Saxon royal family. Maria Theresa was at this stage resolutely opposed to Max Franz's involvement, but as signs of his physical decrepitude multiplied, encouraged by countless failed operations on his knees, Maria Theresa became more and more open to the idea of her youngest son pursuing high ecclesiastical office. The final incentive came when her son Leopold suggested that one of his own offspring, her grandson, be considered for the Cologne election. Finally, Kaunitz, as usual, rose to the occasion with his faultless logic and insisted to Maria Theresa that here was a relatively straightforward way to strengthen Austria's position within the *Reich* and prevent Prussian influence seeping back into Germany.

She had already shown by the machinations around the appointment of Hieronymus Colloredo, the son of another minister, to the prince-archbishopric of Salzburg in 1772 that she, like Joseph, was not averse to interference with the process of ecclesiastical election.[4]

In the case of Cologne, there were military implications which Kaunitz, ever obsessed with the Prussian presence, could not fail to point out to the Empress. Cologne established a bridgehead towards Prussia and therefore would increase Austria's attraction towards France. Moreover, and here was perhaps the argument best suited to secure his Empress's commitment to the project, Kaunitz argued that the removal of Max Franz from Vienna to the wealthy city of Cologne would result in an immediate saving to the Empress's own personal *Gratifikations* funds of several tens of thousands of florins.

Kaunitz did not dwell on the million florins he envisaged it would cost to secure the position for Max Franz, but those funds would come, logically, from the coffers of the state, not the family. The Pope was persuaded in secrecy to give his blessing and the recovering Max Franz entered holy orders in 1780. It was Maria Theresa's last political success. Both London and Constantinople noticed that Frederick and Prussia had suffered a significant reverse. Frederick ranted and raged about the Austrian 'Court whose sole aim is to incorporate one German province after another'. Unlike the War of the Bavarian Succession, a dangerous and expensive project to which Joseph had been fully committed, this enterprise of his mother's was smooth, comparatively cheap and peaceful.

Joseph found the entire business 'petty and expensive'. It was his mother's project, 'the cost of buying the Holy Spirit'. He had not been consulted on the detail and, when it happened, he was travelling in

Russia where he refused to mention it to the Tsarina Catherine because it 'was such a minor matter'.

Undoubtedly, Joseph felt irritated – he rarely enjoyed being found at fault. His mother, in her dying months, had demonstrated through the election of Max Franz that constitutional methods could achieve far more in terms of influence than threats and violence. In the question of Cologne, it was Maria Theresa who had made all the running. Yet for Joseph, the obsessive reformer committed to a centralized monarchy, the provision of younger sons of the dynasty with their own states was almost an *Affront*. The idea was entirely alien to all his thinking, practically and emotionally, while the very idea of ecclesiastical temporal power was of course anathema.

Some historians have seen Maximilian's elevation as just another example of the Empress's obsession with controlling everything her children in any positions of political responsibility attempted to do, but this could never be the case with Maximilian. For a start, the Empress was in declining health when the young Max was installed. By the time he was elected by both cathedral chapters, the Empress had barely three months to live. The charge that she now 'expected him to let her direct him as she pleased' falls also on the fact that her general advice to her son in any event was of such an unspecific character that it could have borne no relevance to any detailed decisions Max was going to have to take. Above all, his election to prince-elector would furnish him with powers and independence which, in her increasingly enfeebled state, she could do very little to influence. In the event, Maximilian's election would not occur until three years after his mother's death.

In any case, Maximilian demonstrated while he was alive that he was perfectly capable of acting without reference to his mother's sensibilities or wishes. As he travelled to Bonn, the young archduke quickly demonstrated that he had, for all his indifference, a mind of his own. He chose, without consulting his mother, to give the Elector of Mainz an expensive brooch of diamonds. It was not the cost which had outraged the Empress but the fact that he had decided on this expensive gift without informing her. It was the secrecy she despised. She was reconciled to his taking independent decisions but she wanted to be consulted: 'I wish you could see me not just as your mother but as your friend and best counsellor . . . such secrecy reveals a lack of trust and it must be stamped out.'

The Empress once again in her dying days had been unable to let go of her children's development, but once again she failed to give them credit for their ability to take for themselves decisions which could prove correct and helpful. In the end, the Prince-Archbishop of Cologne not only satisfied Kaunitz's ambitions admirably in stemming Prussian pretensions on the Rhine, he also introduced several reforms which underlined a sound judgement and moral probity which would have undoubtedly brought a glow to her heart had she lived long enough to witness it.

Maria Theresa's son Ferdinand was always a staunch defender of his brother Max. More communicative than his brother, he became governor-general of Milan in 1771. Born in 1754, he eventually became his mother's favourite son. He was astonishingly apolitical, and was fortunate in enjoying a role within the monarchy's most prosperous region where he was not required to play any part in its governance. He had none of Joseph's quest for esteem and power, none of Maximilian's brusque manner, and concentrated instead on being a 'good Christian and good husband'.

His wife, the domineering Beatrice d'Este, adopted a rather chivvying stance with Ferdinand, but he seemed on the whole to welcome her qual-ities, not least her childbearing capacity and degree of self-discipline which constantly was deployed to impose a certain austerity on her otherwise fun-loving husband. As Ferdinand became older, he resembled more and more the hedonistic side of his father's temperament.

Maria Theresa thought him and his wife exemplary and she wrote to both regularly, openly discussing many aspects of married life. Here were a couple finally behaving in the way she believed a marriage should be conducted. 'Beatrice and Ferdinand are quite in love with each other. She occasionally takes the high line with him but as long as she does not exaggerate, I have nothing against it', wrote Maria Theresa to a friend. Much to the Empress's surprise, Ferdinand was 'managing far better than I could ever have imagined'.

Leopold, who has bequeathed to us many an acerbic pen sketch of his siblings, found Ferdinand less impressive. 'He is,' the Grand Duke wrote, 'a man of mean intelligence and very little talent notwithstanding the rather high opinion he has of himself . . . He is indecisive, unfocused, devious, proud and avaricious. His subjects resent him and his wife completely dominates him.'[5]

Yet Ferdinand seems to have fulfilled his duties most conscientiously. By keeping in the political background and leaving things to his ministers in Milan, he built a degree of trust between the dynasty and populace which was to endure well into the next century when Ferdinand's successor was the equally well-intentioned Archduke Ferdinand Maximilian.[6]

Ferdinand's wife Beatrice was also noted for her vivacity and, when not giving her husband a hard time, was generally shielding him from potential critics. The more educated Milanese noted that 'their' Archduke was 'intellectually somnolent, uninterested in books and even less in ideas' but such a lack of mental agility suited the local patriciate well. In only one respect did Ferdinand and his wife prove disappointing. While procreating in the best tradition of the time and his House, Ferdinand proved incapable of producing a male heir, always a nerve point for Maria Theresa. After the birth of the fifth baby girl, the Empress wrote that she would have preferred an alternative to 'yet another Reserl'.

Arguably, none of Maria Theresa's children had to submit to the degree of 'benign solicitude' which the Empress inflicted on Ferdinand in Milan. As neither he nor his wife destroyed the letters she sent them, we can construct a fairly detailed account of the scale of Maria Theresa's influence and the almost claustrophobic degree of interference in her son's life. Maria Theresa decided virtually everything with Kaunitz regarding Milan: the uniforms of the Milanese Guard, court appointments, the numbers of equerries and even which prisoners were to be released. This was partly the result of Milan's special status within the monarchy and the peculiarly ceremonial role of the Habsburg couple in Lombardy. But Ferdinand, who was nothing if not his father's son, appears to have enjoyed this enforced compliance, aware, as his father had been, that he was probably not up to imposing his personality on high politics.

This was certainly not the case with Leopold, whose comments on his siblings provided Maria Theresa always with valuable insights, and who came to embody much of the pragmatism and moderation which was so foreign to his elder brother Joseph's thinking.

Leopold enjoyed sharing many of his elder brother's Enlightenment ideals but differed in his approach to their implementation. While Joseph was always a man in a hurry, Leopold was far more reflective. The contrast between the two brothers was noted by William Wraxall, who observed: 'if Joseph's reign was one of the most unfortunate and injurious to the house of Austria, Leopold's accession gave Florence a new aspect. Although he repaired to Vienna to see his mother he cared little for the manners of that city while he loved the banks of the Arno . . . He was a man of enlarged capacity, deep reflection and sound judgement.' This compared favourably with Joseph, whom Wraxall dismissed as 'theoretical, precipitate and ambitious, despite his frugality, indefatigable application and renunciation of pleasure'.

Leopold, as we have seen, had been gifted the Grand Duchy of Tuscany on his father's death in 1765. It had long been planned that the duchy would go to a 'second son' but Leopold's inheritance was poor and backward. He was unamused when Joseph peremptorily transferred 2 million Gulden from the Tuscan treasury to the Austrian state treasury. Francis Stephen had organized the finances of the monarchy so well that he left Joseph 22 million Gulden to deploy towards reducing the national debt, but 2 million of that amount belonged to Tuscany. When Leopold protested most vigorously, only Maria Theresa's direct intervention prevented a total family breach.[7]

In return, Leopold found himself enlisted in the arguments between his mother, his brother and Kaunitz. In 1778, faced with his mother's resistance to hostilities with Prussia, Joseph wrote to Leopold in Tuscany suggesting his return to Vienna where he could 'back me up and obtain for me the means to enable the army to do a good job'.

Leopold was too astute to fall into this trap and it was only his mother who could persuade him to return to Vienna in late August 1778 when she offered him his first access to the most secret state papers. Leopold saw immediately the weaknesses in the Austrian system his mother was hoping to preserve for a new era but his brother's prescriptions in their radicalism also horrified him.

The relationship between the two brothers foundered on sibling rivalry, differing temperaments and the growing resentment that Joseph was a 'control freak' determined to subject everyone and everything within his domains to greater centralization. Maria Theresa confided in Leopold that Joseph was determined sooner or later to incorporate the Grand Duchy of Tuscany into the monarchy.[8]

Tuscans to this day regard Leopold (Gran Duca Pietro Leopoldo) as the most benign of all their past rulers. Although never really popular with his Tuscan subjects, he devoted tirelessly all his energy to improving that backward state's finances and infrastructure. The legacy of the Medicis had been mixed and, in terms of modern administrative practice, primitive. They had left behind them an inefficient and corrupt local government, a non-existent financial system, poor local infrastructure, especially roads and canals, and a vacuum of judicial and medical expertise.

For the first five years of his time as Grand Duke, Leopold had to seek his mother's consent to nearly every action of reform he embarked upon. Her councillors and advisers supervised his day-to-day political activity, but after a visit to Vienna in 1770, he was able to govern without too much interference from Vienna and he initiated a series of hallmark reforms. Public works became a priority; roads and canals were all improved while the swampy Val di Chiana was systematically drained and replanted with vines. Slowly but steadily, he brought the duchy into a high state of material prosperity, even though some of his inhabitants were offended by his determination to resist papal interference in his temporal activities. He also, inevitably, annoyed those who had enjoyed the patronage of the Medicis and found the new Austrian regime far too austere for their tastes. The Grand Duke might be portrayed in portraits in Austrian gala white uniform, but he shared all his brother Joseph's disdain of etiquette and ceremonial pomp.

Had he not been recalled to Vienna ahead of the death of his brother Joseph in 1790, it is not to be excluded that Leopold would have even granted Tuscany the first modern constitution of the eighteenth century, pre-dating the American and French efforts by several years. He was committed to empowering a legislative body which could work in cooperation and constructive dialogue with the sovereign.

Nonetheless, in the twenty years during which he ruled Tuscany, he transformed the backward, disease-ridden duchy into a model of enlightened government throughout Europe, in many ways the envy of the Enlightenment world.

His new administration granted the inhabitants a predictable and independent judiciary along Austrian lines. Leopold's reforms included the abolition of capital punishment – the first such act in Europe – and an embryonic constitution which guaranteed basic human rights. He also abolished torture. In 1774 laws on the insane (*legge sui pazzi*) were introduced which radically changed the way mental health was treated, providing a blueprint for the rest of Europe. At the same time, he followed Maria Theresa's policies in public health, making inoculation freely available. A well-resourced new hospital, the *Bonifacio*, transformed the way the mentally ill were housed while other institutions were funded to provide basic medical and emergency healthcare.

Leopold knew he would one day most probably have to succeed his elder brother. The childless Joseph towards the end of his life offered Leopold the chance of joining him as co-ruler, but Leopold was far too fly for such an obvious invitation to share in Joseph's mounting unpopularity.

In barely ten years, Joseph had embarked on so much unbridled interference with the traditions and habits of the nations under his crown that his revolutionary zeal had met with explosive reactions in every corner of the monarchy. Joseph, as we have seen, lacked all his mother's tact and pragmatism, but it was only after her death that, no longer hindered by Maria Theresa's influence, the full extent of his lack of statecraft came to the fore.

Historians of the Enlightenment prefer to dwell on Joseph's 'reforms', especially the Patent of Toleration of 1782 which 'freed the Jews' from Maria Theresa's 'bigotry'. Yet even the 'Great Patent' imposed restrictions in the service of Josephinian centralizing control. Jews might have no longer been persecuted but the insistence that they all speak German and be recognizable by their names arguably institutionalized anti-Semitism more vigorously and permanently in the German-speaking world than anything done by the Great Empress.

Yet it was Joseph's insistence on changing the existing norms of practice in the Austrian Netherlands, Italy and Hungary which brought the monarchy closer to the brink of collapse than at any time since 1740. In Italy, his monastic reforms turned a largely compliant population towards a visceral anti-Austrian sentiment. In modern-day Belgium, the Austrian Netherlands, his attempts to reform the theological faculty and deconstruct the province's autonomy led to a full-blown uprising. The new cadres of administrators he sent to take over were bitterly resented and Joseph's attempts to force the ancient University of Louvain to permit instruction in other faiths and other 'impolitic innovations' proved incendiary.

When Joseph ordered half the university professors to be sacked, clergy and laity linked hands across a sea of Enlightenment troubles and the small Austrian garrison in Louvain found itself confronted by a violent mob led by monks, academics and sacked tax collectors. Joseph might have brought his intellect to bear on this had he not been distracted by a rebellion in Hungary and a full-blown war against the Ottomans, from which only Loudon rescued the honour of Austrian arms by eventually seizing Belgrade.

'Your country has killed me', Joseph wrote to his friend, the Prince de Ligne, but it was the ill-fated Turkish campaign which finally did for Joseph. The empire he bequeathed to Leopold in 1790 was in a desperate situation which only the most perspicacious statesmanship could rescue. Fortunately for Austria, Leopold possessed none of Joseph's fanaticism, and within six months, peace had been made with Turkey and calm reigned again in Louvain and the Hungarian estates.

Leopold reigned for barely two years as pleurisy took him suddenly just as he was getting into his stride. In that time, Austria faced challenges from both east and west and, although he did not live long enough to face the even greater challenge of Napoleon – determined to remake the map of Europe at Austria's expense and drive her from Germany and Italy – his steady, low-key approach to rule brought the monarchy much desperately needed relief after the torrent of Joseph's reign.

It was Austria's tragedy not to have enjoyed Leopold's wisdom as a ruler for longer than two years, but even in that limited time his pragmatism and moderation, qualities inherited from his mother, restored the stability of the Habsburg lands, just in time to confront all the storms about to be unleashed from the direction of France.

CHAPTER 23

Joseph and Josephinism

THE CULT OF JOSEPH and Josephinism (*Josephinismus*) owed its construction to the revolutionary events of 1848. Before then there had been relatively little interest in him, or his mother, but the rise of nationalism and the turbulence of the year of revolutions rekindled interest in Joseph as a 'radical ahead of his time'. Joseph was first and foremost the 'German Emperor'. Then he was the 'bringer of light', the Emperor 'with a Patent of Toleration', the granter of 'press freedom'. The ensuing need after 1849 to keep Hungary happy extended this posthumous approval to Joseph's mother, Maria Theresa, but only in much smaller doses. The revolutionary mob which charged past the Hofburg in 1848 made a special detour to revere the statue of Joseph. There was no monument to Maria Theresa to delay their progress.

Yet Josephinism, as has been pointed out, owed in fact little to Joseph and much to Maria Theresa.[1] The reforms of the 1780s, following Maria Theresa's death, could never have been enacted had it not been for the foundations for change laid down by the Great Empress; she and her ministers established the principles which her son then developed. In many cases, Joseph's radicalism depended entirely on the administrative machine his mother had created. Few of his innovations could have been brought to life without the civil service fashioned three decades earlier by Haugwitz, Van Swieten and later Kaunitz. His two great Patents – on religious toleration and Freemasonry – illustrate well the legacy of his mother's reforms while demonstrating all too clearly the dangers of attempting to develop that legacy too swiftly and without compromise.

Long before Joseph's famous Patent on Freemasonry was issued, Maria Theresa had tolerated the activities of the lodges. Many of her closest advisers were Freemasons. Yet, as we have seen, they were also committed Catholics. Kaunitz described lodge membership as both 'ludicrous and a mere bagatelle', a social and charitable activity which posed no threat to the interests of the state.

Yet by the time Joseph succeeded his mother in 1780, the political atmosphere of the 1770s had changed. First, with the American War of Independence and then with the growing anti-monarchist sentiment in France. We have already seen in Maria Theresa's letters to Marie Antoinette that she feared Europe to be on the brink of immense changes which could easily threaten the privileges of her family and especially her daughter in France. Joseph embarked on his reform programme in such haste largely because this fear of his mother's became for him an almost pathological neurosis. Fed by his many travels incognito, his perception for the need for change became all-consuming. In Joseph's eyes, everything had to be reformed if the imminent political and social explosion which he saw as inevitable was not to occur in the Austrian crown lands.

Joseph's Patents were therefore as much inspired by *raison d'état* as by 'Enlightenment thinking'. Each was an instrument to shore up the state. The Toleration Patent of 1782 not only strengthened the economic activities of the state (there would no longer be unchecked emigration), but it also gave those of his subjects who had hitherto been indifferent towards the lands of their birth a stake in the system. Joseph, with his usual mordant wit, argued that his subjects, once granted freedom of religious practice, might prefer in a crisis to die for their state, rather than for each other. His insistence on Jews speaking German and having German names should be seen in the context of this policy.

Four years later, in December 1785, Joseph confronted another perceived threat to his vision of the cohesive Austrian state: the secret societies. There is no evidence that Joseph, unlike his father and his brother Leopold, was ever admitted into a lodge, but that he felt instinctive sympathy with their activities is undeniable. Yet this sympathy had rigid limits and was always to be subordinated to the interests of the state and his rule.

When, in 1777, Maria Theresa consulted him on the meetings of certain Masonic lodges in the Lowlands which were causing concern in some quarters of her court, Joseph intervened:

I have the honour to relate that whatever methods are employed to prevent and harass such clubs tend only to make them more attractive and, since their innocence is recognized by all sensible persons in society, to bring ridicule on governments and on those who by forbidding things that they believe to be bad simply because they do not know anything about them, endows them with a measure of importance. I therefore very humbly suggest that no action be taken . . . although if she thinks it appropriate, the leaders of Brussels society would be gently informed that we should prefer them not to amuse themselves so publicly with Freemasonry but that they should conceal it better so that the affairs won't cause much talk.[2]

This sympathy could not remain unconditional as the political activities of the lodges began to become more pronounced. While, early in his reign, Joseph had argued in favour of Count Brigado, who was about to go to Galicia as governor, that he should be initiated and promoted into Ignaz Born's lodge at a single meeting, such undiluted enthusiasm could not survive the challenge of rising political tensions. Born probably knew he was enjoying a transient favour when he informed his fellow Masons that 'the Emperor would very much like the heads in each province to be taken into the Order'.[3]

After his mother's death, Joseph moved swiftly to centralize and regulate this part of his inheritance and a Patent tolerating but regulating the activities of the Freemasons was prepared.

One year before this Patent was issued, Count Dietrichstein had negotiated on Joseph's behalf that a single Grand Lodge of Austria be established. In this way Joseph hoped not only to indulge his obsession with centralization but also exclude foreign influences and eliminate the growing opaqueness of the lodges following the establishment in Bavaria, ten years earlier, of the more politically oriented 'Illuminati'.

Dietrichstein was a follower of the Rosicrucians and was, therefore, well aware of the potential within secret societies to multiply into differing sects, each with different agendas. As stronger decrees banning the 'Illuminati' were introduced in Bavaria, the entire fashion for Freemasonry appeared in danger of becoming riven by public as well as private division. Joseph's constitutional reforms met with increasing opposition, especially in Hungary. As all too many of his opponents there were members of lodges, Joseph was convinced it was the right moment to bring their burgeoning activities 'within the remit' of the state.

Joseph seems to have refused to listen to any advice on how to deal with the secret societies and the Patent issued in December 1785 has certainly a highly personal style:

> The so-called societies of Freemasons, about whose secrets I know nothing, as I have never been in the least curious to experience their charlatanries, are growing and spreading even to small towns. These gatherings, if left entirely alone and uncontrolled, can lead to excesses harmful to religion, order and morality. This is especially the case if the people at the top are bound closely by a shared fanaticism, and behave unjustly towards their social inferiors.
>
> In former times in other countries Freemasons were prohibited and punished and their meetings were dispersed because it was not known what their secrets were. Although they are also unknown to me, it is enough for me to know that these Masonic meetings do yield some real benefit to the community, to the poor and for education so that I shall do for them more than any other country has yet done, namely to order that, as long as they do good, they shall be taken under the care and protection of the state and their meetings are to be formally permitted . . . in this manner this brotherhood, which consists of so many upright men well-known to me, can perhaps become truly useful to society and distinguished by learning.[4]

The 'care and protection of the state' came at a high price. The lodges were permitted outside Vienna only to operate in provincial cities, their number in those cities was strictly limited to a single presence, while even in Vienna, only three lodges were allowed. Compared to the unhindered proliferation of lodges in the Vienna of Maria Theresa, these were powerful restrictions on what later historians and apologists for Joseph have described as the 'golden age of Austrian Freemasonry'.

The reduction in lodges in Vienna alone, from at least eight but probably many more, the disappearance of the famous lodge 'True Concord' (*Zur wahren Eintracht*), the obsequiousness towards the Emperor of the surviving lodges' writings and music all point to an intellectual and moral decline in Austrian Freemasonry which was absent during the reign of Joseph's mother.

It did not help that the leading lights of the 'craft' proceeded to fall out with each other in public. Sonnenfels, a member of the controversial Illuminati, and Born, another Illuminato who was also Master of the Lodge *Zur Wohltätigkeit*, refused to speak to each other. Their rivalries and disputes spilt out into the public space. Joseph had wanted to neutralize the attraction of the lodges and his Patent proved more effective than any reactionary government's censure. Within six months of the Patent's proclamation, numbers of Freemasons in Vienna had fallen by a third to 547. Thereafter, they fell rapidly so that by the time of Joseph's death in 1790, there were barely 200. Josephinism, long seen by commentators as synonymous with Enlightenment progress, can be considered here for what it was: the manifestations of autocratic centralization and control in sharp contrast to the less rigidly enforced proscriptions of his mother's reign.

Of the other pillars of Josephinism, reform of civil and criminal law were at first glance little more than a reanimation of a process begun by his mother. But in the *Allgemeines bürgerliches Gesetzbuch* (general civil law handbook) of 1787 the influence of Sonnenfels and Martini can be seen in wordings which register in a more concrete form the oft-expressed wishes and desires of Maria Theresa with regard to the security and protection of her subjects.

The *Gesetzbuch* was *allgemein* and, therefore, enforceable throughout the monarchy, a long-standing wish of Maria Theresa's legislation. Some commentators have dwelt on the 'revolutionary' aspects of Sonnenfels's phrasing but there is little which would not have found wholehearted approval by Maria Theresa: 'Every subject expects from the ruler security and protection. So it is the duty of the prince to lay down clearly the rights of subjects and so to direct their conduct that it furthers both general and individual well-being.'[5]

To describe these provisions as 'genuine anticipations of the French Revolution' is an exaggeration, and apologists for Joseph must concede that the absence of the term 'citizens' is alone enough to show that the political freedom demanded by the French Jacobins had no place there. 'Subjects' and 'prince' are the defining poles of responsibility.[6]

Other provisions were perhaps more tangibly progressive. Joseph moved to prevent the entailing of estates until it was pointed out to him that the Habsburg inheritance was one giant entail. The great land-owners formed up to him and Joseph bowed to the logic (and self-interest) of their arguments.

In 1787 a new criminal code was introduced, formally abolishing the death penalty. In practice, it had already under his mother been consistently commuted. Torture had, as we have seen, also been abolished in 1776 and Joseph's reforms of the *Nemesis Theresiana* in many places simply tidied up legislation already undertaken by Maria Theresa. What struck contemporaries most about the *Josephinismus* elements in the new criminal code was its determined egalitarianism. The aristocracy's previous exemptions were abolished. In a typically Josephinian interpretation of *noblesse oblige*, the nobility were now expected to be penalized more than the ordinary people for offences committed. This again was pushing beyond his late mother's instincts.

Three particular cases made a great impression. The first was of a minor court official, von Zahlheimb, who murdered his fiancée for money. He was, exceptionally, sentenced early in 1786 to be broken on the wheel, the last execution to take place in eighteenth-century Austria. The sentence would have been certainly commuted had the crime been committed by a commoner. In the case of Freiherr von Szekely, another official, who embezzled a substantial sum from his regiment, he was cashiered and paraded for three successive days wearing a placard identifying him as a dishonest servant of the state. The third case was Count Podstatsky-Liechtenstein, who, despite his formidable connections to the greatest of court families, was found guilty of forging banknotes in an attempt to stem his gambling losses.

He was given what was, after the abolition of the death penalty, Austria's cruellest sanction, *Schiffsziehen*, the hard labour of pulling barges up the Danube. Groups of criminals were chained together, and had to wade through swamps and the river. They were forced to sleep in all weathers in the open, forbidden from changing their clothes, and when they collapsed, refused all medical aid and simply left to die. That a member of the high aristocracy could be so treated was a rarity in the pre-revolutionary Europe of the 1780s.

Aristocrats found guilty of crimes were to be automatically demoted to the status of commoners. Maria Theresa's scepticism of the privileges of the aristocracy had in this case inspired Joseph into creating a code which was truly innovative for the time. Britain was still making do with legal commentaries while Joseph's *Gesetzbuch* antedated the Napoleonic code by nearly twenty years. Perhaps more than any of his other reforms, this helped stave off the imminent social explosion which had so preoccupied his mother towards the end of her reign.

Another reform associated with Joseph, which owed its inspiration to Maria Theresa, was the sweeping change the Emperor brought into the administration of the censorship system. We have seen that it was one of Maria Theresa's earliest decisions to take the censorship system out of the monopolistic hands of the Jesuits and widen the existing system under the guidance of a devout Catholic layman, Van Swieten. This laid the foundations for Joseph's later reform of the monarchy's censorship system.

It was not enough that the commission created by his mother had granted educated laymen a formal role in the process. The entire censorship of books and other publications was for Joseph still too arbitrary, obscurantist and intrusive. Joseph was especially outraged by the censorship of foreign texts. It was the height of folly to try to ban these as 'there is not a bad book which has been censored which does not exist in Vienna. Anyone tempted can procure it simply by paying double its price.'[7]

Very early on in his reign, he broached the subject with his advisers and demanded greater centralization so that there could be more consistency in the censorship process. What was the point of a book being banned in Vienna if it was allowed free circulation in Prague? It has been suggested that one of Joseph's motives was promotion of the book trade – he had enjoyed a brief apprenticeship at the Vienna publishing house of Trattner as part of his education as a teenager.

Unsurprisingly, the censorship *Grundgesetz* which was implemented a few years later bears all the signs of Joseph's personal involvement and commitment to a cause close to his mind. The proclamation expresses very clearly his own predilection: 'Is it a bigger mistake if books are admitted which ought to be banned or is it better with maximum severity and disagreeable compulsion to exclude many good books thus obstructing a vital thread of commerce?'[8]

It was for Joseph a point of honour 'to come down strongly against works which contain unbridled obscenities from which no learning nor enlightenment can ever arise'. But it was therefore equally important to 'be all the more indulgent in the case of those in which wisdom, knowledge and understanding are to be found'. It was the language of the Jesuits and his mother: wisdom, knowledge and understanding, three of the seven gifts of the Holy Spirit.

Joseph did not shirk from acknowledging that the books under consideration divided along class and intellectual lines: 'The former are only read by the multitude of weak souls while the latter come into the hands only of those with well-prepared minds and well-established principles.'

Joseph was adamant that works which systematically sought to ridicule or criticize the Church could not be tolerated but 'Protestant' books could be permitted as they were 'unlikely to lead to conversions but provide succour for co-religionists'. Such books should be available but not 'widely diffused'.

The reforms Joseph implemented thus went rather further than his mother might have contemplated, but under Van Swieten's influence she might have acceded to Joseph's tolerance of 'medical, juridical and military' writings being allowed unfettered access to the monarchy's booksellers. She certainly would have been resigned to 'single books' not being enquired into, in contrast to 'books in quantity'.

These changes have often been perceived as a portent of 'press freedom'. A pamphlet published in Vienna in 1781 hopefully concluded: 'The wisest, the best of monarchs has given us the freedom to write what we think.' But this was optimistic. Neither Joseph nor any of his advisers imagined the kind of liberty granted to pamphleteers in London or Holland. Maria Theresa had happily put out of business a Viennese publisher who had dared to print an article indicating that Catherine of Russia was about to face a coup by her son Paul. The limits of tolerance were firmly established under Maria Theresa and Joseph scrupulously followed them. No criticism of foreign rulers was permitted and the clergy remained banned from criticizing, either in their pulpits or in print, any government decree. Plays and operas were subject to censorship, although Joseph might have himself been involved in da Ponte and Mozart's slightly subversive opera *The Marriage of Figaro*. In all cases, the targeted audience governed the strictness of the censorship.

Joseph's deployment of different criteria on the one hand liberalized his mother's regime while on the other redirecting it. Anything which hinted at disagreement with government policy or critique of the Emperor was banned. A profusion of intellectual pamphlets aimed at the well-educated and well-heeled, on the other hand, was permitted. This ambivalence of Joseph was well noted at the time and subsequent biographers have referred to the 'peculiar mixture of liberality and barracks discipline'.[9] As one Princess Liechtenstein pointed out:

We are really in quite a new world . . . It is not enough to tolerate everything, we must also publish it. Everything is to be expected from the Emperor's spirit in this field, from his love of novelty, his perversity, his mania for rousing subordinates against their chiefs and still more from the hardening of his heart and finally abandonment of God.[10]

Unsurprisingly, the Papal Nuncio was more scandalized:

Libertines and the irreligious have considered themselves invited, not to say authorized, to appear before the public. Not a week has passed without the publication, among many other insidious little books, of more or less intemperate attacks on the Church; even the reputation of private individuals has suffered and is suffering though they are identified only by initials. As in England these pamphlets have few pages but are vulgar in tone and have enigmatic titles to attract readers.[11]

Joseph defended himself vigorously against all attacks, focusing as always on the cerebral debate, writing to the Elector (Prince-Archbishop) of Trier, a Saxon prince:

> Fortunately my good Austrians and brave Hungarians are unaware of either Molinos or Jansenius and if you spoke to them they would ask whether they were Roman consuls and admit they had never heard of them. I myself once knew a Molinos, a greyhound who could course and kill his hare single-handed; that is how ignorant we are about the great disputes over grace.

Joseph continued: 'Finally the Vienna censorship causes you some upset. I should feel the same if I had not already seen enough of men to realize that very few of them read and even fewer profit from or remember what they read. I even know some people who do not know what they write.'

He continued: 'With beings so constituted should one not rather fear the prohibition of bad books? For it is only the prohibition which causes them to be read. But for this fatal prohibition which tempted even the father of us all we would still be walking naked in the terrestrial paradise.'[12]

This was not a view likely to commend Joseph to traditionalists and in a later exchange with the Elector (Prince-Archbishop) of Trier he admitted: 'I see that we do not dance to the same tune: you take the form for the substance while in matters of religion I hold strictly to the substance and object only to the abuses which have disfigured its purity.'

It was precisely this intellectual, arrogant point-scoring which Maria Theresa detested in Joseph. She knew how deeply resentful those at the receiving end of such arguments and cerebral sword thrusts felt, and she knew it was no way to win friends and influence people. Reform yes, but a reform which took pleasure in ridiculing others of differing mental capabilities was anathema to Maria Theresa, and for that reason – however strongly she can be seen as the inspiriter of, to use a phrase of Joseph's, the substance of Josephinism – many aspects of its form would have left her cold.

CHAPTER 24

Stocks, Subsidies and Free Trade: The World of Theresian Finance

IT WAS MARIA THERESA's husband, Francis Stephen, who quietly in the background looked after the financial affairs of the monarchy. He was 'good with money' and the healthy state of the Austrian Treasury in 1765, when he died, was testament to his common sense and prudent financial management.

Here he complemented Maria Theresa whose own personal finances were erratic and considerably less well ordered than her eye for detail in public expenditure might suggest. While the Empress, on the one hand, scrupulously moved to eliminate excessive expense in the design and manufacture of her army's uniforms, alone with her generals, she adored whiling away the early hours in games of 'Lu' and Austrian *Bezique* in which more often than not she lost huge sums of money. A contemporary print shows her with Lacy and some other officers playing cards *à quatre*. She is dressed in mourning so we can date the picture to after 1765. Francis Stephen enjoyed frivolities but he would have been pained by the costs incurred by his widow at the card table.

These losses came out of Maria Theresa's own funds, which had been arranged by Francis Stephen long before he died in the so-called *Geheimes Kammerzahlamt*. This department of the Empress's household dealt with 'the financial needs of the sovereign' and included everything from the cost of the court, the education of the children, the needs of relatives, including the Empress's mother, to charitable donations to cripples, wounded soldiers and orphaned children. Six thousand florins was spent annually from these funds just on ladies-in-waiting while thousands of florins went into the *Erziehungsfond* for education, from which not just members of the family but complete strangers such as the young Thugut benefited.

Some of the money was invested and formed the basis of the income which accrued to the *Kammerzahlamt*. While her husband lived, Maria Theresa felt personally able to extend her *Munifizenz* in various directions but as the Empress grew older the funds became open to abuses. Arguments among its officials marred the later era of the department and, without the watchful eye of Francis Stephen, it steadily reduced in asset value. Within a month of his mother's death, Joseph did not hesitate to order the entire department's abolition on 30 December 1780. All payments henceforth had to be personally authorized by him and unsurprisingly these rapidly decreased in number and size.

Another body executing the Empress's expenditure, the Imperial Royal *Commerzialamt*, survived for a little longer, but Joseph insisted that it be brought under the direct control of the imperial treasury. The resulting sudden austerity imposed on the earlier beneficiaries was dramatic and not all adapted seamlessly to the new parsimony.

One important element of Maria Theresa's 'innovations' in the financial world, however, did flourish and still survives to this day: the Vienna Stock Exchange. The wars which Maria Theresa fought always required huge financial expenditure. Had not the great Austrian general of the seventeenth century, Raimondo Montecuccoli, said, 'In order to wage war you need three things: Money, money and money'.[1]

Subsidies from abroad could only account for some of the huge sums needed. In 1742 Vienna began issuing international debt with the help of bankers in Holland and northern Italy. A comprehensive tax reform, initiated by Haugwitz in 1748, on the conclusion of the Austrian Succession wars, encouraged the issuance of domestic debt and these bonds soon found a flourishing secondary market on a newly established Vienna exchange. This exchange was later restructured and formally inaugurated on 14 August 1761.

Another of Maria Theresa's advisers, Karl Zinzendorf, had already, a year earlier, in his *Finanzvorschläge* (financial suggestions), laid down how he envisaged a Vienna Stock Exchange financing at any time up to eighteen months of the Austrian state's obligations. The exchange would control the costs of any wars and ensure that funds never dried up thanks to the issuance of rolling *Staatsanleihen* (state bonds). A sovereign guarantee made these bonds 'gilts' and, as Maria Theresa's prospects improved, they swiftly became bestsellers. The state paper was traded daily in denominations of 25 and 100 florins. To support the trade in these *Bankozettel*, a number of financiers were encouraged to participate in the secondary market and thus a flourishing highly liquid loan business began to develop. A significant figure, Johann Fries, dominated this market and founded the first of many banks in the monarchy.

By the time of Francis Stephen's death in 1765, Fries's banks, together with other financial houses, had been established in Vienna, Linz, Graz, Milan and Trieste. These banks were subject from the beginning to regulation and Maria Theresa oversaw in 1767 the establishment of a banking regulator in the form of a state commission to oversee all activities of the banks, in particular their trading books. By 1769 more than 12 million of the *Bankozettel* were being traded every day. The banks rapidly became vehicles for raising capital. If the banks served as outer spokes of financial investment, the hub of the monarchy's embrace of capitalism was the Vienna exchange. Under Maria Theresa, it was open every day except religious holidays and had two principal trading sessions: from 11 am to 1 pm and 4 pm to 5 pm. It played a key role in ensuring the monarchy was in a far stronger financial position than Prussia when it came to the Seven Years War and the War of the Bavarian Succession.

In time, it would finance the industrialization of the empire and the rebuilding of Vienna and all the important provincial capitals of the Habsburg domains. It would become the heart of financial interests which included some of the most powerful financiers in the world, notably members of the Rothschild family, whose Vienna branch rivalled those of London, Paris and Frankfurt.

The cities which established banks soon prospered mightily. Milan became a leading financial centre and even Graz, which had last flourished under Ferdinand II nearly two hundred years earlier, ceased to be a provincial backwater and laid the foundations of its nineteenth-century bourgeois prosperity as *Pensionopolis*.

Above all, it was the Austrian Netherlands which provided much of the dynamism for the new financial techniques and capital-raising practices. Antwerp was a fulcrum of inventive commercial trading. In Maria

Theresa's father's day, the Ostend East India Trading Company had threatened to rival England's East India Company. It had become an obsession among the politicians of England, especially in Robert Walpole's government, to close it down.

Although the potential of the Ostend East India Company had to be sacrificed, as we have seen, on the altar of the Pragmatic Sanction, many other banking and allied activities flourished in the Austrian Netherlands, giving it a period of material prosperity under the Great Empress which it has arguably never achieved since (even after the ruthless exploitation of the Congo's mineral wealth by King Leopold).

Moreover, when an attempt to revive something of the Ostend East India Company's glory was made in the 1770s under the English adventurer William Bolts, his financial backers came from the empire's bankers, supported by Kaunitz. Bolts went bankrupt but not before one of his backers, Count Karl Proli, had established in Brussels the first insurance company in the empire which, in its first five years of existence, paid its financial backers a handsome 8 per cent dividend.

But it was a city in the eastern Mediterranean, which had always been close to Maria Theresa's father's ambitions, which benefited most from the creation of a banking and financial sector. Unlike Joseph, who was highly protectionist in matters of trade, Maria Theresa was, like her father and the Spanish Habsburgs, a globalist and a staunch defender of free trade. Nothing expressed this more forcefully than her support for Trieste, a city she never visited, but which was to become Austria's window on the eastern world, and the second city of the empire.

CHAPTER 25

Trieste and the Renewal of a Global Presence

WE HAVE SEEN IN earlier chapters how Maria Theresa's father, in his desperate attempts to secure British compliance with the terms of the Pragmatic Sanction, had agreed to close down the Austrian Ostend East India Trading Company. But as the statue of his predecessor, Leopold I, which graces the approaches to Trieste's main square even today still symbolizes, Charles VI was not the first Habsburg to understand the potential of Trieste. Leopold was the first Habsburg to offer Trieste a significant role within his empire. With the end of the long wars against the Ottomans, trade with the Orient became increasingly significant. The closure of the Ostend and related trading companies represented serious concessions with profound effects for the commercial direction of the monarchy. The fact that their existence is barely recalled today should not distract us from their significance at the time.

If Austria might not be encouraged to spread her lines of communication with the Far East, there were plenty of opportunities nearer to home. The agreements with the Ottoman empire which Maria Theresa reached opened up trading opportunities with Vienna's once great rival. As the Adriatic commanded two of the three principal routes to the east, Maria Theresa honoured her father's commitment to the city which together with Venice dominated the 'inmost sea of all the earth'.[1]

By the time of her death in 1780, she had encouraged its status as a Free Port and been instrumental in establishing a confessional tolerance which allowed Jews, Serbs, Greeks and Protestants to settle in the city, giving it a cosmopolitanism which was rare even in the Habsburg domains at that time.

In time, Maria Theresa's encouragement of the Jews in Trieste would become a blueprint for the extension of tolerance of non-Catholic religions throughout the empire. While the Empress held firm to her principle of 'no systematic toleration' of non-Catholic faiths, she could envisage a status for Jews which went far beyond mere sufferance to include corporate legal standing, religious freedoms, extensive economic activity and exemption from humiliating signs, taxes and restrictions. It is worth recalling that several decades before Joseph's Patent of Toleration, Maria Theresa's patents governing Trieste, beginning in 1746, paved the way for the removal of the city ghetto and allowed unfettered public worship for the small but important Jewish community of the city. Whatever her personal distaste for the confessional beliefs of non-Catholics, the Empress saw the merits of Jewish people and the need to vouchsafe them a degree of security and freedom. The assertions of recent writers, notably Derek Beales, that 'historians . . . cannot find a shred of evidence for Maria Theresa's envisaging the measures of toleration for Protestants and Jews that were (later) enacted' and that 'nothing at all was done about tolerating the Jews' vividly falls away in the case of Trieste.[2]

On 29 November 1749, Maria Theresa issued a proclamation of fifty-five pages indicating the lines along which she wished the city of Trieste to develop commercially. A detailed city plan underlined the transformation of a still-medieval town centre into a modern city of broad boulevards, substantial warehouses and city palaces. The *Borgo Teresiano* to this day in Trieste illustrates the scope of the Empress's ambitions. A canal was constructed to divide the new quarter from earlier settlements and Vienna-trained engineers descended on the city to lay out the new quarter under the supervision of a gifted architect, Francesco Saverio de Bonomo. The result, as can be seen today, is a series of grid-like streets with well-proportioned palaces whose architecture is above all a tribute to the commercial purpose of the city. Situated close to the city's harbour, the palace's ground floors were warehouses which stored all the produce of Austria's flourishing trade with the east. Coffee, fruits, spices, textiles, silks were all to be imported and placed in these huge depositories to await onward shipment to various parts of the empire.[3] Above these impressive spaces were apartments whose façades boasted an ornate decoration rich in allegories of classical virtues. They provided living quarters for a new class of commercial traders, largely remote from, and therefore indifferent to, the aristocracy, whose sway over this city was never as strong as in the other great cities of the empire.

No less remote was the Catholic Church. If the territory in every direction from the city was dominated by clergy and an uneducated peasantry, the city began to develop a dynamic which, notwithstanding the strong Jesuit presence in Trieste before the Suppression, was markedly unclerical.

The style adopted throughout the city was an undeniably fashionable 'Enlightenment' classicism. As the fortunes of the many merchants increased during the last years of Maria Theresa's reign, so too did the splendour of their buildings.

The architectural investment was followed rapidly by the arrival of considerable human capital. By the year of Francis Stephen's death, 1765, the population of the city had doubled. The new incomers came from all over the Adriatic and beyond. Aspiring traders from Milan, Modena, Mantova, Ferrara and Friuli competed with Turks, Greeks, Bosnians and Serbs as well as a handful of English, changing traditions of dress, manners and language. Jews driven out of Venice by the parochialism and anti-Semitism of the doges found a safe home in the nearby Austrian port. The Triestine dialect became a lingua franca, acquired and spoken by all nationalities, irrespective of origin. The wealth of immigration brought new skills, new professions and new produce: clocks and soap manufacturers arrived along with glass, and carpenters trained in the best workshops of the monarchy.[4]

The Greeks and Serbs quickly developed trading routes with Istria and Dalmatia. The Jews competed with the Greeks for the trading routes beyond, notably Durazzo, Smyrna and Salonica. By 1768 the number of ships using the port annually had grown from barely 700 in 1753 to nearly 7,000. A visitor to the port, Antonio de Giuliani, estimated a couple of decades later that as many as seven out of every eight inhabitants were foreign-born.[5]

These developments were accompanied by a virtual avalanche of legislation, unseen in any other part of the monarchy, designed to impose predictability and consistency on all commercial activity in the city. In 1755 a regulated Stock Exchange (*Regolamento di Borsa*) was proclaimed while, on 19 January 1758, regulations concerning foreign currency exchange and other commercial trades were brought into force. A year later, the rapidly expanding commodity trading was regulated as to volume, weights and other measures, to which all traders in the city were expected to conform.

The results of these Theresian reforms for Trieste were three-fold. Firstly, they introduced a hitherto unprecedented transparency into all commercial transactions in the city. Secondly, they imposed a consistency and impartial legal framework to act as a backdrop to all trades; and lastly, they encouraged merchants from all over the Mediterranean to settle in Trieste and take advantage of the rules-based commercial life which, free from clerical and political interference, allowed trade to flourish. 'Consoler of the afflicted and refuge of sinners, for emigrants, that is Trieste', wrote Charles-Albert, Comte de Moré, who dubbed the city 'the Philadelphia of Europe'.[6]

The Seven Years War barely arrested the city's progress – Silesia was remote from the Mediterranean – but with the end of the war in 1763 Trieste's seemingly unstoppable ascent took on new energy. Military barracks and stores for ammunition were swiftly converted into commodities warehouses and accommodation for a new burgeoning mercantile class. The small but significant Jewish community was encouraged, and increased five-fold by the end of the 1760s to comprise more than fifty-three households.[7]

In 1776 Maria Theresa reorganized Trieste's constitutional status by appointing a Viceregal Governor, Count Karl Zinzendorf, to oversee the developments in the city. Zinzendorf busied himself first and foremost with the construction of a good road linking the city with Vienna. It stretched from the northern tip of the *Borgo Teresiano* via Laibach (Ljubljana) and Graz to the Austrian capital and was until 1918 the principal road linking the two cities.

Maria Theresa, despite her son's centralizing zeal, realized that if the city was to continue to flourish it would have to enjoy a certain independence. Public works became largely the affair of the local government and a period of hospitals and barracks construction ensued.

Zinzendorf also encouraged a brief revival in Austria's ambitions for maritime mercantile success. In the easy commercial environment of Trieste, where business ideas could be discussed without restriction or constraint, a rough English adventurer, William Bolts, a former employee of the East India Company, suggested a commercial journey to the Orient to take advantage of England's preoccupation with the revolt of her colonies in America. His story illuminates the risks and commercial appetite of Theresian Austria as Trieste flourished.

A ship was bought with the help of Triestine and Belgian capital and renamed *Joseph and Therese* in honour of the imperial family. It was crewed by 25 marines and 155 sailors of various nationalities. To provide a small escort and protection against piracy, a frigate, the *Etruria*, of the navy of the Grand Duchy of Tuscany, under the command of Captain Joseph Acton, was dispatched from Leghorn to accompany Bolts's mission.

On reaching Tristan da Cunha, Bolts established a depository to store commodities, guarded by two small forts which, again in honour of the imperial House, he named Joseph and Therese. By late 1777 he had established himself at Mysore, where the notoriously anti-British Hyder-Ali looked favourably on an Austrian mission, but at Calcutta Bolts was arrested by the British and his ship had to continue its journey under a new name, the *Kaunitz*, in the hope of a degree of diplomatic protection the name might afford. The risks were so great for Bolts that, unescorted back to the Mediterranean, he did not hesitate to hoist an English ensign to navigate Gibraltar.

Back in Leghorn he promptly changed the name of his ship again to *Grand Duke* to procure maximum favour in the Tuscan port. By this time, the statesman Kaunitz, who had from the beginning taken a keen interest and developed Zinzendorf's project, had established with the help of Antwerp capital a Compagnie Imperiale d'Asie rapidly known as 'Compagnie Trieste'.

But this enterprise was as doomed as the ill-fated Ostend East India Company a generation earlier which had so preoccupied the British. With the Empress's death in 1780, her successor proved much more sceptical of the project and when both the company and Bolts became insolvent in 1782, there was no imperial blessing or financial help available. Joseph showed no interest in the project. Count Karl Proli, the Brussels financier, already heavily indebted, committed suicide[8] and Bolts, after coming to an agreement with his debtors, emigrated to Paris where he died in 1808. The Nicobar Islands, where he had established his depository and forts, meanwhile were occupied by a Portuguese raiding force who burnt the depository and demolished the forts.

Of this brief exotic Austrian presence in the Orient all that remained was the white Theresian military coat of one of Bolts's ship's officers which, carefully preserved, was subsequently proudly worn by a native chieftain when greeting the astonished crew of the Austrian naval frigate, *Novara*, visiting the islands eighty years later.[9]

Meanwhile, back in Trieste, with the suppression of the Jesuits in 1773, a large amount of property in the city became available and this formed the nucleus of a new commercial district named, appropriately enough, after Joseph. The *Borgo Giuseppino* was less grand than the *Borgo Teresiano* but was soon reinforced by the streets of another newly laid-out district, later called, after Joseph and Leopold's successor, Francis, the *Borgo Franceschino*.

At the same time, the city began to prosper, not least as a result of its resourceful Jewish population. They received significant reinforcement when nearby Venice passed legislation to expel the Jews from the Venetian ghetto. Many of them came to Trieste and found not only tolerance and patience but countless opportunities to progress their social and economic advancement, opportunities denied to them in the corrupt, declining Serenissima.

By the time Maria Theresa died in 1780, the population of the city was touching twenty thousand. In barely fifteen years it had trebled. The city boasted not only a handsome new quarter of imposing buildings; its population was also industrious, prosperous and increasingly diverse. These trends would culminate in Trieste's golden era more than a century later when the arrival of the spectacular railway linking it with Vienna brought the Alpine and Adriatic worlds into an even closer harmony in the 1850s.

A few years later, the opening of the Suez Canal in 1869 added to the city's financial and trading possibilities in a dramatic way. Austria was the European empire closest to the new canal and the largest private shareholder in the enterprise was a Triestine merchant by the name of Pasquale Revoltella. Revoltella, the son of a Venetian butcher, had emigrated to Trieste. After the increasingly lacklustre, sclerotic Venetian Republic, the Austrian city was a breath of fresh air for Revoltella with its bustling community of intellectuals, artists and merchants from all over Europe. Appropriately enough, when the Suez Canal opened, the first ship to pass through it was Revoltella's, an Austrian cutter named *Trieste*.

CHAPTER 26

Maria Theresa's Italian Inheritance: Lombardy

It was Kaunitz's boast that so untroublesome was Lombardy as a possession of the monarchy that, along with the Austrian Netherlands, he felt he could easily 'deal with the affairs of both of them in the time it takes to put my socks on in the morning'.[1]

Prince Eugene's triumphant entry into Milan on 26 September 1706 had brought the Austrians to Lombardy, ending two hundred years of Spanish sovereignty. The conclusion of the War of the Spanish Succession brought also an end to two hundred years of sclerosis. The city had been treated by the Spaniards as just a source of revenue on the 'Spanish Roads' and it was again Maria Theresa's father, Charles VI, who first saw the potential in the Po valley, and his daughter who took the future development of this rich and fertile territory in hand.

The first feature of the province which needed to be digested by Maria Theresa's advisers was that, unlike most of the possessions of her crown, the ruling class here was not a feudal aristocracy but an urban patriciate. Such a patriciate was at once more sophisticated and less easily dragooned by crude threats. The exigencies of war neutralized their talents and reduced their capacities. Until peace reigned in the monarchy, there could be no real reform.

What is generally referred to as Austrian Lombardy was the area of two duchies, Milan and Mantua, which formed two distinct administrative districts. Kaunitz quickly persuaded Maria Theresa that if reform were to occur in these backward provinces there would have to be more emphasis on persuasion and consensus. This was of course an easier discussion to have with the Empress than with her son, Joseph.

Maria Theresa decided that a representative of the ruling dynasty should be entrusted with the largely symbolic role of representing Habsburg rule. Unlike the situation in Tuscany, where Leopold ruled as Grand Duke, unfettered by any of Florence's local nobility, Lombardy needed to be governed with more representative structures.

The 17-year-old Archduke Ferdinand and his wife Beatrice (the wealthy d'Este heiress of the Duke of Modena) assumed the governor-generalship of the province in 1771 but their arrival was surrounded by modest gestures aiming at cooperation and support. The imperial couple's marriage had occasioned an opera by Mozart (*Ascanio in Alba*) and in general, apart from offering a good-humoured word of encouragement from time to time, Ferdinand carefully focused on cultural and domestic duties rather than Milanese politics.

Ferdinand's role was confined to playing largely a ceremonial function. The business of the province's government was conducted by the Italian department of the state chancellery. There, Count Karl Joseph Firmian worked in close collaboration with Kaunitz and produced a policy of 'light-touch' administration which encouraged the natural diligence of the Lombardy population. This, combined with the resources of the Po valley, led during Maria Theresa's reign to a substantial increase in the prosperity of the region.

Under this mild direction, stability and harmony quicky ensued, not least thanks to the appointment of Count Beltrame Cristiani to oversee the province. Cristiani came from impoverished but highly talented stock. Hunchbacked and unprepossessing in appearance, loyal and unambitious, he was typical of the diligent, intelligent men harnessed to the service of the Empress.

Cristiani's appointment marked a new era for Lombardy, not least because, unlike his predecessors, he was not given the rank of *Statthalter* (Viceroy) but, more appropriate for the proud Milanese, the title of Minister in Kaunitz's newly created *Departimento d'Italia*. Cristiani was enlightened, scrupulously honest and methodical.[2]

Indeed, Cristiani proved so effective that Kaunitz needed to devote very little time to Lombardy in his daily examination of the monarchy's pressure points. It helped that the province was densely populated and relatively wealthy. There was no serfdom to abolish or large estates to pose problems. Cristiani benefited from the fact that many members of the Milanese elite were already highly devoted servants of the Austrian state such as Cesare Beccaria and Pietro Verri. These were already devoted to the Empress, impressed by her tenacity and pragmatism. Moreover, a separation of powers already existed: judicial affairs were the prerogative of the patriciate, and the supreme court was the Lombardy Senate. In spiritual affairs, Catholicism dominated and the area was rich in contemplative orders, especially convents.

Maria Theresa's father had always wished for a *Gran Censimento* to be carried out in the northern Italian provinces but it was only with the end of hostilities in 1748 that Maria Theresa felt secure enough to give the project renewed impetus. The Milanese Cataster was one of the most comprehensive census projects of the eighteenth century and it was not the least of Cristiani's achievement to bring this long-delayed enterprise to a successful conclusion. It served local as well as imperial interests as it afforded a database which could enable Cristiani to hold sway over not only the Church but a Milanese *Giunta economale*. Administered by a class of imperial servant who was instinctively sceptical of clericalism, it had already begun in 1768 to examine critically the finances of monastic houses which had fallen into disrepair and neglect.

Until the virus of nationalism began to infect, nearly seventy years later, the monarchy's Italian inhabitants, the Milanese were the most loyal of the Empress's subjects. Their loyalty was reciprocated. Maria Theresa gave many fine monuments to the city and oversaw the building of the opera house, La Scala, which opened two years before her death. The city's presence within the Habsburg system would not be questioned until long after the advent of revolution.

Today, the Theresian inheritance in the city is rarely referenced, yet arguably the urban patriciate which administered and ruled the city never had greater freedom than under the enlightened governorship of Cristiani and his successor Firmian. The Empress and her advisers exercised a suzerainty which was both benign and distant. The Theresian era of stability would not endure for long after the Empress's death. Joseph's arrival in these provinces as elsewhere spelt change and radical uncompromising reform.

Joseph's knowledge of Lombardy had been highly coloured by his first encounter with the province in 1768. After various gaucheries with a former viceroy, the aged and corrupt Duke of Modena, he astounded a group of minor officials by saying: 'Gentlemen, I am a pupil; you must instruct me.' To their credit, none of the officials present were unsophisticated enough not to recognize immediately Joseph's opening gambit for what it was: cynical insincerity and suspicion thinly disguised as harmless ignorance.

As Pietro Verri observed with typical Milanese perspicacity: 'This journey of Caesar's had been undertaken in order to discover, in maladministration and especially in the favour shown to farmers (under the present system) weapons with which to fight Kaunitz.' It was somehow typical of Verri that his antennae quickly registered Vienna court intrigues. He was too experienced in the higher levels of Italian political science not to predict the outcome as long as Maria Theresa remained alive: 'The Empress, jealous of her authority, will find that the minister, precisely because he is ill-regarded by her son, must be upheld' was his realistic comment and he gave Joseph only the most cautious of receptions.

Verri was quick to see that, although Joseph encouraged contradiction, he was, like many after him, camouflaging a dangerous reconnaissance in the clothing of an academic exercise. He had 'only come to inform himself' and always spoke with 'the greatest respect' of his mother, wanting only 'to get to the bottom' of 'the present system' introduced by Maria Theresa with 'the greatest affability'.

This approach, if it did not fool the Milanese, must have amused Maria Theresa; she knew her son well enough to realize very early on that such techniques of enquiry were always, however courteous, the prelude to an imminent storm of proposals for change.

While Maria Theresa remained alive, she and Kaunitz could neutralize the zeal Joseph wished to apply to Milan and Lombardy and maintain the 'present system' which left important power structures more or less untouched.

Joseph found such easy-going arrangements unfit for the new centralizing era and, with his usual abruptness after he came to rule in 1780, he sent Kaunitz a blistering memorandum on what he considered to be the shortcomings of the Lombardy administration. Entitled ominously 'Observations on the conduct of affairs in the Milan government and the necessary changes to be made to it', it was heavily invested in root-and-branch change.

No longer was Kaunitz to be permitted to think about Lombardy only during his morning *levée*. The relaxed administration of Cristiani and Firmian was to be replaced by a 'council of state', administrative code for a typically Josephinian instrument of total control. In common with other parts of the monarchy, Milan was to have a centralized judicial function separated from the executive. The Senate's judicial role was to be abolished shortly before the Senate itself was eliminated from all formal functions. Lombardy would be divided into eight districts, each of them under the control of an all-powerful governor.

Even the patriciate was not considered immune to the new wave of reforms that swept the province. It was about time, Joseph insisted, that it received a long-overdue injection of new blood. More sensitive to its privileges than any landed aristocracy, the patriciate, unsurprisingly, turned sullen and hostile. Like all patriciates in Italy – Genoa was about to provide another example – they represented a robust provincialism in a form which was to be crossed by remote central government with trepidation. They controlled all the internal lines of communication and they had grown accustomed to running their cities in an enlightened but idiosyncratic manner. Maria Theresa and Kaunitz had understood this and had left well alone, satisfied to have the revenues and happiness of their subjects with Austrian rule as reward enough for their privileges.

On his mother's death, Joseph upturned this stability almost overnight. Of the Lombardy constitution almost nothing remained after Joseph's reforms. By alienating the patriciate, an elite which had never hitherto questioned Austria's rights, Joseph ensured they became within a generation the fiercest of Austria's critics. Their resentment would not be extinguished until 1859 when Napoleon III broke once and for all the Austrian connection Maria Theresa had so successfully developed and, by her pragmatism, so conscientiously upheld.

If Joseph had limited his reforming zeal to just suborning the patriciate of Milan, Habsburg loyalty might have weathered the imminent storms but with his usual energy he set about making Lombardy the heart of his monastic reforms. There were at the time of Maria Theresa's death more than eight hundred monasteries and convents in Lombardy, many of them contemplative. Even the contemplative orders, however, performed vital social functions, looking after the poor and sick. Joseph alienated permanently the Lombard peasantry from the Habsburgs by interfering with these institutions. The resentment was so bitter that when, less than ten years after Joseph's death, Napoleon arrived with his French troops, the Italians flocked to him as a saviour from the tyranny of the Enlightenment's Josephinian dissolution of the monasteries.

Joseph challenged papal authority as vigorously as his mother and his brother Leopold, but in proceeding against the Italian monasteries he helped create something even his Enlightenment imagination could never have contemplated: a papacy which learnt an important lesson from the French Revolution; a papacy which then applied this lesson more successfully than the Josephinian centralizing Austrian state – namely, that real power rested with the 'voice of the people'.

A few years later, post-revolutionary popes began to appeal to the 'masses' to an extent that had not been seen before, and the 'masses' confirmed the papacy as a lonely beacon of hope in a world darkened by over-zealous Enlightenment values. Any chance that a Catholic Enlightenment might ride to the Habsburgs' rescue was dashed by Joseph's failure to translate his vision into a popular movement. Against the reforming zeal of an emperor determined to disband virtually over-night monasteries which had for centuries in Lombardy played a critical role in the infrastructure and daily life of the majority, the peasantry could only turn to revolution.

Napoleon's great victories in Lombardy, culminating in the dramatic Battle of Marengo, are inconceivable without the wholehearted support of the local populace which fed his army and welcomed him like a demi-God of deliverance from the Austrian anti-Christ. It did not help that Joseph, after promising his dying mother that he would always keep one monastery open for members of the orders whose houses had been closed down, reneged on the promise and with almost sadistic pleasure closed that monastery down, too.[3]

The Lombard peasantry not only altered the course of military history, they arguably saved the papacy and a church which seemed to many contemporary observers on the brink of death. By helping Napoleon defeat the Austrians at Marengo, they laid the grounds for the Concordat of 1801 which allowed the First Consul to reverse the de-Christianization of revolutionary France and, in the words of one contemporary, 'suppress an entire church with the stroke of a pen and then reconstitute it on an entirely new basis'.[4]

It is entirely plausible to think that the 'unintellectual', 'bigoted', 'conservative', 'reactionary' Maria Theresa understood this and, while she lived, held off the wholesale reforms of the Italian monasteries which her son enthusiastically endorsed.

The law of unintended consequences was as forceful in the eighteenth century as it is today and it was never Maria Theresa's policy to strengthen the papacy. Yet the consequences of her son's vandalism were far-reaching. Nearly two centuries later, Owen Chadwick, lecturing the Scots on the secularization of the European mind, could point out that the Pope had become a far more threatening figure to Anglican statesmen in England by the time of Gladstone than he had ever been during the reign of Henry VIII. In the late eighteenth century, Napoleon's armies, overrunning Europe, broke the bonds between State and Church which Maria Theresa had long begun to loosen.

Bishops lost their power and their institutional backing. When Napoleon ordered the capture and the imprisonment of Pius VII, he hoped the Bishop of Rome's confinement would crush the reputation of the Church but the opposite was the case. More than anyone else, Pius had personally resisted the Corsican ogre, risking liberty and even his life; he had 'lost almost all in order to keep the papacy from becoming the trump card of French nationalism'. He emerged from incarceration in 1814 as a living martyr, venerated by Catholics throughout the world.

The peace treaty of Luneville in 1801 – negotiated, after his great victories in Lombardy, by Napoleon with the Holy Roman Empire – confirmed the demise of the German churches' elaborate structures of princely archbishops, allowing more secular rulers like the Habsburgs to absorb their property.

It is hard to imagine the peaceful stability of Maria Theresa's Lombardy surviving such dramatic events. Though returned to Austria after the great upheaval of the Napoleonic Wars, the province never regained its easy relationship with Vienna and the breach initiated by Maria Theresa's son was confirmed in 1859 on the killing fields of Solferino and Magenta.

CHAPTER 27

Challenge and Salvation: Hungary

MARIA THERESA WAS FOND of saying that she was a good Hungarian – 'Ich bin eine gute Ungarin' – and the strange compact agreed between the great magnates and the dynasty in the crisis of 1741 left Maria Theresa always conscious of the fact that, unlike any of her other crown lands, Hungary was *sui generis* and completely different in social structures and political outlook. It could simply not be lumped together with her other possessions and it was a tribute to her intuition that she never attempted to impose uniformity on the lands of the crown of St Stephen.[1]

She had gone to Pressburg in 1741 to be crowned under the careful advice of Count Palffy. He had primed her carefully. He had reminded her of the sensibilities and *amour propre* of the people with whom she was dealing. She had delivered the speech of her life to the magnates and demonstrated more powerfully, perhaps than either before or after, the hypnotic power of a female sovereign in distress addressing a high-testosterone male audience. All this had taught her that, when it came to change and Hungary or reform and the Magyars, there were powerful obstacles. If Maria Theresa's reign cemented the link between Austria and Bohemia for more than a century, it equally stabilized for centuries the concept of Hungarian autonomy and its independence from the rest of the monarchy.

By refusing to interfere more than she had to in the internal affairs of her Magyar lands, she gave Hungary a freedom of manoeuvre which would pose a challenge to every one of Maria Theresa's successors right up to and even beyond the end of the monarchy in the twentieth century.[2]

At the same time, like Lombardy, Hungary, arguably, never enjoyed a more stable period than under the rule of their great Queen. Hungary was loyal to the dynasty and this fragile consensus made Maria Theresa always wary of tinkering with the constitutional arrangements of her kingdom. In countless minor ways she also ensured that Magyar resentment was never allowed to get out of hand. She never for a moment thought of moving the crown of St Stephen, the symbol of all authority in the Hungarian lands, from Pressburg castle to Vienna. She was happy to allow the Hungarian aristocracy to speak Latin at court and virtually construct a Hungarian language in the matter of a decade to replace it rather than resort to the German favoured by her son.

Above all, the Hungarian Chancellery enjoyed great freedom of policy and resisted all attempts to centralize its processes of decision-making away from the Magyar capital of Ofen (Buda). The Hungarian Diet and the privileges of the great Hungarian landowners and aristocracy were untouchable. Their number alone made them a formidable entity. Out of a total population of some 8 million, nearly a quarter of a million considered themselves to be nobility.

Maria Theresa was careful not to allow the Haugwitz reforms any freedom of writ in Hungary. The Hungarian tradition of opposition to foreign rule, honed during centuries of Ottoman domination, made them intuitively hostile to external change from above. Maria Theresa's own seminal experiences with the Magyars in 1741 had proved to her time and time again that the Hungarians were better allies than enemies. The proud selfishness, arrogance and volatility of the Magyars was well known to her. But she responded to their warmth and ardour with a loyalty and practicality which gave them a special place in her considerations. She was always ready to indulge them. When Haugwitz's taxation plans were resisted, she moved swiftly to find a compromise which allowed the Magyar nobility to avoid paying taxes to Vienna for almost another century.

Joseph was altogether far less accommodating but, while Maria Theresa lived, his seething desire to get his hands on the Hungarian constitution was always thwarted by his mother. In return, the Magyars were nothing if not sensitive to changes of sovereign and, long before Maria Theresa's death, they expressed their devotion towards her by participating in many ceremonial and military events in her honour. When she died, they recognized immediately that in Joseph they were faced with a man determined to reduce their privileges, centralize their administration, while undoubt-edly increasing their 'burdens' of taxation.

It did not help that Joseph was not prepared to indulge in any conces-sions to the Hungarians at all. Writing shortly after his mother's death, he observed: 'The gentlemen of Hungary are giving me a lot of trouble. They are opposing the introduction of a census idiotically and inso-lently. It may be that I shall be forced to make an example of someone to put an end to their arrogance.'[3]

This was language Maria Theresa would never have used. Rather, she would have accepted that the Magyar arrogance was not something a ruler could eliminate like cutting the rotten branch off a tree but some-thing which had to be worked 'around' and even occasionally harnessed to dynastic ends.

The Magyars suspected, quite rightly, that Joseph's proposals for a census were but a prelude to increasing demands for taxation. After all, Hungary contained half the population of the monarchy but, for this very reason, Maria Theresa, while allowing a census to be carried out during her reign in other crown lands, kept Hungary safe from such intrusions. She well understood the hornets' nest that it would stir up. When, long after her death, Joseph managed to get the census begun in Hungary, it caused such bitterness and resentment that the experiment was not attempted again until 1850.

The experience hardened Joseph's attitude towards the Hungarians, their constitution and their powerful magnates. All attempts to intro-duce a compliant administrative hierarchy failed completely. His mother had tried gingerly to combine financial and civil administration in the lands of St Stephen in 1764 only to retreat rapidly in the face of opposi-tion in the sixty autonomous county assemblies or diets which were the power base of the nobility.

At every turn, the Hungarian constitution with its right to 'resist foreign interference' blocked progress. Even Kaunitz admitted that, however desirable such reforms might be, the 'game was not worth the candle'. The only way to deal with the Hungarians was to simply ignore their structures where they impeded legislation. Thus, Maria Theresa continued to legislate for Hungary over the *Robot* in the *Urbarium* of 1767 without bothering to consult the diet but she was careful in this to avoid challenging openly the diet. Rather, with 'sweet amorous reluctant delay' she simply expressed a desire to call the diet at some indeterminate future date to discuss the matter. A similar tactic was deployed with regard to her educational reforms. In the meantime, she drew some of the more open-minded members of the high aristocracy in Budapest closer to the court in Vienna.

All this contrasted with Joseph, who believed in rule by fiat and was utterly indifferent to the Hungarian Chancellery in Vienna and the Magyar constitution. Yet, as Count Eszterhazy – the long-serving chancellor who had kept Maria Theresa's confidence as a Hungarian with whom she could work – observed: 'the traditional constitution did not just defend the liberty of the aristocracy, it guaranteed the dynasty of powerful reserves of patriotism'.[4] The price for this was consultation, consensus and pragmatism but this was the coinage of Maria Theresa and not her son. With Maria Theresa's death, the bitter arguments went back and forth. In Transylvania, attempts to interfere with the local government structures resulted in open revolt, while in Hungary proper, Joseph's appointed commissars found themselves marginalized by the local nobility and their peasantry.

Joseph had always felt aggrieved, during his travels incognito, that the Hungarian magnate was not averse to going out 'unter dem Volk' (among the people) and buying tobacco and alcohol for local peasants in their nearby inns. This patronage of the lower orders in public was for Joseph 'wholly degrading' for men of 'advanced education'. Yet this relationship between serf and grandee, certainly not an egalitarian one, was nevertheless one of the guarantors of the Magyar social hierarchy and to this day, notwithstanding the inroads of communism and capitalism, remains visible throughout much of Hungary.

By 1787, as, seven years after his mother's death, all Joseph's plans ran into the sands of Magyar resistance, it was left to Kaunitz to point out that in 'our dealings with Hungary we should always be cautious'.[5]

CHAPTER 28

Jewel in the Crown: The Austrian Lowlands

IN THE MAIN CHAMBER of the royal Belgian parliament in Brussels, it may strike a modern visitor as strange that pride of place is given not to any portrait of a Belgian monarch of the twentieth century but to a large imposing portrait of Maria Theresa.

The Empress had a particular fondness for what is called today Belgium but which was known in her day as the Austrian Netherlands. As we have seen, she was fond of pointing out that they supplied her best and favourite domestic servants. But the Austrian Netherlands were a possession which contained many treasures apart from its human capital. They consisted of ten provinces, nearly all of them with medieval constitutions and powerful estates. Of these ten provinces, the most important by far were Flanders and Brabant. Brabant, whose red, yellow and black cockade would, within a few years of Maria Theresa's death, become the symbol of national revolt against her son, was by far the most important. It boasted what has been called 'an especially recalcitrant' constitution, the so-called *Joyeuse Entrée*, which dated from the fourteenth century and had last been revised in the sixteenth century.

From having been a kind of joint stock company with England in the early part of the eighteenth century in the wars against France, Kaunitz's *Renversement* had made the continued possession of the provinces dependent on French military support. The provinces thus cost little to run and were expected to provide a significant surplus on which Vienna could draw for general purposes. Maria Theresa quickly realized from the reports about her viceroy, her brother-in-law, the mediocre commander Charles of Lorraine, that the administration of the provinces left much to be desired.

Charles, it will be recalled, had not distinguished himself militarily, and finally, after his defeat at Leuthen, which more or less guaranteed Silesia remaining a part of Prussia, Lorraine was 'booted upstairs' and made viceroy of the Austrian Lowlands. But while unlucky in battle, Lorraine was to prove exceptionally happy in the Austrian Lowlands as that country entered a period of prosperity which was probably unsurpassed in any other part of Europe in the years before and after the French Revolution. From 1757, when the great *Renversement* made any French military occupation of these territories unlikely until the Battle of Jemappes nearly a half-century later, the Austrian Lowlands, notwithstanding a brief domestic uprising against Joseph, enjoyed only peace, external security and internal wealth.

Lorraine ruled with the lightest of touches. From an early age, he had been accustomed to hunt and this was indeed his main pastime. When Maria Theresa wrote to him asking for an account of how he spent his days, the jovial prince compiled a completely fictitious timetable of his 'working hours' which began by 'rising' at 7.30 am, attending to state papers until 10 am before consulting his political secretary until 11 and, if necessary, until 4 pm 'ou je m'amuse'.

If the prince thought he could deceive his Empress so easily, he was of course mistaken. Throughout her reign, Maria Theresa employed a network of spies to find out what was really going on, not only throughout her domains but in other countries such as France and England. As far as life in Brussels was concerned, she was well aware that Charles spent most of his time hunting at Montplaisir and Mariemont, preferring to visit Brussels only twice a week, on Wednesdays and Sundays. When questioned on this, Lorraine simply retorted that the inhabitants were 'faciles à gouverner' and that his main task as viceroy was to prevent despotic local ministers 'arrête bien des affaires de ce pays'.

The Treaty of Aix-la-Chapelle had confirmed these lands as a domain of the House of Austria and the ensuing prosperity and stability banished all worries in Lorraine's point of view. His table certainly appeared to confirm a commercial opulence unmatched by any other part of the empire. His wines came from Tuscany, Burgundy and Tokay. Barrels of the finest English oysters were shipped from Hamburg every week, while marinated tuna arrived monthly from Venice and poultry fortnightly from the Tyrol. Lorraine spent a huge fortune every week as, in Maria Theresa's phrase, 'Coq du village' and the Belgians loved him for it.[1]

This richest of jewels in the Theresian crown had never at first glance appeared to offer much to commend it. It was the most vulnerable of all Maria Theresa's domains and the furthest from Vienna, and therefore the most difficult on which to impose Haugwitz's centralization plans. For these reasons, Maria Theresa worked hard to ensure that only the highest calibre of imperial servants of the Austrian state were deployed there.

First came Antonio Botta Adorno and then Philipp Cobenzl. Both men were sent to manage affairs in the Palais Egmont. Adorno was especially useful in the financial sphere. Lorraine had long conceded that as a soldier he had understood as much about finance as 'an ox might comprehend different colours'.

Following the imposition in 1746 of heavy duties on the import of English wares, notably cloth and textiles, Adorno encouraged free trade with Scandinavia, abolishing all tariffs on imports of wood from Denmark. To transport the commodity, he set about enlarging the country's network of canals, making them practical not only for trade but also passenger traffic. New canals were built between Bruges and Ostend and Bruges and Ghent. Adorno also set about with energy initiating a programme of road construction. New roads with tarmac were built linking Liège with Aix-la-Chapelle, Brussels with Liège, Namur with Louvain and Bruges with Brussels. What is today Belgium became in Maria Theresa's reign the most easily travelled area of Europe with the finest internal communications on the continent.

Both these improvements in communications spawned new areas of state expertise. An imperial school of hydraulics was established to provide a *corps hydraulique* which could carry out regular inspections of the canals. Engineers, prized by Maria Theresa as the finest in her empire, were trained to inspect the new roads. When Maria Theresa came to the throne, there were only 60 kilometres of highways in the Austrian Lowlands. By the time of her death in 1780, this had risen to more than 900 kilometres.

Between 1749 and 1753, Adorno worked on an agreement with Holland which offered subsidies in return for free trade. The Treaty of Versailles between Austria and France guaranteed the full neutrality of the Austrian Lowlands and this could be exploited commercially by Adorno's successor, Cobenzl, a highly educated German who had married a Palffy and had one of the most prized collections of drawings in Europe.

Both men were representatives of an Enlightenment which permitted a flourishing press. The *Ghendtsche Post*, the *Gazette des Pays-Bas* and the *Gazette von Antwerpen* all commanded high circulation. The official organ of the viceroyalty was the *Pays-Bas Gazette*, which Cobenzl, a formidable bibliophile, allowed to be edited by a Frenchman, Maubert de Gouvest. The editor had so impressed the literary world with his editing of the *Mercure historique* that even Voltaire, no easy judge of writings, had dubbed it the best monthly in Europe.

This contrasted with conditions elsewhere in the monarchy where the 'freedom of the press' was more restricted. This was particularly the case in Vienna during the Seven Years War when Maria Theresa insisted official bulletins of the campaigns be compiled exclusively by members of the *Kriegsrat*. The news of the day was publicly declaimed by the so-called 'newspaper singers' and some handwritten newspapers were circulated in coffee houses but pundit journalism was not encouraged outside the Austrian Netherlands. In 1750 the Empress even banned coffee houses from distributing written material, threatening them with the withdrawal of their business licences in the event of any breach, but the threats were never implemented. Throughout her reign, handwritten newspapers continued to circulate in Vienna and Prague and in the Austrian Netherlands. Unlike printed material, they were not subject to censorship, and indeed only profited from any official tightening of restrictions on printed material.

Nevertheless, outside the Austrian Netherlands, handwritten notes were theoretically banned and a reward of 100 ducats offered to informers. But, as with most things to do with Maria Theresa, the actual enforcement of such draconian measures was frustrated. Matters improved with the appointment of Thomas Trattner as court printer in 1754. Trattner provided a new alternative to the official *Wienerisches Diarium* with the racy *Gazette de Vienne*.

Cobenzl increased the wealth of his responsibilities when, in 1761, he permitted Antonio Calzabigi to introduce a lottery into the empire. Ranieri Calzabigi, Antonio's brother, was a poet and librettist, collaborating on many works with Gluck. There was a small but influential community of Italians in the Austrian Lowlands and Antonio Calzabigi was able to secure not only local financial support but also the backing of Kaunitz. The lottery was held every three weeks and five numbers were chosen from a kind of 'wheel of fortune'.

Like modern Premium Bonds in the United Kingdom, there were prizes of varying value and frequency. The Brussels treasury soon gained considerable new annual revenue. It was estimated that the yearly sum of 3 million florins was brought into its coffers for a cost of 7 per cent of the total. Kaunitz arranged for Baron Fries to stand surety for the initial trial runs which were then guaranteed by bonds issued by the Wiener Stadtbank. Very rarely, the numbers produced winners in such propensity that the capital provided was deemed insufficient, but as the years passed vast sums were quickly accumulated, becoming another reliable source of support for Austrian borrowing during the Seven Years War.

The Austrian Netherlands' lottery survived Calzabigi's defection to the Prussian cause – Frederick was eager to raise large sums for his dwindling sinews of war. The development of the lottery in Austria had underlined Kaunitz's sure hand on the affairs of state in Brussels.

Kaunitz's system in Brussels could survive duds. One envoy was Georg Starhemberg, the chief minister of Lorraine, who as a godson of the English King George I (having been born in London) was described as 'infatuated with his pride'. His incompetence was easily neutralized in Vienna and Starhemberg was soon withdrawn.

At the same time, thanks to the prevailing zeitgeist of meritocracy encouraged by Maria Theresa, there were more gifted talents like Adorno and Cobenzl. Both these men were loyal servants of the Austrian crown and displayed that degree of personal austerity which was the hallmark of the Theresian civil servant. Neither man enriched himself, despite being surrounded by conspicuous wealth wherever they looked. Cobenzl, in fact, had such difficulty keeping up with the grandees of Brussels society that when he died in 1770 his widow was faced with debts amounting to more than half a million ducats.

Maria Theresa did not hesitate to pay off this debt from her own funds but even she blanched when Cobenzl's widow declared herself utterly destitute. The Empress wrote that she wondered how she could support her expenditure after dealing with her late husband's liabilities but with her usual *Milde und Munifizenz* she settled an annual pension of 3,000 ducats on her for life. Mercifully for the imperial coffers, the widow only survived a year and the payments ended in 1771.

After Cobenzl came the entrepreneurial Karl Zinzendorf, whom we have already encountered in Trieste. He built on his Triestine experience and the work of his predecessors. Commercial imperatives were critical. Manufacturing was encouraged, especially in textiles. Mineral deposits were exploited – the first coal mines were opened and domestic salt production encouraged by a tax on all imported salt. The Austrian Lowlands' agriculture was farmed increasingly economically and efficiently. The harmony which reigned between the 'peasantry' who possessed significant rights and the aristocracy enabled both to cooperate on the land in a way that promoted a commonality of interest. Belgian farming techniques became a model for the rest of Europe and a young British attaché, Nathaniel Kent, working with the British diplomats in Brussels, drew up a report for London which proved in time highly influential. His later book, *Hints to Gentlemen of Landed Property*, extolled the virtues of farming in the Theresian Netherlands, though initially to a characteristically indifferent audience.

The prosperity of the region was not entirely the result of internal and external politics. It helped that the Austrian Lowlands, after the year of Maria Theresa's accession, 1740, never experienced a famine. Annual harvests indeed were prodigious and were often more than three times as great as was needed for domestic consumption. The traders of Antwerp quickly disposed of the surplus by selling the excess grain on to England and France.

For Kaunitz, in charge of overall strategic issues with regard to the provinces, the Austrian Netherlands were a smooth-running machine. If the time needed for the donning of his right foot's sock was sufficient for dealings with Lombardy, the left foot's accoutrements accounted for all the time Kaunitz felt he needed to spare for the Netherlands.

Kaunitz, however, was quick to take advantage of new ideas arising from the province. When reports reached him from Starhemberg that it was proving difficult to encourage the local authorities to permit the construction of wind and water mills to facilitate the production of certain processed oils, Kaunitz moved swiftly to order that the local officials be paid a fee of 50 ducats for every new mill erected. The measure bore immediate fruit. Within a year, more than a dozen new mills had been constructed.

It was not only agriculture which flourished; fishing also benefited, although it was in a more parlous state. There were too few harbours. Nieuport and Ostend were the only ones capable of handling the large catches, and the ability to fish off the ports of neighbouring French Dunkirk was hindered by the Dutch, but in 1763 Cobenzl arranged for primitive oyster farming techniques to be introduced from England so that finally a domestic bivalve supply could be established which, to this day, is one of the great attractions of the Belgian coastline.

Kaunitz's great *Renversement* may not have won back Silesia but for the Austrian Lowlands it was a golden age, an era where the lightest of touches on the part of the Austrian chancellor combined with a period of political stability which lasted forty-four years. By the time of Maria Theresa's death, the population of the Austrian Lowlands had grown to more than 3.5 million. The population of Brussels was 112,000 and it was gaining a reputation for becoming a centre of the arts which even rivalled Vienna. A corollary of the population increase and its growing wealth was that the consumption of coffee increased exponentially. In 1762, 196,000 pounds of coffee were drunk throughout the Austrian Lowlands. By the time of Maria Theresa's death, this had risen to more than 5 million pounds.

The Empress even revitalized the illustrious tapestry school which had made Flanders a byword for exquisite hangings. Just as the King of Prussia supported his domestic Meissen porcelain by sending as diplomatic gifts entire dining services, the Empress turned to Brussels and the famous workshops of de Vos to turn out tapestries which could serve as marks of the Empress's munificence to visiting ambassadors and foreign sovereigns. Under her patronage, tapestries were produced which were much-prized presents, destined to find their way to the great houses of St Petersburg, London and Paris.

Attempts to bring these skills of the Flemish craftsmen to other parts of the empire had mixed results. The textile workers of Verviers were encouraged to open a workshop in the little town of Iglau in Bohemia but local opposition drove them to Moravia. There they finally settled in Brünn (Brno) to establish a flourishing textile industry which was one of the most prosperous in the empire and a byword for innovative design right up to the 1950s.

In this atmosphere of *benessere*, there were very few parts of the political landscape which were not harmonious. The coal miners of Charleroi were kept happy with a renaissance in local beer, world famous to this day. More than forty breweries, including such names as have come down to us as Löwenbräu, competed for their custom. Paper mills to produce writing paper and playing cards set new standards of quality, while the empire's insatiable need for black crêpe and mourning dress was met by milliners in Antwerp which became rapidly the imperial home of most black silk.

When the Empress allowed herself to be painted in pink Brussels lace, the fashion caught on in Vienna to such an extent that a shop was opened offering a Viennese alternative, almost indistinguishable from the Brussels original. So fastidious, however, were the ladies of the court that they preferred to order their lace from Brussels rather than benefit from the ease of logistics offered by the local shop which, unsurprisingly, soon closed down for lack of custom.

For most of Maria Theresa's reign, everything was remarkably quiet in the Netherlands. But this did not mean that 'precautions' were not taken by the state 'apparatus'. Because they were detached from the central core of the monarchy, their affairs were administered in local languages and dialects. Although ultimately responsible to Kaunitz and the state chancellery, these were the most vulnerable of Maria Theresa's possessions and the ones with the greatest exposure to outside European influences, especially from the Protestant north. It was therefore hardly surprising that the territory was also an important hub for domestic and external espionage.

The local officer in charge of all postal activity was the former postmaster of Milan, Captain Rainoldi. During Botta Adorno's period of office, Rainoldi had operated a postal surveillance system which had been much admired in Vienna. Given the strategic vulnerabilities of the Netherlands, Rainoldi was summoned from Milan to open a *Postloge* or postal office where all correspondence leaving the empire for France,

England, Holland and Scandinavia could be intercepted. The importance of such capabilities in the eighteenth century cannot be exaggerated and it was surely significant that in Rainoldi's Italian period Adorno had felt it necessary to consult with him at least four times a week.

We know from Maria Theresa's letters to her daughters that she always assumed her correspondence was subject to interference. The post then, as some would argue even today, was an arm of the state. Only the Thurn and Taxis family appeared to guarantee the Habsburgs a reliable postal service, free from interception. They had long organized the Dutch post with great efficiency. During the Seven Years War, although Austria was not at war with England, London was the enemy of France, her ally, so it was natural that correspondence destined for England and from England (Lady Mary Coke's letters, for example) should be read. The internal post was of less immediate concern but the frequency of Adorno's consultations with Rainoldi suggests that there was much of interest to Vienna even in domestic correspondence.

Each of the Austrian Netherlands' ten provinces possessed its own highly complex constitution. Several of them had their own ruling system, separate courts and established privileges which Maria Theresa had sworn to uphold. Brabant was the richest province and there were exceptionally strong restrictions on the ruler's power. The Council of Brabant reserved the right to reject government legislation. Moreover, provincial authorities had to be consulted.

From the beginning of her reign, Maria Theresa and later Kaunitz had strongly maintained their power as the lay ruler of the provinces against all interference from clerical authorities, including the Papal Nuncio and the Archbishop-Primate of Malines. The Church authorities, nevertheless, enjoyed considerable influence and Maria Theresa proceeded warily against clerical conditions and the monasteries. At the same time, in deference to what today might be termed 'local conditions', she exempted the province from the abolition of torture. As in the case of Hungary, she was loath to confront head-on the traditional constitutional arrangements of the territory.

Part of the reason for this approach was the immense wealth of the province. The million florins spent on procuring the archbishopric of Cologne for her son Max Franz had come from revenues arising from the

Netherlands. Taxes were negotiated annually by the sovereign and thus could be diverted for special secret purposes. While her brother-in-law, Charles of Lorraine, was viceroy, these cosy arrangements persisted, much to Joseph's annoyance. Charles lamented to Maria Theresa the peculiarity of the arrangements, but he knew the temper of the Flanders populace well and understood that any attempt at radical change would meet with a violent response. Reform could only come with negotiation and patience. This was especially the case with regard to military conscription in the province where widespread exemptions existed which neutralized the system's effectiveness.

Joseph found this last circumstance especially irksome. In 1777 he was presented with a copy of an atlas of the province which allowed him, so he hoped, to provide a detailed map for an 'army of the Netherlands' based on the potential for conscription. Unfortunately, the map revealed all too clearly the immense complexity of the frontiers of the province with the Dutch Republic and the Archbishopric of Liège. This last could boast no fewer than twenty-six enclaves within the Austrian Netherlands. This elaborate tapestry of fiefdoms defied rational analysis. Joseph bitterly complained to his mother that there was no population census, no taxation survey (cadastre) and, of course, no transparent statement of revenue. Sensibly, he held off visiting the provinces until the viceroy and his mother had both died in 1780.

When he finally arrived, he found a population very different to other parts of his domains. They were not only well-educated, especially in the city of Brussels – a city comparable almost in size to Vienna – they were rather sceptical of Austrian methods. In 1778 reports that Joseph might wish to exchange the Lowlands for Bavaria had not escaped notice in Brussels. Their suspicion that when Maria Theresa died there would be changes ahead was only increased following Joseph's reluctance to visit the provinces while his mother was alive.

When, just before her death, the viceroy died, Joseph tried to insert himself into the affairs of the provinces but Maria Theresa, fearing what might follow, in one of her last acts before death, forbade her son to interfere with the long-standing agreement that her daughter Marie Christine and her husband, Albert of Saxony, would succeed Charles of Lorraine to the viceroyalty.

Nevertheless, the fears of the population were confirmed when Joseph, within a year of his mother's death, stripped his sister and her husband of all executive power in a move designed to bring the governance of the Netherlands under direct imperial control.

The contrast between Joseph's policies and those of his mother was emphasized as her life drew to a close. In her declining weeks, she strove to impress upon her son the wisdom of moderation with regard to the provinces:

> In the essentials of the constitution and form of government of this province I do not believe that anything needs changing. It is our only happy province and it has provided us with so many resources. You know how these peoples value their ancient, even absurd, prejudices. If they are obedient and loyal and contribute more than our impoverished and discontented German lands what more can one ask of them? The governor must have full authority in view of the remoteness and separation of this province and given how powerful are the neighbours. It has already been too much eroded . . . only a shadow of the past remains . . . the results have proved that this branch has been successfully managed, to mutual satisfaction.[2]

That Maria Theresa, in the last few months of her life, was still capable of rejecting Joseph's proposals is testament to her wisdom and confidence in a policy of minimal interference and the virtues of 'light-touch' administration. Her second son, Leopold, had perhaps influenced her in favour of the Netherlands and Hungarian constitutions; he had been studying them and had found clauses to admire in both. Some commentators have seen this letter as a sign that the Theresian reforms had finally exhausted themselves. Yet it is surely a testament to the Empress's instincts that she was able to see so clearly in Joseph's energy and zeal the double threat of destabilization and chaos.

Maria Theresa late — some might say too late — realized that what would follow her reign would not be a constructive addition to her reforms but something that would endanger all the checks and balances she and her statesmen had so carefully erected. She now in these final weeks began to resist almost everything her son suggested. She drew the line at the

wholesale dissolution of the monasteries, the total relaxation of censorship and introduction of full religious toleration but these were minor
skirmishes. As her life drew to a close, she must have seen that all her
efforts to tame and curb her son's dynamism as co-regent had only delayed
rather than neutralized the threat he posed to all her achievements.

Her rearguard action over the Austrian Netherlands was a masterly
effort which preserved the harmony there for a few more years but it was
not a stability that could withstand Joseph's aims for very long. As Maria
Theresa observed, after Joseph had survived a riding accident in 1772, 'I
adore him despite the fact that he torments me.' Maria Theresa's staunch
refusal to abdicate and leave the reins of power entirely in Joseph's hands
illustrates perhaps best of all how determined she was to keep some kind
of lid on his exuberant lust for reform and centralization. Unfortunately,
it was not to produce anything but a brief delay before the convulsions
brought on by Joseph's disavowal of his mother's policies ushered in the
spirit of rebellion to almost every corner of his empire.

When he finally arrived in Brussels, he got off to a bad start when he said
that the celebrated local Carthusian monastery would be just the place
to accommodate a military foundation poorly housed in Antwerp. The
hundreds of contemplative orders in the provinces would soon face the
treatment his mother had spared them but which Joseph was inflicting on
them in Lombardy. Joseph would proceed against them with his usual insen-
sitivity. When he insisted that Protestantism be tolerated in the universities
and theological faculties, the majority Catholics rose up in violent revolt.

'Who would believe that a Catholic Prince would so far have forgotten
himself as to have usurped a spiritual right,' wrote one local observer,
Malingié, adding, 'I fear strongly that all these sudden changes are manifestations of a systematic plan to destroy religion and overthrow the
constitution . . . he has only pernicious intentions.'[3]

CHAPTER 29

Pandours and Lighthouses: Theresian Croatia

AT THE VERY FURTHEST extremity from Maria Theresa's possessions in the Netherlands stood the fastnesses of Croatia, a kingdom which had been a possession of the Habsburgs since the sixteenth century. Although it had formed part of the Kingdom of Hungary, the martial character of its people had always won it special privileges. The title of Ban was granted to its highest-ranking official and this evolved into the rank first of governor and then of viceroy with commensurate prestige. Most of interior Croatia was organized into part of what was known as the Military Frontier, a vast borderland stretching from the fringes of Styria and Carniola, commanding the approaches to Graz, to the Ottoman salient stretching across the eastern edge of the Banat and Serbia.

Croat soldiers became some of the fiercest of Maria Theresa's warriors, notable for their courage and cruelty. The borderlands they occupied were porous so a mixed population of Serbs, Croats, Turks, Romanians, Vlachs and Albanians infused their ethnicity with exotic elements. Nowhere was this more apparent than in the strange irregular force which marched from the eastern fringes of Croatia to Vienna to pledge support for the Queen in her moment of need in 1741.

As we have seen, about a thousand of them had followed their leader Baron Trenck and marched to put themselves at the disposal of Maria Theresa's generals. These *Pandours* fascinated Maria Theresa but she was determined to ensure that they were incorporated into the army as regular soldiers with an order of precedence which would, in her words, 'naturally be after that of my Regular infantry regiments'. The *Pandours* would capture many Prussian standards and guns before her wars were over but they were a constant reminder to Maria Theresa that her domains contained areas which were in a state of almost Oriental primitiveness. The twin engines of Enlightenment reforms she endorsed for her Croatian subjects were the widening of trade, through the Croatian littoral, and the introduction of compulsory education. Because of Croatia's union with the Hungarian crown, both faced opposition from the Hungarian aristocracy but Maria Theresa skilfully placed the Croatian coastal areas under the responsibility of the *Kommerzienrat*. This department, responsible for commerce in the Austro-Bohemian lands, was not answerable to any Hungarian structure and existed solely to promote trade. It had a commercial imperative which invested it with significant discretionary powers.

Gradually, the department extended its commercial influence into the political sphere and, by the time of Maria Theresa's death in 1780, the sliver of Croatian coastline had developed a markedly more socially progressive environment than interior Croatia.

Venetian and Austrian influences gave the small Croatian coastline access to the flow of ideas emanating from western Europe so that by the time, in 1776, the Austrian and Hungarian coastlines were defined more formally, the Croatian littoral around Fiume (Rijeka) and the Quarnero had already embraced many of Maria Theresa's public reforms, obstructed and delayed in other parts of Hungary. To this day, the Croatian population along the Quarnero feels itself to be superior in education to that of the interior of the country.[1]

To safeguard mercantile maritime traffic, Maria Theresa ordered that the safety of her waters be enhanced by the construction of several lighthouses stretching from Trieste to Dalmatia. These were the precursors of the 'string of pearls', the fine classical lighthouses dotted across the Quarnero and Dalmatia, which within a generation would set new standards of design for lighthouses throughout Europe.

The lighthouses were constructed in a stripped neo-classical style with a view to providing accommodation for a duty officer and his family. Although far less comfortable and imposing than the lighthouses built a generation later in the early nineteenth century, the Theresian lighthouse regulations heralded a new era in maritime safety.

Meanwhile, the interior of the country continued to provide plentiful numbers of outstanding officers and generals. For most of Maria

Theresa's reign, her 'Ban' was Ference Nadasti, the legendary Hungarian
cavalry commander whose hussars had struck such terror into the
Prussian supply lines in the 1740s. Croatian soldiers, once incorporated
into the regular army, soon made a name for themselves which spread
across western Europe. The Croatian infantry was instantly recognizable by their tradition of wearing a neckerchief of a different colour to
their usually white uniforms.

During the Seven Years War, their bravery so impressed a French
general that, when he asked the origin of these shock troops, he was told
by their Hungarian commanding officer that they were 'Hrvat', the
Magyar word for Croats. The Frenchman misheard and the term 'cravate'
entered the French language to denote the silk square worn around the
neck. The term stuck and to this day Croats proudly consider themselves the progenitors of the tie, maintaining, even in the extravagant
informality of dress prevalent in the twenty-first century, a healthy
respect for this increasingly rare sartorial flourish.

When Maria Theresa was crowned King of Hungary she had to
vouchsafe the integrity of the Croatian lands as part of her coronation
oath. This implied respect for Croatian traditions and, above all, for
their language and customs within the Magyar kingdom. Her Croat
soldiers had fought so bravely but most knew only a handful of German
words. Attempts to get them to learn more were encouraged but, with
her usual nose for tact and moderation, Maria Theresa refrained from
imposing a general requirement that German be the language of administration in her Hungarian lands. The Croats, let alone the Ruthenes,
Romanians, Slovaks and Serbs, if educated, could use the Latin of the
Magyar nobility and, if uneducated, were unlikely to understand more
than a smattering of German. Here, she showed greater understanding
than her son, Joseph, who within months of his mother's death would
ignite hostility all across Hungary, including Croatia, by his demand
that German be the sole language of administration in the monarchy.

It offended the devout Catholic Croats perhaps as much as their
Magyar overlords that they were to learn German and they took particular exception to Joseph's determination to impose uniformity. But
Joseph, oblivious to his mother's carefully constructed equilibrium,
insisted:

The use of a dead language, like Latin, in all official business is enough to show that the Nation has not yet reached a sufficient level of enlightenment since it implies that either the national language is defective or that no other people can read or write it and that only those who have devoted themselves to the study of Latin are in a position to express themselves adequately in writing, while the nation itself is being ruled and judicial decisions are being handed down in a language which it does not understand. All enlightened peoples have already banned the use of Latin in public business and it retains its old position only in Hungary, and neighbouring kingdoms like the principality of Transylvania and Poland.[2]

Nadasti, as a proud Magyar and as Ban, rallied the Croatian nobility around the magnates but, in an early demonstration of pan-Slavism, the Croats began to develop their own 'Military Frontier German' (*Militägrenzedeutsch*), which well into the twentieth century could be heard with its amalgam of German and Croatian words.

Joseph's views certainly implied that he wished to eradicate the vernacular languages of Hungary, Croatian included, but he continued his mother's practice of issuing proclamations in the languages of the monarchy. Great advances were made in the study of all the languages of the Magyar lands. Ironically, Germanization of official transactions provoked greater interest and study of the Croat language. Not for the first time did the attempt to impose a dominant tongue actually promote the development of the indigenous language.

Maria Theresa had well understood this. The use of Latin in her Hungarian possessions had submerged many problems associated with the various nationalities. Latin was no-one's first language and therefore privileged no particular ethnic group. German, on the other hand, was spoken only by minority groups throughout the eastern part of the empire, such as the Saxons in Transylvania. Its imposition was open to the interpretation of a domineering Germanization in the 1780s, almost as greatly resented as its repetition a hundred and fifty years later in the 1940s.

Yet, thanks to the educational reforms during the earlier part of Maria Theresa's reign, Croatia benefited from a flowering of consciousness

which in many ways foreshadowed the great awakening of Croat nationalism in the writings of Ludwig Gay (Ljudevit Gaj) a half-century later.
By then, Croatia had demonstrated time and again its unflinching loyalty
to the Habsburg dynasty which, in its modern form, could be traced
entirely back to the compact sealed between Maria Theresa and the
exotic *Pandours*.

CHAPTER 30

Twixt Cross and Crescent: The Military Frontier

WE SAW IN THE previous chapter how Maria Theresa's Croat territories supplied some of her finest infantry. They also supplied the backbone of the Military Frontier in the seventeenth century during the almost continuous wars against the Turks.

The Military Frontier bequeathed her a unique patchwork of nationalities harnessed to the defence of the Theresian inheritance. Thanks to Maria Theresa's respect for this tapestry, which defied radical reorganization, its patchwork qualities have persisted to this day in countless mixed communities across the Balkans.

It was, the reader might recall, Kolowrat, one of Maria Theresa's most astute advisers, who counselled her to follow tacitly a policy of settling as many non-Magyar nationalities as possible in Hungary so that the Hungarian predominance might be stealthily diluted by the presence of Serbs, Saxons and others. This was a subtle policy, especially in comparison to the more direct confrontations with the Hungarians initiated by her son. It could also be easily encouraged by the precedent set by the Military Frontier which had long been a vehicle for the movements of population eastwards under the imperatives of strategic defence.

The Military Frontier began as a series of isolated garrison outposts along what military strategists would call today the 'contact line' between Habsburg and Ottoman domains. Following the lifting of the Great Siege of Vienna in 1683, the outposts benefited from the subsequent campaigns which culminated in the Treaty of Karlowitz in 1699, ending centuries of Ottoman power in Europe.

This resulted in a shifting of the Military Frontier several hundreds of miles to the east. The Frontier no longer needed to guard the approaches to Styria or Inner Austria; it was required to secure the fortresses further east of Kopreinitz, Varazdin and Osijek. The garrisons became soldier-settlements with their own customs, legal system and autonomy.

Maria Theresa encouraged this development, not only promoting the settlement of Serbs fleeing westwards after failed revolts against Ottoman suzerainty, but also the immigration of Germans eastwards along the Danube valley. These *Donauschwaben* were to repopulate areas devastated by the Ottoman wars and establish 'modern' agricultural techniques to bring the land's potential to the service of the monarchy. It was Maria Theresa's skill that she could tinker with the ethnicity of the Military Frontier without challenging its traditions. The Germans, like the Croats, Turks, Vlachs and Albanians before them, brought their own habits but it was their organizational skills which were highly prized.

This was only possible by exercising a degree of greater centralized control from Vienna and, just as the *Pandours* were after five years incorporated into regular army units, so was the Military Frontier integrated into the Austrian military and administered from a new headquarters in Zagreb. Thus were the Croats given a new route to discharging their role as 'Ante murale Europae contra immanissimum nominis christiani hoste'.[1]

Maria Theresa's policies of integration, and even those of her son, failed to incorporate completely the military settlements of the Frontier into any deep subordination to the legal system of the emerging Austrian state. A generation later, Marshal Marmont, Napoleon's commander in Dalmatia, could note: 'The regime of military Croatia is a masterpiece in all ways perfected by the incessant resistance to Moslem hordes since 1389 in which everything holds together in this system in which to command or to obey is the exclusive sphere of its conception.'[2]

Maria Theresa ensured that these men were, whatever their origin, 'loyal to the state of Austria'. As Marmont observed, 'they would move to Austria immediately if threatened by any change'.[3] The Empress secured this loyalty in a number of ways. Firstly, she granted the men and families of her *Militärgrenze* special privileges if they were to settle permanently in her borderlands. They were given complete freedom of confessional worship and, to this day, the variety of church buildings to be found on the territory of the former frontier is testament to the lifting of restrictions still prevailing elsewhere in the monarchy. Secondly, she granted them the right to enjoy their own military system of dispensing justice. Thus, a completely parallel set of legal procedures existed to those in force elsewhere in the monarchy. As the men were nearly all soldiers, they were under the jurisdiction of their company commander, who presided over disciplinary tribunals. Finally, the right to property was fixed by the simple expedient of all Military Frontier housing belonging to the crown. Property was occupied on trust by families of the district and could be surrendered instantly in the event of the family dying out or some dishonour falling upon them.

In this environment the 'brotherhood of arms', as a later illustrious child of the Frontier, Josef Jellačič, called it, quickly became 'greater than any race or creed'. Such a spirit was only possible as a result of Maria Theresa's conviction that those who risked their lives for her needed support and reward even if that meant permitting deviation from the all-consuming imperatives of consistency and uniformity. This pragmatism inevitably brought her into conflict with her son. The part of the Military Frontier where the disagreements proved most fractious was that touching Transylvania.

The beautiful land of the 'Seven Castles' was in many ways unique in the monarchy. Roman Catholics, far from being the majority as elsewhere in the monarchy, were here a small minority, barely 150,000 out of a total population of 1.5 million. Maria Theresa recognized that her Transylvanian subjects were beneficiaries of her educational reforms and quickly came to make up a higher-than-average number of her official administrative class. They were diligent, hard-working, fluent in three languages, honest and often possessed a Lutheran austerity which she found increasingly captivating as she grew older.

Of the four non-Catholic recognized denominations, the Lutherans were considered to enjoy a certain primacy, followed by the Calvinists and then, unexpectedly, the Unitarians, and finally, the Greek Catholics. There were 120,000 of these Greek Catholics, so called as they were the product of an agreement of 1700 whereby adherents to the rites of the Greek Orthodox Church could retain them in return for acknowledgement of papal supremacy. This submission was understandably regarded askance by Orthodox churches elsewhere, and the status of the Greek Catholics, so encouraged by Maria Theresa, remains a bone of contention between Rome and the Orthodox world to this day.

Each religion was associated with a particular ethnicity. Thus, the German Saxons, of whom there were roughly a quarter of a million, were Lutheran, the Hungarians who numbered 150,000 were Calvinists, and the Szeklers, virtually indistinguishable from the Magyars but the descendants of a tribe deployed along the frontier, were Unitarians. In addition to these four principal groups, there were significant numbers of Jews and Armenians but by far the largest number were the 700,000 Romanians and Vlachs who were largely Greek Orthodox.

Such an exotic confessional tapestry has been depicted as one of the glories of the Habsburg possessions, but the administrative problems posed by the presence of four nations, each with their own native language and religion, were considerable and while the Military Frontier parts could be governed with discipline, other parts of Transylvania were susceptible to more centrifugal forces. It was this disequilibrium which Joseph was determined to remove through the imposition of uniformity and centralization.

While Maria Theresa lived, much of the potential tension was defused by the conducting of all official business in Latin. This prevented the Saxons, who were by far the most culturally and economically advanced, from appearing to enjoy too much privilege in the event of Latin being replaced by German. In any case, most of the land was owned by the Magyars, while the Romanians and Vlachs were effectively just a nation of tax-paying serfs without any civil rights or education, considered by Austrians, Saxons and Magyars alike to be lawless, corrupt and primitive. This prejudice would survive into the approaching century with a later Austrian chancellor, Metternich, denouncing the Romanians as 'a profession not a nation'.[4]

Maria Theresa was all too aware that conditions in Transylvania were 'deeply unsatisfactory'. From the beginning of her reign, she saw that, as in Croatia, the local sensitivities demanded local solutions. She agreed to the establishment of a Greek Orthodox bishopric to cater for the needs of the majority population and she appointed a Protestant, Baron Samuel Bruckenthal, as governor. Bruckenthal was a Saxon. He was a highly respected bibliophile and partly on this account possessed insights into Transylvanian affairs few other administrators could have enjoyed. But his reports to Vienna only aroused the ire of the Vienna administration which saw Bruckenthal's descriptions of Magyar abuses as vivid illustrations of Hungarian arrogance and exploitation. Yet Maria Theresa held off the confrontation with the Hungarian aristocracy which alone could deliver the reform needed in Transylvania. Instead, in 1773, she dispatched her son Joseph on a fact-finding mission to discover for himself if the reports of Hungarian 'tyranny' were exaggerated or not.

Joseph predictably came back from the province appalled and demanding radical action – 'Things cannot stay as they are. Palliatives will do no good' – but Maria Theresa, ever cautious in dealing with her Magyars, was not ready for the drastic reforms Joseph had in mind. It is hard not to see in her reticence that wise if cynical statecraft designed to preserve a status quo too complex to tinker with. In this case, her instinct appears to have been correct: better to keep the lid on such a combustible part of her domain than risk the explosions that sudden change would, and indeed did after her death, provoke.

That her instincts were proved all too prescient can be seen by what followed within months of her death when Joseph was finally able to try another disastrous experiment in 'revolution from above'. In March 1781 Joseph took a step that his mother would not have contemplated, let alone enacted: he cancelled the rights and privileges of the Saxons, whose communities Maria Theresa had done so much to promote. This may have struck a blow for the embryonic Romanian nation but it upset the carefully constructed Theresian balance which the Empress and Bruckenthal had both worked so hard to preserve. Of course, critics could point to the self-serving elements of this equilibrium, but the alternative proved once again to be highly disruptive. Maria Theresa had only rather reluctantly agreed to the Banat's administration's incorporation into the Kingdom of Hungary in 1778. She resisted doing the same for Transylvania and the deed of incorporation was signed only two years after her death.

On the one hand, this strengthened Joseph, who believed his reforms would now have the advantages of bureaucratic simplicity and Magyar support. On the other hand, the reality was immediately apparent that Magyar opposition to Joseph's policies was significantly strengthened by the increase in their formal influence over the province. An eyewitness to Joseph's second visit to the province provided the following account of Joseph's dismantling of his mother's policies in Transylvania:

> The entire world of Transylvania was now in part hopeful and in part fearful as to what Joseph would do. All was quiet enough for the first few days although the governor, the general officer commanding and the president of the diet were received in audience. Petitioners of all types, high and low, young and old from all the Transylvanian nations but especially Vlachs gathered in front of H.M's lodging and handed in memorials in great numbers which they could easily do as His Majesty only had one sentry and this one was not permitted to deny anyone entrance. As a result the rabble took up the entire staircase . . . the Emperor defended his policies by saying ardently but mildly 'I desire to introduce love and unity and I want everyone to work together' . . . with regard to the Catholic clergy he said they kept putting hindrances in his way: 'I have the devil of a time with them' . . . we were astonished by this statement.[5]

This performance by the Emperor was indeed astonishing but, as his mother would no doubt have pointed out, was a very different choreography from that which enabled her to go among her subjects. Joseph could be praised for his personal courage and his determination to improve Transylvania but he had fallen into the error of many liberal statesmen in confusing personal popularity with support for unpopular policies.

The Hungarians saw matters more critically: Joseph, by introducing language and constitutional change, was in effect trying to overthrow the entire constitutional basis of the Hungarian kingdom. It was not difficult to engineer a popular demonstration against this, and the unhappy transfer of some Romanian peasants' alcohol licences to their Armenian neighbours implausibly but effectively provided the fuse for a full-scale 'peasants' revolt'.

When Joseph attempted to quell this by offering to incorporate more Transylvanian towns into the Military Frontier so that the lowly status of the Romanian peasantry could be elevated in return for service to the crown, the Magyar landowners spread rumours that conscription was imminent and tax increases inevitable. A largely illiterate peasantry could be easily manipulated but this stoking of discontent soon back-fired when the peasantry turned on the manor houses of their masters and began to burn them, killing hundreds of the nobility who were forced to flee for safety to the towns. When some of the Magyar nobles organized a full-scale insurrection by mobilizing their equivalent of the local yeomanry, the stage was set for brutal clashes. In less than a month, Joseph's sincere and well-intentioned policies had created the conditions for an uprising which was repressed with calculated brutality, including the summary execution by the Magyars of thirty-seven peasants captured after one especially sanguinary encounter.

Only the full-scale mobilization of the garrisons along the Military Frontier eventually brought the situation under control. By then, 132 manor houses had been destroyed, 62 villages completely burnt and more than 4,000 members of the aristocracy slaughtered. This was dramatic evidence, if any was needed, of how skilfully his mother had preserved the status quo in Transylvania.

Joseph was bright enough to realize that his own actions, in particular his attempts to listen to all and be 'all things to all men', had played a role in sparking the uprising. Like many 'tolerant' men in positions of power, he switched seamlessly from spurious chumminess to ruthless absolutism. The two main ringleaders of the revolt, despite the aboli-tion of the death penalty, were ordered to be broken on the wheel. Joseph personally ordered that the barbaric executions take place in front of a large, specially assembled crowd so that those who witnessed the spec-tacle could 'learn to obey'. It is impossible to imagine his mother encour-aging this kind of *nemesis Theresiana* while she reigned but, more importantly, it is most unlikely that the situation in Transylvania would have spiralled out of control under her cautious policies.

Following this powerful revolt in Transylvania came reports of disturbances in Lombardy and the Austrian Netherlands. Joseph had gradually turned the relatively stable and calm empire of his mother into a patchwork of seething discontent.

CHAPTER 31

Galicia and Lodomeria

MARIA THERESA HAD, AS we have seen, been reluctant to become involved in the partition of Poland but after she had 'cried but taken', in the Prussian king's phrase, she was determined to put into 'better order' the conditions of the new acquisition which today corresponds to eastern Poland and western Ukraine.

Joseph, travelling in Transylvania in 1772, after the First Partition of Poland, insisted on continuing the journey into Galicia-Lodomeria, lands which only the previous year had formed part of Poland. The new province had more than 2 million inhabitants and a large but impoverished Catholic Polish nobility. Most of the population were, however, Greek Catholic Ruthenes (Ukrainians in today's parlance).[1]

Maria Theresa was apparently horrified that the new province contained nearly a quarter of a million Jews. Her dismay was shared by most Jews in Vienna who, either by origin or through assimilation, considered themselves to be of an entirely different stamp to the Galician or *Shtetl* Jews from the east. Neither Joseph's Patent of Toleration nor the later assimilation of hundreds of Jews into the emerging upper middle classes of Vienna would eradicate this division. Joseph, after visiting Lemberg (Lviv) and encountering tens of thousands of Orthodox Jews, drily observed in a letter to his mother: 'I now understand why one of my titles is King of Jerusalem.'[2]

As with Transylvania and Croatia, Maria Theresa's instincts were to treat the province gently, respecting at all times, where possible, the institutions, structures and attitudes of the inhabitants. She appointed, with Kaunitz's blessing, the enlightened Count Pergen to be governor.

Johann Pergen had implemented important educational reforms in Vienna, notably at the Theresianum, where he had reconstructed it after the suppression of the Jesuits. Before that, he had worked at the Oriental Academy, where he had again organized the post-Jesuit transition. His energetic mindset made him in many ways the obvious candidate to deploy in Galicia but even his talents needed to be used with caution. Maria Theresa wrote to Kaunitz:

> I entirely agree, Pergen should be told to proceed very slowly in all matters, especially as far as concerns the clergy. Over such a stupid, servile people they possess great power. We therefore ought to try to deal tactfully with them, to win them over rather than to impose things on them by force, at least until we are in a position to set up something solid.[3]

So great was Maria Theresa's caution that she even discussed with Kaunitz giving the new province the kind of medieval privileges which pertained in the Austrian Netherlands. Haugwitz's reforms, as we have seen, had been largely limited to Austria and Bohemia; the idea that they might be exported to Galicia struck the Empress as premature. Joseph, predictably, baulked at this policy of procrastination. Galicia should be brought into the modern age as soon as possible. To that end, it was 'out of the question' to make the province part of Hungary, even though Austria's claim to the province rested on an ancient Hungarian title. For Joseph, Galicia was to be made a 'German hereditary province'. Polish customs, dress and attitudes were to be systematically eradicated. Even the Latin language was to be preferred to the prevailing Polish and Russian.

Altogether, Joseph spent more than six weeks travelling around the province, complaining at the prevalence of insects, the absence of roads and the generally mountainous terrain. If it was to be fully exploited for its potential, it had no choice but to become a centrally administered province of the monarchy. Joseph felt that Pergen had been overwhelmed by the province. On his return to Vienna, he persuaded Kaunitz to sack him and establish a department of state within the Austro-Bohemian Chancellery to deal exclusively with Galician affairs. But distance imposed its own delays and Galicia, and later Bukovina, which was added to it in 1775 from the principality of Ottoman-ruled Moldavia, was at the very edge of the Habsburg empire. Even a hundred and fifty years later, Joseph Roth could paint a picture of its isolation and wearying backwardness in his masterpiece *Radetzky Marsch*. The orders from Vienna often were simply lost on the journey. When they arrived, they occasioned such lengthy long-distance disputes that one governor was said to spend far more time exchanging missives with Vienna than implementing orders.

Governors came and went. As Kaunitz swiftly saw it, Galicia was a useful political graveyard for the careers of potential rivals or interfering courtiers. Galicia digested and ruined governors more effectively than Frederick had shredded the reputation of Austrian generals. Count Brigido, the fourth governor in as many years, was suddenly bombarded by Joseph with requests to employ more Slovaks. Maria Theresa had insisted on sending more German administrators to the region, partly to reconcile Joseph to her policies by pandering to his idea of a 'German hereditary province' but, with his usual volatility, Joseph had erupted, 'For God's sake don't send yet more Germans here', adding:

> in just over two months I think six or seven new officials have arrived, all originating from Bohemia and Austria. I testified to you that they were too numerous and useless but this is what happens. If we go on like this, these gentlemen, in order to do nothing, or worse than nothing, while making it appear they are doing something, will cream the revenues of the Estates . . .

Joseph would find several opportunities to visit the far-flung Galicia-Lodomeria, always using it as a staging post when he visited Catherine of Russia, and generally immersing himself in its development, despite Maria Theresa's constant anxiety that the area was unsafe and full of pitfalls which might lead to an indiscretion.

Joseph's encounters with the inhabitants eventually cured him of his anti-Polish sentiments and even his anti-Semitism. By the end of his reign, he had taken the revolutionary step of enacting, in the face of stiff military opposition, provisions allowing Jews to serve in the imperial army. Whatever Maria Theresa's objections to Jews, the Austria she bequeathed to her son found it relatively straightforward to initiate in 1788 legislation more philo-Semitic than that of any other European country, with the possible exception of Holland.

CHAPTER 32

Austria-Bohemia: Consolidating the Austrian Heartlands

If GALICIA-LODOMERIA WAS AT the north-eastern periphery of Maria Theresa's domains, at the very core of her possessions was Bohemia, which included Moravia and the tiny portion of Silesia remaining under Austrian rule after the conclusion of hostilities with Prussia. Its population of 4 million souls paid nearly 40 per cent of the tax revenues of the central crown lands and it occupied a strategic position of unrivalled importance. Bohemia faced Prussia, and its northern foothills approaching the *Riesengebirge* were the traditional Prussian invasion route, not only in the eighteenth century but also later in the nineteenth.

This exposed situation required the maintenance of substantial numbers of troops even in peacetime. Moravia was the headquarters of the Austrian artillery arm, and the embryonic strategic armaments factories of Pilsen and Witkowitz were all situated in the province. Culturally, Moravia linked geographically the Germanic world of beer, sausages and dumplings with the Danubian cosmos of wine and wheat. Unsurprisingly, the prosperity of Bohemia under Maria Theresa become the Empress's priority.

No sooner had the ravages arising from the Seven Years War ended in 1763 than a new horseman of the apocalypse began to stalk the land: famine. The harvests of the late 1760s became progressively smaller until in 1770, they failed in Bohemia entirely. Maria Theresa was desperate. Not only were tax revenues falling as a result but large numbers of her troops needed to be withdrawn, leaving the province theoretically open to Prussian incursions. The Empress banned the export of what little grain was left from Bohemia, extending the ban a few weeks later to the entire monarchy.

She dispatched an official fact-finding mission under a minor but competent official called Kressel. Kressel found conditions which were far from encouraging: high unemployment among skilled labour, desperate shortages of food and all the distortions of profiteering and hoarding among the rich, as well as increasing poverty among the poor.

Kressel noted that the legally enforceable *Robot* (compulsory unpaid service to landowners) gave the poorer inhabitants no chance to earn even enough to buy food. When she was informed of these conditions, Maria Theresa immediately responded with direct interventionist measures. Provision was to be made for seed, corn and potato farming. The programme of planting fruit trees along roads, initiated to help sustain her marching troops during the wars, was to be dramatically extended. Pricing and taxation measures with regard to all foodstuffs were to be overhauled. The troops stationed in Bohemia were to assist in planting and agriculture while ensuring the wider movement of supplies through the construction of new roads.

It was a sign of how important and sensitive these steps were for Maria Theresa that although Joseph badgered his mother constantly, asking for permission to visit the province, Maria Theresa resolutely refused to deploy Joseph in such a fragile crisis environment. Joseph complained to his brother Leopold bitterly:

> I have a great deal of business associated with a mortal grief arising from the news we have just received from Prague where famine has appeared. It was only at the very last minute that we were informed that supplies had run out. The provisional government is making no arrangements and only the military has revealed it . . . I wanted to set out at once, but H.M. has caused me great sorrow by not desiring it. She gave me no convincing reasons and I am left to guess at them . . . You can imagine I have a pretty good idea and [her reasons] are neither flattering nor loving but, however mortifying the vexation of seeing myself prevented from making myself known and taking action at the most crucial moment might be, I have to swallow it, and to set it among the study of a hundred thousand annoyances to which I am condemned by a quite special twist of destiny. Pity me, dear brother, for few things in the world have given me such distress.[1]

Perhaps Maria Theresa understood all too well that Joseph's principal concern might have been the loss of an opportunity to satisfy his own predilection for grandstanding rather than the ultimate well-being of her Bohemian subjects. A year earlier, he had basked in the sensation of what today would be called a 'publicity stunt' when, on the way to visit Frederick in 1769, he had encountered a peasant tilling the soil near Brno in Moravia. Seizing his plough and to the consternation of his entourage, Joseph had proceeded to till the field for an hour. The scene, immortalized in several prints which received wide circulation throughout the empire, might on the one hand have confirmed Joseph's Enlightenment credentials as a 'man of the people', but for Maria Theresa it was shameless exhibitionism. She was exasperated by the superficiality and, in her view, insincerity of the gesture. She knew better than most that, whatever else her son might be, Joseph was not a 'man of the people'.

Yet Joseph's constant nagging about Bohemia reinforced the need for change, and in 1771 Maria Theresa finally removed from the control of the Austro-Bohemian Chancellery in Vienna the ageing and increasingly decrepit Count Chotek. The octogenarian Count Kolowrat was also stood down from the *Gubernium* in Prague. At the same time, she finally relented and allowed Joseph to visit Bohemia, although she ordered that his departure be delayed.

A year later, a satisfactory harvest ended the crisis, but the population of the province had by then fallen by nearly half a million. Joseph insisted that the administration of the province be completely overhauled. As usual, Joseph had a Frederician model in his mind, and he argued forcefully that a system of cantonments along Prussian lines might combat aristocratic indifference. The army had been the only government institution to see the famine coming, and it had been the only arm of the state to react swiftly and effectively to its consequences. The landowners' abuse of the *Robot* was draining Bohemia of its manpower. In northern Bohemia, for every ten men immigrating, more than a hundred emigrated, usually to Prussia.

Lacy wrote a detailed report in July 1771, in which he observed to the Empress: 'the peasants when they turn up for their *Robot* are subjected to blows and rough words by the estate officials. A remarkable proof that time-honoured oppression makes these subjects leave the fatherland.'[2]

The abuses inflicted on the peasantry by many of the landowners became a dominating domestic concern of Maria Theresa's in the closing years of her reign. As Bohemian landownership was largely in the hands of the aristocracy and the Church, the *Robot* meant that in practice most tenants of these estates were in a state of serfdom: they were forbidden to move or marry without the consent of their lord and were bound to do service for him on his land. As taxes rose from central government, the burden of expectation on the peasantry similarly increased because the landlords quickly realized that the easiest way to meet rising tax demands was to make greater use of the free labour available to them.

These abuses had a long history. Attempts by Maria Theresa's father, Charles VI, to introduce some predictability and consistency through the *Urbarium* of 1738 had only strengthened the hold of the landowners over their tenants, and the Empress's initial reforms, a few years later, equally did not offer any solace. Her remodelling of the *contributio* under Haugwitz's oversight led to the peasantry becoming liable to pay additional taxes to their lords as well as offering service. Gradually, it dawned on the Empress that reform aimed at providing the army with a healthy quota of peasantry was only possible if they had not been ground down by landlord exploitation. This military expediency, rather than civil rights, came to the rescue of the peasantry. Already before the famine made the problem acute, Maria Theresa had issued in 1769 the following proclamation to the Austro-Bohemian Chancellery:

> Whenever there is a question of defining the obligations of the peasantry to their landlords, the Chancellery must take as its guiding principle that the first consideration must be to sustain the peasantry: they are the most numerous class of subjects and the foundation and greatest strength of the state.[3]

Here was a typical piece of Theresian realpolitik, unsentimental, practical and progressive. It was also one with far-reaching consequences. She continued: 'They must be maintained in such a condition that they can feed themselves and their families and afford the general taxation in peace and war. Thus, it follows automatically that existing agreements and customs, however old, cannot stand if they are irreconcilable with the aforementioned maintenance of the subjects.'[4] In this way, Maria Theresa guaranteed the survival of an independent peasantry in central Europe, long after it had disappeared from many other European states.

It can be well imagined that the reception of this instruction was – at least among the more traditional of the *Grossgrundbesitzer* – mixed. They tried to corrupt and bribe government officials sent from Vienna to report to the Empress but their dispatches describing the 'tyranny of the *Herrn*' were inescapable.

The Empress was soon in receipt of mounting evidence describing the *Skandur* (scandal) of oppression on the Bohemian estates. Six estates in particular caught the Empress's attention, all in the possession of names redolent of the Thirty Years War. One especially, that of Prince Mansfeld Colloredo, appeared to epitomize the abuses: peasants were forced to buy produce from the prince whose agents flogged or beat them when they failed to comply. The agents also threatened them with incarceration if they did not submit to unreasonable demands of enforced labour. The Empress, on hearing in detail a report of these abuses, ordered that the prince be heavily fined and, notwithstanding the stiff opposition of the Austro-Bohemian chancellor, Count Chotek, deprived him of his rights over all the estates where the 'tyranny' had been prevalent.

This, however, was a rare success. In many other cases, Maria Theresa's attempts at reform, although strongly supported by her co-regent Joseph, ran into a quagmire of passive resistance from the aristocracy. Nevertheless, her determination resulted in progress and, in 1770, she legislated to abolish the worst of the irregularities, notably forced child labour, compulsion of peasantry to buy produce from their landlords at inflated prices, and the requirement of 'gifts' in return for permission to travel and marry. The new legislation outlawed such practices, but enforcement was sporadic and within a year it was clear further measures were required.

With Joseph's help, the Empress now submitted to the Austro-Bohemian Chancellery a memorandum which asked whether the state might not benefit from the complete abolition of serfdom, beginning with the elimination of the *Robot*. The memorandum was innovative, posing questions concerning whether labour should be remunerated and whether the peasants' small private holdings be sold off to them so that their payments to their landlords might be replaced with payment to local military units. The tenor of the memorandum was highly critical of the landowners, underlining their role in exaggerating the effects of the poor harvests by insisting on selling their grain abroad.

In June 1771 a new *Urbarium* was ordered to be established for Bohemia but this foundered on the corruption of some of the local officials who were in the pocket of the aristocracy. Joseph, travelling to Bohemia, contrasted the oppression and brutality he encountered there with the beauty and benign conditions prevailing in adjoining Upper Austria where the estates of the aristocracy were more modest:

> This land is beautiful and well-cultivated and the corn stands upright and the fields are all well-tended. The reason for this is the private property that the peasant in Upper Austria has and the fact that he is not hindered in his operations by forced labour and owes only taxes to his lord.[5]

But neither the Empress's nor her son's sympathy for the oppressed peasantry in Bohemia could make much progress in the teeth of determined opposition on the part of the great landowners. The Estates produced their own proposals for reform but as these involved virtually no change to the status quo, they were quickly seen by Maria Theresa for what they were: cosmetic and irrelevant.

The Empress did, however, make it abundantly clear that those aristocratic families that came to agreements with their serfs received court favour. In Moravia, the Liechtensteins broke ranks with their fellow landowners to reach such an agreement and in Bohemia, another family, the Czernins, followed suit. But these were isolated cases and by 1774 Maria Theresa, without the support of her son Joseph, began arguing firmly for the total abolition of the *Robot*. So determined was she for the abuses of serfdom to end that she told Joseph that this was the 'only thing which keeps me at the helm of the state'.[6]

Yet Bohemia's landowners deployed all their skills at delay and prevarication, at one point agreeing to 'voluntary reform', and then proceeding to dilute systematically the reform proposals in the context of these 'voluntary agreements'. Every estate had its own peculiarities and defied consistent or uniform change. As the attempts at progress became bogged down, the peasantry quickly saw that efforts at reform were running into the sands. In the winter of 1775, the inevitable frustrations spilt over into a violent revolt. Insubordination, combined with attacks on landowners' property and even the emergence of Hussite sentiment, threw rural Bohemia into a state of widespread agitation.

This revolt, coming after years in which Maria Theresa's armies had fought Prussia, Bavaria and France ostensibly to bring good government to Bohemia, shattered the Empress. The uprising subsided quickly but there seemed to be no long-term solution. Writing to Mercy, her ambassador in Paris, the Empress anguished:

> I have sacrificed 35 years to the public. I am worn down, so troubled by the fact that I do more harm than good. The revolt in Bohemia is suppressed but is very far from being extinguished . . . I cannot put things right and I do great harm by my continued presence.[7]

Mercy replied, advocating the Empress remain 'at the helm' and do her best by 'submitting to divine providence'. It was advice which Maria Theresa found compelling and so she returned to the charge to 'settle matters'. She had understandably counted on her son's support in abolishing the distortions and inadequacies of the *Robot* but now found that Joseph was, most strangely for this obsessive reformer, actually opposed to the abolition of the '*Robot* system'. Joseph perhaps foresaw the problems in a fragile pre-revolutionary era of stripping the aristocracy of its fundamental privileges. In any event, on hearing the detail of his mother's proposals, he rounded on her, defending the *Robot*, as 'it forms an essential element in our constitution'. Reform was preferable to abolition. What followed expressed a typical Josephinian over-intellectualization of the problem.

The new *Urbarium* was dated 13 August 1775 and ran to more than eighty pages. It divided all peasants into eleven classes, each with distinct obligations. Implementation was predictably watered down by the landlords but the legislation brought considerable relief to the serfs of Bohemia as, while not abolishing the system entirely, it reduced significantly the obligations of the *Robot* and laid the foundations for its eventual termination.

Maria Theresa determined to push for this and decided to set an example to the aristocracy by experimenting through two estates which had formerly belonged to the Jesuits but were now hers to dispose of as she pleased.

In a highly innovative move, she sold off the land to the peasantry, appointing a minor official by the name of Raab to organize the sale and develop what gradually became known as the 'Raab system' as it was extended to other royal properties. In this way, Maria Theresa demonstrated that as a reformer she could be more radical at times than her son. This did not mean, however, that she favoured shaking the foundations of her monarchy, and a much-quoted letter to her son from this time made the point that she did not hold with 'the annihilation of the existing nobility under the specious pretext of preserving the majority, of which I accept neither the necessity nor still less the advantage'. As elsewhere, Maria Theresa's reform was tied to the strengthening of the state rather than reform for reform's sake. Well might Joseph accuse his mother of displaying an 'absolutely invincible mistrust' towards her son's advice.

The heated arguments over the reform of the *Robot* gave rise to much correspondence. Maria Theresa penned one of her more pointed missives to her son, rich in understanding, affection and maternal love but unyielding in its scepticism with regard to theoretical, abstract, impractical solutions: 'There is a great misfortune in our relations; with the best of intentions we do not understand each other . . . I can never accept lax principles in matters of religion and morals . . . I have every reason to feel alarmed at your precarious situation, and I tremble for the future'. Had she known how close her empire was to come to collapse in less than a decade after her death, she might have trembled even more.

But Joseph remained unyielding on the preservation of the *Robot* and Maria Theresa felt she could not abolish it in the face of the aristocracy's and her co-regent's determined opposition. Writing to another of her sons, she insisted: 'I believe that if the Emperor – I will not say would support me – would merely remain neutral, I should succeed in abolishing serfdom and the *Robot*. Then all would be well. But unfortunately, the Lords, seeing that I'm not taken in by them, have ranged themselves on the Emperor's side, and the spirit of contradiction that reigns here makes my task very hard.'[8]

A few weeks earlier, in a letter dated January 1777, the Empress returned to the challenges of her Bohemian kingdom:

> Bohemian affairs trouble me greatly, the more so as the Emperor and I cannot agree on the means to be adopted. The oppression of these poor people and the tyranny are well known and acknowledged. It is only a question of laying down suitable principles. I had reached the point of success when suddenly the lords, who by the way are all ministers, conspired to weaken the Emperor's resolution and so in a moment undo the work of two years.

By this time, Maria Theresa felt all her efforts were being undermined and that, with increasing age, she was becoming isolated. That she was certainly becoming more strident was attested to by her son, who wrote to his brother in Florence:

> Committees are continually being held to devise something that can be proposed to her, but her ideas are so strong, so ruinous, that it is not possible to find anything which can approximate to them.[9]

> She would like to abolish serfdom . . . change the entire rural economy of the landed classes . . . without paying the slightest regard to the landowner so that he loses at least half his revenues . . . You will not regret being at Florence. I should like to be in the Antipodes.[10]

Historians have chosen largely to ignore this letter which proves beyond any scintilla of doubt whose ideas were more progressive when it comes to apportioning the spoils of the Enlightenment between Joseph and his mother. Maria Theresa detested Voltaire and Frederick of Prussia, yet even these two 'darlings of the Enlightenment' could have never envisaged anything as radical as abolishing serfdom at a stroke. The Great Empress, on the other hand, less than three years before her death, could demonstrate a vision which was more radical, bold and forward-looking than all of these so-called revolutionary minds cobbled together.[11]

CHAPTER 33

Looking West: The Failure of the French Intellectual Connection

WE HAVE SEEN IN the preceding chapter how, barely three years before her death, Maria Theresa, if incapable of pushing through her ideas in the teeth of her son's implacable opposition, was nevertheless tireless in her pursuit of what she considered to be morally and humanely correct. These were not necessarily the two sides of the same coin and we have seen that her sympathy for the peasantry of Bohemia did not extend to allowing them much confessional laxity.

Yet, as her physical and mental strength ebbed away, she redoubled her efforts to fight a rearguard action against what she saw as the most pernicious ideas of her time. Nothing expressed this more vividly than her dynamic with Joseph as he travelled – this time not eastwards on a tour of inspection of the monarchy but westwards and then beyond the frontiers of *Vorderoesterreich*, to the future 'cradle of the Enlightenment', Paris.

The further west Joseph travelled, the more critical he became of the failure of Enlightenment ideas to penetrate western Alpine Austria, especially the provinces of Vorarlberg and Tyrol. These and their attached territories enjoyed, like Hungary, a customs barrier with Austria, which gave them a certain autonomy and remoteness from Viennese administrative control. Maria Theresa adored the Tyrol and, as we have seen, often dreamt of retiring to its wildernesses should the duties of office become unbearable. But for Joseph such remoteness was anathema. Predictably, Tyrol and the other parts of the territory did not survive his scrutiny:

When one looks carefully at this province it becomes obvious that there is very little advantage to be derived from it . . . an expensive and ill-manned administration wastes revenue and causes discontent . . . twenty councillors who with their subordinates cost 140,000 florins in a province that yields in total only 300,000 florins since each of them has to find something to do, examine, invent, question, write and generally exasperate everyone.[1]

Maria Theresa at first resigned herself to these critical observations but she became more concerned when Joseph, travelling as usual incognito, decided to extend his trip to include Paris and 'observe everything interesting that a great monarchy can show in the way of resources, administration, agriculture, finance etc'.

Maria Theresa did her best to discourage her son's push westwards. The Austro-French alliance, which Kaunitz had worked so hard to construct and of which Joseph's sister Marie Antoinette's marriage to the Dauphin was the culmination, was too important to run risks. On the one hand, Joseph would no doubt imbibe the more radical ideas of the French philosophers; on the other, his intellectual appetites would find much of French court life hollow and dull. Either way, the visit was fraught.

'This visit greatly displeases me and I do not anticipate any advantage from it (except perhaps on account of my daughter)', Maria Theresa wrote to her ambassador in Paris. 'His dislike will only grow stronger when he sees the frivolity, absurdity and intrigues of this nation. His entourage will include Nostitz and Colloredo, sworn enemies of France, and there is even the idea of returning through Switzerland to see Voltaire, Tissot, Haller and all those extremists.'[2]

That last leg of the journey, Mercy replied, would 'most likely collapse of its own accord . . . Tissot is a doctor and Haller a poet, neither famous as to deserve the Emperor's attention. . . .' Nevertheless, Maria Theresa fretted over the visit, and it was delayed for three years before, with the crowning of his sister as Queen of France in 1774, Joseph's trip began to assume the importance of a necessary state visit.

A long, defensive and submissive letter from Joseph acknowledged that he would of course be strictly under his mother's orders throughout his time in Paris. Maria Theresa knew better than to forbid the journey, but she hoped the frequent postponements would result in the entire expedition being called off. The journey could not be shorn of its political significance and Joseph was too Prussophile not to enjoy the frisson of unease which the Francophile Kaunitz expressed on hearing the news of the proposed visit.

Joseph, however, agreed to carry out a mission to warn his sister of their mother's foreboding concerning her behaviour. When he finally reached Paris in 1777, he tempered his delight at his sister's company – he found her vivacious, beautiful and amusing – with a severe censure of her taste for 'gambling and other imprudences'.

He had been encouraged by Maria Theresa to wean Marie Antoinette off her seeming addiction to frivolity and his warning could have been uttered by his mother; it was simple and to the point: she was to change her ways, 'otherwise the revolution will be cruel'.[3]

Mercy kept the Empress informed almost daily of her son's progress around the capital, dwelling on his visits to hospitals and other medical institutions which contrasted often unfavourably with facilities in Vienna but which aroused nonetheless Joseph's curiosity. In contrast to the ruling monarch of France, his brother-in-law Louis XVI, who never appeared informally, Joseph adored imitating his mother's removal of the 'forbidden zone'. He loved talking to people who did not recognize him and seeing their astonishment when they found out who he was.

Joseph had hoped to meet Voltaire on his return journey via Switzerland, as we have seen, but this, like his earlier attempts to meet Benjamin Franklin, was a failure, too, less as a result of his mother's vividly expressed reservations than on account of a slight 'misunderstanding' between the two men's intermediaries.

In truth, Joseph was sufficiently loyal to his mother's beliefs to reject Voltaire's contempt for traditional Catholic theology and to remain suspicious of a man whom Kaunitz warned was 'the head of a sect destructive to society and to all good government'. Maria Theresa would have been deeply offended had her son supped with Voltaire and, ultimately, filial duty trumped intellectual curiosity. The affront to the philosopher rankled down the years and even Goethe felt compelled to condemn Joseph's behaviour: 'it would have done no harm to him and his undertakings if he had shown greater respect for the mind'.[4] But on this occasion, Joseph preferred evidently to show even greater respect towards his mother.

Maria Theresa's sensitivity to the fragility of the Austro-French relationship was well-founded. Her efforts ensured that the relationship reached heights it would never afterwards obtain. If the seventeenth century had been one of great power rivalry between Paris and Vienna, the nineteenth century degenerated again into violent estrangement. Maria Theresa's efforts to secure a lasting entente between Paris and Vienna came closer to success than anyone before or after achieved.

A century later, Crown Prince Rudolf would initiate a rapprochement with France which, had it succeeded, would have moved Austria once again towards an understanding with France. To this end, Rudolf engaged with leading French personalities and intellectuals. His efforts foundered, however, less on the conservatism of his father than on the intrigues of his partners. Like Joseph, he realized, a little too late, that there were limits to the tolerance French 'enlightenment' could extend towards a Catholic absolute monarchy.

Yet, even if its political dimension did not survive the challenges of later centuries, its legacy is still audible in twenty-first-century Vienna, and can be heard in the countless French words and phrases which still permeate Viennese dialect and which are still pronounced in an archaic way.[5]

CHAPTER 34

The Borders of Intolerance: Maria Theresa and the Jews

In EXAMINING THE POSITION of Jews in Maria Theresa's monarchy and the legacy of her policies, it is difficult to avoid the prism of the twentieth century so dominated by the unique bestiality of the Holocaust. Not only did the Third Reich's liquidation policies occur in territories formerly belonging to the Habsburgs – Theresienstadt, one of the most notorious death camps, was a city which had even been named after the Empress – Hitler, born an Austrian, who went to school with Wittgenstein in Linz, often referred to his anti-Semitism as something born and nurtured in Vienna. It is hardly surprising, then, that historians have focused on Austria's role as a vector for ingrained hostility towards the Jewish population. The Waldheim affair in the 1980s reinforced this view and Maria Theresa's aversion to Jews, referenced in earlier chapters, has been fitted neatly into a narrative of seemingly seamless Austrian anti-Semitism. Yet a closer examination of Maria Theresa's reign offers a more complex evaluation of the relationship between the Empress and the Jews.

First and foremost, the reader must bear in mind that the position of Jews in Maria Theresa's territories resembled that of non-Catholic Christians. In both cases, freedom of worship and eligibility for public office were at issue but, although Theresian officials might refer to Jews as a 'nation', they were not concerned with the Jewish race as such but only those who adhered to the Jewish faith. In this way, as we have seen, the son of a rabbi, Joseph Sonnenfels, on conversion to Catholicism, could enjoy a meteoric career with all the benefits of Theresian patronage. His rise had a profound effect on the empire's juridical progress.

Maria Theresa accepted unquestioningly that a Jew who had converted to Catholicism attained full civil rights, just as any Protestant who converted became equally open to official favour. There were many around Maria Theresa, notably Bartenstein and Haugwitz, who fell into the latter category. The Empress's own mother had converted from Protestantism to Catholicism on marrying Charles VI, so the concept of conversion was theologically and practically familiar to Maria Theresa.

With both communities of Jews and Protestants there was a fear that the cohesion of the monarchy was threatened by their links with their fellow-confessionals beyond the monarchy. Just as in England, Roman Catholicism was perceived as a link with ultramontane forces beyond the control of the British state, so too were Judaism and Protestantism seen in Austria as capable of breeding disloyalty to the state. Jews, on account of their international links and language skills, were vulnerable to such accusations and, as we have seen earlier, in one infamous case in Prague suffered wholesale expulsion on Maria Theresa's orders. In that case, they had not crossed borders or acted as covert spies but 'systematically' sympathized and collaborated with the occupying forces. Protestants were under arguably even greater suspicion as capable of harbouring secret sympathy for a Lutheran Prussian king.

Before the First Partition of Poland in 1772, there had been far more Protestants than Jews in the monarchy but the incorporation of Galicia-Lodomeria brought 200,000 new Jewish subjects into the monarchy, far more than the estimated 120,000 that had existed in Maria Theresa's domains until that time. The Galician Jews enjoyed a different tradition: on account of their numbers, especially in Galician cities and towns, they were more autonomous, visible and dominant. There were 191 synagogues and more than 200 village communities outside the cities. This contrasted with conditions elsewhere in Austria where Jews could, with few exceptions, only worship in the privacy of their homes.

Maria Theresa was astounded and perplexed when she was first acquainted with the scale of the Jewish population she was acquiring and, as we have seen, her son Joseph on visiting Lemberg (Lviv) was also impressed by the sheer numbers involved.

Inevitably, financial considerations dominated. An elaborate Theresian *Judenordnung* of 1776 attempted to regulate the activities of the Galician

Jews and incorporate them into the taxation system of the monarchy. Maria Theresa's programme made considerable concessions towards Jews which her son Joseph, interestingly, despite his much-acclaimed Toleration Patent, would eventually remove. Maria Theresa's legislation guaranteed the right of the rabbis to control the education of their communities and the exemption from compulsory use of German in their internal affairs. Unlike her son, who later banned the import of books in foreign languages, notably Hebrew, Maria Theresa was perfectly accepting of the need for 'foreign' imported books to be made available for her Jewish communities.

But there can be no escaping the fact that Maria Theresa fully accepted the teachings of her early Jesuit mentors that Jews were responsible for Christ's death and that they were as a result accursed. She certainly believed right up to the end of her days that their numbers should be limited in the heartlands of her domains, even if in Galicia and above all in Trieste her policies were encouraging.

As late as 1777, when a renewed bout of vigour was, as we have seen, investing her policies with regard to serfdom in Bohemia, she issued the following instruction to the Austro-Bohemian *Hofkanzlei*:

> In future no Jews of whatever reputation are to be permitted to remain here without my written permission. I know of no more dangerous plague than this nation who reduce people to beggary by fraud, usury and money-lending, who engage in all the evil business practices that an honourable man would shun. Hence, they should, so far as possible, be kept away from here and their numbers be reduced. Send me every quarter-day a table showing how many Jews are here, where they live and whether they have increased or diminished.[1]

This hyper-sensitivity was paradoxically partly the result of the relatively very small numbers of Jews – in contrast to Prague – who were living in Vienna. By the end of the Seven Years War, there were barely 600 Jews in Vienna, but they included several wealthy families who enjoyed positions of influence as trusted financial advisers and bankers. Some like the Wertheimers had even become agents of the government.

Although Maria Theresa's reign saw even these small numbers reduced, the families who remained continued to enjoy privileges on account of their perceived usefulness in financial matters. Maria Theresa may have held the Jews in moral purdah but she fully understood the value of their support for the economic life of her lands and she encouraged their settling, not only in Trieste but also even in Transylvania and the Banat, in order to foster the economic development of those underpopulated provinces. This paradox would persist throughout the Habsburg monarchy's history until Franz Josef adopted a more openly philo-Semitic stance in the face of the increasing political anti-Semitism arising from German nationalism.

From the earliest days of her reign, Maria Theresa's advisers saw Jews as far more useful than Protestants, but a challenge was posed by the rituals, attire and habits of the empire's Galician Jews, who were increasingly regulated by the state.[2] Their 'privileges' and 'toleration' came directly from the sovereign and not from any provincial diet. No provincial constitution contained any provisions in the Jews' favour.

With the exception of Trieste, in the Austrian crown lands, Jews were not easily granted the privilege of residence and there were in theory therefore no Jews in Styria, Carniola, Carinthia or Upper Austria, though small communities existed in Graz and Laibach. Theirs was in no way comparable with the wealth of the Vienna Jewish community and, although far from being persecuted, they endured considerable restrictions on their movements and numbers.

These included confinement to ghettos in towns, the requirement to stay out of the sight of Christians on Sundays, and exclusion from property ownership and public office. Nearly always, despite Josephinian reforms, they were also encouraged to wear the identifying yellow star and, in some places, men were required to grow beards, although this last feature was often a requirement of the Jewish community. Their tax burden was also heavy, sometimes as much as three times what Gentiles in the same provinces paid. Of these taxes, the most bitterly resented was the so-called *Leibmaut* (body-tax) which equated Jews with animals. Only and exceptionally were the Jews of Trieste recused of these burdens by imperial patents granted by the Empress culminating in the privileges and statutes of 1771.

Elsewhere the implementation of these measures was far from uniform or consistent but in several towns Jews had administrative and judicial authority over the ghetto. In some cases, synagogues were constructed as well as schools. In Vienna, members of the leading Jewish families consorted at theatres and concerts with Christians, provoking the ire not of the Empress but of the Prince-Archbishop of Vienna, Cardinal Migazzi. It had particularly scandalized the Cardinal that one Jew had even been seen wearing a sword in public.

Many Galician Jews moved west after the Partition of Poland, and by the time of Maria Theresa's death, the Jewish population of Bohemia had surpassed 60,000 while there were more than 75,000 in Hungary. The expansion of their numbers in Hungary, coupled with the fact that nearly half of them engaged in money-lending, led to a concomitant rise in anti-Semitism, especially among the extensive minor nobility whose estates were increasingly mortgaged to Jews. This anti-Semitism would infect the Hungarian establishment well into the twenty-first century.

In addition, there were increasing numbers of itinerant Jews, often impoverished, the so-called *Betteljuden*, who had no regular employment and were on the brink of utter destitution. It would be left to Joseph to explore how such people could be 'made more useful' to the state and he would, after Maria Theresa's death, introduce legislation outlawing their language (except during worship) and replacing it with German.

This was a far-reaching change which Maria Theresa never contemplated but it was accompanied by the later abolition of many restrictions, not least the requirement to wear distinctive clothing or signs, which was considered humiliating and divisive in a state with such a significant Jewish population.

Whether, had Maria Theresa lived longer, she might have been forced by her son to go down this route is a moot point. The consensus view of most historians is that her personal prejudices against Jews would have precluded any Patents of Toleration aimed at a programme of civil toleration during her reign. On the other hand, the Partition of Poland changed at a stroke the position of Jews in the monarchy and such large numbers of Jewish subjects must have inevitably resulted in less discriminatory conditions and legislation. In any event, Maria Theresa had, long before her son's majority, granted considerable privileges to the

Jews who had settled in Trieste. Venetian diplomatic reports on the economic life of Venice's emerging rival noted, already in the late 1740s, that a significant number of the merchants of Trieste were Jewish and prospering under Austrian laws and incentives denied to them in Venice.[3]

By the time of Maria Theresa's death in 1780, there were established privileges and rights for certain Jewish communities which afforded autonomy and freedom of worship. When Joseph finally, two years after her death, issued his famous Patent of Toleration, he employed Sonnenfels, his mother's protégé, to draft the legislation and used language which could have come directly from his mother:

> From the beginning of our reign we have shown it to be one of our principal concerns that all our subjects without distinction of nation and religion, as soon as they have been accepted and tolerated in all our states, should take their share in the public prosperity that we desire to increase by our solicitude, should enjoy a legally guaranteed freedom, and encounter no hindrance when seeking in every honour-able way to make their living to contribute by their industry to the general prosperity.

In its reference to an 'honourable way to make their living' and its focus on 'acceptance and tolerance in all our states', the language echoes Maria Theresa's views as expressed formally and informally and can be seen once again as building on Theresian foundations. Jews had in some ways enjoyed under her greater freedoms than Protestants and Orthodox. Hebrew books, for example, had always been more freely allowed to circulate than Protestant publications. It was obvious to Maria Theresa that if Jews were to be allowed into the monarchy at all – and there was no reason to wish to exclude them – then they would have to be allowed to hold their rituals, observe the Sabbath and eat their special food. She would have almost certainly sided with the Jews of Trieste against her son's insistence they give up the city's lingua franca Triestine dialect and replace it with compulsory German.

By retaining, until her dying breath, a scepticism of all religions other than the Catholic faith, Maria Theresa balanced her prejudices widely, and her energetic determination to stamp out crypto-Protestantism in Moravia was arguably considerably more vigorous and decisive than her desire to limit the numbers of Jews in Vienna.

It is certainly the case that once she had died, her son's formal Patents of Toleration gave the Jews formal recognition, but Joseph's simultaneous opening up of the monarchy to Protestantism actually stimulated anti-Semitism in many ways that Maria Theresa's policies avoided. Under Joseph, Jews were forced to participate in state education, forced to learn German and forced to take German names which identified them immediately as Jews as crudely as any visual labelling. These measures would hinder complete assimilation for centuries afterwards. Their books were much more strictly controlled than under Maria Theresa's rule and their customs and rituals and, above all, their languages of Hebrew and Yiddish faced far greater hostility than had ever occurred during her reign. Only the Jews of Trieste on account of their exceptional privileged position under Maria Theresa protested successfully against Joseph's 'Deutschwahn'.

Moreover, Joseph, for all the approbation his groundbreaking Patents have received, shared some of his mother's prejudices about Jews, telling Fanny von Arnstein, the Viennese Jewish salonnière: 'I will do everything I can for them; but I cannot like them.'[4] In both mother and son, personal distaste was overruled by wider ethical considerations tempered with practicality. The Jewish population brought many benefits to those dedicated to strengthening the Austrian state and Maria Theresa was perhaps the first Habsburg to confront the challenge of how, despite theological and other prejudices, to encourage rather than simply tolerate the Jews within her lands.

Long before Maria Theresa died, she had been informed by Kaunitz that many of his best sources of information about Prussia came secretly via Jews. Kaunitz's espionage system would not have been so effective without their help. Moreover, the Empress's own awareness of their critical role in the financing of her empire no doubt reinforced her acceptance of the Jews' utility. Just before her death, Kaunitz had persuaded Maria Theresa to adopt a more liberal line towards the Jews of Mantua and they had discussed her Jewish subjects in a more favourable light. Kaunitz had even said, foreshadowing the developments of a later age, that he looked forward to a time when the Jews of the monarchy would 'change from being a separate nation into a society distinct only in religion'.[5]

The rapidly developing prosperity of Trieste, where Maria Theresa had long permitted Jews to enjoy special privileges, was proof that Jews could be loyal subjects of her empire. When, in the 1770s, the Venetian Republic initiated a series of punitive measures against the Jews, most of the Veneto's Jewish community fled to Austria and, in particular, Trieste. Jews settled under her reign in the city and found that they had the perfect framework to pursue the opportunities which the great port began to offer to all its immigrants, irrespective of creed or race. From 1746, Jews enjoyed a corporate identity recognized by the Empress in her patents of 1747. In 1771 'The Privilege' was presented by the Empress to the Jews of Trieste with the opening:

> We Maria Theresa . . .
>
> The internal happiness of our subjects having been the principal object of the concerns of our reign . . . we have not spared effort or care in making commerce prosper especially in Trieste. The Jewish nation, especially suited to commerce invited by the Patents of our most august parent, arouses our most merciful reflections . . .
>
> We therefore wish to give the Jewish community in Trieste a solemn demonstration of our sovereign approval for the purpose of attracting more such families and individuals . . .[6]

This process was begun under Maria Theresa and it was her, rather than her son's, actions that allowed Jews to prosper within her domains. Like most of her policies aimed at strengthening the state, they were imbued with practical requirements as well as considerations of humanity.

When Maria Theresa died in 1780, the Jewish leaders of Trieste felt they had lost not only a benign sovereign but a protectress. Elia Morpurgo, Trieste's leading silk manufacturer and, as the name implies, a prominent Jew of Ashkenazi descent, composed the following eulogy:

> A woman of valour: how much happiness had she not provided for her subjects? Open ports, better roads, our flag at sea respected and

secure, commerce made flourishing and active, with benefit for her subjects . . . to the admiration of all peoples.[7]

In a later century, it was left to the Jews of Trieste to express again their gratitude to the Great Empress in a speech delivered by the Chief Rabbi of Trieste in April 1845 on the anniversary of the then Emperor Ferdinand I's birth. Referring to Ferdinand as the inheritor of the Habsburgs' devotion and Theresian support for the city, the Chief Rabbi insisted that the Habsburgs treated Jews as a parent might treat their children, rather than as a sovereign moving among their subjects.

Trieste, and in particular her Jewish community, owed its 'dolcezza, benignità [and] affabilità' to the Habsburgs. It also owed them its splendid roads, elegant palaces and happy and contented population. To describe it in more detail had already 'stancaron già tante penne' (exhausted many a pen). If a Habsburg visited Trieste, every Jewish heart beat with palpitations of impatience to see them ('ogni cuore palpitava d'impatienza di vederlo'). This was, on one level, a superficial piece of oratorical ingratiation but, on another, it conformed to a sense of progress and prosperity which the Chief Rabbi associated with Habsburg rule over the city. This was especially noticeable at a time when Italian nationalism was gaining momentum throughout the Italian peninsula barely twenty miles to the west.

Summing up the city and its Jewish community's indebtedness to the Habsburgs and especially Maria Theresa, the Chief Rabbi concluded that fidelity and love towards a sovereign is deeply inculcated into the Jewish mind and the king of kings had brought the Jews to this unique devotion to their Habsburg monarchs. 'Così sia' ('this is how it is and how it will be').[8]

Such loyalty was not widespread in the city just three years before revolution engulfed nearby Venice and Milan but the Jews of Trieste were demonstrating, in this brief *pronunciato* on the occasion of the Emperor Ferdinand's birthday, that they could be counted among the most loyal of the Habsburgs' subjects. Such a loyalty was not lightly or easily bestowed but had developed with many obstacles en route into a modus vivendi which had first borne fruit under the Great Empress.

PART III (ii)

THE LEGACY: CULTURE AND PIETY

CHAPTER 35

The Artistic Parnassus: Vienna

IF TRIESTE'S PROSPERITY INCREASED under the Great Empress, urban living in the monarchy of Maria Theresa was underdeveloped elsewhere. While her possessions in Lombardy and the Austrian Netherlands could boast several cities of importance, barely 5 per cent of the population of Austria and Bohemia lived in settlements with more than 10,000 people. This contrasted with the Austrian Netherlands, where more than 20 per cent of the population lived in towns of that size, and Lombardy, where the urban population accounted for 14 per cent of the inhabitants. Brussels had a population of more than 75,000 and Milan more than 135,000.

Vienna was, in comparison, enormous, with a population in 1775 approaching 230,000. Its development had been rapid once the Great Siege of Vienna had been lifted in 1683. Although the walls which had protected the city still stood, the suburbs beyond the defensive glacis had quickly developed in all directions. Vienna was capital of the empire and the monarchy and its vibrant cultural and political life made it a magnet especially for the German-speaking parts of Europe. The city quickly assimilated these into its everyday patterns of life. Above all, Viennese dialect became a lingua franca for many immigrants, although ironically then, as now, it was the Germans who found the dialect most difficult to acquire. Maria Theresa only spoke Viennese dialect and, right up to her death, to the dismay of visiting Prussian pedants, she never mastered High German grammar.

Under Maria Theresa, censorship was relaxed and a cosmopolitan intelligentsia encouraged. Maria Theresa's own advisers were from all over continental Europe and their cosmopolitan background lent much to the intellectual life of the court and the city.

Maria Theresa took much interest in the organization and governance of her capital and in 1770 ordered the numbering of all houses. Street lighting was introduced in 1776 and each suburb established its own police district with its own archives and constabulary.

In another one of his 'discoveries', Francis Stephen had imported from Lorraine the leading hydro-engineer of his time, Jean-Baptiste Brequin. He quickly set about shoring up the Danube so that its floods became less frequent. He also oversaw the construction of several bridges. The stone bridges were well made but not proof against storms and serious inundations. Terrible flooding was commonplace throughout the 1770s, as Joseph described to his brother:

> Continuous storms on the 29th of July and cloudbursts in the mountains above Pukersdorf have caused such flooding and incalculable damage that it is unbelievable unless one has actually seen it. Many persons, perhaps more than a hundred, cattle and horses have perished. Many houses, all the bridges, large parts of the road have been swept away. In ten minutes, the river Wien rose thirty feet with waves six feet high. I have been everywhere and the only thing to do was to load boats onto carts and get them to the suburbs to save people perched on their roofs.
>
> Luckily, the Danube calmed down and only flooded in the Prater but no-one can cross the bridges in a carriage, while at Schönbrunn the whole of the ground floor has been under six foot of water, along with the corridors, chapel, offices and stables. Lacy and Loudon at Dornbach and Hadersdorf have suffered immensely.[1]

On such occasions, Maria Theresa was always keen to support her son, and the welfare of their capital city was perhaps the one area of policy where mother and son could collaborate without any friction. Both were keen to invite the establishment of entities which might intervene between sovereign and people. Maria Theresa encouraged local government and the local guilds which played such an important part in the city. Chief among these was the bread bakers' guild, whose assembly hall in the Josefstadt to this day contains many prized souvenirs of the Theresian period.

Such guilds were an important part of the fabric of Viennese life and were especially important in the textile industry. Maria Theresa encouraged them not least because they assisted in the collection of taxes and were part of the fabric of local politics.

Architecturally, the city moved forward under Maria Theresa in a number of different directions. There was a plurality of styles but no particular architect could be said to personify any of these styles. Unlike the giants of the earlier generation of high baroque, Fischer von Erlach and Lukas Hildebrandt, there were no figures who represented the apogee of a particular movement. Late baroque, rococo, zopf or pre-neoclassical can all be used to describe individual buildings of Maria Theresa's reign.

Perhaps the architect who expressed the Empress's own thoughts on the subject most faithfully was Nikolaus Pacassi (1716–1790). Maria Theresa once said that she thought he 'understands better than anyone how to express my ideas'. But Pacassi held no such dominance over Austrian architecture as once Erlach or Hildebrandt had enjoyed. Pacassi shared the stage with many other talents, even in Vienna. Among these there was Jean Nicholas Jadot, another 'discovery' whom Francis Stephen had brought with him from Lorraine. Jadot favoured a kind of embryonic Louis XVI style but it took no hold in Vienna. Then there was Balthasar Neumann who arguably created, on paper at least, a Theresian palatial style with a projected new arrangement of the Hofburg in which giant pilasters and relentless symmetry were perhaps the chief hallmarks. This design was never executed.

If this was at one end of the spectrum, in Styria and Tyrol the baroque was enjoying a late flowering. The great Marian shrine of Maria Trost, outside Graz, was only finished a few years before Maria Theresa came to the throne. Its furnishings made no concessions to the new severity beginning to emanate from Vienna.

There, Pacassi had remodelled the Imperial Library's façades and created an austere square in front of them which has been called by one eminent Austrian architectural historian the 'triumph of intellect over clericalism'.[2] Certainly, Pacassi's opening up of the Josefsplatz made a street which normally would have focused on the nearby Augustine church filter pedestrians straight past the entrance of the Imperial Library.

This rather stripped-back style found expression in other cities of the empire, especially where the imperial residence was far less in use. In Prague, Budapest and Innsbruck, Pacassi's architectural language came to symbolize, if not an entirely absent imperial authority, one which was cold and distant.[3] Nowhere was this new restraint perhaps better represented than in the clear lines of the Palais Fries (today Pallavicini) which closed off the austere square in front of the *Hofbibliothek*. Johann Fries was a Protestant banker of Swiss nationality who proved of great support in the financing of Maria Theresa's military reforms, not least by overseeing a complete reorganization of the army's catering arrangements which had up to then been haphazard.

Fries reformed supply and distribution and his son became a trusted adviser at court. In fact, so favoured was the family that they were granted the rare privilege of constructing a new palace barely a stone's throw away from the Hofburg opposite the magnificent baroque Imperial Library of Fischer von Erlach. Everything about the new Fries palace was a statement. It was closer to the Hofburg than the palaces of the Dietrichsteins and Liechtensteins, Palffys and Eszterhazys even though Fries, unlike those families, was not a Catholic. It was monumental but simple, elegant but unfussy, grand yet restrained.

Maria Theresa did not question either the style or the proximity of such a 'Protestant' building to the Hofburg. The architect, Hohenberg, had just completed the Gloriette on the hill above Schönbrunn, a structure which had delighted Maria Theresa in its visually striking celebration of Daun's great victory at Kolin.

Hohenberg later regothicized several of Vienna's churches, including the Augustine, Minorite and St Michael churches, in another striking departure from the architectural language of the Counter-Reformation. But these strands of the new style left Maria Theresa unmoved, and by the time it came to discuss her tomb in the Capuchin crypt, the proposed and accepted design was a fulsome essay in late baroque.

Under Maria Theresa, it was not just architecture which followed different strands of taste; painting also moved in a plurality of directions.

A Theresian taste for rococo's 'triumph of the light' represented one thread. An aesthetic preferring greater sobriety was another. In the art of the ceiling fresco, the former held sway and Austria developed a style which came to express fully the lightness and almost sugary rococo style which, at the start of the twentieth century, would come to epitomize in the popular imagination the Theresian era in Richard Strauss's opera *Der Rosenkavalier*.

Some years before Maria Theresa's birth, Philipp von Hörnigk had coined a phrase which would become a touchstone for later generations of Austrians: 'Oesterreich über alles wenn es nur will' (Austria supreme if only it wishes). The phrase implied that nothing could limit Austria if only the willpower existed to translate commercial ambition into reality, and it might have been invented to express the visual world of the new generation of Austrian fresco artists who had worked during Maria Theresa's reign.[4]

Wealth, commerce, trade: all these increased exponentially under Maria Theresa as court, aristocracy and church all became richer and more interested in demonstrating in their artistic creations a new Austrian confidence. The painters and illusionists of these frescoes were inspirited by the imperial acknowledgement that such an illusionism was perhaps the perfect vehicle for expressing this newfound optimism.

Ceiling frescoes were not simply works of abstract composition. They were the artistic solution par excellence for expressing the unity of heaven and earth and the coexistence of the real and the unreal. In their creations they attempted to represent all the harmonies and contradictions of their sovereign.

Such a creative imperative was fortunate to find its expression during Maria Theresa's reign just as a new and gifted generation of fresco artists was coming to the fore. When Maria Theresa came to the throne in 1740, most of the artists working on ceiling frescoes had trained in Italy or under Italians. Beduzzi and Comazzi were Italians, and Johann Michael Rottmayr (1654–1730) had trained for twelve years in Venice, imitating the sombre colours of Pozzo and the bold contrasts of darkness and light which were the hallmark of Neapolitan *trompe l'oeil*.

As Maria Theresa's reign gathered momentum, however, three younger artists took up the reins of fresco work and struck out in a new direction. They were Daniel Gran (1694–1754), Bartolomeo Altomonte (1702–1783) and Paul Troger (1698–1762). Between them, they broke the dominance of the Austro-Italian school of painting and developed a specific Austrian style which moved away from the Roman and Neapolitan intensity of their predecessors.

Their work was not only brighter and lighter in atmosphere and colour, it also deployed markedly less pathos in its characterizations. The interiors of the garden pavilion at the great Abbey of Melk along the Danube offer perhaps the best example of this work. It was carried out by Troger's most gifted pupil, Johann Bergl (1718–1789). Bergl was born the year after Maria Theresa and thus can be seen to be the fresco artist who best expresses her reign, but one need only look at the astonishing work of his teacher at the monastery of Altenburg, deep in the Waldviertel of Lower Austria, to see that this lightness of style did not lead necessarily to an atmosphere of frivolity. As the depiction of the *Sapientia divina* there demonstrates, the lightness of the Austrian rococo was not incompatible with high-mindedness. At the monastery of Göttweig, Troger created a veritable apotheosis of Maria Theresa's father, Charles VI, who is portrayed as a formidable Apollo.

Another pupil of Troger who carried forward the new style was Franz Anton Maulpertsch (1724–1796). In his work on the interior of the ceiling of the Piaristenkirche in Vienna, he established a dynamic composition which nevertheless exuded a certain calm, in which the urges of a previous generation to create a tangible *Welttheater* had long diminished. By the time of his death in 1796, Maria Theresa had been dead for over fifteen years and the *Illusionismus* which she had promoted during her reign among her fresco painters had drawn to a close, but the scores of frescoes which had been created under her rule were perhaps the most enduring symbols of an optimism which saw in her rule the daily triumph of light over darkness.

Perhaps, in addition to these frescoes, Maria Theresa's greatest artistic bequest to Vienna was her summer palace at Schönbrunn. Here, patron and architect were in aesthetic lockstep. Pacassi once again organized for his Empress a long façade with understatement. However, under the influence of her adviser Tarouca, some elements of Jadot also seemed to creep into the design around the side pavilions and staircase. The summer palace was based on a horseshoe plan whose centre was conceived as the visual climax of the entire ensemble. But as important as the architectural design was, it was the gardens which arguably were to outshine this enduring legacy of the Empress. If Schönbrunn was a Maria Theresa *Schlössl* writ large, a model capable of imitation on a more modest scale throughout Austria, the gardens were truly unique.

No city in Europe possessed as much garden architecture as Vienna, where the removal of the Turkish threat had allowed the suburbs to flourish into a patchwork of small houses and gardens. By the time Maria Theresa came to the throne in 1740, Vienna was the largest baroque garden city in the world and, as has been observed, the aristocracy constructed gardens in imitation and deference towards Schönbrunn, 'like pins to a magnet'.

These *Lustschlösser* spread well beyond the glacis, and while the influence of Versailles and Le Nôtre was apparent in some of them, an indigenous style quickly developed which was unmistakeably Austrian. Geometric paths were disrupted by more intimate spaces. The dominance of symmetry became complemented by elements which took the wanderer away from the feeling that the 'Order' which expressed the dictatorship of higher authority was the only way to enjoy gardens. Maria Theresa introduced the concept of the *Boskett* or shrubbery to create alternative evergreen areas.

The life-blood of such gardens, as always, was water, and Maria Theresa encouraged fountains in the Italian style rather than just simple French-style waterways. These fountains helped choreograph the transition from formal parterre to shrubbery and then to such visual high points as a belvedere.

At Schönbrunn, the visual climax was the sensationally placed Gloriette, a monument to Austrian feats of arms and a striking composition in a classical idiom by Hohenberg, completed in 1775. Its design was the subject of much correspondence between Maria Theresa and her daughter Marie Antoinette while Joseph, too, chipped in on several aspects of the palace and garden designs, most of which he disliked heartily. 'Vous avez raison', the Empress wrote to her daughter after Marie Antoinette had questioned one of the early designs for the monument 'on the hill'. As Maria Theresa later replied: 'Joseph does not like the place and, at my age, should I be really thinking about beginning such a work?'

In the end, it was completed five years before Maria Theresa's death and is perhaps the most instantly recognizable architectural monument, along with the palace it overlooks, of her entire reign.

By the time the Gloriette was finished, Maria Theresa had long had plenty of experience of overseeing garden designs which were invested with powerful symbolic meaning. Following Prince Eugene's death, she had inherited the Upper and Lower Belvedere palaces and had immediately set about employing the Bavarian garden architect Dominique Girard, to soften the Italian lines with 'French' visual effects. The grandiose panorama which is the climax of the gardens represented a new departure from the strict formality of baroque gardens: cascades and statuary appeared at unexpected points, surprising the visitor and making it impossible to judge distances accurately. *Bosketts* abounded and the illusory effect is perhaps best captured by Bellotto's famous painting of a skyline which even today is virtually unchanged.

In addition to the Belvedere, Maria Theresa also inherited Prince Eugene's summer palace at Schloss Hof. As elsewhere, she threw herself wholeheartedly into the garden's designs. The result was not just a triumph of horticulture but a powerful symbol of its former owner's prowess as a military commander. A grand vista, in this case the conquered east which the Prince's military genius had delivered to the monarchy, with its horizons stretching far into the distance, formed the visual climax of the garden's design.

At Schönbrunn, Maria Theresa was able to draw on this experience while adding some significant new innovations. Already in 1752, under the influence of Francis Stephen, a *Tiergarten* was introduced into the grounds with a small pavilion designed in the French manner by his favourite architect Jadot. This became the focal point for many summer encounters the Empress had with her children, as well as meeting places for more political discussions with her advisers. Kaunitz regularly held discussions on high diplomacy in this intimate and picturesque surrounding, interrupted occasionally by the braying of various zoological inmates.

The kiosk became a rendezvous for morning coffee, a ritual for the Empress which was quickly extended to virtually all other ranks of society during her reign. A year later, the horticulturist Adrian van Steckhoven developed another part of the gardens to grow exotic plants imported from Asia. It was about the same time that the Empress granted permission to construct a botanical garden near the Belvedere under the supervision of the renowned botanist Nicholas Jacquin. The creation of such areas of exotic plantation assisted the establishment of *giardini secreti*. The secret garden was an important element in Viennese life, developed to create zones of encounter where conversations in many different forms might be carried on in private. At Schönbrunn, this idea was reinforced by extensive trellising which, when constructed carefully, produced a number of *Saletteln* or small garden 'rooms' where Maria Theresa's children could play undisturbed in the shade of Vienna's hot summers. In time, these came to be seen as the *sine qua non* of the rococo garden, special 'chambers' where the scent of roses predominated, and everything was in half-shadow.

Other innovations in garden design began to flourish under the Empress's benign eye. The picturesque and 'harmonious chaos' began to become aesthetic concepts during Maria Theresa's reign and she embraced many of their aspects, even seeing them in terms of the relaxation of court ceremony. Such devices moved away from the grand parterres of imperial gardens towards more informal, contemplative creations where 'one wanders in and is unaware of quite where one enters or leaves'.[5]

Thus was the dictatorship of the baroque garden finally ended under the Empress. The coup de grâce was undoubtedly another, less visible but equally significant addition to the gardens of Schönbrunn – the classical ruins which suddenly surprise the visitor at the foot of the long ascent to the Gloriette. If the Gloriette gave the gardens of Schönbrunn a focal point of coherence they otherwise might have lacked, the ruins offered an early glimpse into the world of the sublime and melancholy, a forerunner of the Romantic era which Maria Theresa barely lived to see but which in these ruins are powerfully present. The ruins are rich in Enlightenment symbolism, with Masonic and pantheist motifs present throughout. Together with the obelisk commemorating her, these symbols expressed the Empress's commitment to progress and innovation. The beginning of a new era in garden design, an era which ushered in a modesty and intimacy while underpinning imperial authority, was a fitting monument for the Great Empress.

CHAPTER 36

Wills and Laws: *Milde und Munifizenz*

ARGUABLY, IF THE FORMAL gardens of palaces were the most visible and external expression of Maria Theresa's character and thoughts, her most intimate wishes concerning her legendary *Milde und Munifizenz* were enshrined in her last will and testament. Her generosity and determination to honour the obligations of loyalty and affection accumulated over a forty-year reign expressed her character at every turn. They also caused her successor, Joseph, extensive challenges.

Leaving aside for the moment her bequests to her children, it became quickly apparent that the Empress had made provision for countless others whose interests she had helped throughout her reign. She had always had at her disposal a private treasury, the well-funded *Kammerzahlamt* (chamber payment office). It had been set up by Johann von Mayer, a financier of Jewish descent, and then later administered by his son Albert. The sums of money which were deposited originated in many parts of her domains. As with all personal financial affairs of sovereigns, they were shrouded in secrecy but the documents show that the First Partition of Poland brought a significant injection of funds into the *Kammerzahlamt*. The funds, although solely to be deployed at the discretion of the monarch, were nonetheless often used for the service of the state. There is ample evidence that they were used for special political services such as funding missions abroad, an elaborate espionage network, and even the establishment of a code-breaking capability. In addition, many smaller amounts were used to support a handful of poets, artists, architects and musicians.

By far the greatest amount, however, was distributed to families to make gifts and pensions. These families were 'certain distinguished families who earn our full consideration by their birth, devotion and service'. These, first and foremost, included her generals, most of whom came from relatively modest circumstances. Daun who had 'saved Austria' qualified for such largesse, as did Loudon and Lacy. The amounts so distributed provided them with the wherewithal to lead the life of a nobility which was often short of money and burdened by debts but nonetheless expected to maintain appearances.[1]

In addition to these 'high-end' families, Maria Theresa also looked after her servants at all levels, providing where necessary funds for their extended families. The beneficiaries of these stretched into four figures. Another class of recipients were the 115 godchildren Maria Theresa and her daughters had acquired. At another level, Protestants who had converted in her service to Catholicism were similarly rewarded. We have already seen how she funded the education of such strays as Thugut; her munificence extended to many families whom she encountered and felt a sovereign's moral obligation to help. By the end of her reign there were more than four thousand beneficiaries receiving pensions, costing many millions of florins a year.

In her will, Maria Theresa required that all these pensions be continued. Furthermore, she included many new beneficiaries, including her physician and confessor, and even alms to be distributed to the poor in the thirty-two towns where commemoration services were to be held for her. Most extravagant of all, perhaps, was her command that on her death every soldier in her service be given an extra month's wages.

Unsurprisingly, the Empress anticipated that her son Joseph – who usually refused even to be a godfather, as it involved 'private motives' – would seek to reverse the clauses in her will. Consequently, she drafted them as tightly as possible and supplemented them with additional funds. On the night before she died, she instructed that another lavish bequest, amounting to 100,000 florins, be given to a school set up by Felbiger to augment the funds of this *Normalschule* which she feared would otherwise be deprived of pensions.

As in everything, Maria Theresa was consistent. As her son later accused her, she was not of the opinion that state revenues 'should be sacred' but that her system of government was first and foremost 'a family affair'.[2]

Joseph, as the high priest of the glorification of the state (he was just the 'state's first servant'), was unlikely to be convinced. 'Family affairs have nothing to do with the concerns of the state', was his verdict. Within weeks of her death, he had abolished the private treasury and required the orphans and cripples supported by his mother to go into cheaper accommodation. Although defensible on the grounds that the state should establish standardized arrangements for the care of such people, the austerity of Joseph's policies contrasted mightily with those of his mother. There was widespread resentment by officials, aristocrats, as well as the poor at the loss of their perquisites. It did not help that Joseph at the same time reduced the number of court chamberlains from 1,300 to 36 and excluded such powerful families as the Liechtensteins and Palffys.

Only the army was permitted to enjoy the full benefits of Maria Theresa's will but even here Joseph felt compelled to diminish his mother's largesse when announcing the award, by loudly insisting that he would personally make up the shortfall in funds on account of the inadequacy of her estate.

At the time of her death, Maria Theresa still had ten of her sixteen children living. Of these Joseph, Max Franz, the recently appointed archbishop-elector of Cologne, and two daughters, both considered unmarriageable because of physical deformities, were living in Vienna. In addition, Marie Christine was frequently present as she lived only a few hours by boat down the Danube at Pressburg where her husband, Albert of Saxony, was *locumtenens* or governor.

When Francis Stephen had died, he had left an estate in excess of 8 million florins but Maria Theresa had immediately assigned half of that amount to Marie Christine's impoverished husband. Marie Christine, it may be recalled, was the only one of Maria Theresa's daughters allowed to marry for love rather than dynastic or political interests. If the impe-cunious Albert was to have a court at Pressburg worthy of his status it would require considerable funding, hence the transfer of such vast funds.

Marianne entered a convent in Klagenfurt and this required only a far more modest endowment of 80,000 florins a year. Elisabeth required even less in her conventual retreat in Innsbruck. The remaining children were each to receive a comfortable 50,000 florins a year until they were otherwise provided for. By the time of Maria Theresa's death in 1780, one of the children, Josepha, had died, and several had been 'placed' in grand establishments: Maria Carolina was Queen of Naples, Marie Antoinette was Queen of France, Amalia Duchess of Parma, Leopold Grand Duke of Tuscany, Ferdinand heir presumptive to the Duchy of Parma and Max Franz Elector of Cologne.

Most of these arrangements, with minor modifications, had been made on Francis Stephen's death in 1765 and Maria Theresa simply reinforced his generosity. Her will also implicitly confirmed the unifying policy of her father regarding the monarchy. Although she had lost most of Silesia and the eastern marches around Belgrade, most of this inheritance was still guaranteed as a single unit. With Haugwitz's help, and later that of Kaunitz, the central crown lands of Austria and Bohemia (but not Hungary) were brought into an administrative and fiscal uniformity. The legal enforceability of the Empress's will was contingent on this administrative uniformity.

In 1749 Maria Theresa had established a single court of appeal, the so-called *Oberste Justizstelle*, which in her words, 'ensured that the uniformity at which I was aiming should not be interrupted nor any opportunity be left to look back at the harmful old constitution'. Thus did Maria Theresa establish a de facto ministry of justice. In conformity with this policy of establishing uniformity of laws throughout the Austrian and Bohemian lands, she also created a commission to produce a general compilation of legal procedure in civil and in criminal and constitutional law. From 1756 this was known as the Compilation Commission. Its tasks were often technical and complex and it faced opposition nearly everywhere but, with the Empress's unstinting support, Haugwitz and Kaunitz succeeded in presenting Maria Theresa with a draft civil code, the so-called *Codex Theresianus*, in 1766. The same lawyers had also worked on a criminal code, the so-called *Nemesis Theresiana*, on account of its formidable sanctions.

Although it would take six more years, it was Maria Theresa's achievement to succeed in getting her Compilation Commission to draw up a list of procedures which could govern court and judicial practice in all courts in the Austrian and Bohemian lands. The attempt had led to a highly fractious debate. The issues at stake received added adrenaline once Joseph took over the helm of state. The question as to whether an aristocrat needed to be sworn in by oath when giving evidence, rather than being simply asked to give his word of honour, provoked further enormous dispute.

Maria Theresa's will was thus embedded in a legal system which owed its foundation to her reign but was not entirely without inconsistencies, and this enabled Joseph to attack and ignore many elements of it.

Eventually, Joseph drove a consistent programme which abolished many of the exemptions enjoyed by military and clerical courts in a vast Patent which Maria Theresa did not live to see. Paradoxically, her son's reforms would allow a much narrower interpretation of her wishes.

Nevertheless, the foundations of the coherent legal system were laid under her jurisdiction. In particular, the rules governing the appointment of judges – that they have legal training and not receive financial inducements from any of the litigants – were all laid down during her reign. Whatever disputes might arise in the interpretation of her will, the Rule of Law added credibility to any decisions taken.

The establishment of such a system could only survive in the varied domains of the Habsburgs by the enactment of those carefully thought-out compromises which were the hallmark of the Empress's reign.

Maria Theresa well knew from her earliest relations with the *Judex Curiae*, Janos Palffy, that attempts to bring Hungary into line with legal practice in Austria and Bohemia were unlikely to succeed. At the diet of 1764, her proposals for tax increases and greater protection of the serfs against the nobility were rejected after so much bitter argument that Maria Theresa determined never to submit any legislation to this forum again.

Major tax changes could not be imposed on the Hungarians without their approval. A similar problem pertained to the Tyrol and the Austrian Netherlands, both of which had constitutional rights defending them against the sole authority of the monarch.

Even the new Austrian system of conscription ran into the sands in these provinces. Despite the best efforts of Maria Theresa's generals, notably Lacy, the system of military conscription he established in the Austro-Bohemian lands possessed no authority in Lombardy, Tyrol, Hungary or the Austrian Netherlands. The constitutional challenge posed by these districts was familiar to Maria Theresa and she chose always to move cautiously. She had concluded that these provinces needed special handling, however unfair and inequitable it might appear. The differences within the monarchy had to be respected, just as the seemingly infinite gradations of charity in her will needed to be honoured.

As always, the sheer geographical dispersion of Maria Theresa's possessions posed another problem. To execute all the details and provisions of the late Empress's will required tentacles in all the parts of her domains and beyond. The prince-archbishops such as those in Salzburg had both temporal as well as spiritual authority over large parts of the monarchy even though, in Salzburg, they were based outside the Habsburg crown lands.

Austro-Bohemia comprised a coherent bloc. Hungary could be also treated as a bloc but elsewhere the situation was far more complicated. To reach Milan, Austrian representatives had to travel across the Venetian Republic or the Swiss Confederation. To get to the Austrian Lowlands it was necessary to traverse large parts of southern and Middle Germany and, while there were numerous enclaves of Austrian territory en route, it was impossible to avoid passing through independent states such as Bavaria or Trier and Mainz.

Tuscany was arguably even more remote, but it was increasingly, after 1765, no concern of Maria Theresa although, right up to the day of her death, she urged Leopold to stand firm against papal attempts at encroachment on the Grand Duke's authority.

All these factors reinforcing 'variety rather than uniformity' were of course anathema to Joseph, who was especially aggrieved by the Hungarian exemptions and privileges. On her deathbed, Maria Theresa wrote to Joseph advising him to rule Hungary with pragmatism and care but he had years earlier determined to put the monarchy's government on a 'firm footing' in which no differentiation could be tolerated in the face of his absolute power. To this end, he neither summoned the Hungarian Diet nor took a coronation oath. Nor did Joseph honour Maria Theresa's wish before she died that he go to Pressburg for the coronation ceremony. Choosing to largely ignore his mother's will was just a symbol of the much greater determination of Joseph to ignore all her wishes.

Maria Theresa had also been crowned Queen of Bohemia but again her son refused to submit to this dignity, lest it suggest special privileges for Bohemia rather than the *Gleichförmigkeit* which so dominated Joseph's thinking on issues of government. In the 1750s, in addition to her will, Maria Theresa had composed two versions of a *politisches Testament*. This was intended to guide Joseph as her successor. Drawing on the notable reforms of Haugwitz in the Austro-Bohemian lands, she noted that the power of the Estates had been much diminished by these reforms. This document certainly enumerated the priorities of administrative reform which the years after the end of the War of the Austrian Succession had ushered in. When Haugwitz died in 1765, Joseph would inherit many of the great statesman's ideas and concepts of absolute power in a uniform monarchy. Yet the monarchy was, like the Holy Roman Empire in R.J.W. Evans's later words, a 'mildly centripetal agglutination of bewilderingly heterogeneous elements'.

By the time of Maria Theresa's death, the Holy Roman Empire was less than thirty years away from its self-inflicted extinction, hastened by the Napoleonic upheaval but already predicted by Frederick of Prussia. The Austrian empire which replaced it was altogether more important and, thanks to Maria Theresa, it endured all the shocks of revolution and war rather better than most European states.

In her final will and testament, Maria Theresa thus paid tribute in miniature to the structures she had created while at the same time ensuring that, in every clause, the state's obligations which she bequeathed never lacked a humane element. Her son's disregard for it reveals how, in small things as well as great, mother and son were constantly faithful to their own widely divergent values.

CHAPTER 37

Music and Drama: A Subversive Universe

IN PAUL WEIDMANN'S PLAY, *Die schöne Wienerin*, published in 1776 and widely performed during the last years of Maria Theresa's reign, there occurs an interesting exchange between a black servant and his master, Graf Fixstern. The count has just upbraided the servant for some minor peccadillo and receives the potentially for that time subversive response: 'Nature made me free when I was born, as free as you! I am flesh and blood like you. The same sun shines on us; the same earth bears and feeds us; we live and die in the same manner.' This message of universal brotherhood across racial and confessional frontiers was fashionable in the 1770s, if not widely held outside progressive circles. The name Fixstern was also slightly subversive, originating as it did from the oft-repeated oath of that time, *Fix Loudon Stern!*[1]

Theresian court circles would have been familiar with the presence of a 'Court Moor', Angelo Soliman, who had been 'gifted' to Prince Wenzel Liechtenstein but had been 'freed' and emancipated to the extent that he could eventually marry an aristocrat and join the leading Masonic lodge of Maria Theresa's reign, *Zur wahren Eintracht*.

The combination of Soliman's presence in Vienna and the text of *Die schöne Wienerin* suggests that many of what we have become in a later age accustomed to recognizing as the usual neuroses of censorship were not present in Vienna during Maria Theresa's reign. The same lodge Angelo Soliman joined, and later became master of ceremonies in, also boasted Mozart as a member and the slightly subversive text of Beaumarchais's play *The Marriage of Figaro* would have been taken in the Vienna court's stride while Maria Theresa was alive, unlike in Paris, where it was initially banned. Indeed, the censorship in Vienna had long forbidden the portrayal of servants as lowly or ugly in contrast to their elegant aristocratic masters. Even 'anti-aristocratic' comments were permitted during Maria Theresa's reign.

Mozart met the Empress on three occasions in Vienna. The first, at the age of six in 1762, was arguably the most successful. News of the young boy's prodigious musical talents quickly reached the Viennese court, where music was perhaps almost a way of life for Maria Theresa. She had grown up taught to sing and dance. Her ancestors Leopold I and Joseph I had both been music patrons. There was a flourishing court orchestra which Leopold had increased until it numbered 100 and Charles VI further reinforced. There was the imperial choir and another choir directed in St Stephen's Cathedral by the teacher of Haydn, Reutter.

For several decades, Maria Theresa's father had taken an inordinate delight in seeing his offspring perform and he was determined that music assume an important part of court life. He supported Johann Joseph Fux, dubbed the 'Austrian Bach', and paid out of his own purse for the publication of his work *Gradus ad Parnassum*. Each year, while Charles was alive, at least a dozen operas or oratorios were performed, including *Euristeo*, in which Maria Theresa danced, as well as countless arias and duets by Antonio Caldara.

Even though, for a few years, the crisis of 1741–45 put an end to many of these musical festivities, peace, however brief, brought a resumption of the court's interest in music. By 1761 Christoph Willibald Gluck was setting Molière to music and both he and the young Haydn were established composers, the latter thanks to the increasing patronage of the Eszterhazy family in nearby Eisenstadt and Rohrau.

Under Maria Theresa's reign it was not just the conventional world of opera and oratorio which was nurtured; instrumental music came increasingly to the fore. String quartets by Haydn became fashionable along with chamber music and the structure of sonata form. By the time of Mozart's third visit to Vienna in 1773, he had already written his striking Lodi quartet and was absorbing many lessons in musical composition from Haydn. But the traffic went both ways and Haydn's symphonies began to take on certain Mozartian traits, especially in the development of the melodic line.

Maria Theresa presided thus over the musical capital of Europe, a golden era in music which made Vienna a centre of western European culture, unrivalled in musical terms by any other city. Of Mozart's three visits to Vienna, the first was also the most spontaneous. Marie Antoinette took a great shine to the young boy and when she asked him to perform musical tricks, such as playing a work with just one finger, the little boy quickly complied. The visit is immortalized in one of Leopold Mozart's letters in which he describes how his son leapt into the arms of the Empress: 'our little Wolfgang sprang onto the lap of the Empress and put his arms round her neck and vigorously kissed her'.[2]

This demonstration of imperial favour opened the doors of all Vienna's palaces and soon the young Mozart and his sister were being invited to the great houses of the Kinskys, Palffys and Kaunitzs. Kaunitz himself was an accomplished musician and may well have inspired the Empress to send two outfits, previously worn by her own children, and the sum of a hundred ducats to the Mozart children, along with the command that they both appear at court 'as soon as the instruction arrives'.

On 30 October 1762, Mozart again visited the Empress but by then the young boy was ill with fever which cannot have endeared him to Maria Theresa. Nevertheless, a few weeks later, the Empress called out to the Mozarts from her table at a public banquet to which Leopold and his children had been allowed admittance.

By the time of the next visit in 1768, although Mozart and his sister 'made a very great impression' in the words of one eyewitness, his precociousness was a little more strident and his manner more *penetrant*. The Empress had of course recently lost her husband and was in mourning and withdrawn. She saw the family for two hours and commissioned the 12-year-old to write music for the newly constructed orphans' church of which she was a patron. She was by all accounts very pleased by the result.

Leopold was thrilled by this second long audience, writing to his friend in Salzburg: 'You cannot possibly conceive with what familiarity the Empress conversed with my wife, talking partly of the children's smallpox and partly of our grand tour. Nor can you imagine how she stroked my wife's cheek and pressed her hands . . . extraordinary friendliness.'

Again, although any paterfamilias might be moved to embroider such a family encounter with so illustrious an imperial personage, there is no reason to doubt the essentials of this meeting. Its musical and pecuniary advantages were nugatory. Leopold complained that a medal bestowed upon him amounted to little in terms of earnings and the Empress's mourning did not help. As he noted: 'The Empress no longer has concerts in her own apartments; nor does she go to opera or plays and her manner of life is so removed from the world that it would be impossible to describe it with any accuracy.' Moreover, the Emperor, Joseph II, was 'not a man given to expenditure' although fulsome in bestowing praise. Maria Theresa sent the Mozarts an early Christmas present on 14 December and there followed the commission for *Ascanio in Alba* for the marriage of her son, Archduke Ferdinand, to the Duchess of Modena in 1771.

By the time, in August 1773, she received Mozart for the third and last time there could be none of the intimacies of these earlier encounters; she was studiously correct but little more. Mozart's father wrote to his landlord in Salzburg: 'The Empress was very gracious but that is all.' But the Empress supported the composer in many subtle ways, not least encouraging her son Joseph to take an interest in the talented teenager. It was a sign of the social mobility Maria Theresa championed that the provincial boy's talents were more important to her than his modest background but Joseph, as noted above, was notoriously careful with money.

When Maria Theresa's son Maximilian visited Salzburg in April 1775, Mozart composed *Il re pastore* but if he hoped it would lead to imperial commissions, he was disappointed.

By the time of Maria Theresa's death in 1780, Mozart had taken the resolute decision to leave Salzburg behind him and in particular the cantankerous and musically illiterate Prince-Archbishop Colloredo. Colloredo, as a great admirer of Joseph, was so keen to follow Joseph's anti-clerical policies that he was more than happy to reduce the number of sung Masses in the churches of the city, thus more or less forcing Mozart to find pastures new. Historians have praised Colloredo as a leading Enlightenment figure but his aversion to pomp and Latin liturgy had a highly deleterious effect on the young Mozart's finances. If there were no more sung Masses after 1772 in Salzburg, a vital element in his income stream dried up. Moreover, Colloredo was a philistine concerning music and may well have been, unusually for an Austrian, tone-deaf. He certainly viewed the musicians he met as being on a par with his footmen and treated them as such.

Mozart confided his thoughts about Salzburg and Colloredo in a letter in 1777: 'You are well aware how I detest Salzburg. Salzburg is no place for my talent . . . You cannot imagine the low estimation in which musicians are held here.'

In letters to his father, a few years later, he contrasted Vienna and Salzburg even more vividly, describing the so-called 'Enlightenment' figure of Colloredo as 'a tyrant': 'Why should I return to Salzburg when here (Vienna) I am liked and respected by the greatest families while there Colloredo never offered me the slightest remuneration or encouragement since the beginning of his reign, only incessant abuse . . . I shit on Salzburg and the archbishop. . . .'[3]

The Theresian atmosphere of the 1770s in Vienna was more encouraging. From the first moment after he arrived he was inducted into the various lodges of Freemasonry and these gave him access to many potential patrons. Some, like Raimund Planckenstern, the son of a converted Jew by the name of Karl Abraham Wetzlar, came into contact with Mozart through his membership of one of the lodges. Mozart wrote several pieces of music for the lodges, one of which today serves as modern Austria's national anthem.[4]

Like his Enlightenment protégé, Colloredo, Joseph's relationship with Mozart was not wholly benign. One eminent musicologist has written that Joseph's 'negative attitude towards Mozart's music was of catastrophic effect'.[5] The famous exchange between composer and emperor concerning Joseph's opinion that there were 'too many notes', after the premiere of the *Entführung aus dem Serail*, did not help. Mozart's reply, 'just as many notes as are necessary, Your Majesty', was not appreciated by the Emperor.

Certainly, when Mozart finally settled in Vienna, a few months after Maria Theresa's death, the earlier Theresian support seemed to vanish. He found it virtually impossible to find a permanent position at court or in a noble household, or at a monastery or church. He always hoped that imperial patronage would come to his rescue but it never did. His magnificent wind music could only be played by two aristocratic houses which had costly wind instrument establishments: the Liechtensteins and the Schwarzenbergs.

Fortunately, Prague, which had a rich musical life that was not under the direct influence of the court, kept Mozart financially afloat as his prodigious output increased. Shortly before Maria Theresa's death, however, the court composer Salieri returned to Vienna and appears to have ingratiated himself with Joseph to such an extent that both men agreed that the future belonged to Italian not German opera.

Following Joseph's death in 1790, Mozart's attempts to curry favour with the new emperor Leopold in 1791 began, and ended, with *La clemenza di Tito*, an opera based on a fable of monarchical clemency written half a century earlier by Pietro Metastasio. Metastasio was praised by Voltaire, although the Roman poet appears to have had a firm grip on the realities of the times he was living in, writing perceptively long before the French Revolution: 'All great revolutions and changes of ancient systems, even if it were certain that posterity would be benefited from them, are ever fatal to the unhappy mortals who are condemned to be spectators in the conflict.'[6]

Clemenza di Tito may well have been a celebration of an enlightened monarch; it attempts to conjure a new era very different in atmosphere to that prevailing under Maria Theresa. The Mozart opera which gives us the best insight into that world is undoubtedly *Die Zauberflöte* which, commentators have noted, is also the best guide to Mozart's own spiritual values.

Certainly, *Zauberflöte* offers a convincing depiction of aristocratic and Enlightenment values linking arms across a sea of democratic and despotic troubles. So many of the *Singspiel*'s currents of thought and symbolism conjure up the burning issues of the late Empress's last few years. It is almost as if Mozart is consciously harking back to the Theresian era where the contrast between 'lightness and darkness' was more vivid than in the confused and chaotic circumstances of Joseph's reign.

In the Queen of the Night, Maria Theresa was recognizable to a contemporary Vienna audience enjoying the opera when it was first performed. Like Maria Theresa, she appears all-powerful. Like Maria Theresa, she is dressed permanently in black. Like Maria Theresa, she has a dazzling voice and, above all, like Maria Theresa, she is in opposition to her more control-oriented fellow protagonist. Sarastro would to a contemporary audience have been recognizable as Joseph rather than Ignaz Born who was known to relatively very few people.

The *Singspiel*, so often dismissed as a purely Masonic fable, reflects rather the undivided house of faith and reason and carries many rich religious elements. The appearance of the three boys who guide Tamino on his life's journey might have conformed to three angels watching and protecting the Christian's pilgrimage. The concept of evil is clearly embodied in the figure of Monostatos who attempts to rape Pamina. The light of a self-sacrificing female goodness of an almost Marian perfection is reflected in Pamina's great aria in the final act, while 'nichts edlers sei als Mann und Weib' surely represents the Christian ideal of marriage to this day.

Another Christian element is present in the wondrous passage composed by Mozart for the two guards of the temple which introduces a Protestant chorale of great majesty into the score, a gesture towards the *Vielfalt* of religions in the monarchy encouraged by the reforms of Maria Theresa's reign.

By the time Mozart's *Die Zauberflöte* had been composed with the character of Sarastro as a thinly veiled reference to Joseph, Mozart must have realized his professional gamble had failed and that there could be no patronage from either Joseph or Maria Theresa. Both sovereigns were dead and the new Emperor Leopold was altogether too focused on the turbulence within his inheritance to think much about music.

It remains a mystery as to why Mozart should have, in the compositional frenzy of his last months, been so open to these acknowledgements of the Church. Certainly, growing up in Salzburg, the young Mozart would have been exposed to some of the Catholic Enlightenment ideas of Ludovico Antonio Muratori. Muratori's book *The Science of Rational Devotion* was widely available in the city of Paracelsus. A copy of this book was in Mozart's father Leopold's library. In it Muratori expounded on the 'limitations of reason and the necessity of revelation'.[7] Temporal progress was within the bounds of divine providence and the revelatory tradition. Reason was within the bounds of the doctrine of original sin and revelation. That Mozart, like many of the most creative minds in Vienna, subscribed to this is also shown by his letters pitying the 'poor' Jesuits after the Suppression.[8]

Mozart came from a family which was not on the margins of society and his ease of entry into the lodges of Vienna was partly the result of his father's reputation, but in the end the greatest composer of his age, even when expressing in his genius so many of the intellectual preoccupations of the time, found neither the support nor the income which had seemed so assured while Maria Theresa was alive.

In death, genius and diversity went uncelebrated. Mozart was buried in an unmarked grave; an arguably crueller fate awaited the deceased Angelo Soliman, his fellow lodge member. Soliman's body, after his death in 1796, was given over to taxidermists and exhibited in the embryonic Natural History Museum. Like Mozart, Soliman had also experienced the limitations of the Austrian Enlightenment. While in the lodge he could be treated by his master, the Prince of Liechtenstein, as an equal, but not once, on their return journey afterwards, did the prince allow Soliman to share his carriage, and the faithful servant walked home behind dutifully at a respectful distance.

It would be a mistake, however, to think that cultural life in Theresian Vienna revolved only around a few grand families. The Theresian music world was not limited to the few great musicians whose names have given us some of the greatest achievements in the musical canon. Music was truly a part of nearly everyone's daily life in one form or another, largely thanks to the military.

When, in 1741, the *Pandours* had paraded in front of their Queen to pledge their loyalty to the Habsburg cause, they had also brought, along with their famous red cloaks, heart-shaped elbow patches and exotic footwear, their music. This was Ottoman-inspired and consisted of drums and pipes but also some Turkish music with its very different harmonies.

The sight and sound of this music inspired the adoption of musicians into everyday regimental life, at first paid for by the colonels of the regiments and then, 'more democratically', by the officers who, burdened already with debts, were forced to shell out more money for sheet music, instruments and ornate uniforms, it being usual to attire the musicians in the facing colour of the regiment they were attached to.

As the prestige of the army increased under Maria Theresa, the Empress sought, as always, to introduce a degree of uniformity into the *Regimentsmusik*. The costs were shouldered by the embryonic War Ministry, the *Kriegsrat*, and thus was born, under the Great Empress, one of the finest military music traditions in the world.[9]

Just as Mozart's music contained on occasion elements 'alla turca', the marches and other military music were also rich in Orientalisms, so much so in fact that it was described as *Türkische Musik* on many occasions. Gradually, with the development of new technically superior wind instruments, composers such as Mozart began composing more conventional music for the soldiers.

The wind *banda* became a feature of everyday life in Vienna. The regimental musicians, in order to supplement their meagre pay, soon found that they could, with their regimental commander's permission, perform in public at church services, family celebrations and high and feastday events. Thus did the music of the horn, bassoon, oboe and clarinet gain wide currency during the Theresian era, with Mozart writing fine concerti for all of them.

Certain Oriental features of the original Turkish music remained. The dress of the musicians was always exotically ornate, and the *Schellenbaum* – an extraordinary, vertically carried glockenspiel whose decorative features included a crescent-moon-shaped metal crossbar and sometimes a Chinese pavilioned top – reminded everyone of the exotic origins of the regimental bands. With its horsehair plumes and jingling bells, the *Schellenbaum* provided a link between the battlefields of Prince Eugene's greatest victories over the Turks and the baroque village churches of any provincial garrison.

Music played, in Theresian times, a much more central part in the life of the ordinary people than arguably at any time before or after the Great Empress's reign. Thanks to the Theresian military's embrace of the musical traditions of an alien and hostile neighbour, the instrumentalists were available to perform Mozart's magnificent *Gran Partita* and the soloists available to inspire the instrumental music for horn and clarinet which have come down to us as among some of the most inspired works in the repertoire.

In time, the regimental bands of the Austrian army would give rise to a tradition of military music-making second to none. Composers in the next century would make their careers, before becoming household names, by serving as bandmasters of the local 'house' regiment. The two most famous members of the Strauss family and later Franz Lehár began their musical careers in this way. If such a tradition could flourish in the nineteenth century it was largely owing to the Theresian embracing of foreign cultural elements.

By the end of her reign, despite the austerities imposed by her son Joseph, the Austrian army boasted more than a hundred regimental bands and a corpus of compositions which would provide the foundations for the huge repertoire of the next century. Eventually, with the incorporation of four regiments of Bosnians into the imperial and royal army after 1878, the composers of the day would vie with each other to revive more marches in the 'Turkish style'. The immortal results were a tribute to Maria Theresa's embrace of the *Pandours* with their Turkish music, not only 'alla turca' but also 'alla Teresiana'.[10]

CHAPTER 38

Maria Theresa and Tyrol

TYROL ALWAYS OCCUPIED A special place in Maria Theresa's heart. The very idea of the place seemed to offer a kind of spiritual refuge in times of crisis and often did her letters dwell on 'retiring to Tyrol' to see out her final days free from the stresses and strains of court life. This vision was largely imaginative. Innsbruck, of course, featured in her psyche as the place where her beloved husband had suddenly died, but her visits to the glorious mountains around that city had been infrequent.

Yet, along with Hungary and the Austrian Netherlands, Tyrol enjoyed unique privileges. Its nobility was largely exempt from taxation and its Estates Committee remained powerful. Military conscription and a census had both been successfully resisted and such was the force of the Empress's feeling towards Tyrol that, much to her son's chagrin, she had been loath to push for either. Geography and tradition – Tyrol had been often governed separately by a younger archduke – made it impervious to centralizing tendencies. Its frontier with Bavaria and the Archbishopric of Salzburg was considerably longer than with Austria (it only bordered Carinthia). Two powerful prince-bishoprics, Trent and Brixen, were within Tyrol and much of the terrain was mountainous and in winter inaccessible.

Under Maria Theresa, the land's unambivalent Catholicism was encouraged and a flourishing university in Innsbruck was supported by her. She had no intention of subjecting the province to centralizing administrations and even less appetite for attempting to unite the province with Vorarlberg, where the leisurely ways of the Holy Roman Empire combined with Swiss manners and dialect to forge a political tradition which had significant elective elements.

Reports of local government irregularities in Bludenz left Maria Theresa unmoved. She was also happy to tolerate the Tyrolean population's refusal to have their houses, as in the rest of her empire, numbered on the grounds that 'they do not know what it could mean'. This laissez-faire approach to the westerly provinces once again underlined Maria Theresa's convictions that centralization, if carried out without elements of pragmatism, could become counterproductive, impacting on the loyalty of her subjects.

She therefore applied the brakes to her son's attempts to interfere with the local constitutions and arrangements. Such interference always made her uneasy and, while she lived, she preserved as much of the province's autonomy as she could.

Maria Theresa recognized that the Tyroleans were not the easy-going Moravians or Lower Austrians of the Danubian parts of her inheritance. As always, she had a feel for the temper of her subjects and knew that the Tyroleans were fiercely independent in mentality and, like highlanders anywhere, would be quick to resort to violence if they perceived they were losing their rights. Within ten years of her death, her worst fears were realized and Joseph's uncompromising wave of 'reforms' drove both provinces into armed rebellion by 1789.

Yet by the time, a few years later, Napoleon had placed the province under the rule of the detested Bavarians and the Confederation of the Rhine, the Tyroleans had recovered their loyalty to the imperial house and, in the four great battles of Berg Isel, shown their devotion to Austria and the memory of their Great Empress. This devotion survived even the Habsburg refusal to intervene in the execution in Mantua by Napoleon of the great Tyrolean leader Andreas Hofer.

A hundred and twenty years later, the beleaguered Austrian chancellor, Kurt Schuschnigg, would enjoy a brief respite from the agonies of Nazi pressure in a dramatic appeal in Innsbruck for support which briefly seemed to offer some hope of Austria avoiding the *Anschluss*.[1] His speech on 9 March 1938 was considered the high point of Austrian defiance and the unfortunate chancellor's 'finest hour'. Inevitably, he prefaced his oratory with a tribute to the woman who had done so much for Austria and Tyrol, Maria Theresa.

To this day, nobody can be a few hours in Innsbruck without passing through the Maria Theresienstrasse dominated at one end of the street by the triumphal arch erected by its citizens in 1765 in commemoration of Maria Theresa's visit, with her husband, on the occasion of the marriage of Archduke Leopold to the infanta Maria Ludovica. As we have seen, the great festivities were brought to an abrupt halt by the death of Francis so that only the southern side of the arch displays symbols of joy, the northern being decorated with those of sorrow.

CHAPTER 39

Porzellan and Augarten

THE GREAT ABBEY OF Altenburg, hidden in the folds of the *Waldviertel*, close to the Bohemian frontier, boasts a unique insight into the life of Theresian Austria. In 1746, for the eightieth birthday of the abbot, Rainer Köllmann, a magnificent porcelain service was presented to the octogenarian monk celebrating the four great cardinal virtues his life had so vividly expressed: Fortitude, Temperance, Justice and Prudence. In addition, the *Aufsatz* (service) depicted Apollo, Venus and Neptune but it is the additional supporting cast who make this service one of the artistic wonders of the Theresian epoch. There, in all their modest professionalism, are displayed the tradesmen and crafts-women of the age: the wig-maker, the *Bandlkramer* (ribbon-maker), the *Bratlkoch* (meat-chef) and *Luftinspektor* (inspector of air, i.e. good-for-nothing). The porcelain expresses more vividly than many paintings the inclusive temper of the Theresian age and fittingly it was produced by the imperial porcelain manufacturer of Claudius Innocentius Du Paquier.

Eight years after the establishment of a porcelain concern at Meissen in 1710, Du Paquier founded a porcelain factory in the Austrian capital. This porcelain manufacture workshop began life in what is today the Porzellangasse, in the 9th district of Vienna.

The factory's life was virtually contemporaneous with the Empress and she grew up very familiar with its delicate creations from an early age. By 1744 Maria Theresa had granted an imperial licence to the Du Paquier porcelain factory and when, a little later, Du Paquier ran into financial difficulties, she did not hesitate, despite the economic pressures on her purse and treasury, to purchase the factory outright and place it under sovereign patronage.

At the time of its establishment, it was one of only two porcelain manufacturers in Europe – the other being Meissen in Saxony. When the Empress acquired the factory, she renamed it the Imperial State Porcelain Manufacturer and granted it the right to use her personal shield as its emblem. To this day, the horizontally divided Habsburg shield (*Bindenschild*) is the trademark of all the factory's production, housed since 1864 in the palace known as the Augarten. The Empress had allowed the factory to be transferred to her own property but it remained in the 9th district of Vienna, then a leafy suburb beyond the inner-city walls.

The Empress's support was tempered with practical considerations. She was determined that the factory would stop losing money – she immediately covered Du Paquier's debts of 45,559 florins – but she was also determined to introduce efficiencies to boost profitability. To that end, she appointed an administrator, Franz Xaver Mayrhofer, supported by a deputy, Andreas Altomonte, to increase production. In 1764 further administrators and what would be called today 'marketing experts' were brought in to widen the reputation of the brand. Chief of these was Conrad Sörgel von Sorgenthal. Du Paquier, meanwhile, had been deftly removed from the running of the business and granted an annual pension of 600 florins, to be paid, with typical Theresian *Munifizenz*, to his widow after his death in 1751.

New kilns and storage facilities were constructed. A detailed business plan was drawn up with a ten-year timeline. Maria Theresa offered a guaranteed annual subsidy for five years in excess of 5,820 florins. The numbers working at the factory increased to 40 and then by 1757 to 55. A year later, turnover had increased substantially, from barely 7,000 florins in 1745 to nearly 29,000.

During this period there was much demand for *Bisquit* (unglazed porcelain), although Sorgenthal became convinced that it was altogether too expensive and glass-like to produce en masse. Nevertheless, by 1770 the factory's inventory, including substantial items of *Bisquit*, was valued at more than 325,000 florins. Three years later, the Augarten factory had representatives selling their works throughout the empire. 'Branches' of the factory were established in Prague, Lemberg, Buda and Brünn.

The teams of model-makers and painters were also increased. Identifiable by numbers rather than names, they included such talents as Philipp Schindler and Gottfried Klinger. During most of Maria Theresa's reign, the factory produced, under their guidance, works of outstanding quality. The chief modellers included Anton Grassi and Johann Niedermeyer who were both dispatched to Italy to study classical remains. These became increasingly the focus for the porcelain's designs. Often services were commissioned as diplomatic gifts and were frequently used by Kaunitz to express imperial favour or gratitude towards visiting diplomats. Some of these services were exported to Russia and the Ottoman empire and can be found to this day in museums there, fragile adjuncts of Theresian diplomacy.

Inevitably, following the marriage of Marie Antoinette to the Dauphin of France, French stylistic traits began to be deployed more frequently in the Austrian porcelain. At the same time, new 'outlets' and offices to arrange the export of the services were established in Trieste and Carlsbad, expressing Maria Theresa's commitment to free trade.

From the beginning of her involvement with the factory, Maria Theresa was kept abreast of all the important technical challenges. She was particularly keen to find the best sources of kaolin for the porcelain works. New sources of kaolin were found in Bohemia and Styria and the material combined with a taste for a wider colour palette. Ceramics historians describe this period of the factory's output as the 'Plastic epoch' of Augarten. This period, generally considered to have covered the years 1744 to 1784, coincided more or less with the Empress's reign and saw a blossoming in the depiction of figurative works enriched with striking new colours. These included 'Du Paquier purple' and 'rococo gold'. Often a purple-green *rocaille* predominated. A certain sentimentalism, imported from the German Meissen works, also began to make itself felt with such figures as the *verliebter Greis* (love-sick old dolt) or *verliebte Alte* (love-sick old maid).

More in keeping with the Theresian era was perhaps the series of figurines dedicated to the Austrian army, making full use of the *Farbkastel* of facing colours which added such distinction to the plain white tunics of Austrian officers. As these colours represented local regiments they could immediately be invested with regional relevance attractive to specific markets. Thus, yellow facings coincided with the 'House' regiment of Graz, black with that of Linz, sky-blue with Vienna, chocolate with Carinthia and rose with Trieste.

As Kaunitz's and Maria Theresa's diplomacy continued to yield results, more Parisian influences became noticeable during the 1770s. The Parisian style of dressing the hair and the more ornate elements of French costume become evident in the later years of the 'Plastic epoch'. More *galant* scenes, deriving in part from the more formal etiquette of the French court, were also depicted at this time, notably the *Handkuss* and other courtly gestures which in time began to dominate Viennese manners well into the twentieth century.[1]

At the same time, the influence of Asian motifs began to make itself felt. Travellers to Asia and beyond returned to Europe with striking examples of Oriental art. Wiener Porzellan was at the forefront of harnessing these new trends to conventional domestic designs.

The golden era of Wiener Porzellan lasted less than a century. In 1864 further financial difficulties and competition from Hungary's Herend factory led to its closure. It was nevertheless revived in the twentieth century in the Palais Augarten where it still resides. Pieces from those years are among the most collectible items of porcelain in the world and it is an unmistakeable if curious tribute to Maria Theresa that the imperial device that she granted to the factory which marks the base of those masterpieces is today considered to be, along with the crossed swords of Meissen, the most commonly forged identifying mark of the entire porcelain world.

CHAPTER 40

The Art of the *Pittor Turco*: Jean-Étienne Liotard's Visits to Vienna

IN COMMON WITH HER second son, the later Emperor Leopold II, Maria Theresa did not enjoy having her portrait painted. The presence of Martin van Meytens as court *Kammermaler* from 1732, while productive in sheer numbers of regal portraits, never resulted in any works of outstanding psychological penetration, such as could be found at the same time by the remarkable sculptors Messerschmidt and Donner.

Yet portrait painting was not without interest to the Empress. Both her daughters Marie Antoinette and Marie Christine were excellent draughtswomen and the Empress herself was not without gifts in this direction. This artistic inclination combined with the tradition of musical training in the Habsburg family to inspire a flowering of the arts once Maria Theresa came to the throne. Certainly, with her reign, it was no longer possible for Voltaire to observe dismissively that he had always wondered why Prince Eugene had 'spent so much time promoting art and science in a country where both subjects count for so little'.[1]

The entry of the Swiss painter Jean-Étienne Liotard into Austrian court circles demonstrated vividly a striking new openness. His arrival was unconventional, to say the least. In all, the Swiss painter made three visits to Vienna. He had been born in Geneva in 1702 to a family of Huguenot descent but his first appearance in Vienna in 1743 caused something of a sensation. He arrived in the city after a tour of the Ottoman lands where he had so immersed himself in Turkish fashion and culture that he had grown a long beard and dressed himself in Oriental garb including – if a self-portrait from this time is any guide – an extravagantly large turban headdress.[2]

This colourful garb did not prevent access to the court. His pastels were of such an immediate attraction to Maria Theresa that she commissioned him on the spot to produce a portrait of her. She appears to have hit it off instantly with the Swiss. As a foreigner, he was exempt from any Theresian prejudice concerning his non-Catholic confessional status. His very Oriental appearance invested the 'Pittor Turco' with exotic charm.

Under Maria Theresa there came about a veritable flowering of interest in the positive aspects of Turkish culture. In popular publications, such as weeklies and almanacs, the Turks appeared as welcome exotic additions to Austrian tastes. The memory of the Great Siege of 1683 had long receded by the time Maria Theresa ascended the throne. The introduction of coffee during the siege to the Austrian capital, thanks to an imaginative Polish entrepreneur, was the most enduring cultural legacy of the terrible siege and by the 1740s it had certainly eclipsed all the tales of infidel Ottoman horror with which an earlier generation had been raised. Moreover, had not the sanguinary conflicts of the first years of Maria Theresa's reign shown that far more was to be feared from the so-called civilized Prussian than the *soi-disant* barbaric Ottoman? It was partly the King in Prussia's achievement to allow the Viennese to develop a positive view of their eastern neighbours. By the time Maria Theresa had come to the throne and Liotard had paid his first visit to Vienna, the only legacy of the conflicts with the dreaded Janissaries was the (still) commonly deployed oath *Kruzitürken!* (Cross the Turk!)

The Ottoman empire had long ceased to be a threat to the Habsburg domains and the palisades and earthworks of the Military Frontier were security enough against the legendary hordes which had once threatened Graz and Vienna a century earlier. Moreover, in Maria Theresa's struggles, the Sultan had not only guaranteed Turkish neutrality but had even condemned Frederick's invasion of Silesia. By 1763 Maria Theresa could even refer to the Ottomans as 'Our Good Turks'.[3]

The new fashion for all things 'alla turca' would in time become a staple of Mozart's creative genius. Already well before Maria Theresa's death, his fifth violin concerto would be graced with a *Rondo alla turca*. *The Abduction from the Seraglio* and a piano sonata with Turkish harmonies would follow. The fashion quickly established itself in the imperial court and nothing expressed this more vividly perhaps than Liotard's double portrait of Maria Theresa and her daughter Marianne in 'Oriental' costume.

While he was in Vienna, Liotard also produced a portrait of the Empress with Oriental headdress which was much copied and, to this day, can be found in such diverse parts of the former Habsburg domains as Lemberg (Lviv), Cracow and Trieste.

As well as creating this much-reproduced portrait of Maria Theresa, Liotard used his visit to work up other portraits which reflected the Theresian epoch, including the well-known *La Belle Chocolatière* (*The Chocolate Girl*). This portrait of a modest and not especially pretty female servant came to represent Theresian social harmony as well as the tradition – continued to this day in Vienna – of serving coffee or hot chocolate with a glass of ice-cold water on a tray.[4]

The *Chocolate Girl* unsurprisingly caused something of a sensation when it found its way onto the market shortly after Liotard's first visit to Vienna. In 1745 it was purchased by Francesco Algarotti of Venice. He noted:

> I have bought a pastel portrait about three feet high by the celebrated artist Liotard. It shows a young chambermaid carrying a tray with a cup of chocolate and a glass of water. It is almost entirely devoid of shadows with a pale background. The light is provided by two large windows reflected in the glass. It is painted in half-tones with imperceptible gradations of light . . . it could appeal to the Chinese who as you know are sworn enemies of shadows . . . with regard to the perfection of the work it is a Holbein in pastel.[5]

The technical brilliance of the work was no less matched by the meteoric rise of the portrait's sitter, Nandl Baldauf, whose life was yet another illustration of the capacity for social mobility present in the Theresian monarchy. Fräulein Baldauf was the daughter of a Viennese coachman and, despite lacking obvious conventional elegance and beauty, her modesty, good humour and charm made a deep impression on all who met her. She eventually married into the high aristocracy. Her husband,

Moritz Dietrichstein, was well known at court and, as a Count of the Holy Roman Empire, assured that the *belle chocolatière en personne* enjoyed an elevated social status, well beyond the dreams of *Stubenmädchen* (chambermaids) anywhere else in Europe.

The second visit to Vienna by the 'Pastell Holbein' took place in 1762 and was a less sensational event. This time Liotard eschewed Oriental garb and allowed his reputation to develop more conventionally. The portrait of Maria Theresa that has come down to us from this visit is no less accomplished. The Empress's eyes were, in Liotard's words, 'gentle and good' but the expression she wore was 'trop complexe pour être décrite'. This psychologically perceptive portrait is presently in Lemberg (Lviv), in the western part of war-torn Ukraine, an enduring symbol of links with the heart of Europe. When completed, it was received with such pleasure by the Empress that she commissioned Liotard to produce drawings of all her children and gave him a magnificent pink and gold tête-à-tête Wiener Porzellan coffee set.[6]

During this sojourn in the Habsburg capital, Liotard appears to have reinforced his rapport with the Empress enormously. His wife gave birth to a daughter whom he promptly named Marie-Thérèse. It would seem that, during the year of 1762, Liotard struck up a particular friendship with Marie Antoinette. The portrait he executed of her is certainly one of the most successful of Maria Theresa's children. Once Marie Antoinette became Queen of France, Maria Theresa encouraged her daughter to invite Liotard to Paris to produce a pastel of her 'at her desk' but this portrait, finished in 1770, has long since disappeared.

Finally, in August 1777, Liotard paid his third and last visit to Vienna where he also produced portraits of Kaunitz and Baron Fries. This time he brought his son with him. The journey took thirteen days to accomplish from Ulm down the Danube to Vienna. He found Maria Theresa much changed in appearance and dress but her pleasure at seeing him was apparently undiminished. She received him 'avec un bonté extraordinaire' and renewed the 'ancienne connaissance' with much happiness. During his stay, the Empress ensured Liotard was kept well provisioned with plenty of Tokay wine and that father and son enjoyed the run of most of the imperial apartments. They were quartered in Schönbrunn for most of the time. It was, by all accounts, a most happy time when patron and artist could enjoy each other's company without any internal or external jealousy penetrating their time together.

Three years later, in one of her last acts before her final illness, Maria Theresa wrote to her ambassador Mercy in Paris concerning an early painting of her by Liotard, saying that 'je me suis très attachée a ce tableau'. It was a rare admission of her sentimental connection to a portrait of her youth.

That Maria Theresa's favour in portrait-sitting was not lightly given nor widely offered is confirmed by the experience of a local artist, Alexander Roslin, who throughout the late 1770s attempted to paint the Empress but was repeatedly refused a sitting by Maria Theresa, even though he had done portraits of her children.

In her reluctance to sit for a portrait, the Empress rejected the proposal on account of the amount of time it would take up – in this case four sittings in one week of three hours each. The Empress insisted: 'Ich habe nicht genug Zeit 12 Stunden in der Woche zu verlieren' (I do not have enough time to lose 12 hours in the week). But perhaps the reason was more delicate – she added with her usual candour: 'Why would he want to paint something as ugly as a 60-year-old woman?'[7]

CHAPTER 41

Pietas Theresiana

WE HAVE SEEN IN earlier chapters how Maria Theresa's personal piety was first developed by the Jesuits, became enriched by her own conviction that only a miracle had spared her inheritance, and was later reinforced by the refuge of daily prayer intensified by the loss of her husband in 1765. It is now time to consider how that personal piety differed from that of her forefathers and to what extent she here, as elsewhere, ushered in a new era, in which the spiritual and confessional beliefs of her ancestors were modified.

The linkage between the Habsburgs and the Catholic faith possessed an intensity unique to the imperial dynasty. In particular, the relationship to the concept of the 'simple' host containing the 'Body of Christ' was deeply embedded from the very first days of the House of Habsburg.

In 1218 a modest Alpine count, Rudolf, had brought his family out of the Swiss Alpine fastnesses to establish what would become the greatest imperial family in European history. Despite his relative obscurity, he had already developed a personal piety which became a touchstone for later generations of Habsburgs. Shortly after his death in 1291, stories began to circulate about how one day, while travelling through some remote mountain valley, Rudolf had seen a priest quietly marching along carrying the host. Not wishing to 'ride while Our Lord walked', the Habsburg had immediately dismounted and offered his horse to the priest and his sacramental charge who rode off while their benefactor continued his journey on foot.

Variations of this story were already widely prevalent by the end of the fourteenth century and could be seen as cementing the dynasty's special relationship with what would become in time the great Catholic feast of Corpus Christi. It was a relationship grounded in a belief in the benefits and validity of sacramental life. Maria Theresa herself accepted this as one of the foundations of her life and encouraged all her children to participate daily in sacramental life. While she reigned, the magnificent feast of Corpus Christi was always celebrated and the orders, mostly contemplative, that existed specially to venerate the great feast were left untouched. Even her son Joseph, while happy later to suppress the brotherhoods dedicated to Corpus Christi, maintained the annual procession and the dynasty's leading part in it.

If the veneration of the sacrament was one of the foundations of *Pietas Austriaca* – and in years to come there would be many anagrams composed showing the indelible link between Austria and the Eucharist – Marian devotion was another.[1] Here, as we shall later see, Maria Theresa did subtly usher in some slight change.

The Empress never deviated from her devotion to Marian theology. That Marian worship was at the heart of her Jesuitical upbringing was immediately apparent from her father's veneration of the great shrine, the *Magna Mater Austriae, Bohemiae et Ungariae*, high up in the Styrian Alps at Mariazell. Charles VI had stressed the importance of this shrine to his recently converted wife, commending 'the Immaculate Mother of God' as the protector of his House while noting that 'no-one knew better' than he 'the fruits and benefits to be derived from such devotion'.

The shrine's origins were well documented. On 21 December 1157 a young monk was walking through the Styrian Alps with a small figure of Mary. The monk, referred to as Magnus of St Lambrecht, had carved the figure from one piece of wood and was travelling south towards Carinthia where a Benedictine monastery had been founded on land originally belonging to the Hohenstaufens. As the monk struggled up a pass, a vast waterfall barred all further progress. Placing the statue on a rock while he knelt, prayed, paused and pondered his next steps, he was astonished to see that the waterfall suddenly ceased.

The name of Mariazell dates from that encounter which, however open to question in more rational and secular times, is the foundation of the Austrian tradition of Marian shrines. The figure was quickly venerated and covered in a white cloth with a coat lined in red – two colours which in time would assume great significance for Austria and the dynasty.[2]

News of the 'miraculous statue' spread to Moravia and Bohemia. The margrave Heinrich Wladislaw who reigned from 1198 to 1222 was the first illustrious pilgrim, although the precise date of his visit is unknown. The margrave suffered from the excruciating torture of gout. The medical men of the time were powerless to arrest the pain of the ailment and, according to legend, an angel appeared to Wladislaw urging him to make the pilgrimage to Mariazell. Cured almost instantly after a few hours' veneration of the image, the margrave transmitted the news of his cure to King Wenceslaus of Bohemia, who promptly became the second important personage to pay homage to the shrine. By 1266 an altar had been built to shelter the statue. In 1342 Albrecht II, Duke of Austria, erected a new altar just in time for another illustrious visitor, King Lajos the Great of Hungary (Lajos Nagy). The Hungarian king implored the shrine's help in his war against the Turks and the night before his greatest victory he believed that the Marian image had appeared in a dream and even offered him advice on tactics. His thanksgiving pilgrimage anchored the remote mountain altar forever in Hungarian consciousness.[3]

Thus were the crown lands of Maria Theresa's monarchy, whatever their variety and diversity, united in a common tradition of Marian veneration. The Habsburgs had been bound to this shrine already for half a millennium by the time Maria Theresa was born. Ferdinand II, the scourge of heretics, whose policies at the end of the sixteenth century recovered Austria for the faith, first coined the phrase *Magna Mater Austriae*, and the name stuck. Neither the Turkish wars nor the Reformation made much of an impact on the shrine's popularity. The Counter-Reformation injected new dynamism into the old traditions and on the last day of the sixteenth century no fewer than 23,000 pilgrims were led by Cardinal Melchior Khesl to venerate the shrine. Leopold I came six times to Mariazell to pray for deliverance from the threat of the Turks. On his orders, captured Turkish flags were laid at the image's feet. Joseph I gave a priceless gold crown to adorn the image and Maria Theresa's father Charles VI continued this tradition.

The connection with his daughter was established very early with Maria Theresa visiting the shrine as a child and taking her first Holy

Communion there. Even her marriage to Francis Stephen was partly conducted at the foot of the statue which by 1740 had been adorned with a baroque church to house it. In 1757 she took six of her children with her on a pilgrimage there. She would never deviate in her prayer life from the conviction that this link with Mariazell gave her a special place under the protection of the Blessed Virgin. Yet, if her rule rested on veneration of the Eucharist, Corpus Christi and devotion to the Immaculate Conception, the latter's formally majestic dimension was undoubtedly slightly softened during Maria Theresa's reign.

Her father had petitioned the Vatican to elevate both feasts to the rank of what today we would call minor solemnities but were then referred to as 'semi-doubles'. Maria Theresa never hesitated for a moment from her belief that she owed much to Mary and that the Mother of God was the object of her exceptional devotion, but she also encouraged a small shift in perception towards Mary, seeing her increasingly less as a distant sovereign figure, a holy Queen, but rather more as an almost intimate, a Mother of Grace, a *Gnadenmutter*. This was an important step, a slight but significant shift in perception, paralleling the removal of the forbidden zone around her own monarchical presence at court and in her empire. If the Mother of Grace was also the Mother of Mercy, she, too, was no longer remote.

To demonstrate this accessibility, the Empress encouraged the daily recitation of the rosary, appointing a special chaplain to lead the prayers, and stressed to her family and friends that she was 'indeed indebted many times over to our miraculous mother of Mariazell'.[4]

This relationship with Mariazell endured even Joseph's secularizing onslaughts. When, after his mother's death, over-zealous acolytes closed the shrine down, under the pretext of a fire hazard, thinking they might ingratiate themselves with the Emperor, he paid another incognito private visit. He promptly revealed his true identity and sacked all the clergy who had participated in such an 'excess of secularism'.

By banning pilgrimages which lasted more than one day, Joseph nonetheless contributed to a significant curtailing of the annual cycle of veneration which had undoubtedly materially benefited the shrine. Yet even he could not ignore its special significance for his mother and her empire. No Habsburg, right up to the present day, has been able to escape the conviction that the preservation of their House has been partly the result of Marian intervention.

Maria Theresa thus presided over a quite subtle and almost unconscious change in attitude towards the *Magna Mater* which has endured to this day. Mary was still all-powerful, but she was also all-merciful and approachable. No longer was she guarded by the pomp and architectural majesty of the baroque. The plea for help quietly shifted prayers away from the imposing awe of the 'Holy Queen'. Under Maria Theresa, Marian devotion no longer represented an exclusive basis for imperial authority but altogether something far more accessible and even democratic. In this way, the supposedly unintellectual Maria Theresa may have proved the catalyst for progressive theological development.

Joseph was not prepared to be so indulgent towards the contemplative orders which had established themselves over centuries in proximity to the shrine. He dissolved all of them, including the monastery of St Lambrecht, which had always had a special relationship with Mariazell, providing many of the clergy to assist at the larger pilgrimages.

Yet the shrine survived even these measures and, even more traumatic, the occupation of Napoleon's troops a generation later. However, as the immense flowering of pilgrimages from all over eastern Europe after the fall of the Berlin Wall in 1989 more than amply demonstrated, the Theresian ideal of Marian devotion – of the *Gnadenmutter* – has prevailed to this day, and the great shrine of Mariazell is arguably almost as much a monument to the Great Empress as it is to the Holy Queen.

CHAPTER 42

Theresian (Keynesian) Monetary Policy:
The Austrian 'Dollar'

IN JANUARY 1885 A British relief force in the Sudan under the command of
that soldier with arguably the most romantic name in British military
history, Sir Garnet Wolseley, struggled to reach Khartoum where a beleaguered Anglo-Egyptian force under General Gordon faced imminent
destruction at the hands of the fanatical Mahdi.

As most English schoolboys of the post-war generation were taught,
the relief force arrived two days too late and Queen Victoria never
forgave Gladstone's Liberal government for its tardy response towards
Gordon's perilous situation.

What we were not taught was the reason why Wolseley's 'desert
column' arrived too late. It was left not to an historian but to arguably
the greatest economist of the twentieth century, J.M. Keynes, to point
out in an essay published in June 1914 that the reason for Gordon's death
had been the failure of the British relief force to secure enough camels
for their desert column. This shortage of camels, according to Keynes,
had been created by an unfortunate mismatch of currencies. As Wolseley
complained in a dispatch to the British Foreign Office, 'our gold sovereigns command no respect here. All that the Bedouin will accept as
payment for his beasts of burden is the Maria Theresian silver Thaler.'[1]

A telegram was sent by London, immediately upon receipt of this
desperate plea, to that most westerly outpost of the British Levant
consular service, Trieste, where Her Majesty's Consul was no less a
person than the redoubtable explorer and Arabist, Richard Francis
Burton.

Burton stirred himself from his writings and hunted down his contacts in the local banking community and arranged for a merchant ship to sail to the Nile with a supply of no less than 600,000 silver Thalers, enough to conscript an entire Arab camel corps, but this effort came too late. The ship laden with its treasure arrived at Suez a week after Gordon and his men had been slaughtered.

By the time these events took place in a faraway country which had never been colonized by Austria, Maria Theresa had been dead for more than a hundred years. Yet for the Bedouin tribesman and above all for his wives, the image of the Great Empress was all they would accept in their daily barter. How was it possible at the time of the zenith of British world domination that a long-dead Austrian woman could command through her coinage so much respect a century after her death in a land where the British flag had flown for decades?

Why was this 'Great Empress' capable of exerting influence beyond her grave while another Empress still alive and loyally served by the bayonets and pith helmets of her armies watched impotently from afar?

How had this silver coin, first minted a hundred years earlier, come to command such respect that in distant primitive lands where no white woman, and certainly no Austrian *Fräulein* had ever set foot, her image, and hers alone, provided the currency for everyday transactions?

The answer to this question was first articulated by John Maynard Keynes. In June 1914, barely a fortnight before the assassination of the Archduke Franz Ferdinand in Sarajevo ignited the long-awaited fuse to world war, Keynes devoted his thoughts to a review of a book by Marcel Maurice Fischel which attempted to analyse the economics underpinning the enduring use of the Maria Theresa coin in the east.

The 'Austrian dollars' which Wolseley so desperately needed were of course the Maria Theresa Thalers, the silver coins whose name in Viennese dialect, *Dowllar*, soon became synonymous with the American currency that was named after them. The Thalers alone could be used in the Arab world, and thus was the fate of General Gordon sealed by the shortage of a silver coin minted with the image of Maria Theresa on one side and the Habsburg double-headed eagle on the verso.

Keynes noted that the Thaler had been 'turned out for a century and a half as though it were a Bath Oliver biscuit, a thoroughly reliable article, never genuine without the signature of the now long mourned for Mrs M. Therese'.[2]

Keynes's flippancy disguised, as it often did, a significant economic point: namely, that the Austrians had recognized during Maria Theresa's reign an important economic truth, denied to the other great powers of Europe, including England, France and Prussia. That truth was, as Adam Smith had pointed out, that a country's currency was no more and no less than a commodity and therefore subject to the laws of supply and demand.[3]

Now in the case of the Thaler, the demand stretched far beyond the confines of Maria Theresa's empire. Traders in coffee dealing with the Ottomans found that they only wished to sell their commodity in return for the silver coins bearing the Empress's head. This was largely because the Bedouin tribesmen who controlled many of the trading routes had acquired a taste for the Empress, her ample bosom (a symbol of plenty and fertility), her noble profile, her abundant hair, and her sober countenance. Their womenfolk, often the deciding factor in commercial transactions in the Arab world, appeared equally impressed and so it was that the imperial mints of the empire turned out millions of Thalers to keep up with eastern demand.

Between 1751 and 1761, 17 million coins were minted, of which at least 8 million were destined for the Orient to become, in the Viennese parlance of the time, *Levantiners*.

It was the canny Baron Fries, whose palace on the Josephsplatz we have already admired in an earlier chapter, who saw the wider potential of the currency. He quickly established with some fellow merchants a supplementary mint in Günzburg where the coin could be produced under imperial patent. As France, Prussia and England all forbade traffic in their own currencies, the *Levantiners* quickly became an exclusive Austrian monopoly which, despite the absence of any colonial ambitions, dominated the trade of the Levant from the Bosphorus to the Yemen. Other European powers, hamstrung by protectionist policies forbidding the export of their coinage, were unwilling and unable to compete. Under Maria Theresa, 'Austrian economics' – two hundred years later set to dominate the western world with such giants as Mises, Hayek and Schumpeter and such ideas as 'creative destruction' – scored an early victory.

The international dimension soon began to influence the design of the coins. When, after 1765 and the death of her husband Francis Stephen, Maria Theresa began to wear mourning, coins were minted from 1768 with her plentiful hair and body covered. The tribesmen of the east soon expressed their displeasure at this apparent self-effacement of imperial matriarchal vigour and demanded trade be conducted solely in the earlier coinage. As the coins depicting the Empress in 'widow's weeds' were returned, Fries obliged and the imperial mint reverted in 1777 to the earlier image of the Empress with low-cut gown and generous hair. This was, in Keynes's view, an exemplary indication of how Austria, uniquely at that time, freed herself from the protectionist instincts of her European neighbours and adapted practically to the exigencies of supply and demand.

We have already seen how Maria Theresa overruled her son Joseph in promoting free trade over parochial protectionism. The Thaler with her image was and still is a suitable symbol of the validity of the concepts of free trade and its alternatives to the mercantilist protectionist spirit of the eighteenth century. Only Austria under Maria Theresa could generate the supplies of silver coinage needed in the Levant. The other European powers were not only inhibited by their protectionist policies but also, as Keynes pointed out, by the 'unreliable quality of their silver coinage'. Under Maria Theresa, a standard was set to produce a 'handsome uniform coin of a high degree of influence'.

Keynes did not live to see later research on the Thaler in the Arab world which has documented its attraction to women who soon came to prize it as the ultimate personal adornment. But by the time of Keynes's death in 1946, the two-hundred-year-old Maria Theresa silver 'dollar' was already the largest coin in circulation, defying all attempts by the British in the nineteenth century and the Italians in the twentieth to supplant its use in their colonial territories. (Both countries were reduced to minting their own versions, the Italians legally, the British illegally.)

In this way, the Theresian Thaler can be seen as a tangible expression par excellence of that phrase of Hörnigk's uttered just before the beginning of Maria Theresa's reign: 'Austria supreme if only it wishes.' The staggering 66 million examples still estimated to be in circulation in the second quarter of the twenty-first century remain to this day arguably the most widely visible legacy of the Great Empress's reign.

CHAPTER 43

The 'Silver Rose': Theresian Nostalgia

IF THE SILVER THERESIAN Thaler was one enduring legacy of the Empress's reign, a silver rose became for a smaller, more select audience another lasting symbol of her reign. On 10 December 1975, at a special performance of *Der Rosenkavalier* at Covent Garden, a descendant of Hugo von Hofmannsthal, the Austrian librettist of the opera, presented a silver rose to the director of the world-famous opera house to commemorate the one hundredth anniversary year of the writer's birth. The production that evening was spectacular but traditional, comfortably set in the Theresian epoch with costumes, wigs and furnishings glorifying the Austrian rococo with no hint of either modernity or the imposition of modern fashion on the music. The rose would be used – and still is used – for all subsequent productions of *Rosenkavalier* at Covent Garden.

Hofmannsthal had been born nearly a hundred years after the Great Empress had died, but the powerful nostalgia for the fading glory of one of the high points in Austrian history which he immortalized in the language of this greatest of all Richard Strauss operas was very much the zeitgeist of his formative years.

Two years before Hofmannsthal's birth, the great commemorative Maria Theresian hall in the Vienna Arsenal museum of military history had been completed with its frescoes depicting the glorious victories of the Theresian epoch. Eight years earlier, ahead of the completion of this spectacular interior, Professor Arneth had produced the first of his exhaustively researched tomes on the Great Empress. The imposing monument to Maria Theresa on the Ringstrasse was commissioned the year of Hofmannsthal's birth and opened on his sixteenth birthday in a celebration which lasted all day and which must have brought the long-dead Empress to the forefront for the many Viennese who passed, Hofmannsthal included, along this recently completed segment of the Ringstrasse.

As the Danube monarchy entered its final phase, a veritable Theresian renaissance engulfed Vienna undoubtedly influencing the young Hofmannsthal. This neo-Theresian trend influenced fashion in all of the arts. The 'Dritte Rococo' became the official house style of the court. The British embassy in Vienna, then one of London's five most important overseas residences, was promptly constructed in it.[1] A variation on the style was chosen for the remodelling of the Hofburg entrance opposite the Kohlmarkt. Its ornate conservatism contrasted deeply with Adolf Loos's Goldman and Salatsch offices opposite, constructed a few years later in the best *Wiener Moderne* style.

Hofmannsthal grew up in a torrent of nostalgia for the Theresian epoch tempered by some of the most modern influences on art and literature then in existence. After the lukewarm reception of some of their earlier collaborations, Hofmannsthal had determined with Richard Strauss to produce an opera which would have mass appeal and to this end he homed in, with unerring instinct, on the emerging popular cult of Maria Theresa.

Moreover, as we have seen, he did not hesitate to incorporate his own pro-Austrian (and therefore by implication anti-Prussian) views into the libretto. His sentimental fascination with the era comes through in his writings, especially his essay on Maria Theresa which stressed her humanity and intuition: 'In which powers she trusted and in which she did not is not contained in any catechism but from generation to generation was carried in her heart.'[2]

Hofmannsthal deepened his own personal interest in Maria Theresa through his friendship with Hans Schlitter, an Austrian archivist born in Vicenza when the Veneto was still Habsburg, and a distinguished historian of the Theresian epoch. Schlitter's researches into court life and manners undoubtedly helped Hofmannsthal with his libretto.

At the same time, another personality enamoured of the nostalgia for Maria Theresa, Harry Kessler, also influenced the librettist. Kessler had Anglo-Irish roots and a strong affection for Maria Theresa and the

Habsburgs. He was heard to observe when the Hohenzollerns were exiled from Germany: 'The last Habsburg at least died as a gentleman; the last Hohenzollern . . . like a coachman.'

Kessler and Schlitter combined with Hofmannsthal's talents to create a vision of Theresian Austria which would long survive the fall of the monarchy. It was a vision which stressed, above all, her Austrian character and its contrast with Prussian modalities. It also helped Maria Theresa emerge into the twentieth century as the personification of the special relationship Austrians have to the feminine and matriarchal.

Leaving aside the painful and exhausting rigours of eighteenth-century childbirth, Maria Theresa became a paradigm for Austrian motherhood well into the twentieth century. That this was supported by male historians has been well documented.[3] The element of gallantry, however, persists and no scholar of the Empress can fail to see the human frailties which Hofmannsthal works as themes into his great libretto. Handsome Octavian, the older Marschallin (an overt reference to the military campaigns of the era), the Viennese dialect of Mariandl, the 'Chocolate Girl' of the opera, even if it is only Octavian in disguise, and of course the *Zärtlichkeit* of Sophie, are all Hofmannsthal's reflections on a new interpretation of femininity arising out of the era of Maria Theresa.

Although modern opera productions have travelled a long way in an attempt to strip the period of its rococo grace and glamour, the traditional rendering of the Theresian era remains in Vienna and elsewhere always the most popular, conforming as it does to general acceptance of the qualities, material and spiritual, associated with the Great Empress.

But there is more to the opera's genius than just optics. Hofmannsthal could not have been blind to the major debates of his time, and the elevation by the Austrian state of Maria Theresa in the 1880s was inextricably bound up with the growing neurosis surrounding pan-German sentiment.

There is in the unflattering depiction of Baron Ochs a slight undercurrent of anti-German sentiment. The Marschallin and Octavian are the epitome of grace and elegance while the aptly named Ochs is boorish, heavy-handed and even more heavy-humoured. He is in von Hofmannsthal's libretto conspicuously unable to speak Viennese German and the comic aspects of his dialogue with Mariandl would have been recognizable to a Viennese audience as not too subtle lampooning of north German stereotypes of clumsy, unimaginative behaviour.

Of course, Hofmannsthal would not have wished to endanger the success of the opera among German audiences – Strauss was, after all, German – so the contrast, while apparent to any Austrian spectator of the opera, is not given any formal Austrian-versus-German polarity.

In this subtle way, Richard Strauss and Hugo von Hofmannsthal perpetuated in *Der Rosenkavalier* an enduring friction between Austria and Prussia which was the dominant policy challenge of the entire Theresian era. Viewed through this historical prism, the silver rose becomes not only a legacy of Theresian grace and elegance but also – every rose has thorns, after all – of Maria Theresa's determination and defiance.

CHAPTER 44

Courage and Honour: The Maria Theresa Order

In the late winter of 1984 a distinguished old gentleman with grey hair and a double-breasted dark grey suit appeared at one of Vienna's more discreet hotels, not far from the Capuchin crypt where Maria Theresa is buried along with the other Habsburgs. He wore a cream shirt and a midnight-blue tie and, but for the splash of red and white in his buttonhole, might have stepped out of a sepia photograph taken decades earlier.

The buttonhole was the ribbon of Imperial Austria's highest military honour and the man wearing it was Baron Gottfried von Banfield or, to give him his Italian name, Goffredo de Banfield. He had in fact been born a British citizen, Geoffrey Banfield, the son of an Irish naval officer in the Imperial Austrian Navy, Richard Banfield. He had enrolled in the imperial and royal naval cadet school at Fiume (Rijeka) before the First World War and, when hostilities broke out with Italy in 1915, he was in command of the newly established naval air station in Trieste. He was barely 25 years old and had only a handful of planes with which to defend Austrian airspace. His bravery was conspicuous and on several occasions he single-handedly took on superior numbers of enemy aircraft. It was largely thanks to Banfield that Italian, British and French aircraft never enjoyed undisputed air superiority over Trieste until the very end of the war.

For his combination of youthful energy, formidable good looks and unquestionable bravery, Banfield was awarded the Knight's Cross of the Order of Maria Theresa which carried automatic elevation into the junior ranks of the imperial nobility. As he strode through the hotel to the room where a reception was prepared for his memoirs, no-one passing him realized that here was, astonishing to behold, the last living link with Maria Theresa's order of chivalry founded on that day in 1757 when Daun had shattered the myth of Prussian invincibility at the Battle of Kolin.

Banfield was the last survivor of an extinct breed. Appropriately, his life expressed all the internationalism of the Theresian era. Born a British subject in modern Montenegro in 1890, he had become an Austrian in 1910, an Italian in 1926 and an honorary French citizen in 1962. Banfield's award had not guaranteed him an easy life. The Italians admired him but, inevitably as an enemy combatant, he was imprisoned and only released after the good offices of the American consul were deployed to secure his freedom. The Italians had then promptly expelled him and – after a brief but fruitless sojourn in Vienna, where many officers of the old imperial army had gathered to wander aimlessly in search of some remuneration, work or comfort – he had found that his British nationality papers had not been entirely cancelled and that, as he had been born a British subject, he could go to England to find work.

This he had promptly done in Newcastle where he had begun to work as a draughtsman for the armaments firm Vickers. There, his gallantry in the First World War counted for very little but he was soon rescued from this obscurity by a chance encounter with his childhood Triestine sweetheart Maria Tripcovich. The two immediately plighted their troth and were married in Brompton Oratory in 1924. Eventually, Banfield returned to Trieste, becoming an Italian citizen, where he could play a useful role in his wife's shipping company.

The Maria Theresa Order was always prized by him but there were many recipients still alive at that time and the reunion celebrations on 18 June were not events Banfield felt much enthusiasm to attend. He had long become accustomed to hearing the cry 'abbasso Banfield!' (down with Banfield!) when he had attended Italian patriotic events in Trieste. Yet, by 1985, he represented the last living link between the Order and the Great Empress. It would be another year before Banfield's death, at the age of 96, brought the Order to an end more than two centuries after Maria Theresa had established it.

It was Tarouca who suggested, on the news of Daun's great victory, a new medal be struck for bravery, to commemorate not just that campaign but also to reward future generations for exemplary military service. The terms of the award were innovative: 'For exceptional bravery performed by an officer on his own initiative which had an essential impact on the campaign, including acts whose omission would not be construed as representing any neglect of duty.' From the beginning the award was linked to the soldier's individual initiative and boldness.[1]

The award was also innovative socially: it carried automatic elevation to the lower ranks of nobility, and was open to all ethnicities, irrespective of background and social status. A committee of recipients would determine who was eligible for the award and the Order's first grand master was Leopold Daun. The award's motto was *fortitudine* (courage) and that alone was in theory the criterion for its bestowal.

Despite bearing such an intimate connection with the Empress, the medal was of a modest simplicity which delighted the austere tastes of her son: a simple small white enamel cross with the Habsburg *Bindenschild* at its centre carried by a red-white-red ribbon.

Between its inauguration in 1757 and Banfield's death in 1986, the medal was awarded only 1,241 times. At the launch of Banfield's memoirs one early evening in Vienna on 12 March 1984, the doyen of Austrian military historians, Johann Christoph Allmayer-Beck, reminded us of the multiple historical legacies Banfield personified: he was the last man alive to have been personally received in an audience by Franz Josef; he was the last man alive to have been decorated by the Emperor Charles; but, above all, he was the last man alive to have been awarded this most coveted of decorations whose chivalry linked him in unbroken lineage with the Great Empress.

That Maria Theresa should have been invoked that evening was hardly surprising, but that the nonagenarian gentleman standing before us was a link in that unbroken chain stretching back to Maria Theresa and Daun's victory at Kolin could not fail to impress us all. Thus could yet another legacy of Maria Theresa resonate well into the late twentieth century.

With Banfield's death, the Order finally yielded to the dictates of history and ceased to exist. It is today probably the most forgotten of

COURAGE AND HONOUR: THE MARIA THERESA ORDER

Europe's most illustrious military awards for valour, but its legacy lies perhaps less in the context of the roll of honour and battles which its recipients represent and more in the creation by Maria Theresa of a truly inclusive order, promoting not just courage but social mobility. The Maria Theresa Order, long before the Victoria Cross and other awards for gallantry were established, represented a gateway not only into fame but, in keeping with the Empress's enduring commitment to social mobility, the ranks of the aristocracy. Moreover, a lifetime pension for recipients was guaranteed by the Empress although this, unsurprisingly, did not survive the end of the Habsburgs. By the 1960s Banfield's enquiries into the whereabouts of his military pension ran into unyielding bureaucratic sands between Rome and Vienna.

Taken together with the career of Johann Thugut, the social advancement of the 'Chocolate Girl', and the promotion of otherwise obscure musical and artistic genius, the Maria Theresa Order was yet another example of a society dynamic with a firm grasp of the potential of human capital. Maria Theresa had an unerring instinct for quality and, while it lasted, the Maria Theresa Order underlined, not least in its last surviving recipient, the unambivalent promotion of that ideal.

CHAPTER 45

The *Zuckerkönigin*: Rococo Delights

ONE DAY IN THE summer of 1760 Maria Theresa was studying a draft diplomatic communication from Kaunitz. It was late morning and the Empress was at Schönbrunn in a recently constructed pavilion near her husband's projected *Tiergarten*. As she studied her papers, she dipped, as was her custom, a small pastry kipfel into her cup of coffee, and proceeded to eat, not noticing until a few moments later that the coffee had been spilt on Kaunitz's draft. Without hesitating, the Empress took her pen and ringed the offending stain with the words *Verzeihung. Unser' Schuld.* (Excuse me. Our fault.)

This instant admission of guilt is often held up as an example of the Empress's moral rectitude. She might have chosen not to own up to such a small infringement. She might have hoped it would go unnoticed; she might even have thought that her chancellor would be indifferent to such a small blot on his papers. The fact that she immediately chose a confessional route which involved self-criticism was long held by writers to illustrate her sense of personal responsibility.

The anecdote, much related during her lifetime but invested with almost excessive piety after her death, illustrates another perhaps less austere truth about the Great Empress, namely that she was addicted to *Kaffee und Kuchen* (coffee and sweet pastries). Under Maria Theresa the full panoply of rococo sweetmeats became enshrined in Austrian, especially Viennese, everyday life. The *Mehlspeis* (pronounced usually *Murlschpeis* in Viennese dialect) became a staple of all imperial cooking and Schönbrunn's kitchens were rapidly transformed into the epicentre of the Empress's baking world. Under Maria Theresa, sugar, previously a commodity usually stored at pharmacies on account of its expense, became a household product essential for the production of any banquet. At Count Schlick von Bassano's feast in Bohemia, no expense was spared in producing a dessert which incorporated the kipfels and almonds that were so highly prized in Vienna.

It was not just the legendary crescent-shaped kipfel which symbolized the defeat of the infidel Turks at the gates of Vienna in 1683 that was a daily part of Maria Theresa's diet. The rococo era brought new gastronomic creations especially from France and other parts of southern Europe. *Spanische Windbaeckerei* (Spanish air confection) became one of the specialities of the Schönbrunn *Conditorei Kunst*.

Magnificent meringue confections were created, such as the richly layered sugar poodles whose feet and nose were dipped in dark chocolate. Then there were various cakes which long pre-dated the creations of the nineteenth century, including the famous Sachertorte. Maria Theresa might have been denied the opportunity to eat a Sacher cake or a *Rigo-Jancsi* but the multi-layered Eszterhazy and Traunkirchner cakes were certainly known to her.[1]

A particular delicacy which arrived from the Near East was the 'Mohr in Hemd' (Moor in a shirt), a partly baked runny chocolate cake topped with whipped cream which was much prized on feast days for celebrations.[2]

These exotic numbers were reserved for special occasions while the lighter kipfel and the *Guglhupf* sponge cake were more regular elements in the daily menu. The *Guglhupf* in particular was a favourite of Maria Theresa's and, although she rather disapproved of her children eating sugar, she encouraged her daughter Marie Antoinette to introduce the French royal court to its simple ingredients (mostly eggs). It was of course poorly received by Parisian aristocrats who placed more emphasis on the appearance of a cake than its ingredients. The humble simplicity of the *Guglhupf* could not compete with the multi-tiered concoctions of the French patisserie.

A no less enduring example of this relative simplicity was the apple strudel, whose first mention in official Austrian papers can be traced back to a municipal document dated 1687, four years after the lifting of the great Turkish siege of Vienna. The apple strudel appears to have owed its origin to a variation of the Turkish baklava delicacy and enjoyed rapid promotion to a favourite imperial dish under Maria Theresa. It had first been brought to Vienna by merchants operating in the Levant and it quickly gained currency throughout the monarchy.

Prague also developed its own rival delicacies which quickly gained widespread popularity in court circles in the capital. 'Prune plum pockets' or *Powidltatschkerln* in Viennese dialect (*powidla*: Czech/Polish for plum) impressed Maria Theresa when she was offered them for the first time shortly after her husband died in 1765.

Eventually, Czechs in particular would become prized as pastry cooks and their puddings much sought after in Vienna, providing significant employment for Czechs in domestic service throughout Austria during the nineteenth century. Such cakes and other treats also were a daily reminder of the cosmopolitan qualities of the monarchy. If the cakes of Vienna could penetrate even the protectionist mentality of the French, then Austria could be said to stand again for an internationalism, albeit confined largely to the world of baking trays and ovens.

To be a Vienna-trained pastry chef became, under Maria Theresa, for the first time, a badge of honour and the fact that Austrian confectionery enjoys, two hundred years later, the highest of reputations can also be irrefutably laid at the feet of the Great Empress.

Other aspects of Viennese cuisine would in time also find their way to the European capitals, notably the famous *Wiener Schnitzel* which originated in Milan and the equally prized *Tafelspitz* or boiled cut of beef, but it was in her puddings that Maria Theresa bequeathed to Europe the benefits of a gastronomic superpower. Even the whipping of cream (*Schlagobers* – in Vienna usually leavened with icing sugar) became a byword for opulence. If Maria Theresa could demonstrate her moral rectitude and steeliness throughout her reign, and ask her children to avoid eating sugar, a degree of indulgence could on occasion be expected. It was no coincidence that perhaps the most widely adopted gastronomic innovation of her reign was the consumption of *Schlagobers* as a dish in its own right.

Marzipan also became a much-prized luxury during her reign, arriving in Vienna, from the Orient via Trieste, during the second half of the 1770s. The sweetmeat was especially associated with femininity and to this day Triestine dialect knows no greater compliment than to describe a woman as *un marzapan di donna*.

As always, the Empress's interest was accompanied by a highly practical awareness of costs and the need constantly to avoid superfluous
expenditure. She carefully monitored the expenses of the court kitchens
and this led her to realize that she would have to take, even in this seemingly unimportant department of her affairs, certain matters in hand. At
first, she found the details of expenditure almost impossible to fathom.
She was particularly concerned that the costs of the pastry and dessert
elements were lacking entirely in any transparency. When it came to
these, the traditional accounting practices prevalent for estimating the
cost of the purchase of meat and fish appeared to be entirely absent.

In 1744 she ordered the separation of the *Zuckerbäckerei* element of
the *Hofküche* and had it established as a separate entity with its own
Offize. This was a typical Theresian reform introducing greater transparency, significant cost savings as well as greater efficiency and production. In a memorandum she penned at this time, the Empress noted:
'The activities of the *Zuckerbäckerei* cost too much and produce too little.
This must change and a better business made out of it.'[3]

By 1754 it seemed indeed as if a 'better business' had been made out
of it. At a court banquet held in Prince Eugene's former *Schloss* at Hof,
the dessert chefs excelled themselves by producing meringue soldiers
with chocolate facing colours and sugar bearskins. As one eyewitness
noted: 'the martial spirit of the old much mourned Prince Eugene rapidly
turned into a feast of a more pacific note as all the assembled soldiers of
sugar were quickly consumed'. As they disappeared, they bequeathed a
battlefield where 'no military survivors could be any longer surveyed'.
As another one of the guests observed, 'even the weapons and tents of
the armies were digested so that peace could reign supreme'.[4]

Although her son Joseph would cut down extravagantly on the
desserts and puddings produced for court feasts, Maria Theresa at this
time was still a devotee of the rococo or late baroque delight in desserts
of spectacular dimensions. One described in the *Wienerisches Diarium* was
the climax of a celebration commemorating the fiftieth anniversary of
Archbishop Kollonitz's prelature. It left nothing to the imagination as an
example of culinary *Wunderwerk*. It was three feet high, forty-two feet
long and depicted in life size the crowns of Bohemia, Hungary and the
Holy Roman Empire. A vast triumphal arch of meringues made up the

centrepiece, while the four seasons and the high altar of St Stephen's Cathedral were all portrayed in icing sugar and chocolate to create a sweetened and heightened chiaroscuro.

The entire creation was almost certainly the work of a French patisseur by the name of Charles Cuisset. Cuisset had come to Vienna from Lorraine, encouraged by Maria Theresa's husband, Francis Stephen, and he had quickly been promoted to the post, newly established by Maria Theresa, of court sugar cook (*Hof-Zuckerbäcker*).

However, if Maria Theresa might have hoped that under his leadership costs could be made more manageable, they became even less transparent than hitherto. In particular, the frequent disappearance of large orders of fruit suggested that the autonomy granted to the sugar bakers was being exploited in ways which did not reflect exclusively their imperial responsibilities.

Once again, Maria Theresa felt compelled to intervene. She asked for advice and was introduced to the pastry chef of Count Ulfeld, Johann Michael Pleyerl. His creations had impressed both Maria Theresa and her husband. Francis Stephen was especially impressed by Pleyerl's flair with accounting, always a subject close to the Emperor's heart. Pleyerl certainly had an eye for figures. In less than six months, he demonstrated his accounting skills by saving the court culinary treasury the stupendous sum of 8,000 Gulden.

His career at court appeared assured but on closer examination the savings he had introduced were accompanied by a sharp reduction in the amounts of sugar deployed. The resulting alteration in taste did not escape the Empress unnoticed and once again Maria Theresa intervened.

In a detailed memorandum, she concluded, 'Cuisset gefällt mir besser in gusto' (I prefer the taste of Cuisset's creations), and the Frenchman was reinstated in 1760. Perhaps his return fitted into Maria Theresa's plans for ever-greater Austro-French understanding – Marie Antoinette had married the Dauphin two years earlier – or perhaps, as was also rumoured, Cuisset had perfected an attractive hardness in his meringues which allowed them to be eaten in greater quantities on long journeys.

Unfortunately, no sooner had the change of regime in the pastry kitchens been effected than there were new accusations of profligacy and poor accounting. The costs of the sugar department of the imperial kitchens were rising enormously and provoking an 'ungemeinen grossen Aufsehen' (unusually great upset). Once again, significant amounts of time were devoted to finding a long-lasting solution.

Other practical external factors now began to make themselves felt. First of these was an increasing frustration that in hot summers the more elaborate sugary confections were liable to attack from ants, flies and other insects from the nearby Danube. The confections were scaled back drastically after one summer gala lunch at Schloss Hof had seen a swarm of wasps descend on the meringues and candied fruits, much to the discomfort of the imperial guests who had been forced to flee en masse indoors.

If the presence of desserts was inhibited increasingly during the hotter months, it still seemed as if the hold of baroque dessert menus was impregnable during the winter, but here too matters took a turn for a more austere finale to the imperial banquets.

In 1758 Louis XV sent a precious Sèvres service to Vienna as a present to Maria Theresa to celebrate the wedding of Marie Antoinette to his son. The service was enormous: some 185 pieces in total, of which the 38 exquisite *Bisquit* figurines were the chief glory. Coated in contours of silver-plated copper, the pieces were elegant, but fragile. They were not designed or indeed manufactured with the rougher peasant hands of Vienna's pastry chefs in mind and they quickly demonstrated their unsuitability for their deployment as a platform to show off the more extravagant confectionery of the *Hofzuckerbäckerei*.

To the consternation of the Empress, within two months of their arrival, almost half the *Bisquit* pieces had been broken, either during the dinner's preparation or during the post-prandial clearing up when glass and *Bisquit* vied with each other for first place in the damage caused by over-hasty *Tafelsaufsatz* (dining service) deconstruction.[5]

It quickly became apparent that the new rococo style in porcelain figures was requiring a lighter touch and lighter design of desserts. By the time Maria Theresa died in 1780, the tyranny of delicate porcelain had led to the extinction of the once grand desserts of the Empress's youth. With Joseph's arrival as sole monarch the tables of the Hofburg were set with just porcelain and flowers to create visual effects and the dictatorship of the Theresian court *Zuckerbäckerei* was, at least for the moment, over.

CHAPTER 46

Femininity and Feminism: Maria Theresa
as *Landesmutter*

FOR THE MODERN READER, aware of the revolution in attitudes towards women which has progressed during the second half of the twentieth century and gathered momentum in the first decades of the twenty-first, the sentimental pastiche of womanhood traditionally presented by (usually male) biographers of Maria Theresa is no longer, understandably, acceptable.

Yet to examine Maria Theresa from a feminist perspective and through the lens of female agency, to use the modern term, is to invite challenge and paradox. On the one hand, Maria Theresa, unlike her female contemporaries around the courts of Europe, owed her sovereignty to a male system of inheritance. She had not married into kingship like Catherine of Russia nor had she come to wield influence through physical intimacy like Madame de Pompadour. Rather she was the beneficiary of an unambivalently masculine system of dynastic succession. Not once during her reign did she contemplate deploying her power in order to effect any permanent alteration to the essentially male-dominated circumstances which were the source of all her formal power.

Commentators who try to ignore this fact by dwelling on the 'ethos' of a century which, in their view, demanded unhesitating subservience to male dominance and the eighteenth-century 'norms' of female subservience, fail to give credit for the advances in thinking on the role of female sovereigns which, as the century progressed, became a legitimate focus for debate.

It was Montesquieu who – in his treatise *L'Esprit des Lois* on political theory, published in Geneva in 1748, the year the War of the Austrian

Succession ended – noted that nothing inherently prevented women from governing successfully. The great political theorist, who divided systems into the three categories of republican, monarchical and despotic, devoted considerable space to developing the idea of female legitimacy in the exercise of power.

He wrote that women are 'far better suited to government than to running a household'. This was partly, in Montesquieu's view, because government was not the usual route of female activity and it promoted skills *faute de mieux* not usually developed in the female psyche. Through leadership, a woman went against the conditioning of her upbringing and the spirit of the age, namely 'Reason and Nature', two dominant themes of the eighteenth-century Enlightenment. Precisely because of this, Montesquieu argued, affairs of state offered a platform in which a woman could excel and thrive.

Although the writer did not mention Maria Theresa explicitly, it is clear that he could easily have had her in mind when he wrote that the feminine constitution granted women 'exactly the qualities' necessary for good government.

This was partly, in Montesquieu's opinion, the result of female physical factors. 'Weaker bodies' made them 'moderate and gentle'. The physical challenges of childbirth gave them insights into the human condition denied to masculinity. Such female moderation contrasted with the bellicosity and brute strength associated with some male monarchs.

Above all, and this certainly applied to Maria Theresa as we have seen, the perceived and real physical 'weakness' of the female sovereign's frame – the result, in the philosopher's view, of such a monarch's 'softer flesh' – made it imperative for her to consult knowledgeable advisers: men who could 'carry the burden of government'. Delegation and listening to advice were therefore inescapable features of any female sovereign's government even at a time of absolutist politics.

Maria Theresa undoubtedly conformed to this contemporary view. Her daughters, Marie Caroline and Marianne, also expressed these qualities. Although Montesquieu was writing this before the advent of Maria Theresa's most influential advisers such as Kaunitz, Daun and Tarouca, she had already, through Palffy and Haugwitz, learnt to lean heavily on men to 'carry the weight' of government. That Montesquieu could have so ably ventilated the concept of the advantages of a female sovereign without mentioning the Austrian Empress illustrates that ideas of female leadership were a topic of discussion well beyond the crown lands of the Habsburg monarchy.

The difficulty of framing the Great Empress within the parameters of the modern feminist debate is not just apparent when one examines such contemporary male thinking on the subject of female leadership. Maria Theresa's personal life and beliefs offer no easy access to the advocates of overt feminism. The Empress was not, as some have maintained, socially conservative – the career of Thugut and her commitment to social mobility at court and a meritocratic education within her domains is proof enough of that – but she was, as we have seen, undoubtedly devout. Her Jesuitical training and Marian devotion carried as their foundations the concept of service: service to her subjects, service to her state and service to her husband. Such concepts necessarily involved humility, and a degree of submission was an unavoidable corollary of such an outlook. Above all, as she would have learnt from the Jesuits, the sin of pride was the sin from which most other failings flowed and therefore had to be combated at every turn.

Her advice, already noted, to her daughter Marie Antoinette on how she should behave towards her husband the Dauphin shows that, while she was not averse to the reality of 'having the last word' in a relationship, the appearance of a degree of submission was a *sine qua non* of a successful marriage: 'The wife must completely submit to her husband and must have no business other than to please him and obey him.' Such language was meant to be taken literally but it implicitly did not rule out freedom of mental or physical space for the female spouse. Rather, its importance lay in terms of a convention distinct from, but not incompatible with, reality. If the first lesson of Mozart's later work, *Die Zauberflöte*, was not to be taken in by appearances, it was a lesson Maria Theresa, along with much of late eighteenth-century Vienna, had long digested before that work's first performance.

This of course has led to many charges of hypocrisy levelled at Maria Theresa. How could she implore her daughter to submit while she herself ruled with iron determination her own family? Certainly, the undermining of male authority as a guiding principle of marital behaviour was anathema to her but reality and appearance were distinctly separate, if intersected, dimensions.

Equilibrium meant much to Maria Theresa and, in her quest for it politically as well as domestically, she was nothing if not pragmatic, transposing seamlessly some of the practical flexibilities of Jesuitical practice into the marital experience. Within this philosophical universe, the implementation of principles could be matched to circumstances, especially when the first question asked in any crisis was always 'What is it that God expects of me?'

In a post-Christian age such concepts cannot be as easily absorbed as they were in the eighteenth century. The nineteenth and twentieth centuries have eroded for many that sacramental relationship with God that meant so much to Maria Theresa. 'Interior' attitudes were compatible with an outward display of femininity. The Miltonian ideal of 'sweet, reluctant, amorous delay'[1] was one Maria Theresa understood completely, and her recognition of the tactical value of outward femininity with all its perceived frailties was exploited on countless occasions (another capital offence in the eyes of proto-feminists). That she was also permanently pregnant and seemingly indifferent to intellectual discussions were further black marks to be garnered in evaluating the Empress in the context of modern feminist progress.

It has therefore, unsurprisingly, been far easier for biographers, especially in Austria, to avoid simply the emotionally charged feminist debate and place Maria Theresa onto an entirely different neutral platform: that of the *Landesmutter*, the mother of the nation, a kind of temporal guardian angel spreading feminine harmony and maternal protection throughout central Europe but above all for Austria.

In this vision of Maria Theresa, the Great Empress exudes all the great feminine qualities with which her many male biographers have invested her. She is, above all, contrasted in Austria with that other striking female personality of the Habsburgs, the Empress Sissi. Sissi, the unpredictable wife of the emperor Franz Josef a century later, offered another icon for Austrian femininity. Her tragic death, stabbed by an Italian anarchist as she stepped onto a ferry on Lake Geneva, and her restless travels to Corfu and Ireland have given her a lasting if brooding presence in central Europe.[2]

Both Empresses are lodged in the collective psyche of modern Austria but while they were both famous for their copious luxuriant hair, the contrast is vivid. Where Sissi was impulsive, unpredictable and impetuous, Maria Theresa embodied the virtues of common sense and stolid reliability. She is the devoted wife constantly, despite the *difetti piccoli* of her husband, prepared to sacrifice everything to support his career and prestige. This is a model of marital devotion which has not survived in many places in northern Europe but may be still visible in Austria.

By aligning herself with this image, Maria Theresa no doubt was simply following the rules of her upbringing but she could not have known that the image would prove so resilient, reinforcing a notion of womanhood which, for better or worse, has become fundamental to modern Austrian culture despite attempts to deconstruct it.

It has been pointed out that this cult of Maria Theresa and glorification of her womanhood was largely a creation of the late nineteenth century as a response to the political rise of Prussia.[3] Undoubtedly, the cult was given a push as every weapon in the Austrian cultural armoury was deployed in the closing years of the nineteenth century to pinprick Berlin's pretensions, but the cult was firmly embedded in the Viennese subconsciousness long before the Battle of Königgrätz ushered in Prussian blue.

Schönbrunn, the favourite Sunday excursion of the Viennese, the Theresianum, even the countless matriarchal figures organizing and running the cafes and *Gasthäuser* of the capital all subconsciously referenced the Empress. She was present in the Austrian psyche in countless stories on which children were raised, of struggles against the odds, and the frescoes of most churches in some way presented an image of the *Landesmutter* transposed into angelic guise.

The great statue erected on the Ringstrasse reinforced the cult of Maria Theresa and, in one respect, it brilliantly reflected her powerful femininity. She sits imperious but with only a modest tiara adorning her head. In one hand is the famous Pragmatic Sanction. In the other, the sceptre, the symbol of imperial authority. Beneath her, gathered in equestrian and pedestrian loyalty, are her generals and her advisers. In her simple *suffisante* pose, she rises above all these men and yet the document she holds in her right hand, the fount of all her power, is the creation of her father and ultimately the legal source, however disregarded by most of its signatories, of her legitimacy. All this male effort and service is at her disposal, but it is a male world which holds sway over all her privileges.

CHAPTER 47

Triumph of the Modern: Franz Xaver Messerschmidt

IF THE ARTISTIC LEGACY of Maria Theresa gave no particularly dominating personalities in the architectural world to match the giants of the Austrian baroque, the personality of Franz Xaver Messerschmidt offered a new sculptural tradition which was truly groundbreaking in its realism and interpretation of emotional mood. Messerschmidt's creations in the Lower Belvedere are among the most extraordinary works of art produced during the entire Theresian period. His pieces for the imperial couple, the life-size figures of Maria Theresa and Francis Stephen, are overshadowed by the subsequent busts of courtiers and peasants which all display a breathtaking modernity.

Messerschmidt was a pupil of Balthasar Moll, the designer of Francis Stephen's and then Maria Theresa's funerary monuments in the Capuchin crypt. His fame in Austrian court circles and his subsequent meteoric rise was largely attributable to the court painter van Meytens's patronage. The painter recognized the genius and, in 1764, secured the commission for two statues of the imperial couple.

They were both executed in tin and showed the Empress and her consort in their full imperial regalia. Powerful symbols of their imperial authority, the statues were completed a few months after Francis Stephen's sudden death in Innsbruck in 1765.

The career of Franz Xaver Messerschmidt indicates again that capacity for raw talent to rise in the Theresian monarchy irrespective of social background and circumstances. What later generations would call an *Aussteiger* (drop-out), the eighteenth century more neutrally referred to as a *Sonderling* (original). Art historians have only recently confronted this astonishing personality, having previously found the subject too difficult, preferring to relegate the study of the master to the discipline of psychiatry. The renowned 'character heads' are objects which break all eighteenth-century conventional portraiture boundaries but the innovative depiction of human emotions they contain are no less extraordinary than the life of the man who made them.

Messerschmidt had been born near Ulm, the youngest of thirty-three children. His father had been a man of apparently 'Herculean build' and his mother had lived until the age of 97. A distant relation of hers was the sculptor Philipp Straub in Graz and the young Messerschmidt travelled the well-worn cultural highway of Munich–Salzburg–Graz–Vienna. Straub's Graz workshop trained Messerschmidt, and the faces of the Styrian peasantry – distorted by the prevalent cretinism in the remote valleys of Upper Styria which contemporary travellers remarked upon – may well have made a strong impression on him.[1] By the time he reached Vienna and enrolled in the Academy of Fine Arts, Meytens had spotted his talent.

Interestingly, Meytens's support was not enough to get the young Messerschmidt established in Vienna. What propelled his career were the military requirements ahead of the Seven Years War. The Austrian artillery had been reformed under Prince Wenzel Liechtenstein and it was the custom in those times to adorn the barrels of cannon with highly decorative reliefs. The man in charge of this process in Vienna was David Chantelle (or as the Viennese called him – and even wrote to him as – David Schantey). Chantelle had studied his craft in France and was typical of the 'foreign' talent Liechtenstein brought in from all over the continent to improve the monarchy's gunnery.

Stückhauptmann Chantelle commissioned Messerschmidt to make busts of Maria Theresa and Francis Stephen for the ceremonial hall of the Vienna Arsenal, the so-called Kaisersaal. Liechtenstein was so taken by these that he commissioned two more of Joseph and his first wife, Isabella of Parma. When Maria Theresa saw these, she expressly commissioned Messerschmidt to make a terracotta bust of her which was also widely admired.

This imperial commission opened many doors for Messerschmidt. In particular, it aroused the interest of a cousin of Liechtenstein's, the

Duchess of Savoy, the last living relative of the deceased Prince Eugene. The duchess was a loyal and generous patron and Messerschmidt could send considerable sums of money back to his mother's family in Germany while she lived. At one point, over a period of five years, he appears to have earned from her alone more than 5,000 Gulden, a considerable sum in those days for a simple craftsman.[2]

The life-size statues of Maria Theresa and her husband were paid for out of Maria Theresa's personal treasury and cost 12,000 florins each. Half of this amount went to Chantelle while the other half was paid to Messerschmidt. The work was not completed until just after Francis Stephen's death. These tin portraits are striking not just on account of their artistic quality; the choice of regalia for the two sovereigns is also significant. Maria Theresa is wearing the crown of Hungary while Francis Stephen is attired in the imperial regalia he was wearing when Joseph was crowned King of the Romans. Both figures thus display their own distinctive sovereignties. So pleased was Maria Theresa with the execution of the figure of Francis Stephen that she paid Messerschmidt an additional sum and awarded him a large gold medal, two gestures which she very much hoped would 'encourage other artists' (*mit einem Gnadenpfennige und einer grossen goldenen Medaille um anderen Künstler zu ermutigen*).[3]

The work on these figures was interrupted by a study tour of Rome. In 1772 the Vienna Academy of Fine Arts would introduce the prestigious Rome *Stipendium* (scholarship) for talented artists to spend time in the Eternal City studying classical remains. Messerschmidt's sojourn in Rome was well ahead of this development and he returned to Vienna in 1766 where he continued to find imperial patronage. In 1769 the Empress commissioned a bust in gold-plated metal of the eminent physician Gerard van Swieten. Maria Theresa had it adorn the main *Saal* (hall) of the newly established medical faculty of the Vienna University. Imperial patronage began, however, to tail off, and with the death of the Duchess of Savoy, another source of income disappeared.

Messerschmidt turned increasingly to studies of human expression, in particular male grimaces. The study of these wide-ranging emotions appears to have accompanied a mental 'decline' which made the artist increasingly unstable and unpredictable. The visit to Rome had opened his eyes to the cool simplicity of classical sculpture but, despite a few essays in this neo-classical idiom, he seems to have preferred a more real-istic, almost expressionist approach to depicting the human character.

In 1770 Meytens died, depriving him of another powerful supporter. Contemporaries in Vienna found Messerschmidt's sudden rages and mood swings increasingly difficult to handle. It did not help that Messerschmidt had never found the Viennese court manners much to his taste or under-standing. At home in Munich and Salzburg or Graz, where things were judged on how *bodenständig* (reliable) they were, Messerschmidt was ill at ease with the *Schmäh* (froth) and languid frivolity of the Vienna court. His behaviour occasioned criticism and court circles closed ranks against him.

In 1774 Kaunitz, no less, felt compelled to intervene as more and more examples of Messerschmidt's mental turbulence began to emerge. Writing to Maria Theresa in the summer of that year Kaunitz proposed a simple solution: 'I regret the condition of this talented man and that all other persons regard him with hostility but his head is not clear. Therefore, I propose that Your Majesty relieves his misfortune by the grant of a pension of 600 Gulden a year.' A single word, *Placet*, showed Maria Theresa's agreement with this humane course of action.

For a brief time, he resided in Pressburg, enjoying some support from the artistically inclined Marie Christine and her husband. He even had enough money to buy a house, albeit in one of the least salubrious areas of the city. Pressburg, however, offered a plentiful supply of lead and superb foundries for his art. His sculptures of Marie Christine's husband, Albert von Sachsen Teschen, show that he was still capable of producing outstanding conventional portraits but the 'Hogarth of sculpture' was dedicating himself more and more to his character heads, which were moving far beyond the norms of conventional portrait sculpture in their attempts to explore the furthest limits of human emotion and expres-sion. Scientists have since speculated that Messerschmidt's erratic behaviour was the cumulative result of lead poisoning affecting his brain.

The strict frontality and narrowness of silhouette place these works, begun in 1770, in a stylistic environment which can only be described as unashamedly modern. By the time of his death in 1783, barely three years after the death of the Empress, Messerschmidt had bequeathed a series of sculptures which to this day show that, for all the rococo grace and supposed conservatism of her beliefs, Maria Theresa was capable of supporting an artist who truly broke all boundaries and explored the furthest limits of human emotion, more than a century before such depiction of human expression became more widespread.

Two hundred years later, a young American of Austrian Jewish background, Ronald Lauder, recalled seeing for the first time Messerschmidt's work in the Lower Belvedere, after the 'obligatory' tour of the great Klimt portraits hanging in the Upper Belvedere. 'After admiring the wondrous Adele Bloch-Bauer, I stumbled almost by accident into a room full of the most amazing sculptures. They were displayed, it seemed, virtually as a curiosity and I found it almost impossible to believe that they were works of the 18th century, so modern and realistic did they look.' The later US ambassador to Vienna was so impressed by the work that he eventually found two character heads for sale at auction and bid, unsuccessfully, for them, only to secure them from their new owner a year later. They formed one of the centrepieces of an exhibition he organized in New York in 2012 which marked the first serious attempt to understand these remarkable works from an art-historical point of view. As a contemporary critic wrote: 'This exhibition showed that we dismiss ill-advisedly the artistic environment of the era of Maria Theresa as one of innate conservatism: in parallel with the ornate frescoes of Maulpertsch, the bombastic buildings of Hohenberg, there were also the astonishing 64 variations on the male grimace of Messerschmidt's character heads.'[4]

CHAPTER 48

The War on Superstition

THERE CAN BE LITTLE doubt that Catholic piety was open in Maria Theresa's reign, as today, to the accusation of superstition. Yet the idea of eighteenth-century Vienna being somehow in the grip of superstition is very wide of the mark. The Jesuits, far more than any secularist 'enlightenment' thought, attacked superstition with all the intellectual weapons at their disposal. *Abergläubigkeit* was a sin against the very foundations of a church which was built upon the 'rock of truth'.

The Council of Trent had already, in the mid-sixteenth century, attempted to purge Christian theology of superstitious elements. Mendicant orders had attempted to establish criteria for deciding when divine intervention had occurred. Some medieval writers complained that superstitious formulas were mixed with holy and pious words.

A century later, an English priest, Thomas White, had, as president of the English college in Lisbon, answered critics with his study on 'Devotion and Reason' that neither the rosary nor prayers for the dead were 'irrational'. Reason, when deployed free from prejudice, was perfectly compatible with faith. In Maria Theresa's domains, this argument was expressed in a highly sophisticated form by the Hungarian Pauline monk Johann Bartholotti, who wrote a treatise on superstition combining Catholicism with the Enlightenment in an attempt to defeat ignorance and prejudice.

Bartholotti argued that there was no danger to Catholic dogma if the more fantastic stories of miracles were excised from the lives of the saints. Moreover, he insisted that religious fanaticism could be counted as a superstition, since it confused human ideas with divine instruction.

The Catholic Enlightenment, in which Maria Theresa grew up, dismissed fanaticism as an irrational religious force. To insist on the irrelevance of reason was a sacrifice of the intellectual coherence of the faith. Doctrinally irrelevant marginalia should never be advanced to a predominance over rational belief, Bartholotti argued.

A faith which was unintelligible to the Enlightenment world was therefore a distortion. The Jesuits who taught Maria Theresa understood this perfectly, knowing full well that, if the Catholic Church was to retain its relevance, it needed to remain an intellectually serious alternative to secular world views. The twentieth century's later division of the house of reason and faith, best articulated perhaps by Wittgenstein, would have been alien to those around Maria Theresa.[1]

Resistance to papal interference in her temporal affairs was something we have seen Maria Theresa imbibe from an early age. In 1763 the auxiliary bishop of Trier, Nikolaus von Hontheim, wrote a book under the pseudonym of Febronius entitled *On the State of the Church*. In this he argued that the authority of the bishops came not from the Pope but from their status as the successors of the Apostles. The papacy should lead the Church but not understand itself in terms of an absolutist monarchy, because Christ never left the keys to the kingdom of God to a single pope but rather to the entire Church. Church government in this interpretation was collegial not monarchical.[2]

Maria Theresa was familiar with these currents of thought, not least because her monarchy was prone to many examples of papal interference and widespread superstition. For Protestants and secular Enlightenment thinkers, superstition was easily harnessed to the anti-Catholic cause. It was the Protestant German philosopher Immanuel Kant who defined superstition as 'the belief in miracles as a duty'. Enlightenment for him meant a 'liberation from superstition'. As Catholicism was seen to promote belief in the supernatural, Protestantism was carefully aligned with rationality. They did not believe in saints, or ostentatious rituals, and they did not hold with the Corpus Christi celebration of the sacrament.

As we have seen, Maria Theresa's reign shows that this black-and-white depiction of faith versus reason is a gross simplicity. Nothing illustrated this more than the increasing caution, as her reign advanced, with which the Church treated miracles and the veneration of relics and images. At the same time, Maria Theresa's officials waged a relentless war on the myths and superstitions of her most remote provinces.

For the Empress, certain superstitions, such as a belief in witches and vampires, were remnants of pagan beliefs. When, in 1749, a nun from a noble family, Renata Singer von Mossau, had been executed as a witch, Maria Theresa had been horrified at the barbarity of extracting her confession under torture. The hapless woman had confessed to intercourse with the devil, and the bishop of Würzburg had had her beheaded and then her body burnt, save for her head which had been exhibited on a pike. The sentence had been all the more barbaric given that two theologians sent by Pope Benedict XIV to investigate the case had both been highly dubious of the methods deployed to secure the conviction. The Pope told the bishop that killing an elderly nun had brought scandal to the Church. The case convinced many enlightened Catholics that no time could be lost in fighting superstition. It was embarrassing to the Holy Roman Emperor that Germans had executed more witches than the infamous Spanish Inquisition.

A Bavarian priest, Ferdinand Sterzinger, condemned the belief in witchcraft as a 'prejudice'. Pacts with the devil were figments of the imagination along with 'flying broomsticks' and evil spells. The incantation of spells had long been seen by the Inquisition as evidence of heresy but accusations of witchcraft remained in the crown lands and beyond a tangible challenge. In Salzburg, it would remain a penal offence until well after Joseph II's death in 1790. Although the bishop of Würzburg had been responsible for the execution of Renata Singer, it was Catholic reformers, rather than secularists, who had been the first to try to eliminate the scourge of witchcraft.

Yet even the devotees of the Catholic Enlightenment had to tread carefully. No priest could reject entirely the possibility of demons without coming closer to denying the existence of the devil. To deny the existence of Satan was to 'close down half of the gospel of Christ' in the words of one later theologian, Carl Schwarzel.[3] Unlike Catholicism, Protestant theology in the middle of the eighteenth century found the devil a 'mythological' figure. The Lutheran theologian Johann Salomo Selmer denied his existence and attributed Christ's 'casting out of spirits' to purely physical healings. This was unacceptable to Catholic priests who were convinced of the validity of the presence of evil. The Jesuits, particularly, had long seen the battle between good and evil in a stark light. The meditation on the 'Two Standards' in the Spiritual Exercises of St Ignatius provided a vivid contemplation of the existence of the devil which would have been familiar to everyone brought up in the eighteenth century within the Jesuit tradition.[4]

Secular priests followed the Jesuitical line albeit with variations. Although not a Jesuit, Father Joseph Gassner developed a reputation for combining this teaching with scientific methods. He conducted a series of exorcisms, expelled 'devils' and cured the sick just as his contemporary philosophers thought they had convinced people there was no such thing as the devil in either the Old or the New Testament.

Gassner was a difficult target for rationalists as he endorsed the Enlightenment critique of witchcraft while arguing that demonic possession existed but was not caused by spells. He never doubted for a moment that the devil existed, but his exorcisms connected science and medicine with religion. Gassner had arrived at his conclusions through personal experience. He had suffered from chronic headaches and had, as a last resort, performed an exorcism on himself which had cured him. As he toured Germany, he drew large audiences of educated people and by the end of the 1760s had a well-established reputation.

He demonstrated that a person's miseries could be cured in the context of attributing responsibility for the disease to the devil. This sometimes made the illness intelligible and produced a positive mental response. But this was only one strand of Gassner's treatment. By harnessing the latest techniques of medicine and science, Gassner produced a parallel physical response which proved highly efficacious and encouraged many imitators.

Another contemporary confronting similar challenges was Franz Anton Mesmer. He tried to heal similar illnesses with magnets, developing a therapy first advanced by the Jesuit astronomer Maximilian Hell. Mesmer, who has bequeathed to us the verb 'to mesmerize', relied entirely on scientific experiments. His methods at first aroused some suspicion and he moved to Paris, while Gassner's more controversial psychological treatment was tolerated by local officialdom.[5]

Despite efforts to cast him in the role, Gassner cannot be character-ized as an 'anti-Enlightenment' figure, even if part of his cure relied on his patients' imagination. Progress in science and medicine, developed during the reign of the Great Empress, was an integral part of his tech-nique. Gassner used these discoveries so practically that it can even be argued that he contributed to the emergence of 'modernity' in psychic studies. Today, Gassner is hailed by historians of psychiatry and psycho-analysis for taking an important step towards the discovery of the unconscious. His techniques of treating patients and controlling their symptoms remain the foundation of all modern hypnotherapy.

Catholic theologians, while not rejecting the possibility of demons completely, could attempt, like Gassner, to develop a philosophical and theological framework that would impose rational discipline on their actions. Just as miracles became more carefully investigated, so too were reports of magical and demonic activity. Criteria were drawn up to help to ensure that no innocent person was convicted. Deaths supposedly caused by witchcraft were subjected to more and more rigorous exami-nation. Unsurprisingly, German Jesuits were in the forefront of such developments and their thinking was certainly known to Maria Theresa.

Two in particular, Friedrich von Spee and Adam Tanner, favoured an empirical examination of all claims of witchcraft. They both argued in favour of the total abolition of the prosecution of witches on the grounds that it offended the empirical principle; no evidence beyond reasonable doubt, they argued, could be found that a person was a witch.

For Ludovico Muratori, the Modena intellectual trained by the Jesuits, whose theology was, as we have seen, so influential in Theresian Austria, there was a further rational Catholic response to the phenom-enon. In his book *La Forza della fantasia humana*, the Italian priest argued persuasively that hysteria and such illnesses as depression and extreme anxiety were responsible for beliefs in witchcraft and that such beliefs could quickly develop into epidemics if their suggestive power was shared with people who were either ignorant or suffering from similar ailments.

Muratori's ideas were highly influential in court circles among the more important of Maria Theresa's advisers. He harnessed the latest scientific thought to his theology, using modern science to show that in the material world, words alone could not bring about any mental or physical changes in a person. Spells and charms were ineffective. This was precisely what Maria Theresa's Jesuit teachers had taught her and it coincided precisely with the views of her physician Van Swieten.

Neither Van Swieten nor Maria Theresa had any difficulty in digesting Muratori's ideas. Protestant critics were quick to ask: if the Catholic theologian was denouncing the use of words to bring about change, where did this naturalist explanation leave the words uttered in the administration of the sacraments? This was a question Van Swieten and Muratori had no problem in answering. Both the Empress and her trusted adviser shared the Italian's view that the material and spiritual worlds were separate, as indeed even the French philosopher René Descartes had declared a century earlier.

For Muratori, charms and spells only worked in a material world on account of their suggestive power. As an example of this he recounted the story of how the French Renaissance philosopher Montaigne, who certainly did not believe in magic, gave a friend a necklace to help him perform his 'marital duties' on his wedding night. The necklace appeared to have worked, but this illustrated for Muratori the suggestive, not the miraculous.

Van Swieten, with the Empress's support, drew up an edict outlawing all forms of superstitious practice and targeting in particular witchcraft and vampirism but also including all practices which encouraged *Abergläubigkeit*. Van Swieten relied on his Italian contemporary Girolamo Tartarotti, who had long argued that belief in witchcraft was credulous nonsense and that the confessions of witches were worthless as they had been exacted under torture.

In his book *Del Congresso notturno delle Lammie*, which was published in 1749, Tartarotti left open the possibility that alchemy, as practised for example by Paracelsus, was 'real', but he insisted in terms familiar to any Jesuit that the devil and his companions' power had been severely curtailed with Christ's resurrection.[6]

Another significant influence on Van Swieten was the Marchese Scipione Maffei who had travelled widely in Europe, spending time in the Netherlands before Van Swieten departed for Vienna. As a Catholic, it is highly unlikely that he would not have come into contact with Van

Swieten. He took an uncompromising line on all superstitions, including 'erudite magic' such as Paracelsus had practised. In an essay published in 1751, Maffei argued that magic was a 'chimera' and the power of Satan limited since the time of Christ. The resurrection had ended Satan's power over human bodies.

Maria Theresa, like Maffei, expressed a strong criticism of anything associated with magic. The issue of witchcraft could not be allowed to undermine her peoples' confidence. It therefore needed state intervention and the Empress did not shirk from deploying it where necessary. She also moved robustly against vampirism.

Vampirism arguably inspired human fantasy even more than regular witchcraft accusations, since the accused, by definition, were dead. One did not need to apply torture to secure hard evidence; it could be found simply by an examination of a corpse. A community did not need to find a scapegoat or blame one of its own members for the misfortune; the blame rested firmly with the dead.

As witchcraft accusations slowly receded under the onslaught of Theresian measures, cases of vampirism vastly increased. A Spanish monk, Benito Feijóo, sarcastically remarked in 1753 that if the stories about vampires were true then there had been more resurrections of the body in Maria Theresa's lands during her reign than at any time since the death of Christ.

One case infamously claimed the sighting of more than a dozen blood-sucking monsters. In 1755, in the village of Hermersdorf on the Silesian–Moravian border, villagers became obsessed with the idea that the recently deceased Rosa Polakin must be a vampire because several people had testified to weird nightly attacks. The villagers opened her grave and found her body in good condition even though her funeral had taken place several months earlier. There was, the villagers insisted, even blood in her veins. This had to be evidence that she was a vampire, they insisted. The villagers then forced the deceased's family to drag the body out of its grave and burn it. Then, as with witches, the head was removed and displayed on a pike.

When accounts of this barbaric case reached her, the Empress was horrified. Her revulsion was all the more intense on account of the unfortunate theological affinities the myth of vampires had with Catholic doctrine. Both believed in incorruptible bodies. Yet while one saw this as evidence of saintliness, the vampirical credulity described it as proof of evil. Like some medieval saints, the fingernails and hair of vampires continued to grow after their death and their bodies did not decompose. Like saints, vampires seemed to demonstrate a vitality and energy well beyond their earthly demise. Even the blood-sucking seemed to have a parallel in Christianity's rite of Holy Communion which many early modern Christians depicted as a material absorption of Christ's flesh. Vampires appeared in this context to be the negative dark side of a coin whose verso was sanctity.

With Maria Theresa's encouragement, Van Swieten brought the machinery of the state to bear on the cult of vampirism. As with witch-craft, the first duty of the state was to establish an empirical system of investigation. As the majority of accusations of vampirism came from the eastern borderlands of Maria Theresa's empire, in particular the Military Frontier, it seemed best to let the military bring some disci-pline and rigour to the process of investigation.

Van Swieten introduced regulations requiring military doctors to be brought into the cases at the earliest possible moment. Two military physicians were to exhume the body of any person accused of vampirism and to conduct a post-mortem before writing a detailed scientific analysis of the causes of death and the state of the corpse.

Following the compilation of several reports indicating no evidence of any supernatural dimension in the deaths of those accused of vampirism, a Viennese court in 1754 publicly stated that vampirism was a figment of popular imagination. This decision was supported by the Papal Nuncio who expressed Pope Benedict XIV's personal opposition to vampire hunts. But, as with witchcraft, it was often the local bishops who were the most determined to proceed against the phenomenon. Vampirism in remote rural areas was a means of shoring up clerical authority. Yet even this episcopal enthusiasm could not survive the combination of scientific rigour and papal disdain of what Maria Theresa termed these 'outrageous inventions'.

In 1758 legislation was passed attacking not only the myths of witch-craft and vampirism but the entire panoply of superstitious calendars, exorcisms and alchemic practices. By 1766 a further, new law, against the persecution of witches, was passed. With all these measures, the Empress was determined to defend the reputation of the Catholic faith, all too aware that superstition had the potential to put Catholicism in an unflattering light.

The Empress was undoubtedly, like her mentor Van Swieten, a 'Catholic enlightener'. The key to the removal of these abuses was for her, first and foremost, the eradication of the ignorance which kept the belief in vampires and witchcraft alive. Her subjects had to be taught the difference between imagination and reality from an early age. Maria Theresa was resolute in her determination to stamp out the influence of these superstitions. 'The children,' she wrote, 'have been infected from the cradle by these terrible fairytales.'[7]

A twin-track strategy was initiated to deal with the challenge. Firstly, the local clergy and imperial officials were to cooperate to bring about a greater awareness of the natural causes of events. Then, the investigators of any reports of sorcery were legally obliged to consult scientists and experts. It was necessary to establish beyond any reasonable doubt the presence of supernatural magic or demonic worship before any case could proceed.

The application of stricter criteria immediately had an effect. The numbers of accusations declined dramatically and the trials ceased. It is significant that the Theresian laws and their application did not explicitly condemn all magic. Rather, the new rules preferred to dwell on the rigour of investigation before determining whether a particular belief was superstitious. In this way the Empress deliberately appears to have avoided denying explicitly the capacity of Satan to interact with the world. Such Muratorian credentials of balancing faith and reason were exemplary. Moreover, by waging war on superstition, the Empress was removing a stumbling block to progress, especially if the Austrian state was to realize its full economic potential. As long as the population believed such stories and fairytales, they were unable to live and work in a way which could benefit the Austrian state. Yet enlightenment was never to be encouraged at the cost of renouncing the basic tenets of the Catholic faith which included the acknowledgement of the presence of evil.

The Theresian battle against *Abergläubigkeit* is often depicted as the forerunner of the reforms of Joseph II but it would be more accurate to see it rather as an example of the Catholic Enlightenment, emphasizing the intelligibility of the faith.

In this way, Maria Theresa, while sharing the secular Enlightenment's horror of prejudice and superstition, nonetheless rejected a naturalist *Weltanschauung*. Her religious commitments were not deviations from the march of progress but perfectly compatible with the execution of policies designed to banish beliefs which retarded her empire's spiritual and material development.

CHAPTER 49

The Secret World: *Postlogen* and *Geheimziffern*

THAT THE ENLIGHTENMENT WORLD of the eighteenth century never respected for a moment the privacy or secrecy of personal correspondence should come as no surprise. That Maria Theresa's intelligence-collecting operations, both domestic and external, were so sophisticated, however, may come as a jolt to those used to associating the secret police in Austria with the post-revolutionary obsessions of the Austrian chancellor, Metternich.

Yet it was during Maria Theresa's reign that the techniques of the interception of correspondence were perfected. Under previous Habsburg rulers, the Thurn and Taxis family had run an imperial postal service with *cabinets noirs* at critical geographical locations. Prince Kaunitz – aware, like every diplomat, of the importance of such capabilities – expanded this so that by 1755 nearly eighty carriages of mail arrived every month for secret scrutiny in the monarchy's capital.

In fact, here as elsewhere, the Empress was a pioneer.[1] Her imperial authority gave her the right to break all undertakings of postal secrecy in the interests of the state. This was another extension of state power from the individual to the machinery of the administration. Yet such licence could never, then as today, be formally admitted and it was a *sine qua non* of the entire system that such surveillance techniques be shrouded in secrecy at all times.

The postmaster general, Thurn and Taxis, deliberately opted to remain in ignorance of what occurred in his subordinates' bureau so that he could face squarely accusations from other imperial or foreign sources with protestations of ignorance. Such techniques continued and long outlasted the reign of Maria Theresa but she initiated the tradition in central Europe of the ever-watchful eye of the state, long after other countries, notably England and France, had established their own surveillance states. The Theresian variant, while watchful, was rarely as oppressive as it became in central Europe in later centuries.[2]

Domestically, these activities came to the fore when the Empress sought to discourage adultery in the hope that a general, legally imposed restraint ensnaring unfaithful husbands, even from the highest ranks of society, might deter her own husband's predilection for the *Seitensprung* (adulterous affair). Francis Stephen certainly enjoyed the company of handsome women but there is remarkably little evidence to suggest that he had enduring affairs. One of his closest female friends, the widow Beatrice de Ligneville, shared an intimacy entirely confined to written correspondence while the oft-cited Princess Auersperg may also have been mostly just a platonic friendship.

At the heart of Maria Theresa's policies was a conviction that somehow morals had loosened considerably during her reign, compared to that of her father, and that if she did not intervene, an atmosphere of general dissipation would ensue. Yet her formal restrictions were mainly targeted at prostitution which she regarded as the greatest scourge, and reports of an intrusive *Sittenpolizei* have been much exaggerated.[3]

Nevertheless, a small force of freelance spies was recruited to monitor the more outrageous infidelities of the Viennese populace in an attempt to clean up society's morals. There were, by the fifth year of Maria Theresa's reign, more than 16,000 prostitutes working in Vienna, of whom nearly 6,000 were so-called 'high-class ladies' in much demand among aristocrats and foreign diplomats. Increasingly, many of these faced regular interrogation by the authorities and pressure to reveal the identities of their clientele.

The remit of the Imperial Royal Chastity Commission, established by the Empress in 1751, was in theory virtually unlimited. It could break an officer's career and end the promotion chances of anyone in government service. In keeping with Maria Theresa's socially progressive views, rank and status were no defence. Heavy fines were served on scions of some of the greatest families of Vienna, including the Starhembergs and Trautsons. But the penalties for women prostitutes were even more draconian. They risked banishment to the furthermost extremities of the empire or incarceration in a convent for the rest of their lives. As Giacomo Casanova pointed out: 'A legion of vile spies interrogate the girls mercilessly. The Commissioners of Chastity are the tormentors of all pretty girls. The Empress does not seem to practise the sublime virtue of tolerance when it comes to what is termed illegitimate love.'

The Commissioners worked hand in hand with the Vienna police whose presence in the city was greatly expanded under Maria Theresa. In 1752 she approved the establishment of twenty-three new police stations just to work with her 'Chastity Commissioners'. By the end of her reign, the number of police stations in the capital had increased to nearly a hundred, from a modest sixteen at the beginning of her reign.

When it came to external intelligence, the sensitivity of the work created its own dynamics. Central to divining the intentions of foreign agents, ambassadors and statesmen was the interception of their correspondence. Brussels, as we have seen, under the former postmaster of Milan, Rainoldi, was a major hub of interception, allowing all the mail destined for Holland, France and England to be read at leisure by teams of translators and cryptologists.

A *Geheimeziffernkanzlei* (secret code office) had been set up by Maria Theresa's father in the year of her birth 1717 and, under the Empress, this capability was greatly expanded. It was headquartered in Vienna with significant sub-departments in Milan and Brussels. They were so adroit in copying and 'unbuttoning' encoded correspondence that Kaunitz, who ultimately was in receipt of their most important work, felt compelled to urge them to slow down as the sheer weight of deciphered material was leading to information overload: 'all the abundant communication of papers and especially of intercepts produces only confusion and worry', he lamented in a complaint which could have been echoed by many a later spymaster.[4]

The officials who were selected for this work were usually fluent in at least six languages plus their accompanying dialects, establishing a basic standard of linguistic requirement for Austrian servants of the state which would endure until 1918.[5] On account of the political sensitivity of the work, the officials were granted several privileges including early retirement for health reasons. Nearly half of the officials staffing the

Vienna secret cypher office went blind long before the usual retirement age on account of the sheer volume of material they were supposed to get through, involving much work at night in poorly candlelit offices.

The extreme delicacy of the work restricted recruitment to a handful of often interrelated families which tended to bring their own offspring into the service so that the secrets remained 'family secrets'. Often, the information gathered led to some latent frictions becoming more visible, although, as always in such work, the source of the 'enlightenment' could never be admitted.

One of the cases where the interception of a foreigner's correspondence led to serious consequences directly involving the Empress was the example of Lady Mary Coke who, on her second visit to Vienna in the winter of 1771/72, appears to have confided some highly sensitive information about the Empress's finances in a letter to Horace Walpole back in England.

Walpole's father, Robert, as Prime Minister, had often intercepted the correspondence of the Austrian ambassador in London, especially after Count Salm had received instructions from Vienna to make contact with the Tory opposition. The Tories had eagerly accepted evidence provided by the Austrian diplomat that Walpole had taken bribes from the Austrian Ostend East India Company, even though Walpole had made it the priority of his policy towards Austria to have the Ostend Company suppressed and had forbidden Englishmen to invest in the company.

Anything therefore touching the Empress's personal affairs or indeed political views which reached the younger Walpole from Vienna would be deemed 'sensitive'. It was Lady Mary's good fortune to have known the effete Horace Walpole for many years. The Cokes of Holkham were the rival aristocratic family in Norfolk and were close neighbours of the Walpoles at Houghton.

The editor of Lady Coke's journals is rather coy as to the details of what followed but the *Geheimeziffernkanzlei* translated a letter to Horace Walpole from the Englishwoman in which, after admitting that she did not 'answer for the truth of this intelligence', went on to reveal several details of Maria Theresa's monthly private expenditure.

As Lady Mary wrote, 'every anecdote relating to the Empress must I fancy be interesting'. She then went on to describe how every month, the Empress was overdrawn on her personal account of 100,000 Gulden a year. The sum was 'taken each month' but 'by the twentieth of the month' the allowance was 'gone'.[6]

It would be hard to imagine a more delicate matter to be committed to a letter certain to be read by the subject of its contents. Moreover, it implied that Lady Mary had rather overreached herself in her social contacts at court and was developing a taste for harmful gossip. The personal financial affairs of a monarch were then, as today, a state secret whose disclosure merited the severest of sanctions.

The Empress's response was predictable and swift. Nothing was said or explained to the English guest but, within a month of her sending the letter, and its subsequent interception, Lady Mary found herself no longer admitted to the Habsburg court. The love and admiration she had clearly felt for Maria Theresa turned to paranoia and even hatred. Her editor a century later noted: 'an officious foreigner had no business to meddle with the intrigues of court and when the audiences ceased, Lady Mary left Vienna in perfect dudgeon'.[7]

From then on, Lady Mary only referred to Maria Theresa as 'that person' and felt in her subsequent tour of Tuscany that, at every corner, spies were monitoring her activities. The Empress appears, despite her earlier undoubted affection for Lady Mary, to have become convinced that she was at best unreliable and at worst a spy in the service of a hostile country – England had five years earlier been allied to Prussia.

As well as providing useful insights into the personalities of eminent foreigners living in Vienna, the *Geheimeziffernkanzlei* played an important role in assessing foreign state relations with the Ottoman empire. Most mail from northern Europe for Constantinople passed every two weeks through Vienna where the officials of the *Geheimeziffernkanzlei* got to work translating and decrypting anything of interest from London, Paris or Amsterdam.

So professional did the officials become in their work that they soon became a *corps d'élite* in the Theresian apparatus. Eventually, the translation service became, like interpreting, a highly prized skill. Under Maria Theresa and Kaunitz, such interception and intelligence helped to shape the foreign policies of the empire. It did not take long to see from the correspondence heading east that Austria's knowledge of the Orient was significantly superior to that of other parts of western Europe. Improved relations with Constantinople began to become a priority.

CHAPTER 50

Recalibrating Austria's Eastern Flank: Maria Theresa and the Ottomans

AFTER THE BATTLE OF Mohacs in 1526 which had wiped out the flower of the Magyar nobility, the Habsburgs saw their role as the bulwark of Christendom against the onslaught of Islam. The Great Siege of Vienna in 1683, following that of 1529, and Prince Eugene's series of spectacular victories culminating in the storming of Belgrade, only reinforced the dynastic sense of duty. The 'ever-present' Turkish threat was even part of the rationale behind the Pragmatic Sanction. It was the responsibility of a 'powerful central control' to protect German princes from Turkish threats. But, as with France, this particular *Erbfeind* had to be accommodated to see off the threat to the monarchy which came from an altogether different direction, namely Prussia.

For Kaunitz, the diplomatic possibilities of a rapprochement with the Ottoman empire were almost as enticing as better relations with France but Constantinople was probably the least attractive posting in the entire Austrian foreign service. European envoys had no knowledge of Ottoman customs or languages. Unlike other postings, their faith prevented access to large swathes of Ottoman society. They were only permitted to see the Ottoman Sultan twice, once when presenting their credentials and once on introducing their successors.

Interaction with the Grand Viziers was more unpredictable. They often lost their posts and indeed sometimes even their heads. One diplomatic mission setting out from Vienna had to turn back and produce new documentation on being apprised that the original papers of accreditation were no longer valid after a change of office.

In order to ensure that such envoys could make themselves understood, a system of locally employed *Sprachknaben* (lit. language-boys) developed but this proved 'far too costly' and Kaunitz persuaded Maria Theresa to set up an Oriental Academy in Vienna to train a new cadre of translators, dragomen and interpreters. It is hard to imagine that cost was a factor in the decision, although Kaunitz would have known that considerations of cost always played well with the Empress. Rather, the guiding spirit behind the Oriental Academy was partly an ambition to set the entire Austro-Ottoman relationship onto a new footing with a service of highly trained and intelligent diplomats fluent in Oriental languages and customs. Austria was the Ottomans' closest and arguably most important western neighbour. It was therefore an obligation, once harmonious relations were established after the long years of conflict, that Austria send her 'best men' east. Kaunitz set great store by having diplomats who could 'share the Ottoman humour' and not flinch at Ottoman customs.[1]

These were varied and challenging for any European diplomat. Thugut mentioned in one report that, during an all-night negotiation with one Ottoman minister, matters had to be cut short on account of the minister inhaling a huge breath of opium and promptly passing out.

One of the most widespread of Ottoman customs, which the Austrians quickly absorbed, was of course the use of *baksheesh* and bribes. These had to be distributed liberally to the servants of any Ottoman dignitary and Thugut often complained that it cost him 'more than thirty piastres' every time he visited a new vizier. These changed so often that one Austrian resident noted that 'grand viziers change more frequently than the coiffeur of the women of Versailles'.[2]

Though Thugut acquitted himself well and went on to a dazzling career in imperial service, other residents were less fortunate. In 1769 Maria Theresa's envoy, Brognard, found himself recognized in the Islamic quarters gazing at an image of the Prophet held high in a procession. Only the kindness of an Armenian shopkeeper preserved his life.

As Kaunitz made it more and more apparent that he wanted a much closer relationship with the Ottomans, the Austrians were treated with increasing respect. Their Turkish bodyguards, often Albanians, were the finest at the Sultan's disposal. Moreover, in the event of hostilities, the Porte made it clear that, unlike Russian representatives who would be always initially incarcerated in the dreaded 'castle of seven towers', the Austrians could expect to be safely escorted to the frontier.[3]

From the beginning, the Oriental Academy included commercial studies in its curriculum and the Austrians soon became known for their openness to assisting trade between the two countries. For commercial deals the interlocutor on the Turkish side was often one of the so-called *Pfortendolmetscher*, usually of Greek origin. Though often thought of as anti-Austrian, these Greeks helped act as an important intermediary for the Austrians, especially in helping them identify slaves of European descent for whom they had clear instructions from the Empress they were to secure the immediate release.

This could be controversial, but increasingly the manumission of slaves of European or Christian descent became an important part of the Austrian resident staff's 'extra-curricular' activities. The Austrian commitment to emancipating European slaves was borne on Catholic dogma. There were no vast commercial interests at stake here as in other European countries whose colonies provided huge income through slavery. Instead, Austria under Maria Theresa saw itself as the upholder of the 'dignity of man'. If torture and capital punishment were to be abolished for violating these sacred laws, slavery loomed even more beyond the pale. In this way Vienna in the 1770s showed it was more than half a century ahead of other European states.

This Austrian diplomatic consideration for slaves in the Ottoman territories had an interesting counterpoint: while the Austrian resident kept a watchful eye out for European slaves, the Ottoman court and its embassy in Vienna enjoyed the convention of a protective eye over the monarchy's Jewish population. Jews were deemed to have come 'originally' from the east – Ottoman territory.

This strange compact was reflected in how both Vienna and Constantinople hosted each other's embassies. In Constantinople, the Austrians were offered a building in Pera, the European quarter of the city where all the other European embassies were housed. In Vienna, the Austrians gave the Turkish resident a palace in the Jewish quarter, the Leopoldstadt, where the camels and exotic clothing of the Ottoman presence mixed freely with the several hundred Jews who lived in the streets around them. This was considered appropriate as the Ottomans felt they were the 'protecting power' for all peoples of the east.

When Maria Theresa threatened to expel all the Jews of Prague for collaborating with the Prussians and French occupiers, it was the Ottoman resident who felt compelled first to intercede for them, offering them sanctuary in the Ottoman lands. Kaunitz immediately saw a diplomatic quid pro quo and suggested that the order expelling the Prague Jews might be rescinded in return for better treatment of Armenian Christians. Penkler, his envoy in Constantinople, wrote to Vienna saying, 'I see a means to help these people if the Jews of Bohemia are pardoned in the name of Her Royal Majesty.'[4] In the end, as we have seen, Maria Theresa's own clemency, encouraged by the advice of her Bohemian ministers, notably Count Kinsky, together with pressure from London, spared the Jews all the trauma of prolonged persecution and the expulsion order was reversed.[5]

The Oriental Academy turned out, in addition to future dragomen and residents, a cadre of consuls who, under Maria Theresa, began to expand throughout the Levant. By the end of her reign, there were more than a hundred of these consulates spread across the Balkans and the Ottoman territories. They reported to Constantinople from where the resident's carefully edited and summarized dispatches were sent by courier directly to Kaunitz.[6]

Kaunitz's negotiations with the Ottomans introduced him to ever more arcane levels of diplomacy. His earliest instructions to Thugut, the resident, were for the Austrian to secure the Porte's recognition of Francis Stephen's title to the throne of the Holy Roman Empire but this proved rather more difficult than even Kaunitz could have imagined. The main sticking point arose from Francis Stephen enjoying, as a result of his Lorraine heritage, the title of 'King of Jerusalem', a city of course well established in the eighteenth century as part of the Ottoman empire. How could Austrian diplomacy resolve this obviously blatant infringement of Ottoman sovereignty?

In the end, Vienna offered the Sultan a careful compromise, worthy of the theological debates of the Catholic Enlightenment. Kaunitz and Thugut advanced the idea of a distinction between the temporal and the symbolic Jerusalem, the former obviously being part of the Sultan's prerogatives while the latter was applied to Francis Stephen. Both sides could feel that their *amour propre* had been respected and this eventually satisfied Constantinople.

A no less thorny issue arose when Kaunitz sought to enshrine the agreement with the phrase 'permanent and eternal'. 'Eternal', it was pointed out by the Porte, was a religious term and therefore had no place in any secular treaty. The word was promptly struck out by Thugut and replaced with another formula more acceptable to the Turks.

While the *Grand Renversement* has come down to us as Kaunitz's greatest achievement, the study of Austro-Ottoman relations during the reign of Maria Theresa offers ample evidence of his diplomatic skill and, above all, his commitment to saving the monarchy all unnecessary expenditure. When Russia began to make overtures towards Prussia, Kaunitz immediately saw a way of breaking with the centuries-old tradition of Habsburg–Ottoman enmity and – in the interests of the state – making a play for some kind of agreement. When the European chancelleries got wind of what was afoot, they were aghast. Most had been expecting hostilities between the two empires. It was characteristic of Kaunitz's sophisticated mindset that – aware, as he was, that such a treaty could arouse opposition in Austrian and especially Russian circles – he convinced the Ottomans to keep the treaty a state secret so that no-one could accuse either party of bluffing. In this way, a secret treaty was far more useful than a public one.

In another dazzling stratagem, Kaunitz hastened Ottoman compliance by hinting that Russia might be seeking an alliance with Vienna. What were the advantages of all these diplomatic chess moves on the eastern flank of Maria Theresa's domains? The most tangible was that the armies of Austria need no longer be marched across half of Europe from the Austrian Netherlands to Croatia to fortify the Military Frontier. If the Ottomans pledged peace, then the Frontier could be safely left to its own devices and even gradually wound down. This saved the empire considerable amounts of money and left its forces free to deal with Prussia, undistracted by any threats from the east.

Eventually, this carefully erected equilibrium would be disastrously upset by Joseph when he decided in 1788 to go to war with Russia against the Ottomans in the last years of his reign. The war was yet another flashpoint undermining his mother's empire and fortunately for Austria it fizzled out after Joseph's death.

By then, Kaunitz was still in office but no longer in power. Yet his earlier achievement had been remarkable. While Maria Theresa reigned, the Austro-Ottoman rapprochement reflected that it had become accepted that states fought wars against each other for geopolitical reasons rather than on religious grounds. Although it did not long survive her demise, Theresian policy must be given some credit for transforming old enmities into new possibilities.

Not only was an Empress prepared to be painted by Liotard in Turkish costume, she agreed with Kaunitz that 'when the self-preservation of the state was at risk, differences of religion cannot prevail'. For his part, Kaunitz was nothing if not adroit at his messaging. He instructed Thugut to use the word 'concert' rather than 'alliance' in describing the agreement with Turkey. He also urged the Empress to remember that it was saving the monarchy more than 34 million Gulden a year in military expenditure.

When Maria Theresa had come to the throne she had inherited advisers for whom the only response to events on her eastern flank was 'What would Prince Eugene have done?', a question whose useless response more often than not was 'We must act like Prince Eugene'. Kaunitz was not the great Prince of Savoy but he transformed relations between the empire and the Porte and showed, in his diplomatic skill, how the interests of a state led by a Catholic sovereign committed to the defence of Christendom could happily coexist with an Islamic empire once dedicated to that state's destruction.

Conclusion: The Enlightenment Empress

THE HAPPY STATE OF Austro-Ottoman relations showed the Empress's practical and pragmatic approach to her statecraft. It was an approach which demonstrated her ability to detach herself from many of the imperatives of her confessional obligations. Yet the moral dimension of her values and policies was rarely far from the forefront of her decision-making. Unsurprisingly, this has posed challenges for the dispassionate biographer, working in a more secular age, less comfortable with the Empress's spirituality. As Derek Beales has pointed out, major difficulties stand in the way of her acceptance as an Enlightenment ruler by anglophone historiography precisely because of her Catholicism.[1]

Yet, as this book has consistently argued, it is this spirituality which demands perhaps the most forensic of examination in the context of the wider currents of prevailing Catholic dogma which informed so much of Maria Theresa's daily thinking. Her intervention on behalf of European slaves; her commitment to the material, spiritual and educational improvement of her subjects; her reluctance to aggrandize her territories (in contrast to her son Joseph), especially with regard to Bavaria and Poland – all these traits were not conceived solely with the aim of strengthening her imperium at a time of crisis. Underpinning everything was a faith which offered a route-map through life's challenges as well as, in extremis, that refuge 'where nothing could harm her'.

As a prized pupil of the Jesuits, she did not have to meditate her way through all fifty pages of Ignatian spiritual exercises to be open to many of the ideas contained therein. She also certainly knew well the texts of Erasmus, in particular his humanist counterargument to Machiavelli's cynical *The Prince.* When, in 1516, Erasmus composed *The Education of a Christian Prince*, he emphasized the need for a sovereign to be, above all, virtuous and loved, rather than calculating and feared, as Machiavelli had recommended. This was a lesson Maria Theresa took to heart from an early age but she also fully embraced Erasmus's belief in education as a means of self-improvement, and the need for 'moderation, foresight and a zeal for the common good'. Such qualities deeply invested her thinking.[2]

Her letters to Marie Antoinette suggest that she was completely at ease with this Erasmian system of values and that, moreover, they were shared by Van Swieten, Kaunitz, Tarouca and Haugwitz, all of whom were practising Catholics.

In many ways, for all her much-cited absence of intellect, Maria Theresa's mind was daily reconciling faith and reason. In this sense, she was a standard-bearer of an unhesitatingly Catholic Enlightenment, a term once considered a contradiction in terms but now enjoying more dispassionate evaluation.

If these pages prove anything, it is that she far exceeded in achievements, legacy and, above all, virtue, all the other monarchs of the eighteenth century. One need only compare the state of Austria on Maria Theresa's death with that of Prussia and Russia at the time of the demise of their respective contemporary sovereigns to see that she left her responsibilities in far better shape than when she inherited them. The encouragement of free trade, the commercial opening of the Orient, the development of the great multi-confessional port of Trieste, the abolition of the *Robot* and serfdom, the establishment of a social contract – these were all radical progressive policies which she pursued often in the teeth of opposition from her 'enlightened' son Joseph. It was she, not her son, who created the institutional framework for a multi-confessional, polyethnic, cosmopolitan merchant class. It was the Great Empress who permitted formal communal entities to be established in Trieste, first by Jews, then by the Greek Orthodox and the Armenian Uniates. So much for a monarch famous for her negative views of non-Catholics.

For all her well-publicized disdain for abstract mental gymnastics, she was, paradoxically, intuitively at ease in an intellectual world which the Roman moralists had once inhabited. Her belief that 'it is always rational to be moral' came straight from Cicero. In this way she saw far beyond the writings and superficial polemics of Voltaire and his fellow *philosophes*. In her policies towards Judaism and Protestantism she was capable of that quality the ancient world prized above all: *sophrosyne/ σωφροσυνή* (knowing when to stop; moderation).

In Maria Theresa's world, the paradigms of Adam Smith's theories of supply and demand could coexist happily with the religious bestseller of the time, a now largely forgotten tract by Alphonsus of Liguori called in English 'The Glories of Mary' which, translated into eighty languages when it appeared in 1750, offered a hyperbolic veneration of the Mother of Christ certainly understood by Maria Theresa.[3]

Liguori's text also preached the validity of a 'personal encounter' with Christ where emotions and desires were not sealed off during prayers but opened up. It was Liguori's legacy to make such profound truths accessible to ordinary, uneducated people. Such practical anthropology chimed often with Maria Theresa's own spirituality which, like Alphonsus's, demanded gentleness in all things – *Milde und Munifizenz* – even though her emotions sometimes overshadowed such ideals.

Maria Theresa nearly always eschewed the 'hard-hearted' clinical reforming zeal of the secular Enlightenment, personified in her son Joseph. Shrewd contemporary observers, like the musicologist Charles Burney, saw these differences in governance between mother and son with stark clarity: 'Maria Theresa's piety has been thought to border on bigotry,' he ventured in an essay, 'but if we judge its effects by the tranquillity, happiness and affection of her subjects with the turbulence, discontent and detestation of her unprincipled, philosophical and disorganizing successor, we can suppose that too much religion is less mischievous than too little'.[4]

Such piety demanded empathy with the plight of the less fortunate. As Lady Mary Coke in Vienna noticed, 'unlike England', the old, poor and unwell were not shunned. 'Here age is particularly respected and the sick and unhappy always have friends. In England the sick, the unhappy and the old are always neglected.'[5] Perhaps this was what Auden meant when he wrote in one of his later poems, affectionately contrasting Catholic Austria with England: 'No Whig landlord, the landscape vaunts, / Ever empired on Austrian ground.'[6]

The Empress never shared that elitist indifference to the suffering of the underprivileged which was a hallmark of other courts. The accusation that she never challenged the 'plight of the common man', whatever that might be, or the existing hierarchy of social structures has been taken to suggest that she was indifferent to the fate of the poor. Yet time and time again, in countless acts of personal charity and generosity, she demonstrated a fortiori that she was informed by a deep compassion and humanity which, even in her hardest admonitions and criticisms of her family, was never obscured.

This was in stark contrast to the great *philosophes* of her time who, for all their 'impeccable' Enlightenment credentials, hated and feared *das Volk*. For them, the people were always a mob marked by ignorance, anarchy and chaos. For Voltaire, the 'lower orders' were 'always composed of brutes'. For Kant, 'the people consist of idiots', while even Schiller wrote that the 'lower classes only seek animal satisfactions'.[7] In all the acreage of the Empress's writings, one looks in vain for a single disparaging comment about the general behaviour of the poorer mass of her subjects. Quite the opposite, as Lady Mary Coke acknowledged, 'the common people are certainly better than in England; crimes are less frequent, and the Empress is so compassionate that she hates to see anyone put to death'.

To acknowledge these qualities is not a kind of outworn, misplaced male chivalry. By far the finest and most glowing portrait of Maria Theresa was penned by a woman, Lady Mary Coke, divorced scion of the great Leicester family and not known generally for her charitable descriptions of sovereigns. Yet Maria Theresa made a great impression on her even while keeping her distance from the stranger at her court.

Lady Mary, before her fall from grace, showed in the following description that she was second to none in recording a judicious admiration of the Great Empress. 'She is about my height and though very fat is not encumbered by it . . . until she had the smallpox she was extremely handsome but she holds herself well and her air is the most noble I ever saw', opined the Englishwoman from a distance, who also noticed that the Empress possessed 'more spirit and sense in her eyes than I ever saw'.[8]

These externals were just the beginning for Lady Coke. As she gradually came to know the Empress, she fell under her spell: 'I believe there never existed her equal, and her speaking is a kind of witchcraft.' One exchange revealed to the English lady that Maria Theresa was, in at least one respect, a true pupil of the Jesuits: her almost pathological aversion to any pride. In the Ignatian spiritual exercises with which she was brought up, the Empress would have encountered the meditation which demanded a complete renunciation of pride, the sin 'from which so many other sins arose'. When Lady Mary commended a book which praised the Empress, Maria Theresa answered: 'I can never read such things. I look upon praise rather as a reproach which puts me in mind of what one ought to be rather than what one is.'[9]

For Lady Mary, 'beauty, sense and manner' were in 'so great a portion' in the imperial family that any visiting princess must have felt immediately at a disadvantage. Although the English lady would later, as we have seen, 'fall out' with the Empress, sensing, so she thought, her spies and a claustrophobic imperial surveillance as she crossed Europe, these comments were never revised. For this woman, at least, the Empress remained, despite their personal differences, the apogee of the greatest human and regal qualities.

Such personal attributes alone do not constitute greatness, although they go a long way to demonstrate that the Great Empress was far from being just an exceptional 'normal' woman. It is when we come to the political and policy achievements of her forty-year reign that we see a statesmanship far superior to that of any other contemporary European monarch or minister.

Again, the moral dimension informed by Maria Theresa's spirituality was always paramount – hence the endless agonizing over the partition of Poland, hence the carefully concealed policy of defusing the Austro-Prussian tensions over Bavaria. Her virtues of prudence, justice, moderation and courage eventually came to define her politics and contrasted sharply with the lives of many of her contemporaries. But such a disciple of Van Swieten and Muratori could never have been capable of a total dismissal of the ideas in ferment all around her.

If she roundly criticized the sarcasm and 'wit' fashionable among some intellectuals of the time – keen, as intellectuals always are, to sharpen their verbal swords on what they see as outdated dogma or misguided clericalism – Maria Theresa countered them not with academic posturing but the simple verities of her faith. She may not have, in the eyes of Marxists, sought to upend the social system of her reign, but she granted everyone, however exalted or lowly, with whom she came into contact the same consistent kindness and compassion. The words *Deus caritas est* might have been engraved on the Empress's heart. It was this sincerity, born of innermost conviction, which so seduced those who came into contact with her, from Prussian diplomats and English ladies to Tyrolean peasants and Triestine merchants.

The label of 'modern' has rarely been applied to Maria Theresa, yet modern central Europe owes nearly all its institutions to her. But the Theresian legacy is not limited just to central Europe. The shape of the entire continent after the end of the Cold War has come more and more to resemble the Theresian decades of the eighteenth century: a detached Britain, facing dislocation in Scotland and Ireland, an interfering Russia and a temporarily emasculated but unpredictable Berlin. Even the historic lands of Poland are again the subject of potential 'partition', with the former Austrian province of Galicia-Lodomeria and the city of Lemberg (Lviv) a flagship of western values embraced by an insurgent Ukraine whose eastern territories are violently contested. Above all, Austria retains a separate and independent identity from Germany, confirming the 'German dualism' which was the despair of German nationalists in the early twentieth century, but owes its enduring survival first and foremost to the wars Austria fought against Prussia throughout Maria Theresa's reign.

When we survey the legacy of the Great Empress, it is impossible not to be impressed by that combination of vigour and insight which accompanied most of her reign. It left Austria, arguably alone among the great continental powers, in a state whereby it could not only withstand the tempest of revolution which followed less than a decade after Maria Theresa's death but emerge ultimately triumphant, with its future assured for another century.

Such a record was arguably only possible after the long decades of Theresian reform but, as we have seen time and again, both faith and reason played key parts in strengthening Maria Theresa's empire. When discussing her faith, as a later theologian once wrote, it is important to understand 'what we mean by religion'.[10]

Luckily, Maria Theresa's military reforms furnish us with precisely that. Her own thinking is perfectly expressed in the 1769 *Reglement für die Sämmentlich-Kaiserlich Königliche Infanterie*: 'Religion is something you should never speak about. Rather it is something you should strive to live by. Upon pain of severe and unfailing punishment we forbid any behaviour which may create ill-feeling between those of different faiths.'[11]

Just as there were multiple roads to salvation for Maria Theresa, the Empress also clearly believed that there were many routes to progress and that far from being mutually exclusive, Catholicism and the Enlightenment often complemented each other.

To the plethora of terms which have emerged in recent years concerning the Enlightenment – 'radical Enlightenment', 'secular Enlightenment', 'Jewish Enlightenment', to name but a few – the reader will, I hope, having absorbed this study, tolerate the validity of a new, additional term: 'Theresian Enlightenment'. The phrase has been scrupulously avoided by historians, accustomed to asserting that 'we do not think of Vienna as the place where we first look for the Enlightenment'.[12] Yet this study has, it is to be hoped, shown that it is precisely Theresian Vienna which incubated many of the ideas and freedoms which we associate with the Enlightenment, and that arguably nowhere in continental Europe was reasoning exploited with such vigour to advance the cause of a state's progress, including degrees of religious tolerance unknown even in Whiggish England.[13]

Rousset de Missy was one of the more inspired of Maria Theresa's spymasters and the Grand Master of the Dutch Masonic lodge *La Bien Aimée*.[14] He was not a Catholic but he was the most loyal and patriotic of Maria Theresa's agents. Under the Empress, there was no contradiction in such circumstances, and it would be Joseph who developed the rift which opened in subsequent years between the lodges and the state.

The Vatican had moved swiftly in 1738 to denounce Freemasonry. But in Vienna, Maria Theresa, while remaining a devout Catholic, zealously guarded her prerogatives from Vatican interference. In this sense, she personified a Catholic Enlightenment which was sceptical of the papacy's pretensions to temporal power but nonetheless saw the prospect of temporal progress firmly within the bounds of divine providence and revelatory tradition. Her reign illustrates thus a paradox which challenges directly those who continue to see the defining feature of the Enlightenment as a sharp criticism of religion concomitant with a commitment to an exclusively secular enterprise.

Yet the earlier generation of great minds even in the Protestant countries of Europe who were contemporary of or succeeded Galileo – Kepler, Descartes, Barrow, Leibniz, Gilbert, Boyle and Newton – were all deeply and genuinely religious thinkers. These pioneers of the new cosmology based their search into nature on the mystic conviction that there must exist laws behind confusing phenomena. The aspiration to demonstrate that the universe ran like a piece of clockwork was itself initially a religious inspiration.[15] Although this Pythagorean unity did not last very long and a progressive estrangement between faith and reason reasserted itself, there were many pockets of civilized Europe where both coexisted. Atheists during the reign of Maria Theresa were certainly the rare exceptions among her advisers.

Nothing illustrates this paradox more vividly perhaps than the great Mozart *Singspiel*, *Die Zauberflöte*. The work, as noted earlier, exemplifies the Theresian Enlightenment with its combination of religious and Masonic references: the depiction of good and evil residing in the same psyche and soul, and the forces of light's triumphant apotheosis.

Maria Theresa's reign thus combined what have become deeply unfashionable traits with a march of scientific, social and political progress unprecedented in any continental country during the same period. Her reign personified an era where theology and physics had not parted company and still had much to say to each other, even if both sides, as the next century progressed, would become increasingly bored with each other. This tragic divergence, which has led to consequences all too familiar to us from similar, more recent events, still had yet to be proclaimed when the Great Empress died in 1780. By then, as has been noted by some recent Habsburg historians, 'the Habsburg Monarchy had become the locus of the boldest and most ambitious innovations in Europe'.[16]

Timeline of Events

1717	Maria Theresa born (13 May), eldest daughter of Emperor Charles VI and Elisabeth-Christine of Brunswick-Wolfenbüttel
	Foundation of the Grand Lodge of Westminster (Grand Lodge of England)
1719	Charles VI grants status of Free Port to Trieste
1736	Married Francis Stephen, Prince of Lorraine and Grand Duke of Tuscany
1740	Death of Charles VI (20 October)
	Frederick II of Prussia invades Silesia (December)
1741	Defeat of Austrian army at Mollwitz (April)
	Maria Theresa crowned Queen of Hungary
	Elector Charles Albert of Bavaria, supported by France, invades Austria
	Fall of Prague: Charles Albert crowned King of Bohemia
1742	Charles Albert crowned Emperor Charles VII in Frankfurt
	Khevenhueller occupies Munich and later recaptures Prague
	Treaty of Breslau brings armistice but Prussia holds on to most of Silesia
1743	Maria Theresa is crowned Queen of Bohemia
1744	Frederick invades again, seizing Prague
	Maria Theresa orders expulsion of Prague's Jews following reports of collaboration with the Prussian occupiers and other acts of treason
1745	Death of Emperor Charles VII

Francis Stephen crowned at Frankfurt as Holy Roman Emperor Francis I

Treaty of Dresden ends second war for Silesia

Gerard van Swieten appointed Maria Theresa's personal physician

1746   Friedrich Wilhelm Haugwitz establishes *Directorium* to govern Habsburg lands

1747   Maria Theresa approves first Patent of Toleration of Jews residing in Trieste, confirming their right to a public synagogue and school

1748   Maria Theresa permits return of the Jews to Prague

Treaty of Aix-la-Chapelle ends War of Austrian Succession

1749–56 Haugwitz domestic policy reforms progressed

1753   Wenzel Kaunitz-Rietburg becomes Austrian Chancellor

1756   *Grand Renversement des Alliances*: Austria allied to France

Seven Years War opens with Frederick of Prussia invading Saxony

1757   Crushing defeat of Frederick by Daun at Kolin. Hadik occupies Berlin

1758   Destruction of Frederick's forces at Hochkirch

1759   Prussian army annihilated at Kunersdorf

1760   Frederick loses another army at Torgau

1762   Death of Empress Elizabeth of Russia breaks coalition against Prussia

1763   Peace of Hubertusburg ends Seven Years War

1765   Death of Francis Stephen. Maria Theresa's son becomes co-regent Joseph II

1768   Promulgation of Theresian Legal Code (*Nemesis Theresiana*)

1770   Marriage of Maria Theresa's daughter Maria Antonia (Marie Antoinette) to the Dauphin of France

1772   First Partition of Poland: Austria establishes Kingdom of Galicia-Lodomeria

1773   Pope Clement XIV issues Papal Brief *Dominus ac redemptor* suppressing the Society of Jesus (Jesuits)

1774–80 Educational, judicial, economic and public health reforms

1778–9 War of Bavarian Succession

1780   Death of Maria Theresa (29 November)

MARIA THERESA = Francis Stephen of Lorraine
1717–80   1708–65

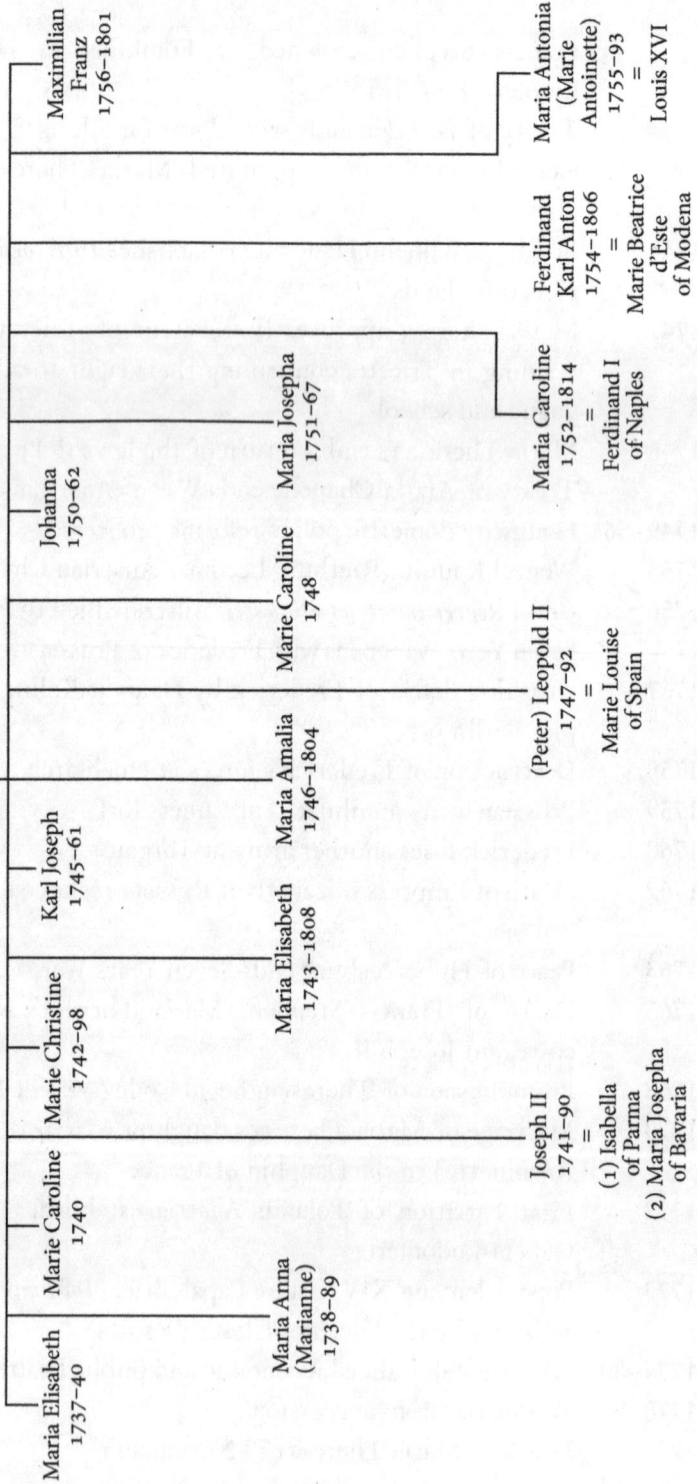

Maria Elisabeth
1737–40

Marie Caroline
1740

Maria Anna (Marianne)
1738–89

Joseph II
1741–90
=
(1) Isabella of Parma
(2) Maria Josepha of Bavaria

Marie Christine
1742–98

Karl Joseph
1745–61

Maria Elisabeth
1743–1808

Maria Amalia
1746–1804

(Peter) Leopold II
1747–92
=
Marie Louise of Spain

Marie Caroline
1748

Johanna
1750–62

Maria Josepha
1751–67

Maria Caroline
1752–1814
=
Ferdinand I of Naples

Ferdinand Karl Anton
1754–1806
=
Marie Beatrice d'Este of Modena

Maximilian Franz
1756–1801

Maria Antonia (Marie Antoinette)
1755–93
=
Louis XVI

Endnotes

INTRODUCTION

1. 'Friedrich der Zweite, den die Deutschen nennen der Grosse' was how Barbara Coudenhove-Kalergi recalled her father referring to him. Barbara Coudenhove-Kalergi to author, 27 May 2023.
2. Hugo v. Hofmannsthal, quoted in Walter Koschatzky (ed.), *Maria Theresia und ihre Zeit* (Vienna 1980), p. 16.
3. Carl Hinrichs (ed.), *Friedrich der Grosse und Maria Theresia: Diplomatische Berichte von Otto Graf Podewils, königl. Preuss. Gesandter am oesterreichischen Hof in Wien* (Berlin 1937), p. 48 ff.
4. For Thugut, see Karl A. Roider, *Baron Thugut and Austria's Response to the French Revolution* (Princeton 1987).
5. A symptom of this legacy is the Viennese dialect which, as the Viennese proudly, and accurately, boast, can be learnt by nearly every immigrant – save the Germans. 'Die einzige Zuwanderer, die nie unsere Sprache lernen, können san di Deitschen'. The late Dr Raimund Kerbl to author, 7 May 2023.
6. Heinrich Ritter v. Srbik, *Gestalten und Ereignisse aus Oesterreichs deutscher Vergangenheit* (Leipzig 1942).
7. Srbik, *Deutsche Einheit* (Munich 1935), pp. 110–31, express these arguments most coherently.
8. This is not the place to trace the development of Freemasonry from its eighteenth-century origins to its nineteenth- and twentieth-century variations, some of which were markedly anti-clerical. The sharper distinctions of a later age were largely absent during Maria Theresa's lifetime. The mid-eighteenth century would have probably found the Vatican's latest (2023) reaffirmation of the incompatibility of Freemasonry and Catholicism surprising.
9. See *Maria Teresa e Trieste* (Udine 2018), essay by Francesca Pitacco, pp. 78–100.
10. Koschatzky (ed.), *Maria Theresia und ihre Zeit*, p. 9.
11. See R.J.W. Evans, 'Josephinism, "Austrianess" and the Revolution of 1848', in *The Austrian Enlightenment and its Aftermath*, ed. Ritchie Robertson and Edward Timms (Edinburgh 2004), p. 145.

CHAPTER 1: THE MAY CHILD

1. The version here as used in the Piaristenkirche, Vienna VIII, 1995.
2. Germanized Anglo-Indian term meaning a native nurse.

3. See William Coxe, *History of the House of Austria*, vol. 3 (London 1888), p. 83.
4. Ibid.
5. Barrister and Habsburg devotee Michael Keane to author, 6 November 1990.
6. Students of linguistics could profitably devote some study as to why French and Italian words continue to prevail in Austrian German while Viennese dialect remains even in the digital age still mostly impervious to Spanish and English. See Reinhold Gayer, *No Kangaroos in Austria* (Salzburg 2014) and Hans Georg Beyr, *Die oesterreichische Provokation: Ein Mahnruf für Deutsche* (Frankfurt 1973).
7. Ludwig Jedlicka (ed.), *Maria Theresia in ihren Briefen und Staatsschriften* (Vienna 1955). See also Otto Krack (ed.), *Briefe einer Kaiserin: Maria Theresia an ihre Kinder und Freunde* (Berlin 1910).
8. Sir Thomas Robinson Corr. and papers, British Library MS 22529/23780.
9. Alvise Pisani, Archivio di Stato Venezia (Pisani dispattti 3/5).
10. Malcolm Davis, *The Masonic Muse: Men, Manners and Songs Associated with Dutch Freemasonry* (Utrecht 1995). Modern Freemasonry dates its formal foundation back to the year of Maria Theresa's birth, 1717, and, by happy coincidence, also two years before Free Port status was conferred on Trieste.
11. See Robinson MS 22529/23780.
12. According to the French ambassador, Francis Stephen put down his pen three times before signing. Quoted in exh. cat, *Maria Theresia und ihre Zeit* (Vienna 1980), Kat. 03.09. Also quoted in Alfred v. Arneth, *Johann Christoph Bartenstein und seine Zeit*, in *Archiv für österreichische Geschichte*, vol. 46 (Vienna 1871), pp. 51–2. See also Friedrich Walter, *Männer um Maria Theresia* (Vienna 1951), p. 19. Bartenstein's 'Keine Abtretung, keine Erzherzogin!' before the 'Offizielle Werbung' of 31 January 1736 is noted in Kat. 03.09 by Dr Selma Krasa-Florian.

CHAPTER 2: THE STRUGGLE FOR THE INHERITANCE

1. See Alex Randa, *Oestereich in Übersee* (Vienna 1966).
2. There are more references to the Ostend Company in the Hansard reports of Parliament in the years leading up to Maria Theresa's accession than of any other factor of Austrian politics. See Hansard 1738–40.
3. Cardinal Fleury, *Mémoires et Documents*, vol. 2 (Paris 1920), p. 46. Quoted in the exh. cat. *Maria Theresia* (Vienna 1930), p. 165.
4. Lord Macaulay, *Essays, Biographies &c*, vol. VIII (London 1897), p. 62.
5. Haus-, Hof- und Staatsarchiv (HHStA), Allgemeine Urkundenreihe (1742 Juli 28).
6. Jedlicka (ed.), *Maria Theresia in ihren Briefen und Staatsschriften*, p. 25.
7. Christopher Duffy, *The Army of Maria Theresa* (London 1977), p. 157.
8. Chancellor Schuschnigg in 1937. See Richard Bassett, *Playing for Time: Guido Schmidt and the Struggle to Save Austria from the Nazis* (London 2022), Chapter 7.
9. The 'Spanish Roads', a formidable sixteenth-century trading route, linked the Spanish Duchy of Milan with the Spanish Netherlands.
10. HHStA, Allgemeineine Urkundenreihe (1742).
11. See Arneth, *Johann Christoph Bartenstein*, pp. 53–4.
12. Quoted in Jedlicka (ed.), *Maria Theresia in ihren Briefen und Staatsschriften*, p. 26.
13. 'Titles can be bought or inherited. Nobility must be earnt': seventeenth-century Hungarian proverb, quoted in Michael O'Sullivan, *Patrick Leigh Fermor: Noble Encounters between Budapest and Transylvania* (Budapest 2018), p. viii.
14. Bratislava (Pozsony in Hungarian).

CHAPTER 3: THE HUNGARIAN CONCORDAT

1. Robinson to Lord Harrington, 28 June 1741. Robinson MS 22529/23780. Also quoted in Coxe, *History of the House of Austria*, vol. 3, p. 268.
2. Ibid.
3. See Krack (ed.), *Briefe einer Kaiserin*, Briefwechsel Maria Theresia mit Franz Ulrich Fuerst Kinsky. Also Alfred von Arneth, *Briefe der Kaiserin an ihre Kinder und Freunde* (Vienna 1881), vol. 1.
4. Robinson MS 22529.
5. Original in Latin: Papier, Kanzleischreiber 1 Folio Wien, HHStA, Ungarische Akten F. 427. Quoted in German in Alfred von Arneth, *Geschichte Maria Theresias*, vol. 4 (Vienna 1868), pp. 85–91.
6. Note the sharp number of explosive consonants in the original.
7. See National Archives of Hungary, Magyar Nemzeti Leveltar: Batthyany papers 46/33/91.
8. *Lieber und getreuer Khevenhueller*, 1741, in Jedlicka (ed.), *Maria Theresia in ihren Briefen und Staatsschriften*.

CHAPTER 4: THE TURNING OF THE TIDE

1. Not to be confused with his kinsman, also named Trenck, who found a home in the Prussian service and whose memoirs were widely read. See Philip Murray (ed.), *The Strange Adventures of Baron Trenck* (London 1927).
2. Arneth, *Briefe der Kaiserin an ihre Kinder und Freunde*, vol. 1, p. 414.
3. Otto Christoph v. Podewils, *Diplomatische Berichte*, ed. Carl Hinrichs (Berlin 1937), p. 36 ff.
4. See *In Praise of Her Most Serene Majesty Maria Theresa upon the Happy Success of Her Arms* (Antwerp 1742).
5. Quoted in Coxe, *History of the House of Austria*, vol. 3, p. 283.
6. Ibid.
7. A much-celebrated event: the last British monarch to lead an army in battle and distinguish himself in a brief cavalry charge. See Maj. Gen. Robin Carnegie, 'Dettingen and British Cavalry' (unpublished manuscript, Ridge, Wiltshire, 2005).
8. The reader may notice that the language is almost identical to that used by Vladimir Putin to justify his invasion of Ukraine in 2022.
9. See Duffy, *The Army of Maria Theresa*, p. 158 ff.
10. Quoted in Coxe, *History of the House of Austria*, vol. 3, p. 306.
11. Duffy, *The Army of Maria Theresa*, p. 159.
12. Ibid.

CHAPTER 5: THE PRUSSIAN RECOVERY

1. See Richard Bassett, *For God and Kaiser: The Imperial Austrian Army 1619–1918* (London 2015), p. 104.
2. Duffy, *The Army of Maria Theresa*, p. 160.
3. Ibid., p. 162.
4. Numbers of Jews in Prague had fallen since the 'Golden Age' of seventeenth-century Prague but in 1745 they comprised nearly a third of the population, considerably more than Vienna.

5. See Aubrey Newman, 'The Expulsion of the Jews from Prague in 1745 and British Foreign Policy', *Transactions & Miscellanies* (Jewish Historical Society of England), vol. 22 (1968–9), p. 30.

CHAPTER 6: THE AGE OF REFORM I: THE NEW MEN

1. Th. G. von Karajan, *Maria Theresia und Graf Sylva-Tarouca* (Vienna 1859) and Krack (ed.), *Briefe einer Kaiserin*.
2. Karajan, *Maria Theresia und Graf Sylva-Tarouca*, p. 28.
3. Ibid.
4. For a recent description of Tarouca's physical appearance, see Hanne Egghardt, *Maria Theresias Männer* (Vienna 2015), pp. 71–6.
5. Ibid, p. 72.
6. Rudolf Graf Khevenhueller-Metsch, *Aus der Zeit Maria Theresias. Tagebuch des Fürsten Johann Josef Khevenhüller-Metsch*, vol. 3 (Vienna 1907–25), pp. 46–59.
7. Letter 32, 17 September 1766, quoted in Karajan, *Maria Theresia und Graf Sylva-Tarouca*, p. 29.
8. Karajan, *Maria Theresia und Graf Sylva-Tarouca*, p. 51.
9. Ibid., p. 57.
10. Ibid.
11. Wandruszka, quoted in Koschatzky (ed.), *Maria Theresia und ihre Zeit*, p. 45.
12. Ibid.
13. Khevenhueller-Metsch, *Aus der Zeit Maria Theresias*, vol. 1, p. 39.
14. See Haugwitz in Walter, *Männer um Maria Theresia*, p. 24. Also Egghardt, *Maria Theresias Männer*, p. 161.
15. MT Politisches Testament 1750/51, 1755/56.
16. Johann Heinrich Gottlob Justi, *Beweis der Universalmonarchie* (Theresianum inaugural lecture, Vienna 1747).
17. 'A complete separation of the Justice workings from the public and political activities of the Länder'. See Werner Ogris, 'Staats- und Rechtsreformen', in Koschatzky (ed.), *Maria Theresia und ihre Zeit*, pp. 59–64.
18. Van Swieten letters, quoted in August Fournier's *Gerhard van Swieten als Censor*, in *Sitzungsberichte der Philosophisch-Historischen Classe der Kaiserlichen Akademie der Wissenschaften*, vol. LXXXIV (Vienna 1877).
19. G. Lessing, quoted by Franz Eybl in *Aufgeklärte Sozietäten, Literatur und Wissenschaft in Mittleuropa* (De Gruyter 2019).
20. Egghardt, *Maria Theresias Männer*, p. 100.
21. See Evelyn Waugh, *Edmund Campion S.J.* (London 1935); Frank T. Brechka, *Gerard van Swieten and his World, 1700–1772* (The Hague 1970).
22. As Owen Chadwick noted in his brilliant series of lectures, *The Secularization of the European Mind in the Nineteenth Century* (Edinburgh 1973), philosophers 'did not ask why belief arose but whether belief was true', ignoring the fact that religion was 'one of the foundations of social and moral life between 1650 and 1750'.
23. John Morley, *Voltaire* (London 1886), p. 69 ff.
24. See Chadwick, *The Secularization of the European Mind*, p. 29.
25. Quoted in Edward Crankshaw, *Maria Theresa* (London 1969), p. 202.
26. This letter to Frederick has not survived but it is quoted in Barbara Stollberg-Rilinger, *Maria Theresia: Die Kaiserin in ihrer Zeit* (Munich 2017), p. 502.

CHAPTER 7: THE AGE OF REFORM II: RELIGION AND EDUCATION

1. Maria Theresa to Ulfeld, quoted in Gustav Otruba, *Die Wirtschaftspolitik Maria Theresias* (Vienna 1963), p. 41.
2. See Chapter 15.
3. Otruba, *Die Wirtschaftspolitik Maria Theresias*, pp. 44–8.
4. Ibid., p. 73.
5. See Chapter 15.
6. The phrase was used in correspondence with Kaunitz. See Arneth, *Geschichte Maria Theresias*, vol. 3, pp. 57–89.
7. Kaunitz, quoted in Walter, *Männer um Maria Theresia*, p. 29.

CHAPTER 8: ENTER KAUNITZ

1. Unlike Francis Stephen, there is no record of Kaunitz having been inducted into an English lodge.
2. *La finta semplice* was mired in intrigue and controversy as it was deemed too sophisticated to have been written by a 'mere' 12-year-old boy and there were many accusations that Mozart's father had partly composed the work. The controversy prevented the work's performance in Vienna but illustrates Kaunitz's finger on the musical pulse. See Georg Kuntzel, *Fürst Kaunitz-Rietberg als Staatsman* (Vienna 1923), pp. 18–32.
3. Podewils, *Diplomatische Berichte*, pp. 101–7. See also *The Letters and Works of Lady Wortley Montagu*, ed. Lord Wharncliffe (London 1887); Caroline Pichler, *Denkwürdigkeiten aus meinen Leben* (Munich 1914), vol. 2.
4. See Alexander Novotny, *Staatskanzler Kaunitz als geistige Personalität* (Vienna 1947).
5. See Franz A.J. Szabo, *Kaunitz and Enlightened Absolutism 1753–1780* (Cambridge 1994), p. 35.
6. It is perhaps particularly difficult for English historians, because of the traditional centuries-old friction between English Freemasonry and ultramontane Roman Catholicism, to accept the degree of compatibility of Austrian Catholicism and Freemasonry in eighteenth-century Vienna.
7. Szabo, *Kaunitz and Enlightened Absolutism*, p. 32.
8. Kriegsarchiv: Kaunitz 1751/3/84.
9. Szabo, *Kaunitz and Enlightened Absolutism*, p. 87.
10. The dreaded *Schablonenmenschen* identified by the later Austrian author Thomas Bernhard. See Thomas Bernhard, *Holzfällen* (Vienna 1984).
11. Arneth, *Geschichte Maria Theresias*, vol. 6, p. 88.
12. For the spiritual dimension of patience, see Richard Clarke S.J., *Patience* (London 1997).
13. Arneth, *Geschichte Maria Theresias*, vol. 6, p. 91.
14. Podewils, *Diplomatische Berichte*, p. 136.
15. Szabo, *Kaunitz and Enlightened Absolutism*, p. 154.
16. See Chapter 15.
17. Szabo, *Kaunitz and Enlightened Absolutism*, p. 240.
18. Ibid. See also Sergio Galimberti and Mariano Malý (eds), *I Gesuiti e gli Asburgo* (Trieste 1995), p. 29 ff.
19. Galimberti and Malý (eds), *I Gesuiti e gli Asburgo*, p. 44.
20. *Der Mann ohne Vorurteil*, in *Moralische Wochenschrift*, vol. 1 (Vienna 1765).
21. HHStA Staatskanzlei, 13.X.1792.

CHAPTER 9: THE *GRAND RENVERSEMENT*

1. J.H. Plumb, *Robert Walpole*, vol. 1 (London 1960), p. 59.
2. Robinson MS 22530.
3. See *Neutralitaetsvertrag zwischen Oesterreich und Frankreich*, HHStA, Allgemeine Urkundenreihe, and Staatskanzlei Vorträge, Kart. 75 fol. 146–53.
4. As noted earlier, Frederick was until 1772 the King in Prussia (König in Preussen). This maintained the court of the Holy Roman Empire's fiction that he was the 'Elector of Brandenburg' and that the title of King, granted at Habsburg intervention, was literally only a courtesy title.
5. A bad omen for the Brühls – architectural nemesis pursued them across Europe: their city palace in Warsaw was torched in 1944. Three ruined arches are all that remain today around the tomb of the Unknown Polish Soldier in the city's main square.
6. See Andrew Bisset (ed.), *Memoirs and Papers of Sir Andrew Mitchell* (London 1850), vol. 2, p. 35.
7. Nepomucene (Ger. Nepomuk) had defied the Bohemian King Wenceslaus IV who had tortured him demanding he reveal what his Queen had said to him in the confessional. Nepomucene, after refusing to disclose a single word, was hurled off the Charles Bridge. Much later, during the Counter-Reformation, he was declared a saint faithful to the 'seal of confession' in 1729. Statues commemorating him can be found on many bridges in Austria, Bavaria, Bohemia and Moravia. The five stars around his head spell the Latin word TACET.

CHAPTER 10: *MATER CASTRORUM*

1. Duffy, *The Army of Maria Theresa*, p. 172.
2. The Austrians lost 13,400, of whom 5,000 were prisoners.
3. J. Gognazzo, *Freymütiger Beytrag zur Geschichte der Oesterreichischen Militärdienstes* (Frankfurt 1799), p. 106.
4. The quote in French still adorns the plinth of the spectacular Habsburg eagle which is the battlefield's principal monument.

CHAPTER 11: AUSTRIA RESURGENT

1. Frederick to Wilhelmina, 3 October 1757, in Johann Gustav Droysen (ed.), *Die politische Correspondenz Friedrichs des Grossen* (Berlin 1879–80), vol. 15, pp. 398–400.
2. With the death of Baron Goffredo (Geoffrey/Gottfried) de Banfield in Trieste in 1986, the Order finally, 228 years after its creation, ceased to exist. See Chapter 44.
3. 'Every time you look at this map, remember the day your father saved the monarchy', 18 June 1758, quoted in Jedlicka (ed.), *Maria Theresia in ihren Briefen und Staatsschriften*, p. 52.
4. J.W. Archenholz, *Geschichte des Siebenjaehrigen Kriegs in Deutschland* (Berlin 1860), vol. 1, p. 20.
5. Frederick to Prince Henry, in Droysen (ed.), *Die politische Correspondenz*, vol. 17, p. 217.
6. Duffy, *The Army of Maria Theresa*, pp. 119–28.
7. Coxe, *History of the House of Austria*, vol. 3, p. 392.
8. Rudolf Ottenfeld, *Die Oesterreichische Armee von 1700–1867* (Vienna 1895), p. 79.
9. *Schvo-ley* – Maria Theresa's Viennese dialectical contraction for her elite *Chevaux-légers* cavalry regiments.

10. Duffy, *The Army of Maria Theresa*, p. 72.
11. *Regulament und Ordnung des gesammten Kaiserlich-Koeniglichen Fuss-Volcks* (Vienna 1749).
12. A division that has not survived in Austria but continues to this day in the British preparatory/public school system.

CHAPTER 12: THE HUMBLING OF FREDERICK

1. Szabo, *Kaunitz and Enlightened Absolutism*, p. 203.
2. Ibid., p. 204.
3. Vienna Kriegsarchiven: Kabinettschreiben 24 July 1759.
4. And beyond. In 2023 an historically literate analyst, substituting Russia for Prussia in Kaunitz's memorandum, would describe well the choices facing the West following Moscow's invasion of Ukraine. Once again, the issue is not just the recovery of territory but the 'unbearable burden and other evil consequences' of not eliminating a factor of disequilibrium in the global equation of power.
5. It would be a descendant of this Prittwitz who would make military history in 1915 by suggesting the victorious German army call its great victory in East Prussia after a distant village named Tannenberg.
6. Frederick to Prince Henry, in Droysen (ed.), *Die politische Correspondenz*, vol. 18, p. 86.
7. Archenholz, *Geschichte des Siebenjaehrigen Kriegs*, vol. 2, pp. 106–8.
8. Frederick to Finckenstein, 10 December 1761, quoted in de Ligne, *Melanges Militaires Letterataires et Sentimentaires* (Dresden 1800), vol. 2, p. 65.
9. Duffy, *The Army of Maria Theresa*, p. 199 – a tactic much imitated by later psychopathic warlords. For Hadik's occupation of Berlin, see *Bericht FML Hadik's ueber die Expedition in die Mark Brandenburg und die Einnahme Berlins*, Kriegsarchiv, Alte Feldakten 1757, Hauptarmee 10/466a.
10. Duffy, *The Army of Maria Theresa*, p. 205.
11. Quoted in C.B.A. (Bette) Behrens, *Society, Government and the Enlightenment: The Experiences of Eighteenth-Century France and Prussia* (London 1985), p. 81.

CHAPTER 13: THE QUEEN OF PEACE

1. Krack (ed.), *Briefe einer Kaiserin*, pp. 97–101 (Maria Theresa to Graefin Walburga Lerchenfeld, 1756).
2. The reader will find much material on this in the current literature. See Ingrid Tague, *Love, Honour, and Obedience: Fashionable Women and the Discourse of Marriage in the Early 18th Century* (Cambridge 2001).
3. Traunkirchner, Eszterhazy and Powidltascherl to name but three.
4. In a similar vein is the portrait of her as Judith holding the head of Frederick as Holofernes.
5. See H.C. Robbins Landon, *Mozart and Vienna* (London 1994). Quoted in full in Emily Anderson (trans. and ed.), *The Letters of Mozart and his Family* (London 1938), vol. 1.
6. See Chapter 21.
7. Arneth, *Briefe der Kaiserin an ihre Kinder und Freunde*, vol. 2, p. 73.
8. Quoted in Arneth, *Geschichte Maria Theresias*, vol. 1, p. 112.
9. See Chapter 23.
10. Charles Joseph Prince de Ligne, *Memoirs, Letters* (London 1899), p. 46.

11. £2.8 million today.
12. HHStA, Familienakten, Kart. 54, fol. 3–6. See also Josef Hrazky, *Mitteilungen des Oesterreichischen Staatsarchivs* (Vienna 1959), vol. 2, p. 199, MC/IP.

CHAPTER 14: THE AUSTRIAN ENLIGHTENMENT

1. 24 June 1717 is usually given as the date of the founding in London of the first Grand Lodge.
2. Ernst Krivanec, *Die Freimauerei in der Theresianischen Epoche* (Vienna 1979), p. 197.
3. Thugut's biographer Roider casts some doubt on the story of the orphan's first encounter with the Empress, but it is beyond doubt that Thugut came from the humblest of origins and captivated Maria Theresa with his boyish charm: see Roider, *Baron Thugut*. A case perhaps of 'se non è vero è ben trovato'.
4. Maria Theresa's final letter to Marie Antoinette, 3 November 1780, in Jedlicka (ed.), *Maria Theresia in ihren Briefen und Staatsschriften*, p. 59.
5. Peter Prosch, *Leben und Ereignisse des Peter Prosch's eines Tyrolers aus Zillerthal* (Munich 1789).
6. See Monika Czernin, *Der Kaiser reist inkognito: Joseph II und das Europa der Aufklärung* (Munich 2021).
7. This would appear to contradict those who argue 'plebeian' access to the Empress was impossible: see Barbara Stollberg-Rilinger, 'Maria Theresa Empress-Queen', 35th Robert A. Kann Memorial Lecture (University of Minnesota), 2020.
8. A common calculation places the value of one fish as the equivalent of £500 in the currency of the early twenty-first century. See Introduction, *Diary and Letters of Lady Mary Coke*, ed. James Home (London 1970).
9. Notably the former imperial and royal suppliers of playing cards Ferdinand Piatnik.
10. See Simon Schaffer, 'Enlightened Automata', in *The Sciences in Enlightened Europe*, ed. William Clark et al. (Chicago 1999).
11. Stefan Seitschek, *Der Wiener Hof im Spiegel der Zeremonialprotokolle 1652–1800* (Innsbruck 2007), p. 357.
12. Lady Mary Coke, *Letters and Journals of Lady Mary Coke* (Edinburgh 1889).
13. In fact, the last English monarch to have performed this ceremony was, predictably, the much maligned Catholic King James II. See Hilaire Belloc, *James II* (London 1928).
14. See Geoffrey Holt S.J., *The English Jesuits in the Age of Reason* (Tunbridge Wells 1993).
15. Unsurprisingly, English historians in the 'Whig tradition' have often been among the most sceptical of the Society.
16. Ernst Wangermann, 'Matte Morgenröte', in Koschatzky (ed.), *Maria Theresia und ihre Zeit*, p. 68.

CHAPTER 15: THE GREAT SUPPRESSION: EDUCATIONAL UPHEAVAL

1. *Dominus ac redemptor*, Rome 21 July 1773.
2. See Holt, *The English Jesuits*, p. 174.
3. Ironically, Pombal had first seen the power of the Jesuits during a visit to Vienna and had developed a personal vendetta against them on account of their studied indifference to his presence. Such *suffisance* offended his pride.
4. See Frances Yates, *The Rosicrucian Enlightenment* (London 1972), p. 290.
5. See Derek Beales, *Joseph II*, vol. 2: *Against the World* (Cambridge 2009), p. 157.

6. Eva Vetter, *Die Finsternis der Unwissenheit aufklären* (Vienna University, guest lecture 17 July 2017).
7. See C.A. Macartney, *Maria Theresa and the House of Austria* (London 1969), p. 127.

CHAPTER 16: PHYSICAL WELL-BEING: THE ARRIVAL OF A PUBLIC HEALTH SYSTEM

1. A regulation still in force in Austrian hospitals.
2. De Ligne, *Fragments de l'histoire de ma vie* (Paris 1927), vol. 1, p. 184.
3. Ibid.
4. Thomas Lau, *Die Kaiserin* (Vienna 2017), p. 346.

CHAPTER 17: THE KING OF THE ROMANS

1. See Beales, *Joseph II*, vol. 2, p. 157.
2. Tim Blanning, *Frederick the Great: King of Prussia* (London 2016), p. 222.
3. J.C. Allmayer-Beck, *Das Heerwesen unter Joseph II* (Melk 1980), p. 61.
4. Ibid.
5. Derek Beales, *Joseph II*, vol. 1: *In the Shadow of Maria Theresa* (Cambridge 1987), p. 108.
6. HHStA, Hofreisen K2-2-1 Reisejournal Banat 11–22.
7. Derek Beales, *Joseph II*, vol. 1, p. 108.
8. Khevenhueller-Metsch, *Aus der Zeit Maria Theresias*, vol. 6, p. 134.
9. Maria Theresa to Kaunitz, 6 June 1766. HHStA, Familien Archiv, Sammelbaende K. 70.

CHAPTER 18: THE TERRIBLE 'BETRAYAL': THE FIRST PARTITION OF POLAND

1. See Norman Davies, *God's Playground* (Oxford 1981), vol. 2, p. 3 ff.
2. Beales, *Joseph II*, vol. 1, p. 364.
3. Camillo Paganel, *Storia di Giuseppe II* (Milan 1843), p. 109.
4. Ibid., p. 87.
5. *Mémoires couronnés et autres mémoires, publiés par l'Academié Royale des sciences et des lettres et des beaux-arts de Belgique*, ed. Kervyn de Lettenhove (Brussels 1869), pp. 25–7.
6. As British diplomats found out in 1914 and 1939.
7. Alfred von Arneth (ed.), *Maria Theresia und Joseph II: Ihre Korrespondenz sammt Briefen Joseph's an seinen Bruder Leopold* (Vienna 1868), vol. 1, p. 344.
8. Szabo, *Kaunitz and Enlightened Absolutism*, p. 67.
9. Duffy, *The Army of Maria Theresa*, p. 210.
10. Suffolk to Keith, 11 June 1773, Secret PRO SP 80/213.

CHAPTER 19: BAYONETS AND POTATOES: THE BAVARIAN SUCCESSION CRISIS

1. HHStA, Kriegsarchiv. Inv. Nr. H III e 207/208.
2. HHStA, Familien Archiv, Sammelbaende, K. 72. See also exh. cat., *Maria Theresia und ihre Zeit*, p. 193.
3. Maria Theresia/Joseph Korrespondenz (12 April 1778–8 June 1778). Oesterr. Nationalbibliothek, Handschriftensammlung Autogr.296/4-7.
4. Maria Theresa to Joseph, 8 June 1778, in Arneth (ed.), *Maria Theresia und Joseph II: Ihre Korrespondenz*.

5. Ibid.
6. Paganel, *Storia di Giuseppe II*, p. 177.
7. Thugut's mission is also described in Adolf Beer, 'Die Sendung Thugut's in das preussische Hauptquartier und der Friede zu Teschen', *Historische Zeitschrift* (1877).
8. Paganel, *Storia di Giuseppe II*, pp. 121–7.
9. Ibid., pp. 177–89.
10. See 'Eigenhaendige Resolution Maria Theresias auf fol.1 v des Originalvortrages Kaunitz vom 6 Mai 1779', in exh. cat., *Maria Theresia und ihre Zeit*, Kat. 32.05.
11. *Resolution Maria Theresias zum Abschluss des Friedens von Teschen Wien 6t Mai 1779.* HHStA, Vortraege. Kart 129.

CHAPTER 20: *KAISERIN, WITTIB*: THE MOURNING EMPRESS AND THE STRUGGLE FOR CONSTANCY

1. Exhibited in Vienna: *Maria Theresia und ihre Zeit*, 1980. See Notizen Maria Theresias über die Dauer ihrer Ehe, Wien, 18 August 1765. Haus-, Hof- und Staatarchiv, Familienurkunden Nr 2011/12 Beilage. See also Gebetbuch fuer Franz Stephan und Maria Theresia, Wien, Oesterr. Nationalbibliothek, Handschriftensammlung, Od.Ser.n3.593.
2. See pp. 215–59.
3. *Judenordnung 5 May 1764*, Niederösterreichisches Landesarchiv H 1 Judensachen Normale outlines extensively the coercive measures to be applied to Jews not in the service of the state.
4. Joseph's attempts to meet with Franklin foundered, it was later said, on Franklin's refusal to meet 'a monarch even if he is enlightened'. The reality is that British diplomacy, ever watchful of any Austro-American rapprochement, intervened to prevent the encounter. See Jonathan Singerton, *The American Revolution and the Habsburg Monarchy*, paper presented to Cambridge New Habsburg Studies Network, March 2022.
5. Joseph to Maria Theresa, June 1777, in Arneth (ed.), *Maria Theresia und Joseph II: Ihre Korrespondenz*, vol. 2, p. 141.
6. Anthony Blunt, *Boromini and the Baroque*, lecture at the Courtauld Institute of Art, London, 4 December 1979.
7. HHStA, Depot Migazzi Kart 6.
8. Oesterr. Nationalbibliothek, Handschriftensammlung, Autogr. 9/49-27.
9. Arneth (ed.), *Maria Theresia und Joseph II: Ihre Korrespondenz*, vol. 2, pp. 170–4.
10. See Dr Michael Philpot, *Dyslexia and the Brain: Studies in Developmental Dyslexia* (unpublished manuscript, London 1998).
11. P. Adolf Innerkofler, *Eine grosse Tochter Maria Theresias: Erzherzogin Marianne in ihrem Haupt-Momente, dem Elisabethinenkloster zu Klagenfurt* (Innsbruck 1910), pp. 32–3.
12. Teresa of Ávila, *Camino de Perfección* (1556).
13. The exchange with Joseph is best rendered in Lau, *Die Kaiserin*, p. 380: *Der Kayser sagte: Ihro Mayst. ligen sehr uebel; ja sagte sie aber gut genug um zu sterben.*

CHAPTER 21: THE MOTHER (I): THE DAUGHTERS

1. There are some who argue Canova's monument in the Venice Frari is superior but, even when dazzlingly restored, as it has been recently by the British charity Venice in Peril, it still betrays the inferior work of Canova's pupils when measured against the Augustinerkirche's masterpiece.

2. See Élisabeth Badinter, *Les conflits d'une mère: Marie-Thérèse et ses enfants* (Paris 2020), p. 42.
3. Maria Theresa to Marie Antoinette, 17 April 1770, in Jedlicka (ed.), *Maria Theresia in ihren Briefen und Staatsschriften.*
4. For this and all subsequent extracts from the correspondence between Maria Theresa and Marie Antoinette, see Georges Girard, *Correspondance entre Marie-Thérèse et Marie-Antoinette* (Paris 1933).
5. The well-known passage in Mozart's *Die Zauberflöte*, 'nichts edlers sei als Mann und Weib', could have been penned by the Empress.
6. Ibid., p. 67.
7. 30 May 1774, in Jedlicka (ed.), *Maria Theresia in ihren Briefen und Staatsschriften*, p. 44.
8. HHStA, Familien Archiv, Sammelbaende, K. 3.
9. Ibid.
10. Ibid.
11. Hilde Knobloch, *Maria Theresia* (Vienna 1946), p. 359. Probably Walpole, then just an MP but destined for higher office.
12. Jedlicka (ed.), *Maria Theresia in ihren Briefen und Staatsschriften.*
13. Paul Christoph (ed.), *Maria Theresia: Geheimer Briefwechsel mit Marie Antoinette* (Vienna 1980), p. 334.
14. Ibid.
15. Jedlicka (ed.), *Maria Theresia in ihren Briefen und Staatsschriften*, pp. 44–5.
16. Joseph II to Maria Theresa, exh. cat. *Marie Antoinette* (Versailles 1955), p. 136.
17. Maria Theresa, 3 November 1780, quoted in Jedlicka (ed.), *Maria Theresia in ihren Briefen und Staatsschriften*, p. 59.
18. Ibid., p. 62.
19. This mutual regard persisted well into the twentieth century and beyond. It is generally accepted for example in Slovenia that it was directly responsible for parts of Carinthia remaining part of Austria despite a sizeable Slovene minority after the two German wars. Professor Edo Ravnikar to author, March 1981.
20. Jedlicka (ed.), *Maria Theresia in ihren Briefen und Staatsschriften*, p. 59.
21. Krack (ed.), *Briefe einer Kaiserin*, p. 55.
22. Quoted in Harold Acton, *The Last Bourbons of Naples 1825–1861* (London 1961), p. 141.
23. Eugenio Lo Sardo, *Napoli e Londra nel XVIII secolo: Le relazioni eonomiche* (Naples 1991).
24. Nathaniel William Wraxall, *Memoirs of the Courts of Berlin, Dresden, Warsaw and Vienna in the years 1777, 1778 and 1779* (London 1806), vol. 1, p. 177.
25. Lady Anne Miller, quoted in Hugh Tours, *The Life and Letters of Emma Hamilton: The Story of Admiral Nelson and the Most Famous Woman of the Georgian Age* (Barnsley 2020), p. 54.
26. *Emma Hamilton: Mistress to Muse*, exh. cat., National Maritime Museum, Greenwich (2015).
27. Raffaele Palumbo, *Maria Carolina Regina delle Due Sicilie, suo carteggio con Lady Hamilton* (Naples 1877). See also Harold Acton, *The Bourbons of Naples* (London 1956), pp. 437–42.
28. See Palumbo, *Maria Carolina Regina delle Due Sicilie*, p. 212.
29. Further indignity was to follow in 1803 when the family were mediatized. For Maria Amalia's antics, see Badinter, *Les conflits d'une mère*, p. 95.

30. Although buried in the great cathedral of St Vitus, her heart, in accordance with Habsburg tradition, was sent to Vienna to the family's *Herzgruft*.
31. Maria Theresa appears to have been always very concerned that her daughters manifest straight frames free of any taint of scoliosis. It was a theme, as we have seen, of one of her letters to Marie Antoinette.
32. Innerkofler, *Eine grosse Tochter Maria Theresias*, pp. 109–10.
33. I am indebted to the Museum of Freemasonry in London for this information.
34. Innerkofler, *Eine grosse Tochter Maria Theresias*, p. 107.
35. Letter to Marquise de Herzelles, 27 October 1763, cited in exh. cat. *Maria Theresia und ihre Zeit*, p. 190 (private collection).
36. Marquis d'Ossun, 16 September 1758, Archives du ministère des Affaires étrangères (MAE), Correspondance politique Naples 58, 75.

CHAPTER 22: THE MOTHER (II): THE SONS

1. The Teutonic Knights had long ceased, with the end of the Crusades, to exercise any temporal functions but the prestige among the high aristocracy of belonging to the order was significant, as can be seen in Vienna to this day in their buildings just behind St Stephen's Cathedral.
2. *Maria Theresia Brief an Maximilian*, April 1774, in Jedlicka (ed.), *Maria Theresia in ihren Briefen und Staatsschriften*, pp. 36–43.
3. Ibid. Also quoted in Krack (ed.), *Briefe einer Kaiserin*, 18 April 1774, BMT 1, p. 271.
4. The Colloredo appointment was supposed to secure the 'Enlightenment' for the clerically dominated Salzburg but, paradoxically, Colloredo interpreted his brief so zealously that he banned performances of orchestral Masses in the cathedral, one consequence of which was to drive Mozart to Vienna. Another admirer of Voltaire (his bust adorned the archbishop's desk), he also banned pilgrimages and devotion to the saints. Mozart detested him, writing to his father, 'I shit on Colloredo who has never offered me any encouragement'. See p. 359.
5. Leopold, *Stato della famiglia*, in Adam Wandruszka, *Leopold II: Erzherzog von Oesterreich, Grossherzog von Toskana, König von Ungarn und Böhmen, Römischer Kaiser* (Vienna 1963–5), vol. 1, p. 353. Zinzendorf notes Leopold was a member of the eighteenth (Rosicrucian) degree of Scottish rite Freemasonry.
6. Sadly, the road to hell is paved with good intentions, as Archduke Ferdinand Maximilian's fate as the brief, ill-starred Emperor of Mexico would vividly demonstrate a hundred years later.
7. The money was repaid to the duchy. See Otruba, *Die Wirtschaftspolitik Maria Theresias*, p. 350.
8. Wandruszka, *Leopold II*, vol. 1, pp. 331–5.

CHAPTER 23: JOSEPH AND JOSEPHINISM

1. See Macartney, *Maria Theresa and the House of Austria*, p. 127.
2. HHStA, Familien Archiv, Sammelbaende, 21 February 1777. See also Christian Rapp (ed.), *300 Jahre Freimaurer: Das wahre Geheimnis* (Vienna 2017), pp. 35–8.
3. See Beales, *Joseph II*, vol. 2, p. 258.
4. See Edith Rosenstrauch-Königsberg, *Freimaurer, Illuminati, Weltbürger* (Berlin 1984), p. 150.
5. HHStA, *Hofakten des Ministerium des Innerens Allgemeines Gesetzbuch 1787*.
6. See Beales, *Joseph II*, vol. 2, Chapter 5.

7. Ibid. See exh cat. *Maria Theresia und ihre Zeit*, pp. 510–15.
8. *Grundgesetz des Censor*, Staatsarchiv Depot Migazzi-Prueschenk-Hardegg Kart 6.
9. Teodora Shek Bernardic, *Hrvatska Stoljece* (Zagreb 2013), pp. 34–6.
10. Liechtenstein papers, Herrschaftsarchiv Steyregg, Maria Elisabeth Nachlass: Briefe 1780.
11. Bernardic, *Hrvatska Stoljece*, p. 134.
12. Quoted in Beales, *Joseph II*, vol. 2, p. 467 ff.

CHAPTER 24: STOCKS, SUBSIDIES AND FREE TRADE: THE WORLD OF THERESIAN FINANCE

1. See Johann Christoph Allmayer-Beck, *Die kaiserlichen Kriegsvölker* (Vienna 1978), p. 150.

CHAPTER 25: TRIESTE AND THE RENEWAL OF A GLOBAL PRESENCE

1. The phrase is Chesterton's – see *Lepanto* (London 1915): 'The inmost sea of all the earth is shaken by his ships.'
2. Beales, *Joseph II*, vol. 1, pp. 465, 473, 478.
3. The Triestine writer Giorgio Voghera remembers as a child before the First World War, growing up in the *Borgo Teresiano* and being able to smell coffee and oranges stored in the ground-floor depositories of the quarter's palaces. Even today, the ground floors of these buildings retain a commercial purpose and remain largely uninhabited. The arrival of the railway, almost a century after the construction of these buildings, initiated a new and more industrial series of warehouse building around the Southern Railway Station, today converted into apartments. See Voghera, *Gli Anni di Trieste* (Gorizia 1989).
4. See Lois C. Dubin, *The Port Jews of Habsburg Trieste: Absolutist Politics and Enlightenment Culture* (Stanford 1999), p. 16.
5. Antonio de Giuliani, *Riflessioni politiche sopra il Porto prospetto attuale della città di Trieste* (Vienna 1785), pp. 289, 333.
6. Charles-Albert, Comte de Moré, *Memoires* (Paris 1828), pp. 221–2, 297–300.
7. For the details of Jewish professions in Trieste and the statistics of dynamic growth in the city see Dubin, *The Port Jews of Habsburg Trieste*.
8. Though not before he had founded the empire's first insurance company in Brussels and Trieste in 1754: the Compagnie Assicurance paid its investors an 8 per cent dividend on a capital outlay which totalled 500,000 Gulden. Eventually, with the Treaty of Paris ending Ostend's mercantile privileges, the insurance baton was picked up by the Triestine plutocracy a century later to create the world-famous Assicurazione Generali.
9. For the best modern account of these events, see Randa, *Oesterreich in Übersee*, p. 73 ff.

CHAPTER 26: MARIA THERESA'S ITALIAN INHERITANCE: LOMBARDY

1. Quoted in Beales, *Joseph II*, and Szabo, *Kaunitz and Enlightened Absolutism*, among other sources. Originally in HHStA, *Kaunitz Nachlass, Briefe an M.T.*, 14 January 1770.
2. Once again, Maria Theresa's ability to select outstanding servants of state appears to have been the direct result of eschewing ambitious, opinionated, showy, materialist and conventionally splendid personalities.

3. Provoking from Kaunitz the acid observation that Joseph's zeal went even further than that of Henry VIII, who 'after all' had only dissolved the monasteries once. HHStA, Handschriftensammlung, Autogr.9/49-1 Kaunitz Nachlass 1786 Briefe Firmian 'Zweimal aufgehoben'.
4. Thugut Nachlass HHStA 1801 Serie D.

CHAPTER 27: CHALLENGE AND SALVATION: HUNGARY

1. A policy whose perspicacity has proved remarkably elusive.
2. Viz. the last Habsburg emperor, Charles's failed attempts at restoration in the 1920s. See G. Brooke-Shepherd, *The Last Emperor* (London 1968), Chapter 15, for the obstacles facing Charles's return to Hungary.
3. Beales, *Joseph II*, vol. 2, p. 67.
4. HHStA, Eszterhazy Nachlass, p. 33.
5. HHStA, Kaunitz Nachlass 1787, Memorandum to J.II.

CHAPTER 28: JEWEL IN THE CROWN: THE AUSTRIAN LOWLANDS

1. The phrase was directed by the Empress at Lorraine's frequent adventures in the bedchamber but the Belgian affection for their 'Coq' was genuine. When Jacobins tore down a statue of the prince after the outbreak of the French Revolution, it was quickly restored with the inscription: 'Ainsi périssent les despotes, Renversés par les sans-coulottes.'
2. Maria Theresa to Joseph, 25 July 1778, in Jedlicka (ed.), *Maria Theresia in ihren Briefen und Staatsschriften*, p. 50.
3. Quoted in Suzanne Tassier, 'Léopold II et la révolution brabançonne: la déclaration du 2 mars 1790', *Revue d'histoire moderne et contemporaine*, vol. 4, no. 20 (1929).

CHAPTER 29: *PANDOURS* AND LIGHTHOUSES: THERESIAN CROATIA

1. And culturally distinctive from the Dalmatian population south of Zara (Zadar).
2. Joseph memorandum 1780, quoted in Beales, *Joseph II*, vol. 2, p. 56.

CHAPTER 30: TWIXT CROSS AND CRESCENT: THE MILITARY FRONTIER

1. 'The soldiers who in the name of Christ guard the walls of Europe against the countless hordes'.
2. Marmont, Duc de Raguse, *Voyages en Hongrie* (Paris 1847).
3. M. Hartley, *The Man who Saved Austria* (London 1929), p. 86.
4. Heinrich (Ritter von) Srbik, *Metternich: Der Staatsman und der Mensch* (Munich 1957), vol. 2, p. 455.
5. Quoted in Beales, *Joseph II*, vol. 2, p. 367, and in Czernin, *Der Kaiser reist inkognito*, p. 43.

CHAPTER 31: GALICIA AND LODOMERIA

1. Different in confession and outlook from Ukrainians living in Russian territory before 1989 who tended towards the Greek Orthodox/Russian Orthodox confession. The Ukrainian war of independence beginning in 2022 appeared to complete the welding of the two traditions into one fervently Ukrainian movement.

2. The title came with the Lorraine inheritance of Joseph's father and has remained ever since one of the many Habsburg titles.
3. HHStA, Alte Kabinettsakten Kart 1. See also Arneth, *Geschichte Maria Theresias*, vol. 3, pp. 86–8.

CHAPTER 32: AUSTRIA-BOHEMIA: CONSOLIDATING THE AUSTRIAN HEARTLANDS

1. Joseph to Leopold, quoted in Beales, *Joseph II*, vol. 2, p. 89.
2. J. Kalousek (ed.), *Archiv český*, vol. XXIX (Prague 1913), p. 510.
3. *Codex Theresianus* 1769, Oesterreichische National Bibliothek, Inv 226 970-D.
4. Beales, *Joseph II*, vol. 2, pp. 68–9.
5. Arneth, *Maria Theresia und Joseph II: Ihre Korrespondenz*, vol. 10, p. 50.
6. HHStA, Familienkunden Nr 2013 1.2.
7. Maria Theresa to Mercy, in Jedlicka (ed.), *Maria Theresia in ihren Briefen und Staatsschriften*, p. 56.
8. Maria Theresa to Ferdinand, 13 February 1777, in ibid.
9. François Fejtö, *Joseph II: Un Habsbourg révolutionnaire; Portrait d'un despote éclairé* (Paris 1953), p. 140.
10. Quoted in Krack (ed.), *Briefe einer Kaiserin*.
11. Voltaire shied away from such seismic reform in his writings: see Morley, *Voltaire*, pp. 89–101. For Frederick's lack of spine in such matters, see *Essai sur les forms de gouvernement* (1777) in Preuss, *Oeuvres de Frédéric*, vol. IX, pp. 205–6. Rousseau also opposed the abolition of serfdom: see C.E. Vaughan, *The Political Writings of Jean Jacques Rousseau* (2 vols, Cambridge 1915), vol. 2, pp. 497–9.

CHAPTER 33: LOOKING WEST: THE FAILURE OF THE FRENCH INTELLECTUAL CONNECTION

1. Quoted in Beales, *Joseph II*, vol. 2, p. 96.
2. Maria Theresa to Mercy, in Jedlicka (ed.), *Maria Theresia in ihren Briefen und Staatsschriften*, p. 78.
3. Arneth, *Réflexions*, p. 14.
4. Naples, 5 March 1787: Goethe, *Letters from Italy*, trans. W.H. Auden and Elizabeth Mayer (London 1962).
5. See Patrick Leigh Fermor, *A Time of Gifts* (London 1977), p. 257. (For example, Chopin = 'Chopern' rather than 'Chopan'; Jacquin = 'Jaquern' rather than 'Jaquan'.)

CHAPTER 34: THE BORDERS OF INTOLERANCE: MARIA THERESA AND THE JEWS

1. This text is published in A.F. Pribram, *Urkunden und Akten zur Geschichte der Juden in Wien* (2 vols, Vienna 1918), vol. 1, pp. 425–6.
2. The Josephinian Enlightenment ironically left a far from progressive legacy with regard to the relations between Jews and Gentiles in central Europe as the use of name-labelling reinforced rather than eliminated the divide. See 23 July 1787 Edict imposing German surnames on the Jews: *Wir Joseph der Zweite . . . die Judenschaft in allen Provinzen . . .* (Vienna 1787) (Kerbl Privatbesitz Groedig).
3. See Pitacco, *Maria Teresa e Trieste*, p. 87 ff.

4. Hilde Spiel, *Fanny von Arnstein* (Oxford 1991), p. 67. Also letter from Hilde Spiel to author, 28 April 1986.
5. J. Karniel, *Die Toleranzpolitik Josephs II* (Gerlingen 1982), p. 387.
6. Maria Fausta Maternini Zotta, *L'ente communitario ebraico: La legislazione negli ultimi due secoli* (Milan 1983), p. 215.
7. Elia Morpurgo, *Orazione funebre in occasione della morte dell'Eroina della Germania S.S.C.R.A.M. Maria Teresa Imperadrice e Regina* (Gorizia 1781), pp. 11–12.
8. Address of the Chief Rabbi of Trieste 1845 in Documenti, Archivio della comunità israelitica di Trieste.

CHAPTER 35: THE ARTISTIC PARNASSUS: VIENNA

1. HHStA, Familien-archiv Sammelbände Karton 15.
2. Renate Wagner Rieger in Koschatzky (ed.), *Maria Theresia und ihre Zeit*, p. 263.
3. The Plečnik renovations at Hradčany in Prague made during the 1920s have certainly not diminished this impression.
4. Philipp von Hörnigk's treatise was the most widely read economic text before the advent of Adam Smith. Published in 1684, a year after the raising of the second siege of Vienna of 1683, it became a European classic, though now largely forgotten. See Hörnigk, *Oesterreich ueber alles wann es nur will: Wohlmeynender Fuerschlag* (1685), Bayerische Staatsbibliothek.
5. See Koschatzky (ed.), *Maria Theresia und ihre Zeit: Gartenanlage* 127.01, pp. 520–2.

CHAPTER 36: WILLS AND LAWS: *MILDE UND MUNIFIZENZ*

1. This practice was by no means unique to Austria. In England, as the two French flags annually presented to the sovereign at Windsor Castle indicate and which are a token of the peppercorn 'rent' owed by the 'soldier' dukes Wellington and Marlborough, such monarchical munificence was not confined to the Habsburgs.
2. HHStA, Familien Archiv, Sammelbaende, K. 15, Allegato 1.

CHAPTER 37: MUSIC AND DRAMA: A SUBVERSIVE UNIVERSE

1. *Fix Loudon Stern* derives from an eighteenth-century curse damning Loudon for his late arrival, presumably on the battlefield: 'Verflüchteter Laudon!' (confounded Laudon). I am indebted to the late Reinhold Gayer for this information. Fixstern also suggests a star which is incapable of movement.
2. This story neatly underlines the informality of the Austrian court once the court ceremonial had been penetrated, which many other observers confirmed (Coke, Wraxall, Montagu, to name but three English observers). There is no need to dispute the proud father's account, although Maria Theresa's affection for the little boy did not stand the test of time. See Anderson, *The Letters of Mozart and his Family*, vol. 1.
3. See ibid., letters from W.A. Mozart to Leopold Mozart, 12 May 1781 and 12 July 1783.
4. *Maurerlied*, K. 623a.
5. See H.C. Robbins Landon, *1791: Mozart's Last Year* (London 1999), p. 8.
6. Pietro Metastasio, *Opere drammatiche e sacri* (Rome 1737). See *Maria Theresia und ihre Zeit*, Kat. 81.20, p. 375.
7. See also Ludovico Antonio Muratori, *Della pubblica felicità* (Modena 1749).

8. See W.A. Mozart, letter to L. Mozart, 4 September 1773: 'Now it is all up with the poor Jesuits . . . the public is very much distressed', in Anderson, *The Letters of Mozart and his Family.*
9. Gottfried Pils, with Eugen Brixen and Gustav Martin, *Das ist Österreichs Militärmusik* (Graz 1982) is the standard and unsurpassed work.
10. 'Die Bosniaken kommen' is perhaps the most celebrated of these. For the full list of regimental marches dating back to the reign of Maria Theresa and their incorporation into each of the regiments of the later Habsburg armies, Pils, Brixen and Martin is again invaluable: ibid.

CHAPTER 38: MARIA THERESA AND TYROL

1. See Richard Bassett, *Playing for Time* (London 2022).

CHAPTER 39: PORZELLAN AND AUGARTEN

1. It was the journalist Anton Kuh who noted that, at the celebrated *Conditorei* Demel's in 1920s Vienna, the *Handkuss* still offered one Theresian tradition which defied all republican sanctions. In polite society in Vienna, Graz and Salzburg, it is, even in the twenty-first century, an enduring convention. See Anton Kuh, *Lenin und Demel* (Vienna 2016).

CHAPTER 40: THE ART OF THE *PITTOR TURCO*: JEAN-ÉTIENNE LIOTARD'S VISITS TO VIENNA

1. Voltaire, quoted in Morley, *Voltaire*, p. 48.
2. A good thirty years before Joshua Reynolds's turbaned Omai caused an almost equal sensation in London.
3. See Karl A. Roider, *Austria's Eastern Question 1700–1789* (Princeton 1982).
4. It is interesting to note that none of Liotard's paintings for his English patrons, while frequently containing coffee cups, ever contained the Viennese addition of the glass of iced water.
5. See Koschatzky (ed.), *Maria Theresia und ihre Zeit*, Kat. 61.47, p. 313. Also Renée Loche and Marcel Roethlisberger, *L'Opera completa di Liotard* (Milan 1979), No. 70.
6. See National Gallery exh. cat. *Liotard and the Lavergne Family Breakfast* (London 2023).
7. Koschatzky (ed.), *Maria Theresia und ihre Zeit* (Christine Reinwetter, *Maria Theresia als Witwe*), Kat: 33.03, p. 197.

CHAPTER 41: *PIETAS THERESIANA*

1. Perhaps the most famous of these anagrams was: EUCHARISTIA: Hic est Au(st)ria.
2. The Austrian flag today bears only these two colours (as does that of another Catholic bastion, Poland). The colours have also been linked to the Norman standard which flew over fourteenth-century Naples. See Duffy, *The Army of Maria Theresa*, p. 15 ff.
3. Hungarian pilgrimages occurred throughout the communist interregnum, not least on account of the communist-persecuted Cardinal Mindszenty's tomb. Its return to Hungary following the end of communism has only slightly impacted the numbers of Hungarian pilgrims.
4. Kurt Dieman, *Magna Mater Styriae* (Graz 1977), p. 17.

CHAPTER 42: THERESIAN (KEYNESIAN) MONETARY POLICY: THE AUSTRIAN 'DOLLAR'

1. J.M. Keynes, 'Some Notes on the Austrian Thaler', *Economic Review* (June 1914).
2. Ibid.
3. The British soon caught up with the theory and 'imperial preference' and the 'sterling area' featured well into the twentieth century. See Robert Skidelsky, *John Maynard Keynes*, vol. 3: *Fighting for Freedom 1937–46* (London 2000).

CHAPTER 43: THE 'SILVER ROSE': THERESIAN NOSTALGIA

1. Prompting a later ambassador (Michael Alexander) to exclaim (to author, 9 June 1984): 'If this is third rococo where is first and second?'
2. Hofmannsthal, quoted in Koschatzky (ed.), *Maria Theresia und ihre Zeit*, p. 8.
3. See Stollberg-Rilinger, *Maria Theresia: Die Kaiserin in ihrer Zeit*, pp. xiv–xxviii (*Maennerphantasien*).

CHAPTER 44: COURAGE AND HONOUR: THE MARIA THERESA ORDER

1. One English recipient, the Earl of Uxbridge, later Marquess of Anglesey, famously led the impetuous cavalry charge which almost cost Wellington the Battle of Waterloo and forced him onto the defensive for the entirety of the remaining battle. Wellington, too, received the decoration and it is displayed (in a later replica form) at Apsley House along with the gold and brown velvet baton of an Austrian field marshal.

CHAPTER 45: THE *ZUCKERKÖNIGIN*: ROCOCO DELIGHTS

1. The Sachertorte was the invention of Eduard Sacher, a pastry chef at the Hotel Sacher in Vienna, an institution which did not exist in Theresian times. The story of *Rigo-Jancsi* is more prosaic. The cake is named after 'Gypsy John', a violinist who played so entrancingly that he caught the attention of Clara Ward, an American heiress married to a Belgian, Count de Caraman-Chimay. The music sent the Belgian to sleep and when he woke up he was informed that his wife had eloped with 'Gypsy John' but that a chocolate cake had been ordered by her for her husband as a small 'douceur', from that time onwards known as a *Rigo-Jancsi*.
2. The once near-obligatory 'Negerschuss' of hot chocolate sauce became politically unacceptable throughout most of Austria in the third decade of the present century.
3. HHStA, OMeA Prot 17 1741–43.
4. See *Maria Theresias Kulturwelt*, Documenta Austriaca, vol. 2 (Hildesheim 2014).
5. The increasing robustness of Bohemian crystal impacted adversely the demand for the more fragile *Bisquit*. See Koschatzky (ed.), *Maria Theresia und ihre Zeit*, Kat 70.

CHAPTER 46: FEMININITY AND FEMINISM: MARIA THERESA AS *LANDESMUTTER*

1. John Milton, *Paradise Lost*, Book IV (London 1678), lines 295–311.
2. As I write, there are monuments to her, preserved or planned, in Vienna, Prague, Trieste, Marienbad and Budapest.
3. Notably Adam Wandruszka, *Die grosse Kaiserin* (Vienna 1980), p. 18 ff.

CHAPTER 47: TRIUMPH OF THE MODERN:
FRANZ XAVER MESSERSCHMIDT

1. See for example J.G. Kohl's *Austria* (London 1843), pp. 394–5.
2. The 'average' family of four had to make do on less than 300 Gulden a year. See Gustav Otruba, *Österreischische Fabriksprivilegien vom 16. bis ins 18. Jahrhundert* (Brill 1981).
3. See Maria Malikowa, 'Die Portraetplastik von F.X. Messerschmidt', *Mitteilungen der Osterr. Galerie*, vol. 9, no. 53 (1965), p. 11. Also Koschatzky (ed.), *Maria Theresia und ihre Zeit*, Kat 44.01.
4. See exh. cat. *Franz Xaver Messerschmidt* (Neue Galerie New York 2012).

CHAPTER 48: THE WAR ON SUPERSTITION

1. See Ludwig Wittgenstein, *Tractatus Logico-Philosophicus* (London 1922), 4.116.
2. See Justini Febronii, *De Statu Ecclesiae* (Frankfurt 1765).
3. Ulrich L. Lehner, *The Catholic Enlightenment: The Forgotten History of a Global Movement* (Oxford 2018), p. 140.
4. Thomas Corbishley S.J. (trans.), *The Spiritual Exercises of St Ignatius* (London 1963), pp. 52–5.
5. See Lehner, *The Catholic Enlightenment*, p. 142 for a detailed description of Gassner's exorcism techniques.
6. Tartarotti is often depicted as anti-Jesuit but his ideas show he had absorbed, although not unquestioningly, many of their ideas. This did not prevent his book, although widely available in Vienna, being placed on the Index.
7. See Franz Leander Fillafer, *Aufklärung habsburgisch: Staatsbildung, Wissenskultur und Geschichtspolitik in Zentral Europa 1750–1850* (Göttingen 2020), p. 117 ff.

CHAPTER 49: THE SECRET WORLD:
POSTLOGEN AND *GEHEIMZIFFERN*

1. Sixteenth-century England was of course the model par excellence, familiar to Maria Theresa through her Jesuit tutors whose order had, after all, been the principal target of the Elizabethan surveillance state.
2. See Lau, *Die Kaiserin*, p. 203.
3. Ibid. Lau convincingly demonstrates that the 'crackdown' on public morals was, in reality, another typically Theresian compromise.
4. HHStA, Kaunitz Corr. Penkler.
5. See, for example, Goffredo Banfield in Trieste 1985, Richard Bassett, *Last Days in Old Europe* (London 2019), pp. 49–50.
6. Lady Mary Coke, *Letters and Journals*.
7. Ibid., vol. 1, p. civ.

CHAPTER 50: RECALIBRATING AUSTRIA'S EASTERN
FLANK: MARIA THERESA AND THE OTTOMANS

1. The enthusiastic consumption of sheep's brains and eyes at state banquets being perhaps one of the most common.
2. See Roider, *Austria's Eastern Question*.
3. Yedikule Hisari was both the most impressive and most feared of Constantinople's prisons.

4. HHStA, Türkei 8, Penkler to Kaunitz, 11 August 1745.
5. Ironically, it would be Austria which became the protecting power of Jews in Palestine 150 years later in the early twentieth century, as most of the Jews settling there from central Europe were subjects of the Habsburg empire.
6. This system was copied a century later by the British, whose Levant Consular Service reported to the embassy in Constantinople before 1914.

CONCLUSION: THE ENLIGHTENMENT EMPRESS

1. Derek Beales argues that even Joseph II's Catholicism impeded generous evaluation by British and American historians. See Derek Beales, 'Joseph II: An Enlightened Despot?', in *The Austrian Enlightenment and its Aftermath*, ed. Ritchie Robertson and Edward Timms (Edinburgh 2001), p. 186.
2. See Erasmus (ed. Lisa Jardine), *The Education of a Christian Prince* (Cambridge 1997), p. 17.
3. See Alphonse de Liguori (ed. Duffy), *Glories of Mary* (Georgetown 1981), based on original of 1762 Rome.
4. See Charles Burney, *The Present State of Music in Germany, the Netherlands and the United Provinces* (London 1772).
5. Lady Mary Coke, *Letters and Journals*, vol. 4, p. 29.
6. W.H. Auden, 'Prologue at Sixty (for Friedrich Heer)', in W.H. Auden, *Collected Poems* (London 1978), p. 622.
7. See Nicholas Till, *Mozart and the Enlightenment* (London 1986), pp. 190–1.
8. Lady Mary Coke, *Letters and Journals*, vol. 3, pp. 353–61.
9. Ibid., p. 372.
10. A.N. Whitehead, *Science and the Modern World* (Cambridge 1953), pp. 233–8.
11. *Reglement fuer die Saemmentlich-Kaiserlich Koenigliche Infanterie 1769*. See Bassett, *For God and Kaiser*, p. 124 ff.
12. Margaret Jacob, *The Secular Enlightenment* (Princeton 2019), p. 157.
13. The persecution of Catholics was only ended formally after the Napoleonic Wars with the passing of the highly controversial Catholic Emancipation Act of 1829. Jews were similarly discriminated against well into the nineteenth century.
14. Gilbert W. Daynes, 'The Duke of Lorraine and English Freemasonry in 1731', *Ars Quatuor Coronatorum*, vol. 37 (1924), pp. 107–28.
15. See Herbert Butterfield, *The Origins of Modern Science* (Cambridge 1949), p. 105.
16. Szabo, *Kaunitz and Enlightened Absolutism*, p. 5.

Select Bibliography

The English reader is poorly served by the present historiography on the Great Empress. Unlike Frederick of Prussia, whose career is the focus of one adulatory study after another, there is a dearth of literature in English on Maria Theresa. In recent years, there has been only one English biography of the Empress of note, Edward Crankshaw's 55-year-old tome which, while eminently readable, has become something of a period piece, refreshingly (or obsolescently, depending on your point of view) indifferent to the obscurantism of much modern academic history writing.

We are, nonetheless, fortunate to have Barbara Stollberg-Rilinger's vast scholarly biography which was published in Germany to universal acclaim in 2017; while adequately translated into English, it remains, at over a thousand pages, a formidably dense read. It is indispensable for modern scholars and shows a superb mastery of sources but its very brilliance makes it, paradoxically, somewhat inaccessible.

The scholar of Theresian studies is fortunate to have at his or her disposal the archives of the Austrian State Haus-, Hof- und Staatsarchiv and these cast an exceptionally interesting light on Maria Theresa's relations with her advisers, especially Kaunitz, and the discussions around her diplomatic and domestic policies. For those who attempt to come to a closer understanding of Maria Theresa, the available primary material is immense. Once the Austrian establishment decided to commemorate, in the late nineteenth century, the Great Empress with a monument on the Wiener Ringstrasse, serious work was begun on the editing and collating of her papers. A score of researchers in the imperial archives were encouraged to produce a reasonably transparent compilation of the available relevant documents. The first fruits of this gargantuan undertaking occurred with Arneth's immense publication.

Alfred Ritter von Arneth's ten volumes (Vienna 1863–79) were supplemented by his beautifully edited editions of the Empress's correspondence in seven additional volumes. These include *Briefe der Kaiserin Maria Theresia an ihre Kinder und Freunde* (4 volumes, Vienna 1881) and *Maria Theresia und Joseph II: Ihre Korrespondenz* (Vienna 1868).

The indispensable supplement to the Arneth volumes is the diary of Count Rudolf Khevenhueller-Metsch, the Empress's chamberlain, published in six volumes in Vienna between 1907 and 1925. An earlier useful selection from this journal is offered in *Aus dem Hofleben* edited by Adam Wolf in 1859 in Vienna. Maria Theresa's own political writings were edited with an introduction by Josef Kallbrunner in Vienna, 1952.

Successive anniversaries have built on these massive foundations. The year 1980 produced a magnificent exhibition in Austria (*Maria Theresia und ihre Zeit*) with a fine accompanying catalogue, rich in scholarship. A contemporaneous series of essays edited by the tireless Walter Koschatzky, *Maria Theresia und ihre Zeit* offers perhaps the most accessible route into the sheer breadth of the Empress's achievement. Koschatzky followed the general line of unquestioning adulation for the Empress, a judgement which was conspicuously missing in more recent anniversary celebrations. As one would expect from the editorship of the then director of the Albertina, there are fine essays on architecture, garden design, Liotard and fresco painting. Serious political analysis comes mainly from Adam Wandruzka whose own biography of the Great Empress is full of insights and those fine, often ironic, historical connections which were once the delight of the academic historian but appear to have become deeply unfashionable to the new 'miniaturist' school of historians.

Although much discredited for his pan-German sentiments, which certainly brought him into a compromising position with regard to the Nazis who seized Austria in 1938, the writings of Heinrich Ritter von Srbik on Maria Theresa repay reading. His rather dry account of trade under Maria Theresa is compensated for by a superb and, from a German nationalist point of view, highly favourable account of Maria Theresa's reign in his *Deutsche Einheit*, a study of, in his view, the woeful effects of German *Dualismus*. The book should be seen in its context. It was published in 1935 and aimed to provide some academic justification for an eventual Austrian *Anschluss* with Nazi Germany, although, like many Austrian Nazis, it is unlikely Srbik envisaged that event in the way it actually occurred.

Recently, studies of the Empress have led the educated lay reader into many excursions into the obstetrical arcana of childbirth and what is termed (but usually unexplained) as 'systematic cameralistics'. Two masterpieces of clarity which are exceptions to this are Karl Roider's fascinating *Austria's Eastern Question* (Princeton 1982) and Nicholas Till's *Mozart and the Enlightenment* (London 1992), both of which I have drawn on in the section assessing the Great Empress's cultural legacy.

By the time it came to celebrate Maria Theresa's three-hundredth anniversary in 2017, the passionate hagiography of Koschatzky's great work had dimmed into a more sceptical questioning of the Great Empress's achievement, reflecting the trends of the time. There was, nonetheless, a flurry of publications. Marxism might have been put to the sword in Europe nearly thirty years earlier, but a vein of inspired criticism of imperial social structures and class consciousness imbued some of the major Austrian contributions to the literature at that time. A notable exception was Élisabeth Badinter's study of the Empress and even more insightful study of Maria Theresa as a mother, *Marie-Thérèse d'Autriche et ses enfants* (Paris 2020). Mme Badinter's study revealed a fascinating new seam of original primary sources in the form of the Bentinck correspondence archived in Holland.

Symposia and exhibitions also marked the anniversary year in Trieste, Zagreb and Budapest, all of which produced fascinating papers of lasting significance to Theresian studies, from which I have quoted frequently in the text. Over the last ten years there has been a revival in interest in Wiener Porzellan, as well as several exhibitions in the Augarten Palais in Vienna under the inspired curatorial direction of Dr Claudia Lehner-Jobst, the current Director of the Augarten Porzellansammlung. The significant history of the Jews of Trieste whose privileges and rights dispel the widely accepted view that Maria Theresa was not at times a benefactor of her Jewish subjects is definitively dealt with by Lois C. Dubin's wonderful study of *The Port Jews of Habsburg Trieste* (Stanford 1999).

An exhibition in 2017 on Freemasonry in the Vienna State Library reminded us that it was formally inaugurated in the year of Maria Theresa's birth, 1717, and offered in its catalogue many insights into some of the men who advised Maria Theresa. Theodore von Karajan's study of the correspondence between Tarouca and the Empress, published in Vienna in 1859 (*Maria Theresia und Graf Sylva-Tarouca*) is probably still one of the most helpful in providing insights into Maria Theresa's supporting cast.

For the men of war, Daun, Lacy and Loudon and the Empress's other generals, Christopher Duffy's groundbreaking study, *The Army of Maria Theresa* (London 1977), has still never been bettered and its interpretation is shared by my own *For God and Kaiser* (London 2015), the first and still, perhaps surprisingly, the only comprehensive history of the Habsburg army to have been published in English.

Both Haugwitz and Kaunitz have been the subject of major studies in recent years. Franz Szabo's study, *Kaunitz and Enlightened Absolutism*, is now the standard text while Friedrich Walter's essay on Haugwitz remains still the best we have on that enigmatic statesman. Walter has also written on Van Swieten. The Prince de Ligne's character foibles and interaction with the Vienna court have been well described by the writer Philip Mansel in *The Prince of Europe* (London 2003).

Studies of Francis Stephen remain still rather sparse. Despite his many undoubted qualities, he has never emerged from the shadow of the Great Empress but his role and life are well documented in studies of the Holy Roman Empire, notably those of Joachim Whaley at Cambridge and the indefatigable Fräulein Stollberg-Rilinger.

The literature on Frederick of Prussia is predictably immense and rich in new biographies which occur with the same regularity almost as the change of the seasons. Fine studies by Tim Blanning, Giles MacDonogh and David Fraser have all enriched the bookshelves in recent years. The reports of Frederick's ambassador to the court of Vienna are masterly and well presented in *Otto Graf Podewils: Diplomatische Berichte* which were first published in Berlin in 1937.

For the arts, in addition to the essays in Koschatzky's commemorative tome mentioned above, there are several studies of the architecture of the period. The late Renate Wagner-Rieger wrote extensively on Hohenberg in her *Wiens Architektur im 19ten Jahrhundert* (Vienna 1970), while for those wishing to acquaint themselves with the earlier baroque period, Sedelmayr's great study of Fischer von Erlach (Salzburg 1956), despite the pan-German sympathies of the author, is still, perhaps inevitably, the standard work. For the early stages of neo-classicism, there is probably no better introduction in the English language than Hugh Honour's classic work on the subject published in 1976.

For musical life, there is Charles Burney's *Musical Tours in Europe*, including *The Present State of Music in Germany*. Mozart, following the 250th anniversary of his birth in 2006, seems to have faded from concert programmes and literature but the classic life of Mozart is contained in the trilogy of H.C. Robbins Landon, usefully supplemented by Nicholas Till. The highly revealing letters of Mozart, which contain so many insights into the temper of the Austrian Enlightenment, are contained in three volumes superbly translated and edited by the late and formidable Emily Anderson.

Contemporary memoirs include the indispensable William Wraxall, *Memoirs of the Courts of Berlin, Dresden, Warsaw and Vienna* published in 1806, Lady Mary Coke's diaries and journals published in 1889 as well as the letters and works of Lady Mary Wortley Montagu.

Since the publication of the second volume of Derek Beales's study of Joseph II, the serious scholar has needed to look no further when wishing to examine in more depth the dynamic between son and mother, or the thorny issue of which elements of the Enlightenment Joseph embraced and which he enthusiastically discarded. Thanks to this and other scholarly works of recent years, the world of eighteenth-century Vienna has been opened up to a wider range of readers than was the case even ten years ago. Professor Beales astutely noted the difficulty with which Anglo-Saxon historiography has coped with the Great Empress and her son.

The recent gradual awakening of interest in Maria Theresa's world has gone consciously, or unconsciously, hand in hand with a new interest in what is now widely perceived to have been a 'Catholic Enlightenment'. The pioneering work here is Ulrich Lehner's *The Catholic Enlightenment: The Forgotten History of a Global Movement*, published less than ten years ago. This has encouraged renewed interest in many contemporary writings of Catholic reformers such as Muratori and the Jesuit 'natural philosophers' of the time. Geoffrey Holt S.J.'s *The English Jesuits in the Age of Reason* is one standard work; Marcus Hellyer's study of *Catholic Physics* is another.

The spiritual world of the Great Empress was informed from the earliest age by the religious writing of her time. Her second name bound her umbilically with the mysticism and prayers of the great St Theresa of Avila, and St Theresa's 'bookmark' must have been one of the most inescapable of the Empress's devotions. She avidly read spiritual and religious texts and urged her children to put aside a few minutes each morning before talking to anyone to immerse themselves in the writing of the saints. The reader wishing to delve more deeply into these should perhaps first acquaint themselves (preferably with some Jesuitical guidance) with the *Spiritual Exercises* of St Ignatius which were the backbone of Maria Theresa's spiritual formation, and then with the writings of Theresa of Avila which were the foundation of her faith. Other writers, notably Alphonsus of Liguori, could also be approached. A modern and highly accessible Jesuit volume immensely helpful in understanding the practicality and fecundity of the Jesuit approach is the late Anthony Meredith S.J.'s *Faith and Fidelity*.

Austro-British relations in the eighteenth century are still best viewed through Archbishop Coxe's three-volume history of the House of Austria and Sir Jack Plumb's biography of Robert Walpole. Both Edward Crankshaw and A.J.P. Taylor wrote general studies of the Habsburg empire which highlight the incompatibility of the British monarchical system with the absolutist system of the Habsburgs. More recent social-historical studies of the Habsburg empire, notably by Peter Judson and Martin Rady, have the merit of acquainting a younger readership with the eccentricities of the Habsburg world in a digestible and readable form. C.A. Macartney's short *Maria Theresa and the House of Austria* is still a masterpiece of insightful brevity.

The personalities of Maria Theresa's children have also recently been the source of new studies. Antonia Fraser has produced a highly readable biography of Marie Antoinette, bringing much of the material contained in Stefan Zweig's biography of the Dauphine to a wider English audience. Nancy Goldstone's *In the Shadow of the Empress* has several entertaining anecdotes concerning the younger children of Maria Theresa but is light on Maria Carolina and the two fascinating spinsters, Elisabeth and Marianne. For the latter we still must use Fr. Adolf Innerkofler's informative but outdated *Eine grosse Tochter Maria Theresias* (Innsbruck 1910).

Lighter works on Joseph II also appear to be capturing the German appetite for racy accounts of enlightened despots. Monika Czernin's delightful *Der Kaiser reist inkognito* (Munich 2021) has built on earlier studies of Joseph and maintains the cult of his personality as a darling of the Enlightenment.

Most encouraging of all has been the revival of interest in the Empress in the former crown lands. Recently unveiled statues and monuments to her are now to be

SELECT BIBLIOGRAPHY

found in Trieste, Prague and Budapest and there has been a sharp increase in interest in her role in the Balkans with plans for new monuments in Croatia and Slovenia. A flurry of publications emerged from Zagreb and Trieste following the recent 2017 anniversary and this renewed attention of local scholars can only further establish Maria Theresa's reputation in the former crown lands, where the communist empire so long banned any public reference to the Great Empress.

ARCHIVAL SOURCES

Austria

Haus-, Hof- und Staatsarchiv (HHStA)
  Allgemeine Urkundenreihe
  Archiv des Dr Raimund Kerbls Grödig I
  Familienkorrespondenz A (FKA 23–39)
  Grosse Korrespondenz: 180–185
  Hausarchiv (HausA)
  Kabinettsarchiv Nachlass Zinzendorff Handschriften 87–93
  Kabinettsarchiv Nachlass Haugwitz 1–7
  Kabinettsarchiv Nachlass Ezsterhazy 1–4
  Kabinettsarchiv Nachlass Kaunitz 4, 23, 32–69
  Kriegsarchiv (1751–53) 2.33.6
  Länderabteilungen (LA) Belgien DD-B blau 1–5
  Ministerialkorrespondenz Karton 10–14
  Nachlass Alfred von Arneth 8b-1
  Staatenabteilungen England Varia 10–18
  Staatenabteilungen France Varia 33–39
  Staatenabteilungen Neapel Varia 11–15
  Staatskanzlei (StK) Diplomatische Korrespondenzen Preussen
  Staatskanzlei Vorträge 49–118
  Türkische Urkunden Mai 7 1775

Czech Republic

Clary-Aldringen Alfons Státní archiv v Litoměřicích
National Archives (Národní archiv)
RAM-Acta Clementina 11:1/20, 1/21, 2/23/25/26
Moravský zemský archiv v Brně
Salm-Reifferscheidt Family archive (Rodinný archiv Salm-Reifferscheidt) G150: 26–150 (Brno)
Tarouca Family archive (Rodinný archiv Sylva-Tarouca) G 445: 12 24-A-1 86 23-B-3
Kaunitz Family archive (Rodinný archiv Koudinice) G 86: 7–29
State Archives Litoměřice (Státní oblastní archiv v Litoměřicích) Lobkowitz papers P16/19; P 16–17

France

La Courneuve, Archives du ministère des Affaires étrangères (MAE)
  Correspondance politique Naples 58, 75
  Correspondance politique Autriche vol. 22 (supplément) 242–344

SELECT BIBLIOGRAPHY

Hungary

Magyar Országos Levéltár
  Vegyes Iratok Pálffy P299-I.6
  Vegyes Iratok Nasdadi N1-7

Italy

Archivio di Stato di Parma, Carteggio Borbonico Germania 96–99
Archivio storico della comunità Israelitica di Trieste Catalogo General, Curiel Riccardo
  1942

Netherlands

Arnheim, Gelders Archief, 0613 Bentinck/Aldenburg Bentinck 629–653

United Kingdom

National Archives
  Thomas Robinson (Baron Grantham) papers SP 87/26 series
  Correspondence of Thomas Robinson Ne C705/1–4
  Gordon of Khartoum records FO633
Nottingham University, Papers of Lady Mary Coke
Holkham Hall, Norfolk, Family Papers

PRINTED SOURCES

Acta Publica und verschiedene andere Schrifften die Sucession in denen Oesterreischischen Erb-Landen und jetztregierender Röm. Kayserl. Majetät darüber errichtete Pragmaticam (Frankfurt a. M. 1732)

Acta Publica oder Sammlung aller Staatsschriften welche seit denen im Jahr 1756 zu London und Versailles geschlossenen Allianz Tractaten an das Licht gekommen sind und noch kommen werden (4 vols, Vienna Prague 1756–58)

Adelung, Johann Christoph, *Pragmatische Staatsgeschichte Europens von dem Ablebn Kaiser Carls 6 an* (Gotha 1763)

Allgemeine Schulordnung für die deutschen Normal-Haupt- und Trivialschulen in sämmtlichen Kaiserlich Königlichen Erbländern d.d. Wien den 6ten December 1774

Betrachtung über des Deutschen Reichs-Staats besondere Beschaffenheit bei des Kaysers Carls de VI. Ableben den gesammten Reich-Ständen zu weiterer Prüfung übergeben, November 1741

Bourgoing, Jean-François de, *Pius VI und sein Pontifikat: Eine historische und philosophische Schilderung* (Hamburg 1800)

Der Heldentempel Oesterreichs zum Nachruhme des k.k. Feldmarshalls Grafen Leop. V Daun besungen von M. Denis aus der G.J. Lehrer am k.k. Thresiano (Vienna 1766)

Exercitium für die sämmentlich Kaiserl.-Königl Infanterie (Vienna 1769)

Geschichte und Thatten der Allerduchlauchtigsten u. Grossmächtigsten Fürstin und Frau Maria Theresa jetztregierende Königinin Hungarn un Böheim mit unpartheyischer Feder pragmatisch beschrieben und hin und wieder mit nützlichen Anmerkungen erläutert (1743)

Gognazzo, J., *Freymütiger Beitrag zur Geschichte der Oesterreischichen Militärdienstes* (Frankfurt 1799)

Holzmayer, Wolfgang, *Rede auf die höchstbeglückte Genesung Ihro kais. Königlich Apostol. Majestät Maria Theresia: bey dem feyerlichen Dankfeste welches von den Verordneten einer Hohöbl. Landschaft Oesterreich sob der Enns den 19 Heumonats gehalten wurde* (Linz 1767)

SELECT BIBLIOGRAPHY

In Praise of Her Most Serene Majesty Maria Theresa upon the Happy Success of Her Arms (Antwerp 1742)

Kriegs- und Heldenthaten des Freyherrns Gideon von Laudon (Vienna 1723)

Metastasio, Pietro, *Opere drammatiche e sacri* (Rome 1737)

Muratori, Ludovico Antonio, *Della pubblica felicitá* (Modena 1749)

Prosch, Peter, *Leben und Ereignisse des Peter Prosch's eines Tyrolers aus Zillerthal* (Munich 1789)

Redlich, Karl Julius, *Ueber den Tod der Kaiserin* (Vienna 1781)

Regulament und Ordnung des gesammten Kaiserlich-Koeniglichen Fuss-Volcks (Vienna 1749)

Regulament und Ordnung für Gesammte Kaiserl. Koenigl. Husaren Regimenter (Vienna 1751)

Reglement für das Kaiserlich Königlich Gesammte Feld-Artilleriecorps (Vienna 1757)

Reglement für die sämmentlich Kaiserlich Königlich Infanterie (Vienna 1769)

Robotpatent für das Königreich Böhmen von den 13 Tage des Monats August 1775 (Vienna 1775)

Vortreffliche Anekdoten zur Erläuterung der Geschichte Theresiens und Friedrichs (Leipzig 1762)

Wien(n)erisches Diarium 1740–49

Wiennerische Beleuchtungen oder Beschreibung Aller deren Triunph- und Ehren-Gerüsten, Sinn-Bildern, Gemählden und andern sowol prächtig als kostbar und unvergleichlichen Auszierungen (Vienna 1746)

Wurz, Ignaz, *Trauerrede auf Franz den Ersten, Röm. Kaiser* (Vienna 1765)

SECONDARY SOURCES

Acton, Harold, *The Last Bourbons of Naples 1825–1861* (London 1961)

Ahrens, Annette, 'Warum Maria Theresia keine 44 Gläserkühler in Sèvres bestellte? Das Wiener Porzellan unter Maria Theresia', in *Maria Theresias Kulturwelt*, ed. Pierre Behar (Hildesheim 2011)

Allmayer-Beck, Johann Christoph, *Militär, Geschichte und politische Bildung* (Vienna 2003)

———, *Das Heer unter dem Doppeladler 1718–1848* (Munich 1981)

———, 'Der Aufbau des Oesterreischischen Heerwesens', in exh. cat. *Maria Theresia und ihre Zeit* (Vienna 1980)

Anderson, Emily (trans. and ed.), *The Letters of Mozart and his Family* (London 1938)

Archenholz, Johann W., *Geschichte des Siebenjaehrigen Kriegs in Deutschland* (Berlin 1860)

Aretin, Karl Otmar von, *Das Reich: Friedensordnung und europäisches Gleichgewicht 1648–1806* (York 1998)

Arneth, Alfred von (ed.), *Maria Theresia und Marie Antoinette: Ihr Briefwechsel* (Leipzig 1866)

———, *Maria Theresia und Joseph II: Ihre Korrespondenz sammt Briefen Joseph's an seinen Bruder Leopold* (Vienna 1868)

———, *Johann Christoph Bartenstein und seine Zeit*, in *Archiv für österreichische Geschichte*, vol. 46 (Vienna 1871)

———, *Briefe der Kaiserin Maria Theresia an ihre Kinder und Freunde* (4 vols, Vienna 1881)

———, *Die Relationen der Botschafter Venedigs über Oesterreich im 18ten Jahrhundert* (Vienna 1863)

———, *Geschichte Maria Theresias* (10 vols, Vienna 1863–79)

——— (with M.A. Geffroy), *Correspondance Secrète entre Marie Therese et le Comte de Mercy-Argenteau* (Paris 1874)

Auden, W.H., *Collected Poems* (London 1978)

Avila, Teresa of, *Philosophiae memoria (Camino de perfección)* (Avila 1556)

Badinter, Élisabeth, *Isabelle de Bourbon-Parme: "Je meurs d'amour pour tois', Lettres 1760–1763 à L'archiduchesse Marie-Christine* (Paris 2008)

———, *Le pouvoir au féminin: Marie-Thérèse d'Autriche 1717–1780, L' imperatrice, reine* (Paris 2016)

———, *Les conflits d'une mère: Marie-Thérèse d'Autriche et ses enfants* (Paris 2020)

Bassett, Richard, *For God and Kaiser: The Imperial Austrian Army 1619–1918* (London 2015)

Baud-Bovy, Daniel, *Peintres Genevois 1702–1817, Liotard* (Geneva 1903)

Beales, Derek, *Joseph II*, vol. 1: *In the Shadow of Maria Theresa* (Cambridge 1987)

———, *Joseph II*, vol. 2: *Against the World* (Cambridge 2009)

Beer, Adolf, *Die Zusammenkünfte Josefs II und Friedrichs II zu Neisse und Neustadt* (Vienna 1871)

———, 'Die Denkschriften des Fürsten Wenzel Kaunitz-Rietberg', *Archiv für österreischiche Geschichte*, vol. 48, no. 1 (1872)

———, 'Die Sendung Thugut's in das preussische Hauptquartier und der Friede zu Teschen', *Historische Zeitschrift* (1877)

——— (ed.), *Aufzeichnungen des Grafen Bentinck über Maria Theresias* (Vienna 1871)

——— (ed.), *Joseph II, Leopold II und Kaunitz: Ihr Briefwechsel* (Vienna 1873)

Behrens, C.B.A., *Society, Government and the Enlightenment: The Experiences of Eighteenth-Century France and Prussia* (London 1985)

Belloc, Hilaire, *James II* (London 1928)

Bergl, J., 'Das Exil der Prager Judenschaft von 1745–1748', *Jahrbuch der Gesellschaft für Geschichte der Juden in der Čechoslovakischen Republik* (1929)

Bernhard, Thomas, *Holzfällen* (Vienna 1984)

Bissett, Andrew (ed.), *Memoirs and Papers of Sir Andrew Mitchell* (London 1850)

Blunt, Anthony, *Borromini and the Baroque* (Lecture, 4 December 1979, Courtauld Institute of Art, London)

Brechka, Frank T., *Gerard van Swieten and his World, 1700–1772* (The Hague 1970)

Browning, Reed, *The War of the Austrian Succession* (New York 1995)

Burney, Charles, *The Present State of Music in Germany, the Netherlands and the United Provinces* (London 1772)

Butterfield, Herbert, *The Origins of Modern Science* (Cambridge 1949)

Chadwick, Owen, *The Secularization of the European Mind in the Nineteenth Century* (Edinburgh 1973)

Christoph, Paul (ed.), *Geheimer Briefwechsel mit Marie Antoinette* (Vienna 1980)

Coke, Lady Mary, *Letters and Journals of Lady Mary Coke*, ed. James Home (4 vols, Edinburgh 1889)

Coreth, Anna, *Pietas Austriaca* (Munich 1982)

Coxe, William, *History of the House of Austria* (3 vols, London 1847–88)

Crankshaw, Edward, *Maria Theresa* (London 1969)

Czernin, Monika, *Der Kaiser reist inkognito: Joseph II und das Europa der Aufklärung* (Munich 2021)

Da Costa Kauffmann, Thomas, *Painterly Enlightenment: The Art of Franz Anton Maulpertsch 1724–1796* (Princeton 2006)

Davies, Malcolm, *The Masonic Muse: Men, Manners and Songs Associated with Dutch Freemasonry* (Utrecht 1995)

Davies, Norman, *God's Playground* (Oxford 1981)

Daynes, Gilbert W., 'The Duke of Lorraine and English Freemasonry in 1731', *Ars Quatuor Coronatorum*, vol. 37 (1924)

D'Elvert, Christian, 'Das Zauber und Hexenwesen: dann der Glauben an Vampyre in Mähren und Schlesien', in D'Elvert Christian (Hrsg): *Schriften der historisch-statistischen Sektion der k.k. mährisch-schlesischen Gesellschaft des Ackerbaues, der Natur und Landeskunde*, ed. Christian D'Elvert, vol. 12 (Brünn 1859)

Dickson, Peter George Muir, *Finance and Government under Maria Theresa 1740–1780* (2 vols, Oxford 1987)

Droysen, Johann Gustav (ed.), *Die politische Correspondenz Friedrichs des Grossen* (18 vols, Berlin 1879–80)

Dubin, Lois C., *The Port Jews of Habsburg Trieste: Absolutist Politics and Enlightenment Culture* (Stanford 1999)

Duffy, Christopher, *The Army of Maria Theresa* (London 1977)

————, *Sieben Jahre Krieg: Die Armee Maria Theresias* (Vienna 2003)

Egghardt, Hanne, *Maria Theresias Männer* (Vienna 2015)

Erasmus, Desiderius (trans. Neil M. Cheshire and Michael J. Heath, ed. Lisa Jardine), *The Education of a Christian Prince* (Cambridge 1997)

Evans, R.J.W., 'Maria Theresa and Hungary', in *Enlightened Absolutism in Later Eighteenth-Century Europe*, ed. H.M. Scott (London 1990)

Fata, Marta, *Migration im kameralistischen Staat Josephs II: Theorie und Praxis der Ansiedlungspolitik in Ungarn, Siebenbürgen, Galizien und der Bukowina von 1768–1790* (Münster 2014)

Feil, Joseph, *Sonnenfels und Maria Theresia* (Vienna 1858)

Fejtö, François, *Joseph II: Un Habsbourg révolutionnaire; Portrait d'un despote éclairé* (Paris 1953)

Fillafer, Franz Leander, *Aufklärung habsburgisch: Staatsbildung, Wissenskultur und Geschichtspolitik in Zentral Europa 1750–1850* (Göttingen 2020)

Fischer, Robert-Tarek, *Österreich im Nahen Osten: Die Grossmacht der Habsburgermonarchie im Arabischen Orient 1633–1918* (Munich 1999)

Fleury, Cardinal André-Hercule de, *Mémoires et Documents* (Paris 1920)

Fournier, August, *Gerhard van Swieten als Censor* (Vienna 1877)

Galimberti, Sergio and Mariano Malý (eds), *I Gesuiti e gli Asburgo* (Trieste 1995)

Gates, Rebecca, 'Court and Cottage: The Public Image of Maria Theresa's Government during the Transdanubian Unrest 1765–1767', *Austrian History Yearbook*, vol. 21 (1985)

Gérard, Jo, *Marie-Thérèse: Imperatrice des Belges* (Brussels 1987)

Girard, Georges, *Correspondance entre Marie-Thérèse et Marie Antoinette* (Paris 1933)

Godsey, William, 'Adelsautonomie, Konfession und Nation im oesterreichischen Absolutismus 1620–1848', *Zeitschrift für Historische Forschung*, vol. 33 (2006)

Göllner, Carl, *Die Siebenbürgische Militärgrenze: Ein Beitrag zur Sozial- und Wirtschaftsgeschichte 1762–1851* (Munich 1972)

Gooch, George P., *Maria Theresa and Other Studies* (London 1951)

Grasberger, Franz, 'Ein goldenes Zeitalter der Musik', in *Maria Theresia und ihre Zeit*, ed. Walter Koschatzky (Vienna 1980)

Grimm, Gerald, *Die Schulreform Maria Theresias 1747–1775. Das oesterreichische Gymnasium zwischen Standesschule und allgemeinbildender Lehranstalt im Spannungsfeld von Ordenschulwesen, theresianischem Reformabsolutismus und Aufklärungspädagogik* (Frankfurt 1987)

Grothaus, Maximilian, *Der Erbfeindt christlichen Namens: Studien zum Türkenfeindbild in der Kultur der Habsburgermonarchie zwischen 16. und 18. Jahrhundert* (Graz 1986)

Grünberg, Karl, *Die Bauernbefreiung und die Auflösung der gutsherrlich-bäuerlichen Verhältnisse in Böhmen, Mähren und Schlesien*, vol. 1 (Leipzig 1893)

Grünmayer, Brigitte, *Chinoise Blaumalerei der Wiener Porzellanmanufaktur von 1718–1820* (Vienna 2009)

Hackl, Bernhard, 'Die staatliche Wirtschaftspolitik zwischen 1740 und 1792: Reform versus Stagnation', in *Josephinismus als Aufgeklärter Absolutismus*, ed. Helmut Reinalter (Vienna 2008)

Hainisch, Erwin, *Der Architekt Johann Ferdinand Hetzendorf von Hohenberg* (Innsbruck 1949)

Hartley, M., *The Man who Saved Austria* (London 1929)

Hartl, Friedrich, 'Humanität und Strafrecht. Zum 200 jährigen Jubiläum der Aufhebung der Folter in Oesterreich', *Oesterreichische Juristen-Zeitung*, vol. 6 (1976)

Hasquin, Hervé, *Diplomate et espion autrichien dans la France de Marie-Antoinette, le comte de Mercy-Argenteau* (Waterloo 2014)

Hausmann, Friederike, *Herrscherin im Paradies der Teufel: Maria Karolina, Königin von Neapel* (Munich 2014)

Herre, Franz, *Maria Theresia: Die grosse Habsburgerin* (Cologne 1994)

Hersche, Peter, *Der Spätjansenismus in Oesterreich* (Vienna 1977)

Hinrichs, Carl (ed.), *Friedrich der Grosse und Maria Theresia: Diplomatische Berichte von Otto Graf Podewils, königl. Preuss. Gesandter am oesterreichischen Hof in Wien* (Berlin 1937)

Hirtenfeld, Jaromir, *Der Militär-Maria-Theresien-Orden und seine Mitglieder* (Vienna 1857)

Hochedlinger, Michael, *Austria's Wars of Emergence: War, State and Society in the Habsburg Monarchy* (London 2003)

Holt, Geoffrey, S.J., *The English Jesuits in the Age of Reason* (Tunbridge Wells 1993)

Hrazky, Josef, *Mitteilungen des oesterreichischen Staatsarchivs*, vol. 2 (Vienna 1959)

Ibby, Elfriede and Alexander Koller, *Schönbrunn* (Vienna 2007)

Innerkofler, Adolf P., *Eine grosse Tochter Maria Theresias: Erzherzogin Marianne in ihrem Haupt-Momente, dem Elisabethinenkloster zu Klagenfurt* (Innsbruck 1910)

Jacob, Margaret, *The Secular Enlightenment* (Princeton 2019)

Jedlicka, Ludwig (ed.), *Maria Theresia in ihren Briefen und Staatschriften* (Vienna 1955)

Jessen, Hans (ed.), *Friedrich der Grosse und Maria Theresia in Augenzeugenberichten* (Düsseldorf 1965)

Justi, Johann Heinrich Gottlob, *Beweis der Universalmonarchie* (Vienna 1747)

Kann, Robert A., *A History of the Habsburg Empire* (Berkeley 1974)

Karafiol, Emile, *The Reforms of the Empress Maria Theresa in the Provincial Government of Lower Austria 1740–1765* (Cornell University PhD thesis 1966)

Karajan, Th. G. von, *Maria Theresia und Graf Sylva-Tarouca* (Vienna 1859)

Keynes, J.M., 'Some Notes on the Austrian Thaler', *Economic Review* (June 1914)

Khevenhueller-Metsch, Rudolf Graf, *Aus der Zeit Maria Theresias. Tagebuch des Fürsten Johann Josef Khevenhueller-Metsch* (6 vols, Vienna 1907–25)

Klarwil, Victor, *Der Fürst von Ligne: Errinerungen und Briefe* (Vienna 1920)

Klingenstein, Grete, 'Was bedeuten "Oesterreich' und "oesterreichisch" im 18. Jahrhundert?', in *Was heisst Oesterreich? Inhalt und Umfang des Oesterreichbegriffs vom 10. Jahrhundert bis heute*, ed. Richard G. Plaschka, Gerald Stourzh and Jan Paul Niederkorn (Vienna 1995)

Klingenstein, Grete, with Eva Faber and Antonio Trampus (eds), *Europäische Aufklärung zwischen Wien und Triest: Die Tagebücher des Gouverneurs Karl Graf Zinzendorf* (4 vols, Vienna 2009)

Koestler, Arthur, *The Sleepwalkers* (London 1959)

Kohlrausch, Frederick, *A History of Germany* (London 1844)

König, Peter R., *Maria Theresia. Ein Europäischer Mythos in Oesterreich in Geshcichte und Literatur* 58 (Vienna 2024)

Koschatzky, Walter (ed.), *Maria Theresia und ihre Zeit* (Vienna 1980)

Kriele, Johann Ludwig, *Der Schlacht bei Kunersdorf und Frankfurt am ersten August 1759* (Berlin 1801)

Krivanec, Ernst, *Die Freimauerei in der Theresianischen Epoche* (Vienna 1979)

Krummholz, Martin, '"Zu unaussprechlicher Freude allhöchsten Herrschaften wie auch zum höchsten Troste allhiesiger Inwohner": Zwei Iluminationen vor dem Wiener Stadtpalais Schwarzenberg anlässlich der Geburt der ältesten Söhne Maria Theresias', *Orbis atrium*, vol. 1 (2009)

Kulenkampff, Angela, *Oesterreich und das alte Reich: Die Reichspolitik des Staatskanzlers Kaunitz unter Maria Theresia und Joseph II* (Vienna 2005)

Kuntzel, Georg, *Fürst Kaunitz-Rietberg als Staatsman* (Vienna 1923)

Lau, Thomas, *Die Kaiserin* (Vienna 2017)

Lehner, Ulrich L., *The Catholic Enlightenment: The Forgotten History of a Global Movement* (Oxford 2018)

Lettenhove, Kervyn de, *Mémoires couronnés et aucuns mémoires publiés par L'Académie Royale des Beaux-Arts de Belge* (Brussels 1869)

Lever, Evelyne, *C'était Marie Antoinette* (Paris 2010)

Ligne, Charles Joseph de, 'Mémoire sur Frederic II, Roi de Prusse', in *Mémoires et Mélanges historiques* (Paris 1827)

Lukowski, Jerzy, *The Partitions of Poland* (New York 1999)

Macartney, C.A., *Maria Theresa and the House of Austria* (London 1969)

Macaulay, Thomas Babington, *Essays*, vol. 6 (London 1897)

Mansel, Philip, *The Life of Charles-Joseph de Ligne 1735–1814* (London 2003)

Marmont, Duc de Raguse, *Voyage en Hongrie* (Paris 1847)

Meredith S.J., Anthony, *Faith and Fidelity* (Leominster 2000) Mitchell, Leslie, *The Whig World* (London 2005)

Montesquieu, Charles-Louis de Secondat, *L'Esprit des Lois* (Geneva 1748)

Morley, John, *Voltaire* (London 1886)

Newman, Aubrey, 'The Expulsion of the Jews from Prague in 1745 and British Foreign Policy', *Transactions & Miscellanies* (Jewish Historical Society of England), vol. 22 (1968–9), pp. 30–41

Novotny, Alexander, *Staatskanzler Kaunitz als geistige Personalität* (Vienna 1947)

Otruba, Gustav, *Die Wirtschaftspolitik Maria Theresias* (Vienna 1963)

Ottenfeld, Rudolf, *Die oesterreichische Armee von 1700–1867* (Vienna 1895)

Paganel, Camillo, *Storia di Giuseppe II* (Milan 1843)

Pfister, Kurt, *Maria Theresia: Mensch, Staat und Kultur der spätbarocken Welt* (Munich 1949)

Pichler, Caroline, *Denkwürdigkeiten aus meinem Leben* (Munich 1914)

Pils, Gottfried, with Eugen Brixen and Gustav Martin, *Das ist Österreichs Militärmusik* (Graz 1982)

Pitacco, Francesca, 'Tracce teresiane a Trieste: piccole storie di grandi mutamenti urbani e sociali nella Trieste del XVIII secolo', in *Maria Teresa e Trieste: Storia e culture della città e del suo porto* (Trieste 2018)

Plaggenborg, Stefan, 'Maria Theresa und die böhmischen Juden', *Bohemia*, vol. 39 (1998)

Plumb, J.H., *Robert Walpole* (2 vols, London 1960)

Podewils, Otto Christoph von (ed. Carl Hinrichs), *Diplomatische Berichte* (Berlin 1937)

Pribram, A.F., *Urkunden und Akten zur Geschichte der Juden in Wien* (2 vols, Vienna 1918)

Randa, Alexander, *Oesterreich in Übersee* (Vienna 1966)

Rapp, Christian (ed.), *300 Jahre Freimaurer: Das wahre Geheimnis* (Vienna 2017)

Reinalter, Helmut, *Der Jakobinismus in Mitteleuropa* (Stuttgart 1983)

Robbins Landon, H.C., *Mozart and Vienna* (London 1994)

Roider, Karl A., *Austria's Eastern Question 1700–1790* (Princeton 1982)

————, *Baron Thugut and Austria's Response to the French Revolution* (Princeton 1987)

Rosenstrauch-Königsberg, Edith, *Freimauerei, Illuminati, Weltbürger* (Berlin 1984)

Rothe, Carl (ed.), *Die Mutter und die Kaiserin: Briefe der Maria Theresia an ihre Kinder und Vertraute* (Vienna 1968)

Sardo, Eugenio Lo, *Napoli e Londra nel XVIII secolo: Le relazioni economiche* (Naples 1991)

Schilling, Lothar, *Kaunitz und das Renversement des alliances: Studien zur aussenpolitischen Konzeption Wenzel Anton Kaunitz* (Berlin 1994)

Schünemann, Konrad, *Oesterreichs Bevölkerungs Politik unter Maria Theresia* (Berlin 1936)

Schuschnigg, Kurt von, *Austrian Requiem* (London 1946)

Seiffert, Eckhardt, *Paul Joseph Riegger (1705–1755). Ein Beitrag zur theoretischen Grundlegung des josephinischen Staatskirchenrechts* (Berlin 1973)

Seitschek, Stefan, *Der Wiener Hof im Spiegel der Zeremonialprotokolle 1652–1800* (Innsbruck 2007)

Singerton, Jonathan, *The American Revolution and the Habsburg Monarchy* (Charlottesville 2022)

Spiel, Hilde, *Fanny von Arnstein* (Oxford 1991)

Srbik, Heinrich Ritter von, *Gestalten und Ereignisse aus Oesterreichs deutscher Vergangenheit* (Leipzig 1942)

————, *Metternich: Der Staatsman und der Mensch* (Munich 1957)

Steiner, Stephan, *Rückkehr unerwünscht. Deportationen in der Habsburgermonarchie in der Frühen Neuzeit und ihr europäischer Kontext* (Vienna 2014)

Stollberg-Rilinger, Barbara, *Maria Theresia: Die Kaiserin in ihrer Zeit* (Munich 2017)

Szabo, Franz A.J., *Kaunitz and Enlightened Absolutism 1753–1780* (Cambridge 1994)

Tague, Ingrid, *Love, Honour and Obedience: Fashionable Women and the Discourse of Marriage in the Early 18th Century* (Cambridge 2001)

Telesko, Werner, *Maria Theresia: Ein europäischer Mythos* (Vienna 2012)

Till, Nicholas, *Mozart and the Enlightenment* (London 1986)

Vaughan, C.E., *The Political Writings of Jean Jacques Rousseau* (2 vols, Cambridge 1915)

Vehse, Carl E., *Memoirs of the Court, Aristocracy and Diplomacy of Austria* (London 1856)

Vetter, Eva, *Die Finsternis der Unwissenheit aufklären* (Vienna University, guest lecture, 17 July 2017)

Villermont, Antoine de, *Marie-Thérèse 1717–1780* (2 vols, Paris 1895)

Voghera, Giorgio, *Quaderno d'Israele* (Milan 1967)

————, *Gli Anni di Trieste* (Gorizia 1989)

Voltaire, M. de (François-Marie Arouet) (ed. Theodore Besterman), *Correspondence and Related Documents* (Geneva 1970)

Wakefield, André, *The Disordered Police State: German Cameralism as Science and Practice* (Chicago 2009)

Wandruszka, Adam, *Leopold II: Erzherzog von Oesterreich, Grossherzog von Toskana, König von Ungarn und Böhmen, Römischer Kaiser* (2 vols, Vienna 1963–65)

Waugh, Evelyn, *Edward Campion S.J.* (London 1935)

Whitehead, A.N., *Science and the Modern World* (Cambridge 1953)

Wittgenstein, Ludwig, *Tractatus Logico-Philosophicus* (London 1922)

Wolf, Adam, *Der Wiener Hof in den Jahren 1746, 1747 & 1748. Diplomatische Relationen des Grafen von Podewils, bevollmächtigen Minister in Wien an Friedrich II König in Preussen* (Vienna 1850)

————, *Oesterreich unter Maria Theresia* (Vienna 1885)

Wortley Montagu, Lady (ed. Lord Wharncliffe), *The Letters and Works of Lady Wortley Montagu* (London 1887)

Wraxall, Nathaniel William, *Memoirs of the Courts of Berlin, Dresden, Warsaw and Vienna in the years 1777, 1778 and 1779* (London 1806)

Yates, Frances, *The Rosicrucian Enlightenment* (London 1972)

Zech, Heike, *Kaskaden der deutschen Gartenkunst des 18 Jahrhunderts* (Berlin 2010)

Zedinger, Renate, *Franz Stephan von Lothringen (1708–1765)* (Vienna 2008)

Illustrations

PLATES

ILLUSTRATIONS

FIGURES

Index

MT stands for Maria Theresa.
HRE stands for Holy Roman Emperor.
'Joseph' stands for Joseph II, son of MT and later HRE.
Non-English titles and phrases are entered in strict alphabetical order so that definite articles (such as 'la' or 'il') are not inverted and form part of the filing order.

Frederick enters 196
Frederick leaves 199
Illuminati 262
menacing Vienna 45
occupies Linz 42–3
occupies Prague 32
Papacy supports 88
progress along the Danube valley 40
succession crisis 191–201, 249, 271
   other countries adopt positions 194
Treaty of Nymphenburg 38
Bayreuth 193, 197, 200
Beales, Derek 274, 436
Beatrice d'Este 253–4, 280
Beaumarchais, Pierre-Augustin Caron de 359
Beccaria, Cesare 281
Bedouin 386–8
Beitel, Karl 7
Belgium (Austrian Netherlands) 102, 192–4, 257, 277, 290, 292, 295
   see also Austrian Netherlands
Belgrade 24, 355, 430
Belgrade, Treaty of 33
Belle-Isle, Marshal 29, 40
Bellotto, Bernardo 350
Belvedere palaces 350–1, 410, 414
Benedict XIV, Pope 88, 167, 417, 422
Benedictines 6, 11
Beneš, Edvard 77
Bentinck, Lady 96
Berg Isel 370
Bergl, Johann 348
Berlin 135–7
Berlin Wall 385
Bertoli, Daniele 16
Bestuzhev, Count Alexey 115
Betteljuden 335
Bevern, Duke of 113
Bezique 16, 269
Bismarck, Count Otto von 109, 115
Bisquit 373, 403, 464n5
Black Eagle, Order of the 136
Blunt, Anthony 205
Boerhaave, Herman 79
Bohemia 318–26
   Austria and the Battle of the White Mountain 72–4, 76–7
   demographics 343

electing a new Emperor 30
Elector of Bavaria crowned 32
expulsion of Germans 77
famine 187
Frederick invades 115–16
Jews of 60
Joseph II's tour 179
MT as king of 59
MT determined to save 46, 48
Protestants in 204
Prussian invasions 52–3, 112
recognised by Holy Roman Empire xi
tax receipts fall 161–2
Bolts, William 24, 272, 277–8
Bonomo, Francesco Saverio de 274
books 84, 165, 265–8
Borgo Giuseppino 278
Borgo Teresiano (Trieste) 208, 274, 459n3
   see also Trieste
Born, Ignaz von 245
Boskett 349–50
Bosnians 368
Bourbon, House of 50, 51, 219
Brabant 290, 298
Brady 172
Brandenburg, Electors of 25
Brandenburg, Margrave of 59
Brandenburg, miracle of 136
Brequin, Jean-Baptiste 344
Breslau 26, 39, 40, 48, 122
Breslau, Treaty of 50
bridges 344
Brigado, Count 261
Britain
   Austrian Netherlands 94
   East India Company 23
   embassy in Vienna 391
   fickleness of policy denounced 49–50
   Fontenoy disaster 56
   MT's husband 20
   obsessive trade conflict with France 106
   pillage and burning by 60
   Pragmatic Army 51–2
   Silesia 98
   Sudan relief force 386
   supporting Austria 107
Broglie, Duke of 40, 51
Brognard 431

INDEX